T0350900

Handbook of Intelligent and Sustainable Smart Dentistry

With the exponential growth of science and technology, the delivery of dental care has shifted from conventional methods to intelligent techniques. In addition to adapting intelligent techniques, sustainable dental practice is of the utmost importance. Eco-friendly dentistry, sustainable dentistry, or green dentistry are approaches that reduce the environmental impact of dental practice and help safeguard planetary and community well-being. This handbook provides the latest and most comprehensive evidence-based guidance on intelligent and sustainable approaches in dentistry.

Handbook of Intelligent and Sustainable Smart Dentistry: Nature and Bio-Inspired Approaches, Processes, Materials, and Manufacturing highlights how Dentistry 4.0 has come to the rescue after COVID-19 and how it has helped in providing needed e-healthcare. This handbook bridges the gap between research and development in the field of smart dentistry for professionals and clinicians. Intelligent materials, equipment, instrumentation, and the latest behavior management techniques and how these techniques provide superior care and treatment to society are explored in detail. The scope of nature-inspired techniques and procession, along with green solutions, are also discussed in this one-of-a-kind handbook.

This valuable handbook is a single-stop solution for practitioners, researchers, scholars, students, academicians, and clinicians interested in updating their knowledge on intelligent and sustainable dentistry. The handbook will bestow the readers with not only theoretical knowledge but will equip them with clinical skills as well.

Advancements in Intelligent and Sustainable Technologies and Systems

Series Editor: Ajay Kumar

This book series aims to provide a platform for academicians, researchers, professionals, and individuals to participate and to provide novel systematic theoretical, experimental, computational work in the form of edited text or reference books, monographs in the area of intelligent and sustainable technologies and systems from engineering, management, applied science, healthcare, etc. domains. This book series will educate and inform the readers with a comprehensive overview of advancements in intelligent and sustainable techniques and systems with novel intelligent tools and algorithms to move industries from different domains from a data-centric community to a sustainable world. The book series covers ideas and innovations to help the research community and professionals to understand fundamentals, opportunities, challenges, future outlook, layout, life-cycle, and framework of intelligent and sustainable technologies and systems for different sectors. It serves as a guide for computer science, mechanical, manufacturing, electrical, electronics, civil, automobile, industrial engineering, biomedical, healthcare, and management professionals.

If you are interested in writing or editing a book for the series or would like more information, please contact Cindy Carelli, cindy.carelli@taylorandfrancis.com

5G-Based Smart Hospitals and Healthcare Systems: Evaluation, Integration, and Deployment
Edited by Arun Kumar, Sumit Chakravarty, Aravinda K., and Mohit Kumar Sharma

Handbook of Intelligent and Sustainable Smart Dentistry: Nature and Bio-Inspired Approaches, Processes, Materials, and Manufacturing
Edited by Ajay Kumar, Namrata Dogra, Sarita Rathee, Surbhi Bhatia Khan, and M. S. Sidhu

Handbook of Intelligent and Sustainable Manufacturing: Tools, Principles, and Strategies
Edited by Ajay Kumar, Parveen Kumar, Yang Liu, and Rakesh Kumar

Handbook of Intelligent and Sustainable Smart Dentistry

Nature and Bio-Inspired Approaches, Processes, Materials, and Manufacturing

Edited by
Ajay Kumar
Namrata Dogra
Sarita Rathee
Surbhi Bhatia Khan
M. S. Sidhu

CRC Press
Taylor & Francis Group
Boca Raton London New York

CRC Press is an imprint of the
Taylor & Francis Group, an **informa** business

Designed cover image: ShutterStock – anatoliy_gleb

First edition published 2025
by CRC Press
2385 NW Executive Center Drive, Suite 320, Boca Raton FL 33431

and by CRC Press
4 Park Square, Milton Park, Abingdon, Oxon, OX14 4RN

CRC Press is an imprint of Taylor & Francis Group, LLC

© 2025 selection and editorial matter, Ajay Kumar, Namrata Dogra, Sarita Rathee, Surbhi Bhatia Khan and M. S. Sidhu; individual chapters, the contributors

Library of Congress Cataloging-in-Publication Data
Names: Ajay, editor. | Dogra, Namrata, editor. | Rathee, Sarita, editor. | Bhatia, Surbhi, 1988- editor. | Sidhu, M. S. (Maninder Singh), 1964- editor.
Title: Handbook of intelligent and sustainable smart dentistry : nature and bio-inspired approaches, processes, materials, and manufacturing / edited by Ajay Kumar, Namrata Dogra, Sarita, Surbhi Bhatia, and M S Sidhu.
Description: First edition. | Boca Raton, FL : CRC Press, 2025. | Includes bibliographical references and index.
Identifiers: LCCN 2024006248 (print) | LCCN 2024006249 (ebook) | ISBN 9781032517254 (hardback) | ISBN 9781032520247 (paperback) | ISBN 9781003404934 (ebook)
Subjects: MESH: Dentistry--trends | Dental Care | Smart Materials | Computer Simulation
Classification: LCC RK240 (print) | LCC RK240 (ebook) | NLM WU 100 | DDC 617.600285--dc23/eng/20240515
LC record available at https://lccn.loc.gov/2024006248
LC ebook record available at https://lccn.loc.gov/2024006249

ISBN: 978-1-032-51725-4 (hbk)
ISBN: 978-1-032-52024-7 (pbk)
ISBN: 978-1-003-40493-4 (ebk)

DOI: 10.1201/9781003404934

Typeset in Times
by MPS Limited, Dehradun

Contents

Preface

Around 3.5 billion people are affected by oral diseases worldwide. Providing quality dental care is of utmost importance for the overall well-being of the human race. The advancements in the field of science and technology have resulted in the adaptation of intelligent techniques in providing dental care. These intelligent techniques would provide the best treatment results and superior quality care to the patients. Artificial intelligence (AI), which is a technology that utilizes machines to mimic intelligent human behavior, has great potential in preventing postoperative complications, providing improved quality of life, improving decision-making, and decreasing the number of unnecessary procedures. In addition to adapting intelligent techniques, sustainable dental practice is of utmost importance. Eco-friendly dentistry/Sustainable dentistry or green dentistry is an approach that reduces the environmental impact of dental practice and helps in safeguarding planetary and community well-being. This book is expected to provide the latest and comprehensive evidence-based guidance on Intelligent and Sustainable approaches in dentistry. It will provide an insight into the latest Artificial Intelligent techniques in dentistry like Digital Twin, Big Data Analytics in Dentistry, IODT (Internet of Dental Things), and Nature-Inspired and Bio-Inspired Approaches. The readers will be familiarized with the clinical applications of digital dentistry in diagnosis, prognosis, and accurate treatment planning. Novels and the latest materials in dental applications will be covered in detail. The readers would be engrossed with Innovative techniques for improving oral health care and learning innovative techniques of behavior management. The aim of the book is to equip the clinicians with detailed knowledge in order to upgrade their daily practice. Moreover, the book will incorporate the applications of Dentistry 4.0 in providing efficient dental care and E-learning during the COVID era. The coverage of this book, with inputs from worldwide R&D scholars, academicians, and clinicians, will become a revolutionary and unique compendium in the field of providing quality dental care to the society.

The book consists of 16 chapters that describe perspectives of Intelligent and Sustainable Dentistry. Chapter "Internet of Things: A New Perspective to Digital Dentistry" provides an overview of the IoDT, which enables productivity and patient management tools for oral wellness, risk assessments, and research and aids patients in various dental fields, saving time and increasing efficiency. Chapter "Intelligent Prosthodontics, Intelligent Implantology, Intelligent Full Mouth Rehabilitation" discusses Intelligent prosthodontics that harnesses AI, 3D printing, dental robots, and digital tools to revolutionize dental care, offering precision, esthetics, and accessibility while incorporating data analytics and machine learning for personalized treatment. Chapter "Cryotherapy: A New Paragon in the Field of Endodontics" focuses on varied applications of cryotherapy in the field of endodontics such as after peri-radicular surgeries and during root canal treatment to minimize postoperative pain and inflammation.

Chapter "Design and FEA Analysis of Customized Temporomandibular Joint Implant" is related to biomechanical analysis of novel designed temporomandibular joint implant using finite element analysis software (Ansys workbench). Chapter "Latest Intelligent and Sustainable Materials for Dental Application" provides a comprehensive review of intelligent and sustainable materials used in dentistry, integrating digital technology in dentistry 4.0. The focus is on improving patient outcomes and experiences through the use of environmentally friendly and biocompatible materials. Chapter "Recent Advances in Sintering Techniques in Dental Ceramics" emphasizes the principles of speed-sintering and its applications in dental zirconia and advanced dental glass-ceramics. Chapter "Navigating Endodontic Irrigants: Applications and Advancements for Successful Root Canal Therapy" emphasizes a variety of solutions that have been advocated for irrigation during endodontic treatment such as saline, sodium hypochlorite, EDTA, and antiseptics. Chapter "Recent Advances in Newer Generation Composite Resin" discusses the ten recent advances in newer generation composite resin. Chapter "Materials for Tissue Engineering and Their Applications in Dentistry" explores the advances in materials science and engineering that make it possible to engineer and regenerate damaged oral soft and hard tissues. Chapter "Use of Bioinspired and Nanostructured Materials from Nature in Dentistry" describes the role of bioinspired and nanostructured materials like curcumin, chitin, chitosan, totarol, catechol, collagen, and nacre materials in dentistry to remodel dental implant materials and their surface to increase the lifespan of implants. Chapter "Dentistry 4.0's Role in COVID 19: Telemedicine and Online Education" emphasizes the significant obstacles, some of which have never been faced before, confronting dental education today. Chapter "The Era of Telemedicine: Current Applications" deals in depth with the use of technologies to aid in the attainment of health goals and to alter how health services are delivered all over the world. Chapter "Virtual Reality Distraction as an Effective and Intelligent Tool for Effective Behaviour Management" explores virtual reality (VR) that is set to become an essential component of a wide range of fields aimed at improving behaviour and decision-making in individuals of all ages and backgrounds. Chapter "Sustainable and Innovative Techniques for Improving Dental Health: Towards Effective Behavior Management" provides a comprehensive overview of the latest and most effective techniques for managing patient behavior during dental procedures. Chapter "A Mobile Application for Malocclusion Classification and Segmentation in Dental Images Using a Deep Learning Ensemble" focuses on developing an application for detecting malocclusions in the teeth through a deep learning model to mobilize door-to-door dentistry and democratize dental accessibility. Chapter "Doctor's Assistive System Using Augmented Reality Glass" describes AR glasses that display vital information, alerting doctors of abnormal conditions and storing medical records for future retrieval.

This book is intended for both the academia and the industry. Postgraduate students, Ph.D. students, and researchers in universities and institutions who are involved in the areas of **Intelligent and Sustainable Dentistry** will find this compilation useful.

The editors acknowledge the professional support received from CRC Press and express their gratitude for this opportunity.

Reader's observations, suggestions, and queries are welcome.

Editors
Ajay Kumar
Namrata Dogra
Sarita Rathee
Surbhi Bhatia Khan
M. S. Sidhu

Acknowledgments

The editors are grateful to the CRC Press for showing their interest in publishing this book in the buzz area of Intelligent and Sustainable Dentistry. The editors express their personal adulation and gratitude to Ms. Cindy Renee Carelli, (Executive Editor) CRC Press, for giving consent to publish our work. She undoubtedly imparted great and adept experience in terms of systematic and methodical staff who have helped the editors to compile and finalize the manuscript. The editors also extend their gratitude to Ms. Kaitlyn Fisher, Editorial Assistant, CRC Press, for supporting during her tenure.

The editors, Prof. (Dr.) Ajay Kumar, Dr. Namrata Dogra, Ms. Sarita Rathee, Dr. Surbhi Bhatia Khan, and Prof. M. S. Sidhu, wish to thank all the chapter contributors/authors for contributing their valuable research and experience to compile this volume. The chapter authors, corresponding author in particular, deserve special acknowledgments for bearing with the editors, who persistently kept bothering them with deadlines and with their remarks.

Finally, the editors dedicate this work to the divine creator and express their indebtedness to the "ALMIGHTY" for gifting them the power to yield their ideas and concepts into substantial manifestation. The editors believe that this book will enlighten the readers about each feature and characteristic of smart dentistry.

Prof. (Dr.) Ajay Kumar
Dr. Namrata Dogra
Ms. Sarita Rathee
Dr. Surbhi Bhatia Khan
Dr. M. S. Sidhu

About the Editors

Dr. Ajay Kumar is currently serving as a professor in the Department of Mechanical Engineering at School of Engineering and Technology, JECRC University, Jaipur, Rajasthan, India. He received his Ph.D. in the field of Advanced Manufacturing from Guru Jambheshwar University of Science & Technology, Hisar, India, after B.Tech. (Hons.) in mechanical engineering and M.Tech. (Distinction) in manufacturing and automation. His areas of research include Biomedical, Incremental Sheet Forming, Artificial Intelligence, Sustainable Materials, Additive Manufacturing, Mechatronics, Smart Manufacturing, Industry 4.0, Industrial Engineering Systems, Waste Management, and Optimization Techniques. He has over 80 publications in international journals of repute including SCOPUS, Web of Science, and SCI indexed database and refereed international conferences. He has organized various national and international events including an international conference on Mechatronics and Artificial Intelligence (ICMAI-2021) as conference chair. He is currently organising international conference on Artificial Intelligence, Advanced Materials, and Mechatronics Systems (AIAMMS-2023) as conference chair. He has more than 20 national and international patents to his credit. He has supervised more than 8 M.Tech and Ph.D. scholars and numerous undergraduate projects/thesis. He has a total of 15 years of experience in teaching and research. He is a guest editor of many reputed journals. He has contributed to many international conferences/symposiums as a session chair, expert speaker, and member of the editorial board. He has won several proficiency awards during the course of his career, including merit awards, best teacher awards, and so on. He has also co-authored and co-edited more than 15 books and proceedings. He has also authored many in-house course notes, lab manuals, monographs, and invited chapters in books. He has organized a series of Faculty Development Programs, International Conferences, workshops, and seminars for researchers, PhD, UG, and PG-level students. He is associated with many research, academic, and professional societies in various capacities.

Dr. Namrata Dogra is currently working as an associate professor, Department of Orthodontics, Faculty of Dental Sciences, SGT University. She has experience of 9 years in academics and patient care. She graduated from Santosh Dental College, Ghaziabad, in 2011, and completed her Post Graduation from the prestigious SGT Dental College, Gurugram, in 2015. She has presented various papers and posters at national and international conferences. Recently, she was awarded the research excellence award in July 2023 for her outstanding contribution in the field of research. She has more than 50 publications including articles and book chapters in various indexed (Scopus, Web of Science) national and international journals. She also holds a patent in her name entitled "Three Dimensional Facial Assessment Device". The main areas of interest include expansion appliances and CBCT. She is a life member of the Indian Orthodontic Society

Sarita Rathee is currently serving as an assistant professor in the Department of Electronics and Communication Engineering, School of Engineering and Technology, JECRC University, Jaipur, Rajasthan, India. She received her M.Tech (Distinction) in the field of Electrical and Electronics Engineering from Maharshi Dayanand University, Rohtak, India, after B.Tech. (Hons.) in electrical engineering. Her areas of research include artificial intelligence (AI), Internet of Things (IoT), cloud computing, Industry 4.0, and optimization techniques. She has over 15 publications in international journals of repute including Scopus and Web of Science database and refereed international conferences.

She has more than 7 national and international patents to her credit. She has supervised more than 4 M.Tech scholars and numerous undergraduate projects/thesis. She has a total of 5 years of experience in teaching and research. She has won several proficiency awards during the course of his career, including merit awards, best teacher awards, and so on.

She has also authored many in-house course notes, lab manuals, monographs, and invited chapters in books. She has attended a series of Faculty Development Programs, International Conferences, workshops, and seminars for researchers, PhD, UG, and PG-level students. She teaches the following courses at the graduate and postgraduate levels: instrumentation engineering, IOT, FACTS devices, power electronics, electric vehicles, and so on. She is associated with many research, academic, and professional societies in various capacities.

Dr. Surbhi Bhatia Khan has a doctorate in Computer Science and Engineering in machine learning and social media analytics. She is listed in the top 2% researchers released by Stanford University, USA. She earned Project Management Professional Certification from reputed Project Management Institute, USA. She is currently working in the Department of Data Science, School of Science, Engineering and Environment, University of Salford, Manchester, United Kingdom. She holds research positions at Lebanese American University. She also enjoys an adjunct professor position at Shoolini University, Himachal Pradesh, India. She has more than 12 years of academic and teaching experience in different universities. She has published 100+ papers in many reputed journals in high-indexed outlets. She has around 12 international patents from India, Australia, and the USA. She has successfully authored and edited 12 books. She has completed research-funded projects from Deanship of Scientific Research, Ministry of Education in Saudi Arabia and India. She is working in the research projects with UKRI, EU, RDIA, and also with King Salman Disability research programme. She is a senior member of IEEE, a member of IEEE Young Professionals, and ACM. She has chaired several international conferences and workshops and has delivered over 20 invited and keynote talks across the globe. She is serving as an academic editor, associate editor, and guest editor in many reputed journals. She is the awardee of the Research Excellence Award given by King Faisal University, Saudi Arabia, in 2021. Her areas of interest are information systems, sentiment analysis, machine learning, databases, and data science.

Dr. M. S. Sidhu graduated from Dr. Ahmed Dental College & Hospital, Calcutta University, in 1987. He topped in Calcutta University in three of the four University Examinations and won Honours and Gold Medals in all four professional years. He was awarded the prestigious Dr. R Ahmed Gold Medal for the best graduate for the batch of 1987. Dr. Sidhu received the prestigious Shri Mohan Wig Gold Medal for the Best Clinical Research work done at AIIMS as a postgraduate for the year 1990 presented by Shri Shankar Dayal Sharma, The President of India. Dr. J.G. Kannapan's Best Thesis Award in Orthodontics was presented in 1991 by the Indian Orthodontic Society.

He was the director Post Graduate Studies and professor and head of the Department of Orthodontics in Faculty of Dental Sciences at SGT University, Gurgaon. He is also a member of Board of Advisors of Indian Journal of Health Sciences and Care, SGT University, Gurgaon, and a member of Academic Council, Board of Management at the same university. He is an examiner and paper setter at postgraduate level for large number of universities including AIIMS, New Delhi. He is also a visiting professor at University of Detroit, Mercy School of Dentistry, Michigan, USA.

He was awarded the Best Teacher Award from SGT University, Gurgaon, in 2014, and P.P. Jacob's Award for the Best Scientific Paper Published in the Journal of Indian Orthodontic Society in 2014. He has 32 National & International Publications to his credit. He was also awarded for his contributions to the Indian Orthodontic society by Orthodontic study group of Delhi in April'15.

He was awarded Fellowship of prestigious National Academy of Medical Sciences, New Delhi. He is one of the pioneers to have obtained Diplomate in Indian Board of Orthodontics in 2006 for achieving excellence in Clinical Orthodontics. He is a member of American Association of Orthodontics, a fellow at World Federation of Orthodontics and Pierre Fauchard Academy, and the National Expert Committee of Dental Materials (Bureau of Indian Standard) B.I.S. of Dental Material. He is also a subject expert with J&K Public Service Commission.

He was the dean of Research & Development, Faculty Development and Institutional Planning and Development at SGT University.

He has been the director of IQAC at SGT University, Gurugram, for more than two years, where he was undertaking an exercise for NAAC accreditation of the whole University. Presently, he is in full-time private practice after being in academics and teaching for more than 3 decades.

Contributors

Ashtha Arya
Department of Conservative Dentistry
and Endodontics
SGT Dental College, Hospital and
Research Institute
Gurugram, Haryana, India

Wided Askri
Restorative Dentistry and Endodontics,
University Hospital Farhat Hached,
Faculty of Dental Medicine of
Monastir
University of Monastir
Monastir, Tunisia

M.S. Cholaathiraj
Department of Artificial Intelligence
and Machine Learning
Bannari Amman Institute of
Technology
Sathyamangalam, Tamil Nadu, India

Firas Chtioui
Restorative Dentistry and Endodontics,
University Hospital Farhat Hached,
Faculty of Dental Medicine of
Monastir
University of Monastir
Monastir, Tunisia

Deepika Dahiya
Department of Orthodontics
Shri Guru Gobind Singh Tricentenary
University
Budhera, Gurugram, Haryana, India

Namrata Dogra
Department of Orthodontics
Shri Guru Gobind Singh Tricentenary
University
Budhera, Gurugram, Haryana, India

K.R. Don
Department of Oral Pathology &
Microbiology
Sree Balaji Dental College and
Hospital, Bharath Institute of Higher
Education & Research (BIHER)
Bharath University
Chennai, Tamil Nadu, India

Sivaranjani Gali
Department of Prosthodontics
Faculty of Dental Sciences
M.S. Ramaiah University of Applied
Sciences
Bangalore, Karnataka, India

Imen Gnaba
Restorative Dentistry and Endodontics,
University Hospital Farhat Hached,
Faculty of Dental Medicine of
Monastir
University of Monastir
Monastir, Tunisia

Nilay Gupta
Center for Artificial Intelligence
ZHAW School of Engineering
Zurich, Switzerland

Prakash Chandra Gupta
School of Pharmaceutical Sciences
C.S.J.M. University
Kanpur, Uttar Pradesh, India

Roua Habachi
Restorative Dentistry and Endodontics
University Hospital Farhat Hached
Faculty of Dental Medicine of Monastir
University of Monastir
Monastir, Tunisia

Hayet Hajjami
University Hospital Farhat Hached,
  Faculty of Dental Medicine of
  Monastir
University of Monastir
Monastir, Tunisia

Labjar Houda
Faculty of Sciences and Technology
University Hassan II Casablanca
Mohammedia, Morocco

Archana Jaglan
Department of Orthodontics
Shri Guru Gobind Singh Tricentenary
  University
Budhera, Gurugram, Haryana, India

Sanjoli Jain
Department of Conservative Dentistry
  and Endodontics at SGT University
Gurugram, Haryana, India

Kalpana
School of Pharmaceutical Sciences
C.S.J.M. University
Kanpur, Uttar Pradesh, India

Manisha Khanna
Department of Orthodontics
Shri Guru Gobind Singh Tricentenary
  University
Budhera, Gurugram, Haryana, India

Serghini-Idrissi Malika
Laboratory of Spectroscopy, Molecular
  Modeling, Materials, Nanomaterials,
  Water and Environment
(LS3MN2E-CERNE2D)
Department of Chemistry, Faculty of
  Sciences
Mohammed V University in Rabat
Rabat, Morocco

Monalisa Mishra
Neural Developmental Biology Lab
Department of Life Science
NIT Rourkela
Rourkela, Odisha, India

Priyanka Mishra
School of Pharmaceutical Sciences
C.S.J.M. University
Kanpur, Uttar Pradesh, India

Reena Mittal
Prosthodontics and Crown & Bridge
Kothiwal Dental College and Research
  Centre
Moradabad, Uttar Pradesh, India

Subrata Mondal
Department of Mechanical Engineering
National Institute of Technical
  Teachers' Training and Research
  (NITTTR) Kolkata
Kolkata, West Bengal, India

Labjar Najoua
Laboratory of Spectroscopy, Molecular
  Modeling, Materials, Nanomaterials,
  Water and Environment
(LS3MN2E-CERNE2D), ENSAM
Mohammed V University in Rabat
Rabat, Morocco

K.R. Padma
Department of Biotechnology
Sri Padmavati Mahila Visvavidyalayam
  (Women's University)
Tirupati, Andhra Pradesh, India

Deepak Kumar Panda
Neural Developmental Biology Lab
Department of Life Science
NIT Rourkela
Rourkela, Odisha, India

Sujata Pandey
Prosthodontics and Crown & Bridge
Kothiwal Dental College and Research
    Centre
Moradabad, Uttar Pradesh, India

P. Kanaga Priya
Department of Computer Science and
    Engineering
KPR Institute of Engineering and
    Technology
Coimbatore, Tamil Nadu, India

A. Reethika
Department of Electronics and
    Communication Engineering
Sri Ramakrishna Engineering College
Coimbatore, Tamil Nadu, India

Kawthar Bel Haj Salah
Restorative Dentistry and Endodontics,
    University Hospital Farhat Hached,
    Faculty of Dental Medicine of
    Monastir
University of Monastir
Monastir, Tunisia

Sapana
Department of Conservative Dentistry
    and Endodontics
SGT University
Gurugram, Haryana, India

Mouadh Selmi
Restorative Dentistry and Endodontics,
    University Hospital Farhat Hached,
    Faculty of Dental Medicine of
    Monastir
University of Monastir
Monastir, Tunisia

Deepak Sharma
Department of Mechanical and
    Industrial Engineering
Indian Institute of Technology, Roorkee
Roorkee, Uttarakhand, India

Nisha Sharma
School of Pharmaceutical Sciences
C.S.J.M. University
Kanpur, Uttar Pradesh, India

Shruti Sharma
Department of Conservative Dentistry
    and Endodontics
SGT University
Budhera, Gurugram, Haryana, India

Mamta Singla
Department of Conservative Dentistry
    and Endodontics at SGT University
Gurugram, Haryana, India

Sanya Sinha
Department of Electronics and
    Communication Engineering
Birla Institute of Technology Mesra
    Patna Campus
Patna, Bihar, India

Lakhloufi Soraya
Laboratory of Spectroscopy, Molecular
    Modeling, Materials, Nanomaterials,
    Water and Environment,
    (LS3MN2E-CERNE2D), ENSAM
Mohammed V University in Rabat
Rabat, Morocco

El Hajjaji Souad
Laboratory of Spectroscopy, Molecular
  Modeling, Materials, Nanomaterials,
  Water and Environment
(LS3MN2E-CERNE2D)
Department of Chemistry, Faculty of
  Sciences
Mohammed V University in Rabat
Rabat, Morocco

Gourav Thapak
Department of Conservative Dentistry
  and Endodontics
SGT Dental College, Hospital and
  Research Institute
Gurugram, Haryana, India

1 Internet of Things

A New Perspective to Digital Dentistry

Nisha Sharma, Prakash Chandra Gupta,
Priyanka Mishra, and Kalpana
School of Pharmaceutical Sciences, C.S.J.M. University,
Kanpur, Uttar Pradesh, India

1.1 INTRODUCTION

The mouth and teeth are crucial components of human anatomy, supporting and facilitating vital physiological processes, and the mouth is a key element of individual identification. Based on the concepts already in place, oral health can be described as having multiple dimensions, covering the physical, psychological, emotional, and social realms crucial to a healthy lifestyle [1]. A person's oral health is subjective and progressive, allowing them to eat, speak, smile, and interact with others without experiencing pain, discomfort, or humiliation. A person's capacity to adjust to physiological changes as they occur throughout life and to take care of their teeth and mouth via individual self-care is reflected in their oral health [2]. Oral diseases are extremely common across the life cycle and have a significant detrimental impact on people, communities, and society as a whole, even though they are largely preventable.

The growing incidence of dental problems in many low- and middle-income nations, which can be attributed to broader social, economic, and commercial trends, is of special concern as a worldwide public health issue [3]. The frequency and severity of oral illnesses are strongly and consistently correlated with socioeconomic status. As an early sign of population ill health associated with lack, oral illnesses might thus be seen as a sensitive clinical measure of socioeconomic disadvantage [4].

The oral health disparities and prevalence of oral illnesses throughout the community can be attributed to broader social and economic factors, which serve as underlying causes. The quality of lifestyle for persons impacted by oral disorders is significantly reduced because they are amongst the most prevalent illnesses in the world that cause substantial health and financial consequences [5].

The soft and hard tissues of the oral cavity are susceptible to a variety of diseases and conditions, including a variety of craniofacial disorders, congenital deformities, traumas, and different infections [6]. Dental caries, periodontal disease, tooth loss, and cancer of the lips and mouth are among the well-known and dangerous mouth disorders

DOI: 10.1201/9781003404934-1

in humankind. Worldwide, oral illness is thought to impact close to 3.5 billion individuals [7]. To provide patients with high-quality care, emerging innovations are integrating a variety of alternatives into dentistry practices. As a result, digitalization in dentistry has been incorporated into every facet of dental care.

1.2 COMMON ORAL DISEASES

Oral ailments are degenerative, chronic ailments that harm the oral cavity and teeth. One of the most prevalent disorders in people is oral disease. The concept of oral wellness encompasses the absence of pain, cancer, infections, blisters in the mouth, periodontal disease, decay and loss of teeth, and other ailments that restrict the capability for biting, gnawing, smiling, talking, and psychosocial well-being. The most typical problems of the mouth are bad odor, gum disease, mouth sores, decay and tooth loss, difficulty with wisdom tooth, and unpleasant smiles [8]. Figure 1.1 shows the frequently encountered oral diseases.

1.2.1 DENTAL CARIES

The phrase "dental caries" was first documented in 1634 and originated from the Latin term "Caries" signifying to decay and the old Irish arachrinn, it decays. Dental caries (tooth decay), as described by the World Health Organisation (WHO), is the breakdown of the tooth's enamel layer by acidic byproducts generated by the activity of bacterial metabolism on dietary sugars [9]. It is well recognized that tooth decay constitutes amongst widely spread chronic infectious pediatric diseases and is a preventable oral health issue [10]. Dental caries has a significant impact on a substantial portion of the global population, affecting more than 2.4 billion individuals, which accounts for approximately 36% of the worldwide populace [11] and causes the loss of primary teeth in over 530 million children worldwide [12].

Dental caries is a multifaceted phenomenon that arises from a confluence of factors, encompassing host vulnerability, bacterial presence, nutritional factors, and the passage of time. The interplay between bacteria and a diet rich in sugars generates acid, which contributes to the formation of cavities in teeth [13]. Acid damages the enamel surface as a consequence, and if the damage is not noticed, the tooth will gradually deteriorate. Tooth pain, pulpitis, tooth loss, dental discoloration, and Ludwig angina are only a few of the consequences associated with dental caries [11].

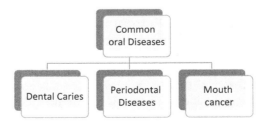

FIGURE 1.1   Types of common oral diseases.

1.2.1.1 Pathophysiology of Dental Caries

i. Role of Microbes

Streptococcus mutans is a species of acidogenic-aciduric bacteria that is well-known for being significantly engaged in cariogenic actions, such as childhood caries, enamel carious scars, cavitated lesions, or carious dentine. Numerous epidemiological and *in vitro* research urge that *S. sobrinus* might be cariogenic to a greater extent than *S. mutans* under undetermined conditions. The network of microbial organisms involved is extremely complex and diverse and includes bacteria, *saccharolytic yeasts* (like *Candida albicans*), Archaea (which speeds up fermentation by consuming byproducts like CO_2 and H_2), and bacteriophages (which speed up lateral gene transfer and consequently evolution).

Each cavity may have a unique demineralizing consortium of living things and genes, but the following direct rules apply to all cavities:

a. Existence of acidogenic-aciduric microbes and its capacity to adhere to the pellicle-laminated exterior of teeth, as well as their potential positive effects on other microorganisms such as bifidobacteria and lactobacilli [14].
b. Environmental factors such as the presence of low-molecular sugary foods, such as sucrose, plus a concurrent low redox potential, contribute to favorable conditions for the establishment of this particular species. Low oxygen and high sugar produce acid quickly during fermentation. With these concepts, it is feasible to determine carious tissue and the need for excavation of tissue to stop further disintegration.

ii. Demineralization and Remineralization

Biofilm bacteria metabolize carbs that can ferment into organic acids, mainly lactic acid. The accumulation of metabolic by-products from bacteria within the fluid phase of the biofilm results in a reduction in pH and demineralization of dental enamel.

The pathophysiology of dental caries involves several stages:

a. **Demineralization:** This is the initial stage of dental caries, where acid producing bacteria residing in the dental plaque cause the demineralization of the enamel surface of the tooth.
b. **Formation of a cavity:** As the demineralization continues, the enamel surface breaks down and a cavity is formed in the tooth.
c. **Spread of caries:** If the cavity is not treated, caries can progress to the underlying dentin and eventually to the pulp, which contains the nerves and blood vessels. This can lead to toothache and infection.
d. **Inflammation and necrosis:** As the caries spreads, the pulp becomes inflamed and may eventually die, resulting in abscess formation.
e. **Tooth loss:** If left untreated, dental caries might ultimately lead to the extraction of the affected tooth.

1.2.1.2　Types of Dental Caries

1.2.1.2.1　Primary Caries (Incipient Caries)

The early phases of demineralization, also known as primary carious lesions, exhibit vulnerability to either reversal, cessation, or advancement toward cavitation. The observed dental abnormalities are characterized as white spot lesions or smooth surface caries, which are considered active lesions confined solely to the enamel layer [15]. The bacteria that invade the growing lesion penetrate both the dentin-penetrating lesion and the innermost layers of enamel in not having any of cavities, extending up to the amelodentinal junction.

The most promising methods for early dental caries detection are those based on optical qualities (fluorescence, ultrasonic system, tracer dye, transillumination, etc.) [16]. As the porosity beneath the enamel surface increases, light is scattered and enamel translucency is lost, giving the incipient lesion a white or brown spotlike appearance, especially when dried. The white, powdery tint will go away after rehydrating.

Active lesions are commonly observed in locations with plaque stagnancy and near the gingival border. From a clinical perspective, it is observed that arrested lesions often have smooth surfaces reflecting light, hence creating a shining effect [17].

1.2.1.2.2　Secondary Caries (Recurrent Caries)

The term "lesions at the edges of existing restorations" [18] or "caries caused by restorations or sealants" has been used to describe secondary (or recurring) caries. Secondary caries pathogenesis implies a similar idea as other caries lesions. Secondary caries presents a multifaceted and demanding mechanism that encompasses several factors associated with "typical" caries, along with unique attributes related to the repair and restoration materials [19].

Secondary caries may be

a. directly linked to inadequate restoration due to several factors, namely the presence of spaces in the repair and the tooth. These spaces create an opportunity for acidic fluids or microbes to infiltrate the junction, leading to negative outcomes,

b. randomly connected with an intact restoration (e.g., through a poor buffering effect of the restoration in contrast to tooth hard tissue), or

c. not directly linked with the restoration but rather with primary caries adjoining to prevailing restorations (primarily when the cavities are small and the restorations are not in contact with the tooth). But in each of the three scenarios, the well-known risk factors for caries – a cariogenic colony, availability of fermentable carbohydrates, an unbalanced loss in minerals, and a loss of tooth hard tissue must be present [20,21].

There have been a lot of *in vitro* investigations utilizing different secondary caries models, and the results show that the admissible gap measures of the anomaly range from 60 to 1,000 m [22,23] with in-situ testing supporting the validity of the range of measured gap widths.

Regardless of the restoration material, up to 90% of secondary carious lesions are located around the gingival margin of restorations [24,25]. Patients with high-risk caries have a much higher probability of unsuccessful restoration owing to secondary caries than with low-risk caries [26]. There is proof that secondary caries and restoration longevity are related to socioeconomic level [27,28]. The caliber of the repair used is correlated with secondary caries to some extent. Screening of secondary caries may be achieved by employing a variety of methods, such as inspections that are visible, tactile, radiographic, optical fluorescence, etc. quantitatively based on light-augmented fluorescence [29]. To prolong the life of the restoration, identified secondary caries can be changed or, if deficient to some extent, can be taken into consideration for repair or resealing.

1.2.1.2.3   Arrested Caries

Clinical indicators of arrested caries in dentine include a hard surface with a yellow to dark brown color. Arrested carious lesions are more frequently observed on the lingual and labial surfaces of teeth than on interproximal. Large crystals obstruct the dentinal tubules in the region amongst the soft and hard dentine in cases of caries that have gotten arrested.

Stages of Arrested Caries
  a. **First stage:** The mineral in the vicinity of intertubular dentine is dissolved by the approaching bacteria's acids. A saturation of calcium, magnesium, and phosphate ions occurs in the tubule fluid. If the bacterial metabolic activity is not decreased, the lesions will worsen. If there is less acid production, the second step may happen.
  b. **Second stage:** Tricalcium phosphate crystals of enormous sizes form as the saturated solution precipitates. Despite being relatively soluble, these crystals nonetheless clog the tubule.
  c. **Third stage:** Collagen is secreted into the dentin tube by the odontoblast process, which is shielded by the large crystals obstructing the tubule. Hydroxyapatite accumulates in small, plate-like crystals that are more potent tubule blockers than tricalcium phosphate because they are less soluble. Crystallization also simultaneously takes place in tubular dentine. Such caries is unlikely to be halted in high-risk patients [30].

1.2.1.3   Interventions to Prevent and Treat Dental Caries

  a. **Oral hygiene:** Regular elimination of plaque by brushing, flossing, and rinsing constitutes the best strategies to avoid oral cavity and periodontal disease. This is because dental caries cannot advance without the bacteria found in dental plaques.
  b. **Fluoride application:** By inhibiting demineralization of the crystal framework within the tooth and promoting remineralization, fluoride helps to prevent dental cavities. The remineralized surface is acid-resistant. Fluoride also prevents the activity of bacterial enzymes [31].
  c. **Pit and fissure sealants:** Tooth caries predominantly forms in the pits and fissures of teeth throughout early childhood. Pits and fissures are more

likely to develop oral cavities due to the anatomical tendency for plaque deposition and their size, which makes oral care difficult. Filling anomalies with flowable repair material reduces morphological vulnerability [32].

d. **Xylitol:** Higher consumption of sucrose is linked with an elevated vulnerability to dental caries, a widely acknowledged oral health condition mostly attributed to the consumption of sugar. To lower the risk of cavities, sugar alternatives like xylitol are used. Xylitol is both non-cariogenic and anti-cariogenic with a sweet flavor similar to sugar. It prevents sucrose molecules from interacting with *Mutans streptococci* (MS), preventing the metabolic process. Additionally, it lessens the prevalence and adhesion capacity of MS [33].

e. **Vaccine:** Efforts have been undertaken to develop a vaccine for dental caries, as it is recognized as an infectious microbiological disease. Protein-carbohydrate conjugates, recombinant peptides, and DNA-established vaccines have been useful. Targeting MS receptors or inhibiting glucosyl transferases can trigger an immunological response. While oral fluids are difficult to produce and retain high antibody levels, neither of these vaccines has reached the market [34].

1.2.2 PERIODONTAL DISEASES

An infection of the periodontium causes periodontitis. While "perio" denotes the gingiva and other tissues around teeth, "dont" refers to a tooth, and "itis" to inflammation. Therefore, the term "periodontitis" as a whole denotes chronic gingival inflammation, dental cement, alveolar bone, and periodontal ligaments. According to the WHO, this particular ailment is classified as a chronic condition that exhibits a high risk for worldwide dissemination [35]. Dental plaque accumulates in the vicinity of the teeth, resulting in the formation of microbial biofilms comprising bacteria. Subsequently, this process leads to the development of localized gingival irritation. Failure to take this aspect into account leads to the development of a persistent periodontal disease condition. The periodontal framework undergoes degradation through the action of detrimental byproducts and enzymes released by periodontal biofilms of leucotoxins, collagenase, fibrinolysis, and different Bacteroids spp. like *B. intermedius*, *B. gingivalis*, and fusiform organisms like *Actinobacillus actinomycetem* comitans, *Wollina recta*, and Eikenella spp.; *Porphyromonas gingivalis*; Taneerella for synthesis; various bacilli and cocci; spirochetes; and amoebas and trichomonads [36,37]. The phrase "Periodontal Pocket" denotes the anatomical space that arises across the gingiva and the tooth [38].

Plaque on the teeth is primarily the cause of gingivitis and periodontitis. Around 150 different species of bacteria have been found in a single human, while 800 different species have been found in tooth calculus. Gram-negative anaerobic bacteria, spirochetes, and even viruses are among the species. When these microorganisms are out of balance, it creates a "pathogenic unit," which leads to persistent periodontal disease [39].

1.2.2.1 Different Forms of Periodontitis

a. **Gingivitis:** Gingivitis, also known as gum inflammation, can be effectively managed by the implementation of proper dental hygiene practices.

b. **Chronic periodontitis:** Persistent periodontitis is characterized by symptoms such as bleeding during oral hygiene practices, pronounced halitosis, and continuous swelling of the gums. The permanent degeneration of bone, ligaments, and epithelial tissue. The clinical manifestations of serious periodontitis are identical to those observed in cases of chronic periodontitis [40].

c. **Necrotizing ulcerative gingivitis:** It primarily affects those who have HIV infection, are undergoing suppressive immune therapy, or are experiencing nutritional deficiency. Necrosis refers to the process of cellular or tissue death in living organisms. This phenomenon predominantly develops when individuals do not receive a sufficiently nutritious diet.

d. **Peri-implant mucositis:** It is a clinical manifestation characterized by inflammation of the soft tissues about the dental implants, without concomitant evidence of bone resorption. The gingival tissue around dental implants may exhibit erythema or tenderness, and the act of brushing may induce bleeding [41].

e. **Systemic chronic periodontitis:** It is a type of chronic periodontal disease commonly observed in patients with systemic syndromes. Various systemic disorders, like cardiovascular disease, diabetes, and lung disease, have the potential to induce inflammatory processes in the gums [42].

1.2.2.2 Treatments of Periodontal Disease

The treatment plan for periodontal diseases is categorized into three phases which are specified in Table 1.1.

1.2.2.3 Oral Cancer

Oral carcinoma is a category of carcinoma of head and neck, affecting mostly the anterior two-thirds of the tongue, the gums, the mucous membranes of the lips and cheeks, the sublingual base of the oral cavity, the hard palate, and the tiny retromolar area. The existence of a lump or non-healing sore or ulcer that has

TABLE 1.1

Treatments of Periodontal Disease [43]

Initial Treatment and Non-surgical Treatments	Corrective Therapy or Surgical Treatments	Supportive Therapy
• Brushing teeth and cleaning between teeth	• Flap surgery, soft tissue grafting, bone grafting,	• Routine examinations of the patient
• Pharmacological additive agent	• tissue-stimulating proteins,	• track their periodontal health and re-educate them
• Scaling, Root planning, and Antibiotics	• reconstructive surgery, reactive surgery, regenerative surgery, and other surgeries.	• maintaining good oral hygiene and preventing plaque buildup

persisted for more than 14 days, soft red, white, or dotted patches in red or white in the oral parts, trouble speaking, chewing, or jaw movement, malocclusion or ill-fitting prosthetic teeth, and abrupt loss in weight are all indications of oral cancer. In total, 90% of oral carcinomas are histologically squamous cell carcinomas, making them the sixth most typical cancer in the world by prevalence [44]. In severe instances, the five-year survival rate is around 50%, with women having a better prognosis. The prognoses of these individuals are consistently impacted by factors such as age, lymph node contribution, and the dimensions and position of the initial malignancy. Premalignant conditions, tobacco, betel nut, alcohol consumption, inadequate oral hygiene, UV rays, Epstein-Barr virus, and Human Papillomavirus (HPV), particularly HPV 16 and 18, are the most prevalent risk factors. By grading the malignancy, the degree of oral cancer spread is estimated [45]. The TNM (Tumor, Lymph nodes, metastasis) system, is the most widely used staging approach for oral cancer size. Tumor size is further categorized from 1 to 4; a higher number denotes a larger size. N indicates the extent to which cancer has progressed to lymph nodes close to the organ. Additional classifications include N0 (no spread), N1, N2, and N3. The N1–N3 displays the number and location of lymph nodes that are implicated. Cancer that advances to various parts of the body through lymphatic or blood vessels is known as metastasizing [46].

Despite the serious consequences of oral disorders, the majority of individuals are afraid to go to the dentist or just underestimate how much valuable is dental health. Additionally, the screening and diagnosing procedures tend to be expensive when patients do visit. People are subsequently discouraged from continuing with the recommended follow-ups as a result. In the end, this leads to people putting off taking care of their dental health until it gets too late. It is not surprising that experts in the area are seeking new methods to give patients a more comfortable experience throughout the full dental care procedure since dentistry has evolved into a technologically driven healthcare domain. Due to the prevalent skepticism and anxieties related to visiting the dentist, the dental care sector was motivated to come up with innovative techniques to decrease patient suffering, provide improved outcomes, speed up appointments, and establish satisfactory visits for patients. IoT in dentistry is mainly focused on early detection approaches by identifying the source of orthodontic problems as quickly as possible by continually communicating data among the patient and the dentist.

1.3 DIGITALIZATION IN DENTISTRY

Digital dentistry is the practice of doing dental treatments without the use of traditional electrical or mechanical tools and instead employing dental innovations or gadgets.

The use of different innovations, such as digital radiographs (DR), digital scans [47], cone beam computed tomography (CBCT for imaging of hard tissues), 3D printing [48], augmented (AR), and virtual reality technology (VR) supported dental replacement procedures, has allowed the world to adapt to a variety of intelligent digital technologies [49].

This section seeks to summarize the fundamentals of the IoT idea and its dental applications.

1.3.1 INTERNET OF THINGS (IoT)

IoT represents the newest and most clever ideas to emerge. IoT is a method of machine-to-machine communication.

IoT transforms the globe into a smarter world and establishes an emblem in practically all industries by handling large data. There are many uses for IoT, and it is essential in the age of robotics. In addition, it can be applied to industries including robotics, agriculture, dentistry, medicine, the military, and government work [50]. Integrating sensors along with other technological gadgets into the internet is a key component of the IoT. These gadgets can be watched over and managed from any location around the world. In essence, the data collected from the sensor or gadget is forwarded to the core server, where it is made accessible to the end user. The information is handled following the client's requests [51].

IoT is a notable breakthrough in technology, i.e., a combination of multiple technologies like Artificial Intelligence, Cloud Computing, Data Science, Internetworking, Security, etc. (Figure 1.2) that quickly gained momentum in tele-communication to give solutions. The IoT possesses a significant impact on several attributes of normal life and possible user activities, which undoubtedly constitutes its primary advantage. The differentiation of the impact and market demand of the IoT can be delineated by considering many criteria, including user categorization (private versus commercial). For private users, the demand for the IoT is most pronounced in areas like "convalescent home," "e-Health," "e-education," etc. Likewise, the impact of commercial and business users may be seen in fields such as "robotization," "business management process," "industrial production," "artful transportation of people/goods," etc. [52].

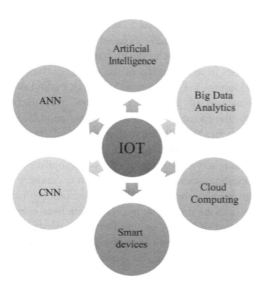

FIGURE 1.2 Combination of multiple technologies IoT.

(IoT, is a blend of AI, Big data analytics, cloud computing, ANN, CNN, smart devices, etc.)

On a never-before-seen scale, it has encroached upon every sector of the economy, particularly "Health-Care." The IoMT is an approach of IoT for medical and health-related procedures (such as data collecting, research analysis, and precise monitoring). IoMT has thus been referred to as "Smart-Healthcare" due to the inclusion of technology and its ongoing improvements for marketing a digitized system with readily accessible "Medical-Sciences" resources [53].

IoT has many advantages for the medical industry, including tracking fitness (with smart bands), alerting emergency systems, and more. These health-checking tools can range from simple ones that measure blood pressure and heart rate to sophisticated ones that can keep track of complex implants like pacemakers. IoT has expanded into dentistry as well as the medical field, giving rise to the IoDT. IoT has an extensive scope in the dental industry, which has significantly changed how diagnoses and treatments are carried out. IoT has altered the way that biomechanical treatment is practised in medicine in addition to altering the face of ideology [54].

1.3.2 INTERNET OF DENTAL THINGS IoDT

Dental professionals are genuinely searching for novel technologies to enable them to deliver precise diagnoses and efficient interventions; therefore, the IoT is rapidly evolving into a crucial component of dentistry. IoDT and IoMT work together to create an "IoT Cloud" that is important for dentistry. IoT is described as "a worldwide network for the Information Society that aims at permitting sophisticated services by bringing together (physical and virtual) things based on, current and progressive, compatible information and communication technologies" by the International Telecommunication Union, which views it as a far-reaching perception with technological and social repercussions. IoT can be broadly defined as the anytime, anywhere connectedness of anything. IoDT solutions can be widely accessed as a result of the development and expansion of inexpensive connections in developing and underdeveloped nations. This will improve dental health in remote areas of the world and reduce the need for dental care as a whole. The industrial IoT, sometimes known as the Industrial Internet, was one of the first implementations of IoT in the industry (manufacturing) domain. The machinery or objects in the factories converse with one another.

The IoT of Vehicles, Health IoT, Internet of Personal Health (IoPH), Internet of M-health Things (M-IoT), and Agriculture IoT are some of the other domains where there is adoption, according to the industrial sector's accomplished adoptions. One of the most untapped, yet appealing markets for IoT adoption is dentistry. In dentistry, there is a lot of investigation being done on intelligent instruments (smart brushes, smart brackets). IoT is going to make it possible to collect data from connected mouthwashes, flossers, brackets, and other devices. One can forecast a person's oral health using the data from these devices in conjunction with the pathological parameters gathered by wearable technology, and afterwards decide on the person's future treatment plan [55].

1.3.3 ARTIFICIAL INTELLIGENCE (AI)

AI describes several techniques used to program machines to function intelligently like humans. Building independent devices involves fusing vast amounts of information with cutting-edge algorithms. AI improves existing systems and speeds up break-throughs in healthcare. In addition to being applied to diagnose patients and examine prospective therapies, it is also utilized to evaluate the effects on public health [56].

An increasing number of industries stand to gain from the use of AI, such as the field of surgical (e.g., smart systems for supported surgery, video-surgery, automated medical diagnosis (e.g., verdict support diagnosis mechanisms out of images, and newly invented personalized medicine, offering the predisposition to diseases, diagnosis, and selection of the most effective therapy for a particular patient [57,58]. Although it might not appear that developments in AI have had much of an influence on dentistry, there have been major developments in domains like image-based automatic recognition of illnesses as well as diagnosis-assistant systems, image splitting for computational recognition of oral characteristics, and betterment of resolution of dentistry-related images. On the robotics front, some developments have made it possible to use robotic assistance in dentistry. In any case, the new digital dentistry paradigm leaves many aspects of dentistry open to the use of AI approaches [59].

Towards the 3D design of the dental prosthesis, preliminary simulations predicted on the basis of convolutional neural networks (CNNs) and 2D and 3D imaging have been created with extremely promising outcomes. A library of knowledge can be developed to aid in devising optimized medical care using big data and AI techniques due to industrial attempts to electronically archive data from a lot of patients for subsequent analysis. Many articles linking AI and Machine learning (ML) to dentistry have recently been published. Researchers explored the subject from a clinical perspective, concentrating either on particular AI working areas of dentistry, or on particular AI research fields of dentistry (dental and maxillofacial radiology, orthodontics, dental caries forensic odontology) [60–62].

1.3.4 Artificial Neural Networks (ANNs)

ANNs are learning algorithms designed to mimic how biological neural networks operate. They have been utilized to address a wide range of issues and apply to supervised, unsupervised, and reinforcement learning challenges. An ANN's basic building block is a system of interlinked layers with active neurons; the term "deep" denotes an ANN with a significant number and neurons per layer.

One of the most captivating domains of research is the utilization of deep learning (DL) within the field of dentistry. These techniques have the capability to identify certain attributes from large image databases derived from various biological signals or additional sources of information, thereby contributing to the development of decision-making support systems with outstanding accuracy [63].

1.3.5 Applications of Deep Learning/IoT

It emphasizes three segments of applications: Ailments or damage recognition, image partitioning and utilization, and image improvement employing the implementation of Generative Adversarial Neural Networks. CNNs have generated encouraging outcomes in the discipline of diagnosis and prediction, particularly in the domains of radiology and pathology.

Several radiographic formats, clinical characteristics, near-infrared trans-illumination pictures, and periapical imaging have all been employed efficiently by ANNs to diagnose dental caries [64,65]. The detection of carcinoma of mouth has also benefited from the use of DL, whether via the usage of hyperspectral or photographic pictures, other medical image categories, or clinical data [66]. To identify and diagnose dental cavities in the premolar and molar teeth, a particular study employed a beforehand trained Google Net Inception v3 CNN network [67]. Transfer learning (TL) was trained on a dataset consisting of 3,000 periapical radiography images. The published rate of accurateness for diagnosing dental caries in premolars and molars were 89.0% and 88.0%, respectively. In recent times, a study revealed that taking advantage of radiography pictures facilitated the implementation of a CNN-based model known as U-Net for the purpose of caries diagnosis. The model demonstrated a noteworthy reliability rate of 80% [68]. Before caries excavation, the use of clinical information on deep feedforward neural networks (FFNNs) has been examined for the estimation of post Streptococcus mutations and the existence of caries. CNNs were utilized to examine and predict oral cancer, with a 7-fold cross-validation accuracy of 91.4% using hyperspectral pictures as the input. To achieve a 92.3% accuracy rate, photographic photos and TL were combined with a big database of more than 40,000 images [69]. With fewer successes, other studies have concentrated on CNN models utilizing different forms of imaging (histopathological, x-ray, or CBCT scans), or deep ANNs employing clinical characteristics [70].

To season a CNN system for the identification and projection of periodontally weakened teeth using radiographic pictures of different diseases, TL was employed. When the DL algorithm was used for the periapical dataset (which had a total of 1,840 samples), the accuracy of the examination of periodontal disease was found to be 81.0% for premolars and 76.7% for molars. In addition, several methods, such as shallow FFNNs and CNNs, have been utilized to arrive at a diagnosis of gingivitis illness. Gingivitis was diagnosed by employing an extreme learning machine, which is an easy method of training a model by making use of arbitrarily generated variables [71]. This machine was trained on a basic ANN design with characteristics that were manually retrieved. The contrast-limited adaptive histogram equalization and the gray-level concurrence array were the computational methods that were utilized to extract the features. The dataset that the scientists worked with had a total of 93 digital photos, 58 of which were taken from gingivitis patients, while the remaining 35 were taken from healthy patients serving as controls. The methodology was devised by expanding the already existing research, and the findings showed improvements, with the accuracy reaching 74%, the sensitivity reaching 75%, and the specificity reaching 73%. CNNs were also utilized for the early diagnosis of the condition in intraoral imaging, with very successful outcomes [72].

A smart IoDT platform was suggested which makes use of the Mask-regional-based CNN (RCNN) network for the identification and categorization of seven distinct oral disorders, and it achieves an accuracy level of 93.6% on average [73].

Radiographs are helpful in the diagnosis of periodontal bone loss, osteoporosis, maxillary cyst-like lesions, periapical illness, apical lesions, lesions identification, and root fractures. Other conditions that can be diagnosed with radiographs include osteoporosis and maxillary cyst-like lesions [74].

1.3.6 FUTURE SCOPE OF IoT-BASED DENTAL TREATMENT

1.3.6.1 Oral Disease Prevention

It gives people an easy way to test themselves. With the help of AI analysis, dental conditions can be found and stopped beforehand, and people's knowledge of how to safeguard their teeth can be raised.

1.3.6.2 Intelligent Analysis

Employing a machine learning algorithm, AI can efficiently and precisely find oral conditions in oral images. This helps doctors make diagnoses and saves time on therapy.

1.3.6.3 Remote Medical Service

It facilitates a scheduled visit to the doctor nearby to them and tells them how to get medical care quickly and cheaply. This novel internet approach allows the use of tools that aren't being used for dental diagnostics. Patients have the opportunity to address their oral health concerns at a reduced cost due to two factors. Firstly, the intelligent oral imaging technology is available at a lower price point. Secondly, the technology has successfully engaged vacant dental clinics to accommodate patients [73].

1.4 CONCLUSION

Oral ailments are complex, multifaceted conditions that can be treated with traditional methods as well as modern technologies. Oral wellness has been shown to have both a direct and indirect impact on general health. The pervasiveness and severeness of oral illnesses can be prevented and reduced with the help of dentists.

Early oral disorders are caused by a variety of etiological factors, including dietary carbohydrate intake, oral biofilm, biofilm pH, fluoridation use, and irregular dental hygiene practices. Intraoral sensors, newer smartphones with app integration, IoDT, and cloud servers may all readily track these variables daily. It is simple to monitor cariogenic parameters such as biofilm pH, biofilm presence, and oral cavity temperature using intraoral sensors attached to appliances. This information is continuously gathered from the patient's mouth and sent to a cloud server via a smartphone or tablet app. The IoDT, AI, and telemedicine are used to analyse data. IoDT is a cutting-edge technology that was developed to prevent dental cavities [54].

This IoDT-based oral care approach could be implemented with ease in the oral data collecting stage and clinical monitoring procedure. Additionally, it offers data analysis, early dental caries identification, and avoidance of causes. At the community level, this concept may be simply implemented. There are currently few concrete examples supporting the IoDT notion. Therefore, additional investigation on IoDT will substantially enhance the detection and management of periodontitis, carcinoma of head and neck, and additional mouth disorders, as well as the diagnosis of dental caries. IoDT is going to be crucial in the years to come for data collecting and monitoring in the oral dental industry, and it could assist dentists in creating cutting-edge safety evaluation techniques.

1.5 ACKNOWLEDGMENT

The authors are grateful to Prof. Vinay Kumar Pathak, Vice-Chancellor, C.S.J.M. University for his consistent motivation and support.

REFERENCES

1. Kassebaum, N.J., A.G.C. Smith, E. Bernabé, T.D. Fleming, A.E. Reynolds, T. Vos, C.J.L. Murray, et al. 2017. "Global, Regional, and National Prevalence, Incidence, and Disability-Adjusted Life Years for Oral Conditions for 195 Countries, 1990–2015: A Systematic Analysis for the Global Burden of Diseases, Injuries, and Risk Factors." *Journal of Dental Research* 96 (4): 380–387. 10.1177/002203451 7693566

2. Petersen, Poul Erik, Denis Bourgeois, Hiroshi Ogawa, Saskia Estupinan-Day, and Charlotte Ndiaye. 2005. "The Global Burden of Oral Diseases and Risks to Oral Health." *Bulletin of the World Health Organization* 83 (9): 661–669. https://apps. who.int/iris/handle/10665/269475

3. Yee, Robert, and Aubrey Sheiham. 2002. "The Burden of Restorative Dental Treatment for Children in Third World Countries." *International Dental Journal* 52(1): 1–9. 10.1111/j.1875-595X.2002.tb00589.x

4. Guan, Min, Ola A. Nada, Juan-juan Wu, Jiang-ling Sun, Na Li, Li-ming Chen, and Tai-ming Dai. 2021. "Dental Caries and Associated Factors in 3–5-Year-Old Children in Guizhou Province, China: An Epidemiological Survey (2015–2016)." *Frontiers in Public Health* 9 (September). 10.3389/fpubh.2021.747371

5. Hegde, Dr Mithra N, Dr Priyadarshini Hegde, Dr Raksha Bhat, Dr Ravi Dahiya, and Dr Lakshmi Nidhi Rao. 2011. "Prevalence of Dental Caries in Anterior Teeth in South Canara Population – a Three Year Epidemiological Study." *Indian Journal of Applied Research* 4 (2): 32–34. 10.15373/2249555x/feb2014/127

6. Chapple, I. L. C. 2014. "Time to Take Periodontitis Seriously." *British Medical Journal* 348 (apr10 1): g2645–g2645. 10.1136/bmj.g2645

7. Shitie, Anguach, Rahel Addis, Abebe Tilahun, and Wassie Negash. 2021. "Prevalence of Dental Caries and Its Associated Factors among Primary School Children in Ethiopia." *International Journal of Dentistry* 2021 (March): e6637196. 10.1155/2021/6637196

8. Yap, Adrian. 2017. "Oral Health Equals Total Health: A Brief Review." *Journal of Dentistry Indonesia* 24 (2). 10.14693/jdi.v24i2.1122

9. WHO. 2017. "Sugars and Dental Caries." *World Health Organisation*, Geneva, Switzerland.

10. Syreen, Dr Shagufta. 2018. "Prevalence of Dental Caries among Children Residing in Muslim Dominated Area of Laheriasarai, Darbhanga." *Journal of Medical Science and Clinical Research* 6 (12). 10.18535/jmscr/v6i12.131

11. Yadav, Khushbu, and Satyam Prakash. 2016. "Dental Caries: A Review." *Asian Journal of Biomedical and Pharmaceutical Sciences* 6 (53): 01–07. 10.15272/ ajbps.v6i53.773

12. WHO. 2020. "Oral Health." *World Health Organisation*, Geneva, Switzerland.

13. Chugh, Vinay K, Kushal K Sahu, and Ankita Chugh. 2018. "Prevalence and Risk Factors for Dental Caries among Preschool Children: A Cross-Sectional Study in Eastern India." *International Journal of Clinical Pediatric Dentistry* 11 (3): 238–243. 10.5005/jp-journals-10005-1518

14. Conrads, Georg, and Imad About. 2018. "Pathophysiology of Dental Caries." *Caries Excavation: Evolution of Treating Cavitated Carious Lesions*, 1–10. 10.1159/0004 87826

15. Featherstone, J.D.B. 2004. "The Continuum of Dental Caries—Evidence for a Dynamic Disease Process." *Journal of Dental Research* 83 (1): 39–42. 10.1177/1544 05910408301s08

16. Barberia, Elena, Myriam Maroto, Marcela Arenas, and Cristina Cardoso Silva. 2008. "A Clinical Study of Caries Diagnosis with a Laser Fluorescence System." *Journal of the American Dental Association* 139 (5): 572–579. 10.14219/jada.archive.2008.0217

17. Mount, Graham J. 2005. "Defining, Classifying, and Placing Incipient Caries Lesions in Perspective." *Dental Clinics of North America* 49 (4): 701–723. 10.1016/j.cden. 2005.05.012

18. Kidd, Edwina A. M. 2001. "Diagnosis of Secondary Caries." *Journal of Dental Education* 65(10): 997–1000. 10.1002/j.0022-0337.2001.65.10.tb03476.x

19. Mjor, I.A., and F. Toffenetti. 1985. "Secondary Caries: A Literature Review with Case Reports." *Quintessence International* 31 (3): 165–179. [PMID: 11203922]

20. Schwendicke, F., M. Kern, U. Blunck, C. Dorfer, J. Drenck, and S. Paris. 2014. "Marginal Integrity and Secondary Caries of Selectively Excavated Teeth in Vitro." *Journal of Dentistry* 42 (10): 1261–1268. 10.1016/j.jdent.2014.08.002

21. Ferracane, J.L. 2016. "Models of Caries Formation around Dental Composite Restorations." *Journal of Dental Research* 96 (4): 364–371. 10.1177/002203451 6683395

22. Kuper, N.K., F.H. van de Sande, N.J.M. Opdam, E.M. Bronkhorst, J.J. de Soet, M.S. Cenci, and M.C.D.J.N.M. Huysmans. 2015. "Restoration Materials and Secondary Caries Using an in Vitro Biofilm Model." *Journal of Dental Research* 94 (1): 62–68. 10.1177/0022034514553245

23. Maske, Tamires T., Nicolien K. Kuper, Maximiliano S. Cenci, and Marie-Charlotte D.N.J.M. Huysmans. 2017. "Minimal Gap Size and Dentin Wall Lesion Development Next to Resin Composite in a Microcosm Biofilm Model." *Caries Research* 51 (5): 475–481. 10.1159/000478536

24. Mjor, I A. 1985. "Frequency of Secondary Caries at Various Anatomical Locations." *Operative Dentistry* 10 (3): 88–92. [PMID: 3865152]

25. Mjor, Ivar A. 2005. "Clinical Diagnosis of Recurrent Caries." *Journal of the American Dental Association* 136 (10): 1426–1433. 10.14219/jada.archive.2005.0057

26. Opdam, Niek J.M., Ewald M. Bronkhorst, Joost M. Roeters, and Bas A.C. Loomans. 2007. "A Retrospective Clinical Study on Longevity of Posterior Composite and Amalgam Restorations." *Dental Materials* 23 (1): 2–8. 10.1016/j.dental.2005.11.036

27. Correa, Marcos B., Marcos A. Peres, Karen G. Peres, Bernardo L. Horta, Aluisio J. Barros, and Flavio Fernando Demarco. 2013. "Do Socioeconomic Determinants Affect the Quality of Posterior Dental Restorations? A Multilevel Approach." *Journal of Dentistry* 41 (11): 960–967. 10.1016/j.jdent.2013.02.010

28. Laske, Mark, Niek J.M. Opdam, Ewald M. Bronkhorst, Joze C.C. Braspenning, and Marie Charlotte D.N.J.M Huysmans. 2016. "Longevity of Direct Restorations in Dutch Dental Practices. Descriptive Study Out of a Practice Based Research Network." *Journal of Dentistry* 46 (March): 12–17. 10.1016/j.jdent.2016.01.002

29. Gordan, V. V., J. L. Riley, R. M. Carvalho, J. Snyder, J. L. Sanderson, M. Anderson, and G. H. Gilbert. 2011. "Methods Used by Dental Practice-Based Research Network (DPBRN) Dentists to Diagnose Dental Caries." *Operative Dentistry* 36 (1): 2–11. 10.2341/10-137-cr

30. Wilding, R.J., and Solomon CS. 1996. "Arrested Caries: A Review of the Repair Potential of the Pulp-Dentine." *Journal of the Dental Association of South Africa* 51 (12): 828–833. [PMID: 9462047].

31. Mansur, Eman Khalifa Mohammed. 2020. "Primary Prevention of Dental Caries: An Overview." *International Journal of Clinical Preventive Dentistry* 16 (4): 143–148. 10.15236/ijcpd.2020.16.4.143

32. Lee, Y. 2013. "Diagnosis and Prevention Strategies for Dental Caries." *Journal of Lifestyle Medicine* 3 (2): 107–109. Epub 2013 Sep 30. PMID: 26064846; PMCID: PMC4390741.
33. Riley, Philip, Deborah Moore, Farooq Ahmed, Mohammad O Sharif, and Helen V Worthington. 2015. "Xylitol-Containing Products for Preventing Dental Caries in Children and Adults." *Cochrane Database of Systematic Reviews*, March. 10.1002/14651858.cd010743.pub2
34. Smith, D. J. 2012. "Prospects in Caries Vaccine Development." *Journal of Dental Research* 91 (3): 225–226. 10.1177/0022034511425928
35. Preshaw, Philip M., and Susan M. Bissett. 2013. "Periodontitis." *Endocrinology and Metabolism Clinics of North America* 42 (4): 849–867. 10.1016/j.ecl.2013.05.012
36. Yucel-Lindberg, Tulay, and Tove Bage. 2013. "Inflammatory Mediators in the Pathogenesis of Periodontitis." *Expert Reviews in Molecular Medicine* 15. 10.1017/erm.2013.8
37. Abusleme, Loreto, Amanda K. Dupuy, Nicolas Dutzan, Nora Silva, Joseph A. Burleson, Linda D. Strausbaugh, Jorge Gamonal, and Patricia I. Diaz. 2013. "The Subgingival Microbiome in Health and Periodontitis and Its Relationship with Community Biomass and Inflammation." *The ISME Journal* 7 (5): 1016–1025. 10.1038/ismej.2012.174
38. Holland, Caroline. 2019. "Rethinking Perio Classification for the 21st Century." *BDJ Team* 6 (3): 24–27. 10.1038/s41407-019-0014-9
39. Kato, Tomotaka, Natsuki Fujiwara, Ryutaro Kuraji, and Yukihiro Numabe. 2020. "Relationship between Periodontal Parameters and Non-Vital Pulp in Dental Clinic Patients: A Cross-Sectional Study." *BMC Oral Health* 20 (1). 10.1186/s12903-020-01103-9
40. Dietrich, T., P. Ower, M. Tank, N. X. West, C. Walter, I. Needleman, F. J. Hughes, et al. 2019. "Periodontal Diagnosis in the Context of the 2017 Classification System of Periodontal Diseases and Conditions – Implementation in Clinical Practice." *British Dental Journal* 226 (1): 16–22. 10.1038/sj.bdj.2019.3
41. Herrera, David, Belén Retamal-Valdes, Bettina Alonso, and Magda Feres. 2018. "Acute Periodontal Lesions (Periodontal Abscesses and Necrotizing Periodontal Diseases) and Endo-Periodontal Lesions." *Journal of Clinical Periodontology* 45 (June): S78–S94. 10.1111/jcpe.12941
42. Tonetti, Maurizio S., and Mariano Sanz. 2019. "Implementation of the New Classification of Periodontal Diseases: Decision-Making Algorithms for Clinical Practice and Education." *Journal of Clinical Periodontology* 46 (4): 398–405. 10.1111/jcpe.13104
43. Dubey, Pragati, and Neelam Mittal. 2020. "Periodontal Diseases – A Brief Review." *International Journal of Oral Health Dentistry* 6 (3): 177–187. 10.18231/j.ijohd.2020.038
44. Wang, Laura, and Ian Ganly. 2014. "The Oral Microbiome and Oral Cancer." *Clinics in Laboratory Medicine* 34 (4): 711–719. 10.1016/j.cll.2014.08.004
45. Gupta, Neha, Ritu Gupta, Arun Kumar Acharya, Basavaraj Patthi, Venkatesh Goud, Somanath Reddy, Anshul Garg, and Ashish Singla. 2017. "Changing Trends in Oral Cancer – a Global Scenario." *Nepal Journal of Epidemiology* 6 (4): 613–619. 10.3126/nje.v6i4.17255
46. Scully, C., and S. Portar. 2001. "Oral Cancer." *Western Journal of Medicine* 174 (5): 348–351. 10.1136/ewjm.174.5.348
47. Sehrawat, Sonam, Ajay Kumar, and Mona Prabhakar. 2023. "Substitute for Orthognathic Surgery Using Bioprinted Bone Scaffolds in Restoring Osseous Defects." In *Advances in Additive Manufacturing: Artificial Intelligence, Nature-Inspired, and Biomanufacturing*. Edited by: Kumar Ajay, Haleem Abid, Mittal Ravi Kant. 335–347. 10.1016/B978-0-323-91834-3.00029-6

48. Sehrawat, Sonam, Ajay Kumar, Seema Grover, Namrata Dogra, Jasmine Nindra, Sarita Rathee, Mamta Dahiya, and Ashwini Kumar. 2022. "Study of 3D Scanning Technologies and Scanners in Orthodontics." *Materials Today: Proceedings* 56: 186–193.

49. Sultan, Amina. 2023. "Digitalization in Dentistry: An Ongoing Revolution Shaping the Future of Dentistry." *International Journal of Maxillofacial Imaging* 9 (1): 1–2. 10.18231/j.ijmi.2023.001

50. Gupta Kumar, Manoj, Tarun Gupta, Dharamvir Mangal, Prashant Thapliyal, and Don Biswas. 2022. "Study and Analysis of IoT (Industry 4.0): A Review." In *Handbook of smart manufacturing: Forecasting the future of Industry 4.0*. Edited by: Ajay, Hari Singh, and Parveen, Bandar AlMangour. 29–38. CRC Press, Taylor & Francis. 10. 1201/9781003333760-2

51. Balaji Ganesh, S., and K. Sugumar. 2021. "Internet of Things—A Novel Innovation in Dentistry." *Journal of Advanced Oral Research* 12 (1): 42–48. 10.1177/23202 068209802

52. Kaushal, B., A.K. Sharma, and A. Sharma. 2019. "Iot with Dentistry: Promising Digitalization of Diagnosis in Dental-Health to Enhance Technical Dexterity." *International Journal of Innovative Technology and Exploring Engineering. Blue Eyes Intelligence Engineering and Sciences Engineering and Sciences Publication - BEIESP* 9 (2): 4472–4476. 10.35940/ijitee.b8131.129219

53. Aceto, Giuseppe, Valerio Persico, and Antonio Pescape. 2020. "Industry 4.0 and Health: Internet of Things, Big Data, and Cloud Computing for Healthcare 4.0." *Journal of Industrial Information Integration* 18 (June): 100129. 10.1016/j.jii.2020.100129

54. Salagare, Smita, and Ramjee Prasad. 2022. "Internet of Dental Things (IoDT), Intraoral Wireless Sensors, and Teledentistry: A Novel Model for Prevention of Dental Caries." *Wireless Personal Communications* 123: 3263–3274. 10.1007/s11277-021-09287-1

55. Leason, Isobel, Nicholas Longridge, and Farnaz Nickpour. 2023. "Application and Evolution of Design in Oral Health: A Systematic Mapping Study with an Interactive Evidence Map." *Community Dentistry and Oral Epidemiology*. 10.1111/cdoe.12892

56. Park, Wook Joo, and Jun-Beom Park. 2018. "History and Application of Artificial Neural Networks in Dentistry." *European Journal of Dentistry* 12 (4): 594–601. 10.4103/ejd.ejd_325_18

57. Sun, Mengzhe, Yuanhao Chai, Gang Chai, and Xiaohu Zheng. 2020. "Fully Automatic Robot-Assisted Surgery for Mandibular Angle Split Osteotomy." *Journal of Craniofacial Surgery* 31 (2): 336–339. 10.1097/scs.0000000000005587

58. P, Rajendra, Kumari, Mina, Rani, Sangeeta, Dogra, Namrata, Boadh, Rahul, Kumar, Ajay, Dahiya, Mamta. 2022. Impact of Artificial Intelligence on Civilization: Future Perspectives. *Materials Today: Proceedings in International Conference on Materials, Machines and Information Technology* 56: 252–256. 10.1016/j.matpr.2022.01.113

59. Grischke, Jasmin, Lars Johannsmeier, Lukas Eich, Leif Griga, and Sami Haddadin. 2020. "Dentronics: Towards Robotics and Artificial Intelligence in Dentistry." *Dental Materials* 36 (6): 765–778. 10.1016/j.dental.2020.03.021

60. Hung, Kuofeng, Carla Montalvao, Ray Tanaka, Taisuke Kawai, and Michael M. Bornstein. 2019. "The Use and Performance of Artificial Intelligence Applications in Dental and Maxillofacial Radiology: A Systematic Review." *Dentomaxillofacial Radiology*, August, 20190107. 10.1259/dmfr.20190107

61. Khanagar, Sanjeev B., Satish Vishwanathaiah, Sachin Naik, Abdulaziz A. Al-Kheraif, Darshan Devang Divakar, Sachin C. Sarode, Shilpa Bhandi, and Shankargouda Patil. 2021. "Application and Performance of Artificial Intelligence Technology in Forensic Odontology – A Systematic Review." *Legal Medicine* 48 (February): 101826. 10.1016/j.legalmed.2020.101826

62. Asiri, S.N., L.P. Tadlock, E. Schneiderman, and P.H. Buschang. 2021. "Applications of Artificial Intelligence and Machine Learning in Orthodontics." *APOS Trends in Orthodontics* 10 (1): 17–24. 10.25259/APOS_117_2019

63. Schmidhuber, Jurgen. 2015. "Deep Learning in Neural Networks: An Overview." *Neural Networks* 61: 85–117. 10.1016/j.neunet.2014.09.003

64. Cantu, Anselmo Garcia, Sascha Gehrung, Joachim Krois, Akhilanand Chaurasia, Jesus Gomez Rossi, Robert Gaudin, Karim Elhennawy, and Falk Schwendicke. 2020. "Detecting Caries Lesions of Different Radiographic Extension on Bitewings Using Deep Learning." *Journal of Dentistry* 100 (September): 103425. 10.1016/j.jdent.2020.103425

65. Singhal, Ayush, Manu Phogat, Deepak Kumar, Ajay Kumar, Mamta Dahiya, and Virendra Kumar Shrivastava. 2022. "Study of Deep Learning Techniques for Medical Image Analysis: A Review." *Materials Today: Proceedings in International Conference on Materials, Machines and Information Technology* 56: 209–214. 10.1016/j.matpr.2022.01.071

66. Martino, Francesco, Domenico D. Bloisi, Andrea Pennisi, Mulham Fawakherji, Gennaro Ilardi, Daniela Russo, Daniele Nardi, Stefania Staibano, and Francesco Merolla. 2020. "Deep Learning-Based Pixel-Wise Lesion Segmentation on Oral Squamous Cell Carcinoma Images." *Applied Sciences* 10 (22): 8285. 10.3390/app10228285

67. Szegedy, Christian, Vincent Vanhoucke, Sergey Ioffe, Jon Shlens, and Zbigniew Wojna. 2016. "Rethinking the Inception Architecture for Computer Vision." *2016 IEEE Conference on Computer Vision and Pattern Recognition (CVPR)*, June. 10.1109/cvpr.2016.308

68. Olaf Ronneberger, Philipp Fischer, and Thomas Brox. 2015. "U-Net: Convolutional Networks for Biomedical Image Segmentation." *ArXiv (Cornell University)*, May. 10.48550/arxiv.1505.04597

69. Fu, Qiuyun, Yehansen Chen, Zhihang Li, Qianyan Jing, Chuanyu Hu, Han Liu, Jiahao Bao, et al. 2020. "A Deep Learning Algorithm for Detection of Oral Cavity Squamous Cell Carcinoma from Photographic Images: A Retrospective Study." *E Clinical Medicine* 27 (October): 100558. 10.1016/j.eclinm.2020.100558

70. Das, Dev Kumar, Surajit Bose, Asok Kumar Maiti, Bhaskar Mitra, Gopeswar Mukherjee, and Pranab Kumar Dutta. 2018. "Automatic Identification of Clinically Relevant Regions from Oral Tissue Histological Images for Oral Squamous Cell Carcinoma Diagnosis." *Tissue and Cell* 53: 111–119. 10.1016/j.tice.2018.06.004

71. Wen, Li, Yiyang Chen, Leiying Miao, Mackenzie Brown, Weibin Sun, and Xuan Zhang. 2018. "Gingivitis Identification via Grey-Level Cooccurrence Matrix and Extreme Learning Machine." *Advances in Social Science, Education and Humanities Research* 250: 486–492. 10.2991/emim-18.2018.98

72. Alalharith, Dima M., Hajar M. Alharthi, Wejdan M. Alghamdi, Yasmine M. Alsenbel, Nida Aslam, Irfan Ullah Khan, Suliman Y. Shahin, Simona Dianišková, Muhanad S. Alhareky, and Kasumi K. Barouch. 2020. "A Deep Learning-Based Approach for the Detection of Early Signs of Gingivitis in Orthodontic Patients Using Faster Region-Based Convolutional Neural Networks." *International Journal of Environmental Research and Public Health* 17 (22): 8447. 10.3390/ijerph17228447

73. Liu, Lizheng, Jiawei Xu, Yuxiang Huan, Zhuo Zou, Shih-Ching Yeh, and Li-Rong Zheng. 2020. "A Smart Dental Health-IoT Platform Based on Intelligent Hardware, Deep Learning, and Mobile Terminal." *IEEE Journal of Biomedical and Health Informatics* 24 (3): 898–906. 10.1109/jbhi.2019.2919916

74. Watanabe, Hirofumi, Yoshiko Ariji, Motoki Fukuda, Chiaki Kuwada, Yoshitaka Kise, Michihito Nozawa, Yoshihiko Sugita, and Eiichiro Ariji. 2021. "Deep Learning Object Detection of Maxillary Cyst-like Lesions on Panoramic Radiographs: Preliminary Study." *Oral Radiology* 37 (3): 487–493. 10.1007/s11282-020-00485-4

2 Intelligent Prosthodontics, Intelligent Implantology, and Intelligent Full Mouth Rehabilitation

Sujata Pandey and Reena Mittal
Prosthodontics and Crown & Bridge, Kothiwal Dental College
and Research Centre, Moradabad, Uttar Pradesh, India

2.1 INTRODUCTION

Intelligent prosthodontics utilizes advanced technologies like artificial intelligence, 3D printing, and digital imaging to create precise and customized dental prostheses. This approach improves the accuracy, esthetics, and functionality of prosthetic restorations, resulting in faster treatment and better patient outcomes. Digitalization in dentistry, including AI (Artificial Intelligence) and 3D modeling, enhances diagnosis and treatment planning, while materials like CAD/CAM (Computer-Aided Designing and Computer-Aided Machining) restorations and 3D-printed prosthetics offer improved esthetics and function. Furthermore, digital tools and tele-dentistry improve accessibility and patient communication, making dental care more convenient and inclusive. Overall, intelligent tools and digitalization are transforming dentistry by enhancing outcomes, efficiency, and patient accessibility. Additionally, intelligent prosthodontics also involves the integration of data analytics and machine learning algorithms to analyze patient data and optimize treatment planning, leading to more personalized and effective dental care.

Digitization has several applications in prosthodontics such as investigation and treatment planning, design and fabrication of prosthesis, quality control, patient communication, and in dental education.

2.2 INTELLIGENT PROSTHODONTICS IN INVESTIGATION AND TREATMENT PLANNING

AI can analyze patient data such as medical history, imaging, and clinical records to develop customized treatment plans. This approach can result in more efficient and effective treatment, reducing errors and improving patient outcomes.

DOI: 10.1201/9781003404934-2

2.2.1 Use of Digital Radiologic Imaging in Investigation

Various areas in prosthodontics in which radiologic imaging can be applied are as follows [1].

- Implant dentistry
- Evaluation of the temporomandibular joint (TMJ)
- Analysis of defect for craniofacial reconstruction
- Analysis of the craniofacial region and airway
- Development of comprehensive treatment plans for patients with overdentures

2.2.1.1 Implant Dentistry

Digital radiographic imaging technology has greatly impacted the field of oral implantology, particularly in the surgical and prosthetic phases. Precise evaluation of radiographic data is essential for successful dental implant treatment planning. Historically, diverse imaging methods have been employed to assess bone quantity, quality, and the location of anatomical structures in proximity to potential implant sites. However, traditional two-dimensional (2D) radiographic modalities have limitations. Three-dimensional (3D) imaging has revolutionized the field of implantology, offering several advantages over traditional two-dimensional (2D) imaging. With the advent of Cone Beam Computed Tomography (CBCT), implant clinicians now have access to a new era of radiographic imaging technology for all stages of implant patient evaluation. These technological advancements provide dentists with better information for dental treatment planning and surgery [2]. Radiologic imaging plays a vital role in implantology with numerous applications, such as

- Pre-Surgical Imaging
- Intraoperative Implant Imaging
- Postsurgical Imaging

2.2.1.1.1 Pre-surgical Imaging

The CBCT imaging has become the gold standard for dental implant treatment planning. In this phase of imaging, the primary goals are to acquire essential surgical and prosthetic information necessary to assess the quantity, quality, and angulation of the bone [2]. Additionally, imaging aims to identify the proximity of vital structures to the potential implant sites and evaluate the presence or absence of pathological finding in the proposed surgical locations shown in Figure 2.1.

2.2.1.1.2 Intra Operative Implant Imaging

The imaging process includes capturing images during surgery and while inserting implants, with the aim of aiding both the surgical and prosthetic aspects of the patient's treatment as shown in Figure 2.2. The main objectives of this imaging phase are as follows:

- To assess the surgical sites during and immediately following the surgery.
- Aid in the precise placement and orientation of dental implants.

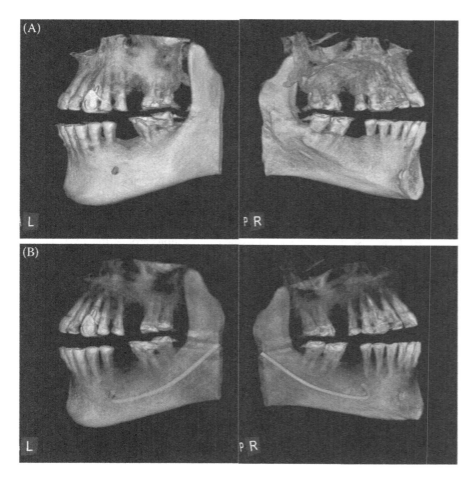

FIGURE 2.1 (A) Anatomical location for inferior alveolar nerve. (B) Proximity to the ridge poses a risk of neurosensory impairment through tissue retraction or transection during reflection.

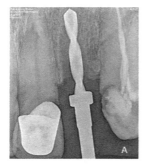
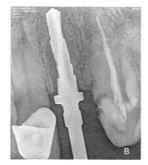
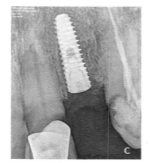

FIGURE 2.2 Intraoral radiographs. (A) Initial pilot showing correct orientation and angulation. (B) Final depth drill during osteotomy preparation. (C) Ideal implant placement radiograph. Note perpendicular orientation of X-ray beam as all threads are seen without distortion.

- To evaluate the healing and integration process of implant surgery.
- To verify the accuracy of abutment position and prosthesis fabrication.

2.2.1.1.3 Post-surgical Imaging

This phase begins immediately after the placement of the prosthesis and continues for as long as the implants last. Its primary objectives are to monitor the long-term stability and function of the implants, by measuring the levels of crestal bone around each implant, and to assess the implant prosthesis as shown in Figure 2.3.

2.2.1.2 Temporomandibular Joint Imaging

CBCT is a highly effective imaging technology that can precisely locate the condyle within the glenoid fossa, revealing any disk dislocation and the degree of condylar translation. Moreover, it allows for simple measurement of the glenoid fossa's roof and offers a vivid 3D view of the relationship between the condylar head and the glenoid fossa. CBCT can also easily detect soft tissue calcifications around the TMJ [1].

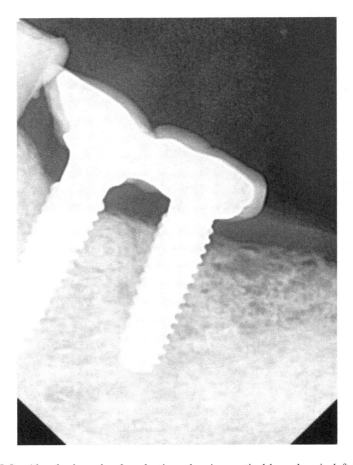

FIGURE 2.3   Alveolar bone level evaluation: showing vertical bone loss in left implant.

2.2.1.3 Analysis of Defect for Craniofacial Reconstruction

CBCT has emerged as the preferred imaging technology for craniofacial defect reconstruction planning. With the use of CBCT (Cone Beam Computed Tomography) (DICOM—Digital Imaging and Communications in Medicine) data software volume rendering can generate 3D augmented virtual models of the patient's face, bony structures, and dentition, which are valuable for treatment planning. The DICOM data transfer protocol that has been universally adopted ensures rapid, undistorted, and unalterable data transfer, thus minimizing the risk of malpractice. Virtual planning using CBCT allows for the precise determination of the shape and position of the graft in the defect area, facilitating virtual reconstruction of the defect before the actual surgery. This technology can enhance the accuracy and predictability of surgical outcomes while minimizing the risks associated with the procedure. By providing a detailed and comprehensive visualization of the defect and surrounding structures, virtual planning ensures that the surgical intervention is customized to the patient's specific requirements, leading to better overall outcomes and patient satisfaction. Additionally, implant placement onto the graft can be planned, and CAD/CAM units can accurately mill obturators for cleft closures, streamlining the clinical process of obturator construction [1].

2.2.1.4 Analysis of Craniofacial Region and Airway

The identification of airway obstruction can be challenging for healthcare professionals. Various methods, including nasopharyngoscopy, cephalometry, nasal airway resistance, and polysomnography, have been used for this purpose. Lateral and frontal radiographs are commonly used to evaluate pharyngeal obstruction [1]. However, CBCT has emerged as a powerful diagnostic tool due to its minimal error and ability to provide a three-dimensional view of the airway and surrounding structures. This allows for precise volumetric analysis and visualization of the airway. CBCT is particularly efficient in detecting both focal and diffuse narrowing of the airway, making it an indispensable tool for healthcare professionals in diagnosing and treating airway obstruction.

2.2.1.5 Development of Comprehensive Treatment Planning for Patients with Overdenture

The idea of keeping some roots to support overdentures is not a new concept and has been described for over 150 years. In the 1950s, researchers found that tooth extraction led to continuous resorption of the remaining alveolar bone, leaving little support for complete dentures and making them challenging to wear. Multiple studies have examined edentulous patients wearing complete dentures and found that resorption is an irreversible and cumulative process. Although the rate of resorption varies due to biological and mechanical factors, it is highest in the first six months after tooth extraction. Furthermore, the mandible tends to experience four times more bone loss than the maxilla, with an average loss of 9–10 mm of vertical height after 25 years of denture use, compared to 2.5–3 mm in the maxilla [1].

To enhance the prognosis of such dentures, CBCT scans can be used for initial assessment and follow-up during a 4-year review. CBCT imaging provides precise information that helps identify changes in the alveolar bone and improves the accuracy of diagnosis and treatment planning.

2.2.2 USE OF INTRAORAL SCANNER IN INVESTIGATION

Data acquisition of jaw and tooth structures is done by using a variety of technologies, including optical sensors and X-ray imaging. These scanners then transform these images into digital data sets, which can be used to create accurate 3D models of a patient's teeth and surrounding structures. These 3D models can be used in various dental procedures, such as orthodontics, prosthodontics, restorative dentistry, and oral and maxillofacial surgery.

Intraoral scanners are used in dentistry to create a digital 3D representation of a patient's teeth and oral cavity. These scanners use advanced imaging technology to capture images of the teeth and gums, allowing dentists to create accurate digital models that can be used for a variety of purposes, such as creating dental restorations, orthodontic treatments, and implant placement.

Intraoral scanners are gaining widespread use in dentistry due to their numerous advantages over traditional impression methods, resulting in better patient care and treatment outcomes as described in Table 2.1 [3].

TABLE 2.1
Advantages and Disadvantages of Intraoral Scanners

Advantages	Disadvantages
Less patient discomfort: • Decreases patient discomfort. • It eliminates the need for materials and impression trays.	**Difficulty detecting deep marginal lines of prepared teeth:** • Deep marginal lines and bleeding can make it difficult for IOS (Intra Oral Scanner) and optical impressions to detect finishing lines, especially in esthetic areas. Proper attention, speed, highlighting strategies, and good oral hygiene can help clinicians achieve good optical impressions in challenging cases.
Time-efficient: • Time-efficient compared to conventional impressions, mainly due to the elimination of subsequent steps such as pouring stone casts and obtaining physical plaster models. • Dental clinics equipped with chair-side CAD/CAM can import optical impression files into CAD software, which can then be transferred to CAM software for milling.	**Learning curve:** • Adopting IOS in the dental clinic requires attention to the learning curve, which may be easier for younger dentists with more experience with technology and computers, while older clinicians may find it more complex.

TABLE 2.1 *(Continued)*
Advantages and Disadvantages of Intraoral Scanners

Advantages	Disadvantages
Simplified clinical procedures: Simplifies impression-making in complex cases and can be edited and recaptured without repeating the entire procedure, which is time-saving.	**Purchasing and managing costs:** • Cost effective.
Better communication with the dental technician: • IOS enables real-time assessment of impression quality by clinicians and technicians. • Technicians can request another impression if necessary, simplifying communication and saving time.	
Better communication with the patients: • Improves patient engagement and communication, resulting in better treatment outcomes such as improved compliance to oral hygiene. • Also, enhances patient communication and marketing efforts.	

2.2.3 INTELLIGENT PROSTHODONTICS IN DESIGNING AND FABRICATION OF PROSTHESIS

CAD/CAM technology has revolutionized prosthodontics, providing numerous benefits to dental professionals and patients alike. It enables dentists to create highly accurate and precise prostheses. Also, it has been known to provide superior efficiency in creating dental restorations compared to traditional methods thereby giving more predictable, long-lasting results. Hence, it improves patient outcome and higher level of patient satisfaction. It also allows for the customization of a prosthesis which needs specific characterization or according to the need of each patient, resulting in a more comfortable and functional outcome. Although the initial investment in CAD/CAM technology may be significant; in the long run, it can be a cost-effective solution. This is because CAD/CAM technology allows for the creation of restorations with greater accuracy and efficiency, reducing the need for rework or additional appointments. CAD/CAM includes the following components shown in Figure 2.4.

2.2.3.1 Scanner

In dentistry, Intraoral scanners (IOS) use light sources (lasers or structured light) to capture direct optical impressions of the dental arches, including prepared teeth and implant scanbodies, eliminating the need for traditional impression materials [4].

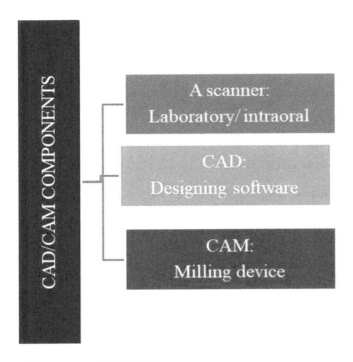

FIGURE 2.4   Components of CAD/CAM.

Three types of workflows are available for dental impressions:

* The traditional workflow.
* The former digital workflow.
* The rapid digital workflow.

2.2.3.1.1   Traditional Workflow

The process of digital prosthesis fabrication involves several steps:

1. Impression of the maxillary and mandibular arches is made in a conventional manner using elastomeric impression material.
2. Cast is obtained by pouring the impression with gypsum product.
3. After that, using extraoral scanner scan the obtained cast to get 3D virtual digital model of the maxillary and mandibular arches by the technician.
4. Designing of the prosthesis is performed using CAD software and transfer the obtained file to milling machine.
5. Using CAM final prosthesis is milled and checked in patient's mouth for occlusal adjustments by the dentist.

Workflow for Digital Prosthesis Fabrication has also been depicted in Figure 2.5.

Traditional workflow for dental impressions.

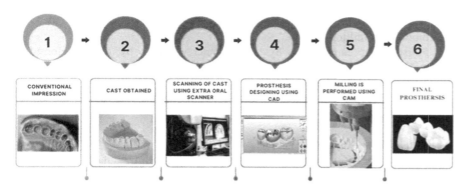

FIGURE 2.5 Traditional workflow for dental impression.

2.2.3.1.2 Former Workflow

The process of digital prosthesis fabrication comprises several stages, as illustrated in Figure 2.6.

1. Digital impression is captured by an intraoral scanning device.
2. Send the acquired digital impression file to a laboratory.

FIGURE 2.6 Former digital workflow for dental impression.

3. The laboratory retrieves the digital file and utilizes specialized software to create digital models of the die and accurately demarcate the margins.
4. The CAD/CAM systems are used to create a Sterlieothography (SLA) model and milling is done.
5. Finishing is carried out by the technician either by their preferred technique like hand layered porcelain, pressing with wax patterns, or by means of CAD/CAM systems.
6. The final restoration is then tried by the dentist in the patient's mouth and cemented.

2.2.3.1.3   Rapid Digital Workflow

The steps for fabrication of prosthesis using in-office milling unit are as follows:

1. Capture the digital impression using an intraoral scanning device.
2. The design of the restoration is done by the dentist, and the software automatically generates the milling unit's program.
3. The milled prosthesis is then ready to be delivered to the patient.

2.2.3.2   CAD/CAM (Computer-Aided Designing and Computer-Aided Machining)

Computer-aided machining (CAM) procedures in dentistry involve the use of digital technology and software to automate and control various manufacturing processes related to dental restorations. The manufacturing processes involved in computer-aided machining (CAM) procedures in dentistry can include the following [5,6]:

Milling: This process uses a milling machine to remove material from a solid block or disc of dental material, such as ceramic or composite, based on the instructions provided by the CAM software. The milling machine's cutting tools precisely carve out the desired shape and contours of dental restorations like crowns, bridges, or implant components.

3D Printing: Also known as additive manufacturing, 3D printing builds dental restorations layer by layer using digital designs and materials such as resin or metal powders. The CAM software provides the instructions for the 3D printer to deposit or solidify the material in a controlled manner, gradually creating the desired dental restoration [7,8].

Laser Sintering: This process is commonly used for metal-based restorations. It involves using a high-powered laser to selectively fuse metal powders, layer by layer, to create complex and precise dental structures, such as implant abutments or frameworks. The CAM software controls the laser sintering process based on the digital design.

Stereolithography (SLA): This is a type of 3D printing that uses a liquid resin that is cured by a laser or other light source. The CAM software guides the light source to selectively solidify the resin layer by layer, creating highly accurate and detailed dental restorations.

2.2.3.2.1 Computer-Aided Designing and Computer-Aided Machining for Complete Dentures

Digital denture manufacturing offers the advantage of time-saving during treatment and digital storage of patients' data. There are two protocols available for digital denture production:

1. The four-visit protocol, and
2. The two-visit protocol.

1. **The four-visit protocol:** Steps to be followed in the four-visit protocol for digital complete denture fabrication are presented in Figure 2.7.
2. **The two-visit protocol:** The protocol for digital complete denture fabrication, spanning two visits, entails the following sequential stages exhibited in Figure 2.8.

Computer-Aided Designing for Complete Denture

In the process of generating distinct orders for each cast, the CAD software is used and the "Full denture design with PMMA (Polymethyl Methacrylate) material" option is selected. After that, the software imports the STL (Sterlieothography) files of the master casts and jaw relation records, and the two are virtually mounted and superimposed together using the "Best fit match" function [9].

The models are evaluated involving the following steps: Firstly, by selecting three control points the occlusal plane is established. Two points are placed at the maxillary tuberosity, one point is placed at the incisive papilla, and two additional points are placed in the maxillary right and left canine areas. Similarly, three points are assigned

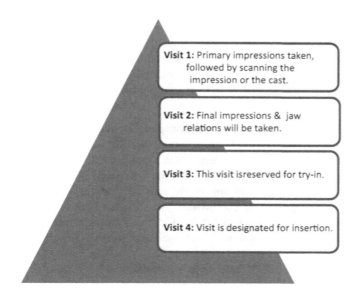

FIGURE 2.7   Four-visit protocol for digital complete denture fabrication.

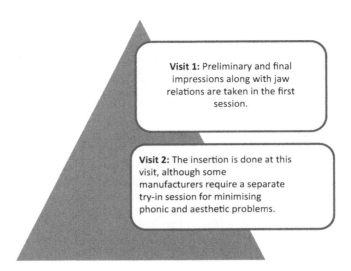

FIGURE 2.8   Two-visit protocol for digital complete denture fabrication.

for each retromolar pad region and two points are assigned in the mandibular right and left canine areas for defining the mandibular points. The "Draw outline button" is used to trace the borders of the maxillary and mandibular casts.

Then, the surveying process for the denture is carried out automatically using specialized software. The software provides a library of teeth sets from which a suitable one is chosen. The software then generates a denture base for both the maxillary and mandibular dentures. These denture bases are further modified by adjusting the position of specific points as needed. For denture characterization, the gingiva is enhanced by applying additional material at the base of the teeth and refining the surfaces. After completion, the data is saved, and four separate STL files are exported. Two files are allocated for the maxillary and mandibular denture bases, while the remaining two files are designated for the maxillary and mandibular teeth. These files are then prepared for the manufacturing of the denture shown in Figure 2.9.

Computer-Aided Manufacturing for Complete Denture
The production of dentures can be accomplished through either an additive or subtractive manufacturing process, using four separate STL files that can be printed independently. Two files are allocated for the maxillary and mandibular denture bases, while the other two files are for the maxillary and mandibular teeth. After importing the STL files into CAD software, the software generates supporting arms automatically, as shown in Figure 2.10. Finally, new files are exported for the denture bases and teeth, now with the included support structures depicted in Figure 2.11 [9].

Once the supporting arms have been generated using CAD software, the next step is to send the STL files for the denture bases with support structures and the denture teeth with support structures to separate 3D printers. The 3D printer

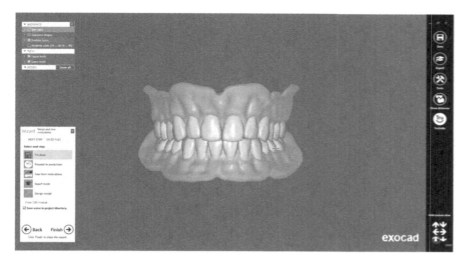

FIGURE 2.9 Final design of CAD/CAM dentures.

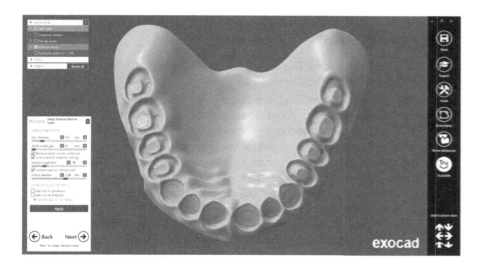

FIGURE 2.10 CAD design of denture base.

that will be used for the denture bases is filled with pink denture base printing resin, while the printer that will be used for the teeth is filled with white teeth printing resin.

Once printing is completed, finishing touches are added by removing the support arms using a carbide disc, followed by rinsing them in alcohol. A minimal amount of polishing is performed on the denture bases and teeth. Subsequently, the denture teeth are placed into the corresponding recesses of the denture bases to attach them

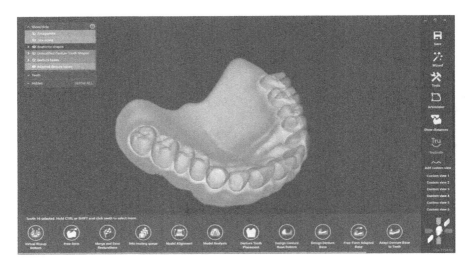

FIGURE 2.11   Denture teeth with support structures on CAD software.

together. The remaining resin is utilized to bind them securely. The final dentures are then cleaned, dried, and placed into a post-curing unit for 15 minutes to ensure the hardening and stabilization of the materials.

2.2.3.2.2   Computer-Aided Designing and Computer-Aided Machining for Fixed Dental Prosthesis

In the realm of modern dentistry, computer-aided design and machining play a pivotal role in the fabrication of fixed dental prosthesis. This section delves into the process of computer-aided designing, encompassing the generation of three-dimensional representations and seamless integration within the oral anatomy.

CAD software is utilized to generate a three-dimensional image of the die that can be viewed from multiple angles. Using the software, the crown form can be designed by selecting the appropriate tooth element from a library and modeling the crown to fit seamlessly with the adjacent teeth [10].

This intricate process is exemplified in Figures 2.12–2.16, showcasing the transformation from digital design to tangible dental prosthesis.

In the domain of CAM technologies, the methodologies employed can be classified into three primary groups: Subtractive technique, additive technique, and solid free-form fabrication [10].

1. The subtractive technique involves cutting the contour out of a prefabricated solid block of various materials using milling units. This technique possesses limitations in terms of the size of the FDP (Fixed Dental Prosthesis) that can be produced.
2. The additive technique, on the other hand, involves dry pressing alumina or zirconia on the die, followed by milling and sintering to achieve the desired shape.

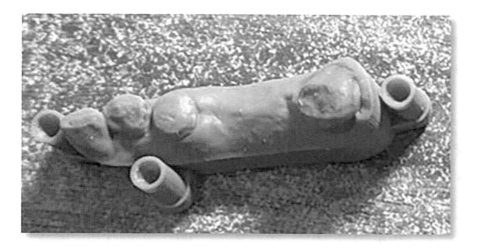

FIGURE 2.12   Die preparation.

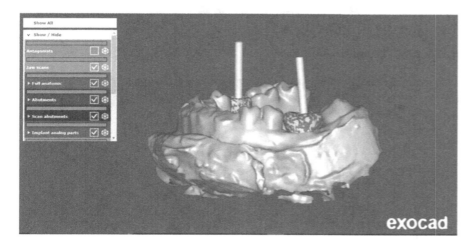

FIGURE 2.13   Graphic presentation of scanned die.

3. Solid free-form fabrication is a modern technology adapted from rapid prototyping, which can create 3-D restorations using various methods including stereolithography and selective laser sintering.

To fabricate the coping, a milling device is used consisting of a rotatory drilling element with interchangeable bores of varying shapes and diameters, along with a mobile platform where the dummy is fixed. The platform can be precisely moved in three dimensions to mill the coping accurately. The milling process is carried out in three steps: Rough milling of the inside of the coping to remove the bulk of the material, fine inside milling to enhance precision, and rough external milling.

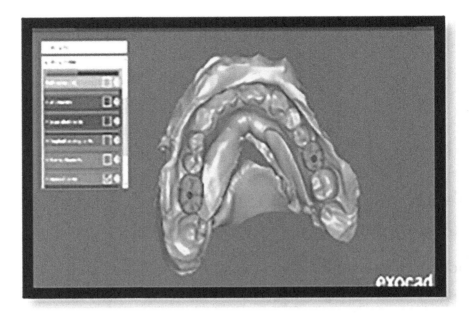

FIGURE 2.14   Digital crown in place.

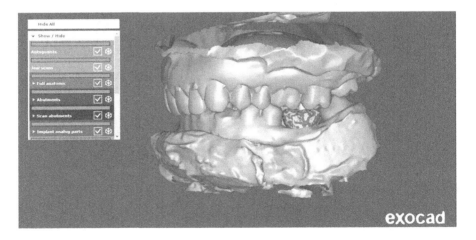

FIGURE 2.15   Digital crown in occlusion.

2.2.3.2.3 Computer-Aided Designing and Computer-Aided Machining for Removable Partial Denture

Introducing a systematic and innovative approach to the design and production of removable dental prostheses, this workflow encapsulates a fusion of advanced computer-aided techniques with traditional dental craftsmanship. Drawing from established protocols and exemplified in Figure 2.17, the subsequent phases

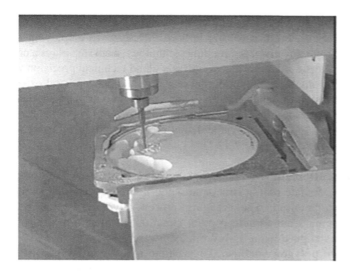

FIGURE 2.16 Milling procedure.

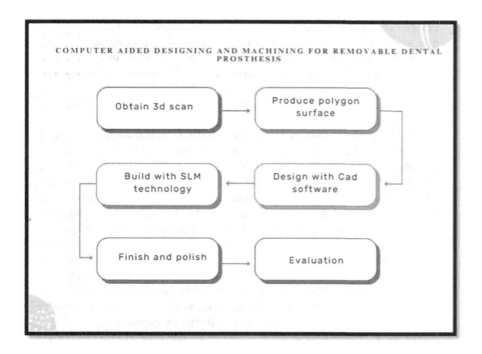

FIGURE 2.17 Workflow for CAD/CAM of removable dental prosthesis.

intricately illuminate the process of translating elaborate 3D scans into finely designed prosthetic solutions. From capturing intricate 3D scans to employing cutting-edge CAD software and selective laser melting technology, each step plays a crucial role in delivering prosthetic solutions that seamlessly blend technical precision with esthetic excellence. The amalgamation of digital dexterity and conventional expertise underscores the evolution of dental prosthesis fabrication into an intricate dance between modern technology and time-honored craftsmanship.

Detailed workflow for removable dental prosthesis produced using CAD/CAM, further summarized in Figure 2.17 [11].

1. **Obtain 3D scan:** To obtain a three-dimensional scan of the patient's partially dentate cast, a structured white light digitizer such as the Comet 250 can be used. The scanning process involved capturing multiple overlapping scans to collect point cloud data. Afterward, the point cloud data was aligned using PolyWorks software.

2. **Produce polygon surface:** To generate a polygon surface in STL file format, Alias-Wavefront's Spider software can be utilized.

3. **Design with CAD software:** The SensAble Technologies' FreeForm CAD package is preferred due to its ability to create intricate and precisely defined shapes necessary for designing personalized prosthetic devices that must conform to the human anatomy. The CAD software has tools analogous to those used in physical sculpting and allows electronic surveying to be completed. The software uses a haptic interface that incorporates positioning in 3D space, allowing the operator to feel the object being manipulated in the software. The combination of tools and force feedback sensations mimics working on a physical object.

4. **Build with SLM (Selective Laser Melting) technology:** An SLM Realizer 2 machine is utilized to manufacture the RPD (Removable Partial Denture) metal framework through Selective Laser Melting (SLM) technology. Adequate supports were created using Materialise's Magics software to provide a firm base for the part to be built onto while separating the part from the substrate plate. In addition, the supports conduct heat away from the material as it melts and solidifies during the build process. The RPD framework was oriented in a way that the supports avoided the fitting surface of the RPD so that the resultant framework would not be affected or damaged by the supports or their removal.

5. **Finish and polish:** Traditional dental laboratory procedures are utilized to finish and polish the RPD metal framework, ensuring that the final product meets the desired specifications and is esthetically pleasing.

6. **Evaluation:** A prosthodontic consultant evaluates the RPD framework on the physical cast to ensure the quality of fit according to recommended practices.

2.2.3.2.4 Computer-Aided Designing and Computer-Aided Machining for Maxillofacial Prosthesis

The role of Computer-Aided Design (CAD) and Computer-Aided Machining (CAM) in maxillofacial prosthesis is indispensable, revolutionizing the field with their precision, efficiency, and customization capabilities. This advanced technology streamlines the entire process of designing and fabricating maxillofacial prostheses, offering significant benefits across various aspects: Patient-Specific Design, Accuracy and Precision, Time Efficiency, Customization, Complex Geometries, Collaboration, Digital Record, CAM Fabrication, Material Optimization, Quality Control, Patient Confidence.

In essence, the integration of CAD and CAM in maxillofacial prosthesis creation has transformed the field by enhancing precision, reducing production time, and allowing for personalized solutions that significantly improve patient's quality of life and self-esteem.

Within the realm of modern medical science, the fabrication of maxillofacial prostheses emerges as an intricate convergence of sophisticated technologies and meticulous design strategies which has been discussed below [12]:

1. Obtain defect data through medical scans or surface scans, including CT, CBCT, MRI, surface scanners, or photogrammetry.
2. Convert the data into digital models in the DICOM (Digital Imaging and Communications in Medicine) format or 3D surface models of the patient's face.
3. CAD programs and software suites are utilized to create a design for the external or internal component of maxillofacial prosthesis, taking into account the patient's unique anatomical features and requirements.
4. Choose the appropriate material, such as silicone-based elastomers or acrylic resins.
5. Rapid prototyping techniques, including additive manufacturing, can be utilized to produce the final maxillofacial prosthesis. This can be done indirectly by first obtaining a model or mold of the prosthesis, followed by conventional anatomic part processing, or directly through 3D printing with appropriate materials.
6. Finish the prosthesis, if necessary, by applying color, texture, and other features to match the patient's natural appearance.

2.3 VIRTUAL FACEBOW AND ARTICULATORS

The terminal hinge axis (THA) is a pivotal point around which the mandible rotates when it's in centric relation. Facebow transfer is a technique used to record the THA and transfer it to the articulator, ensuring that it coincides with the arc of closure or hinge axis of the articulator. This alignment ensures that restorations are free of interferences and provide stability to the stomatognathic system. With the integration of technology in dentistry, virtual facebow transfers and articulators are now available, providing a remarkable advancement in the field [13].

The integration of digital technology in dentistry provides a precise and consistent method for digitally transferring the position of the maxillary dental arch to a virtual articulator. This eliminates the need for mounting casts on a mechanical articulator, allowing for a fully digital workflow. By replicating real patient data, the virtual articulator enables a thorough evaluation of static and dynamic occlusion, as well as jaw relation, surpassing the capabilities of traditional mechanical articulators. This technology has the potential to revolutionize prosthetic restorative dentistry [14].

In prosthodontics, virtual interocclusal records are employed to determine the horizontal jaw relation and position the maxillary and mandibular casts accurately. The integration of digital technology in this field presents a promising opportunity for more efficient and streamlined treatment planning. With the increasing affordability and accessibility of technology, there is great potential for significant time and effort reduction in prosthodontic treatments.

2.3.1   WORKING OF VIRTUAL FACEBOW

Virtual facebow recording can be performed in two phases described in Figures 2.18 and 2.19 [14].

2.3.2   WORKING OF VIRTUAL ARTICULATORS

In Figures 2.20 and 2.21, designing and working of virtual articulators are discussed below:

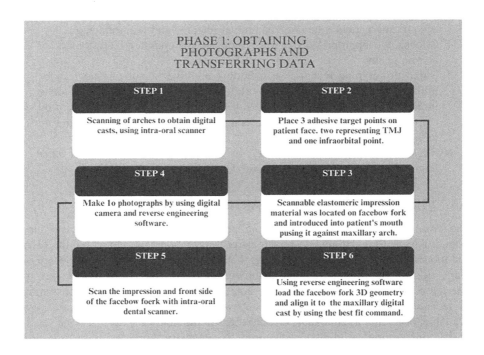

FIGURE 2.18   Obtaining photographs and transferring data.

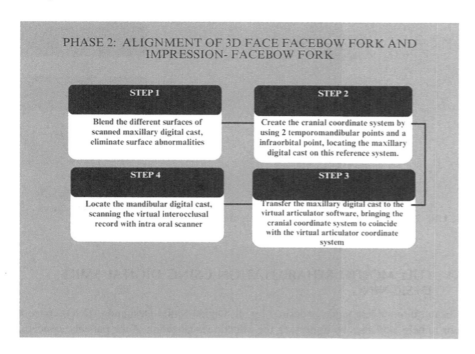

FIGURE 2.19 Alignment of 3D facebow fork and impression—facebow fork.

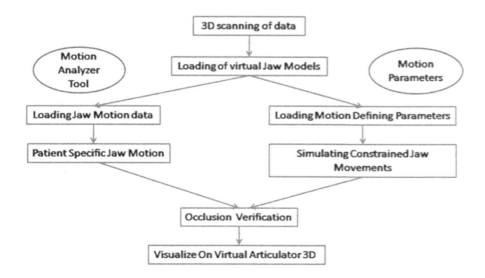

FIGURE 2.20 Virtual articulator designing method.

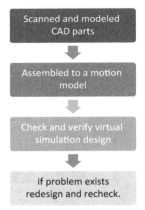

FIGURE 2.21   Virtual articulator functioning method.

2.4 FULL MOUTH REHABILITATION USING DIGITAL SMILE DESIGNING

A beautiful confident smile is desired by all. Digital Smile Designing (DSD) concept aims to help clinicians by improving the esthetic visualization of the patients' concern, giving understanding of the possible solution therefore educating and motivating them about the benefits of the treatment and increasing the case acceptance. It is a digital mode that helps us to create and project the new smile design by attaining a simulation and pre-visualization of the ultimate result of the proposed treatment. A design created digitally involves the participation of the patients in the designing process of their self-smile design, leading to customization of smile design as per individual needs and desires that complements the morpho psychological characteristics of the patient, relating patient to an emotional level, increasing their confidence in the process and resulting in better acceptance of the anticipated treatment [15].

2.4.1 Requirements of Digital Smile Designing

An accurate photographic documentation is essential as complete facial and dental analysis rests on preliminary photographs on which changes and designing are formulated; a video documentation is required for dynamic analysis of teeth, gingiva, lips, and face during smiling, laughing, and talking in order to integrate facially guided principles to the smile design.

2.4.2 Photography Protocol

Photographs taken should be of utmost quality and precision, with correct posture and standardized techniques, as facial reference lines like the commissural lines, lip line, and inter-pupillary line which form the basis of smile designing are established on them. Poor photography misrepresents the reference image and may lead to an improper diagnosis and planning.

The following photographic views in fixed head position are necessary:

a. **Three frontal views:**
   - Full face with a wide smile and the teeth apart,
   - Full face at rest, and
   - Retracted view of the full maxillary and mandibular arch with teeth apart.
b. **Two profile views:**
   - Side profile at rest
   - Side profile with a full smile
c. A 12 o'clock view
   with a wide smile and incisal edge of maxillary teeth visible and resting on lower lip
d. An intra occlusal view

of maxillary arch from second premolar to second premolar.

2.4.3 VIDEOGRAPHY PROTOCOL

For ideal development of the facially guided smile frame, four videos from specific angles should be taken:

1. A facial frontal video with and without retractor smiling.
2. A facial profile video with lips at rest and wide smile.
3. A 12 o'clock video above the head at the most coronal angle that still allows visualization of the incisal edge.
4. An anterior occlusal video to record maxillary teeth from second premolar to second premolar with the palatine raphe as a straight line.

2.4.4 PROCEDURE OF CARRYING DIGITAL SMILE DESIGNING

1. Take extra- and intraoral digital photographs.
2. Analyze facial features using reference lines to determine the ideal horizontal plane and vertical midline.
3. Conduct dento-gingival analysis to determine the gingival display and establish a smile curve by correlating the curvature of the incisal edges of the maxillary anterior teeth.
4. Mark three reference lines on the teeth: A straight horizontal line from canine tip to canine tip, another horizontal line on the incisal edges of central incisors, and a vertical line passing through the dental midline (interdental papillae).
5. Draw additional lines to aid in dental analysis, such as the gingival zenith and joining lines of the gingival and incisal battlements.
6. Incorporate the ideal size of dental width to length ratio for adequate teeth dimension.
7. Use a digital ruler to make required changes.
8. Present digitally approved smile design to the patient as illustrated in Figure 2.22.

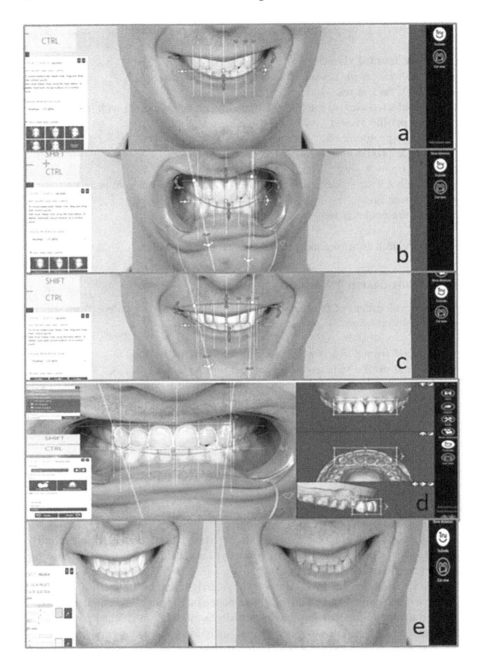

FIGURE 2.22 Digital smile designing process on Exocad 3D software. **a & b** shows drawing of facial and intraoral reference lines. **c** shows integration of facial with dental analysis. **d** represents incorporation of ideal dental contours in 3D. **e** shows digital designed smile compared with original smile.

9. Create a physical mockup for esthetic and phonetic evaluation before performing the final procedures.

2.5 ARTIFICIAL INTELLIGENCE IN PROSTHODONTICS

The application of computer-assisted pre-operative procedures, such as CAD/CAM, has been well-established in dental implantology. However, the utilization of robots for the surgical phase is a relatively new advancement. Several prototype systems have been developed by various institutions, including the University of Kentucky, Ecole des Mines de Paris, Umea Universitet, University of Coimbra, and University of Duesseldorf, as documented in a study [16].

In recent years, a new model has been proposed by researchers at the Finnish Center for Artificial Intelligence (FCAI), the University Hospital of Tampere, Planmeca, and the Alan Turing Institute. This model aims to accurately and automatically identify the precise position of the mandibular canal for dental implant operations [17].

In 2012, an autonomous robotic system with 6 Degrees of Freedom (DOF) was developed, employing a volume-decomposition-based system to place root-shaped dental implants [18,19]. Subsequently, a 3-DOF robotic system equipped with a stereo camera was created, capable of detecting and modulating the dental handpiece. This system ensures implant placement in accordance with the preoperative protocol. The planned surgical procedure is automatically applied by the computer, ensuring precise cutting and appropriate applied force at the designated site [19].

2.5.1 NAVIGATIONAL IMPLANT SURGERY

The first commercially available and state-of-the-art robotic system for dental implantology, named Yomi HJN was developed by Neocis Inc., USA, and approved by the FDA in 2017 (U.S. Food and Drug Administration, 2017). Dental implantology using computerized navigational system intended to provide assistance in both the planning (pre-operative) and the surgical (intra-operative) phases of dental implantation surgery [16,20].

Yomi enables dentists to bridge the digital imaging preoperatively into their operating environment through the use of haptic robotic technology [21]. They receive real-time physical and visual guidance throughout the surgery. This provides accuracy and reliability without the need to manufacture a custom plastic guide or worry about performing an unguided freehand approach shown in Figure 2.23.

2.5.2 AI IN TOOTH PREPARATION

Despite being standard work for professionals with years of clinical training, tooth preparation for a crown or bridge is nonetheless difficult. The main difficulty is to reduce the tooth sufficiently to create room while causing the good tooth substance the least amount of damage. The idea of a robotic device being used for tooth preparation appeals to dentists as being practical and alluring.

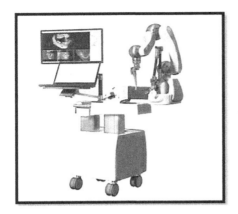 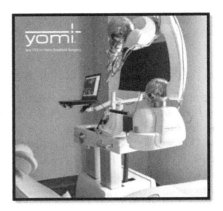

FIGURE 2.23   Yomi dental implantology robotic system.

An in vitro testing of a mechatronic system has been conducted to aid the clinician in tooth drilling. The report demonstrated good outcomes; however, its validation has not been performed so far in the clinical setup. With a mechatronic system, the accuracy of the clinician's position was 53% more efficient than without it [19].

Yuan et al. described a robotic tooth preparation system with:

1. An intraoral 3D scanner (TRIOS, 3Shape A/S, Copenhagen, Denmark) to obtain the 3D data of the patient's target tooth, adjacent teeth, opposing teeth and the teeth fixture;
2. A computer-aided design (CAD)/computer-aided manufacturing (CAM) software for designing the target preparation shape and generating a 3D motion path of the laser;
3. An effective low-heat laser suitable for hard tissue preparation;
4. A 6-DOF robot arm;
5. A tooth fixture connecting the robotic device with the target tooth and protecting the adjacent teeth from laser cutting, designed using Solid works software.

A system with micro robots, controlling a picosecond laser showed a preparation accuracy that met clinical needs, the error was about (0.089 ± 0.026) mm. Another tooth preparation system for veneers with a rotating diamond instrument mounted on a robotic arm was compared to hand crown preparation and showed better results than the tooth preparation carried out by the dentist. The average repeatability of the system was about 40 m [21].

2.5.3   AI IN REMOVABLE PROSTHODONTICS

The most significant step in the (manual) conventional method of creating complete dentures is inserting artificial teeth into a tooth pad in the proper orientation. This can only be done effectively by specialized dentists and trained technicians. Robotic production of denture systems has now supplanted the conventional method. The size of the teeth, how each tooth is positioned and oriented in relation to the others, and how the teeth arch curve differ significantly amongst complete dentures.

The advantage of a robot is its operational flexibility and can be adapted for handling the manufacture of complete dentures [21].

Robotic assistance may also be helpful in supporting the dental technician. A novel system that generates the dental arch has been developed. The system can be used to fabricate full dentures. A study on this tooth-arrangement robot showed that it was very accurate [21].

For the fabrication of a complete denture, Canadian scientists developed a single-manipulator robotic system utilizing a 6-DOF CRS robot [19]. This system was then adapted for the manufacture of complete dentures. A single-manipulator robotic system for tooth-arrangement of complete dentures is composed of the following parts shown in Figure 2.24(a) to (c) [21].

a. Light-sensitive glue
b. Light source device
c. Denture base
d. Control and motion planning

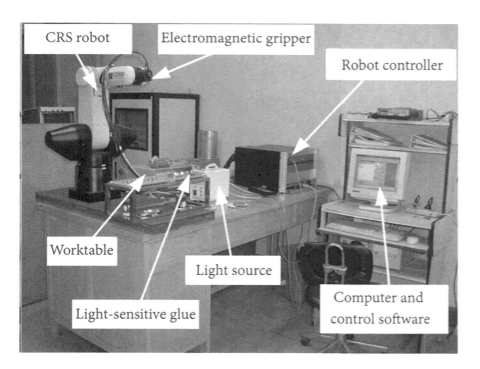

FIGURE 2.24   a. Single-manipulator tooth-arrangement robot system for complete denture. **b.** Structure of the 84-DOF multi-manipulator tooth-arrangement robot. **c.** Complete denture made by the 50-DOF multi-manipulator tooth-arrangement robot system.

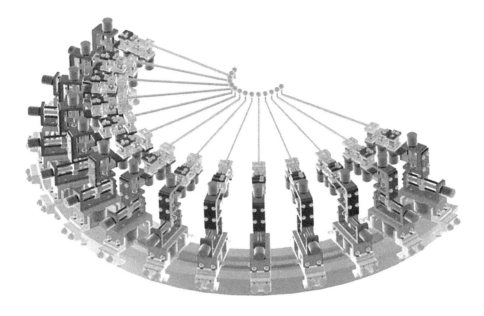

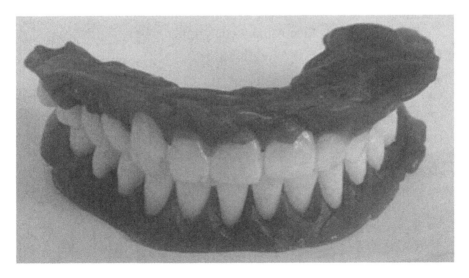

FIGURE 2.24   (*continued*)

  e. Robot modulation software for arranging tooth and a core control system
     having tooth-arrangement
  f. Computer
  g. Electromagnetic gripper.

A much improved 50-DOF tooth-arrangement robotic system was then designed with 14 independent manipulators, a dental arch generator, and a slipway mechanism as its components. Dental arch generator creates the dental arch curve and matches with the one from patient's oral cavity. The slipway mechanism is used to control the dental arch generator.

2.5.4 AI IN ORAL AND MAXILLOFACIAL PROSTHESIS

The bionic eye, developed in the United States, has already been tested in a dozen patients with vision damages. Without the need for surgery, these devices can benefit the people in attaining vision with the help of artificial intelligence.

Due to amputation of limbs, patients can lose the sensory capacity in those areas. Artificial skin developed by researchers from the California Institute of Technology (USA) and the Federal Polytechnic School of Zurich (Switzerland) is changing this scenario [17].

Artificial olfaction plays a crucial role in robotics by mimicking the human olfactory structure that can identify different smells that compare to a range of fields, together with environmental monitoring, disease diagnosis, public security affairs, agricultural production, and food industry [21].

Malignant lesions of the oropharynx are not always readily accessible, and conventional treatment must often resort to radiotherapy and/or chemotherapy. Salvage surgery is usually conducted through mandibulectomy with mandibular displacement and lip split. However, robotic oral and maxillofacial surgery has become an attractive possibility, especially in the treatment of oropharyngeal carcinoma [21]. In 2009, the US FDA approved the da Vinci system for transoral treatment of selected malignant diseases and all non-malignant lesions of the oropharynx, even when located at the base of the larynx and the tongue [19].

In 2010, Vicini et al. first proposed transoral robotic surgery for treating obstructive sleep apnoea. They reported that robot-assisted surgery resulted in minimal morbidity and was well-tolerated by the patients. Moreover, the apnoea-hypopnea index was significantly improved in all participants [22].

A 6-DOF robotic arm was proposed as a surgeon aid during orthognathic surgery. Established on 3D information obtained from a CT, positioning must be performed by the surgeon before surgery [23]. A jawbone skull phantom was used to perform preliminary experiments for the orthognathic surgery [24]. The available software needs to be upgraded and hardware safety improved before automated orthognathic surgery is investigated in human trials [19].

2.5.5 MISCELLANEOUS

2.5.5.1 Dental Hygiene Application

A robot system has been developed that simulates 3D brushing movements as a function of time [21]. The in-vitro results revealed the capability of the robotic system to exhibit reproducible significant differences in the cleaning efficacies of powered toothbrushes. A recent study proposed the application of micro-robots with catalytic ability to destroy biofilms within the root canal and tested the system in-vitro [19].

2.5.5.2 Dental Education

The idea of a dental training robot was first described in 1969. The application of a humanoid in dental education was tested in 2017. A humanoid, a full-body patient simulation system (SIMROID) [21]. "Hanako," the SIMROID stands 165 cm tall. It comes with a metal skeleton and vinyl chloride-based gum pattern of skin shown in Figure 2.25.

Tanzawa et al. introduced a medical emergency robot with the aim of helping dental students to get familiar with emergency situations. Another robotic educational equipment described in the literature is the ROBOTUTOR. This tool was developed as an alternative for a clinician to demonstrate tooth-cleaning techniques to patients. It is a robotic device to train and show brushing techniques [21]. A clinically validated robot toothbrushing program has been developed for reproducible and fast in vitro testing of tooth cleaning [19].

Virtual Reality (VR) laboratories with haptic devices are becoming more and more part of the regular curriculum in dental education and have been found to improve student's learning efficiency and effect.

2.5.5.3 Dental Assistance and Dental Material

Robotics finds application to standardize simple endoral radiographs to analyse CBCT and to compare the bone volumes to match the bone pre- and post-augmentation

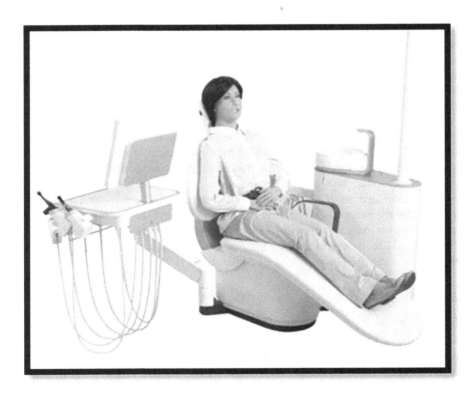

FIGURE 2.25 Simroid-patient simulation system for dental education.

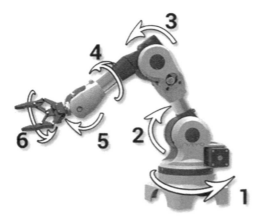

FIGURE 2.26   6-DOF robot arm.

procedure. A study examined the probability of active robot assistance during dental procedures by exchanging instruments through a multi-nodal communication model designed for clinicians as consumers. It consisted of visual gestures, speech input, touch display input, and bilateral physical robot-human communication. In this study, the researchers utilized a state-of-the-art sensitive, collaborative, and safe 7-DOF robotic system and performed a user study to investigate the possibility of varying robot-human communication dental procedures.

Robotic mastication or dental wear simulators are suggested to analyse dental implant materials or tooth-filling materials [21]. A 6-DOF robot exemplified in Figure 2.26 drove one of the systems. Another report described the testing of dental impression material utilizing a robotic arm [19].

2.6   ADVANTAGES AND DISADVANTAGES

Advantages

- Extremely high accuracy and precision.
- Stable and untiring, and hence can be used repeatedly without rest.
- Able to accurately process and judge quantitative information fed into the system.

Disadvantages

- No judgment of the situation and hence unable to use any qualitative information.
- Continuous monitoring of an experienced dentist is always required.
- These devices still remain very expensive and are out of reach of the common man.

2.7 LIMITATIONS

In theory, there are no restrictions on how AI can be used in prosthodontics. However, in many situations, it is monetary factors that drive the development and widespread adoption of new AI technologies in the most commercially lucrative areas and tend to restrict interesting dental applications since a market appears to be limited for the dental sector. Nevertheless, future developments and research on AI can be eagerly awaited.

AI was heavily dependent on datasets. These datasets should be appropriately classified and filtered for excellent model training. The drawback is that most data are in paper format and due to lack of awareness in follow up treatment, data consolidation was not done correctly. In the present scenario, the medical sector has started digitalizing the diagnosis and reports but still has a long way to go for accurate data that can be used in model training.

Furthermore, robotic systems are complex and require expertise for their proper operation and function. Another vital aspect might be the unknown patient acceptance and compliance among dentists. The point regarding the input of data is very critical.

Presently, in dentistry, two main facets can be seen—those that are performed very well via meticulous preoperative planning and implementation, and those carried out very inefficiently by the inexperienced and uninformed personnel resulting in unfavorable results [25]. The results would only be as good as the personnel incorporating the data into the robotic system.

2.8 FUTURE SCOPE

The use of AI in dentistry is said to increase precision, repeatability, and reliability throughout the literature; yet, the volume of robotic dentistry research is constrained by the absence of readily available systems. Additionally, there is a lack of proficiency to program and regulate robotic systems. Therefore, research in this area depends on effective collaboration between dentists and engineers. This might alter shortly since the robotics community investigates innovative communication strategies and programming paradigms.

A majority of the interdisciplinary research merging dentistry and engineering in robotic dentistry is focused on dental implantology, though the invasive nature of this technology might undermine the acceptance of this application among dentists and patients. Thus, these invasive technologies are less appropriate as forerunners. Hence, research in the domain of assistive robotic dentistry appears to have more potential than the conventional methods to support the presentation of this contemporary robotic-enabled era.

Moreover, research on dental educational robotics in university setup appears to be a potential propagator to introduce robotic dentistry and for removing the hindrance of acceptance of robotic systems among future dentists.

2.9 CONCLUSION

The application of AI in healthcare holds promise for the future since it would decentralize the treatment process. AI lets medical workers deliver remote care more effectively. Thanks to artificial intelligence (AI), future illness diagnosis will be more accurate as it will be able to forecast outcomes and combine them with human diagnoses to increase the likelihood of accurate identification [26].

All robot applications described in this chapter, from teeth arrangement for complete dentures, to dental material testing or tooth preparation, have an innate potential to progress dentistry into a new era where digitalization supports the management of our real world. Overall, the level of technological readiness is still low, and more research is required to be performed to produce a worth of robotic dentistry. Hence, the pace of research in this domain should increase in the coming years.

REFERENCES

1. George Puthenpurayil John, Tatu Elenjickal Joy, Justin Mathew and Vinod R. B. Kumar. "Applications of Cone Beam Computed Tomography for a Prosthodontist." The Journal of Indian Prosthodontic Society 16, no. 1 (Jan–Mar 2016): 3–7, 10.4103/0972-4052.161574
2. Randolph R. Resnik. Contemporary Implant Dentistry (4th ed., pp. 275–330). Elsevier, 2021.
3. Francesco Mangano, Andrea Gandolfi, Giuseppe Luongo and Silvia Logozzo. "Intraoral Scanners in Dentistry: A Review of the Current Literature." BMC Oral Health 17, no. 149 (December 2017): 1–11, 10.1186/s12903-017-0442-x
4. Silvia Logozzo, Elisabetta M. Zanetti, Giordano Franceschini and AriKilpelä Anssi Mäkynen. "Recent Advances in Dental Optics – Part I: 3D Intraoral Scanners for Restorative Dentistry." Optics and Lasers in Engineering 54 (March 2014): 203–221, 10.1016/j.optlaseng.2013.07.017
5. Kianoosh Torabi, Ehsan Farjood and Shahram Hamedani. "Rapid Prototyping Technologies and Their Applications in Prosthodontics, a Review of Literature." Journal of Dentistry, Shiraz University of Medical Sciences 16, no. 1 (March 2015): 1–9, PMID:25759851.
6. Abbas Azari and Sakineh Nikzad. "The Evolution of Rapid Prototyping in Dentistry: A Review." Rapid Prototyping Journal 15, no. 3 (March 2009): 216–225, 10.1108/13552540910961946
7. A. Kumar, P. Kumar, RK. Mittal, and H. Singh. "Printing File Formats for Additive Manufacturing Technologies." In Advances in Additive Manufacturing Artificial Intelligence, Nature-Inspired, and Biomanufacturing (pp. 87–102). Elsevier, 2023, 10.1016/B978-0-323-91834-3.00006-5
8. S. Sehrawat, A. Kumar, S. Grover, N. Dogra, J. Nindra, S. Rathee, et al. "Study of 3D Scanning Technologies and Scanners in Orthodontics." Materials Today: Proceedings 56 (2022): 186–193, 10.1016/j.matpr.2022.01.064
9. El Galil, Shaimaa L. Mohamed, Fardos N. Rizk, Marwa E. Sabet and Eman G. Abd. "Evaluation of Two Computer-Aided Design Software on the Adaptation of Digitally Constructed Maxillary Complete Denture." The Journal of Indian Prosthodontic Society 21 (November 2021): 383–390, 10.4103/jips.jips_137_21
10. Aalap Prajapati, Anchal Prajapati, Dhawal R. Mody and Anuraag B. Choudhary. 2014. "Dentistry Goes Digital: A Cad-Cam Way – A Review Article." IOSR Journal of Dental and Medical Sciences (IOSR-JDMS) 13, no. 8 (August 2014): 53–59, 10.9790/0853-13845359
11. R. J. Williams, Richard Bibb, Dominic Eggbeer and John Collis. "Use of CAD/CAM Technology to Fabricate a Removable Partial Denture Framework." The Journal Of Prosthetic Dentistry 96, no. 2 (August 2006): 96–99, 10.1016/j.prosdent.2006.05.029

12. Corina Marilena Cristache, Ioana Tudor, Liliana Moraru, Gheorghe Cristache, Alessandro Lanza and Mihai Burlibasa. "Digital Workflow in Maxillofacial Prosthodontics- An Update on Defect Data Acquisition, Editing and Design Using Open-Source and Commercial Available Software." Applied Sciences 11, no. 3 (January 2021): 973, 10.3390/app11030973

13. Shetty Shilpa. "Virtual Articulators and Virtual Facebow Transfers: Digital Prosthodontics!!!" The Journal of Indian Prosthodontic Society 15, no. 4: 291, 10.4103/0972-4052.171825

14. Y. Satya Sai Sruthi, B. Lakshmana Rao, Satyanarayana S V Tammineedi, G. Sirisha and C. Pallavi. "Reweigh of Classification of Face Bows and Articulators with Virtual Reality – An Innovation for Perfection." Journal of Pharmaceutical Sciences and Research 13, no. 3 (March 2021): 149–154.

15. Zeba Jafri, Nafis Ahmad, Madhuri Sawai, Nishat Sultan and Ashu Bhardwaj. "Digital Smile Design – An Innovative Tool in Aesthetic Dentistry." Journal of Oral Biology and Craniofacial Research 10 (April 2020): 194–198.

16. S. Sreelekshmi, Kurian Varghese, Joshy P Abraham and Jaysa J. J. "Applications of Robotics in Prosthodontics—A Review." International Journal of Innovative Research and Advanced Studies 4, no. 5 (May 2017): 38–41.

17. Shajahan P A, Rohit Raghavan and Neha Joe. "Application of Artificial Intelligence in Prosthodontics." International Journal of Science & Healthcare Research 6, no. 1 (Jan–March 2021): 57–60.

18. Xiaoyan Sun, Yongki Yoon, Jiang Li, and Frederic D. "McKenzie. Automated Image-Guided Surgery for Common and Complex Dental Implants." Journal Medical Engineering & Technology 38, no. 5 (May 2014): 251–259, 10.3109/03091902.2014.913079

19. Paras Ahmad, Mohammad Khursheed Alam, Ali Aldajani, Abdulmajeed Alahmari, Amal Alanazi, Martin Stoddart and Mohammed G. Sghaireen. "Dental Robotics: A Disruptive Technology." Sensors 21, no. 10: 1–15, 10.3390/s21103308

20. Jin-gang Jiang, Yong-de Zhang, Chun-ge Wei, Tian-hua He and Yi Liu. "A Review on Robot in Prosthodontics and Orthodontics." Advances in Mechanical Engineering 7 no. 1 (January 2015): 1–11.

21. Sujata Pandey, Ragini Pandey, Soumitra Agarwal and Aniket Mone. "Extending Arms In Prosthodontics: Artificial Intelligence." Chronicles of Dental Research 11, no. 2 (December 2022): 4–12.

22. Claudio Vicini, Iacopo Dallan, Pietro Canzi, Sabrina Frassineti, Andrea Nacci, Veronica Seccia, Erica Panicucci, Maria Grazia La Pietra, Filippo Montevecchi and Manfred Tschabitscher. "Transoral Robotic Tongue Base Resection in Obstructive Sleep Apnoea-Hypopnoea Syndrome: A Preliminary Report." Head Neck 34 (2012): 15–24, 10.1002/hed.21691

23. SY. Woo, S J. Lee, J Y. Yoo, J J. Han, S J. Hwang, K H. Huh, S S. Lee, M S. Heo, S C. Choi, and W J. Yi. "Autonomous Bone Reposition around Anatomical Landmark for Robot-Assisted Orthognathic Surgery." Journal of Cranio-Maxillofacial Surgery 45 (2017): 1980–1988.

24. S. Sehrawat, A. Kumar, M. Prabhakar, and J. Nindra. "The Expanding Domains of 3D Printing Pertaining to the Speciality of Orthodontics." Materials Today: Proceedings (2021), 10.1016/j.matpr.2021.09.124

25. A. Singhal, M. Phogat, D. Kumar, A. Kumar, M. Dahiya, and V.K. Shrivastava. "Study of Deep Learning Techniques for Medical Image Analysis: A Review." Materials Today: Proceedings 56 (2022): 209–214.

26. P. Rajendra, M. Kumari, S. Rani, N. Dogra, R. Boadh, A. Kumar, and M. Dahiya. "Impact of Artificial Intelligence on Civilization: Future Perspectives." Materials Today: Proceedings 56 (2022): 252–256.

3 Cryotherapy

A New Paragon in the Field of Endodontics

Sanjoli Jain and Mamta Singla
Department of Conservative Dentistry and Endodontics at
SGT University, Gurugram, Haryana, India

3.1 INTRODUCTION

3.1.1 WHAT IS CRYOTHERAPY?

The terms from which the word cryotherapy is obtained are the two Greek words "cryo" meaning "cold" and "therapeia" meaning "cure" [1–6]. It refers to bringing tissues' temperatures either lower or higher for purposes of treatment in physiotherapy. The concept of cryotherapy does not entail cooling the target tissue; instead, it means transferring heat from the tissue of higher temperature to the tissue of lower temperature [2–5].

It has mostly been utilized for treating pain and swelling following hip or knee replacement surgery, runner's knee, arthritis pain, etc. Additionally, it has been employed for the removal of dysplastic tissue. The National Cancer Institute referred to it as cryosurgery for this reason [3].

The duration of the exposure, the thermal conductivity of the tissues, the amount of heat or cold applied, and the type of thermal agents used to apply the heat or cold all serve a role in the extent of the temperature changes and biophysical changes in the tissues in this therapy [2–4].

Applying cold via various methods, such as ice packs, ice chips, etc., appears to reduce the conduction velocity of nerve signals, hemorrhage, edema, and local inflammation and is therefore effective in reducing musculoskeletal pain, muscular spasm, and connective tissue distension [1,3].

Following the application of either heat or cold, the three basic physiological responses are as follows:

i. an increase or decrease in local blood flow,
ii. an increase or decrease in cellular metabolic activity, and
iii. stimulation or inhibition of neural receptors in the skin and subcutaneous tissues.

DOI: 10.1201/9781003404934-3

Cryotherapy also affects the conduction capacity of nerves. Specialized nerve endings called nociceptors are triggered when tissue is injured. Thermoreceptors, which are temperature-sensitive nerve endings that are activated by variation in tissue temperature, are another type of pain receptor. Cryotherapy may interrupt nociception in the spiral cord by activating these thermoreceptors [2–6].

The use of this therapy was first confined to treating oral cavity and lip cancer. Its application in managing various benign skin growths and malignant lesions in the head and neck area is currently ubiquitous. Additionally employed during periodontal surgery, extractions, implant, and intraoral excisional surgeries, it has been shown to be useful in suppressing inflammation, pain, and arthritis of temporomandibular joint [4].

Management of pain pre and post root canal treatment is one of the most challenging and difficult part for the treatment in the field of endodontics and is often considered a standard of the clinician's skills as it leads to distress to both the patient as well as the dentist [5].

There are several reports of postendodontic therapy pain, with occurrence rates ranging from 3 to 58% [6]. To improve patient comfort and increase the efficiency of the work done by the dentist, researchers continually search for novel and innovative therapies. Numerous factors, including the condition of the pulp and peri radicular tissues, pre-operative pain, and the presence of periapical radiolucency, are thought to influence postoperative endodontic pain [4–6].

Hypothetical mechanisms that may be responsible for swelling and/or pain during endodontic therapy have been presented by many authors. These include chemical, mechanical, or microbial injury to the peri-radicular tissue, etc. [2,7–9].

Various strategies have been proposed to reduce postoperative pain, like drugs that include prophylaxis in the prescription, administration of long-lasting anesthesia with proper technique, for cleaning and shaping of root canal the technique that is best accepted is crown-down technique, and occlusal reduction of the tooth that has pain [2,7–9]. However, every strategy mentioned above has its own limitations. But as the field of endodontics keeps expanding, practitioners are increasingly incorporating cryo-treatment into their clinical procedures.

Cryotherapy has been employed in endodontics to treat root canals and during peri-radicular procedures to minimize postoperative pain and inflammation [10,11]. Deep cryotherapy of nickel-titanium (NiTi) endodontic files is another application of cryotherapy in endodontics that improved the instruments' resistance to cyclic fatigue and reduced the probability of file separation [3].

Recently, cryotherapy was also successfully tried in vital pulp therapy as an adjunct for hemostasis in conjunction with bioceramic materials like biodentine and MTA [3,4]. It has also been reported that temperature changes also influence the mechanical properties of dentine [11].

However, numerous research studies should be conducted so as to evaluate the further benefit of cryotherapy so that better treatment can be delivered to patients.

3.2 HISTORY

In around 2500 BCE, the Egyptians used decreased temperatures to cure an array of diseases. During a historic retreat from Moscow, Dominique-Jean Larrey,

Napoleon's renowned surgeon, utilized it as a supplement for amputations [1]. Dr. James Arnott reported on the positive effects of using a reduced temperature regionally to treat a variety of conditions, such as headaches and neuralgia, between 1845 and 1851 [1–3].

The invention of an expansion system for cooling gases initially began in 1877 by Frenchmen Cailletet and Swissmen Picet [1]. The first vacuum flask, invented by James Dewar in 1892, made it simpler to store and handle liquid gases. In 1895–1896, Von Linde introduced commercial air liquefaction [1].

Dr. William Pusey introduced solidified carbon dioxide ($-78.5°C$) into clinical practice [1]. Solid carbon dioxide was the most widely used cryogenic agent in the early 1900s, while liquid air was occasionally employed after 1910 [1–4].

Irving and Turnacliff treated warts, lichen planus, and other skin conditions with liquid oxygen ($-182.9°C$) which was introduced for clinical use during the 1920s. However, after some time it was reported that the liquid oxygen had hazardous properties since it was highly flammable [1].

Liquid $N2(-196°C)$ was widely used after World War Two. The use of cryogen for the treatment of keratoses, verrucae, and a variety of other non-neoplastic diseases was first introduced into clinical practice in 1950 by Dr Ray Allington [11]. Irving Cooper, and Arnold Lee collaborated to establish modern cryosurgery [1].

Between 1961 and 1970, further cryosurgical equipment were developed utilizing liquified nitrogen and a variety of other cryogenic agents, such as nitrous oxide, carbon dioxide, argon, ethyl chloride, and fluorinated hydrocarbons [1].

Cryosurgery was used by Torre to treat several kinds of cancers, including benign lesions and squamous cell and basal cell carcinomas. Setrag Zacarian [1] unveiled a hand-held self-pressurized device in 1967. Together, they reported on the development and use of a handheld liquid nitrogen spray system in 1968 while he was working with Michael Bryne.

Cryotherapy has emerged in recent years as an effective treatment for a variety of benign and malignant skin diseases, with new applications constantly being described.

3.3 EFFECT AND PATHOPHYSIOLOGY OF CRYOTHERAPY

3.3.1 Freezing/Thawing Effects

Freezing of tissue has been extensively researched, with a few hypotheses on how freezing results in cell destruction and death. The primary theory involves direct cellular injury from the extracellular space, because of high concentrations of extracellular ice causing cell dehydration. This occurs through two mechanisms: slow cooling rates resulting in freezing in the extracellular space causing the cells to dehydrate themselves through osmosis, and membrane destabilization during the freezing and thawing cycles [9].

An additional mechanism likely involves intracellular ice formation, disrupting the organelles within the cell as well as the membrane of the cell. A second theory involves an immunological response to freezing, with the immune system becoming reactive to destroyed frozen tissue, which then results in the immune system reacting to any remaining residual tissue. The final theory suggests that damage to

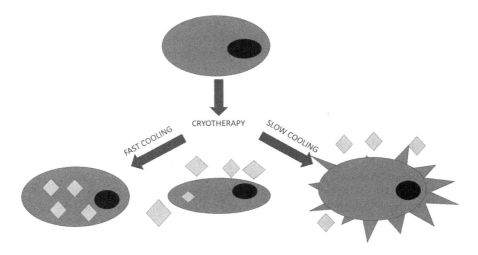

FIGURE 3.1   Thawing effect.

the blood vessels of the lesion through freezing results in loss of blood flow, leading to tissue damage and death [9].

As explained in Figure 3.1, the thawing of these lesions has varying effects, but they are determined by the cooling rate. Slow thawing after cryotherapy is performed allows for the maximum amount of ice to form, thereby causing the greatest effects on the cells. Completely thawing the lesion before re-freezing is essential, as this creates further ice formation and allows for the recrystallization of the ice crystals.

Recrystallization within cells occurs when smaller crystals thaw, then form larger and larger crystals over time and eventually result in punctures to the cell membrane. Rapid cooling and rapid thawing, however, have also proven to be effective, by creating smaller ice crystals within the cells. This then allows for further recrystallization. Previous studies have shown that cells near the center of the probe experience the lowest temperature and fastest cooling rates, whereas the tissue along the outer edge of the lesion typically has near-normal body temperature [9,12].

3.3.2   Pathophysiology

In cryotherapy, biophysical alterations in the tissues and the magnitude of the temperature change depending on the difference between the application of low or high temperature, time for which the tissue is exposed to altered temperature, the temperature that the object possesses, and form of agent used to apply heat or cold, etc. A pack of ice, gel-pack, ice shavings, melted ice water, are some of the ways via which cold application can be done [2].

A decrease in the speed of nerve signal transmission, edema, hemorrhage, and local inflammation could be achieved by applying cold through various means, and this is effective in reducing musculoskeletal pain, muscular spasm, and connective tissue distension. This is supported by clinical as well as physiological evidence [2,3].

TABLE 3.1

Physiological Effects of Cryotherapy

Three basic physiological tissue effects of cryotherapy (2–4)

- Vascular,
- Neurologic, and
- Tissue metabolism

The three basic physiological effects of cryotherapy are mentioned in Table 3.1:

After 15 minutes of prolonged exposure to low temperatures, a tissue experiences reflex vasoconstriction, which is then followed by cold-induced vasodilation. The release of the histamine-like molecules "H" causes vaso-dilation. Vasoconstriction and vasodilation are again triggered by the subsequent passage of warmed blood in the area. As explained in Figure 3.2, the "Hunting Response" is a term given to this continuous, repetitive cycle of vasoconstriction and vasodilation [3].

The adrenergic chemicals of the blood vessels initiate a neurological reaction of vasoconstriction followed by vasodilation and reduce vascular permeability. Decreased permeability is a main factor that reduces the quantity of fluid that leaks as an exudate or a transudate into the peri-radicular tissues, thereby decreasing edema and swelling, which mostly occurs in periapical tissue after chemo-mechanical preparation [3,4].

Applying cold prevents the local blood flow, which inhibits the rebound phenomena that occurs after using local anesthetics that contain vasoconstrictors. Analgesia is closely correlated with the nerve conduction velocity of the nociceptive sensory nerve fibers in terms of the neurologic effect [3].

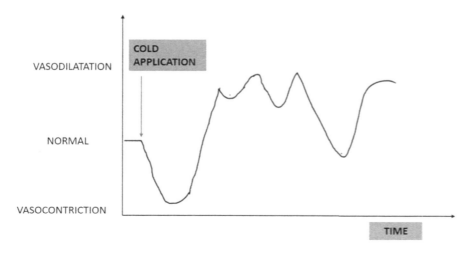

FIGURE 3.2 Hunting response.

Analgesia can be brought on by cryotherapy by lowering the rate of nerve conduction. However, Franz and Iggo's research demonstrates that this effect is more potent in myelinated nerve fibers (A-delta fibers) compared to unmyelinated fibers (C fibers) because the former deactivates at a higher temperature, around 7°C, than the latter, which deactivate at a lower temperature, around 3°C. The analgesic effect of cryotherapy has also been attributed to the gate control theory, which proposes that faster sensory input from the larger myelinated A-fibers causes the gate to momentarily close and prevent the transmission of the more painful impulses from the unmyelinated C fibers [2–4].

Additionally, the cold treatment may cause analgesia by stimulating endorphin release. Endorphins minimize the transmission of nociceptive impulses to the central nervous system by binding to opioid receptors in the medullary dorsal horn [3].

Additionally, a cold treatment may lower the activation threshold of tissue nociceptors, producing a cold-induced neuropraxia, a localized anesthetic effect [5,6]. Thus, both a decreased release of chemical pain mediators and a slower transmission of brain pain signals result in the analgesic action of cooling.

Inflammatory response and endothelial dysfunction are exacerbated by cold by reducing the number of leukocytes that migrate to the affected area [7,8]. Cryotherapy has an impact on the metabolism of the tissue in that it causes the damaged tissue to tend to utilize more oxygen, which leads to tissue hypoxia and necrosis, subsequently. More than 50% of the tissue blood flow and cell metabolism is decreased by cryotherapy. This reduces the amount of oxygen consumption, slows down metabolic activities, hinders the production of free radicals in tissues, and shields against hypoxia and additional tissue damage [3,5].

Table 3.2 summarizes the pathophysiologic effects of cryotherapy.

The category of tissue to be targeted determines the ideal dosage for cryotherapy [8]. The treatment has effects on vascular and neurologic systems both locally and at the spinal cord level. Topical cold therapy lowers the activation threshold of tissue nociceptors and the conduction velocity of pain nerve impulses by lowering skin temperature and that of the underlying tissues to a depth of 2–4 cm [12]. Cold-induced neuropraxia, a local anesthetic effect, results from this.

TABLE 3.2
Pathophysiologic Effects of Cryotherapy [13]

	Cold	Heat
Pain	↓	↓
Spasm	↓	↓
Metabolism	↓	↑
Blood flow	↓	↑
Inflammation	↓	↑
Edema	↓	↑
Extensibility	↓	↑

An ice wrap on one leg for 20 minutes reduced arterial blood flow by 38%, soft tissue blood flow by 26%, and bone uptake, which indicates changes in bone blood flow and metabolism, by 19%, according to a study implementing bone scanning. In the aftermath of an acute traumatic injury to a significant joint, this study supports the use of ice to treat both soft tissue and bone. It has been demonstrated that ongoing cryotherapy has a protective effect on damaged tissue [12].

Although the mechanism of action and efficacy of cryotherapy have been extensively researched in the literature [14], there is a lack of good data that supports its conclusions, in addition to the standardization of key elements such the time, length, form of application, and cold agent employed. To understand the potential benefits of the treatment and apply it clinically, studies are also necessary.

3.3.3 Complications of Cryotherapy

Applying cryotherapy close to superficial nerves requires caution, especially if the cold and compression are combined. After cryotherapy, there have been reports of peroneal neuropathy, and ulnar, axillary, and lateral femoral cutaneous nerve injuries. Cryotherapy has also been linked to heart problems (bradycardia), Raynaud's syndrome, cold urticaria, frostbite, and slower wound healing due to decreased metabolic activity [12].

3.4 EFFECT OF CRYOTHERAPY ON ROOT CANAL IRRIGATION AND REDUCTION OF POST OPERATIVE PAIN

Endodontic treatment's main objective is the eradication of infection using an adequate cleaning and shaping technique, followed by obturation to create a hermetic seal and hasten the healing of the peri-radicular space. Even when the patients receive the treatment with the utmost care, they nevertheless endure discomfort or flare-ups. Postendodontic pain, or PEP, is typically the appearance of symptomatic apical periodontitis [13,14].

The health of the pulp and peri-radicular tissues, microbial components, the effects of inflammatory chemical mediators, immune system-mediated phenomena, psychological variables, preoperative pain, gender, the type of tooth involved, and the pressure in the periapical tissue are among the many of the reasons of PEP [10,12–14]. Other factors like inadequate root canal instrumentation, hyper-occlusion, failure to recognize additional/accessory canals, presence of periapical pathology, etc. also contribute to PEP.

Pain is thought to be an unreliable indicator of long-term effectiveness since it may be brought on by a sudden inflammatory reaction in the peri-radicular tissues [9,14].

Therefore, managing and preventing this postendodontic pain is an important aspect of endodontic treatment. However, in clinical settings, this PEP can be prevented by taking very stringent precautions while performing the endodontic therapy.

Other PEP management methods include the administration of long-lasting anesthesia, occlusal reduction, and premedication with prophylactic analgesics and corticosteroids before endodontic treatment [9,12–14]. PEP prevalence increased in the first six hours and gradually decreased after one week, according to Pak and White, who discovered it was 40% at 24 hours, 11% at one week, and peaked at 40% at 24 hours [9,14].

Although cryo-treatment has advantages for several intraoral surgical procedures, there isn't sufficient proof to support the literature's explanation of the way it functions. However, only a few investigations have investigated and/or demonstrated the use of intracanal cryotherapy for reducing postoperative pain in endodontics in the past few years [9].

For example, Vera et al. were the first to shed light on cryotherapy in endodontics. After a final irrigation with 2.5°C cold saline and Endovac (Kerrdental, KerrHawe SA, Bioggio, Switzerland), they assessed the temperature change on the exterior root surface of tooth that was extracted. They came to the conclusion that any decrease in external root surface temperature of more than 10°C maintained for 4 minutes might be sufficient to have a local anti-inflammatory effect in the peri-radicular tissues [2,3,6].

The EndoVac instrument was used to transport the irrigant up to the apical third because irrigating solutions are rarely able to reach the root apices due to the apical vapor lock. Because of differences in dentine qualities including mineralization and dentin width from coronal and apical thirds, the propagation of cold temperatures to the periodontium varies from the coronal to the apical third of the root. The cervical third of the root dentin contains an increased amount of larger dentinal tubules, which may complicate the transmission of a therapeutic effect. In contrast, apical root dentin has fewer dentinal tubules, is denser and more calcified, and facilitates more effective cold transmission to the surrounding tissues [2,10].

In their latest study, Al-Abdullah et al. assessed the effectiveness of cryotherapy in treating postoperative pain in teeth with vital single roots and single canals that had undergone two distinct types of preparation. For groups receiving cold saline, there were no PEP levels throughout any of the monitoring intervals. Except for the first week of the research, there was a significant difference (p 0.05) between the ProTaper Universal preparation groups that used cold saline and those that did not. According to Vera et al., intracanal cryotherapy successfully decreased PEP, which could possibly be explained by the likelihood that the periapical area's colder temperature began to have a local anti-inflammatory effect by means of lowering edoema [9,15–17].

Cryotherapy reduced postoperative pain after the use of a side-vented, positive-pressure 31-G Navi Tip needle in a different study which evaluated the effect of 2.5°C cold saline irrigation as the final irrigant on postoperative pain following single-visit root canal treatment of teeth with vital pulps [2–4].

According to a study by Al Nahlawi et al., postendodontic pain after single-visit RCTs can be eliminated by using the intracanal cryotherapy approach with negative pressure irrigation. Another study concluded that the last irrigation of the canal with saline, either at room temperature or cold, was effective in minimizing postendodontic discomfort [2,3].

Sodium hypochlorite was cryo-treated at a temperature of 2.5°C–4°C and used to irrigate each canal for 4 minutes in a study by Nandakumar M et al. The use of sodium hypochlorite can be justified by its antimicrobial and tissue-dissolving abilities. When compared to regular sodium hypochlorite, the antibacterial activity of cryo-treated sodium hypochlorite significantly reduced the prevalence of Enterococcus faecalis. According to the study's conclusions, the cryotherapy group significantly reduced postoperative pain levels at the time points tested—6 hours, 24 hours, and 48 hours—and devoured lower analgesic medication at the 6-hour mark. This may be attributable to the cold-treated irrigant's synergistic action, which reduces the external root surface temperature and causes an anti-inflammatory response in the peri-radicular tissues [15].

Another study demonstrated that sodium hypochlorite stored in the refrigerator produced significantly more free chlorine than it did when maintained at room temperature. This finding suggests that higher percentages of active chlorine may have greater antibacterial activity.

Sadaf carried out a randomized clinical trial to investigate the effects of extraoral, intraoral, and intracanal cryotherapy on the PEP in patients receiving root canal therapy for symptomatic apical periodontitis (SAP). The main outcome for postoperative pain was reported using a 100-mm VAS score on days 1, 3, 5, and 7. After receiving cryotherapy (intracanal, intraoral, and extraoral) treatment, patients reported less postoperative discomfort overall than those in the control group [9].

The effect of various irrigation procedures on postoperative pain and interleukin 6 expressions in patients with symptomatic apical periodontitis was investigated by Emad et al. (Thesis, 2020) in a recent unpublished study. In comparison to room temperature irrigation, all irrigation procedures that used 2–5 mL of cold irrigant had considerably reduced pain scores. Additionally, from the beginning to the end of cleaning and shape, irrigation with 2 to 5 mL of cold sodium hypochlorite resulted in the least quantity of interleukin 6 expressions [3].

In a single-visit endodontic procedure, another study assessed the effects of normal saline used as a terminal irrigant at room temperature along with low temperatures on postoperative pain. Only the asymptomatic patients were included in this study. Normal saline at room temperature was discovered to be comparable to cryotherapy in terms of reducing postoperative pain in asymptomatic patients. A clinical trial concluded that cryotherapy reduced the incidence of PEP and as a result, it could assist with chemo-mechanical preparation and minimize the need for drug prerequisite in patients with vital pulp [9].

According to research by Duaa S. Bazaid et al., after 24 and 48 hours postoperatively, cryotherapy brought about a statistically significant reduction in postoperative discomfort for those with irreversible pulpitis and apical periodontitis in comparison to the use of normal saline. This can be explained by the fact that cold saline serves as a local anti-inflammatory in the apical area to reduce edoema and inflammation. Intracanal cryotherapy did not significantly reduce postoperative pain in patients with irreversible pulpits who were not diagnosed with apical periodontitis as compared to normal saline. In these circumstances, the source of the inflammation was removed in both the control and study groups since the inflammatory pulp tissues had previously been removed. As a result of this, the peri-apical tissues had no effect and the inflammation was restricted to the root canal.

This may help to explain why the cold saline did not cause a response which was beyond the usual [2,3].

Therefore, we can infer that cryo-irrigation is quite significant in reducing periapical inflammation reducing postoperative pain. However, further studies need to be conducted to formulate a definite protocol for cryo-irrigation.

3.5 ROLE OF CRYOTHERAPY ON FRACTURE RESISTANCE OF ENDODONTICALLY TREATED TOOTH

In a study on teeth that had undergone endodontic treatment, Keskin et al. evaluated the effect of intracanal cryotherapy on the teeth' resistance to fracture. A four-minute in vitro study found that intracanal cryotherapy lowers the external root surface temperature by 10°C. Variations in temperature have been reported to affect the mechanical properties of dentin. However, there's not much study on the use of intracanal cryotherapy and how it affects the fracture resistance of teeth that underwent endodontic treatment [9,18,19].

In comparison to the reference group, they ultimately came to the opinion that the resistance to vertical fracture had considerably reduced after using intracanal cryotherapy as the last used irrigant. The use of cold saline directly within the pulp space may cause high articulated thermal stress in the dentin component due to the distinctive tubular microstructure of the dentin which lies closer to the pulp space and insufficient structure of the enamel [9].

Thermal change is another factor that can cause mechanical stress in the tooth structure. According to studies, the amount of stress is influenced by factors such as the difference of temperature between the medium and the tooth which is being treated, and also the shape and structure of the tooth, its thermal transfer coefficient, and its physical features, such as past exposure to mechanical stress and aging [18].

According to a prior study, applying cold water to a tooth's outer surface generates excess thermal-related stresses in the structure of the tooth, notably tensile stresses present inside the enamel and compressive stresses present inside the dentine, which can cause deformation of the structure in as less as one second after the exposure. However, during clinical operations, it would be anticipated that cold water administered to the teeth would rapidly [3,18]

Therefore, we can infer that utilization of cold saline or other cryo-treated solution for the irrigation might lead to decrease in the overall pain and might affect the mechanical properties of the tooth.

However, we need furthermore studies in order to inculcate this technique/procedure in normal clinical practice.

3.6 ANTIMICROBIAL EFFICACY OF CRYO-TREATMENT AGAINST ENTEROCOCCUS FAECALIS

Because of its several virulent features, Enterococcus faecalis is the species that is most frequently linked to persistent root canal infections. It accounts for 6% of the total microflora in the canals and exists in almost 22–77% of retreatment cases of root canal [20].

After chemo-mechanical preparation, it has been commonly observed that bacteria can still survive in the canal system. As a result, endodontics has used a range of irrigant treatments as well as other techniques to reduce or get rid of the bacterial load. Currently, the most used irrigant in endodontics is NaOCl [20].

But even after frequent irrigation with NaOCl, residual bacteria are present in roughly 50% of teeth at the time of filling material placement. Numerous irrigation approaches have been suggested for enhancing the efficacy of NaOCl and eliminating the microorganisms present in the root canal [4,20].

Yamamoto and Harris have described how liquid nitrogen used in cryotherapy affects microorganisms. The cell wall destruction, the release of components that are present intracellularly, and changes in the protein structure (confirmational changes) have all been linked to process of freezing and thawing. The gold standard irrigant, sodium hypochlorite, has been used experimentally in multiple investigations against the cryogenic fluid, which has demonstrated a higher effectiveness in antimicrobial action due to the fact that it can reach the appropriate depth and instantly freeze bacteria, followed by cryo-destruction [4].

According to Nandakumar and Nasim (2020), cryo-treated NaOCl helps in lowering postoperative pain and edoema. According to one study, keeping sodium hypochlorite at a concentration of 6% in a refrigerator is the best way to prevent an apparent decrease of active chlorine. The antibacterial action increases as the free chlorine level increases [7].

Cryotherapy and 5% NaOCl was examined by Mandras et al. to determine the probable microbicidal effects against Enterococcus faecalis. A dental instrument with a duct and an attachment for liquid nitrogen was used for cryotherapy, and the cryogenic fluid was administered using a cooling needle. Cryo-instrumentation and NaOCl irrigation significantly (p 0.01) lowered the amount of Ent. faecalis in the root channel. Therefore, compared to a typical NaOCl, it appeared to have an enormous effect on the decrease in microorganisms [9,20].

After 24 hours, NaOCl + cryo treatment significantly improved root canal disinfection infection with Ent. faecalis (P 0.01): a significant decrease in the number of bacteria in the root canal was found to be lower than 2 logs as when they are compared to positive control group and lesser than 1 log when compared only to NaOCl. In the negative control group, there was no growth of bacteria on any of the roots. In comparison to the positive controls and the specimens treated with 9% NaOCl solution, no statistically significant difference was seen [20].

As a result, this study arrived at the notion that cryo-treatment tends to have a more potent impact on the decrease in bacteria than traditional NaOCl irrigation. On the clinical result following cryotherapy, the impact of root canal therapy caused by statistical bacterial load reduction is still unknown. Clinical investigations targeted at developing an appropriate irrigation technique should be conducted in order to further study the intriguing potential of cryotherapy.

3.7 EFFECT OF CRYOTHERAPY ON ENDODONTIC INSTRUMENTS

The most important part of root canal therapy is believed to be biomechanical preparation [2–5]. In curved canals, rotating endodontic instruments are subjected to compressive and tensile strains. The point of curvature is where this stress is concentrated. It has been demonstrated that a continuous cycle of tensile and compressive forces in the canal's area of curvature, to which NiTi rotary instruments are exposed, results in an extremely destructive sort of loading, leading to cyclic fatigue and ultimately fracture of the instrument. It has been stated that 50–90% of mechanical failures have been attributed to cyclic fatigue [21,22].

The unexpected separation of rotary instruments during instrumentation is a significant barrier to successful root canal therapy [3,7].

Flexural fracture (cycle fatigue fracture) and torsional fracture are the two fracture mechanisms reported for NiTi instruments. Sometimes, when the file gets engaged in the apical region during instrument rotation, torsional fatigue failure causes ductile fracture. The constant phase transition between the austenitic and martensitic phases of NiTi, on the other hand, causes cyclic fatigue failure, which results in cyclic fatigue and fracture that is referred to as brittle fracture when it surpasses the unrecoverable plastic deformation state, inside a curved root canal. Up to 90% of fractures are brought about by this mechanism. To increase the cutting effectiveness, cyclic fatigue resistance, and wear resistance of rotary files, numerous surface treatment techniques have been suggested. These include cryogenic processing, electropolishing, thermal nitridation, physical vapor deposition of titanium nitride, and boron ion implantation, etc. [3].

Historically, cryogenic treatment of metal during manufacturing had been recommended to increase its surface hardness and thermal durability. It is a supplementary procedure that involves cooling highly elastic NiTi and stainless steel to below-freezing levels before allowing the metal to gradually reach its normal temperature. Shallow cryogenic treatment and deep cryogenic treatment have been defined based on the treatment temperature. Deep cryogenic treatment is preferable to traditional shallow cryogenic treatment [2].

The main advantage of the dry deep cryogenic treatment (DCT) is that the temperature is gradually increased or decreased to avoid thermal shock, which could lead the instrument to become brittle. The advantages of deep cryogenic treatment over conventional shallow cryogenic treatment include improved cutting performance, better metal strength overall, and the release of alloy internal tensions due to plastic transformation caused by cryogenic treatment. In contrast to surface methods of treatment, cryogenic treatment affects the full cross-section of the metal rather than just the surface. Cryogenic therapy may therefore be effective for enhancing the durability of rotary endodontic instruments. Numerous theories have been brought out to explain how cryogenic therapy improves specific features. These include:

- the emergence of titanium nitride on the surface as a result of an interaction between nitrogen and titanium atoms.,
- NiTi alloy's atomic lattice is subjected to nitrogen atom deposition, which strains the structure.
- a more thorough martensitic transition from the NiTi alloy's austenite phase.; and
- the precipitation of smaller carbide particles all across the crystal structure.

Cryogenic changes in steel alloys have been explained by the latter two explanations. The fourth mechanism is right away ruled out because the NiTi alloy contains no carbon. Which mechanism is accountable is a matter of controversy. Endodontic literature has reported on two research that investigated cryogenic therapy on stainless steel endodontic instruments. While Bramipour et al. found no effect of cryogenic treatment on the cutting efficiency of stainless-steel endodontic instruments (Flex R files; Midwest Dental Equipment & Supply, Oklahoma City, OK, and Hedstrom files), Berls found no appreciable improvement in wear resistance of the stainless-steel hand instruments (S-type and K-type).; Kerr Dental, Kerr Hawe SA, Bioggio, Switzerland). Kim et al. investigated into how cryogenic treatment affected the microhardness and cutting effectiveness of superelastic NiTi endodontic instruments. Although a rise in microhardness was seen, neither the surface nor the internal structure of the metal changed significantly or in a way that could be quantified.

According to Vinoth Kumar et al., cryogenic treatment of super-elastic NiTi files considerably improved cutting effectiveness but preserved wear resistance. The time and type of cryogenic treatment may be responsible for this variance. In the first experiment, instruments were completely submerged in liquid nitrogen for 10 minutes; in the second, dry DCT therapy was carried out for 24 hours. The dry DCT treatment greatly enhances the cyclic fatigue resistance of super-elastic NiTi files as compared to the untreated files [21,23].

The main benefits of utilizing cryogenic treatment can therefore be seen as improving wear resistance and decreasing internal stresses. This favorable effect of dry DCT on the cyclic fatigue resistance of rotating NiTi files was criticized by Yazdizadeh et al.'s study, which found no improvement in cyclic resistance when the files were entirely submerged in 2196°C for 24 hours. NiTi alloys used for endodontic instruments can be divided into two groups based on their crystalline makeup and austenite finish temperature [21].

At body temperature, the first group of instruments—conventional superelastic NiTi, M-Wire, and Rphase—primarily exist in the austenite phase. Due to the stress-induced martensite transition, they have superelastic characteristics and frequently recover their original shape following deformation. The other class of NiTi instruments, which includes Gold and Blue heat-treated NiTi files and CM-Wire, mostly exist in the martensite phase at body temperature. Due to the reorientation of the martensite variations, these martensitic instruments are easily deformed and exhibit a shape memory effect when heated.

Despite the high degree of flexibility of martensite group, further cryogenic processing was done to increase the amount of martensite and enhance cycle fatigue resistance and cutting efficiency, especially for smaller-sized instruments. DCT was administered at 2185°C for 24 hrs and 6 hrs of soaking, respectively [21,23].

With a 24-hour soaking duration, DCT significantly improved cycle fatigue resistance by 13%, but only by 1% with soaking time of 6 hours. The soaking time did not, however, have a similar impact on cutting effectiveness. This might be primarily a result of sufficient time being available for the full transformation of martensite from retained austenite [21,23].

3.8   EFFECT OF CRYOTHERAPY ON VITAL PULP THERAPY AND PERI RADICULAR SURGERY

When reversible or irreversible pulpitis in a carious tooth is found and excavation of caries leads to pulp exposure which might be direct or indirect, partial pulpectomy or pulp capping procedures are recommended treatments. But it is important to assess each case carefully because vital pulp therapy is not recommended for pulps that have partial necrosis of the pulp due to a diagnosis of necrosis which was done before commencing the treatment. It is important to keep in mind that pulpal bleeding could serve as a clinical indicator of how severe pulpal inflammation is. Hemorrhaging in pulps seems to stop when a pre-treatment diagnosis of mild or reversible pulpitis is made, and it is easily controlled by the application of ice [2,3].

The procedure can be carried out on teeth with diagnosis of the pulp reversible pulpitis or symptomatic irreversible pulpitis as well as on teeth with peri radicular pathology of normal or symptomatic apical periodontitis [lesion].

It is crucial to keep in mind that to conduct the cryotherapy of vital pulp requires that the tooth be substituted with a composite restoration as soon as possible and it is not recommended to place a temporary filling or prepare a tooth for a crown after the vital pulp cryotherapy has been done [11].

The final radiograph after the definitive restoration in actuality has a similar appearance to the final radiograph following regenerative endodontic therapy. When compared to the final radiograph obtained after vital pulp therapy with calcium hydroxide, the vital pulp cryotherapy radiograph exhibits improved radiopacity and can reveal more material accumulation on the coronal part of the pulp [24–29].

When using the cryo-technique, shaved- sterile ice is placed on vital pulp tissue that was exposed by the carious lesion either directly or indirectly [2,3]. Cryotherapy to preserve vital pulp has been employed for treating pulpal bleeding. If there is significant bleeding, it may be necessary to perform a partial pulpectomy to eliminate the inflammatory tissue of the pulp, before applying sterile ice shavings and administering the cryotherapy [4].

The pulpal tissue and the entire tooth were immersed in sterile water ice shavings (0°C) whether the pulp was exposed directly or indirectly. The sterile water was frozen to create shaved ice, which was then put in an ice-shaving equipment. It was removed with a high-speed suction after about a minute, and when the melted ice had been removed or eliminated, the exposed area was rinsed with 17% EDTA [2,4,9].

It was noted that teeth continued to be functional, vital, and asymptomatic for the following several months. In order to evaluate the long-term prognosis of cryotherapy in vital pulp therapy, more clinical study is advised [9].

Since EDTA has been proven to produce a number of growth factors that encourage matrix secretion, odontoblastic differentiation, and tertiary development, EDTA irrigation should be preferred over sodium hypochlorite irrigation. In addition, it promotes the adhesion, migration, and differentiation of stem cells from dental pulp. A bio-ceramic material was applied onto the pulp that had been exposed or indirectly and after it had been treated with EDTA and shaved sterile ice. Finally, a permanent restoration was placed over it. After two weeks, the treated teeth were symptom-free and at 12- to 18-month of follow-up, the teeth were still vital, symptom free, and functional.

As a result, it can be assumed that this chapter presented a novel vital pulp cryotherapy technique that entails the use of cryotherapy, EDTA, bio ceramics, and composite restoration on a pulp tissue that was either directly or indirectly exposed.

The patient should be put on a two-week recall following a vital pulp cryotherapy surgery in order to determine postoperative pain. In the first two weeks or at any time after the first two weeks following a vital pulp cryotherapy treatment, if the patient presents with either no change in preoperative pain, the emergence of postoperative pain, or necrotic pulp, the treated tooth should be reevaluated for conventional endodontic therapy. To determine the long-term prospects of pulp after vital pulp cryotherapy, more clinical research must be done. However, more clinical research is needed to assess how vital pulp cryotherapy is going to perform over the long term [24,25,30].

- **Effect On Peri Radicular Surgery:** the use of local anesthetics containing vasoconstrictors causes a bounce-back phenomenon that is neutralized by the postoperative cold administration, which narrows the local bloodstream. In consideration of this, the recommended standard in postsurgical steady therapy is to reduce the temperature of the surgical site using cold application [9].

3.9 APPLICATION OF CRYOSURGERY IN MAXILLOFACIAL LESIONS

Patients generally endure cryotherapy well because it causes minimal to no pain, no bleeding, and minimal to no scarring. The ease of use, maintenance of the inorganic bone structure, and exceptionally low infection rates are all clinical advantages. Compared to radiotherapy or chemotherapy, it has a more localized effect and can be repeated without causing future ill effects. Its usefulness for patients in which surgery cannot be performed because of age or medical history might be the greatest advantage. Cryotherapy has disadvantages, such as swelling and a lack of depth and area management. Also, it depends extensively on the knowledge and experience of the operator [31,32].

Keratotic, hyperplastic, granulomatous, vascular, pigmented, and salivary gland lesions have all been treated using cryotherapy.

Although biopsy before cryotherapy can compromise the outcome for clinically diagnosable lesions such as mucoceles and hemangiomas, histological analysis is typically necessary to establish lesion diagnosis.

3.9.1 BENIGN LESIONS

1. Melanin problems

The use of cryosurgery to treat mucosal lesions is not a subject that is frequently covered in proof-based writing. Gingival melanin pigmentation is a common disorder that affects people of all races, sexual orientations, and ethnicities equally.

Yeh [33] treated 20 patients who had presented with gingival hyperpigmentation using q-tips which were submerged in liquid nitrogen for about 20–30 seconds. This method is an alternative to lasers and medical procedures for depigmenting the gingiva. Excellent outcomes were observed, and patients were generally extremely satisfied and appreciated. Yeh [34,35] also thought about how such cold temperatures would affect macules which were melanotic macules. These were placed on the vermilion border of the lip, giving the patients an unsightly look and leading them to worry.

He gave the same 30-second treatment to 15 patients using fluid nitrogen, and the recovery time was 7 days. Six individuals had noticeable regimentation, which was eliminated in a similar manner to achieve 100% reduction. Following treatment, the labial mucosa developed a slight erythema, which was promptly followed by a white sludge that could be removed from the underlying tissue and appeared after 4 days. None of these patients experienced any postoperative pain, discharge, contamination, or scarring [34].

2. Inflammatory papillary hyperplasia

Incendiary papillary hyperplasia is a disorder that causes wearers of dental prostheses a constant discomfort.

As a result of the difficulty of the situation for both the dentist and the patient, a number of treatments have been tried thus far, including medical procedures, CO_2 laser removal, [36] cryosurgery [31,37,38] and electrocautery.

The treatment for this condition that has been available for some time is cryotherapy, which has had excellent results with fewer recurrences. Amaral et al. placed a cotton instrument that had absorbed fluid nitrogen onto the hyperplastic tissue for 12 to 30 seconds. Complete involution was achieved through administration of two to four medications weekly in intervals. Freon, a fluid cryogen, was applied to the hyperplastic tissue for 45 seconds at a temperature of 50°C to 60°C [32,36].

This entire hyperplastic tissue required to be treated over the course of several times. He said that cryosurgery was preferred to electrocautery since it caused less patient discomfort and no offensive stench.

3. Pyogenic granuloma

In a study [39] used nitrous oxide shut-frame therapy to treat three pyogenic granulomas and one fibroma in order to reach a test temperature of 70°C. Two minutes of freezing and 4 minutes of defrosting were carried out. For their entire relapse, every lesion required two sessions. In conjunction with routine, careful treatment for both wounds, cryosurgery resulted in a bloodless field with minimal scarring.

4. Hemangioma

In the past, hemangiomas were typically treated with an open cryosurgery method, eliminating the need for a more advanced method. According to Leopard, two cycles of 1.5 minute freeze-defrost of cryosurgery can completely relapse large hemangiomas [40].

Gongloff et al. used nitrous oxide (89°C), which was delivered via an intriguing nitrous oxide cryosurgical mechanical assembly. And nearly 10 patients who had received cryosurgery with nitrous oxide showed minimal blood loss and discomfort.

Traditional procedures for careful extraction failed to take into consideration useful faults or distortions that could have been seen [41]. Yeh used a q-tip nitrogen framework to treat hemangiomas for 60–70 seconds throughout the course of 2–4 subsequent treatments and discovered no repetition.

3.9.2 Malignant

1. Leukoplakia

Sako et al. estimated that 20% of leukoplakia patients had repeat cryosurgery procedures throughout the same decade [42,43]. At the same time, Poswillo expressed concern about the employment of toluidine blue to represent the leukoplakic patches before using cryotherapy in order to deliver an adequate freeze-defrost cycle for an area. Presently also, for oral leukoplakia cryosurgery is a potential treatment option. The results of the therapy, as shown by Yu et al., are significantly superior, despite the necessity for more precise mechanical assembly. Every one of the 54 patients who received cryogen cryotherapy on their 60 injuries witnessed a complete recurrence. In contrast, only a few treatments (mean 3.1) were necessary for the complete recovery of the injury compared to the 60 sores treated with q-tip cryotherapy (mean 6.3).

Fluid nitrogen was applied to the sores for 7–10 seconds before allowing them to thaw after 20 seconds. They claimed that the q-tip's inadequate supply of fluid nitrogen is insufficient to keep the treated oral leukoplakia lesional tissues at a consistently low temperature. As a result, the treatment is less effective and needs to be administered more frequently to see results [44–48].

2. Lichen planus

Effective steroids, lasers, antifungal mouthwashes, careful extraction, and cryosurgery have all been used to treat them. Ten patients were treated with cryosurgery in a study [41] using a nitrous oxide apparatus and two freeze-defrost cycles in each zone. 1.5 minutes were spent freezing, followed by a 3-minute thaw. The number of cycles necessary varied according to the size of the lesion.

As a result, he suggested that although cryosurgery does not completely cure lichen planus, it is a good therapy option. Thirty patients with two-sided OLP injuries were the subject of Amanat et al.'s [49] treatment plan that included cryosurgery and steroids. For a single session of cryotherapy using nitrous oxide gas, one sore from each patient was randomly chosen, and the other sore was treated with triamcinolone acetonide 0.1% salve in orabase. At the end of the treatment, they determined that nitrous oxide cryosurgery was as effective as steroid application.

Cryosurgery is an excellent option for managing patients who have underlying allergies or diseases that make the use of steroids contraindicated. Another advantage of cryosurgery is that it does not result in supra-infections like candidiasis. Thus, we can deduce that cryotherapy is currently an efficient therapeutic option for various types of lesions.

Compared to surgery, cryotherapy offers some distinct advantages and is significantly more well-tolerated by patients. Therefore, it might be the best course of action for patients who are worried, newborns, or for whom other treatments are contraindicated. Even though some suspicious lesions could be clinically diagnosable by experienced professionals with an oral medicine background, general practitioners should always seek a definitive diagnosis for any suspicious lesion.

3.10 CONCLUSION

In recent years, cryotherapy has been shown to have an excellent likelihood of being used as a therapeutic boon in endodontics by exhibiting outstanding promising results with its utilization.

Cryo-irrigation has been studied to see the extent to which it works in minimizing periapical inflammation, postoperative pain, and its antibacterial effects. Cryotherapy has additionally proven to be a successful supplement to vital pulp therapy. It is also remarkable how cryotherapy has affected the mechanical characteristics of the current generations of nickel-titanium rotary instruments.

Different oral injuries can be treated in an out-patient facility using cryosurgery, which is a safe, easy to understand and generally inexpensive technique. Unlike conventional medical procedures, it is a non-traumatic type of treatment. For a variety of oral lesions, such as pyogenic granulomas, angiomas, actinic cheilitis, keratoacanthoma, fibromas, HPV-related injuries in HIV and non-HIV patients, hypertrophic lichen planus, verrucous carcinoma, and bodily fluid, fluid nitrogen splash or cryoprobe have been used alone or in conjunction with other careful strategies.

In any case, more in-depth study should be conducted promptly to investigate the possible advantages in regard to this approach in the treatment of various pulpal and peri-radicular conditions and to produce solid evidence that will support its efficacy as a form of therapy in the field of endodontics.

Additionally, research into inflammatory indicators in patients who had intracanal cryotherapy may provide additional insight into the mechanism of action and the prospective applications of cryotherapy in endodontics.

REFERENCES

1. Korpan, Nikolai N. "A history of cryosurgery: its development and future." Journal of the American College of Surgeons 204, no. 2 (2007): 314–324.
2. Gade, Vandana, Digesh Barfiwala, Reema Asani, Rachana Gawande, and Jaykumar Gade. "Cryotherapy: An emerging trend in the field of endodontics." International Journal Of Drug Research And Dental Science 2, no. 3 (2020): 70–76.
3. Fayyad, Dalia Mukhtar, Nelly Abdelsalam, and Nasr Hashem. "Cryotherapy: a new paradigm of treatment in endodontics." Journal of Endodontics 46, no. 7 (2020): 936–942.
4. Vats, Shivangi, and Vinod Jathanna. "Cryotherapy as an adjunct to cleaning and shaping in endodontics: A review." Indian Journal of Forensic Medicine & Toxicology 14, no. 4 (2020): 515–518.

5. Gundogdu, Eyup Candas, and Hakan Arslan. "Effects of various cryotherapy applications on postoperative pain in molar teeth with symptomatic apical periodontitis: a preliminary randomized prospective clinical trial." Journal of Endodontics 44, no. 3 (2018): 349–354.

6. Keskin, Cangül, Özgür Özdemir, İsmail Uzun, and Buğra Güler. "Effect of intracanal cryotherapy on pain after single-visit root canal treatment." Australian Endodontic Journal 43, no. 2 (2017): 83–88.

7. Nandakumar, Mahalakshmi, and Iffat Nasim. "Effect of intracanal cryotreated sodium hypochlorite on postoperative pain after root canal treatment-A randomized controlled clinical trial." Journal of Conservative Dentistry 23, no. 2 (2020): 131.

8. Gupta, Alpa, Vivek Aggarwal, Alka Gurawa, Namrata Mehta, Dax Abraham, Arundeep Singh, Sucheta Jala, and Nishant Chauhan. "Effect of intracanal cryotherapy on postendodontic pain: a systematic review and meta-analysis of randomized controlled trials." Journal of Dental Anesthesia and Pain Medicine 21, no. 1 (2021): 15.

9. Shreya, Praveen S., Vipul Srivastava, Raju Chauhan, and Kishan Agarwal. "Cryotherapy: A comprehensive review on physiology, advent and implications in Endodontics." International Journal of Experimental Dental Science 10, no. 1 (2021): 36–40.

10. Fernandes, Ighor Andrade, Anna Catharina Vieira Armond, and Saulo Gabriel Moreira Falci. "The effectiveness of the cold therapy (cryotherapy) in the management of inflammatory parameters after removal of mandibular third molars: a meta-analysis." International Archives of Otorhinolaryngology 23 (2019): 221–228.

11. Algafly, Amin A., and Keith P. George. "The effect of cryotherapy on nerve conduction velocity, pain threshold and pain tolerance." British Journal of Sports Medicine 41, no. 6 (2007): 365–369.

12. Nadler, Scott F., Kurt Weingand, and Roger J. Kruse. "The physiologic basis and clinical applications of cryotherapy and thermotherapy for the pain practitioner." Pain Physician 7, no. 3 (2004): 395.

13. Sadaf, Durre, Muhammad Zubair Ahmad, and Igho J. Onakpoya. "Effectiveness of intracanal cryotherapy in root canal therapy: a systematic review and meta-analysis of randomized clinical trials." Journal of Endodontics 46, no. 12 (2020): 1811–1823.

14. Balasubramanian, Saravana Karthikeyan, and Divya Vinayachandran. "'Cryotherapy.' A panacea for post-operative pain following endodontic treatment." International Journal of Dental Research and Oral Sciences 2 (2017): 10–12.

15. Vera, Jorge, Jorge Ochoa, Monica Romero, Marino Vazquez-Carcano, Cesar Omar Ramos-Gregorio, Ruben Rosas Aguilar, Alvaro Cruz, Philippe Sleiman, and Ana Arias. "Intracanal cryotherapy reduces postoperative pain in teeth with symptomatic apical periodontitis: a randomized multicenter clinical trial." Journal of Endodontics 44, no. 1 (2018): 4–8.

16. Vieyra, J. P., F. J. J. Enriquez, F. O. Acosta, and J. A. Guardado. "Reduction of postendodontic pain after one-visit root canal treatment using three irrigating regimens with different temperature." Nigerian Journal of Clinical Practice 22, no. 1 (2019): 34–40.

17. Bazaid, Duaa S., and Laila MM Kenawi. "The effect of intracanal cryotherapy in reducing postoperative pain in patients with irreversible pulpitis: a randomized control trial." International Journal of Health Sciences and Research 8, no. 02 (2018): 83–88.

18. Keskin, Cangül, Evren Sariyilmaz, Ali Keleş, and Duygu H. Güler. "Effect of intracanal cryotherapy on the fracture resistance of endodontically treated teeth." Acta Odontologica Scandinavica 77, no. 2 (2019): 164–167.

19. Gage, A. A., J. M. Baust, and J. G. Baust. "Experimental cryosurgery investigations in vivo." Cryobiology 59, no. 3 (2009): 229–243.

20. Mandras, Narcisa, Valeria Allizond, A. Bianco, Giuliana Banche, Janira Roana, L. Piazza, P. Viale, and A. M. Cuffini. "Antimicrobial efficacy of cryotreatment against Enterococcus faecalis in root canals." Letters in Applied Microbiology 56, no. 2 (2013): 95–98.

21. Sabet, Yazdan, Samira Shahsiah, Mohammad Yazdizadeh, Sana Baghamorady, and Mansour Jafarzadeh. "Effect of deep cryogenic treatment on cyclic fatigue resistance of controlled memory wire nickel-titanium rotary instruments." Dental Research Journal 17, no. 4 (2020): 300.

22. Olson, Jane E., and Vincent D. Stravino. "A review of cryotherapy." Physical Therapy 52, no. 8 (1972): 840–853.

23. George, Gingu Koshy, Kavitha Sanjeev, and Mahalaxmi Sekar. "An in vitro evaluation of the effect of deep dry cryotreatment on the cutting efficiency of three rotary nickel titanium instruments." Journal of Conservative Dentistry 14, no. 2 (2011): 169.

24. Poornima, Prabhavathi, Atul UR, and B. S. Prasad. "Cryotherapy–A glimpse of hope in endodontics." Asian Journal of Dental Sciences 5, no. 4 (2022): 18–23.

25. Valsan, Dhanya. "Cryotherapy and its applications in endodontics." International Journal of Dental Sciences 2, no. 3 (2020): 15–17.

26. Jain, Shreya, Shraddha Chokshi, Zarana Sanghvi, Pooja Trivedi, Purav Mehta, and Aanjan Parikh. "Effect of intracanal cryotherapy on fracture resistance of teeth that have undergone endodontic treatment-An in vitro study." Journal of Advanced Medical and Dental Sciences Research 9, no. 1 (2021): 31–34.

27. Gurucharan, Ishwarya, Mahalaxmi Sekar, Saravanakarthikeyan Balasubramanian, and Srinivasan Narasimhan. "Effect of precooling injection site and cold anesthetic administration on injection pain, onset, and anesthetic efficacy in maxillary molars with symptomatic irreversible pulpitis: a randomized controlled trial." Clinical Oral Investigations (2022): 1–6.

28. Vera, Jorge, Jorge Ochoa-Rivera, Marino Vazquez-Carcaño, Monica Romero, Ana Arias, and Philippe Sleiman. "Effect of intracanal cryotherapy on reducing root surface temperature." Journal of Endodontics 41, no. 11 (2015): 1884–1887.

29. Rosenberg, Paul A. "Clinical strategies for managing endodontic pain." Endodontic Topics 3, no. 1 (2002): 78–92.

30. Yadav, Varnika, Vandita Shreya, Praveen Singh Samant, and Raju Chauhan. "Endodontic cryotherapy: A review of current status, potential sequelae, and call for action." Dent Poster Journal 10, no. 2 (2021): 1–2.

31. Amaral, William J., John R. Frost, William R. Howard, and Joe L. Cheatham. "Cryosurgery in treatment of inflammatory papillary hyperplasia." Oral Surgery, Oral Medicine, Oral Pathology 25, no. 4 (1968): 648–654.

32. Carneiro, José Thiers, Ana Paula Guerreiro Rodrigues Couto, and Aline Semblano Dias Carreira. "Use of gas combination cryosurgery for treating ameloblastomas of the jaw." Journal of Cranio-Maxillofacial Surgery 40, no. 8 (2012): e342–e345.

33. Yeh, Chin-Jyh. "Cryosurgical treatment of melanin-pigmented gingiva." Oral Surgery, Oral Medicine, Oral Pathology, Oral Radiology, and Endodontology 86, no. 6 (1998): 660–663.

34. Yeh, Chin-Jyh. "Simple cryosurgical treatment of the oral melanotic macule." Oral Surgery, Oral Medicine, Oral Pathology, Oral Radiology, and Endodontology 90, no. 1 (2000): 12–13.

35. Dawber, Rodney PR, Graham Colver, and Arthur J. Jackson. Cutaneous Cryosurgery: Principles and Clinical Practice. Martin Dunitz, (1992).

36. Hausamen, Jarg-Erich. "The basis, technique and indication for cryosurgery in tumours of the oral cavity and face." Journal of Maxillofacial Surgery 3 (1975): 41–49.

37. Getter, Lee, and Bienvenido Perez. "Controlled cryotherapy in the treatment of inflammatory papillary hyperplasia." Oral Surgery, Oral Medicine, Oral Pathology 34, no. 2 (1972): 178–186.

38. Bekke, J. P. H., and J. A. Baart. "Six years' experience with cryosurgery in the oral cavity." International Journal of Oral Surgery 8, no. 4 (1979): 251–270.

39. Narula, Ravi, and Bhavna Malik. "Role of cryosurgery in the management of benign and premalignant lesions of the maxillofacial region." Indian Journal of Dental Sciences 4, no. 2 (2012).

40. Leopard, P. J. "Cryosurgery, and its application to oral surgery." The British Journal of Oral Surgery 13, no. 2 (1975): 128–152.

41. Venkataram, Mysore. Textbook on Cutaneous and Aesthetic Surgery. JP Medical Ltd, 2012.

42. Sako, Kumao, Frank C. Marchetta, and Richard L. Hayes. "Cryotherapy of intraoral leukoplakia." The American Journal of Surgery 124, no. 4 (1972): 482–484.

43. Poswillo, David. "Evaluation, surveillance and treatment of panoral leukoplakia." Journal of Maxillofacial Surgery 3 (1975): 205–211.

44. Hassan, Shaik Ali, Sumit Bhateja, Geetika Arora, and Francis Prathyusha. "Cryo surgery in dentistry." IP Journal of Surgery and Allied Sciences. 2, no. 3 (2020): 67–71.

45. Brignardello-Petersen, Romina. "Cryotherapy may increase the success rate of inferior alveolar nerve block in patients with symptomatic irreversible pulpitis who undergo endodontic treatment." The Journal of the American Dental Association 150, no. 12 (2019): e221.

46. Bose, Sagorika, Nishita Garg, Lumbini Pathivada, and Ramakrishna Yeluri. "Cooling the soft tissue and its effect on perception of pain during infiltration and block anesthesia in children undergoing dental procedures: a comparative study." Journal of Dental Research, Dental Clinics, Dental Prospects 13, no. 3 (2019): 159.

47. Aminabadi, Naser Asl, and Ramin Mostofi Zadeh Farahani. "The effect of pre-cooling the injection site on pediatric pain perception during the administration of local anesthesia." Journal of Contemporary Dental Practice 10, no. 3 (2009): 1–9.

48. Jayasuriya, Nadeena Sri Swarnagupta, Indika Danuka Weerapperuma, and Malagoda Gamage Chathura Kanchana Amarasinghe. "The use of an iced cotton bud as an effective pre-cooling method for palatal anaesthesia: a technical note." Singapore Dental Journal 38 (2017): 17–19.

49. Amanat, Dariush, Hooman Ebrahimi, Maryam Zahed Zahedani, Nasim Zeini, Sara Pourshahidi, and Zahra Ranjbar. "Comparing the effects of cryotherapy with nitrous oxide gas versus topical corticosteroids in the treatment of oral lichen planus." Indian Journal of Dental Research 25, no. 6 (2014): 711.

4 Design and FEA Analysis of Customized Temporomandibular Joint Implant

Deepak Sharma
Department of Mechanical and Industrial Engineering,
Indian Institute of Technology, Roorkee, Roorkee,
Uttarakhand, India

4.1 INTRODUCTION

The temporomandibular joint (TMJ) is the movable joint in the human body that can act as both a rotating and translation joint (Figure 4.1). This joint plays a significant function in the body while talking, eating, swallowing, and providing airway support. It may move up to 2,000 times each day [1–9]. But, TMJ disorders caused by accidental situations and diseases such as osteoarthritis, ankylosis, etc., can halt the normal functioning of TMJ joints.

TMJ disorder symptoms can be detected in 20–25% of the population. However, only 3–4% seek therapy [7]. Temporomandibular disorders may be caused by an injury to the temporomandibular joint, head, and neck muscles [10]. The TMJ disorder's severity can be quantified using Helkimo Clinical Dysfunction Index. This index is based on signs and symptoms which cause TMJ dysfunction [11]. This index is graded from severe dysfunction to clinically symptom-free according to a score from 0 to 25 [12].

TMJ disorders can be treated with physical, non-surgical, and surgical therapies [10]. It was found that mild TMJ problems can be treated with non-surgical treatments, but there are no treatments to deal with severe TMJ dysfunction. In extreme situations, surgeries are performed where the TMJ implant is attached to the mandible bone by titanium (pure or alloy) screws [6].

TMJ implants can be categorized into customized implants and stock implants. Commercially available stock prosthetic TMJ components cannot adjust to the immense diversity of jaw morphologies and bone pathologies. Brown et al. [13] study confirmed that stock TMJ implant has only an adaptation rate of 74%. These problems can be solved by using customized implants instead of stock. However, only two TMJ implant systems have been approved by the United States Food and Drug Administration: TMJ Concepts (Ventura, CA, USA) and Zimmer Biomet (Jacksonville, FL, USA) [14].

DOI: 10.1201/9781003404934-4

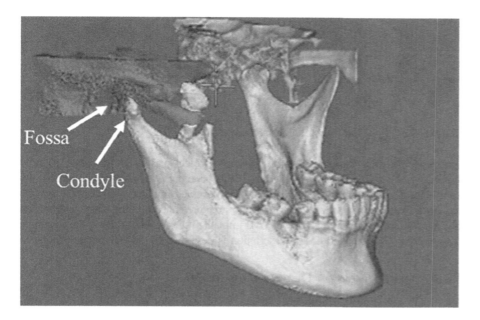

FIGURE 4.1 The temporomandibular joint.

Short-term follow-up studies on these types of metal-based TMJ implants have revealed a success rate of 67 to 97% [10]. There are also few mid to long-term studies conducted on customized TMJ implants [3]. It was revealed that micromotion between the host bone and the implant induced early screw loosening, resulting in implant failure. So, there is still a need to improve the design parameters of customized TMJ implants to achieve durability and safety of the TMJ implant. It was also found that most of the finite element analysis (FEA) studies were done on Ti alloy implants, and very little work was reported on the cobalt-based alloy.

This study aimed to show how to design and analyze a novel customized cobalt-based TMJ implant that ensures an anatomical fit between bone and implant to prevent harmful strain induced in bone. The anatomical fit feature of this implant can minimize the risk of micromotion and enhance the chance for bio integration. This chapter depicted the methodology required for developing a new patient-specific implant design. The new design of the TMJ implant was created by using Mimics software. TMJ implant was made to precisely match the unique anatomical features of mandible bone. So, this design doesn't need shimming or modifying the device or the host bone to get primary stability. The screws can tightly fasten this implant's components to the host bone. Finally, FEA was conducted on the designed implant using Ansys software by simulating the forces during mastication.

4.2 MATERIAL AND METHODS

For this study, a computed tomography (CT) scan of a patient with a condyle injury was taken in digital imaging and communications in Medicine (DICOM) file format. The CT

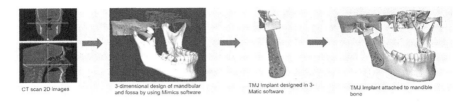

CT scan 2D images　　3-dimensional design of mandibular and fossa by using Mimics software　　TMJ Implant designed in 3-Matic software　　TMJ Implant attached to mandible bone

FIGURE 4.2　Steps followed to design the novel TMJ implant.

scan was analyzed through Mimics software, which was used to create a three-dimensional (3-D) model of mandible bone. This bone provided anatomical features that were helpful in creating the TMJ implant. The designed implant was attached to bone, and the final design was used to perform static structure analysis in the Ansys workbench. The methodology for creating a novel TMJ implant system was laid out in the schematic in Figure 4.2. The detailed design description is described in the following sections.

4.2.1 THREE-DIMENSION DESIGN OF THE MODEL

As mentioned above, this study used a CT scan of a skull with a spatial resolution of $0.38 \times 0.38 \times 0.38$ mm. The analysis of this CT scan was done through Mimics Research 18.0 software. The CT images of the front, top, and sagittal planes are shown in Figures 4.3a, b, and c, respectively. This research

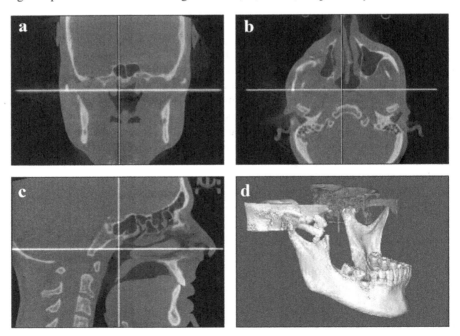

FIGURE 4.3　CT- scan images using a) Front plane; b) Top plane; c) Sagittal plane; and d) 3-D image of mandible and temporal bone.

used CT images to generate the 3-D mandible bone (Figure 4.3d). Algorithms such as interpolation, threshold, and region growth were used in Mimics to recover volumetric data from two-dimensional images. After that, the 3-D design of the temporal and the mandible bone was transferred into 3-Matic research 10.0 software, which helped to create anatomical features for patient-specific TMJ implant.

4.2.2 IMPLANT DESIGN

The damaged part of the TMJ joint (host bone) was cut through the 3-D trim method in 3-Matic software. The customized (patient-specific) TMJ implant was designed in 3-Matic software using the anatomical feature of mandible bone, as shown in Figure 4.4. The lower component of the condyle was made 2.5 mm thick [7]. This was fastened to a condyle head with a diameter of 8.0 mm. There were 13 screw holes with a diameter of 2.9 mm on the condyle component, and the screw hole pattern was inclined at 45 degrees. The fossa part was designed using the temporal bone's anatomic features. The thickness of the fossa part of the implant was 2.5 mm. The fossa part was provided with seven screw holes with a diameter equal to 2.2 mm.

Finally, the designed implant was assembled into the 3-D model of the mandible bone, as shown in Figure 4.5. This 3-D assembly of the condyle and mandible was created using designing tools available in 3-Matic workspaces. The final 3-D model was exported in a suitable design format for FEA analysis.

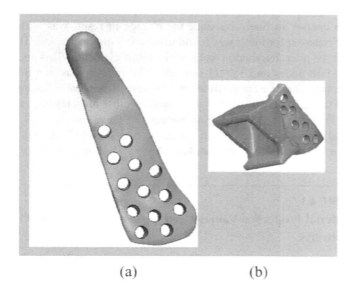

(a)   (b)

FIGURE 4.4 TMJ implant: a) Condyle part; b) Fossa part.

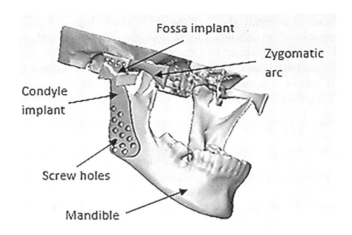

FIGURE 4.5   Assembly of patient-specific implant and bone.

4.2.3 FINITE ELEMENT ANALYSIS OF TMJ IMPLANT

In finite element analysis, the first step was the assignment of material properties for different parts of the model. All materials were assumed to be isotropic and linearly elastic. The condyle part of the implant was updated with Co-Cr-Mo properties. The ultra-high molecular weight polyethylene (UHMWPE) material properties were allocated to the fossa component. The material properties values that were applied to different parts are shown in Table 4.1.

Finite element meshing was performed on Ansys Workbench. The mesh was refined from coarser to finer size until the change in result was within 5%. The convergence criterion for mesh was found using a 0.5 mm mesh size. The FE model meshed with 10-node tetrahedral volumetric mesh elements. This meshed model contained 34,648 nodes and 18,993 elements. For the analysis purpose, only four significant muscle forces were considered: Masseter, Temporalis, Lateral Pterygoid, and Medial Pterygoid because forces generated by other muscles (suprahyoid) were very small [3]. Table 4.2 shows the magnitudes of these forces.

P_x, P_y, and P_z are force vectors in the X, Y, and Z directions. All these forces were taken in the static structure module of Ansys. The top portions of the left and

TABLE 4.1

Material Properties Values Used in Ansys Workbench (FEA Software)

Materials	Young's Modulus in GPa	Poisson's Ratio
Bone [1]	14.5	0.30
Co-Cr-Mo [3]	210	0.29
UHMWPE [6]	1.258	0.33

TABLE 4.2

Muscle Forces on the Left and Right-Side Muscles while Incisal Biting

Muscle Name	Force Components (N)		
	P_x	P_y	P_z
Med. Pterygoid (right side)	−147.525	−113.225	240.11
Med. Pterygoid (the left side)	147.525	−113.225	240.11
Lateral Pterygoid (right side)	−90.965	−100.695	−16.045
Lateral Pterygoid (left side)	90.965	−100.695	−16.045
Masseter (right side)	60.91	−54.175	185.785
Masseter (left side)	−60.91	−54.175	185.785
Temporalis (right side)	8.435	10.91	41.705
Temporalis (left side)	−8.435	10.91	41.705

right condyle head were made fixed, as shown by positions J and K. Muscle forces were applied at points such as A, B, C, D, E, F, G, H, and I, as shown in red color in Figure 4.6. The incisal biting force of 285 N was applied for a 3-D model [3]. Ansys developed a mathematical model for all these boundary conditions and predicted the stress and deformation for the applied conditions.

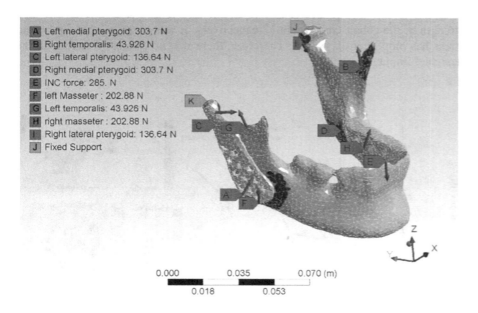

FIGURE 4.6 Application point of muscle forces with 285 N incisal teeth force in a downward direction.

4.3 RESULTS

4.3.1 Maximum Principal Stress and Equivalent Stress on Condyle Component

The principal stress varied from −62 to 385 MPa, below the yield strength (480 MPa) of Co-Cr-Mo alloy. The principal stresses in areas of interest, such as the condyle's anterior, middle, and posterior areas, were 27.3, −5.69, and 73.8 MPa, respectively. It was discovered that posterior and anterior condyle areas caused tensile stress. In contrast, compressive stress was produced in the central area of the condyle.

In Figure 4.7, the graph shows principal and von Mises stress values on seven different points. This graph reveals that the principal stress was initially tensile at the condyle's posterior. After that, it changed to a compressive nature at the middle position of the condyle, and again, it became tensile near the anterior region of the condyle head. The graph showed the maximum value at the posterior region. So, while designing the condyle part of the implant, special care should be given to the posterior part of the condyle as it has to bear larger stress than other areas. After that, there was a decline in the magnitude of principal stress except at the anterior position.

It is well known that Co-Cr-Mo is a ductile material, so von Mises stress criteria can be used to determine whether the material would fail. It was also discovered that von Mises equivalent stresses ranged from 0.0348 MPa to 303 MPa. These stress levels equated to approximately 0.007% and 63% of the yield strength of the cobalt-chrome alloy, respectively. It was observed that equivalent stress has only a tensile nature. Therefore, there was no chance of fatigue in the designed implant.

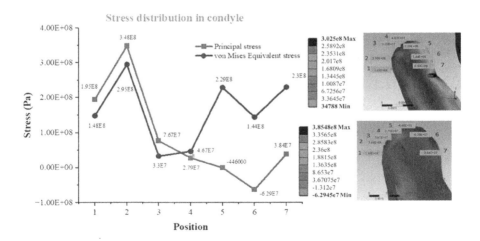

FIGURE 4.7 The graph between stress induced and seven different positions on the condyle.

4.3.2   Maximum Principal Stress and Equivalent (von Mises) Stress on the Fossa

The fossa component was constrained entirely on the upper side. The maximum principal stress dispersals on the fossa contact surface ranged from 37,611 to −19,839 Pa. In the fossa, maximum principal stress was developed near the screws hole, so this area was prone to failure first if the working stress value acceded to the yield strength. However, stress developed in the designed fossa was within the yield strength of UHMWPE (24.1 MPa).

The maximum von Mises stress varies from 2.75E-06 to 38,235 Pa. In the fossa, both tensile and compressive stresses were developed, making it susceptible to fatigue failure. Figure 4.8 depicts a graph of the equivalent stress at seven distinct places in the region of interest. It was found that only equivalent tensile stress was developed in these points, which increased firstly up to the middle area and then decreased in the anterior contacting regions of the fossa.

4.3.3   Total Deformation on Condyle and Mandible

Total deformation induced due to these stresses in the mandible bone and condyle part of the implant is shown in Figure 4.9. The maximum value of total deformation of magnitude 0.756 mm was observed below the incisal teeth of the mandible bone. In the condyle part, the maximum value of total deformation was 0.2641 mm around the screw areas. It was also observed that deformation decreased upward and became minimal near the condyle region.

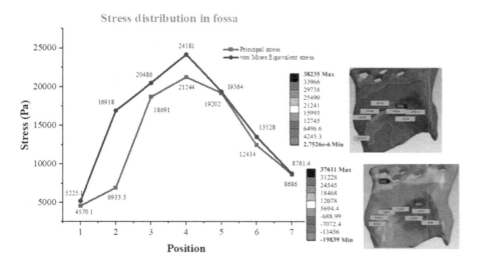

FIGURE 4.8   The graph between stress and position of condyle surface.

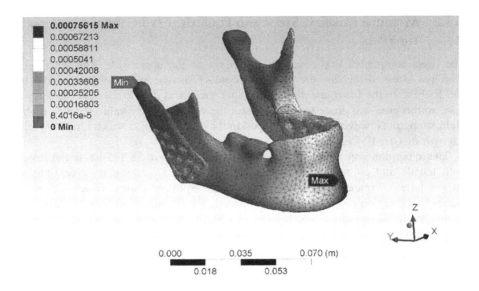

FIGURE 4.9　A contour representation of deformation in the assembly of condyle and mandible.

4.4　DISCUSSION

FEA studies have shown high potential to solve the complex biomechanics of TMJ implants. FE models are beneficial in predicting stress behavior under various loading scenarios [15–18]. The biomechanical characteristics of the TMJ implant have been investigated in this study. The condyle part of the TMJ implant was supported by mandible bone, and the fossa part was supported by temporal bone. A spherical condyle head was designed in the condyle part of TMJ implants because a spherical condylar component can control condylar movement more effectively than other shape designs [3]. Screws are generally used to fix the condyle with the ramus of the mandible to provide primary stability. Ramos et al. [9] indicated that the implant could also be made stable to the bone by fixing just three screws. The fossa component of a TMJ implant can permanently be fixed with 4 to 6 screws. However, in this research, the condyle part and the fossa part were made fixed to the ramus of the mandible (bone) by providing bonded contact between the screw hole circumference and host bone surface in the Ansys workbench.

The FEA predicted that both tensile and compressive stresses were developed in the designed TMJ implant. Therefore, the normal chewing process, talking, etc., may induce fatigue. It was also found that the maximum value of stress developed in the fossa part was much lower than in the condyle part. So, the condyle part should always be designed with bio-compatible material having higher mechanical strength than the fossa part. Ansys study revealed that the posterior part of the condyle head experienced significant stress compared to other regions. This increased stress was because of the opening of the mouth or the lowering of the mandible bone due to the hinge connection made between the condyle head and fossa. For largemouth openings, the condyle head translated slightly over the fossa part. After reaching the fossa's middle position, there was no further translation due to obstruction provided by the fossa part geometry. This led to large stress generation at the middle portion of the fossa. This hinge connection helped to give rotational motion between these two parts.

FEA analyses have shown that mandible bone has experienced maximum deformation of 0.756 mm, less than fracture strain (approximately 3 mm). According to mechanostat theory given by H. M. Frost, bone resorption occurs if the strain in bone is less than 100 μm. Bone formation and resorptions are the same if the strain ranges from 100 to 1,500 microstrain, and bone experiences plastic deformation in the range of 1,500 to 3,000 microstrain. There will be a bone fracture if the strain at any point in the bone exceeds 3,000 microstrains. These strain values are beneficial in the active region of bone, which is within 1.5 mm around the TMJ implant [19]. It was observed that bone experienced an approximate 420-microstrain in the active area, so this strain will help to maintain the balance between bone formation and absorption.

Nowadays, researchers are extensively working on the design of stable TMJ implants. It was found that 15 countries are trying to develop 27 TMJ systems, of which 21 are custom-made [20]. A few studies in the past have also been conducted on different shapes of customized TMJ implants. E. Tanaka et al. [2] reported principal stresses developed in the condyle part were -1.642 MPa, -0.543 MPa, and 0.664 MPa in the anterior, middle, and posterior areas, respectively, on the application of resultant force 500 N. In this process of predicting the stress, D.C. Ackland et al. [1] recorded that maximum stress in the condyle surface of the Biomet TMJ implant was 244.0 MPa for the chewing bite force of 259.6 Pa. Similarly, on applying 150 N force in incisal teeth, a maximum von Mises stress of 148.5 MPa was developed at the condylar component, and a maximum von Mises stress having a magnitude of 0.36 MPa was induced on the fossa component [6].

This research has used FEA to understand the biomechanical behavior, strength, and durability of tailored TMJ Implants. A new design of TMJ implant was made in this research, ensuring stability for the long term. The analysis of stress distribution using the FEA approach is trustworthy. It saves both money and time. FEA study of the designed implant can also improve postoperative clinical results. This biomechanical research will likely help develop patients' specific TMJ implants using bio-compatible material in the future.

4.5   FUTURE SCOPE

Future studies will involve a more in-depth examination of several manufacturing routes for this designed TMJ implant. This implant may be fabricated using additive manufacturing technologies like selective laser sintering, selective laser melting, directed energy deposition, etc. The desired mechanical and surface properties tests, in-vivo and in-vitro analysis, can be done to check the biocompatibility and cytocompatibility of this designed TMJ implant.

4.6 CONCLUSIONS

The Ansys study uncovered important information on the biomechanics of designed TMJ implant as follows:

- The stress values are within the permissible limit (yield stress) for both the customized implant and the supporting bone. The designed cobalt-based TMJ implant is strong against worst-case biting force (285 N).
- The maximum stress generated on the fossa is 19,839 Pa, much less than the stress (385 MPa) developed on the implant's condyle component. As a result, the condyle component should outperform the fossa in terms of mechanical qualities.
- This novel patient-specific designed TMJ implant provided accurate anatomical fit, which helped to reduce the chance of micromotion between the implant and host bone.

ACKNOWLEDGMENT

The author would like to express his gratitude to the Department of Production and Industrial Engineering at Punjab Engineering College, Chandigarh for providing me with the resources and assistance I required to conduct this research.

Author contributions
Deepak Sharma: Conceptualization, Software, Methodology, Data curation, Writing original draft, Supervision, Visualization, Investigation, Validation, Reviewing, and Editing.

Conflicts of Interest: None
Funding: None
Ethical Approval: Not required

REFERENCES

1. Ackland, David C., Dale Robinson, Michael Redhead, Peter Vee Sin Lee, Adrian Moskaljuk, and George Dimitroulis. 2017. "A Personalized 3D-Printed Prosthetic Joint Replacement for the Human Temporomandibular Joint: From Implant Design to Implantation." Journal of the Mechanical Behavior of Biomedical Materials 69 (December 2016): 404–411. 10.1016/j.jmbbm.2017.01.048.
2. Tanaka, Eiji, Kazuo Tanne, and Mamoru Sakuda. 1994. "A Three-Dimensional Finite Element Model of the Mandible Including the TMJ and Its Application to Stress Analysis in the TMJ during Clenching." Medical Engineering and Physics 16 (4): 316–322. 10.1016/1350-4533(94)90058-2.
3. Pinheiro, Manuel, Robin Willaert, Afaq Khan, Anouar Krairi, and Wim van Paepegem. 2021. "Biomechanical Evaluation of the Human Mandible after Temporomandibular Joint Replacement under Different Biting Conditions." Scientific Reports 11 (1): 1–12. 10.1038/s41598-021-93564-3.
4. Rodrigues, Y.L., M.T. Mathew, L.G. Mercuri, J.S.P. da Silva, B. Henriques, and J.C.M. Souza. 2018. "Biomechanical Simulation of Temporomandibular Joint Replacement

(TMJR) Devices: A Scoping Review of the Finite Element Method." International Journal of Oral and Maxillofacial Surgery 47 (8): 1032–1042. 10.1016/j.ijom.2018.02.005.

5. Abel, Eric W., André Hilgers, and Philip M. McLoughlin. 2015. "Finite Element Analysis of a Condylar Support Prosthesis to Replace the Temporomandibular Joint." British Journal of Oral and Maxillofacial Surgery 53 (4): 352–357. 10.1016/j.bjoms. 2015.01.016.

6. Vignesh, U., D. Mehrotra, S.M. Bhave, R. Katrolia, and S. Sharma. 2020. "Finite Element Analysis of Patient-Specific TMJ Implants to Replace Bilateral Joints with Simultaneous Correction of Facial Deformity." Journal of Oral Biology and Craniofacial Research 10 (4): 674–679. 10.1016/j.jobcr.2020.07.013.

7. Arabshahi, Zohreh, Jamal Kashani, Mohammed Rafiq Abdul Kadir, and Abbas Azari. 2011. "Influence of Thickness and Contact Surface Geometry of Condylar Stem of TMJ Implant on Its Stability." Physics Procedia 22: 414–419. 10.1016/j.phpro.2011.11.065.

8. Ramos, António, and Michel Mesnard. 2014. "Load Transfer in Christensen* TMJ in Alloplastic Total Joint Replacement for Two Different Mouth Apertures." Journal of Cranio-Maxillofacial Surgery 42 (7): 1442–1449. 10.1016/j.jcms.2014.04.008.

9. Ramos, A., R.J. Duarte, and M. Mesnard. 2015. "Prediction at Long-Term Condyle Screw Fixation of Temporomandibular Joint Implant: A Numerical Study." Journal of Cranio-Maxillofacial Surgery 43 (4): 469–474. 10.1016/j.jcms.2015.02.013.

10. Ingawalé, Shirish, and Tarun Goswami. 2009. "Temporomandibular Joint: Disorders, Treatments, and Biomechanics." Annals of Biomedical Engineering 37 (5): 976–996. 10.1007/s10439-009-9659-4.

11. Oikarinen, K.S., A.M. Raustia, and J. Lahti. 1991. "Signs and Symptoms of TMJ Dysfunction in Patients with Mandibular Condyle Fractures." Cranio – Journal of Craniomandibular Practice 9 (1): 58–62. 10.1080/08869634.1991.11678350.

12. Helkimo, Martti. 1974. "Studies on Function and Dysfunction of the Masticatory System: IV. Age and Sex Distribution of Symptoms of Dysfunction of the Masticatory System in Lapps in the North of Finland." Acta Odontologica Scandinavica 32 (4): 255–267. 10.3109/00016357409026342.

13. Brown, Z.L., S. Sarrami, and D.E. Perez. 2021. "Will They Fit? Determinants of the Adaptability of Stock TMJ Prostheses Where Custom TMJ Prostheses Were Utilized." International Journal of Oral and Maxillofacial Surgery 50 (2): 220–226. 10.1016/j.ijom.2020.05.009.

14. Guarda-Nardini, L., D. Manfredini, and G. Ferronato. 2008. "Temporomandibular Joint Total Replacement Prosthesis: Current Knowledge and Considerations for the Future." International Journal of Oral and Maxillofacial Surgery. International Association of Oral and Maxillofacial Surgery. 10.1016/j.ijom.2007.09.175.

15. Chen, Xuzhuo, Yexin Wang, Yi Mao, Zhihang Zhou, Jisi Zheng, Jinze Zhen, Yating Qiu, Shanyong Zhang, Haiyi Qin, and Chi Yang. 2018. "Biomechanical Evaluation of Chinese Customized Three-Dimensionally Printed Total Temporomandibular Joint Prostheses: A Finite Element Analysis." Journal of Cranio-Maxillofacial Surgery 46 (9): 1561–1568. 10.1016/j.jcms.2018.06.018.

16. Jaglan, A., N. Dogra, A. Kumar, and P. Kumar. 2023. "Finite Element Simulation Approach in Incremental Sheet Forming Process." In Handbook of Flexible and Smart Sheet Forming Techniques (eds Ajay, Parveen, H. Singh, V. Gulati and P.K. Singh) 129–139. 10.1002/9781119986454.ch7.

17. Kumar, A., P. Kumar, N. Dogra, and A. Jaglan. 2023. "Application of Incremental Sheet Forming (ISF) Toward Biomedical and Medical Implants." In Handbook of Flexible and Smart Sheet Forming Techniques (eds Ajay, Parveen, H. Singh, V. Gulati and P.K. Singh) 247–263. 10.1002/9781119986454.ch13.

18. Kumar, A., R.K. Mittal, and A. Haleem. 2022. Advances in Additive Manufacturing: Artificial Intelligence, Nature-Inspired, and Biomanufacturing. Elsevier, New York.

19. Liu, Bowen, Wei Xu, Mingying Chen, Dongdong Chen, Guyu Sun, Ce Zhang, Yu Pan, Jinchao Lu, Enbo Guo, and Xin Lu. 2022. "Structural Design and Finite Element Simulation Analysis of Grade 3 Graded Porous Titanium Implant." International Journal of Molecular Sciences 23 (17). 10.3390/ijms231710090.
20. Elledge, R., L.G. Mercuri, A. Attard, J. Green, and B. Speculand. 2019. "Review of Emerging Temporomandibular Joint Total Joint Replacement Systems." British Journal of Oral and Maxillofacial Surgery. British Association of Oral and Maxillofacial Surgeons. 10.1016/j.bjoms.2019.08.009.

5 Latest Intelligent and Sustainable Materials for Dental Application

Lakhloufi Soraya and Labjar Najoua
Laboratory of Spectroscopy, Molecular Modeling, Materials, Nanomaterials, Water and Environment, (LS3MN2E-CERNE2D), ENSAM, Mohammed V University in Rabat, Rabat, Morocco

Labjar Houda
Faculty of Sciences and Technology, University Hassan II Casablanca, Mohammedia, Morocco

Serghini-Idrissi Malika and El Hajjaji Souad
Laboratory of Spectroscopy, Molecular Modeling, Materials, Nanomaterials, Water and Environment, (LS3MN2E-CERNE2D), Department of Chemistry, Faculty of Sciences, Mohammed V University in Rabat, Rabat, Morocco

5.1 INTRODUCTION: OVERVIEW OF THE LATEST INTELLIGENT AND SUSTAINABLE MATERIALS FOR DENTAL APPLICATIONS

Dental materials have been used for thousands of years, with evidence of dental fillings made from various materials such as beeswax, resin, and even gold found in ancient Egyptian, Greek, and Roman civilizations. However, it wasn't until the 19th century that modern dental materials began to emerge, with the introduction of amalgam fillings and porcelain dentures. In the early 20th century, new dental materials such as acrylic resins and composite fillings were developed. By the mid-20th century, ceramics and dental adhesives had been introduced, making dental materials more sophisticated. In the 21st century, researchers and manufacturers are focused on creating intelligent and sustainable dental materials that can respond to their environment, are biocompatible, and have a reduced environmental impact. Examples of these materials include Antibacterial and Biomaterials, Nanomaterials, Bioplastics, and Natural Resins [1]. These new materials are revolutionizing the field of dentistry by improving esthetics, durability, biocompatibility, and environmental sustainability [2]. In the past, dental materials were primarily focused on function rather than esthetics. In the era of Dentistry 4.0, the emphasis has changed towards achieving restorations that

DOI: 10.1201/9781003404934-5

possess both optimal functionality and seamless integration with the patient's natural dentition. Among the notable trends in dental materials, the utilization of recycled dental composite resins stands out as an environmentally conscious choice, effectively reducing the ecological footprint associated with composite fillings [3]. Composite resins are tooth-colored and can mimic the natural translucency, color, and shape of teeth, providing superior esthetic properties compared to amalgam fillings, which can be unsightly and discolor over time [4]. The progress in biomaterials has resulted in the emergence of novel materials that possess excellent biocompatibility and facilitate the natural regeneration of tissues [5]. Scientists are currently investigating the application of Nanomaterials in the construction of bone regeneration scaffolds, aiming to minimize the reliance on conventional bone grafts [6]. 3D printing technology is being utilized to fabricate patient-specific scaffolds for bone tissue engineering, offering customization to match the unique anatomy of each patient [7]. The advent of digital technology, including digital imaging and computer-aided design and manufacturing (CAD/CAM) systems, enables the precise and comfortable creation of custom dental restorations such as crowns, bridges, and veneers. Zirconia, a ceramic material, has gained increasing popularity for its excellent esthetic properties and durability in fabricating dental restorations like crowns and bridges [8]. Developing dental materials that possess both biocompatibility and sustainability, along with a focus on environmental friendliness, stands as a key hurdle in the realm of dental materials [9]. Another challenge is to create materials that are highly esthetic while also being durable and functional like dental ceramics [10]. This requires a shift towards the use of non-toxic, easily recyclable materials that do not release harmful substances into the environment. Another challenge is to create materials that are highly esthetic while also being durable and functional, such as dental ceramics [11]. Promising prospects within the dental materials realm encompass leveraging digital technology in the manufacturing phase, encompassing CAD/CAM systems and 3D printing, to produce exceptionally precise and personalized restorations. Additionally, considerable opportunities lie in the advancement of biomaterials that stimulate natural tissue regeneration and facilitate healing. These possibilities include employing Nanomaterials and other cutting-edge materials to fabricate bone regeneration scaffolds, as well as developing bioactive materials that foster the regeneration and healing of soft tissue [12]. The field of dental materials presents significant challenges and opportunities, and continued research and development are necessary to address these challenges and capitalize on these opportunities to improve patient outcomes and enhance the overall dental experience. This chapter provides a comprehensive overview of the latest intelligent and sustainable materials for dental applications. It covers the evolution of dental materials from ancient times to modern materials, including their properties, advantages, and limitations, and their applications in various areas of dentistry. The chapter also explores the integration of artificial intelligence, Dentistry 4.0, and Biofabrication in dental materials and their potential impact on the field of dentistry. The chapter will be valuable to dental professionals, researchers, and students interested in the latest developments and trends in dental materials technology.

5.2 LITERATURE REVIEW: CURRENT TRENDS AND STATUS IN DENTAL MATERIALS IN DENTISTRY 4.0

Recent years have seen significant progress in dental materials, thanks to Dentistry 4.0. Today's trends in dental materials focus on creating materials that are durable, biocompatible, esthetically pleasing, and conformable. One key trend is the incorporation of nanotechnology, which can enhance the characteristics and composition of dental materials, both in terms of their physical and chemical properties, improve their antimicrobial properties, and enable drug delivery and tissue regeneration [13]. A major breakthrough in dental materials under Dentistry 4.0 is the growing use of 3D printing and recently 4D printing [14]. This technology enables the creation of highly precise dental prosthetics and restorations that can be tailored to meet each patient's unique needs, such as denture fabrication, surgical drill guides, smart dental implants, orthodontic devices, crowns, bridges, surgical tools, simulation models for training, etc. The utilization of programmable smart materials enables the creation of components with dynamic physical attributes and responsive behavior to external stimuli, allowing for variations over time in their characteristics and responses. Additionally, the future prospects for 3D/4D printing in the realm of dental prostheses are promising, and the technology is predicted to become increasingly popular in dentistry in the years to come. Furthermore, 3D/4D printing has given rise to new materials such as ceramic resin composites, which have superior mechanical properties compared to traditional materials [15]. Nevertheless, there are still gaps in research regarding the long-term performance of Nanomaterials within the oral environment, which necessitates further investigation. There is also ongoing research into developing alternative materials that are more sustainable and eco-friendly, such as bio-based and biodegradable polymers [16]. The selection of dental materials is influenced by several factors, encompassing the patient's oral health condition, the specific placement of the restoration, and the preferences and expertise of the dentist. Each type of dental material possesses distinct strengths and weaknesses, presenting a range of advantages and disadvantages. Ceramic materials, for instance, offer excellent biocompatibility and esthetic properties, but can be brittle and prone to breakage. Composites are versatile and can be matched to the patient's tooth color, but their wear resistance and durability may be compromised. Metals are strong and durable, but may not offer the same level of esthetics as ceramic or composite materials. Another important trend in dental materials is the increasing use of nanotechnology. Enhancing the characteristics of dental materials, including strength, durability, and antimicrobial activity, can be achieved by integrating nanoparticles into their composition [12]. For example, composite resins can incorporate silver nanoparticles, which effectively hinder the proliferation of bacteria responsible for dental caries and periodontal disease, thereby preventing tooth decay [17]. Nanoparticles have also been studied for their potential in drug delivery systems in dentistry, enabling drugs to be delivered to specific sites in the oral cavity with improved efficacy and fewer side effects [18]. Biocompatibility is a crucial factor to consider when selecting dental materials. Materials that are biocompatible do not cause any adverse reactions or tissue damage when they come into contact with the body. Due to their remarkable biocompatibility and strength, biomaterials like zirconia, titanium, and hydroxyapatite are widely employed in dental implant procedures [19]. While there have been notable advancements in dental materials, additional research is required to bridge existing knowledge gaps and enhance their properties and sustainability. Future research should focus on developing novel materials and procedures that enhance the quality and efficiency of dental restorations and treatments while minimizing their environmental impact. Additionally, patients increasingly desire natural-looking restorations, making esthetics an important factor in dental materials. Lithium disilicate and zirconia are highly esthetic materials that can be used to create lifelike restorations that blend seamlessly with natural teeth. Recent advances in bonding agents and adhesives have also improved the longevity and durability of restorations, ensuring that they remain strong and esthetically pleasing for years to come [20].

5.2.1 ADVANCES IN DENTAL MATERIALS TECHNOLOGY AND PROS AND CONS OF DENTAL MATERIALS

Recent decades have seen remarkable progress in the field of dentistry, particularly in materials technology. As discussed earlier, they have evolved to become more effective and esthetic, and these improvements have been fueled by the advent of Dentistry 4.0. With the integration of digital technology, materials development, testing, and implementation have been revolutionized. This involves the utilization of computer-aided design and manufacturing (CAD/CAM) systems to produce highly precise dental restorations, alongside digital radiography for enhanced diagnostic accuracy [21]. Additionally, biomimetic materials, which aim to replicate the structure and characteristics of natural teeth, exhibit exceptional biocompatibility and provide enhanced bonding and resistance to wear when compared to conventional materials. Moreover, the utilization of nanotechnology involves the integration of nanoparticles into composites, cements, and ceramics, enhancing their mechanical properties such as increased strength, durability, and resistance to wear [22]. 3D printing has allowed for the development of highly precise and custom-made dental restorations, such as crowns, bridges, and dentures, and smart materials are being developed for use in dental restorations that can detect and respond to changes in temperature, pH, and moisture. This includes materials that can release fluoride to prevent decay and others that can release antibiotics to treat infections [23]. These have emerged as notable improvements in dental materials technology. These new materials offer improved properties and functionality and imitate or replicate the characteristics and structure of the patient's original tooth. However, as indicated in Table 5.1, each material has its pros and cons, and factors such as esthetics, strength, and durability should be considered when choosing a material for a restoration. It is important to consult with a dental professional to determine which type of material is most suitable for each individual case, taking into account factors such as the location and size of the filling, the patient's oral health, and their esthetic preferences.

5.2.2 RESEARCH AND GAP AREAS FOR FUTURE EXPLORATION

As Dentistry 4.0 transforms the field of dentistry, there are exciting developments and advancements in dental materials. Recent research indicates that by integrating dentistry, dental engineering, and materials engineering, modern dental technology,

TABLE 5.1

Pros and Cons of Different Types of Dental Materials

Dental Material	Pros	Cons	Common Uses
Composite Resin	Esthetically pleasing and can be color-matched to teeth; Strong and durable; Less tooth structure needs to be removed to place composite resin fillings than amalgam fillings; Can be used for a variety of restorations	Can shrink during the curing process leading to gaps between the filling and tooth; More expensive than amalgam; May require more time to place; Can stain or discolor over time; May not be suitable for larger restorations	Fillings, inlays, onlays, veneers
Amalgam	Strong and long-lasting; More affordable than composite resin; Resistant to wear and tear; Easy to place	Not as esthetically pleasing as composite resin fillings; Concerns about mercury content; Requires removal of more tooth structure than composite resin fillings.	Fillings, crowns
Porcelain/ Ceramic	Natural appearance; Strong and durable; Can withstand daily chewing.	More expensive than other materials; May require more tooth reduction; Can be brittle and prone to fracture	Crowns, veneers
Metal	Strong and long-lasting; Easy to place; Good thermal and electrical conductivity	Not as esthetically pleasing as other materials; May cause issues with thermal and electrical conductivity; May require more tooth reduction	Crowns, bridges, inlays, onlays

including 3D virtual modeling, has the potential to align with the principles of Sustainable Development of Dentistry (SDD) [24]. This approach has successfully treated complex cases of dentofacial deformities through a combination of SF orthognathic surgery and Invisalign orthodontic treatment, resulting in improved patient quality of life [25]. Additionally, cone beam tomography (CBCT) combined with computer-aided manufacturing has been employed for the development of dental prostheses [26]. Nevertheless, potential research gaps and unexplored avenues exist in this domain. An area necessitating further examination is the influence of 3D printing on the advancement and application of dental materials. With the increasing popularity of 3D printing technology in dentistry, it is important to investigate how this technology affects the properties of dental materials and how to optimize the 3D printing process for dental materials. Furthermore, it is imperative to explore the development of novel materials designed explicitly for the purpose of 3D printing [27]. An additional area requiring further investigation is the application of biomaterials in the dental field. While biomaterials have great potential for use in dental applications due to their biocompatibility and other unique properties, there is a need for further research to investigate their efficacy and safety. This could include the development of new biomaterials specifically for dental use, as well as investigations into the long-term effects of biomaterials on oral health [28]. Moreover, there is a necessity to investigate the advancement of intelligent dental materials. These materials possess the capability to adapt to variations in their surroundings, rendering them exceptionally valuable in dental contexts. Smart materials could be used to release drugs or antimicrobial agents in response to the presence of bacteria or other pathogens [29]. Further research is needed to develop and optimize these materials, as well as to investigate their potential uses in various dental applications. The investigation of digital technologies' influence on dental materials is a crucial field of study. The proliferation of digital technologies, including computer-aided design and manufacturing (CAD/CAM), has substantially transformed the development and utilization of dental materials [30]. Future research in dentistry could focus on the impact of digital technologies on dental materials and how to optimize materials for use with these technologies. Additionally, it is important to consider patient preferences when selecting and developing dental materials for patient-centered care. Although considerable progress has been made in dental materials technology, there are still areas within the field that require further research. These include conducting long-term clinical studies, establishing standardized testing methods, assessing the environmental implications of dental materials, exploring new material development, integrating dental materials with digital technologies, and optimizing materials for specific applications. Addressing these gaps through research will drive innovation and improve patient outcomes in the future of dentistry.

5.3 SUSTAINABLE AND ECO-FRIENDLY MATERIALS IN DENTISTRY: A "GREEN" APPROACH

Sustainable and eco-friendly materials in dentistry are those that minimize negative environmental effects and maintain natural resources. These materials may be derived from renewable resources, have a low carbon impact, and be recyclable or biodegradable. In dentistry, the utilization of environmentally friendly and sustainable materials can effectively reduce waste generation, energy usage, and pollution levels. They must satisfy functional and economic criteria while also having a low environmental impact. Sustainable and eco-friendly dental materials are closely related as they both aim to decrease the negative environmental repercussions of dental procedures, conserve natural resources, and are made from renewable sources [31]. Examples of such materials include biocomposites made from natural fibers and biodegradable resins, which are lightweight, strong, and biodegradable, making them an excellent alternative to traditional materials like metal and plastic [32]. Additionally, dental instruments, packaging materials, and even toothbrushes can be made from renewable sources such as bamboo, which is lightweight, durable, and has a low environmental impact [33]. However, it is important to note that not all materials marketed as sustainable or eco-friendly are environmentally friendly. Therefore, careful evaluation of materials and their environmental impact is necessary to ensure that sustainable and eco-friendly choices are made in the dental industry. Table 5.2 outlines the advantages and disadvantages of sustainable and eco-friendly dental materials and provides a useful reference for dental professionals to make informed decisions about which materials to use. One of the main obstacles to the adoption of sustainable and eco-friendly materials is their cost, which can be significantly higher than traditional

TABLE 5.2
Advantages and Disadvantages of Using Sustainable and Eco-Friendly Materials in Dentistry

Advantages of Using Sustainable and Eco-Friendly Materials	Disadvantages of Using Sustainable and Eco-Friendly Materials
Reduced environmental impact: Sustainable and eco-friendly materials are usually produced using environmentally friendly processes and are biodegradable, which reduces their impact on the environment.	Higher cost: Eco-friendly materials are often more expensive than traditional materials, which can make them less accessible to some patients.
Improved patient safety: Some traditional dental materials, such as amalgam fillings, contain potentially harmful materials such as mercury. Using eco-friendly materials can eliminate these risks and improve patient safety.	Limited availability: Some eco-friendly materials are not widely available and may only be offered by certain dental practices or suppliers.
Better esthetics: Eco-friendly materials, such as composite resins, can be designed to match the color of the natural teeth, resulting in a more esthetically pleasing outcome.	Reduced durability: Some sustainable materials may not be as durable as traditional materials, which can result in a shorter lifespan and the need for more frequent replacements.
Higher patient satisfaction: Patients are becoming more environmentally conscious and prefer treatments that align with their values. Using sustainable and eco-friendly materials can increase patient satisfaction and loyalty.	Complexity of use: Some eco-friendly materials require more specialized training or equipment, which can make them more difficult to use and require more time to complete procedures.

materials. Availability and regulatory barriers can also make it difficult to adopt new materials. Nonetheless, the use of sustainable and eco-friendly materials in dental practice can reduce waste generated by traditional materials and improve patient outcomes.

- Examples of sustainable and eco-friendly dental materials include:
  - Bioactive ceramics: Bioactive ceramics can mimic the natural structure of teeth and promote the growth of new tooth structure, reducing the risk of secondary decay [34,35].
  - Resin composites: Resin composites are esthetically pleasing and less damaging to the tooth structure than traditional amalgam fillings [36].
  - Glass ionomers: Glass ionomers can be used for filling cavities or cementing crowns or bridges and release fluoride to help prevent decay [37].

5.3.1 ADVANTAGES AND DISADVANTAGES OF SUSTAINABLE AND ECO-FRIENDLY MATERIALS

These materials have a lower environmental impact than traditional materials and are biocompatible and safe for use in the mouth. By choosing materials that are biocompatible, free from harmful additives, and produce less waste during manufacturing, dental professionals can provide high-quality care while also being mindful of their environmental impact. However, before making a decision, it is crucial to carefully consider the advantages and disadvantages of sustainable and eco-friendly materials, as outlined in Table 5.2.

5.3.2 CASE STUDIES OF DENTAL PRACTICES IMPLEMENTING SUSTAINABLE AND ECO-FRIENDLY MATERIALS

These case studies of dental practices that have implemented sustainable and eco-friendly materials provide concrete examples of how a "Green" approach in dentistry can be achieved [38]. By using digital radiography instead of traditional X-rays, practices can reduce their reliance on toxic chemicals and reduce their energy usage. Energy-efficient lighting and appliances, such as LED lighting and low-flow faucets and toilets, can also significantly reduce the practice's energy consumption [39]. Biodegradable products, such as toothbrushes made from bamboo and dental floss made from silk, can replace traditional plastic products that contribute to pollution and environmental damage [40]. In addition, these dental practices are reducing waste by implementing recycling programs and using reusable products, such as cloth patient bibs and sterilization pouches. The Eco Dentistry Association has played a key role in promoting sustainable practices in dentistry and providing resources and education for dental practices looking to adopt these practices [41]. The Association has also encouraged practices to use eco-friendly building materials, such as bamboo flooring and low VOC paint; this can lead to the promotion of a more healthful indoor environment for both patients and medical personnel. These case studies demonstrate that a "Green" approach in dentistry is not only possible, but can also benefit the practice's bottom line by reducing costs associated with energy usage and waste disposal. By implementing sustainable and eco-friendly practices, dental practices can make a positive impact on the environment and promote a healthier and more sustainable future [42,43]. Several dental practices around the world have implemented sustainable and eco-friendly measures in their operations by employing biodegradable products, digital waste-reduction technologies, and energy-efficient equipment and lighting. To decrease paper waste, these practices employ eco-friendly materials, digital X-rays, paperless charting, and electronic communication, as well as energy-efficient equipment and lighting. For dental uses, novel materials such as antimicrobials, biomaterials, and nanoparticles are being investigated.

5.4 NOVEL MATERIALS FOR DENTAL APPLICATIONS: ANTIBACTERIAL, BIOMATERIALS, AND NANOMATERIALS

As dental technology advances, so does the creation of new materials for dental purposes. The objective of these groundbreaking materials is to enhance the functionality, esthetics, and durability of dental devices and restorations, while simultaneously addressing crucial aspects such as safety, biocompatibility, and sustainability issues [44]. Intelligent materials, such as nanoparticles, are rapidly advancing dentistry by improving the accuracy, precision, and efficiency of dental treatments. Antibacterial materials are essential for oral health, preventing dental disorders caused by bacterial colonization and biofilm formation. Biomaterials mimic natural dental tissues, promoting tissue regeneration and replacing damaged or lost dental tissues [44]. In the following paragraphs, we present an overview of these innovative materials, including their characteristics, uses, and challenges. Our investigation aims to explore the latest trends in dental materials and their impact on dental practice, aiming to improve patient outcomes and the quality of care.

5.4.1 Novel Dental Materials

Dentistry 4.0 implies a significant transformation in the delivery of dental treatment, with a focus on the integration of digital technology, data analytics, and artificial intelligence. This strategy aims to improve patient outcomes by utilizing the power of technology to provide more efficient, customized, and proven treatments [45]. Novel materials are crucial for Dentistry 4.0, allowing digital technologies to create precise, durable, and esthetically pleasing restorations. Antibacterial materials, containing agents like silver nanoparticles, prevent bacterial growth and infections after dental procedures, effective against oral bacteria such as Streptococcus mutans, which causes dental caries [46]. Nanomaterials exhibit distinct characteristics that improve the mechanical, optical, and biological properties of dental materials, resulting in enhanced precision and efficiency during dental implant placement and decreased occurrences of post-operative complications. A study published in the International Journal of Biomaterials revealed that adding nanoparticles like ZrO_2, TiO_2, and SiO_2 to dental composites increased wear resistance and flexural strength [47]. Additionally, researchers at the University of California, San Diego have developed a novel nanomaterial-based dental adhesive that can bond to both wet and dry surfaces, providing a more reliable bond than traditional dental adhesives. Similarly, the application of antibacterial materials can help prevent the development of biofilms and reduce the risk of caries and periodontal disease [48]. Biomaterials are emerging as an essential component of Dentistry 4.0, as they can replace or repair damaged tissue in the mouth. They are biocompatible materials that can be used for dental implants, bone grafts, and periodontal tissue engineering. By imitating the properties of natural dental tissues, biomaterials can help restore the teeth and gums' structure and function, promoting long-term oral health [49]. A study published in the Journal of Functional Biomaterials examined the use of silk fibroin scaffolds for adipose tissue engineering. The study revealed that the silk fibroin scaffolds exhibited a compressive modulus comparable to adipose tissue, rendering them well-suited for adipose tissue applications. Moreover, the research underscores the ecological advantages of silk as a viable substitute for conventional approaches in adipose tissue engineering [50]. The development of new dental materials is an important aspect of Dentistry 4.0, allowing for a more sustainable and patient-centered approach to dental care. Antibacterial, Biomaterials, and Nanomaterials are being studied and refined for their potential to improve the performance of dental devices and restorations. Ongoing research and innovation in this field can help us provide better outcomes for patients and advance the principles of Dentistry 4.0.

5.4.2 Properties and Applications of Antibacterial, Biomaterials, and Nanomaterials

Antibacterial, Biomaterials, and Nanomaterials are important components of Dentistry 4.0, which refers to the incorporation of advanced digital technologies and materials in dental practice. These materials exhibit distinctive characteristics that render them suitable for diverse applications within the field of dentistry. In this response, we will discuss the different properties and applications of each material.

- Antibacterial materials: Antibacterial materials are essential for preventing oral diseases such as periodontitis and caries, which are caused by bacteria. For these materials to be effective, they must possess specific properties, including high antimicrobial efficacy, non-toxicity, and long-lasting antibacterial properties. High antimicrobial efficacy is vital to ensure that the material can kill or inhibit bacterial growth effectively. However, it is also essential that the material does not harm the human body or cause any harmful side effects. In addition, the material should maintain its properties for an extended period to provide continued protection against bacterial growth [51]. The applications of antibacterial materials in dentistry are numerous, from dental implants to orthodontic appliances [52]. Antibacterial coatings can be applied to dental implants to prevent bacterial colonization and infection, which is important due to the implants' proximity to the oral cavity. Antibacterial agents can also be added to composite resin restorative materials to prevent recurrent caries [53]. Antibacterial materials are useful in preventing biofilm formation on orthodontic appliances like brackets and wires, which can cause various oral diseases. This is important since biofilm formation can lead to recurrent caries or other complications that can result in the need for more extensive restorative procedures [54].
- Biomaterials: Biomaterials are materials designed to interact with biological systems and are often used to replace or repair damaged or missing tissue. When designing biomaterials, several properties need to be considered, including biocompatibility, bioactivity, and mechanical properties [55]. Biomaterials must be biocompatible, meaning they should not cause any adverse reactions or be rejected by the human body. Secondly, some biomaterials have bioactive properties that can stimulate tissue regeneration and promote healing [56]. In dentistry, biomaterials have various applications, including dental implants, bone grafting, and root canal filling materials [57]. Dental implants, for example, are made of biomaterials such as titanium because of their biocompatibility and mechanical properties. Titanium is also known for its ability to fuse with bone tissue, making it an ideal material for dental implants [58]. Biomaterials such as hydroxyapatite are used in bone grafting procedures to promote bone regeneration in cases of bone loss due to trauma or disease. Hydroxyapatite is a bioactive material that stimulates bone growth and can help restore lost bone tissue [59]. Bioceramic materials are used as root canal filling materials due to their biocompatibility and

bioactivity. Bioceramics help to seal the root canal system, prevent bacterial growth, and promote tissue healing [60].

- Nanomaterial: Nanomaterials are a rapidly growing field of materials science with immense potential for various applications in different fields. Nanomaterials have exhibited significant potential in the dental field, primarily attributed to their exceptional characteristics that render them suitable for diverse applications [61]. The high surface area to volume ratio of Nanomaterials stands out as a prominent benefit and contributes significantly to their overall advantages. This property makes them highly reactive and thus ideal for drug delivery applications. Engineered nanoparticles effectively treat oral diseases by precisely delivering drugs to specific sites in the mouth. Nanomaterials can be modified to enhance biomaterial properties, such as strength and bioactivity [62]. This makes them ideal for use in dental restorative materials, such as dental implants. Nanoparticles can function as contrast agents in CT and MRI imaging techniques [63]. This is because they have unique optical, magnetic, and electronic properties, which make them ideal for use in diagnostic imaging. Despite their numerous advantages, there are concerns about the potential risks associated with the use of Nanomaterials. This is because their small size means that they can easily penetrate the skin, mucous membranes, and other biological barriers, which could lead to toxic effects [64]. Nevertheless, it is crucial to acknowledge that the utilization of these materials must adhere to ethical considerations and regulatory frameworks [65]. The potential risks of Nanomaterials must be thoroughly assessed and addressed to ensure their safety and effectiveness in clinical use. Antibiotic-resistant bacteria pose a significant concern, emphasizing the need for cautious and limited use of antibacterial materials, with proper monitoring, only when clearly indicated [66]. The potential risks of Nanomaterials must be thoroughly assessed and addressed to ensure their safety and effectiveness in clinical use. Antibiotic-resistant bacteria pose a significant concern, emphasizing the need for cautious and limited use of antibacterial materials, with proper monitoring, only when clearly indicated.

As we proceed, a comprehensive overview in Table 5.3 will outline the advantages and disadvantages of integrating these novel dental materials, shedding light on the opportunities and challenges they bring to modern dentistry.

5.4.3 CURRENT RESEARCH AND DEVELOPMENT OF NOVEL DENTAL MATERIALS

Novel dental materials have garnered significant attention due to their potential to revolutionize dental care, as evidenced by ongoing research and development efforts showcased in Table 5.4. Among these advancements, antibacterial materials such as quaternary ammonium compounds (QACs) stand out. These materials have demonstrated a remarkable ability to impede bacterial growth and thwart the formation of biofilms on dental surfaces. Notably, this breakthrough holds promise for reducing the incidence of secondary caries among patients with dental restorations. The dynamic landscape of innovative dental materials underscores the continuous pursuit of enhanced

TABLE 5.3

A Summary of Advantages and Disadvantages of Using Novel Dental Materials in Dentistry

Advantages	Disadvantages
Enhanced mechanical properties, esthetics, and antibacterial activity: Novel dental materials frequently have enhanced mechanical properties, esthetics, and antibacterial activity, which can increase the durability and performance of dental restorations [67]. Resin composites, for example, have grown more durable and resistant to wear, while ceramics and zirconia can provide better esthetics and strength than traditional metal • based restorations [68]	Cost: Because novel dental materials can be more expensive than standard materials, they may be beyond of reach for some patients. For example, zirconia-based restorations can be more expensive than metal-based options, making them less accessible to individuals with low financial means [69].
Better patient outcomes: New dental materials can enhance patient outcomes such as function and esthetics, pain and sensitivity reduction, and oral health improvement. New adhesive solutions, for example, allow for more conservative tooth preparation, minimizing the need for extensive drilling and maintaining a more natural tooth structure [70].	Long-term data: Because certain innovative dental materials have not been used in clinical practice for a long time, long-term evidence of their safety and efficacy may be lacking [71]. This might make it difficult for dentists to make educated selections regarding the materials to utilize for specific procedures.
Customization: Some innovative dental materials, such as 3D-printed prostheses and orthodontic equipment, may be tailored to individual patients' needs, enhancing treatment outcomes [72]. This enables a more tailored approach to therapy, which can lead to higher patient satisfaction and compliance.	Technical complexity: Some innovative dental materials, like as 3D printing and smart materials, need specific equipment and knowledge, making their application more difficult and time-consuming. This can raise the cost of treatment and limit access to specific dental services [73].
Ability for tissue regeneration and repair: Some innovative dental materials, like as regenerative materials, have the ability to stimulate tissue regeneration and repair, hence boosting the long-term effectiveness of dental therapies [74]. Growth factors and stem cells, for example, can be employed to stimulate bone and tissue regeneration, which is especially advantageous in situations of bone loss or periodontal disease.	Unexpected complications: Unexpected problems or adverse responses to novel dental materials can have an influence on patient outcomes and safety. Some resin composite materials, for example, have been linked to undesirable effects such as allergic reactions and post-operative sensitivity [75].

patient care and improved treatment outcomes [76]. Biomaterials such as hydrogels, scaffolds, and growth factors have been used for tissue regeneration and repair in dentistry [77]. Nanomaterials have also been used to enhance the mechanical properties and esthetics of dental restorations. However, it's important to note that not all novel dental materials have been extensively studied, and limited long-term data on safety and efficacy means that potential risks and limitations should be carefully considered before

TABLE 5.4
Examples of Current Research and Development of Novel Dental Materials

Novel Dental Materials Technology	Applications	Current Research
3D printing of dental restorations	Advances in 3D printing technology have allowed for the creation of highly customized dental restorations, such as crowns, bridges, and dentures. Researchers are exploring new materials and techniques for 3D printing of dental restorations, with the goal of improving their accuracy, strength, and esthetics [79].	Researchers are developing new materials for 3D printing of dental restorations, such as ceramics and resins with improved mechanical properties and esthetics. For example, a recent study demonstrated the use of a ceramic resin for 3D printing of dental restorations with high strength, fracture toughness, and wear resistance. Additionally, 3D printing is being explored for the fabrication of customized orthodontic appliances, such as clear aligners and retainers [79,80].
Antibacterial materials	Researchers are developing new antibacterial materials that can inhibit bacterial growth and biofilm formation on dental surfaces. These materials may have the potential to reduce the incidence of secondary caries and other dental infections [81].	Researchers are investigating the use of various materials and formulations for their antibacterial properties, such as silver nanoparticles, quaternary ammonium compounds, and bioactive glass. For example, In a recent investigation, the application of a composite resin composed of bioactive glass and a quaternary ammonium compound was found to effectively prevent bacterial growth and the formation of biofilms on dental surfaces [82].
Regenerative materials	Biomaterials such as hydrogels, scaffolds, and growth factors are being investigated for their potential to stimulate tissue regeneration and repair in the oral cavity. Researchers are exploring.	Biomaterials such as hydrogels, scaffolds, and growth factors are being studied for their potential to regenerate dental tissues, such as dentin and pulp. For example, a recent study demonstrated the use of a scaffold made from collagen and hydroxyapatite for regenerating dentin-like tissue in vitro and in vivo. Additionally, researchers are exploring the use of stem cells and growth factors for regenerating dental pulp and promoting root development [83].
Smart materials	Smart materials are materials that can respond to changes in their environment, such as temperature, pH, or moisture. Researchers are	Researchers are developing various types of smart materials for dental applications, such as materials that can release drugs or growth factors in

(*Continued*)

TABLE 5.4 *(Continued)*

Examples of Current Research and Development of Novel Dental Materials

Novel Dental Materials Technology	Applications	Current Research
	investigating the use of smart materials in dentistry, such as materials that can release antimicrobial agents in response to bacterial infection, or materials that can change color to indicate the presence of tooth decay or other dental issues [84].	response to bacterial infection or tissue damage. Recent studies demonstrated the use of a smart resin that can release calcium and phosphate ions in response to acid attack, promoting remineralization of enamel [85].
Nanomaterials	Nanomaterials are being studied for their potential to improve the mechanical properties and esthetics of dental materials, as well as their antibacterial activity [86].	Researchers are exploring the use of various types of nanomaterials in dentistry, such as nanotubes, nanoparticles, and nanofibers. For example, A recent study highlighted the effectiveness of a nanotube-modified dental implant coating in improving bone integration and reducing bacterial infection [87]. Additionally, researchers are investigating the use of Nanofibers for periodontal regeneration [88].

use. Novel dental materials can enhance restorations, promoting tissue regeneration and repair [78]. Dental professionals and patients should work together to weigh the potential benefits and drawbacks of using these materials in specific treatment scenarios, taking into account their specific needs and circumstances.

Dental material research focuses on improving performance, safety, and adaptability. Areas of interest include antimicrobial, biomaterial, and nanomaterial research, offering benefits like enhanced mechanical properties, antibacterial activity, and regenerative potential. Although studies have demonstrated their utility in dentistry, long-term clinical studies are needed to assess their safety and effectiveness [89]. The accessibility of these materials can be limited due to specialized equipment and knowledge requirements. Therefore, careful evaluation is necessary when implementing innovative dental materials in clinical practice to improve patient outcomes and advance dentistry.

5.5　APPLICATIONS OF NOVEL MATERIALS IN DENTISTRY: RESTORATIVE DENTISTRY, IMPLANTOLOGY, ORTHODONTICS, AND ENDODONTICS

The field of dental materials science is experiencing rapid growth, encompassing the exploration, experimentation, and practical implementation of a wide range of dental materials. These materials include polymers, ceramics, metals, composites, and bioactive substances, all aimed at enhancing the overall effectiveness, durability, and biocompatibility of dental restorations, implants, orthodontic appliances, and various devices used in the oral cavity [49,56]. This critical field is essential in various dental specialties such as Restorative Dentistry, Implantology, Orthodontics, and Endodontics. It focuses on the development of novel materials and scientific methodologies to improve the efficiency, safety, and esthetics of dental treatments. Ultimately, it aims to enhance the quality of life for patients with dental disorders. Several factors contribute to the demand for innovative materials in dentistry, including the necessity to survive the severe climate of the oral cavity, be biocompatible, and mimic the natural properties of dental tissues such as color, translucency, and hardness. Dental specialties use different materials and procedures to address their specific challenges and goals. Restorative dentistry uses composite resins and ceramics to repair decayed or damaged teeth [90], while implantology uses titanium alloys [91] and ceramic coatings [92] to replace missing teeth and support bone tissue. Orthodontics uses shape-memory alloys [93] and thermoplastic materials to correct crooked teeth and improve occlusion [94], and endodontics uses bioceramics and sealers to disinfect and fill root canals [95]. Research and innovation promote the creation of innovative materials in dentistry, which requires collaboration among materials scientists, dental practitioners, and industrial partners. Nanotechnology, biotechnology, and computational modeling advances are projected to lead to the creation of increasingly more advanced materials and devices that can enhance dental patients' results and experiences.

5.5.1 Restorative Dentistry

Restorative dentistry is a dental specialty focused on the restoration and repair of decayed, damaged, or missing teeth using various materials and techniques. Recent advancements in dental technology have led to the emergence of novel materials and procedures for tooth restoration. These cutting-edge materials offer improved physical and esthetic properties, increased durability, and enhanced bio-compatibility, providing patients with long-lasting and visually appealing dental restorations [96]. Direct and indirect restorations are essential components of modern dentistry, allowing practitioners to preserve and restore the functionality and appearance of damaged or decayed teeth [97]. Over the years, dental materials and techniques have evolved significantly, with novel materials such as resin composites, ceramics, and glass ionomers emerging as popular options for restoring teeth. Each of these materials offers unique benefits and drawbacks, and under-standing these properties is important for dental practitioners to provide the best possible treatment for their patients. Different dental materials have unique benefits and limitations in direct and indirect restorations. Resin composites provide excellent esthetic outcomes and versatility for various restoration sizes, but are susceptible to wear, shrinkage, and discoloration. Ceramics offer superior strength and durability for indirect restorations, but require careful handling and are more prone to fracture. Glass ionomers are biocompatible and release fluoride ions, but have lower strength and may not be suitable for large restorations or areas of high stress [97]. The selection of the most appropriate material for a restoration depends on factors such as location, size, occlusal forces, and patient preferences, requiring dental practitioners to consider the pros and cons of each material.

5.5.1.1 Latest Materials Used in Direct and Indirect Restorations

Gaining a profound comprehension of the scientific underpinnings governing contemporary dental restoration materials, including resin composites, ceramics, and glass ionomers, holds paramount importance for dentists. This comprehension equips them to judiciously select the optimal material for each specific case, meticulously weighing its merits and demerits, as succinctly outlined in Table 5.5. This strategic approach to material selection underlines the pivotal role of informed decision-making in ensuring successful and enduring dental restorations. Resin composites are a popular choice for restorations due to their versatility, strength, durability, and excellent esthetic properties [98]. These materials are composed of a resin matrix and inorganic fillers, which undergo a curing process via free-radical polymerization upon light exposure. Typically, they are formulated with Bisphenol A glycidyl methacrylate (Bis-GMA), urethane dimethacrylate (UDMA), or other methacrylate monomers as their constituents [99]. The inorganic fillers, made of silica, alumina, or zirconia particles, provide the composite with wear resistance and strength. Resin composites offer a versatile solution for both anterior and posterior dental restorations, and their esthetic appeal stems from their capacity to seamlessly blend with the natural color and translucency of the tooth, ultimately resulting in a polished and natural-looking appearance. Ceramics for indirect restorations consist of a glassy matrix for bonding and esthetics and a crystalline or amorphous phase for strength. They can be made of various materials and fabricated through milling, pressing, or sintering. While ceramics provide superior esthetic properties, they require cautious handling and are more susceptible to fracture or chipping. Glass ionomers consist of fluoroaluminosilicate glass powder and a polycarboxylic acid solution, which chemically react to form a matrix of crosslinked carboxylate ions that adhere to the tooth surface via ionic and covalent bonds. They release fluoride ions to prevent tooth decay, but have lower strength and may not be appropriate for large restorations or high occlusal stress areas [100]. Table 5.5 provides a comprehensive overview of the materials and techniques used in dental restorations. In direct restorations, materials such as resin composites, glass ionomers, compomers, amalgam, giomers, bioactive materials, silver diamine fluoride, and increased filler loadings in resin composites are commonly used. Indirect restorations, on the other hand, utilize materials like ceramics, metals, resin-based composites, hybrid materials, adhesive cements, bulk fill composites, bioceramics, and various advancements in dental materials. In terms of techniques, indirect restorations benefit from CAD/CAM systems, 3D printing, digital impression systems, novel ceramic materials, high-strength zirconia materials, lithium disilicate materials, biomimetic materials, layering techniques, guided implant placement, laser-assisted dentistry, intraoral scanning, self-adhesive materials, and minimally invasive dentistry techniques. It's important to note that certain materials and techniques overlap between direct and indirect restorations, depending on their specific applications such as inlays and onlays. This table serves as a valuable reference for dental professionals in selecting the appropriate materials and techniques for different types of dental restoration.

TABLE 5.5

Summary of Latest Materials and Techniques for Direct and Indirect Dental Restorations

Materials	Direct Restorations	Indirect Restorations
Resin composites	Yes	Yes (used for inlays and onlays)
Glass ionomers	Yes	No
Compomers	Yes	No
Amalgam	Yes	No
Giomer	Yes	No
Bioactive materials	Yes	Yes
Silver diamine fluoride	Yes	No
Ceramics	No	Yes
Metals	No	Yes
Resin-based composites	No	Yes (used for inlays and onlays)
Hybrid materials	No	Yes(Resin modified glass ionomers)
Advancements in dental materials		
Increased filler loadings in resin composites	Yes	Yes
Improved bonding agents	Yes	Yes
Novel ceramic materials and processing techniques	No	Yes
High-strength zirconia materials	No	Yes
Lithium disilicate materials and manufacturing techniques	No	Yes
Biomimetic materials	Yes	Yes
Adhesive cements	Yes	Yes
Glass carbomer cement	Yes	No
Bulk fill composites	Yes	Yes
Bioceramics	Yes	Yes
Techniques		
CAD/CAM	No	Yes
3D printing	No	Yes
Digital impression systems	No	Yes
Layering techniques	Yes	No
Bulk-fill techniques	Yes	Yes
Sonic filling	Yes	No
Minimally invasive dentistry techniques	Yes	Yes
Guided implant placement	No	Yes
Laser-assisted dentistry	Yes	Yes
Intraoral scanning	Yes	Yes
Self-adhesive materials	Yes	Yes

5.5.1.2 Case Studies of Successful Implementation of Novel Materials in Dental Practices

Advancements in recent years have significantly improved the materials used for dental restorations, enhancing both functionality and esthetics. Several successful implementations of novel materials in dental practices have contributed to improved patient outcomes. Zirconia-based ceramics [101] are increasingly popular in dental restorations due to their strength, biocompatibility, and esthetics. Resin-based composites, known for their esthetic qualities and versatility, are now the standard for dental restorations [47]. Titanium implants have a high success rate of 97.3% after 10 years [102]. Glass fiber-reinforced composites are successful in restoring teeth with severe structural damage, with a survival rate of 78% after 5 years [103]. Zirconium-reinforced lithium silicate ceramics are effective for restoring anterior teeth, with a survival rate of 97.6% after 5 years [104]. Improved dental materials have enhanced the quality of dental restorations, but successful outcomes depend on the dentist's skill and regular maintenance. Patients should consult with their dentist to determine the best material for their dental needs.

5.5.2 IMPLANTOLOGY

Implantology has revolutionized dentistry by providing durable tooth loss solutions. Dental implants are artificial tooth roots placed in the jawbone to support prosthetic teeth or bridges [28]. The success of dental implants largely depends on the biomaterials and surface modifications used. Biomaterials used for dental implants require biocompatibility, mechanical strength, and durability [19]. Titanium and its alloys are frequently employed in various applications due to their exceptional biocompatibility and impressive strength-to-weight ratio, making them a popular choice [91]. Zirconia ceramics have exhibited encouraging outcomes in relation to biocompatibility and esthetic aspects when used for dental implants [60]. Surface modifications of dental implants are also critical for their success. Surface roughness and topography can influence the biological response of the surrounding tissues, affecting the osseointegration of the implant [87]. Various surface modification techniques such as sandblasting, acid etching, and plasma spraying have been used to modify the implant surface and improve osseointegration. Despite the successes of dental implants, there are still challenges that need to be addressed. One of the major challenges is the development of peri-implantitis, which is a bacterial infection that can cause bone loss and implant failure. To address this issue, research has focused on developing antimicrobial coatings and surface modifications to prevent bacterial colonization. Techniques such as bone grafting and guided bone regeneration have been developed to address limited bone availability in some patients, enabling successful implant placement. Biomaterials and surface modifications that can promote tissue regeneration and improve implant stability will be crucial in the future. The application of computer-aided design and manufacturing (CAD/CAM) technology to customize implants and improve their fit and esthetics will also play a significant role in implantology [105]. Overall, advances in biomaterials and surface modifications have contributed to the success of dental implants, and future research will continue to address challenges and explore new directions in this field.

5.5.3 ORTHODONTICS

Orthodontics is a dental specialty that deals with the diagnosis and treatment of misaligned teeth and jaws. Over time, the field has seen advancements in materials and techniques, providing practitioners with more options to correct different types of malocclusions. New materials like shape-memory alloys and clear aligners have emerged, each with its own strengths and weaknesses. There have been significant improvements in the design, composition, and performance of orthodontic materials in recent years. These advances have allowed orthodontic practitioners to provide more efficient and effective treatment to their patients, with greater patient comfort and satisfaction [106]. In a study by Bichu et al. [107], it was found that the third generation of aligners, which were introduced in 2010, incorporated advanced features like SmartForce™. These aligners utilized optimized attachments automatically designed and placed by commercial software, along with indentations in the polyurethane plastic. These enhancements exerted targeted pressure on specific areas of the tooth to achieve desired torque and root control. Additionally, the sixth-generation aligners, introduced in 2014, implemented SmartStage™ technology to enhance vertical control and root parallelism. This technology optimized the progression of tooth movement, especially in planned extraction treatments, ensuring maximum anchorage. The latest generation aligners, released in late 2020, made notable improvements in correcting deep bite issues. This was achieved through the activation of SmartForce™ aligners for anterior intrusion and enhancements in the ClinCheck software for leveling the Spee curve. These advances have enabled orthodontists to provide more accurate and effective treatments for their patients [107]. One major area of advancement in orthodontic materials is the development of shape-memory alloys. Nickel-titanium alloys are extensively utilized in orthodontic treatment for their unique ability to exert a gentle, continuous force on teeth. This results in faster and more efficient tooth movement, while reducing discomfort and the need for frequent adjustment appointments [108]. Composite materials have also been used for orthodontic purposes. For instance, composite brackets offer several advantages over traditional metal brackets, such as increased esthetics, lower friction between the wire and the bracket, and reduced treatment time. Similarly, tooth-colored wires made of composite materials are less visible than traditional metal wires [109]. The advances in orthodontic materials have allowed for more precise, efficient, and comfortable treatment. The use of shape-memory alloys and clear aligners has transformed orthodontics by providing a wider range of options for individualized treatment plans [110]. Nickel-titanium wires are an example of shape-memory alloys that have unique properties that allow them to return to their original shape when heated, resulting in faster, more efficient tooth movement and reduced discomfort for the patient. These wires require fewer adjustment appointments and reduce the overall treatment time compared to traditional wires. As technology continues to improve, further advancements in orthodontic materials and treatment techniques are expected to improve patient outcomes and satisfaction [111]. Clear aligners are custom-made, removable aligners made from clear, thermoplastic material that gradually moves teeth into the desired position [112]. They offer advantages over traditional braces such as improved esthetics, oral hygiene, and eating without restrictions, as well as fewer appointments and less chair time. Shape-memory alloys, such as nickel-titanium wires, are also used in orthodontic treatment to exert a gentle, continuous force on the teeth, causing them to move gradually [113]. They require fewer adjustments than traditional wires, resulting in faster, more efficient tooth movement and reduced discomfort. The use of clear aligners and shape-memory alloys has transformed orthodontic treatment, and further advancements in orthodontic materials and treatment techniques are expected to improve patient outcomes and satisfaction.

5.5.4 ENDODONTICS

Endodontics focuses on dental pulp and periapical diseases. Root canal therapy involves removing damaged pulp tissue from the root canal system and filling it with suitable material to prevent infection or inflammation [114]. The progress in endodontic materials and techniques has resulted in the emergence of innovative substances like bioceramics, gutta-percha, and irrigants. These advancements have played a crucial role in enhancing the effectiveness of root canal therapy, leading to improved treatment outcomes [115]. Root canal treatment plays a vital role in contemporary endodontics, serving to safeguard and rehabilitate teeth impacted by diverse ailments. The success of this therapy depends on the materials and techniques used, along with the expertise of the endodontist [116]. Bioceramics, improved gutta-percha, and innovative irrigants are some of the latest materials and methods used in root canal therapy. In the past, Gutta-percha has been widely utilized as a filling material in root canal therapy. However, advancements in the field have resulted in the emergence of new materials, including bioceramics, which offer innovative alternatives for this procedure [117]. Advancements in gutta-percha formulations, like thermoplasticized gutta-percha, have been developed to improve the limitations of traditional gutta-percha, including better adaptation to canal walls and reduced risk of underfilling [118]. New irrigants like sodium hypochlorite, chlorhexidine, and EDTA, along with techniques such as passive ultrasonic irrigation, have enhanced debris removal and root canal disinfection. These advancements improve dental professionals' ability to clean and disinfect root canals, promoting overall oral health [119]. Root canal therapy is a common procedure performed by endodontists to treat diseased or damaged teeth. The success of the procedure relies on several factors, including the quality of the materials and techniques used during the procedure. Fortunately, recent developments in endodontic materials and methods offer promising options for improving the success rates of root canal therapy and promoting the long-term preservation of teeth. Endodontists can optimize their approach to root canal therapy by understanding the advantages and limitations of these latest materials and techniques, which are essential for making informed decisions when selecting the most appropriate materials for each case. By doing so, they can increase the success rate of the procedure and improve patient outcomes. Advantages and disadvantages of using novel materials in restorative dentistry, implantology, orthodontics, and endodontics [120]. The field of materials science has witnessed remarkable

TABLE 5.6

Advantages and Disadvantages of Novel Materials in Various Areas of Dentistry

Area of Dentistry	Advantages	Disadvantages
Restorative Dentistry	Novel composite materials offer improved esthetics, physical properties, and reduced polymerization shrinkage.	They are typically more expensive than traditional materials, require technique-sensitive placement, and have limited availability of shades and translucencies.
Implantology	Novel implant materials offer improved biocompatibility, increased osseointegration, and reduced risk of peri-implantitis.	They are typically more expensive than traditional implants, have limited long-term clinical data, and limited availability.
Orthodontics	Novel orthodontic wires offer greater strength and flexibility, reduced treatment time, and more precise tooth movement.	They are typically more expensive than traditional wires, require a higher level of skill for placement, and have limited availability.
Endodontics	Novel endodontic materials offer improved disinfection of root canals, reduced risk of failure, and increased efficiency.	They are typically more expensive than traditional materials, have limited availability, and limited long-term clinical data.

progress, leading to the development of novel dental materials that exhibit improved biocompatibility, increased efficacy, and reduced failure rates, making them suitable for diverse dental procedures. Nonetheless, these cutting-edge materials are not without limitations, including elevated costs, restricted accessibility, and a learning curve for dental professionals. Therefore, it is crucial for dental practitioners to carefully evaluate the benefits and drawbacks of these materials and make informed decisions based on their patients' needs before implementing them into routine practice. Table 5.6 summarizes the benefits and drawbacks of adopting innovative materials in restorative dentistry, implantology, orthodontics, and endodontics, providing valuable information for dental practitioners to make educated selections depending on their patients' individual requirements. Although these technologies have the potential to enhance patient outcomes and revolutionize dentistry practice, it is essential to carefully weigh their benefits and drawbacks before integrating them into everyday practice.

5.6 ADVANCES IN ALGINATE IMPRESSION MATERIALS AND DENTAL RESTORATIVE MATERIALS

Modern dentistry heavily relies on two types of materials: Alginate impression materials and tooth restorative materials. Alginate impression materials are derived from a seaweed extract and are used to create precise molds of teeth and oral structures. They are easy to use, affordable, and have been used in dentistry for many years [121]. In contrast, dental restorative materials serve the purpose of repairing or replacing teeth that have been compromised or lost for different reasons. Commonly utilized options include amalgam, composite resins, ceramics, and gold alloys [122]. Recent advancements in both types of materials include hydrophilic alginate impression materials, resin-based composites, nanotechnology, CAD/CAM technology, and biocompatible materials. Dental practitioners need to stay up-to-date with these advancements to provide the best possible treatment to their patients, taking into account factors such as the location and extent of the damage, esthetic considerations, and the patient's overall health. Both alginate impression materials and dental restorative materials play a crucial role in maintaining good oral health and replacing damaged or missing teeth.

5.6.1 RECENT ADVANCES IN ALGINATE IMPRESSION MATERIALS AND DENTAL RESTORATIVE MATERIALS

Advancements in alginate impression and restorative materials have enhanced accuracy, esthetics, and longevity. Hydrophilic alginate materials absorb moisture for improved quality, while resin-based composites provide better esthetics and strength [123]. CAD/CAM technology enables faster and more precise restorative construction, while nanotechnology has created antibacterial and wear-resistant materials. Biocompatible materials like zirconia and titanium are commonly used in implants. These breakthroughs have increased patient comfort and satisfaction, and dental practitioners must stay up-to-date to deliver optimal care. Understanding the science behind material production is crucial for selecting appropriate materials and delivering excellent treatment.

5.6.2 ADVANTAGES AND DISADVANTAGES OF USING ALGINATE IMPRESSION MATERIALS AND DENTAL RESTORATIVE MATERIALS

Advantages of alginate-based imprint materials include low cost, simplicity of mixing, and flexibility, which allows for precise impressions. They are also safe for patients and compatible with the majority of dental materials. However, they have drawbacks such as lower accuracy when compared to other impression materials, susceptibility to temperature and humidity fluctuations, and allergy concerns in some individuals. Furthermore, with time, alginate-based impressions can get deformed, resulting in mistakes in dental restorations [124]. Table 5.7 encapsulates both the advantages and disadvantages associated with alginate-based impression materials, offering valuable insights for dental professionals who are seeking to make well-informed material choices.

Dental restorative materials provide durability, tooth protection, and customization options for patients. However, some materials may contain mercury, posing risks. They can be expensive, require specialized equipment, and may cause tooth sensitivity over time, necessitating replaceable element. Table 5.8 outlines the advantages and disadvantages of dental restorative materials.

TABLE 5.7
Advantages and Disadvantages of Alginate-Based Impression Materials

Advantages of Alginate Impression Materials	Disadvantages of Alginate Impression Materials
Relatively inexpensive	Limited accuracy compared to other materials
Easy to mix and set quickly	Shrinking and distortion over time
Flexible and elastic	Sensitivity to temperature and humidity changes
Compatible with most dental materials	Unsuitable for use in high anatomical detail areas
Safe and non-toxic	Allergic reactions in some patients

TABLE 5.8
Advantages and Disadvantages of Dental Restorative Materials

Advantages of Dental Restorative Materials	Disadvantages of Dental Restorative Materials
Available in a wide range of materials	Some materials contain harmful substances
Durable and long-lasting	Can be expensive depending on material used
Easy to shape and manipulate	Special equipment and techniques may be required
Can be color-matched to surrounding teeth	May cause tooth sensitivity or complications
Safe and non-toxic	Wear down over time and may need replacement

When planning dental care, it's important for dental professionals to assess the advantages and disadvantages of alginate impression materials and dental restorative materials. This evaluation enables them to provide optimal care for their patients by leveraging the benefits and addressing any drawbacks associated with each material.

5.6.3 Case Studies of Successful Implementation of Alginate Impression Materials and Dental Restorative Materials

A dental clinic in a rural area used alginate impression materials for their patients, as they were affordable and easily available. The clinic treated many patients from low-income families who could not afford more expensive materials. Despite the limitations of alginate impression materials, the dentists were able to use them to make accurate impressions of their patients' teeth, which allowed them to create well-fitting dental restorations. The dental clinic successfully delivered cost-effective, top-notch dental treatment to its patients.

- Case study of successful implementation of dental restorative materials: Alginate impression materials and dental restorative materials are widely used in dentistry. Here are some examples of successful implementation of these materials:

- Alginate impression material: A study reported on the successful use of alginate impression material for the fabrication of complete dentures. The study involved 100 edentulous patients who were treated using a conventional denture technique with alginate impressions. The researchers found that alginate impressions provided adequate detail for the fabrication of complete dentures and were a cost-effective alternative to other impression materials [125].
- Dental restorative material: A case report described the use of a resin-based composite material for the restoration of a patient's teeth. The material was used to restore the patient's front teeth, which had been damaged. The researchers found that the use of the resin-based composite material provided a strong and esthetic restoration that closely matched the color and shape of the patient's natural teeth [126].

These case studies demonstrate the successful implementation of alginate impression materials and dental restorative materials in clinical practice, highlighting their cost-effectiveness, esthetic properties, and good mechanical properties.

5.7 INTELLIGENT MATERIALS IN DENTISTRY: SMART AND RESPONSIVE MATERIALS FOR ENHANCED PATIENT CARE

Intelligent materials are a type of material that may change its characteristics in reaction to external stimuli such as temperature, light, moisture, or pH. These organisms possess the ability to perceive alterations in their environment and react in a consistent and controlled manner, rendering them highly advantageous for diverse purposes. Intelligent materials can even have self-healing or self-regenerating qualities in some situations, allowing them to fix damage without the need for human interaction. Smart materials possess the capability to revolutionize various industries, such as healthcare, electronics, and energy, through enhancements in performance, longevity, and functionality. These intelligent materials have the potential to bring about significant advancements in these sectors [127].

5.7.1 Properties and Applications of Smart and Responsive Dental Materials

Intelligent dental materials, referred to as smart and responsive dental materials, belong to a category of substances capable of altering their characteristics when exposed to various external factors like temperature, moisture, pH, or light. These materials have the potential to revolutionize dentistry by providing improved performance, comfort, and esthetics to patients. Here are some properties and applications of smart and responsive dental materials [128]:

- Self-repairing properties: Some smart dental materials have the ability to repair themselves when damaged, reducing the need for frequent replacements. These materials can extend the lifespan of dental restorations and reduce the overall cost of dental care.

- Stimuli-responsive drug delivery systems: These drug delivery systems have the ability to release medications based on particular triggers, such as variations in pH or temperature. They find applications in oral care products like toothpaste and mouthwash, facilitating the targeted delivery of therapeutic substances to the gums and teeth.
- Shape memory alloys: These materials can change shape in response to temperature changes. They are used in orthodontics to create shape memory wires that apply a constant force to teeth, allowing them to move into the correct position over time [93].
- Smart restorative materials: These substances have the ability to recognize and adapt to variations in the mouth's conditions, such as pH and temperature, and subsequently release therapeutic substances to inhibit additional harm. In addition to their esthetically pleasing appearance, they effectively guard against tooth decay and other oral complications [85].
- Light-cured dental composites: These materials can be cured using light, making them easy to use and highly effective. They are used in dental restorations such as fillings, crowns, and bridges, providing a natural-looking and long-lasting restoration [98].

Advanced dental materials with intelligent and adaptable properties possess the capability to enhance the functionality, longevity, and visual appeal of dental restorations, thus reducing the necessity for frequent replacements and enhancing patient comfort. Nonetheless, further investigation is necessary to comprehensively ascertain the safety and efficacy of these materials prior to their widespread implementation in clinical settings.

5.7.2 ADVANTAGES AND DISADVANTAGES OF USING INTELLIGENT DENTAL MATERIALS

Intelligent dental materials offer several benefits compared to regular dental materials, including increased functionality such as self-repairing capabilities, stimuli-responsive medication delivery, and antibacterial properties, as well as improved esthetics [129]. These materials can reduce the need for frequent dental restoration replacements, lower costs, and improve patient comfort. However, there are also drawbacks to using these materials, including higher costs, unknown long-term safety and efficacy, difficulty in use requiring specific training, and potential adverse reactions in some individuals. Intelligent materials in dentistry offer promise to improve patient care by enhancing performance, longevity, and esthetics of restorations while reducing replacements and improving convenience. The cost, limited research, complexity, and potential adverse reactions should be carefully considered. As research and development progress, practitioners and patients should remain informed and evaluate the benefits and risks of using these materials.

5.7.3 Current Research and Development of Intelligent Dental Materials

Intelligent dental materials research and development focuses on materials that can adapt to changes in their surroundings, including smart dental composites, self-repairing materials, and antibacterial materials. Smart dental composites release fluoride and remineralize teeth, while self-repairing materials use microcapsules to heal when broken. Antibacterial materials aim to destroy oral bacteria and prevent biofilm development [52]. Additionally, oral sensors that monitor pH and temperature levels in real time can aid in identifying oral health issues earlier. Smart dental materials have the potential to revolutionize dentistry and improve oral health outcomes.

5.8 BIOFABRICATION IN DENTISTRY: ADDITIVE MANUFACTURING, TISSUE ENGINEERING, AND BIOINSPIRED MATERIALS

Biofabrication is a developing area of research focused on employing biomimetic materials and methodologies to produce living tissues or artificial organs with enhanced functionality [130]. Biofabrication in dentistry involves the development of biofabricated dental implants, tooth replacements, drug delivery systems, and tissue engineering scaffolds. These applications demonstrate the versatile use of biofabrication techniques in oral healthcare. Biofabrication in dentistry involves using biomaterials with controlled surface roughness to enhance the bond strength between dental restorations and teeth. By incorporating regulated surface characteristics, this technique aims to improve the adhesive properties of the biomaterials used [131]. By employing biofabrication techniques, dental restorations can be enhanced in terms of durability and longevity, minimizing the risk of debonding or detachment by replicating the natural surface topography of tooth enamel. Various dental materials, such as ceramics, composites, and metals, can benefit from biofabrication methods, ultimately leading to improved treatment outcomes and increased patient satisfaction. The incorporation of advanced technologies like 3D printing and CAD/CAM enables the creation of personalized dental restorations and implants, highlighting the role of biofabrication in modern dentistry [132]. The procedure commences by obtaining digital scans of the patient's gums and teeth, which are utilized to generate a virtual representation of the desired dental restoration or implant. This digital model serves as a guide during the fabrication process, which may employ a range of biomaterials such as polymers, ceramics, and metals. Utilizing 3D printing technologies, intricate dental restorations can be produced with complex designs and geometries that surpass the limitations of conventional fabrication methods [130,131]. Biofabrication techniques can create dental tissue scaffolds for regeneration, revolutionizing dental treatment design and fabrication. With advancing research, widespread adoption of Biofabrication methods is expected, leading to improved dental care and patient outcomes [132].

5.8.1 The Applications of Biofabrication in Dentistry

Biofabrication in dentistry involves the use of advanced technologies, such as 3D printing and CAD/CAM, to create customized dental restorations and implants, as well as tissue engineering scaffolds for the regeneration of dental tissues. Biofabrication is being used in dentistry to create customized dental implants with precise dimensions and geometries tailored to individual patient needs [132]. This results in better fitting and functioning implants and improved patient outcomes. CAD/CAM technology is also used to design and fabricate biofabricated dental restorations, such as crowns and bridges, with high precision and accuracy. These restorations can be made from a variety of biomaterials for enhanced functionality and durability [12].

5.8.2 Properties and Applications of Additive Manufacturing, Tissue Engineering, and Bioinspired Materials

- Additive manufacturing: Additive manufacturing (AM) is an advanced technology that has revolutionized the manufacturing industry by allowing the production of intricate geometries that were previously unattainable through traditional manufacturing methods [133]. By creating items only where they are needed, rather than chopping away material from a bigger block, this approach can decrease material waste and expenses. AM is particularly advantageous in terms of speed and on-demand manufacturing, which may considerably reduce lead times and inventory requirements. The technique is commonly utilized in product prototype, customization, and small batch production of specialty items like medical implants or hearing aids [2,55,111,134].
- Tissue engineering: Tissue engineering, a fast-developing discipline within biomedical engineering, focuses on the creation of viable, functional tissues to address tissue damage or disease. As an illustration, the Green Composite in Bone Tissue Engineering represents an environmentally sustainable strategy that generates functional bone tissues for repair and replacement purposes. This groundbreaking technique imitates the inherent structure of natural bone, providing tailored remedies for patients and potential applications in areas such as transplantation, wound healing, and drug testing. By highlighting eco-conscious practices, it actively contributes to a more environmentally friendly trajectory in the realm of biomedical engineering [32].
- Bioinspired materials: In the field of dentistry, bioinspired materials have gained significant attention for their ability to replicate the natural structure and characteristics of teeth. These materials, such as dental composites, offer esthetic benefits by closely resembling the appearance of natural teeth. Additionally, they provide enhanced mechanical properties, improving the durability and functionality of dental restorations [135]. Bioinspired materials can be used to develop antimicrobial coatings for dental implants and other dental materials [136], reducing the risk of infection and promoting improved oral health outcomes. The properties of bioinspired materials, such as self-healing and environmental friendliness,

make them attractive options for use in the development of dental materials that are both functional and sustainable. Ongoing research in the field of bioinspired materials is expected to lead to continued advancements in the development of innovative dental materials with improved performance, durability, and patient outcomes.

5.8.3 Advantages and Disadvantages of Using Biofabricated Dental Materials

Biofabricated dental materials offer numerous advantages over standard materials, including customization, biocompatibility, regeneration, efficiency, and esthetics. Customizable materials can be adjusted to meet the unique requirements of individual patients, ensuring enhanced accuracy and suitability of dental restorations and prostheses. They are made of biocompatible biological materials, which can promote tissue regeneration and healing. Biofabricated dental materials can be produced faster and more effectively than traditional methods, saving time and expenses. They also have a more natural and esthetically pleasing appearance [135]. However, there are some disadvantages, including the high cost, limited availability, regulatory approval requirements, unknown long-term durability, and specific training requirements for manufacture and use. Further research and development are necessary to make biofabricated dental materials more widely available and cost-effective.

5.8.4 Current Research and Development of Biofabrication in Dentistry

The field of biofabrication is experiencing rapid progress as it incorporates cutting-edge technologies like 3D printing to fabricate intricate biological structures including organs, tissues, and cells. Within the realm of dentistry, biofabrication is being investigated as a means to develop personalized dental implants, prostheses, and other devices that align more effectively with the specific requirements of each patient [135]. Bioprinting in dentistry is a promising research area focused on utilizing advanced printing technology to create teeth and oral tissues. This innovative technique shows great potential for advancements in the field of dentistry. Bioprinting involves using specialized printers to deposit cells and other biological materials in a precise pattern to create a specific tissue or structure. Researchers are also exploring the use of bioactive materials in dental implants to promote tissue growth and healing [134]. These substances have the potential to enhance the efficacy of dental implants, minimizing the likelihood of issues like infection. Another focus of research involves the advancement of novel materials applicable to dental restorations, surpassing the durability, biocompatibility, and esthetic appeal of conventional options like metal and ceramics. The field of biofabrication holds immense promise in revolutionizing dentistry, enabling the production of personalized dental devices tailored precisely to meet individual patients' needs [27]. While there is still much research to be done in this area, the progress being made is promising and could lead to significant advancements in dental care in the coming years.

5.9 INTEGRATION OF ARTIFICIAL INTELLIGENCE, DENTISTRY 4.0, AND BIOFABRICATION IN DENTAL MATERIALS

Dentistry has made remarkable progress with advanced technologies like artificial intelligence (AI), Dentistry 4.0, and Biofabrication. These innovations have revolutionized the field, pushing the boundaries of dental care and treatment. By integrating AI, Dentistry 4.0, and Biofabrication, dentistry has achieved transformative advancements for more efficient procedures and improved patient care. These technologies improve dental materials, treatment options, and outcomes. AI analyzes patient and imaging data to create personalized treatment plans and precise dental restorations, including implants. This customization reduces complications and enhances treatment effectiveness [105]. This integration, along with Dentistry 4.0, is a major advancement in the field. Dentistry 4.0 incorporates digital technology and automation, including 3D printing, intraoral scanning, and CAD/CAM software. Using this approach enables the creation of accurate digital models of patients' teeth and gums, enhancing the design and production of dental restorations and prostheses [136]. Biofabrication plays a vital role in creating biocompatible dental materials for tissue regeneration. Integrating optimization and dentistry 4.0, it enhances personalized treatment plans and improves patient outcomes [136–139]. As these technologies continue to advance, we can anticipate further innovative and profound applications in dentistry. The most recent advances include:

- AI Applications in Dentistry [140–143]:
    a) AI algorithms analyze dental images to detect tooth decay, gum disease, and other conditions, aiding faster and accurate diagnoses. b) AI analyzes patient data to develop personalized treatment plans based on medical history, genetics, and lifestyle factors. c) AI-powered chatbots and virtual assistants assist with routine dental inquiries and appointments, freeing up dental staff for complex cases.
- Dentistry 4.0 Applications [27,68,142]:
    a) Digital dentistry: This involves using digital technologies, such as 3D printing, intraoral scanners, and CAD/CAM systems, to design and manufacture dental restorations and prostheses. b) Tele-dentistry: This allows dentists to consult with patients remotely, using video conferencing and other communication technologies. c) Patient management systems: These systems can help dental practices manage patient records, appointments, and billing more efficiently.
- Biofabrication Applications in Dentistry [10,27,144,145]:

3D bioprinting creates dental tissue engineering scaffolds (e.g., bone, cartilage, dental pulp). Biofabrication develops biocompatible materials for dental restorations (e.g., crowns, bridges, implants). Regenerative dentistry employs biofabrication to create biodegradable scaffolds releasing growth factors for oral tissue regeneration.

The following Table 5.9 may be used to weigh the benefits and downsides of introducing artificial intelligence, Dentistry 4.0, and Biofabrication into dental practice. When deciding whether to embrace new dental technology, it is critical to examine these issues.

TABLE 5.9

Advantages and Disadvantages of Using AI, Dentistry 4.0, and Biofabrication in Dental Materials

Technology	Advantages	Disadvantages
Artificial intelligence (AI)		
	AI can help dentists make more accurate and efficient diagnoses and treatment plans, leading to better patient outcomes.	There is a risk that AI could lead to a reduction in the need for human dentists, which could have negative social and economic impacts.
	AI-powered dental robots can perform certain procedures with greater precision and consistency than human dentists.	AI is not yet perfect and there is always a risk of errors or biases in the algorithms.
	AI can help dentists manage patient data more effectively and securely.	
Dentistry 4.0		
	Digital technology has the potential to enhance the precision and effectiveness of dental treatments, resulting in improved patient results and cost savings.	The cost of implementing digital technology can be high, which may make it less accessible to some patients and dental practices.
	CAD/CAM technology allows for the creation of precise dental restorations that fit more accurately and require less adjustment.	There is a learning curve associated with using new technology, which could lead to mistakes or errors in the early stages of adoption.
	Intraoral scanners eliminate the need for messy dental molds and reduce patient discomfort.	
Biofabrication		
	3D-printed dental materials can be customized to fit each patient's unique anatomy, leading to better outcomes and reduced complications.	Early-stage biofabrication technology raises concerns about the long-term safety and effectiveness of these materials.
	Biofabrication has the potential to revolutionize dental implant technology, making implants more biocompatible and longer-lasting.	The cost of biofabricated dental materials may be higher than traditional materials, which could make them less accessible to some patients and dental practices.
	Biofabricated dental pulp tissue could potentially be used to regenerate damaged or diseased teeth, eliminating the need for traditional restorative procedures.	

Artificial intelligence (AI) improves the precision of diagnosis and treatment and enhances the management of patient data. However, there is a concern that it may lead to the replacement of human dentists, which has significant societal and economic implications. Dentistry 4.0 integrates digital technology in dental practice to enhance the accuracy and efficiency of dental procedures, including the elimination of messy dental molds. Nonetheless, the deployment cost may be unaffordable for some patients and dental clinics. Biofabrication may revolutionize dental implant technology by removing the need for conventional restorative treatments, but their long-term safety and efficacy are still unknown. The high cost of biofabricated dental materials may also limit accessibility. As a result, these technologies must be carefully assessed before being implemented in regular dental practice.

5.9.1 FUTURE IMPLICATIONS AND CHALLENGES IN THE INTEGRATION OF THESE TECHNOLOGIES IN DENTISTRY

The integration of artificial intelligence, Dentistry 4.0, and biofabrication technologies in dentistry holds great promise for improving patient care and outcomes. In a recent study by Chau et al. [146], AI was used to design biomimetic dental crowns with acceptable accuracy. The AI system, based on a generative antagonist network (GAN), achieved an average Hausdorff distance of 0.633 mm and a true reconstruction rate of 60%. This highlights the potential of AI in dentistry and the need for further algorithm development and diverse participant involvement to explore its applications in the field [146]. However, there are also significant challenges and implications that need to be considered. Table 5.10 presents some future implications and challenges in the integration of these technologies in dentistry.

TABLE 5.10

Future Implications and Challenges in the Integration of These Technologies in Dentistry

Challenge/Implication	Description
Training and Education	Training dental professionals to effectively use and interpret data from emerging technologies is vital. Developing specialized education programs is necessary to ensure their proficiency in integrating these technologies into their practices.
Cost	The high cost of implementing these technologies in dentistry may make them inaccessible to some patients and practices. Cost-effective solutions and alternative financing models need to be explored.
Regulatory Framework	Governments need to develop regulatory frameworks to ensure safe, effective, and reliable use of these technologies in dentistry.
Data Security	Dental practices must prioritize secure handling of patient data generated through technologies, ensuring ethical collection, storage, and usage.
Ethical and Legal Implications	The use of these technologies raises ethical and legal implications, such as patient privacy, consent, and liability. These issues need to be carefully considered and addressed for safe and ethical use of these technologies.

The integration of artificial intelligence, Dentistry 4.0, and biofabrication technologies in dentistry has the potential to transform the field and improve patient care. However, it will be important to address these challenges and implications to ensure that these technologies are used safely, ethically, and effectively.

5.10 CONCLUSION: OPPORTUNITIES AND CHALLENGES IN THE FIELD OF DENTISTRY AND THE POTENTIAL IMPACT OF INTELLIGENT AND SUSTAINABLE MATERIALS

The field of dentistry is rapidly evolving with the integration of advanced technologies, such as Artificial Intelligence, Dentistry 4.0, and Biofabrication. These technologies offer new opportunities for dental professionals to provide better patient care and outcomes, with more efficient, accurate, and personalized treatments. There are also significant challenges that need to be addressed, such as training and education, cost, regulatory frameworks, data security, and ethical and legal implications. These challenges require collaboration among stakeholders, including dental professionals, technology developers, governments, and patients, to ensure the safe and effective implementation of these technologies. Moreover, intelligent and sustainable materials are also emerging as a potential game-changer in the field of dentistry. These materials are not only biocompatible but also more durable, cost-effective, and environmentally friendly than traditional materials. They have the potential to revolutionize the way dental restorations and implants are made, offering a more sustainable and efficient alternative. The integration of advanced technologies and intelligent and sustainable materials in dentistry holds great promise for improving patient care and outcomes. However, it is crucial to address the challenges and implications of these technologies to ensure their safe and ethical use. By doing so, we can create a more sustainable and equitable future for dental care.

5.10.1 KEY CHALLENGES AND OBSTACLES IN IMPLEMENTING THESE MATERIALS IN DENTAL PRACTICES

Implementing intelligent and sustainable dental materials in dental practices presents several challenges and obstacles. Some of the key challenges include: 1) Cost: The cost of intelligent and sustainable dental materials is often higher than that of traditional materials, which can make them less accessible to patients. 2) Regulatory requirements: New materials and technologies often require regulatory approval before they can be used in clinical practice. 3) The regulatory process can be time-consuming and expensive and may limit the availability of new materials. 4) Education and training: Dental professionals need to be trained on how to use new materials and technologies, which can be a significant barrier to adoption. Education and training programs need to be developed to ensure that dental professionals are equipped to use these materials effectively. 5) Integration with existing systems: Integrating new materials and technologies with existing dental practice systems can be challenging. Dental practices may need to invest in new equipment and software to integrate these materials effectively. 6) Long-term performance and safety: The long-term performance and safety of new materials and technologies are often unknown. It can take years of clinical testing to establish the safety and efficacy of new materials. 7) Ethical and legal issues: The use of intelligent and sustainable dental materials raises ethical and legal issues, such as privacy and data security. Dental practices need to ensure that patient data is protected and that they are complying with ethical and legal requirements.

Implementing intelligent and sustainable dental materials in dental practices presents several challenges and obstacles. These challenges need to be addressed through education, training, regulatory frameworks, and ongoing research to ensure that these materials can be used effectively and safely in clinical practice.

5.10.2 FUTURE DIRECTIONS FOR RESEARCH AND DEVELOPMENT IN THE FIELD OF INTELLIGENT AND SUSTAINABLE DENTAL MATERIALS

The rapidly evolving field of intelligent and sustainable dental materials focuses on enhancing the performance, biocompatibility, and sustainability of dental restorations and implants. Future research and development directions include: 1) Integrating materials with digital technologies, such as intraoral scanners, 3D printers, and artificial intelligence, to enhance precision, efficiency, and customization of dental restorations and implants. 2) Developing multifunctional materials with antibacterial, remineralizing, and self-cleaning properties to enhance the longevity and performance of dental restorations and implants. Enhanced biomaterials: Advancements in biomaterials, such as bioactive and biodegradable substances, offer opportunities to enhance the compatibility, strength, and longevity of dental restorations and implants. 3) Eco-friendly materials: The development of sustainable dental materials, including biodegradable and recyclable options, has the potential to mitigate the environmental impact caused by dental restorations and implants. 4) Tailored materials: Personalized dental materials, designed to match each patient's unique oral environment and requirements, have the potential to enhance the performance and durability of dental restorations and implants. 5) Cutting-edge manufacturing techniques: Progress in state-of-the-art manufacturing methods, like 4D printing and nanomanufacturing, holds the potential to revolutionize dental procedures by providing precise, effective, and personalized solutions that cater to individual patient needs. Continuing investigations and advancements in the domain of intelligent and eco-friendly dental materials strive to enhance the effectiveness, biocompatibility, and sustainability of dental implants and restorations. Such progress holds promise for revolutionizing the field of dentistry and enhancing overall oral health results for individuals.

REFERENCES

1. Arifa Mando K., Rena Ephraim, and Thiruman Rajamani. 2019. "Recent Advances in Dental Hard Tissue Remineralization: A Review of Literature." International Journal of Clinical Pediatric Dentistry 12 (2): 139–144. 10.5005/jp-journals-10005-1603
2. Javaid Mohd, Abid Haleem, Ravi Pratap Singh, Rajiv Suman, and Shanay Rab. 2021. "Role of Additive Manufacturing Applications towards Environmental Sustainability." Advanced Industrial and Engineering Polymer Research 4 (4): 312–322. 10.1016/j.aiepr.2021.07.005

3. Mulligan Steven, Paul V. Hatton, and Nicolas Martin. 2022. "Resin-Based Composite Materials: Elution and Pollution." British Dental Journal 232 (9): 644–652. 10.1038/s41415-022-4241-7

4. Shinya Akikazu. 2023. "Dental Material Research in Prosthodontics—Towards Developing Better and Efficient Biomimetic Materials." Journal of Prosthodontic Research 67 (2): vi–vii. 10.2186/jpr.JPR_D_23_00081

5. Kharouf N., S. Sauro, L. Hardan, Y. Haikel, and D. Mancino. 2023. Special Issue "Recent Advances in Biomaterials and Dental Disease" Part I. Bioengineering 10: 55. 10.3390/bioengineering10010055

6. Gronwald Barbara, Lidia Kozłowska, Karina Kijak, Danuta Lietz-kijak, Piotr Skomro, Krzysztof Gronwald, and Helena Gronwald. 2023. "Nanoparticles in Dentistry — Current Literature Review." Coatings 13 (102): 1–20. 10.3390/coatings13010102

7. Sikder Prabaha, Phaniteja Nagaraju, and Harsha P. S. Naganaboyina. 2022. "3D-Printed Piezoelectric Porous Bioactive Scaffolds and Clinical Ultrasonic Stimulation Can Help in Enhanced Bone Regeneration." Bioengineering 9 (11): 1–25. 10.3390/bioengineering9110679

8. Branco Ana Catarina, Rogério Colaço, Célio Gabriel Figueiredo-Pina, and Ana Paula Serro. 2023. "Recent Advances on 3D-Printed Zirconia-Based Dental Materials: A Review." Materials 16 (5): 1–34. 10.3390/ma16051860

9. Mulimani P. 2017. "Green Dentistry: The Art and Science of Sustainable Practice." British Dental Journal 222 (12): 954–961. 10.1038/sj.bdj.2017.546

10. Kocjan Andraž. 2022. Advances in Applied Ceramics Structural, Functional and Bioceramics. 10.1080/17436753.2022.2139047

11. Doryab Ali, and Jürgen Groll. 2023. "Biomimetic In Vitro Lung Models: Current Challenges and Future Perspective." Advanced Materials 35 (13): 1–6. 10.1002/adma.202210519

12. Iftikhar Sundus, Noureen Jahanzeb, Mehvish Saleem, Shafiq ur Rehman, Jukka Pekka Matinlinna, and Abdul Samad Khan. 2021. "The Trends of Dental Biomaterials Research and Future Directions: A Mapping Review." Saudi Dental Journal 33 (5): 229–238. 10.1016/j.sdentj.2021.01.002

13. Barot Tejas, Deepak Rawtani, and Pratik Kulkarni. 2021. "Nanotechnology-Based Materials as Emerging Trends for Dental Applications." Reviews on Advanced Materials Science 60 (1): 173–189. 10.1515/rams-2020-0052

14. Javaid Mohd, Abid Haleem, Ravi Pratap, Shanay Rab, Rajiv Suman, and Lalit Kumar. 2022. "Significance of 4D Printing for Dentistry: Materials, Process, and Potentials Journal of Oral Biology and Craniofacial Research Significance of 4D Printing for Dentistry: Materials, Process, and Potentials." Journal of Oral Biology and Craniofacial Research 12 (3): 388–395. 10.1016/j.jobcr.2022.05.002

15. Kantaros A., T. Ganetsos, and D. Piromalis. 2023. "3D and 4D Printing as Integrated Manufacturing Methods of Industry 4.0." American Journal of Engineering and Applied Sciences 1: 12–22. 10.3844/ajeassp.2023.12.22

16. Moshood Taofeeq D., Gusman Nawanir, Fatimah Mahmud, Fazeeda Mohamad, Mohd Hanafiah Ahmad, and Airin AbdulGhani. 2022. "Sustainability of Biodegradable Plastics: New Problem or Solution to Solve the Global Plastic Pollution?" Current Research in Green and Sustainable Chemistry 5 (100273): 1–18. 10.1016/j.crgsc.2022.100273

17. Roshan Mojtaba Esmailpour. 2023. "An Overview of the Application of Nanotechnology (Nanoparticles) in the Treatment of Dental Caries and Control of Oral Infections." Insights of Clinical and Medical Images Review, 1–10.

18. Pokrowiecki R., J. Wojnarowicz, T. Zareba, and I. Koltsov. 2023. "Nanoparticles and Human Saliva: A Step Towards Drug Delivery Systems for Dental and Craniofacial." International Journal of Nanomedicine ISSN 9235–9257. 10.2147/IJN.S221608

19. Haugen Håvard J. 2022. "Is There a Better Biomaterial for Dental Implants Than Titanium?—A Review and Meta-Study Analysis." Journal of Functional Biomaterials 46 (13): 1–19. 10.3390/jfb13020046
20. Wen Zhou, Shiyu Liu, Xuedong Zhou, Matthias Hannig, Stefan Rupf, Jin Feng, Xian Peng, and Lei Cheng .2019. "Modifying Adhesive Materials to Improve the Longevity of Resinous Restorations." International Journal of Molecular Sciences 20: 1–20. 10.3390/ijms20030723
21. Elhelbawy Nahla Gamal, Rehab F. Ghouraba, and Fatma A. Hasaneen. 2022. "A Comparative Evaluation of the Radiopacity of Contemporary Restorative CAD/CAM Blocks Using Digital Radiography Based on the Impact of Material Composition." International Journal of Biomaterials 2022: 1–8. 10.1155/2022/4131176
22. Rao Megha, Vanamala Narayana, B S Keshava Prasad, and Bushra Almas. 2022. "Recent Advances in Biomimetic Materials Used in Restorative Dentistry: An Updated Review." Asian Journal of Dental Sciences 5 (4): 56–65. https://www.sdiarticle5.com/review-history/87863
23. Maloo Labdhi M., Aditya Patel, Sumeet H. Toshniwal, and Ashutosh D. Bagde. 2022. "Smart Materials Leading to Restorative Dentistry: An Overview." Cureus 14 (10): 1–8. 10.7759/cureus.30789
24. Dobrzański Leszek A., Lech B. Dobrzański, Anna D. Dobrzańska-Danikiewicz, and Joanna Dobrzańska. 2020. "The Concept of Sustainable Development of Modern Dentistry." Processes 8 (12): 1–86. 10.3390/pr8121605
25. Althagafi Dr. Malak Yousef, and Dr. Mohammed Korayem. 2020. "Dentofacial Deformity: Treated with Combined Orthodontic and Orthognathic Surgery Treatment." Saudi Journal of Oral and Dental Research 05 (05): 254–261. 10. 36348/sjodr.2020.v05i05.004
26. Malara P., and L. B. Dobrzański. 2015. "Computer-Aided Design and Manufacturing of Dental Surgical Guides Based on Cone Beam Computed Tomography." Archives of Materials Science and Engineering 76 (2): 140–149.
27. Tian Yueyi, Chun Xu Chen, Xiaotong Xu, Jiayin Wang, Xingyu Hou, Kelun Li, Xinyue Lu, Hao Yu Shi, Eui Seok Lee, and Heng Bo Jiang. 2021. "A Review of 3D Printing in Dentistry: Technologies, Affecting Factors, and Applications." Scanning 2021: 1–19. 10.1155/2021/9950131
28. Cheng Mei Shuan, Eisner Salamanca, Jerry Chin Yi Lin, Yu Hwa Pan, Yi Fan Wu, Nai Chia Teng, Ikki Watanabe, Ying Sui Sun, and Wei Jen Chang. 2022. "Preparation of Calcium Phosphate Compounds on Zirconia Surfaces for Dental Implant Applications." International Journal of Molecular Sciences 23 (12): 1–15. 10.3390/ijms23126675
29. Montoya Carolina, Lina Roldan, Michelle Yu, Sara Valliani, Christina Ta, Maobin Yang, and Santiago Orrego. 2023. "Smart Dental Materials for Antimicrobial Applications." Bioactive Materials 24 (November 2022): 1–19. 10.1016/j.bioactmat.2022.12.002
30. Spagnuolo Gianrico, and Roberto Sorrentino. 2020. "The Role of Digital Devices in Dentistry: Clinical Trends and Scientific Evidences." Journal of Clinical Medicine. 10.3390/jcm9061692
31. Mahapatra Somalee, Manoranjan Dash, Priyanka Debta, Saswati Siddhartha, Subhashis Mohanty, Histopathology Consultant, and Sum Ultimate Medicare. 2023. "Dental Waste Management for Environmental Sustainability – Review of Literature in Systematic Manner." Social Science Journal 13 (1): 3589–3596.
32. Jouyandeh Maryam, Henri Vahabi, Navid Rabiee, Mohammad Rabiee, Mojtaba Bagherzadeh, and Mohammad Reza Saeb. 2022. "Green Composites in Bone Tissue Engineering." Emergent Materials 5 (3): 603–620. 10.1007/s42247-021-00276-5

33. Martin Nicolas, and Steven Mulligan. 2022. "Environmental Sustainability Through Good-Quality Oral Healthcare." International Dental Journal 72 (1): 26–30. 10.1016/j.identj.2021.06.005

34. Kaou Maroua H., Zsolt E. Horváth, Katalin Balázsi, and Csaba Balázsi. 2023. "Eco-Friendly Preparation and Structural Characterization of Calcium Silicates Derived from Eggshell and Silica Gel." International Journal of Applied Ceramic Technology 20 (2): 689–699. 10.1111/ijac.14274

35. Rodrigues Alisson Mendes, Gelmires De Araujo Neves, and Romualdo Rodrigues Menezes. 2022. New Environmentally-Friendly and Sustainable Materials. New Environmentally-Friendly and Sustainable Materials. 10.3390/books978-3-0365-3117-5

36. Worthington Helen V., Sara Khangura, Kelsey Seal, Monika Mierzwinski-Urban, Analia Veitz-Keenan, Philipp Sahrmann, Patrick Roger Schmidlin, Dell Davis, Zipporah Iheozor-Ejiofor, and María Graciela Rasines Alcaraz. 2021. "Direct Composite Resin Fillings versus Amalgam Fillings for Permanent Posterior Teeth." Cochrane Database of Systematic Reviews 2021 (8). 10.1002/14651858. CD005620.pub3

37. Ivana Miletić, Zalba José, and Khandelwal Piyush. 2022. "Solution Found: The Evolution of Glass Ionomer Cement Technology." Advances 4: 1–23.

38. Khanna Sunali S., and Prita A. Dhaimade. 2019. "Green Dentistry: A Systematic Review of Ecological Dental Practices." Environment, Development and Sustainability 21 (6): 2599–2618. 10.1007/s10668-018-0156-5

39. Connie M., Kracher M. D., Connie M., and Kracher M. 2024. "Digital Imaging in Dentistry: Intraoral, Extraoral, and 3D Technology" www.dentalcare.com/en-us/professional-education/ce-courses/ce512.1-20

40. Abed Rawan Hussein. 2022. "Environmental Sustainability of Oral Health Interventions Study." UCL Eastman Dental Institute. 15–201.

41. Duane Brett, Kim Croasdale, Darshini Ramasubbu, Sara Harford, Inge Steinbach, Rachel Stancliffe, and Devika Vadher. 2019. "Environmental Sustainability: Measuring and Embedding Sustainable Practice into the Dental Practice." British Dental Journal 226 (11): 891–896. 10.1038/s41415-019-0355-y

42. Zhu Xiao-yong, Hua Zhang, and Zhi-gang Jiang. 2019. "Application of Green-Modified Value Stream Mapping to Integrate and Implement Lean and Green Practices: A Case Study." International Journal of Computer Integrated Manufacturing 00 (00): 1–16. 10.1080/0951192X.2019.1667028

43. Al-thunian Felwah Fahad, Roula S. Al-bounni, Navin Anand Ingle, and Mansour K. Assery. 2020. "Evaluation of Green Dental Practice Implementation among Dental Practitioners Worldwide – A Systematic Review." JDOH 7. 10.17303/jdoh.2020.7.104

44. Dobrzanski Leszek A. Dobrza, Joanna Dobrzanska, Anna D. Dobrzanska-Danikiewicz, and Lech B. Dobrzanski. 2020. "The Concept of Sustainable Development of Modern Dentistry." Processes 8 (1605): 1–86. 10.3390/pr8121605

45. Alshadidi A. A. F., A. A. Alshahrani, L. I. N. Aldosari, S. Chaturvedi, R. S. Saini, S. A. B. Hassan, M. Cicciù, and G. Minervini. 2023. "Investigation on the Application of Artificial Intelligence in Prosthodontics." Applied Science 13: 5004. 10.3390/app13085004

46. Wassel Mariem O., and Mona A. Khattab. 2017. "Antibacterial Activity against Streptococcus Mutans and Inhibition of Bacterial Induced Enamel Demineralization of Propolis, Miswak, and Chitosan Nanoparticles Based Dental Varnishes." Journal of Advanced Research 8 (4): 387–392. 10.1016/j.jare.2017.05.006

47. Azmy Emad, Mohamed Reda Zaki Al-Kholy, Mohamed Fattouh, Laila Mohamed Mohamed Kenawi, and Mohamed Ahmed Helal. 2022. "Impact of Nanoparticles Additions on the Strength of Dental Composite Resin." International Journal of Biomaterials 2022: 1–9. 10.1155/2022/1165431

48. Jain Pooja, Uzma Farooq, Nazia Hassan, Mohammed Albratty, Md Shamsher Alam, Hafiz A. Makeen, Mohd Aamir Mirza, and Zeenat Iqbal. 2022. "Nanotechnology Interventions as a Putative Tool for the Treatment of Dental Afflictions." Nanotechnology Reviews 11 (1): 1935–1946. 10.1515/ntrev-2022-0115

49. Zhang, Kai, Bin Ma, Kaiyan Hu, Bo Yuan, Xin Sun, Xu Song, J. García, Antonios G. Mikos, James M. Anderson, and Xingdong Zhang. 2022. "Bioactive Materials Evidence-Based Biomaterials Research." Bioactive Materials 15 (February): 495–503. 10.1016/j.bioactmat.2022.04.014

50. Roblin Nathan V., Megan K. DeBari, Sandra L. Shefter, Erica Iizuka, and Rosalyn D. Abbott. 2023. "Development of a More Environmentally Friendly Silk Fibroin Scaffold for Soft Tissue Applications." Journal of Functional Biomaterials 14 (4): 1–19. 10.3390/jfb14040230

51. Ercole Simonetta D., Francesco De Angelis, Virginia Biferi, Chiara Noviello, Domenico Tripodi, Silvia Di Lodovico, Luigina Cellini, and Camillo D. Arcangelo. 2022. "Antibacterial and Antibiofilm Properties of Three Resin-Based Dental Composites against Streptococcus Mutans." Materials 1891 (15): 1–12. 10.3390/ma15051891

52. Widjaja Gunawan, Universitas Krisnadwipayana, and Yasser Fakri Mustafa. 2021. "Study on the Role of Nano Antibacterial Materials in Orthodontics (a Review)." Brazilian Journal of Biology 84 (2024): 1–7. 10.1590/1519-6984.257070

53. Firoozmand L. M., and Y. Alania Ak. 2022. "Development and Assessment of Bioactive Coatings for the Prevention of Recurrent Caries around Resin Composite Restorations." Operative Dentistry 47 (3): 152–161. 10.2341/20-299-L

54. Siva Suvetha, Shreya Kishore, Priyanka, and Aadhirai Gopinath. 2022. "A Systematic Review on Nano Coated Orthodontic Brackets and Its Antibacterial Effects." Journal of Clinical and Diagnostic Research 16 (2): ZE18–ZE22. 10.7860/jcdr/2022/52649.16020

55. Omiyale Babatunde, and Temitope Olugbade. 2022. "Influence of Mechanical Properties of Biomaterials on the Reconstruction of Biomedical Parts via Additive Manufacturing Techniques: An Overview." In Biotechnology – Biosensors, Biomaterials and Tissue Engineering, (june): 1–11. 10.5772/intechopen.104465

56. afari Nazanin, Mina Seyed Habashi, Alireza Hashemi, Reza Shirazi, Nader Tanideh, and Amin Tamadon. 2022. "Application of Bioactive Glasses in Various Dental Fields." Biomaterials Research 26 (1): 1–15. 10.1186/s40824-022-00274-6

57. Mahesh KP, Meenakshi Srinivasa Iyer, Raghavendra Swamy KN, Karthikeya Patil, and N. Raghunath. 2021. "Biomaterials and Their Applications in Dentistry—A Literature Review." Journal of Evolution of Medical and Dental Sciences 10 (26): 1940–1947. 10.14260/jemds/2021/399

58. Erwin Nina, Debashish Sur, and G Bahar Basim. 2022. "Remediation of Machining Medium Effect on Biocompatibility of Titanium-Based Dental Implants by Chemical Mechanical Nano-Structuring." Journal of Materials Research, no. May: 1–12. 10.1557/s43578-022-00553-x

59. Wang Xinhua, Chengpeng Wan, Xiaoxia Feng, Fuyan Zhao, and Huiming Wang. 2021. "In Vivo and In Vitro Analyses of Titanium-Hydroxyapatite Functionally Graded Material for Dental Implants." BioMed Research Internationa 2021: 1–14. 10.1155/2021/8859945

60. Lin Hua, Cuilan Yin, and Anchun Mo. 2021. "Zirconia Based Dental Biomaterials: Structure, Mechanical Properties, Biocompatibility, Surface Modification, and Applications as Implant." Frontiers in Dental Medicine 2 (August): 1–7. 10.3389/fdmed.2021.689198

61. Dr. Keerthi and Dr. Sahana Purushotham. 2022. "Nanomaterials – The Modern Age Frontier in Implant Dentistry." Journal of Medical Sciences 3 (2): 113–115. 10.47310iarjms.2022.v03i02.017

62. Nematollahzadeh Ali. 2023. Nanomaterials in Dental Medicine. Edited by Sabu Thomas and R. M. Baiju. 10.1007/978-981-19-8718-2

63. Zhu Derong, Fuyao Liu, Lina Ma, Dianjun Liu, and Zhenxin Wang. 2013. "Nanoparticle-Based Systems for T1-Weighted Magnetic Resonance Imaging Contrast Agents." International Journal of Molecular Sciences 14: 10591–10607. 10.3390/ijms140510591

64. Angrisano, Mariarosaria, and Francesco Fabbrocino. 2023. "Recent Progress in Materials the Relation between Environmental Risk Analysis and the Use of Nanomaterials in the Built Environment Sector: A Circular Economy Perspective." Recent Progress in Materials 5 (1): 1–17. 10.21926/rpm.2301005

65. Mardani Amir, Maryam Nakhoda, Alireza Noruzi, and Ehsan Shamsi-gooshki. 2019. "Ethical Considerations in the Biomedical Research: Analysis of National Biomedical Research Ethics Guidelines in Iran." Journal of Medical Ethics and History of Medicine 12 (4): 1–25. 10.18502/jmehm.v12i4.767

66. Gao Lingyan, Haojie Wang, Bo Zheng, and Feihe Huang. 2021. "Combating Antibiotic Resistance: Current Strategies for the Discovery of Novel Antibacterial Materials Based on Macrocycle Supramolecular Chemistry." Giant 7 (100066): 1–28. 10.1016/j.giant.2021.100066

67. Cao Weiwei, Yu Zhang, Xi Wang, Qiang Li, Yuhong Xiao, Peili Li, Lina Wang, Zhiwen Ye, and Xiaodong Xing. 2018. "Novel Resin-Based Dental Material with Anti-Biofilm Activity and Improved Mechanical Property by Incorporating Hydrophilic Cationic Copolymer Functionalized Nanodiamond." Journal of Materials Science: Materials in Medicine 29 (162): 1–13. 10.1007/s10856-018-6172-z

68. Zhi Li, Tissiana Bortolotto, and Ivo Krejci. 2016. "Comparative in Vitro Wear Resistance of CAD/CAM Composite Resin and Ceramic Materials." Journal of Prosthetic Dentistry 115 (2): 199–202. 10.1016/j.prosdent.2015.07.011

69. Laumbacher Harald, Thomas Strasser, Helge Knüttel, and Martin Rosentritt. 2021. "Long-Term Clinical Performance and Complications of Zirconia-Based Tooth- and Implant-Supported Fixed Prosthodontic Restorations: A Summary of Systematic Reviews." Journal of Dentistry 111 (103723): 1–10. 10.1016/j.jdent.2021.103723

70. Ayari Naima, Ibtissem Grira, and Nabiha Douki. 2023. "Endocrown Restorations: A Conservative Approach to Restore Extensively Damaged Endodontically Treated Teeth." EAS Journal of Dentistry and Oral Medicine 5 (02): 53–59. 10.36349/easjdom.2023.v05i02.006

71. NA Fernandes, Zunaid Vally, and Leanne Sykes. 2015. "Longevity of Restorations-a Literature Review." Clinical Review 70 (9): 410–413.

72. Chhikara Komal, Sarabjeet Singh Sidhu, Shubham Gupta, Sakshi Saharawat, and Chitra Kataria. 2023. "Development and Effectiveness Testing of a Novel 3D-Printed Multi-Material Orthosis in Nurses with Plantar Foot Pain." Prosthesis 5: 73–87. 10.3390/prosthesis5010006

73. Rezaie Fereshte, Masoud Farshbaf, Mohammad Dahri, Moein Masjedi, Reza Maleki, Fatemeh Amini, Jonathan Wirth, Keyvan Moharamzadeh, Franz E. Weber, and Lobat Tayebi. 2023. "3D Printing of Dental Prostheses: Current and Emerging Applications." Journal of Composites Science 7 (2): 1–24. 10.3390/jcs7020080

74. Zhang Lei, Guojing Yang, Blake N. Johnson, and Xiaofeng Jia. 2019. "Three-Dimensional (3D) Printed Scaffold and Material Selection for Bone Repair." Acta Biomaterialia 84 (November): 16–33. 10.1016/j.actbio.2018.11.039

75. Schmalz Gottfried, and Kerstin M. Galler. 2017. "Biocompatibility of Biomaterials – Lessons Learned and Considerations for the Design of Novel Materials." Dental Materials 33 (4): 382–393. 10.1016/j.dental.2017.01.011

76. Vereshchagin Anatoly N., Nikita A. Frolov, Valentine P. Ananikov, Ksenia S. Egorova, and Marina M. Seitkalieva. 2021. "Quaternary Ammonium Compounds

(QACs) and Ionic Liquids (ILs) as Biocides: From Simple Antiseptics to Tunable Antimicrobials." International Journal of Molecular Sciences 22 (6793): 1–82.

77. Matichescu Anamaria, Lavinia Cosmina Ardelean, Laura-cristina Rusu, Dragos Craciun, Emanuel Adrian Bratu, Marius Babucea, and Marius Leretter. 2020. "Advanced Biomaterials and Techniques for Oral Tissue Engineering and Regeneration—A Review." Materials 13 (5303): 1–37. 10.3390/ma13225303

78. Liu Chao, Atilim Eser, Thomas Albrecht, Vasiliki Stournari, Monika Felder, Siegward Heintze, and Christoph Broeckmann. 2021. "Strength Characterization and Lifetime Prediction of Dental Ceramic Materials." Dental Materials 37 (1): 94–105. 10.1016/j.dental.2020.10.015

79. Mayinger Felicitas, Marlis Eichberger, Elena Reznikova, and Lisa Marie. 2021. "Mechanical Properties of Thermoplastic Polymer Materials." Journal of the Mechanical Behavior of Biomedical Materials 119 (January): 1–7. 10.1016/j.jmbbm.2021.104544

80. Sehrawat, S., A. Kumar, M. Prabhakar, and J. Nindra. 2021. "The Expanding Domains of 3D Printing Pertaining to the Speciality of Orthodontics." Materials Today: Proceedings. 10.1016/j.matpr.2021.09.124

81. Fakhruddin Kausar Sadia, Hiroshi Egusa, Hien Chi Ngo, Chamila Panduwawala, Siripen Pesee, and Lakshman Perera Samaranayake. 2020. "Clinical Efficacy and the Antimicrobial Potential of Silver Formulations in Arresting Dental Caries: A Systematic Review." BMC Oral Health 20 (160): 1–14. 10.1186/s12903-020-01133-3

82. Ladino Luis Gabriel, Alejandra Bernal, Daniel Calderón, and Diego Cortés. 2021. "Bioactive Materials in Restorative Dentistry: A Literature Review." SVOA Dentistry 2 (2): 74–81.

83. Chen, R.-S., S.-H. Hsu, H.-H. Chang, and M.-H. Chen. 2021. "Challenge Tooth Regeneration in Adult Dogs with Dental Pulp StemCells on 3D-Printed Hydroxyapatite/Polylactic Acid Scaffolds." Cells 10: 3277. 10.3390/cells10123277

84. Krasniq Zana, D. Lila-Krasniqi, Rrezarta Bajrami Halili, Valeza Hamza, and Sokol. 2022. "Evaluation of Antimicrobial Effectiveness of Dental Cement Materials on Growth of Different Bacterial Strains." Medical Science Monitor Basic Research 28 (2325–4416): 1–6. 10.12659/MSMBR.937893

85. Sebastian Ronin, Santhosh T. Paul, Umme Azher, and Divya Reddy. 2022. "Comparison of Remineralization Potential of Casein Phosphopeptide: Amorphous Calcium Phosphate, Nano-Hydroxyapatite and Calcium Sucrose Phosphate on Artificial Enamel Lesions: An In Vitro Study." International Journal of Clinical Pediatric Dentistry 15 (1): 1–5.

86. Larissa Pavanello, Benjamin Gambrill, Rafaela Durrer, Parolina De Carvalho, Mayara Zagui, Dal Picolo, Vanessa Cavalli, Letícia Cristina, and Cidreira Boaro. 2023. "Development, Characterization and Antimicrobial Activity of Multilayer Silica Nanoparticles with Chlorhexidine Incorporated into Dental Composites." Dental Materials 39 (5): 469–477. 10.1016/j.dental.2023.03.005.10.1016/j.dental.2023.03.005

87. Souza, Julio C. M., Mariane B. Sordi, Miya Kanazawa, Sriram Ravindran, Bruno Henriques, Filipe S. Silva, Conrado Aparicio, and Lyndon F. Cooper. 2019. "Nano-Scale Modification of Titanium Implant Surfaces to Enhance Osseointegration." Acta Biomaterialia 94: 112–131. 10.1016/j.actbio.2019.05.045

88. Santos, Mafalda S., and Marta S. Carvalho. 2023. "Recent Advances on Electrospun Nanofibers for Periodontal Regeneration." Nanomaterials 13 (1307): 1–22

89. Agarwalla, Shruti Vidhawan, Adline Princy Solomon, Prasanna Neelakantan, and Vinicius Rosa. 2020. "Novel Materials and Therapeutic Strategies against the Infection of Implants." Emergent Materials 3 (4): 545–557. 10.1007/s42247-020-00117-x

90. Zhou, Xinxuan, Xiaoyu Huang, Mingyun Li, Xian Peng, Suping Wang, Xuedong Zhou, and Lei Cheng. 2019. "Development and Status of Resin Composite as Dental Restorative Materials." Journal of Applied Polymer Science 136 (44): 1–12. 10.1002/app.48180

91. Baltatu Madalina Simona, Petrica Vizureanu, Andrei Victor Sandu, Nestor Florido-suarez, Mircea Vicentiu Saceleanu, and Julia Claudia Mirza-rosca. 2021. "New Titanium Alloys, Promising Materials for Medical Devices." Materials 14 (5934): 1–15. 10.3390/ma14205934

92. Dobrzański L. A., L. B. Dobrzański, and A. D. Dobrzańska-Danikiewicz. 2020. "Manufacturing Technologies Thick-Layer Coatings on Various Substrates and Manufacturing Gradient Materials Using Powders of Metals, Their Alloys and Ceramics." Journal of Achievements in Materials and Manufacturing Engineering 99 (1): 14–41. 10.5604/01.3001.0014.1598

93. Shukla, Uddeshya, and Kamal Garg. 2023. "Journey of Smart Material from Composite to Shape Memory Alloy (SMA), Characterization and Their Applications-A Review." Smart Materials in Medicine 4 (September 2022): 227–242. 10.1016/j.smaim.2022.10.002

94. Albilali A. T., Baras B. H., Aldosari M. A.. 2023. "Evaluation of Mechanical Properties of Different Thermoplastic Orthodontic Retainer Materials after Thermoforming." Polymers (Basel) 15: 1–15.

95. Zovi, Nevi Yanti, Widi Prasetia. 2016. "Effect of Different Irrigation Techniques and Solvents on the Cleanliness of the Apical Thirdroot Canal in Endodontic Retreatment with Bioceramic Based Sealer (in Vitro)." Journal of Molecular & Clinical Medicine 9 (08): 1–23.

96. Yamaguchi, Satoshi, Hefei Li, and Satoshi Imazato. 2023. "Materials Informatics for Developing New Restorative Dental Materials: A Narrative Review." Frontiers in Dental Medicine 4 (January): 1–5. 10.3389/fdmed.2023.1123976

97. Sâmira Ambar Lins, Áquira Ishikiriama, Fabio Antonio Piola Rizzante, Adilson Yoshio Furuse, José Mondelli, Sérgio Kiyoshi Ishikiriama, and Rafael Francisco Lia Mondelli. 2015. "Use of Restorative Materials for Direct and Indirect Restorations in Posterior Teeth by Brazilian Dentists." RSBO 11 (3): 238–244. 10.21726/rsbo.v11i3.854

98. Palacios T., C. Abad, G. Pradíes, and J. Y. Pastor. 2019. "Evaluation of Resin Composites for Dental Restorations." Procedia Manufacturing 41: 914–921. 10.1016/j.promfg.2019.10.015

99. Lopes-Rocha Lígia, Lara Ribeiro-Gonçalves, Bruno Henriques, Mutlu Özcan, Maria Elizabeth Tiritan, and Júlio C.M. Souza. 2021. "An Integrative Review on the Toxicity of Bisphenol A (BPA) Released from Resin Composites Used in Dentistry." Journal of Biomedical Materials Research—Part B Applied Biomaterials 109 (11): 1942–1952. 10.1002/jbm.b.34843

100. Imazato Satoshi, Toshiyuki Nakatsuka, Haruaki Kitagawa, Jun Ichi Sasaki, Satoshi Yamaguchi, Shuichi Ito, Hiroki Takeuchi, Ryota Nomura, and Kazuhiko Nakano. 2023. "Multiple-Ion Releasing Bioactive Surface Pre-Reacted Glass-Ionomer (S-PRG) Filler: Innovative Technology for Dental Treatment and Care." Journal of Functional Biomaterials 14 (4). 10.3390/jfb14040236

101. Zhang Y., and B. R. Lawn. 2017. "Novel Zirconia Materials in Dentistry." Journal of Dental Research in Oral Biology & Medicine 97: 1–8. 10.1177/0022034517737483

102. Altuna P., E. Lucas-Taulé, J. Gargallo-Albiol, O. Figueras-Álvarez, F. Hernández-Alfaro, and J. Nart. 2016. "Clinical Evidence on Titanium-Zirconium Dental Implants: A Systematic Review and Meta-Analysis." International Journal of Oral and Maxillofacial Surgery 45 (7): 842–850. 10.1016/j.ijom.2016.01.004

103. Safwat, Engie M., Ahmad G. A. Khater, Ahmed G. Abd-Elsatar, and Gamal A. Khater. 2021. "Glass Fiber-Reinforced Composites in Dentistry." Bulletin of the National Research Centre 45 (1): 1–9. 10.1186/s42269-021-00650-7

104. Sorrentino, Roberto, Gennaro Ruggiero, Maria Irene Di Mauro, Lorenzo Breschi, Stefania Leuci, and Fernando Zarone. 2021. "Optical Behaviors, Surface Treatment, Adhesion, and Clinical Indications of Zirconia-Reinforced Lithium Silicate (ZLS): A Narrative Review." Journal of Dentistry 112 (103722): 1–34. 10.1016/j.jdent.2021.103722

105. Alshadidi, Abdulkhaliq Ali F., Ahid Amer Alshahrani, Lujain Ibrahim N. Aldosari, Saurabh Chaturvedi, Ravinder S. Saini, Saeed Awod, Bin Hassan, Marco Cicci, and Giuseppe Minervini. 2023. "Investigation on the Application of Artificial Intelligence in Prosthodontics." Applied Sciences 13 (5004): 1–17.

106. Ribeiro Madalena Prata, Filipa Marques, Raquel Travassos, Catarina Nunes, Francisco Caramelo, Anabela Baptista Paula, and Francisco Vale. 2022. "Application of Three-Dimensional Digital Technology in Orthodontics: The State of the Art." Biomimetics 7 (23): 1–14.

107. Bichu Yashodhan M., Abdulraheem Alwafi, Xiaomo Liu, James Andrews, Björn Ludwig, Aditi Y. Bichu, and Bingshuang Zou. 2023. "Advances in Orthodontic Clear Aligner Materials." Bioactive Materials 22 (September 2022): 384–403. 10.1016/j.bioactmat.2022.10.006

108. Jokanović Vukoman, Božana Čolović, and Marija Živković-Sandić. 2019. "The Main Characteristics and Application of the Shape Memory Alloys in Orthodontics and Endodontics." Serbian Dental Journal 66 (1): 29–35. 10.2478/sdj-2019-0004

109. Alzainal Ali H., Ahmed Shehab Majud, Abdulfatah M. Al-Ani, and Adil O. Mageet. 2020. "Orthodontic Bonding: Review of the Literature." International Journal of Dentistry 2020: 1–10. 10.1155/2020/8874909

110. Gangil Namrata, Arshad Noor Siddiquee, and Sachin Maheshwari. 2020. "Towards Applications, Processing and Advancements in Shape Memory Alloy and Its Composites." Journal of Manufacturing Processes 59 (June): 205–222. 10.1016/j.jmapro.2020.09.048

111. Wen Shifeng, Jie Gan, Fei Li, Yan Zhou, Chunze Yan, and Yusheng Shi. 2021. "Research Status and Prospect of Additive Manufactured Nickel-Titanium Shape Memory Alloys." Materials 14 (4496): 1–14. 10.3390/ma14164496

112. Robertson Lindsay, Harsimrat Kaur, Nathalia Carolina Fernandes Fagundes, Dan Romanyk, Paul Major, and Carlos Flores Mir. 2020. "Effectiveness of Clear Aligner Therapy for Orthodontic Treatment: A Systematic Review." Orthodontics and Craniofacial Research 23 (2): 133–142. 10.1111/ocr.12353

113. Uysal Idil, Bengi Yilmaz, Aykan Onur Atilla, and Zafer Evis. 2022. "Nickel Titanium Alloys as Orthodontic Archwires: A Narrative Review." Engineering Science and Technology, an International Journal 36 (101277): 1–12. 10.1016/j.jestch.2022.101277

114. Hosseinpour Sepanta. 2022. "A Critical Analysis of Research Methods and Experimental Models to Study Biocompatibility of Endodontic Materials." 55 (February): 346–369. 10.1111/iej.13701

115. Mohammadi, Fatemeh, Abbas Abbaszadegan, and Ahmad Gholami. 2020. "Recent Advances in Nanodentistry: A Special Focus on Endodontics." Micro and Nano Letters 15 (12): 812–816. 10.1049/mnl.2019.0747

116. Burns Lorel E., Jimin Kim, Yinxiang Wu, Rakan Alzwaideh, Richard McGowan, and Asgeir Sigurdsson. 2022. "Outcomes of Primary Root Canal Therapy: An Updated Systematic Review of Longitudinal Clinical Studies Published between 2003 and 2020." International Endodontic Journal 55 (7): 714–731. 10.1111/iej.13736

117. Zhekov Kostadin I., and Vessela P. Stefanova. 2020. "Retreatability of Bioceramic Endodontic Sealers: A Review." Folia Medica 62 (2): 258–264. 10.3897/folmed.62.e47690
118. Chauhan Ankur, Sameer Makkar, Nisha Garg, and Abhijeet Khade. 2021. "Comparison of the Apical Sealing Ability of Gutta-Percha by Three Different Obturation Techniques: Lateral Condensation Technique, Single Cone Root Canal Obturation Technique and Injectable Thermoplasticized Gutta-Percha Technique (System B)." Annals of the Romanian Society for Cell Biology. 25 (6): 873–879.
119. Abdelhafeez, Manal M. 2020. "Scanning Electron Microscopic Evaluation for the Ability of Endovac and EnoActivator in Cleaning Root Canal Space Using EDTA and QMixTM." Journal of International Dental and Medical Research 13 (2): 469–474.
120. Cintra, Luciano Tavares Angelo, Maximiliano Schünke Gomes, Cristiane Cantiga da Silva, Flávio Duarte Faria, Francine Benetti, Leopoldo Cosme-Silva, Renata Oliveira Samuel, et al. 2021. "Evolution of Endodontic Medicine: A Critical Narrative Review of the Interrelationship between Endodontics and Systemic Pathological Conditions." Odontology 109 (4): 741–769. 10.1007/s10266-021-00636-x
121. Alaghari, Sahithi, Surekha Velagala, Rama Krishna Alla, and Ramaraju Av. 2019. "Advances in Alginate Impression Materials: A Review Advances in Alginate Impression Materials: A Review." International Journal of Dental Materials 1 (2): 1–6. 10.37983/IJDM.2019.1203
122. Kalotra Jatinder, Gaurav Kumar, Jasmeet Kaur, Debashis Sethi, Gautam Arora, and Diksha Khurana. 2020. "Recent Advancements in Restorative Dentistry: An Overview." Journal of Current Medical Research and Opinion 3 (07): 522–530. 10.15520/jcmro.v3i07.311
123. Cho Kiho, Ginu Rajan, Paul Farrar, Leon Prentice, and B. Gangadhara Prusty. 2022. "Dental Resin Composites: A Review on Materials to Product Realizations." Composites Part B: Engineering 230 (2022): 1–66. 10.1016/j.compositesb.2021. 109495
124. Hurtado Alejandro, Alaa A. A. Aljabali, Vijay Mishra, Murtaza M. Tambuwala, and Ángel Serrano-Aroca. 2022. "Alginate: Enhancement Strategies for Advanced Applications." International Journal of Molecular Sciences 23 (4486): 1–45. 10. 3390/ijms23094486
125. Zupancic Cepic, Lana, Reinhard Gruber, Jaryna Eder, Tom Vaskovich, Martina Schmid-Schwap, and Michael Kundi. 2023. "Digital versus Conventional Dentures: A Prospective, Randomized Cross-over Study on Clinical Efficiency and Patient Satisfaction." Journal of Clinical Medicine 12 (434): 1–11. 10.3390/jcm12020434
126. Lima P., Ewald M. Bronkhorst, Luuk Crins, Shamir B. Mehta, and C. Loomans. 2021. "Clinical Performance of Direct Composite Resin Restorations in a Full Mouth Rehabilitation for Patients with Severe Tooth Wear: 5. 5-Year Results." Journal of Dentistry 112 (May): 1–8. 10.1016/j.jdent.2021.103743
127. Stef Corina Laura, Lavinia Simona, Marius Florentin Popa, Agripina Zaharia, and Rodica Maria Murineanu. 2023. "Applied Sciences Intelligent Materials for Labeling Dentures in Forensic Dental Identification—A Pilot Study." Applied Sciences 13 (5574): 1–11.
128. Tiwari M., S. Tyagi, M. Nigam, M. Rawal, S. Meena, and A. Choudhary. 2015. "Dental Smart Materials." Journal of Orofacial Research 5(4): 125–129
129. Gupta Vertika. 2018. "Smart Materials in Dentistry: A Review." International Journal of Advance Research and Development 3: 89–96.
130. Kim Jangho, and Kyunghoon Kim. 2020. "Applied Sciences Editorial Introduction to the Special Issue." Applied Sciences 10 (6388): 1–3.
131. Sehrawat S., A. Kumar, S. Grover, N. Dogra, J. Nindra, and S. Rathee. 2022. "Study of 3D Scanning Technologies and Scanners in Orthodontics." Materials Today: Proceedings 2214-7853: 1–9. 10.1016/j.matpr.2022.01.064

132. Xing Fei, Jiawei Xu, Peiyun Yu, Yuxi Zhou, Man Zhe, Rong Luo, Ming Liu, Zhou Xiang, Xin Duan, and Ulrike Ritz. 2023. "Recent Advances in Biofabrication Strategies Based on Bioprinting for Vascularized Tissue Repair and Regeneration." Materials & Design 229 (111885): 1–43. 10.1016/j.matdes.2023.111885

133. Bhardwaj A., A. Bhatnagar, and A. Kumar. 2023. Chapter 29—Current trends of application of additive manufacturing in oral healthcare system, in Advances in Additive Manufacturing (eds. Kumar, A., Mittal, R. K., and Haleem, A.). Elsevier, pp. 479–491. 10.1016/B978-0-323-91834-3.00010-7

134. Kumar A., R. K. Mittal, and A. Haleem eds. 2022. Advances in Additive Manufacturing: Artificial Intelligence, Nature-Inspired, and Biomanufacturing. Elsevier.

135. Martínez-Vázquez F. J., E. Sánchez-González, O. Borrero-López, Pedro Miranda, Antonia Pajares, and Fernando Guiberteau. 2021. "Novel Bioinspired Composites Fabricated by Robocasting for Dental Applications." Ceramics International 47: 21343–21349. 10.1016/j.ceramint.2021.04.142

136. Elliott, Drew T., Russell J. Wiggins, and Rupak Dua. 2021. "Bioinspired Antibacterial Surface for Orthopedic and Dental Implants." Journal of Biomedical Materials Research—Part B Applied Biomaterials 109 (7): 973–981. 10.1002/jbm.b.34762

137. Dobrzański, Leszek A., and Lech B. Dobrzański. 2020. "Dentistry 4.0 Concept in the Design and Manufacturing of Prosthetic Dental Restorations." Processes 8 (525): 1–52. 10.3390/PR8050525

138. Javaid, Mohd, Abid Haleem, Ravi Pratap Singh, and Rajiv Suman. 2021. "Dentistry 4.0 Technologies Applications for Dentistry during COVID-19 Pandemic." Sustainable Operations and Computers 2 (February): 87–96. 10.1016/j.susoc.2021.05.002

139. Rajendra P., M. Kumari, S. Rani, N. Dogra, R. Boadh, A. Kumar, and M. Dahiya. (2022). "Impact of Artificial Intelligence on Civilization: Future Perspectives." Materials Today: Proceedings 56: 252–256. 10.1016/j.matpr.2022.01.113

140. Kreulen Cees M., A M J Crins Luuk, J M Opdam Niek, A C Loomans Bas, and L A M J Crins. 2022. "Rehabilitation of Worn Dentition with CAD-CAM Restorations: A Case Report." The Journal of Adhesive Dentistry 24: 187–194. 10.3290/j.jad.b2916447

141. Pillai, Sangeeth, Akshaya Upadhyay, Parisa Khayambashi, Imran Farooq, Hisham Sabri, Maryam Tarar, Kyungjun T. Lee, et al. 2021. "Dental 3d-Printing: Transferring Art from the Laboratories to the Clinics." Polymers 13 (1): 1–25. 10.3390/polym13010157

142. Joda, Tim, Michael M. Bornstein, Ronald E. Jung, Marco Ferrari, Tuomas Waltimo, and Nicola U. Zitzmann. 2020. "Recent Trends and Future Direction of Dental Research in the Digital Era." International Journal of Environmental Research and Public Health 17 (6): 1–8. 10.3390/IJERPH17061987

143. Kumar, Ajay, Deepak Kumar, Parveen Kumar, V.D. 2020. Optimization of incremental sheet forming process using artificial intelligence-based techniques, in Nature-Inspired Optimization in Advanced Manufacturing Processes and Systems (eds. Ganesh M. Kakandikar and Dinesh G. Thakur). CRC Press, pp. 113–130.

144. Mohd, N., M. Razali, M. J. Ghazali, and N. H. Abu Kasim. 2022. "Current Advances of Three-Dimensional Bioprinting Application in Dentistry: A Scoping Review." Materials (Basel) 15: 1–25. 10.3390/ma15186398

145. Gregory D. A., L. Tripathi, A. T. R. Fricker, Emmanuel Asare, Isabel Orlando, Vijayendra Raghavendran, Ipsita Roy. 2021. "Bacterial Cellulose: A Smart Biomaterial with Diverse Applications." Materials Science & Engineering R: Reports 145: 100623. 10.1016/j.mser.2021.100623

146. Chun R Chau W, Richard Tai-Chiu Hsung, Colman McGrath, Edmond Ho Nang Pow, Walter Yu Hang Lam. 2023. "Accuracy of Artificial Intelligence-Designed Single-Molar Dental Prostheses: A Feasibility Study." The Journal of Prosthetic Dentistry 1–7. 10.1016/j.prosdent.2022.12.004

6 Recent Advances in Sintering Techniques in Dental Ceramics

Sivaranjani Gali
Department of Prosthodontics, Faculty of Dental Sciences,
M.S. Ramaiah University of Applied Sciences, Bangalore,
Karnataka, India

6.1 SINTERING MECHANISMS IN DENTAL CERAMIC SYSTEMS

Understanding recent advances in dentistry holds immense importance for dental professionals to provide patients with the most effective and advanced treatments available. This knowledge enables them to offer better care, improving patient outcomes and experiences. Secondly, advancements in technology and techniques often lead to more efficient and less invasive procedures, reducing discomfort and recovery times for patients. Additionally, keeping abreast of the latest developments fosters continuous learning and professional growth among dental practitioners, ensuring they remain at the forefront of their field. Additive manufacturing, a vital component of Industry 4.0, has profoundly transformed the realm of dentistry. This advanced method allows for the creation of intricate dental implants, prosthetics, and models with unparalleled precision and tailored customization. In dentistry, 3D printing has revolutionized the manufacturing process of dental prostheses, scaffolds, and aligners, providing personalized solutions perfectly suited to individual patients. Its impact extends beyond mere prosthetics, encompassing the production of precise surgical guides and anatomical models for educational purposes. This technology's ability to streamline workflows, decrease production timelines, and elevate patient outcomes signifies a significant evolution in dental healthcare, showcasing the immense potential of additive manufacturing [1–6].

With this background of advanced technologies, advances in sintering technologies for dental ceramics have vastly improved the strength, precision, and appearance of dental restorations. Innovations focus on refining heating processes and optimizing parameters like temperature and pressure. These advancements result in denser, more durable materials with better esthetics, meeting both functional and cosmetic needs in restorative dentistry.

Metal-ceramic restorations are one of the most commonly used prosthetic systems for partially edentulous conditions. Typically, tooth-colored ceramic is sintered on the strong metal framework, arriving at the best combination of both

DOI: 10.1201/9781003404934-6

esthetics and strength. Sintering has been the traditional method of processing dental ceramic restorations. Sintering is a process of heating closely packed particles below their melting temperatures, promoting diffusion across the particles and densifying the mass. With an increase in temperature, the sintered glass steadily courses plugging the air spaces. Traditional feldspathic porcelains are typically fabricated through the condensation method and are further sintered in a vacuum furnace. Mechanical vibration and blotting are the first attempts in sintering dental porcelains in diminishing the volume portion of porosity. Proper condensation with dense packing of porcelain particles is done to promote low porosity and firing shrinkage [7–12]. In typical air-fired sintering, voids between the powder particles are occupied by atmospheric pressure during initial temperatures. As the sintering temperature increases, the particles come close and densification of porcelain occurs. However, with an increase in temperature, as viscous porcelain prevents air from escaping, air-fired feldspathic porcelains are retained with porosities [13].

Veneering ceramics such as fluorapatite glass-ceramics are sintered and crystallized at low temperatures. Glass-ceramics such as lithium disilicate (marketed as Empress, IPS e.max Press) are typically processed through lost wax technique and pressing followed by sintering. Machinable glass-ceramics (IPS e.max CAD) are processed through two-stage crystallization, wherein lithium metasilicate accommodates easy machining due to its low hardness and partial crystallized state. Second stage sintering of the milled glass-ceramic leads to complete crystallization with the formation of lithium disilicate with better mechanical properties. Dental zirconia is often soft-milled and subject to sintering at high temperatures of 1,300–1,500°C, with slow heating and cooling rates [13].

With the limitations to manually build the complex structures of dental prosthesis and the procedure of sintering, being technique sensitive, new CAD/CAM-based ceramic materials with alternate methods of emerging sintering techniques are being explored to improve clinical productivity for efficient patient treatment.

6.2 ADVANCES IN SINTERING TECHNIQUES IN DENTAL CERAMICS

Alternate sintering techniques for processing dental ceramics have been explored for dental ceramics such as microwave-sintering, spark-plasma sintering, laser-sintering, vacuum-sintering, and speed-sintering. The following sections discuss the fundamentals of each of the sintering mechanisms with their merits and demerits.

6.2.1 Microwave-Sintering

Microwave-sintering has the merits of being energy-efficient and cost-effective due to its fast and uniform heating resulting in fine microstructures with minimal porosity [7,14]. It works on the interaction of electromagnetic waves with the dielectric properties of the material. Microwave-sintering has been explored on dental glazes, feldspathic porcelain, and zirconia.

Microwave-sintering of dental glazes showed superior surface finish, color stability, and flexural strength with less time required (6 min) compared to conventional sintering (12–15 min) in the dental laboratory [15–17]. Microwave-sintering of dental feldspathic porcelain was affected by control of the heating rate and resulted in a higher modulus of rupture than conventional sintering [18]. The application of microwave-sintering to dental zirconia has led to a decrease in both sintering temperature and sintering time, resulting in improved mechanical properties, particularly hardness and fracture toughness [19–21]. In these studies, microwave-sintering conditions typically included a frequency of 2.45 Hz and a power output ranging from 1.25 to 2 kW. For a detailed overview of studies on the microwave-sintering of dental ceramics, please refer to Table 6.1.

6.2.2 SPARK-PLASMA SINTERING (SPS)

Spark-plasma sintering (SPS) is a powder-metallurgy method that combines electric current and pressure [22–28]. SPS produces dense ceramics in shorter sintering times compared to conventional sintering processes. The applied pressure affects the densification and microstructure of ceramics. SPS has been explored for refining microstructures in dental glass-ceramics such as IPS e.max CAD and IPS e.max Press (machinable and pressable glass-ceramics) [29]. SPS has been explored for its effect on temperature on densification, microstructure, and phase assemblage of zirconia mica-based glasses for dental restorations [30]. The advantage of SPS is that it offers short dwell time at low temperatures resulting in densified microstructures and better mechanical properties. However, they have the limitation of the inability to produce patient-specific dimensions and discoloration due to contamination of the graphite layer during sintering and formation of oxygen vacancies.

6.2.3 LASER-SINTERING

Conventional sintering of dental ceramics is time-consuming and subtractive methods of fabricating dental ceramic restorations such as CAD/CAM have limitations of wastage of material, additional tool cost and the inability to precisely machining of undercuts [31–33].

Selective Laser-sintering (SLS) technology is a type of additive manufacturing (AM) technology that offers design flexibility and customizes patient-specific dental restorations in a relatively short time. SLS are classified as direct and indirect SLS. Direct SLS sintering, with a high-temperature gradient and short scanning time, creates cracks in the ceramics [34–37]. In contrast, indirect SLS can be done at low temperatures, wherein the polymers are used to bind the ceramic particles. After laser-sintering, the green part is sintered to burn off the binder. However, SLS-sintered ceramics do not densify due to the low-packing density of SLSed green parts and hence, present with sub-optimal mechanical properties. Therefore, it is recommended for isostatic pressing at 150–200 MPa for pre-densification and sintered at 1,450–1,550°C for achieving the compact shape and dimensions of dental restorations [37–44].

6.2.4 VACUUM-SINTERING

Vacuum firing helps in reducing porosity with air pressure being reduced to one-tenth of atmospheric pressure. As the particles sinter, closed pores are formed with air trapped and separated from the furnace atmosphere. With the sintering

TABLE 6.1
Studies on Microwave-Sintering of Dental Ceramics

Author & Year	Frequency (GHz)	Power Output (kW)	Dental Ceramics	Sintering Time	Build of a Microwave Furnace	Parameters Evaluated
Akanksha 2022[16]	2.45	0.4	Vita Vmk Master & IPS Classic	9 min to reach 903°C and holding time for 1 min	Cober electronics Inc, Norwalk, Conn	Better surface finish
Sanal[14] 2019	2.45	1.25	Vita Vm9/ Vm 13/ Vmk 29 & IPS e.Max Ceram	A few minutes less than conventional sintering	CeralabII Meac	Better color stability
Vaderhobli 2016[17]	2.45	2	Noritake	7–13 min	Microwave Research and Applications, INC (Model number BP 210/211)	High hardness and fracture toughness
Prasad[15] 2009	2.45	1.25	Omega 900 & IPS d.Sign	6 min	ThermWave1.3; Ceralink, Inc, Troy, NY	Smooth surface
Menezes 2007[18]	2.45	Not reported	Feldspathic dental porcelain	6–8 min Heating rate: 65°C/min to 25°C/min	Cober electronics, MS6K	High Modulus of rupture
Presenda 2015[19]	2.45	Not reported	Zirconia	10 min (100°C/min)	Experimental microwave system	Microwave-sintering is feasible
Monaco 2015[20]	2.45	0.5–3	Zirconia	Multi-mode: 6–25 min Single mode: 4–6 min	CEM-MAS 7000 multi-mode applicator (CEM Corporation, Matthews, NC)	Reduced time is possible

temperature reaching close to 55°C less and with the release of the vacuum, there is an increase in pressure on the porcelain by a factor of 10. As the pressure increases, pore size gets reduced by one-tenth of their original size and thus, the total volume of porosity of dental porcelain is reduced with vacuum-sintering compared to the air-fired method [6]. Utilizing a vacuum furnace for sintering enhances the bi-axial flexural strength of zirconia. However, it's worth noting that sintering under a vacuum environment provides minimal benefits when applied to partially and fully stabilized zirconia [45].

6.2.5 SPEED-SINTERING

Conventional sintering of dental zirconia is time-consuming due to its gradual heating and cooling rates required to reach the sintering temperatures of 1,350–1,550°C with a dwell time of 2–5 hrs. This delayed sintering process requires an additional appointment and the necessity of an interim restoration [46].

Advancements in sintering techniques have made it possible to achieve zirconia densification within a brief dwell time of 25 minutes and at a sintering temperature of 1,540°C, resulting in optimal mechanical properties, including flexural strength and grain size [47]. Speed- and high-speed-sintering methods have garnered increasing attention as promising alternatives to traditional sintering techniques. They offer several advantages, such as reduced clinical time, cost-effectiveness, and enhanced patient comfort. Currently, active research is focused on the development of high-speed-sintering furnaces and protocols specifically designed to sinter small fixed dental prostheses (FDPs) in as little as 10 to 20 minutes, as detailed in [42–50]. You can find comprehensive studies on the speed-sintering of dental zirconia and comparative evaluations of various sintering approaches in Tables 6.2 and 6.3.

6.3 THE IMPACT OF ACCELERATED SINTERING ON DENTAL CERAMICS' CHARACTERISTICS

Speed-sintering on dental zirconia has been a subject of investigation in numerous studies, as documented in Table 6.2. These studies have delved into various aspects, such as the microstructure, grain size, and several properties including mechanical, wear, optical, and low-temperature degradation characteristics of zirconia [45, 47–54].

The microstructure and grain size of zirconia are significantly affected by factors such as sintering temperature, sintering time, stabilizer content, and the presence of impurities. For example, a rapid sintering process at 1,580°C for 10 minutes has been found to improve the translucency of InCoris TZI Sirona while maintaining small grain sizes. Furthermore, it has been demonstrated that elevating the sintering temperature can effectively decrease porosity, boost material density, and consequently minimize light diffusion, thereby improving light penetration. Nevertheless, when examining 3Y-TZP zirconia, it was observed that the grain size exhibited an upward trend as the sintering temperature surpassed 1,300°C, reaching its maximum at 1,700°C. This rise in grain size exhibited a notable adverse association with both flexural strength and the contrast ratio (p < .001). On the other hand, a high sintering temperature combined with a short sintering duration improved the

TABLE 6.2

Studies on Speed-Sintering of Dental Zirconia

Author & Year	Brand of Dental Ceramic	Sintering Temperature	Mechanical Properties
Balladares 2022[50]	InCoris TZI	Speedfire: 18 min at 1,600°C Slow sintering: 1,650°C for 8 h	Fracture strength did not make a significant difference. Speed-sintered zirconia is less reliable.
Jerman 2020[51]	TZP Ceramill ZI (3Y TZP) Ceramill Zolid HT+(4 UZP)	Speedfire: 1,580°C 10 min Control: 1,450°C 120 min	Among the tested materials, ZI (3Y-TZP) demonstrated the highest flexural strength, while HT+ (4Y-TZP) exhibited the lowest. It appeared that the specific sintering process employed did not have a significant impact on flexural strength, with the exception of non-aged HT+ (4Y-TZP). In general, flexural strength tended to increase after undergoing artificial thermo-mechanical aging, with the noteworthy exception of high-speed-sintered HT+, where this aging process negatively affected the Weibull Modulus within the high-speed-sintered group.
Jansen Ulrich 2019[52]	3 Y-TZPs (ZI, ZD) and the 4 Y-TZP (HT+)	Final temperature of either 1,570°C or 1,590°C and maintaining this temperature for 10 minutes. Control: Final temperature of 1,450°C and a holding time of 120 minutes, served as a control in the study.	High-speed-sintering maintained the flexural strength, but it resulted in a reduction in transparency for ZD and HT+.
Lawson 2019[53]	Katana STML Block, Prettau Anterior, and Zpex Smile	Customary (7 hours) or high-speed-sintering of (18 or 30 minutes).	Prettau and Zpex became less translucent and less strong with a high-speed-sintering program, whereas Katana STML Block was unaffected.

(Continued)

TABLE 6.2 (Continued)
Studies on Speed-Sintering of Dental Zirconia

Author & Year	Brand of Dental Ceramic	Sintering Temperature	Mechanical Properties
Li 2018[48]	ST-3Y-TZP (UPCERA, China)	R-1: Heating at 400°C/min to 1,200°C. Further heating at 190°C/min to 1,580°C. Dwell at 1,580°C for 2 minutes. Cooling at 310°C/min to room temperature in 12 minutes. R-2: Heating at 400°C/min to 1200°C. Dwell at 1,200°C for 5 minutes. Further heating at 190°C/min to 1,580°C. Dwell at 1,580°C for 10 minutes. Cooling at 310°C/min to room temperature in 25 minutes. R-3: Heating at 400°C/min to 1,200°C. Dwell at 1,200°C for 10 minutes. Further heating at 190°C/min to 1,580°C. Dwell at 1,580°C for 20 minutes. Cooling at 310°C/min to room temperature in 40 minutes.	Flexural strength of 1151 MPa, hardness of 13.3 GPa and fracture toughness of 5.92 MPa.m$^{1/2}$. R3 fared better. In 20 min, long dwell time improves translucency.
Kauling 2018[49]	CEREC Zirconia Medi S A2,	Speedfire: 25 min followed by glaze of 9 min. Sirona: 4hrs followed by 10 min glazing	Speed-sintered FPDs had comparable values of fit and fracture load than conventional sintering.

| Kaizer 2017[54] | InCoris TZI, Sirona | Super-speed (1,580°C, dwell time 10 min), Speed (1,510°C, dwell time 25 min), and Long-term (1,510°C, dwell time 120 min). | Crowns produced through a rapid sintering process displayed increased translucency. All groups exhibited signs of both minor and significant wear on the zirconia surface. The transformation from a tetragonal to a monoclinic phase, induced by the wear caused by sliding, was evident in each of the three groups. |
| Li Jiang 2011[46] | Nano-sized zirconia powders partially stabilized with 3 mol. % yttria. | 15 mm inner diameter, pressed at 20 MPa for 30 seconds, and subsequently compacted at 200 MPa for 1 minute using a cold isostatic pressing machine. Following this, the powders were subjected to sintering at various temperatures, specifically 1,350°C, 1,400°C, 1,450°C, and 1,500°C. | Sintered densities and transmittances consistently increased when elevating the temperature in the range of 1,350 to 1,500°C. Y-TZP (yttria-stabilized tetragonal zirconia polycrystal) achieved nearly complete density and approximately 17–18% light transmittance when sintered at a final temperature between 1,450°C and 1,500°C. It's worth noting that 40-nanometer powders exhibited higher sintered density and transmittance compared to the 90-nanometer powders. This indicates that meticulous control of the sintering temperature and primary particle size can enhance the transparency of Y-TZP dental ceramics. |

TABLE 6.3
Comparison of Sintering Techniques

Type of sintering	Merits	Demerits
Microwave	Energy-efficient and cost-effective	Microwave radiation absorption and heating control
Spark plasma	Densification at low temperatures with less dwell time	Inability to produce patient-specific dimensions and contamination of the graphite layer during sintering
Laser	Design flexibility and customizes patient-specific dental restorations in a short time	Lack of good densification with low mechanical properties
Vacuum	Reduces porosity and pore size	Time-consuming and not much effect on flexural strength
Speed-sintering	Less chairside time	Effect on mechanical properties and translucency of zirconia

flexural strength of zirconia. Therefore, the current research findings do not provide a clear consensus on the connexion between sintering temperature and the flexural strength of zirconia.

6.4 PRINCIPLE BEHIND SPEED-SINTERING, SPEED FIRE FURNACES, AND CAD-CAM SYSTEMS

Typically, zirconia discs are manufactured at 50% density to facilitate ease of milling dental restorations. Zirconia has the unique property of isotropic sintering unlike alloys and other ceramics, wherein zirconia tends to uniformly shrink in all dimensions regardless of the center of mass. Unlike zirconia, dental casting alloys tend to shrink in the pontic regions most where the mass is the highest resulting in distortion of metal three-unit bridges [45].

Traditional furnaces using molybdenum disilicide heating elements house large and multiple trays with beads in the furnace. Such furnaces can therefore handle long-span multi-unit bridges. Sintering times are long with slow heating and cooling rates. Molybdenum disilicide heating elements have the advantage of producing a large amount of heat per square centimeter with high temperatures. In contrast, silicon carbide heating elements offer low working temperatures with minimal power output [55]. Speed-sintering furnaces use silicon carbide heating elements to quickly process single units of zirconia with fast heating and cooling rates. However, silicon carbide furnaces do not provide enough heat for shade development [55].

CEREC SpeedFire furnace is the smallest and fastest sintering furnace that can sinter zirconia crowns in 14 minutes. The furnace can accommodate dental ceramic systems ranging from glass-ceramics to zirconia such as CEREC Tessera, CEREC Zirconia, CEREC Zirconia meso for screw-retained implant prosthesis, Celtra Duo,

CEREC Bloc C and PC feldspathic porcelain blocks. Other than zirconia, advanced glass-ceramics such as Vita Supranity DC and CEREC Tessera, wherein crystallization and glazing can be done in the SpeedFire furnace. Furnaces created for the heat treatment of dental glass-ceramics, specifically for the crystallization process following the initial machining, have been equipped with faster crystallization settings and compact thermal chambers. Examples of such furnaces include the Programat™ P310 by Ivoclar-Vivadent™ in Liechtenstein and the SpeedFire™ by Dentsply-Sirona™ in Bensheim, Germany. These furnaces are equipped with computer-aided design (CAM) software and a thermal unit that calculates the required crystallization time for the restoration, depending on the material used [56–58].

REFERENCES

1. A. Kumar, P. Kumar, R. K. Mittal, V. Gambhir (2023). Chapter 12—Materials processed by additive manufacturing techniques, Editor(s): A. Kumar, R. K. Mittal, A. Haleem, In Additive Manufacturing Materials and Technologies, Advances in Additive Manufacturing, Elsevier, pp. 217–233.
2. A. Kumar, P. Kumar, N. Dogra, A. Jaglan (2023). Application of incremental sheet forming (ISF) toward biomedical and medical implants. In Handbook of Flexible and Smart Sheet Forming Techniques (eds Ajay, Parveen, H. Singh, V. Gulati and P. K. Singh). 10.1002/9781119986454.ch13
3. S. Sehrawat, A. Kumar, M. Prabhakar (2023). Chapter 21—Substitute for orthognathic surgery using bioprinted bone scaffolds in restoring osseous defects, Editor(s): A. Kumar, R. K. Mittal, A. Haleem, In Additive Manufacturing Materials and Technologies, Advances in Additive Manufacturing, Elsevier, pp. 335–347.
4. A. Bhardwaj, A. Bhatnagar, A. Kumar (2023). Chapter 29—Current trends of application of additive manufacturing in oral healthcare system—Editor(s): A. Kumar, R. K. Mittal, A. Haleem. In Additive Manufacturing Materials and Technologies, Advances in Additive Manufacturing, Elsevier, pp. 479–491.
5. Smart Manufacturing and Industry 4.0. L. Kumar, A. Kumar, R. Kumar Sharma, P. Kumar Publication date 2023/7/14 Handbook of Smart Manufacturing: Forecasting the Future of Industry 4.0.
6. Handbook of Smart Manufacturing: Forecasting the Future of Industry 4.0 edited by Ajay, Hari Singh, Parveen, Bandar Al Mangour. CRC Press. (2023). 10.1201/9781 003333760
7. K. C. Cheung, B. W. Darvell (2002). Sintering of dental porcelain: effect of time and temperature on appearance and porosity. Dent Mater. 18(2):163–173. 10.1016/s0109-5 641(01)00038-0
8. R. K. McGeary (1961). Mechanical packing of spherical particles. J Amer Ceram Soc. 44(10):513–522.
9. S. T. Rasmussen, W. Nagaji-Okumu, K. Boenke, W. J. O'Brien (1997). Optimum particle size distribution for reduced shrinkage of a dental porcelain. Dent Mater. 13(1):43–50.
10. J. R. Gill (1932). Methods and results in condensation of dental porcelain. J Amer Dent Assoc. 19:1147–1154.
11. D. B. Evans, N. Barghi, C. M. Malloy, A. S. Windeler (1990). The influence of condensation on porosity and shade of body porcelain. J Prosthet Dent. 63(4):380–389.
12. Phillips Science of Dental Materials, Anusavice (2014). Chapter: Dental Ceramics, First South-Asia Edition, pp. 445.

13. D. E. Clark, W. H. Sutton (1996). Microwave processing of materials. Annu Rev Mater Sci. 26:299–331.

14. F. A. Sanal, M. Kurt (2020). Could microwave glazing be considered as an alternative to conventional surface finishing methods of ceramic materials in terms of color stability? Int Journ Prosthodont. 3:328–332.

15. S. Prasad, EA Jr. Monaco, H. Kim, E. L. Davis, J. D. Brewer (2009). Comparison of porcelain surface and flexural strength obtained by microwave and conventional oven glazing. J Prosthet Dent. 101(1):20–28. 10.1016/S0022-3913(08)60284-X

16. A. Sachdeva, N. Prabhu, B. Dhanasekar, I. N. Aparna (2018). Effect of conventional and microwave glazing on surface roughness of metal ceramics: An atomic force microscopy analysis. Indian J Dent Res. 29(3):352–357. 10.4103/ijdr.IJDR_397_16

17. Vaderhobli, Saha (2015). Microwave-sintering of dental ceramics: Part 1. 5:7. 10.41 72/2161-1122.1000311

18. R. R. Menezes, P. M. Souto, RHGA. Kiminami (2007). Microwave hybrid fast sintering of porcelain bodies. J Mater Process Techno. 190(1–3):223–229.

19. Presenda A., María D. Salvador M, Felipe L. Peñaranda-Foix, Rodrigo M., Amparo B. (2015). Effect of microwave-sintering on microstructure and mechanical properties in Y-TZP materials used for dental applications. Ceram Intern. 41:7125–7132.

20. C. Monaco, F. Prete, C. Leonelli, L. Esposito, A. Tucci (2015). Microstructural study of microwave sintered zirconia for dental applications. Ceram Internat. 41:1255–1261.

21. K. Biswas, J. Q. He, I. D. Blum, C. I. Wu, T. P. Hogan, D. N. Seidman, V. P. Dravid, M. G. Kanatzidis (2012). High-performance bulk thermoelectrics with all-scale hierarchical architectures. Nature 489:414–418.

22. G. D. Zhan, J. D. Kuntz, J. L. Wan, A. K. Mukherjee (2003). Single-wall carbon nanotubes as attractive toughening agents in alumina-based nanocomposites. Nat Mater. 2:38–42.

23. Y. F. Liu, D. H. Liebenberg (2017). Electromagnetic radio frequency heating in the pulsed electric current sintering (PECS) process. MRS Commu. 7:266–271.

24. J. Fu, J. C. Brouwer, I. M. Richardson, M. J. M. Hermans (2019). Effect of mechanical alloying and spark-plasma sintering on the microstructure and mechanical properties of ODS Eurofer. Mater Des. 177:107849.

25. C. L. Cramer, J. W. McMurray, M. J. Lance, R. A. Lowden (2020). Reaction-bond composite synthesis of SiC-TiB2 by spark plasma sintering/field-assisted sintering technology (SPS/FAST). J Eur Ceram Soc. 40:988–995.

26. N. S. Weston, B. Thomas, M. Jackson (2019). Processing metal powders via field assisted sintering technology (FAST): a critical review. Mater Sci Technol. 35:1306–1328.

27. H. Gan, C. B. Wang, Q. Shen, L. M. Zhang (2019). Preparation of La2NiMnO6 double perovskite ceramics by plasma activated sintering. J Inorg Mater. 34:541–545.

28. A. F. Mansour, N. Kharpukhina, S. Grasso, R. M. Wilson, M. J. Reece, M. J. Cattell (2015). The effect of spark-plasma sintering on lithium disilicate glass-ceramics. Dent Mater. 31:e226–e235.

29. S. Gali, S. Gururaja, S. Srikari (2022). Spark plasma sintered zirconia-mica glass-ceramics for dental restorations. Dent Mater. 38:1. 10.1016/j.dental.2021.12.058

30. N. A. Mortadi, D. Eggbeer, J. Lewis, R. J. Williams (2012). CAD/CAM/AM applications in the manufacture of dental appliances. Am J Orthod Dentofac. Orthop. 142:727e733.

31. G. Davidowitz, P. G. Kotick (2011). The use of CAD/CAM in dentistry. Dent Clin North Am. 55:559e570.

32. G. Bosch, A. Ender, A. Mehl (2014). A 3-dimensional accuracy analysis of chairside CAD/CAM milling processes. J Prosthet Dent. 112:1425e1431.

33. J. J. Beaman, C. R. Deckard (1990). Selective laser-sintering with assisted powder handling. US Patent no 4938816.
34. J. Deckers, J. Vleugels, J. P. Kruth (2014). Additive manufacturing of ceramics: a review. J Ceram Sci Technol. 5:245e260.
35. I. Shishkovsky, I. Yadroitsev, P. Bertrand, I. Smurov (2007). Alumina-zirconium ceramics synthesis by selective laser-sintering/melting. Appl Surf Sci. 254:966e970.
36. H. Yves-Christian, W. Jan, M. Wilhelm, W. Konrad, P. Reinhart (2010). Net shaped high performance oxide ceramic parts by selective laser melting. Phys Procedia 5:587e594.
37. K. Shahzad, J. Deckers, J. P. Kruth, J. Vleugels (2013). Additive manufacturing of alumina parts by indirect selective laser-sintering and post processing. J Mater Process Technol. 213:1484e1494.
38. A. N. Chen, J. M. Wu, K. Liu, J. Y. Chen, H. Xiao, P. Chen, C. H. Li, Y. S. Shi (2018). High performance ceramic parts with complex shape prepared by selective laser-sintering: a review. Adv Appl Ceram. 117:100e117.
39. E. C. Hammel, O. L. R. Ighodaro, O. I. Okoli (2014). Processing and properties of advanced porous ceramics: an application based review. Ceram Int. 40:15351e15370.
40. K. Shahzad, J. Deckers, S. Boury, B. Neirinck, J. P. Kruth (2012). Preparation and indirect selective laser-sintering of alumina/PA microspheres. Ceram Int. 38:1241e1247.
41. K. C. R. Kolan, M. C. Leu, G. E. Hilmas, M. Velez (2012). Effect of material, process parameters, and simulated body fluids on mechanical properties of 13-93 bioactive glass porous constructs made by selective laser-sintering. J Mech Behav Biomed. Mater. 13:14e24.
42. K. Liu, Y. S. Shi, C. H. Li, L. Hao, J. Liu, Q. S. Wei (2014). Indirect selective laser-sintering of epoxy resin-Al2O3 ceramic powders combined with cold isostatic pressing. Ceram Int. 40:7099e7106.
43. J. Deckers, K. Shahzad, J. Vleugels, J. P. Kruth (2012). Isostatic pressing assisted indirect selective laser-sintering of alumina components. Rapid Prototype J. 18:409e419.
44. T. A. Sulaiman, A. A. Abdulmajeed, T. E. Donovan, P. K. Vallittu, T. O. Närhi, L. V. Lassila (2015). The effect of staining and vacuum-sintering on optical and mechanical properties of partially and fully stabilized monolithic zirconia. Dent Mater J. 34(5):605–610. 10.4012/dmj.2015-054
45. W. M. Ahmed, T. Troczynski, A. P. McCullagh, C. C. L. Wyatt, R. M. Carvalho (2019). The influence of altering sintering protocols on the optical and mechanical properties of zirconia: A review. J Esthet Restor Dent. 31(5):423–430. 10.1111/jerd.12492
46. L. Jiang, Y. Liao, Q. Wan (2011). Effects of sintering temperature and particle size on the translucency of zirconium dioxide dental ceramic. J Mater Sci: Mater Med 22:2429–2435. 10.1007/s10856-011-4438-9
47. N. Al-Haj Husain, M. Özcan, N. Dydyk, T. Joda (2022 Aug 20). Conventional, speed-sintering and high-speed-sintering of zirconia: a systematic review of the current status of applications in dentistry with a focus on precision, mechanical and optical parameters. J Clin Med. 11(16):4892. 10.3390/jcm11164892
48. L. Li, C. Zhao, Z. Du, Y. Qiu, W. Si (2019). Rapid-sintered dental zirconia for chair-side one-visit application. Int J Appl Ceram Technol. 16:1830–1835. 10.1111/ijac.13228
49. A. Elisa Kauling, J. F. Güth, K. Erdelt, D. Edelhoff, C. Keul (2020). Influence of speed-sintering on the fit and fracture strength of 3-unit monolithic zirconia fixed partial dentures. J Prosthet Dent. 124(3):380–386. 10.1016/j.prosdent.2019.09.003
50. A. Ordoñez Balladares, C. Abad-Coronel, J. C. Ramos, B. J. Martín Biedma (2022). Fracture resistance of sintered monolithic zirconia dioxide in different thermal units. Materials (Basel). 15(7):2478. 10.3390/ma15072478

51. E. Jerman, F. Wiedenmann, M. Eichberger, A. Reichert, B. Stawarczyk (2020). Effect of high-speed-sintering on the flexural strength of hydrothermal and thermomechanically aged zirconia materials. Dent Mater. 36(9):1144–1150. 10.1016/j.dental.2020.05.013

52. J. U. Jansen, N. Lümkemann, I. Letz, R. Pfefferle, B. SenerSener, B. Stawarczyk (2019). Impact of high-speed-sintering on translucency, phase content, grain sizes, and flexural strength of 3Y-TZP and 4Y-TZP zirconia materials. J Prosthet Dent. 122(4):396–403. 10.1016/j.prosdent.2019.02.005

53. N. C. Lawson, A. Maharishi. (2020). Strength and translucency of zirconia after high-speed-sintering. J Esthet Restor Dent. 32(2):219–225. 10.1111/jerd.12524

54. M. R. Kaizer, P. C. Gierthmuehlen, M. B. Dos Santos, S. S. Cava, Y. Zhang (2017). Speed-sintering translucent zirconia for chairside one-visit dental restorations: Optical, mechanical, and wear characteristics. Ceram Int. 43(14):10999–11005. 10.1016/j.ceramint.2017.05.141

55. Speed-sintering: how fast can zirconia be sintered or how fast should zirconia be sintered?c271ffd0-829d-492c-bdcf-7ec06a926897.pdf (constantcontact.com). Accessed on 2-06-2023.

56. Which type of heating elements in sintering furnaces is better? Which Type of Heating Elements in Sintering Furnaces is Better? (whipmix.com). Accessed on 2-06-2023.

57. Dentsply-Sirona™. Operating Instructions CEREC Speed Fire™.; Sirona Dental Inc.: Bensheim, Germany, (2016); pp. 1–56. Available online: https://www.dentsplysirona.com/en/explore/cerec/cerec-speedfire.html (accessed on 3 March 2021).

58. C. Abad-Coronel, A. Ordoñez Balladares, J. I. Fajardo, B. J. Martín Biedma (2021). Resistance to fracture of lithium disilicate feldspathic restorations manufactured using a CAD/CAM system and crystallized with different thermal units and programs. Materials (Basel). 4(12):3215. 10.3390/ma14123215

7 Navigating Endodontic Irrigants

Applications and Advancements for Successful Root Canal Therapy

Ashtha Arya and Gourav Thapak
Department of Conservative Dentistry and Endodontics,
SGT Dental College, Hospital and Research Institute,
Gurugram, Haryana, India

Sapana
Department of Conservative Dentistry and Endodontics,
SGT University, Gurugram, Haryana, India

7.1 INTRODUCTION

"The triad of biomechanical preparation, chemotherapeutic sterilization (disinfection) and three dimensional obturation are the hallmark of endodontic success."

Micro-organisms along with their end products are one of the main factor contributing to development of pulpal and periapical pathologies. Hence in every endodontic case the organisms and their substrates should be estimated.

Mechanical instrumentation alone is insufficient to achieve the above objectives. It is important to note that shaping is development of a "logical" cavity preparation which aids in irrigants cleaning of root canal system.

Irrigation is a word derived from Latin "Irrigace" which simply means "to flush out."

7.2 HISTORY OF ROOT CANAL IRRIGANTS

- Detergents (Zephiron chloride—0.1 to 1.0% and sodium lauryl sulphate) have been used commonly as an endodontic irrigant earlier.
- Panight and Jacquot recommended 0.5% Bardac-22(quaternary ammonium derivative) solution to be used as root canal irrigant.

DOI: 10.1201/9781003404934-7

- D Shrivastava and Chandra recommended the use of 2% chlorhexidine
- Phosphoric acid and sulphric acids have also been used as an irrigant.
- Ciprofloxacin (20%)
- Alcohols (70–90%) are also used as final irrigants for drying the canals before obturation.
- EDTAC (quaternary ammonium bromide) decreases the surface tension leading to deeper penetration of the irrigant.
- Normal saline is used to irrigate the root canals for decades and is still being used.
- Polyacrylic acid (40%), DURELON / FUJI II LIQUID are also employed as agents to irrigate root canal.

7.3 IDEAL REQUIREMENTS OF ROOT CANAL IRRIGANTS

1. *Gross Debridement*
   The irrigant should be capable of mechanically flushing away the pulpal debris and the dentin slurry from the root canals.
2. *Sterilization or atleast disinfection*
   The irrigant should possess broad spectrum antimicrobial properties.
3. *Ability to dissolve debris or remnant tissues*
   In the areas which are hard to reach by the root canal instruments, the irrigants should dissolve/ disrupt any debris of soft tissue or hard tissue.
4. *Non Toxicity*
   Should be non injurious to periradicular tissues.
5. *Lesser Surface Tension*
   Low surface tension allows the irrigant to enter in areas which are hard to access.
6. *Lubricating action*
   Property of irrigant to act as lubricant helps the instruments to glide down the root canal.
7. **Removal of smear layer**
8. *Bleaching Action*
   So that they lighten the teeth discolored by trauma or silver amalgam restoration.
9. *Dilution / Concentration*
   Irrigant should be "minimum concentration with maximum efficacy."
10. **Viscosity**
    Viscosity of the irrigant should be kept minimal so that they can easily enter the non instrumentable areas.
11. *Duration of Action*
    The irrigant should remain active for a longer duration.
12. *Effectiveness*
    The irrigant should be effective enough to produce the desired results.
13. *Other Factors*
    Other factors include wider availability, cost effectiveness, user friendliness, convenient to use, long shelf life, and ease of storage. Other essential

prerequisite is that the irrigant should not be easily neutralized in the pulp space to maintain its efficacy for a longer duration.

7.4 FUNCTIONS OF ROOT CANAL IRRIGANTS

1. **Gross debridement**
   Main goal of irrigation is to clear the debris of pulp and dentin slurry out of the root canal system.
2. *Elimination of microbes*
   Irrigant fluids have a minimum antimicrobial effect, but they decrease the microbial count in an infected root canal [1].
3. *Dissolution of pulpal remnants*
   If the pulpal tissue is necrosed, then it is readily dissolved and if the pulp is vital, then it takes longer time to dissolve [1].
4. *Smear layer clearance*
   As smear layer is calcified, its effective removal is possible by mildly acidic agents like Ethylene diamine tetraacetic acid (EDTA) [1].
5. *Bleaching action*
   Some irrigants like Hydrogen Peroxide have an additional bleaching action by virtue of which they lighten the discoloration of the teeth that is either traumatized or by extensive silver amalgam restoration and also reduce incidence of post operative darkening [1].
6. *Cleaning of the root canal instrument*
   Irrigants restrain the clogging of the debris to the instrument surface.
7. *Removal of food particles*
   Irrigants are also employed to flush out debris of food from canals that are open and left to drain.

7.5 TYPES OF ROOT CANAL IRRIGANTS

7.5.1 NORMAL SALINE

Baker et al. (1999) [2] proposed using saline in physiological concentration.

Irrigation with saline as shown in Figure 7.1 accomplishes dual goals of gross debridement and lubrication [3].

Saline irrigation causes chemical destruction of microbiologic matter and dissolves the tissues which are mechanically inaccessible as in accessory canals and isthmus regions

Isotonic saline should not be the only solution to be used to irrigate the root canals as it is too mild for thorough cleaning. Rather it should be used complementary to chemical disinfection, in which the chemical irrigant provides the disinfecting, and dissolution properties and the saline helps in the mechanical debridement.

It is also used to finally flush the root canal to remove any residual chemical irrigants in the canal after the biomechanical preparation.

The advantage of using isotonic saline is that even if it is inadvertently extruded out of the canal during irrigation it is less likely to produce any adverse reaction.

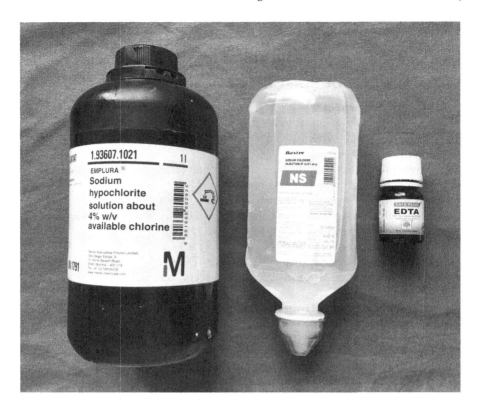

FIGURE 7.1 Endodontic irrigants (left to right): sodium hypochlorite, saline, liquid EDTA.

7.5.2 Sodium Hypochlorite

0.5% Sodium Hypochlorite (NaOCl) is known as Dakin Solution

In 1919 aqueous NaOCl was first used by Coolidge in Endodontics

Sodium hypochlorite irrigant as shown in Figure 7.1, rapidly eliminates even vegetative bacteria, sporogenous bacteria, fungus, protozoa, and majority of viruses (including HIV, herpes simplex 1 and -2, HAV and HBV viruses) [4–6].

Mechanism of action:

$$NaOCl + H_2O \rightarrow NaOH + \underset{\text{Hypochlorous}}{HOCl} \rightarrow Na^+ + OH^- + H^+ + \underset{\text{Hypochlorite}}{OCl^-}$$

Hypochlorous acid is more bactericidal than hypochlorite

pH more than 7.6 – Hypochlorite 7.6—Hypochlorite form

pH below 7.6—hypochlorous form

NaOCl causes dissolution of organic and fat molecules causing their dissolution which degrades fatty acids and changes them into fatty acid salts (soap) and glycerol (alcohol)—sSaponification, which reduces the surface tension of the remaining solution.

Sodium hypochlorite causes neutralization of amino acids thus leading to formation of salt and water—Neutralization reaction. As hydroxyl ions are removed, there is a reduction in pH.

Sodium hypochlorite solution, on contact with organic tissue, releases chlorine that in turn combines with the amino group(NH_2) forming chloramines—Chloramination reaction. Hypochlorous acid (HOCl) and hypochlorite ions (OCl-) degrades and hydrolyse amino acids.

Chloramines formed as a result of chloramination reaction impedes with the cell metabolism. Chlorine has a potent antimicrobial action owing to its oxidant property. It inhibits enzymes released by bacteria as it irreversibly oxidizes their SH groups (sulphydryl group).

The alkaline pH of sodium hypochlorite disrupts the cell membrane along with irreversible inhibition of enzymes. It also causes biosynthetic alterations in cellular metabolism and negatively affects lipidic peroxidation thus causing degradation of phospholipids.

Saponification reaction results in organic tissue dissolution, wherein sodium hypochlorite causes degeneration of fatty acids and lipids leading to formation of glvcerol and soap.

Concentration of NaOCl

• 5.25% NaOCl

Spangberg et al. opined that sodium hypochlorite in 5% conc. is toxic for routine clinical use [7].

Forceful irrigation into periapical tissues may cause leakage through rubber dam causing irritation.

Sim et al. assessed the outcomes of NaOCl treatment on the structure and chemo-mechanical properties of root dentine [8]. They opined that NaOCl reduces the elastic modulus and flexural strength of root dentine, the amount of reduction depending upon the concentration of NaOCl used. Carbon and nitrogen content of dentin was reduced but there was no effect on inorganic dentine components.

Siqueira et al. assessed bacteria in root canal following instrumentation and further irrigating with NaOCl in increasing concentrations of 1%, 2.5% and 5.25% and the results demonstrated no significant differences amongst the three concentrations [9].

Clarkson et al. studied the tissue dissolving capability of different conc. of NaOCl in pulp of incisors of pig. They concluded that greater concentration caused more speedy dissolution of tissue [10].

• At lower concentration

When NaOCl in contact with organic material consume Cl and reduces its antibacterial activity but in higher conc. this doesn't happen.

Frequent and plentiful irrigation with weaker NaOCl concentration maintains a chlorine reserve that is sufficient to eliminate compensating effects of concentration [9,11].

How to increase efficiency of NaOCl?

Increasing the temperature of low concentration NaOCl enhances its tissue dissolving capacity [12,13]. Bactericidal property of NaOCl solution increases by more than two folds for every 5°C rise in temp. in a range of 5–60°C.

Capacity of NaOCl at 1% strength at temperature of 45°C to dissolve pulp was found to be equivalent to that of 5.25% solution at 20°C [14].

Ultrasonic activation of NaOCl—

Ultrasonic energy produce heat which increases the efficacy of NaOCl. An instrument that freely oscillates causes more ultrasound effects than using file that binds to the canal [15,16].

Injection of NaOCl beyond the apex

Symptoms [17]:

- Perception of pain that is immediate in onset and severe in intensity.
- Oedema of surrounding soft tissues that is immediate in onset.
- Oedema may extend over the affected ipsilateral face, upper lip and infraorbital regions.
- Excessive bleeding from the canal.
- Skin and mucosal haemorrhage/ecchymosis.
- Chlorine taste and throat irritation due to inadvertent maxillary sinus entry.
- Canal may be secondarily infected.
- Possibility of anaesthesia or paraesthesia that are reversible.

Emergency treatment of accidental damage due to hypochlorite

- Eye Injuries
  Eyes should be washed with normal saline / water
  Opthalmology referral
- Skin Injuries
  Thorough and gentle washing under running tap water or with normal saline.
- Injuries To Oral Mucosa
  Immediate rinsing with water
  Analgesics may be advised
  Antibiotics to prevent occurrence of secondary infection
  If case of suspicion of inhalational injury or ingestion immediately refer to emergency department.
- Inoculation Injuries
  Ice packs applied to swelling for first 24 hrs
  Heat fomentation is done thereafter
  Analgesics
  Prophylactic antibiotics to cover any secondary infection
  Maxillofacial department referral for any adjuvant management

Measures for prevention:

- Use of plastic drapes over patient's clothing for protection
- Protective goggles over eyes for both patient and dentist
- Rubber dam isolation
- Using Luer-lok irrigation needles with side lock
- Irrigating 2 mm short of working length
- Avoid wedging of needle into root canal
- Avoiding application of excessive pressure while irrigating

7.5.3 Chlorhexidine

Cationic bis-biguanide, commercially available as gluconate salt

Composition:
Mainly consists of a base of chlorhexidine gluconate along with water, glycerine, alcohol, flavoring agent and saccharine.

pH 5.5–7

2% chlorhexidine gluconate as shown in Figure 7.2, is used as an intracanal irrigant and has broad spectrum antibacterial activity against G +ve and G -ve bacteria, both aerobes and anaerobes, viruses, spores and fungi [18].

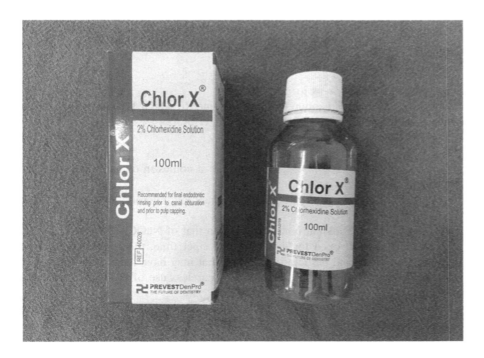

FIGURE 7.2 2% Chlorhexidine endodontic irrigant.

Chlorhexidine causes damage to outer layers of cell wall of bacteria by electrostatic binding to their negatively charged surface. This makes the cell wall permeable causing precipitation of cytoplasm [19].

Its action is bacteriostatic at lower concentration, whereas at higher concentrations it is bactericidal.

They have good antibacterial (E. faecalis) efficacy.

Studies illustrate that irrigation with chlorhexidine was more effective at 2% concentration rather than at 0.2% [20].

Substantivity

Due to its cationic properties they bind and adsorbed to the anionic substrates hydroxyapatite in tooth they act as reservoir and is gradually released as its conc. in the surroundings decreases [21].

Advantages

- relatively nontoxic.
- used in patients that are allergic to sodium hypochlorite, and
- teeth with open apices.

Disadvantage:

It lacks the ability to dissolve necrotic pulp tissue.

6%NaOCl and 2% chlorhexidine have equally effective antifungal (Candida albicans) efficacy which is superior to that of MTAD and 17% EDTA [12].

7.5.4 Hydrogen Peroxide

Commonly used conc 3% as irrigant.

1 ounce of 30% H_2O_2 is poured into a container to which 11 ounces of distilled water are added thus making 12 ounces of 3% H_2O_2.

Two modes of action [22]

- Effervescence of solution produced when it comes in contact with tissue foams debris from canal.
- Release of oxygen destroys obligatory anaerobic microorganisms.

Efficacy of H_2O_2 as a solvent is much less than that of NaOCl.

When teeth are left open for drainage for longer time, the effervescent action effectively removes food particles and debris that may have lodged in the canal.

Tissue emphysema sometimes results from careless use of H_2O_2 for root canal irrigation.

Distilled water or pure water should be used as an irrigant to eliminate H_2O_2 in the canal.

Usually, NaOCl is used as the final irrigant in root canal irrigation. Because of possibility of development of pressure due to O_2 liberation, H_2O_2 must always be neutralized by NaOCl.

NaOCl reacts with H_2O_2 and liberates the remaining oxygen and then the canal can be dried with a paper point so that if there is any remaining irrigant, it is absorbed.

7.5.5 Chelators

Chelation is a physico-chemical reaction leads to rapid uptake of polyvalent anions by specific chemicals. In root dentine, various agents react with calcium ions present in hydroxyapatite crystals. This leads to transformation in dentinal micropattern and alterations in Ca:P ratio.

7.5.5.1 Liquid Chelators

7.5.5.1.1 EDTA

Smear layer is colonized by a variety of microorganisms and also interferes with the formation of an effective seal with the obturating material.

EDTA—Ethylene diamine tetraacetic acid as shown in Figure 7.1, is widely used as an irrigant during root canal procedures and Table 7.1 describes the composition.

Introduced by Nygard Ostby 1957 EDTA (15%) solution at neutral pH (7.3). EDTA shows 20–30 μm demineralization zone after 5 minutes. Studies measuring the quantity of phosphors released after exposure to EDTA solutions for duration of 1–15 min with varied conc 10% and 17% at Ph 7.5 and 9, have shown that efficiency is more at pH of 7.5 than at pH of 9.0 [24]. Exposure time of 1 minute was effective in smear layer removal. Dentin erosion was seen severe after 10 min exposure. It was observed that increased conc. and increased time lead to increased amount of liberated phosphors from dentin [25,26].

Working Time of Chelators:
Goldberg et al. observed 15 min latent period before optimal cleaning effect was achieved [27].

It was concluded that EDTA shows best possible results when working time is between 1 and 5 minutes [24,28,29].

Antibacterial effects of EDTA:
It has limited antibacterial effect. Antibacterial effect is superior to saline and much less than paramonochlorphenol. It has poor antifungal efficacy [30].

TABLE 7.1
Composition of EDTA [23]

Constituent	Quantity
Disodium salt of EDTA	17 gm
Aqua dent	100 ml
Sodium hydroxide	9.25 ml

The US Army Institute of Dental Research showed that it is better to alternately use 15% EDTA and 5.25% sodium hypochlorite so that both organic and inorganic component are removed.

If the apical constriction has been opened, it may leak into the surrounding tissues and damages the periapical bone. So irrigation with sodium hypochlorite should be done before completing the procedure.

EDTA should not be filled in glass syringes as it reacts with glass.

The most commonly used chelators used as endodontic irrigants are Tublicid, EDTA, EDTAC, File-Eze, and RC Prep, which have EDTA as the active component.

7.5.5.1.2   EDTAC

Hill in 1959 improvised EDTA by addition of cationic surfactant Cetavlon (0.84 gm, cetlytrimethylammonium bromide), which lowered the surface tension and was bacteriostatic in nature. It causes inflammatory reaction to soft tissues.

Goldberg et al. suggested optimum working time is of EDTAC 15 min, so renewal of EDTAC solution every 15 min is recommended [27].

7.5.5.1.3   REDTA (Roth Mfg Co Chicago)

Composition:
17% solution of EDTA
0.84 g cetrimide—to reduce surface tension
Sodium hydroxide is added as a buffer in an aqueous solution to achieve pH 8.

Irrigating regimen for REDTA:
REDTA is used during instrumentation subsequent to 10 ml flush of REDTA, followed by flushing with 10 ml NaOCl.

7.5.5.1.4   EGTA

Ethylene glycol-bis (amino-ehtylether) NNNN—tetraacetic acid

Semra et al. compared effects of EGTA and EDTA on smear layer removal [24].

EDTA + NaOCl $\rightarrow$ removed smear layer completely but lead to severe erosion of tubules

EGTA + NaOCl $\rightarrow$ smear layer partially removed no erosion of intertubular and peritubular dentin.

Accidental leakage of EGTA in periapical space not only leads to decalcification of periapical bone but also inhibits phagocytic activity of macrophages, changing the inflammatory and immunological responses reactions in periapical tissues.

7.5.5.1.5   EDTA-T

Addition of Tergentol (sodium lauryl ether sulphate) to 17% EDTA increases penetrability of the solution due to decreased surface tension. Deeper penetration results in more effective removal of smear layer.

7.5.5.1.6   CDTA

1% Cyclohexane -1,2-diaminetetra acetic acid

CDTA solution also shows chelating properties and can be used to eliminate smear layer [23].

Studies have revealed that EDTA, EGTA, EDTAC, and Tetracycline-HCl resulted in calcium loss from root canal dentin whether or not there is a subsequent NaOCl irrigation [31].

Single use

1 min—EDTA > EDTAC > EGTA > Tetracycline – HCl = NaOCl > distilled water

Used in combination

1 min—EDTA + NaOCl > EDTAC + NaOCl > EGTA + NaOCl > tetracycline HCl + NaOCl > NaOCl > distilled water

7.5.5.1.7 Calcinase

Composition:
17% sodium edetate
with sodium hydroxide acting as stabilizer
and purified water

7.5.5.1.8 Largal Ultra (Septodont, Paris)

Composition:
15% EDTA solution(disodium salt)
0.75% cetrimide
sodium hydroxide to achieve pH value of 7.4

7.5.5.1.9 Tubulicid Plus

Table 7.2 describes the composition of Tubulicid Plus which is a chelating agent used as an endodontic irrigant.

7.5.5.1.10 Decal (Viekko Auer, Finland)

Composition:
oxyl-acetate 5.3%
ammonium oxyl-acetate 4.6%
cetrimide 0.065%

TABLE 7.2
Composition of Tubulicid Plus

Constituent	Quantity
Amphoteric-2 (38%)	1.5 gm
Benzalkoniumchloride	0.5 gm
Disodium EDTA	3 gm
Phosphate buffer solution	

7.5.5.1.11 Tetra Clean (Oana Laboratories, Italy)

Composition:
Doxycycline at lower conc than MTAD
Citric acid
Detergent

7.5.5.1.12 SmearClear

Composition:
17% EDTA with detergent

7.5.5.1.13 Salvizol

Salvizol (N1-decamethylene-bis-4-aminoquinald-inium-diacetate) is a detergent and a chelating irrigant.

Salvizol at neutral pH has bactericidal activity against wide spectrum of bacteria and actively chelates calcium.

Salvizol induces irritation of tissue but less than NaOCl or quaternary ammonium compounds (Zephiran).

7.5.5.1.14 Citric Acid

Use of citric acid was recommended by Tidmarsh in 1978

Wayman et al. in 1979 recommended the use of lactic acid and citric acid as an effective endodontic irrigant [32].

Citric acid in conc. of 10%, 25%, and 50% removed smear layer when used as an irrigant but they cause erosion, decrease hardness of dentin when compared to EDTA [33].

7.5.5.1.15 Tetracycline Hydrochloride (HCl)

An acidic solution with bacteriostatic properties.

Tetracyclines are antibiotics with broad spectrum antimicrobial activity. They act by binding directly to demineralized dentinal surfaces. Antimicrobial activity is activity is maintained by drug being subsequently released. Haznedaroğlu et al. showed 1% tetracycline HCl and 50% citric acid removed smear layer completely. But tetracycline HCl caused less erosion of tubules than citric acid [34].

Tetracycline group of drugs can chelate with calcium and cause staining of teeth [34].

7.5.5.2 Paste Type Chelators

Chelators are also available in paste form as shown in Figure 7.3 that act as lubricant during biomechanical preparation of the teeth.

7.5.5.2.1 Calcinase Slide (Ledge artis, Germany)

Composition:
Sodium EDTA 15% and water 58–64%
pH value is alkaline in range of 8–9

7.5.5.2.2 RC-Prep (Premier Dental, USA)

Developed by Stewart et al. in 1969

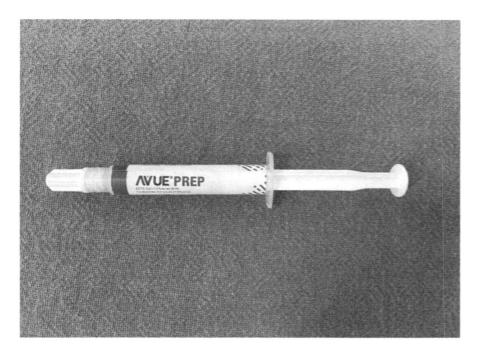

FIGURE 7.3   Paste type chelators.

Composed of 15% EDTA, 10% urea peroxide and glycol

10% urea peroxide generates hydroxyl radicals and leads to oxidation of SH groups and ultimately lead to cell death. Stewart et al. has claimed that, urea peroxide maintains its antibacterial efficacy even in the presence of blood [35].

Oxygen is released when RC-prep reacts with NaOCl, which causes removal of pulpal remnants and blood coagulant.

Glycol – in addition to being the base, acts as a lubricant also. It also prevents EDTA from being oxidized by urea peroxide.

Study by Zubriggen et al. has shown that residues of RC-Prep persist in the root canals even after cleaning and irrigation [36,37].

7.5.5.2.3   Glyde File (Dentsply)

Composition:

15% EDTA and 10% urea peroxide in aqueous solution

When used with NaOCl it releases oxygen from urea peroxide and the effervescence facilitate removal of dentin particles and pulpal remnants.

7.5.5.2.4   File Care EDTA (VDW Antaeous Munich, Germany)

Composition: 15% EDTA and urea peroxide

7.5.5.2.5   File-Eze (Ultradent products, USA)

Water based aqueous solution having 19% EDTA

7.5.5.3   MTAD

Composition:

- 3% doxycycline hyclate - broad spectrum bacteriostatic, low pH
- 4.25% citric acid
- 0.5% polysorbate detergent (Tween-80)

pH 2.15

Placing a barbed broach wrapped with MTAD soaked cotton ensures that the apical portion of the canal has adequate volume of irrigant that enhances debridement of the dentinal wall.

Using conventional in vitro microbiological procedures, the antibacterial effectiveness of MTAD was compared to that of NaOCl and EDTA and found to be much better.

The main drawbacks of using EDTA include its erosive effects on coronal two thirds of radicular dentin and its narrow antimicrobial spectrum [38].

Studies evaluating effect of varied conc. of NaOCl on ability of MTAD to get rid of smear layer have demonstrated no discernible difference between the capacities of 1.3%, 2.6%, 5.25% NaOCl when used to irrigate root canals with MTAD utilized as a last flush for elimination of smear layer [39].

Irrigating regimen is: 1.3% NaOCl for 20 min followed by 5 min irrigation with 5 ml of MTAD.

Potential iatrogenic staining (due to tetracycline) of endodontically treated teeth via NaOCl/MTAD [40]

Without light NaOCl + MTAD → yellow precipitate

Under light NaOCl + MTAD → red purple precipitate

This is due to oxidation reaction involving doxycycline and NaOCl. 1 M oxygen is absorbed for each mole of absorbed doxycycline. It leads to formation of a purplish red product {4-alpha,12-alpha-anhydro-4-oxo-4-dedi-methylaminotetracycline (AODTC)}

Addition of a reducing agent like ascorbic acid can prevent the formation of this product due to oxidation.

Formation of yellow precipitate is significantly reduced if NaOCl treated dentin is rinsed with water before applying MTAD.

There is no discernible difference between the groups in terms of the antimicrobial effectiveness against E. faecalis when comparing NaOCl/Biopure MTAD and NaOCl/EDTA [41].

Study examining the impact of irrigants on Epiphany sealer's shear bond strength to dentin, has demonstrated:[42]

GP 1 – sterile water for 10 min and final rinse with 10 ml sterile water for 1 min.
GP 2 – 2% CHX for 10 min and final rinse with 10 ml of CHX
Gp 3 – 6% NaOCl for 10 min and rinsed with 10 ml of saline
Gp 4 – 6% NaOCl for 10 min and final rinse with 17% EDTA for 1 min
Gp 5 – 1.3% NaOCl for 10 min and final rinse 5 min MTAD

Results: The results of the study did not confirm the manufacturer's claim that NaOCl has negative impact on the bond strength.

Study was done to determine how MTAD and EDTA, when used as final rinses, affected the shear bond strength of three root canal sealers to dentin [43].

Gp I—1.3% NaOCl + 17% EDTA for 1 min
 Subgp—AH plus, Apexit, ZOE sealer
 Gp II—1.3% NaOCl + MTAD for 5 min
 Sub gp—AH plus, Apexit, ZOE sealer
 Gp III—saline (control)
 Subgp—AH plus, Apexit, ZOE sealer

Results:

Gp I—high bond strength due to complete removal of smear layer
 Gp II—decreased bond strength due to formation of precipitate which interfered, although smear layer was removed, all sealers showed adhesive failures
 Gp III—higher bond strength when compared to Gp II

7.5.5.4 HEBP

HEBP—(1-hydroxyethylidene-1,1-bisphosphonate)
 It is a decalcifying agent and removes smear layer efficiently.
 It shows only little short-term interference with NaOCl and is possible alternative to EDTA and citric acid [44,45].

7.5.6 Castor Oil Based Irrigants

Endoquil (castor oil detergent) is a natural product derived from a tropical plant, *Ricinus communis*.

It results in notable reduction in the number of colony forming units for anaerobic microorganisms S. *mutans* and streptococci [46].

7.5.7 Ozonated Water as Root Canal Irrigant

Ozone is a gas formed by ionization of oxygen either by the action of UV light or a strong electric field. It is highly reactive form of oxygen.

It has potent antimicrobial activity against wide spectrum of bacteria, viruses, fungi, and protozoa.

Oxidation mediated by ozone (in gaseous or aqueous phase) damages the cell wall and plasma membranes of various microbes. Oxidative damage to the membrane causes increase in its permeability and molecules of ozone can now easily gain entry into the cells.

Antimicrobial activity of ozonated water is almost comparable to that of 2.5% NaOCl [47].

Method:

1. Oxidising gas is introduced into the open and instrumented root canal through a needle such that it does not escape the root canal.
2. In conjunction with NaOCl—first the root canal is flushed with NaOCl and then ozone is bubbled through it for 20–40 sec. This is repeated several times.

Advantages:

- Less toxic than NaOCl.
- Ozonated water has been shown to damage the fibroblasts.
- Ozone rapidly degrades after coming in contact with organic compounds, and this is one of its significant environmental advantage.
- Further research is required.

7.5.8 OXIDATIVE POTENTIAL WATER (OPW)

It has good antimicrobial and antiviral activities.

Oxidative potential water is created electrochemically, highly acidic water that has accumulate in anode compartment after NaCl (adding for consuming the OH$^-$ ions) is added to water.

In Cathode

- Alkaline water is formed after water has consumed H$^+$ ions
- pH more than 11
- Oxidation-reduction potential < -800 mV
- Have strong cleaning and detergent effect

In Anode

- Electrolysis of NaCl by device forms acidic and oxidative electrolyzed water
- pH < 2.7
- Oxidative—reduction potential is > +1100 mV
- Have good anti microbial effect
- Once prepared it should be used within 48 hrs.
- Effectively debrides the canals, it is bactericidal and has potential for removal of smear layer.
- It has better toxicity profile and low potential to irritate the soft tissues.
- Maintains acidic pH on reaction with photosensitive and/or organic substances.
- But it was observed that it's antibacterial efficacy was not as good as NaOCl [48].

7.5.9 CariSolv

It is a substitute to NaOCl for immature root canals and is used for chemomechanically removing infected and carious dentine.

* Available in two syringes

1st syringe—0.5% NaOCl
2nd syringe—amino acids, gel substance, sodium chlorite, sodium hydroxide and a color indicator (erythrocin)
Upon mixing, the amino acids react with chlorine leading to formation of chloramine which has alkaline pH and possess disinfectant and tissue solvent properties.

7.5.10 Solvidont (BDA)

Bis-dequaliniumacetate (BDA)
Advantages:

* better toxicity profile
* acts as lubricant
* potent disinfectant
* decreases surface tension
* acts as chelator
* lesser incidence of post-treatment pain

Advocated as a good alternative for NaOCl in patients having hypersensitivity to the latter.

7.5.11 Herbal Irrigants

7.5.11.1 Morinda Citrifolia Juice
It has antibacterial, antiviral, antifungal, antiprotozoal, antiinflammatoty, hypotensive and positive immune modulating effects [49].
It contains compounds L-asperuloside and alizarin which possess antibacterial properties.
Minimum inhibitory conc. is 6%
Study: When combined with EDTA, 6% Morinda citrifolia juice was found to be more effective than 2% CHX and as effective as NaOCl at removing the smear layer from instrumented radicular walls infected with E. faecalis [49].
Advantages:

* biocompatible antioxidant
* less likely to result in serious injuries, that may frequently happen in NaOCl-related accidents.

But further clinical trials are required.

7.5.11.2   Green Tea Polyphenols (GTP)

These are made from freshly picked Camellia sinensis (tea) leaves. They have substantial antimicrobial action in E. faecalis biofilms [50,51].

7.6   INTERACTIONS BETWEEN IRRIGANTS

7.6.1   Interaction between NaOCl and H₂O₂

Grossman (1943) made an observation that mixing of H_2O_2 and NaOCl leads to release of oxygen.

$$OCl^- + H_2O_2 \rightarrow O_2 + H_2O + Cl^-$$

Nascent oxygen kills anaerobes, and effervescence would lead to floating of debris from root canal system.

However, Cl^- is in inert form in solution and H_2O_2—hypochlorite mixture does not possess any of desired hypochlorite effects like bactericidal action and dissolution of necrotic debris. So they should be used separately [52].

7.6.2   Interaction between NaOCl and CHX

CHX is dicationic acid (pH 5.5–6) has proton donating property.

NaOCl takes protons from dicationic CHX and has an alkaline pH. The product of this proton exchange is reddish brown precipitate, which contains p-chloroaniline, formed by hydrolysis of CHX, and are insoluble and neutral [53].

PCA when leached is carcinogenic and exposure for a shorter duration causes cyanosis, and leads to methaemoglobin formation.

To minimize formation of PCA, wash residual sodium hypochlorite with EDTA or alcohol prior to CHX application [54].

7.6.3   Interaction between Sodium Hypochlorite and EDTA

When these solutions are mixed it causes decrease in Cl^- ions availability as NaOCl interacts with hydrogen of EDTA and leads to chlorine gas evaporation.

But the action of EDTA is not inhibited by NaOCl.

These combination also decrease antibacterial efficacy of NaOCl [55].

7.7   IRRIGATING REGIMENS

- **Alternatively using NaOCl and EDTA during instrumentation and final rinse with NaOCl.**
- To prevent chelating effect of EDTA against mineralized radicular dentin and to neutralize action of EDTA before obturation, final flush with NaOCl is recommended to rinse out EDTA [55].

Inactivation of EDTA is achieved through oxidation reaction by NaOCl.

Controversy:

Final flush of NaOCl to inactivate EDTA

Final flush with NaOCl is not indicated (to deactivate EDTA by its oxidizing property), at least for a time period that is clinically acceptable and realistic [56]. In fact it may hasten the dentin erosion, which acts as a matrix for the 3D filling of the pulp space.

a. **When is NaOCl needed as final rinse??**

If calcium hydroxide is given as intracanal medicament, final rinse with NaOCl is used as both the chemicals are perfectly complementary [12].

b. **EDTA as a final rinse**

During instrumentation 1% NaOCl is followed by final rinse with 17% EDTA for 1 minute.

Study: Effect of EDTA on smear layer removal after 1 and 10 min application.

*   1 min EDTA irrigation effectively removed smear layer without erosion.
*   10 min caused peri and intertubular erosion [38].

Use of EDTA for final rinse removes smear layer, exposes dentinal tubules and collagen,

helps in sealer penetration and increases the bond strength.

Disadvantage:

*   exposure of collagen leads to binding of E. faecalis
*   EDTA exposes dentine extracellular matrix proteins (MMP2), during cleaning and shaping if debris extrude, MMPs alter cellular behavior and modulation of biological active molecules, interfere with local homeostasis and delay healing of periapical lesions [57].

c. **CHX as final rinse**

Zehnder et al. proposed an irrigating regimen with NaOCl throughout instrumentation followed by use of EDTA and CHX for final irrigation [12].

2% CHX as final irrigant leads to significant reduction in bacterial load in root canals that had been irrigated with NaOCl while doing BMP. Most needed in retreatment cases with high colony count of Gram +ve bacteria in the root canal system.

Suggested Irrigation Regime

1.3% NaOCl is to be used copiously during instrumentation which is followed by flushing with 5–10 ml of 17% EDTA for 1 min in each canal to remove the smear layer and final flush with 2% CHX. 2% CHX is the most promising antimicrobial endodontic irrigant, with the property of substantivity, which can be used as a final flush especially in retreatment cases.

7.8 DELIVERY SYSTEMS

There are two different opinions in comparison of the irrigants with respect to their disinfecting and cleaning attributes.

- According to the first, chemical properties of the irrigant are given more significance such as sodium hypochlorite.
- The counter opinion places more weight on the mechanical action of the solution to flush out the debris.

7.8.1 TYPES OF SYRINGES

Syringes in the early 20th century were totally composed of metal. With time syringes made up of glass barrel having metallic plunger became popular. Then in 1940, glass syringes with interchangeable pistons were introduced. The breech loading syringe, also called cook syringe, came to horizon in the 1920s but took another decade to become popular amongst dental professionals. Many varieties of disposable syringes made of plastic are available now a days. Most frequently used needle is the 27-G needle having a notched tip, which allows for backflow of irrigant. Glass syringes with metal tips are also available.

Other delivery systems available are Monoject endodontic needles, CaviEndo systems ProRinse probes, Micromega 1500, Max-I-Probe as shown in Figure 7.4, Canal Clean as shown in Figure 7.5, the Endo-Eze system and Irrivac.

Several syringes provide for aspiration of irrigating solution as well as deposition of the solution within the tooth, and they range from simple adaptations of tubing

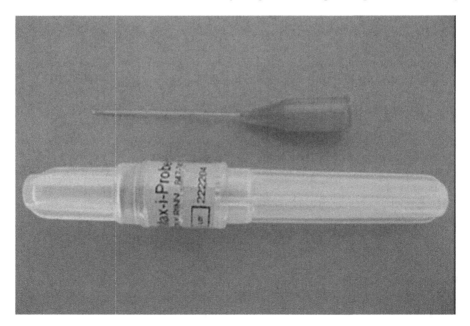

FIGURE 7.4   Max-i- probe needle.

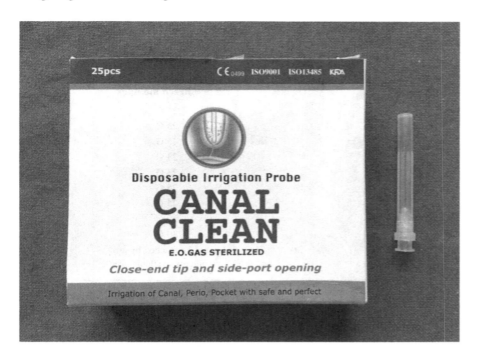

FIGURE 7.5   Close end tip and side-port opening irrigation needle.

connected to saliva ejectors (for aspiration) to sophisticated patented devices that inject and aspirate.

7.8.2 REQUIREMENTS OF DELIVERY SYSTEMS

a. **Length of needle**: It should be long enough so that it can reach up to the apical portion of the root canal so that irrigant can be dispensed up to maximum depth of the canal without much pressure.

b. **Gauge and shape of the needle.**

   Table 7.3 describes the size of apical canal preparation and the largest needle size that can reach the apex.

   • Monoject endodontic needles (Tyco/Kendall, Mass, Mansfield): 23 and 27 G needles with a notched tip which eliminates pressure.

   • Prorinse (Dentsply/Tulsa Dental; Tulsa, Okla): 25-, 28-, and 30-G probes. It has a blunt tip, with the lumen 2 mm proximal to the tip. Turbulence is created around and beyond the probe end as the solution is released from the lumen. Prorinse needle irrigate through a side vent.

   • CaviEndo ultra simple endodontic irrigating system—consists of a disposable syringe made of plastic and needle.

   • The Max-i-Probe Endodontic Irrigating Probe as shown in Figure 7.4, is a needle with a specially designed smooth, closed, rounded side-window dispersal port. Various "probe" sizes range from 30-gauge

TABLE 7.3
Different Sizes of Needles Used in Canals

Canal Size	Largest Needle Size that Can Reach the Apex
80	21 G
70	23 G
60	23 G
55	23 G
50	23 G
45	25 G
35	25 G
30	30 G
25	30 G
20	Cannot be reached by any commonly available needle

(equivalent to a #30 file) to 21-gauge (equivalent to a #80 file). The probes deliver irrigant to the apical third without risk of apical puncture and with less likelihood of apical extrusion.

- The Endo-Eze system is a series of disposable miniature capillary and bendable irrigating tips. These irrigate and dry canals as well as deliver material. One of the capillary tips rapidly vacuums out excess canal fluid when it is attached to a Luer Vacuum Adapter.

c. **Penetration of needle**

- It is advisable to place the needle close to the apex without binding.
- If the needle is near the apical foramen, there is more chance of extension of fluid into periradicular tissues.
- According to some authors, needle tip should be placed in the canal till we feel resistance from the canal walls, then the tip is withdrawn by a few mm and irrigant is dispensed.
- Salzgeber and Brilliant demonstrated that instrumentation beyond size 35 allows irrigant to penetrate beyond the apex into periapical tissues [12,58].

d. **Pressure with which the irrigant should be delivered**

- Average clinical pressure on the plunger, using a 23-gauge needle, should be such that approximately 5 ml of solution is discarded by the syringe in 18 sec.
- The solution must be introduced *very slowly* until the chamber is almost completely filled and avoid wedging of needle in the canal.
- The hand holding the irrigating syringe should be in motion while delivering the irrigant to avoid inadvertent wedging of the needle in the canal.

While treating the posterior teeth or in teeth having smaller canals, the solution is deposited in the chamber. The file carries the irrigant into the canal, and by capillary action of the narrow canal diameter much of the solution is retained.

Kahn et al. described the use of the Irrivac, which provides both aspiration and irrigation with the same instrument. A 25-gauge needle is inserted through Teflon tubing attached by way of a bypass to the saliva ejector. The irrigant is expressed through a syringe into the canal and aspirated out the tubing.

Technological advancements have led to development of in office air pressurized bottles that deliver different irrigants (Vista Dental Products, Racine). The clinician can select solution of his choice with just a push of a button.

7.8.3 ENDOVAC SYSTEM

EndoVac system as shown in Figure 7.6, is based on negative pressure principle.

The system suctions up fluid, creates a vacuum which is automatically filled with irrigation fluid.

Advantages:

- fluid does not have to be forced into canal with syringe with positive pressure
- System suctions out fluid and debris from as far as the actual apical terminus using cannula [59].

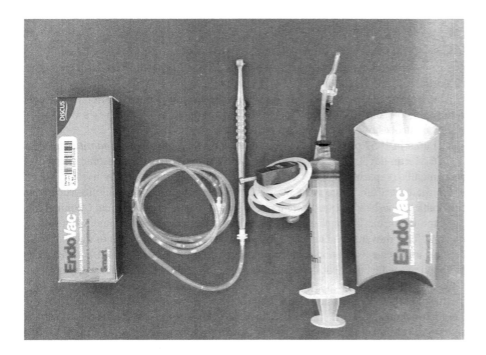

FIGURE 7.6   EndoVac system.

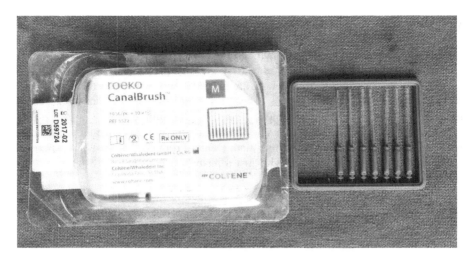

FIGURE 7.7   Rotary activated microbrushes.

7.8.4   ROTARY ACTIVATED MICROBRUSHES

Rotary-activated microbrushes, as shown in Figure 7.7, are quite efficient in cleaning of the canal. These microbrushes are used at 300 rpm speed, and the root canal is effectively debrided of all residues by the helical bristles in a coronal direction.

7.8.5   ULTRASONIC SYSTEM

Endosonics, denotes a device which imparts high intensity sinusoidal vibrations to a root canal instrument in the range which is either ultrasonic (20–42 kHz) or is within the audible threshold range (20 kHz).

They consist of a driver with an endosonic file clamped onto it, often at an angle of between 60 and 90 degrees to the driver's long axis. The driver's oscillation pattern controls how the associated file moves.

Richman in 1957 pioneered the idea of utilizing ultrasound in **endodontic therapy**. In 1976 Martin developed a system harnessing the properties of ultrasonic energy for mechanically preparing the root canal. It is now being commercially used.

Tronstadt et al. in 1985, were the firstly reported the use of a sonic instrument in endodontics. These techniques were termed as **Endosonics** by Martin and Cunningham.

At the ultrasonic frequencies used, the main driver oscillates longitudinally, and its back and forth movement generates a transverse wave along the length of the endosonic file. This transverse oscillation is characterized by a series of *Nodes* and *Antinodes* along the length of the file, the nodes representing sites of minimum oscillation or displacement of the file and the antinodes representing sites of maximum oscillation or displacement. The file tip will oscillate totally unrestrained with the greatest displacement from rest. This file motion almost certainly causes abrasion (filing) of the canal walls due to vertical motion of instrument within the canal. If the file is constrained within a tightly fitting canal the oscillatory pattern will be reduced or even eliminated. This is inefficient and more likely to occur in curved canals than straight ones.

7.8.6 Endosonic Chemical Disinfection

Sonic instruments depend on the passing of air which is pressurized via the handpiece of the instrument in order to generate oscillation in the working tip. Two types are frequently used, which operate at either 3–6 kHz or at 16–20 kHz.

The sonic instruments, Endoactivator as shown in Figure 7.8, have a main driver, which in contrast to the ultrasonic driver produces an elliptical pattern of oscillation during activation.

Biophysical Effects of Endosonics
Cavitation

Cavitation is the term used to describe the development and rapid collapse of a tiny gas-filled pre-existing inhomogeneity in the bulk fluid.

Immersion of a vibrating object in a fluid sets up oscillations which cause local changes in fluid pressure manifesting as either increase (compression) or decrease (rarefaction). At a specific pressure amplitude during the rarefaction phase, the liquid may fail due to sonic stress and produce cavitation bubbles. These cavities, which are largely filled with vapor, implosively collapse during the next positive pressure phase, producing radiating shock waves.

Acoustic Streaming

Acoustic streaming means generation of steady unidirectional circulation of fluid which is independent of time, surrounding a small vibrating object.

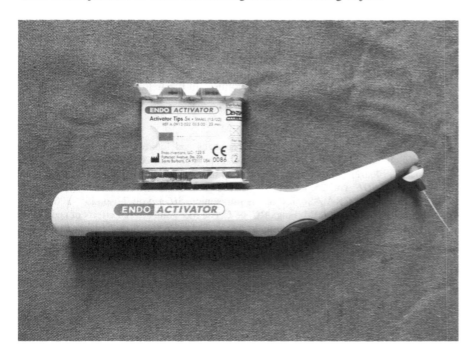

FIGURE 7.8   Endoactivator.

Immersion of a vibrating file into the fluid leads to generation of a streaming fluid which has two components: the *Primary field*, which consists of quickly moving eddies in which the fluid element oscillates around a mean location, and a superimposed *Secondary field*, which consists of patterns of relatively sluggish, time independent flow. Typically, the fluid is transported from the apical end to the coronal end.

Sodium hypochlorite when activated with endosonics makes a potent synergistic combination for the efficient debridement of the pulp space [60].

7.9 FUTURE SCOPE

The future of endodontic irrigants holds promise with the integration of nano-technology for targeted disinfection, development of bioactive irrigants for enhanced tissue regeneration, and utilization of smart delivery systems for controlled drug release. Advancements in material science may lead to novel irrigant formulations with improved antimicrobial efficacy and reduced cyto-toxicity. However, comprehensive research is required to ensure the safety and effectiveness of these innovations in shaping the future of root canal therapy.

7.10 CONCLUSION

In conclusion, endodontic irrigants play a pivotal role in successful root canal treatments. Through their antimicrobial, tissue dissolution, chelating and debris flushing properties, they aid in disinfection and cleanliness of the root canal system. Sodium hypochlorite, EDTA and chlorhexidine remain primary choices, each with distinct advantages. However, a balanced approach is crucial to minimize potential adverse effects. Ongoing research aims to refine irrigant formulations and techniques, ensuring improved treatment outcomes and patient comfort in the field of endodontics.

REFERENCES

1. Boutsioukis C, Arias-Moliz MT, "Present status and future directions – irrigants and irrigation methods," *IEJ*, vol. 55, no. Suppl. 3, pp. 588–612, 2022. doi: 10.1111/iej.13739
2. Buck R, Eleazer DD, "In vitro disinfection of dentinal tubules by various endodontic irrigants," *JOE*, vol. 25, pp. 786–788, 1999. doi: 10.1016/S0099-2399(99)80297-0
3. Parameswaram GKA, "Sonics versus ultrasonic," *JIDA*, vol. 72, p. 255, 2001.
4. Siqueira JF Jr, Batista MM, Fraga RC, de Uzeda M, "Antibacterial effects of endodontic irrigants on black-pigmented gram-negative anaerobes and facultative bacteria," *J Endod*, vol. 24, pp. 414–416, 1998. doi: 10.1016/S0099-2399(98)80023-X
5. Siqueira JF Jr, Machado AG, Silveira RM, Lopes HP, de Uzeda M, "Evaluation of the effectiveness of sodium hypochlorite used with three irrigation methods in the elimination of Enterococcus faecalis from the root canal in vitro," *Endod J*, vol. 30, pp. 279–82, 1997. doi: 10.1046/j.1365-2591.1997.00096.x.
6. Rutala WA, "Uses of inorganic hypochlorite (bleach) inhealth-care facilities," *Clin Microbiol Rev*, vol. 10, pp. 597–610, 1997. doi: 10.1128/CMR.10.4.597
7. Spang berg L, Engstrom B, "Biologic effects of dental materials. III. Toxicity and antimicrobial effect of endodontic antiseptics in. vitro. 1973; 36:856-71," *Oral Surg*, vol. 36, no. 856–71, 1973. doi: 10.1016/0030-4220(73)90338-1

8. Sim TP, Knowles JC, Ng YL, Shelton J, "Effect of sodium hypochlorite on mechanical properties of dentine and tooth surface strain," *Int Endod J*, vol. 34, no. 2, pp. 120–132, 2001. doi: 10.1046/j.1365-2591.2001.00357.x

9. Siqueira JF Jr, Rôças IN, Favieri A, "Chemomechanical reduction of the bacterial population in the root canal after instrumentation and irrigation with 1%, 2.5%, and 5.25% sodium hypochlorite," *J Endod*, vol. 26, no. 6, pp. 331–334, 2000. doi: 10.1097/00004770-200006000-00006.

10. J. R. Clarkson RM, Moule AJ, Podlich H, Kellaway R, Macfarlane R, Lewis D, "Dissolution of porcine incisor pulps in sodium hypochlorite solutions of varying compositions and concentrations," *Aust Dent J*, vol. 51, no. 3, pp. 245–251, 2006. doi: 10.1111/j.1834-7819.2006.tb00437.x

11. Cai C, Chen X, Li Y, "Advances in the role of sodium hypochlorite irrigant in chemical preparation of root canal treatment," *Biomed Res Int*, vol. 13, 2023. doi: 10.1155/2023/8858283

12. Zehnder M, "Root canal irrigants," *J Endod*, vol. 32, no. 5, pp. 389–398, 2006. doi: 10.1016/j.joen.2005.09.014.

13. Dioguardi M, Gioia GD, Illuzzi G, Laneve E, Cocco A, "Endodontic irrigants: Different methods to improve efficacy and related problems," *Eur J Dent*, vol. 12, no. 3, pp. 459–466, 2018. doi: 10.4103/ejd.ejd_56_18

14. Sirtes G, Waltimo T, Schaetzle M, "The effects of temperature on sodium hypochlorite short-term stability, pulp dissolution capacity, and antimicrobial efficacy," *J Endod*, vol. 31, no. 9, pp. 669–671, 2005. doi: 10.1097/01.don.0000153846.62144.d2

15. Zeltner, M, Peters, OA, Paqué, "Temperature changes during ultrasonic irrigation with different inserts and modes of activation," *J Endod*, vol. 35, no. 4, pp. 573–577, 2009.

16. Mohammadi Z, Shalavi S, Giardino L, Palazzi F, "Impact of ultrasonic activation on the effectiveness of sodium hypochlorite: a review," *Iran Endod J*, vol. 10, no. 4, pp. 216–220, 2015. doi: 10.7508/iej.2015.04.001

17. AL-Zahrani MS, "Sodium hypochlorite accident in endodontics: an update review," *Int J Dent Oral Health*, vol. 2, no. 2, pp. 1–4, 2016. doi: 10.16966/2378-7090.168

18. Josic U, Maravic T, Mazzitelli C, Del Bianco F, Mazzoni A, "The effect of chlorhexidine primer application on the clinical performance of composite restorations: a literature review," *J Esthet Restor Dent*, vol. 33, no. 1, pp. 69–77, 2021. doi: 10.1111/jerd.12701

19. Davies A, "The mode of action of chlorhexidine," *J Periodontal Res Suppl*, vol. 12, pp. 68–75, 1973. doi: 10.1111/j.1600-0765.1973.tb02167.x

20. María Ferrer-Luque C, Teresa Arias-Moliz M, Ruíz-Linares M, Elena Martínez García M, Baca P "Residual activity of cetrimide and chlorhexidine on Enterococcus faecalis-infected root canals," *Int J Oral Sci*, vol. 6, pp. 46–49, 2013. doi: 10.1038/ijos.2013.95.

21. White RR, Hays GL, "Residual antimicrobial activity after canal irrigation with chlorhexidine," *J Endodon*, vol. 23, pp. 229–31, 1997.

22. Mohammadi Zahed, Shalavi, "Hydrogen peroxide in endodontics: a mini-review. 8," *Int J Clin Dent*, vol. 8, no. 2, pp. 171–179, 2015.

23. Hülsmann M, Heckendorff M, "Chelating agents in root canal treatment: mode of action and indications for their use." *Int Endod J*, vol. 36, no. 12, pp. 810–30, 2003. doi: 10.1111/j.1365-2591.2003.00754.x

24. Serper A, "The demineralizing effects of EDTA at different concentrations & pH," *JOE*, vol. 28, no. 7, pp. 501–502, 2002. doi: 10.1097/00004770-200207000-00002

25. Baruwa Ao, Martins Jnr, Maravic T, Mazzitelli C, Mazzoni A, Ginjeira A, "Effect Of endodontic irrigating solutions on radicular dentine structure and matrix metallopro-teinases—a comprehensive review," *Dent J*, vol. 10, no. 12, p. 219, 2022. doi: 10.3390/dj10120219

26. Khoroushi M, Ziaei S, Shirban F, "Effect of intracanal irrigants on coronal fracture resistance of endodontically treated teeth undergoing combined bleaching protocol: an in vitro study," *J Dent (Tehran)*, vol. 15, no. 5, pp. 266–274, 2018.

27. Goldberg CSF, "The effect of EDTAC and the variation of its working time analyzed with scanning electron microscopy," *Oral Surgery, Oral Med Oral Pathol*, vol. 53, no. 1, pp. 74–77, 1982.

28. Akhlaghi NM, Behrooz E, and Saghiri MA, "Efficacy of MTAD, Glyde and EDTA in debridement of curved root canals," *IEJ*, vol. 4, no. 2, pp. 58–62, 2009.

29. Scelza MF, Teixeira AM, "Decalcifying effect of EDTA-T, 10% citric acid, and 17% EDTA on root canal dentin," *Oral Surg Oral Med Oral Pathol Oral Radiol Endod*, vol. 95, no. 2, pp. 234–236, 2003. doi: 10.1067/moe.2003.89

30. Yoshida T, Shibata T, Shinohara T, Gomyo S, "Clinical evaluation of the efficacy of EDTA solution as an endodontic irrigant," *JOE*, vol. 21, no. 12, pp. 592–593, 1995.

31. Sayin TC, Serper A, Cehreli ZC, "Calcium loss from root canal dentin following EDTA, EGTA, EDTAC, and tetracycline-HCl treatment with or without subsequent NaOCl irrigation," *J Endod*, vol. 33, no. 5, pp. 581–584, 2007. doi: 10.1016/j.joen.2006.12.010.

32. Wayman BE, Kopp WM, Pinero GJ, "Citric and lactic acids as root canal irrigants in vitro," *J Endod*, vol. 5, no. 9, pp. 258–65, 1979.

33. Kaushal R, Bansal R, "A comparative evaluation of smear layer removal by using ethylenediamine tetraacetic acid, citric acid, and maleic acid as root canal irrigants: an in vitro scanning electron microscopic study," *J Conserv Dent*, vol. 23, no. 1, pp. 71–78, 2020. https://www.jcd.org.in/text.asp?2020/23/1/71/297678

34. Haznedaroğlu F, "Tetracycline HCl solution as a root canal irrigant," *J Endod*, vol. 27, no. 12, pp. 738–740, 2001. doi: 10.1097/00004770-200112000-00006

35. Stewart George G, "A scanning electron microscopic study of the cleansing effectiveness of three irrigating modalities on the tubular structure of dentin," *JOE*, vol. 24, no. 7, pp. 485–486, 1998. doi: 10.1016/S0099-2399(98)80052-6.

36. Zurbriggen T, del Rio CE, Brady JM "Postdebridement retention of endodontic reagents: a quantitative measurement with radioactive isotope," *JOE*, vol. 1, no. 9, pp. 298–299, 1975. doi: 10.1016/S0099-2399(75)80137-3

37. Cruz A, Vera J, Gascon G, Palafox-Sánchez CA, Amezcua O, "Debris remaining in the apical third of root canals after chemomechanical preparation by using sodium hypochlorite and glyde: an in vivo study," *JOE*, vol. 40, no. 9, pp. 1419–1423, 2014. doi: 10.1016/j.joen.2014.05.013

38. Calt S, "Time-dependent effects of EDTA on dentin structures," *JOE*, vol. 28, no. 1, pp. 17–9, 2002. doi: 10.1097/00004770-200201000-00004.

39. Torabinejad M, Cho Y, Khademi AA, Bakland LK, "The effect of various concentrations of sodium hypochlorite on the ability of MTAD to remove the smear layer," *JOE*, vol. 29, no. 6, p. 424, 2003. doi: 10.1097/00004770-200304000-00001

40. Tay FR, Mazzoni A, Pashley DH, Day TE, Ngoh EC, "Potential iatrogenic tetracycline staining of endodontically treated teeth via NaOCl/MTAD irrigation: a preliminary report," *JOE*, vol. 32, no. 4, pp. 354–8, 2006. doi: 10.1016/j.joen.2005.11.006.

41. Kho P, Baumgartner JC, "A comparison of the antimicrobial efficacy of NaOCl/ Biopure MTAD versus NaOCl/EDTA against Enterococcus faecalis," *JOE*, vol. 32, no. 7, pp. 652–655, 2006. doi: 10.1016/j.joen.2005.11.004.

42. Wachlarowicz AJ, Joyce AP, Roberts S, "Effect of endodontic irrigants on the shear bond strength of epiphany sealer to dentin," *JOE*, vol. 33, no. 2, pp. 152–5, 2007. doi: 10.1016/j.joen.2006.09.011.

43. Gopikrishna V, Venkateshbabu N, Krithikadatta J, "Evaluation of the effect of MTAD in comparison with EDTA when employed as the final rinse on the shear bond strength of three endodontic sealers to dentine," *Aust Endod J*, vol. 37, no. 1, pp. 12–17, 2011. doi: 10.1111/j.1747-4477.2010.00261.x.

44. Zehnder M, Schicht O, Sener B, "Reducing surface tension in endodontic chelator solutions has no effect on their ability to remove calcium from instrumented root canals," *JOE*, vol. 31, no. 8, pp. 590–592, 2005. doi: 10.1097/01.don.0000152300.44990.6d.

45. Zehnder M, Schmidlin P, Sener B, "Chelation in root canal therapy reconsidered," *JOE*, vol. 31, no. 11, pp. 817–820, 2005. doi: 10.1097/01.don.0000158233.59316.fe

46. Leonardo MR, da Silva LA, Filho MT, Bonifácio KC, "In vitro evaluation of the antimicrobial activity of a castor oil-based irrigant," *JOE*, vol. 27, no. 12, pp. 717–9, 2001. doi: 10.1097/00004770-200112000-00001.

47. Broadwater WT, Hoehn RC, "Sensitivity of three selected bacterial species to ozone," *Appl Microbiol*, vol. 26, no. 3, pp. 391–393, 1973. doi: 10.1128/am.26.3.391-393.1973.

48. Hata G, Hayami S, Weine FS, "Effectiveness of oxidative potential water as a root canal irrigant," *Int Endod J*, vol. 34, no. 4, pp. 308–317, 2001. doi: 10.1046/j.1365-25 91.2001.00395.x

49. Murray PE, Farber RM, Namerow KN, Kuttler S, "Evaluation of Morinda citrifolia as an endodontic irrigant," *J Endod*, vol. 34, no. 1, pp. 66–70, 2008. doi: 10.1016/ j.joen.2007.09.016

50. Prabhakar J, Senthilkumar M, Priya MS, Mahalakshmi K, Sehgal PK, Sukumaran VG, "Evaluation of antimicrobial efficacy of herbal alternatives (triphala and green tea polyphenols), MTAD, and 5% sodium hypochlorite against Enterococcus faecalis biofilm formed on tooth substrate: an in vitro study," *JOE*, vol. 36, no. 1, pp. 83–6, 2010. doi: 10.1016/j.joen.2009.09.040.

51. Topbas C, Adiguzel O, "Endodontic irrigation solutions: a review," *Int Dent Res*, vol. 7, pp. 54–61, 2017. doi: 10.5577/intdentres.2017.vol7.no3.2

52. Heling I, "Antimicrobial effect of irrigant combinations within dentinal tubules," *Int Endod J*, vol. 31, no. 1, pp. 8–14, 1998.

53. Bui TB, Baumgartner JC, "Evaluation of the interaction between sodium hypochlorite and chlorhexidine gluconate and its effect on root dentin," *J Endod*, vol. 34, no. 2, pp. 181–5, 2008. doi: 10.1016/j.joen.2007.11.006.

54. Mortenson D, Sadilek M, Flake NM, Paranjpe A, Heling I, Johnson JD, "The effect of using an alternative irrigant between sodium hypochlorite and chlorhexidine to prevent the formation of para-chloroaniline within the root canal system," *Int Endod J*, vol. 45, no. 9, pp. 878–882, 2012. doi: 10.1111/j.1365-2591.2012.02048.x.

55. Grawehr M, Sener B, Waltimo T, "Interactions of ethylenediamine tetraacetic acid with sodium hypochlorite in aqueous solutions," *Int Endod J*, vol. 36, no. 6, pp. 411–417, 2003. doi: 10.1046/j.1365-2591.2003.00670.x.

56. Grande NM, Plotino G, Falanga A, Pomponi M, Francesco S, "Interaction between EDTA and sodium hypochlorite: A nuclear magnetic resonance analysis," *J. Endod*, vol. 32, no. 5, pp. 460–464, 2006. doi: 10.1016/j.joen.2005.08.007

57. Sum CP, Neo J, "What we leave behind in root canals after endodontic treatment: some issues and concerns," *Aust. Endod. J*, vol. 31, pp. 95–100, 2005. doi: 10.1111/ j.1747-4477.2005.tb00312.x

58. Huiz Peeters H, Suardita K, Mooduto L, "Extrusion of irrigant in open apex teeth with periapical lesions following laser-activated irrigation and passive ultrasonic irriga- tion," *Iran Endod J*, vol. 13, no. 2, pp. 169–175, 2018. doi: 10.22037/iej.v13i2.17150.

59. Versiani MA, Alves FR, Andrade-Junior CV, Marceliano-Alves MF, Provenzano JC, Rôças IN, Sousa-Neto MD, "Micro-CT evaluation of the efficacy of hard-tissue removal from the root canal and isthmus area by positive and negative pressure irrigation systems," *Int Endod J*, vol. 49, no. 11, pp. 1079–1087, 2016. doi: 10.1111/ iej.12559.

60. Agarwal A, Deore RB, Rudagi K, Nanda Z, Baig MO, "Evaluation of apical vapor lock formation and comparative evaluation of its elimination using three different techniques: An in vitro study," *J Contemp Dent Pr. 2017*, vol. 18, no. 9, pp. 790–794, 2017. doi: 10.5005/jp-journals-10024-2128.

8 Recent Advances in Newer Generation Composite Resin

Imen Gnaba, Kawthar Bel Haj Salah, Firas Chtioui, Mouadh Selmi, Roua Habachi, and Wided Askri
Restorative Dentistry and Endodontics, University Hospital Farhat Hached, Faculty of Dental Medicine of Monastir, University of Monastir, Monastir, Tunisia

Hayet Hajjami
University Hospital Farhat Hached, Faculty of Dental Medicine of Monastir, University of Monastir, Monastir, Tunisia

8.1 INTRODUCTION

In the context of minimally invasive dental procedures, composite resin has become the most important modern biomaterial used in direct restoration of dental defects. It has also become the most commonly used esthetic material in dentistry thanks to its ability to restore both esthetics and function of biological tissue. However, composite resin presents some problems, such as polymerization shrinkage, subsequent marginal leakage, sensitivity, and secondary caries. Thus, as a way to improve the properties of composite resin and to protect healthy tooth structure, newer generation composite resins have been developed. This chapter discusses the ten recent advances in newer generation composite resin.

8.1.1 SPIRO-ORTHO CARBONATES EXPANDING MONOMERS

Dental restorations are a common solution for treating dental caries and other dental problems. However, a common issue with dental restorations is marginal leakage, which can lead to secondary caries and other complications. Expanding monomers have been developed as a potential solution to this problem. One promising group of expanding monomers is spiro-ortho carbonates. Studies have shown that spiro-ortho carbonates can improve the mechanical properties of dental restorations and help seal the restoration to the tooth structure, thus reducing the risk of marginal leakage [1–3]. Additionally, spiro-ortho carbonates have been demonstrated to have antibacterial properties and to prevent biofilm formation. Herein, we provide a comprehensive

DOI: 10.1201/9781003404934-8

review of the use of spiro-ortho carbonates expanding monomers in dental applications, while focusing on recent studies.

8.1.1.1 Synthesis

Spiro-ortho carbonates expanding monomers can be synthesized by a set of reactions involving spiro-ortho carbonate and diacrylate or dimethacrylate monomer. The resulting copolymer can be used in various dental applications, such as composites, cements, or adhesives. The properties of the monomer can be tailored by adjusting the ratio of spiro-ortho carbonate to diacrylate or dimethacrylate and the molecular weight of the monomers. Many recent studies [3,4] have shown the effect of spiro-ortho carbonate monomer content on the mechanical properties of dental composites and announced that increasing spiro-ortho carbonate content improves the flexural strength and modulus of the composites.

8.1.1.2 Properties

Spiro-ortho carbonates expanding monomers have a unique set of properties that make them a promising option for use in dental restorations. One of the key properties of these monomers is their ability to undergo expansion upon polymerization, which can aid in sealing the restoration to the tooth structure, thus reducing the risk of marginal leakage. Several studies [2–5] have extensively investigated this property, and they reported that spiro-ortho carbonates containing composites have better sealing ability compared to traditional composites.

In addition to their expansion properties, spiro-ortho carbonates improve the mechanical properties of dental restorations. The effect of spiro-ortho carbonate monomer content on the mechanical properties of dental adhesives and composite resins has been investigated by many. These studies found that increasing spiro-ortho carbonate content improves the flexural strength and modulus of elasticity of the materials.

Furthermore, spiro-ortho carbonates have been shown to have antibacterial properties and therefore to prevent biofilm formation. Marx et al. [3] and Duarte et al. [4] studied the antibacterial properties of dental materials containing spiro-ortho carbonates and reported that they exhibit an antibacterial effect against *Streptococcus mutans*.

Overall, the unique properties of spiro-ortho carbonates make them a promising option of dental restorations [3–5]. However, further investigations seem essential to better understand the properties of these materials and develop their use in clinical applications.

8.1.1.3 Applications

Spiro-ortho carbonates expanding monomers have diverse applications in dental restorations, such as composites, cements, and adhesives. Recent research has focused on the potential use of these monomers in novel applications, such as injectable composite materials and dental resin-based coatings.

One potential application of spiro-ortho carbonates is in injectable composite materials. These materials can be used to fill difficult-to-reach areas in the mouth, such as root canals or interproximal spaces. Studies demonstrated that spiro-ortho carbonates containing composites have good injectability and setting properties, making them a promising option for this application.

Another potential application of spiro-ortho carbonates is in dental resin-based coatings. These coatings can be used to protect the tooth surface and to prevent the recurrence of caries. Indeed, ortho carbonates containing coatings, have excellent mechanical properties, adhesion, and antibacterial properties, making them a promising option for this application.

Additionally, spiro-ortho carbonates can be used in the development of dental cements. These cements can be used in various applications, such as luting or bonding restorations. Spiro-ortho carbonates containing cements have good mechanical properties and biocompatibility, making them a promising option for this application.

To sum up, spiro-ortho carbonates expanding monomers have significant potential for use in dental applications. These monomers have the ability to expand during polymerization, which can aid in dental restoration sealing, thus reducing the risk of marginal leakage. They also possess the potential to upgrade the mechanical properties of dental restorations and to prevent biofilm formation. More studies are called for to explore the potential of these monomers and to optimize their use in clinical settings.

8.1.2 SILORANES

Traditional methacrylate-based composites have certain limitations that can affect their clinical performance. To overcome these limitations, silorane-based composites were developed as an alternative resin matrix material. Herein, we provide an overview of silorane used in dentistry, including its properties, advantages, clinical applications, and limitations.

8.1.2.1 Advantages

Silorane-based composites have a unique chemical structure consisting of a siloxane backbone and an oxirane ring. This unique structure gives them several advantages over methacrylate-based composites. Indeed, they have lower polymerization shrinkage, which reduces the risk of marginal gaps and secondary caries [6,7]. Silorane-based composites have also shown improved mechanical properties, such as flexural strength and modulus, which enhances their durability and resistance to fracture [8,9]. They also have higher wear resistance and lower susceptibility to staining, which improves their esthetic performance and longevity [10,11]. Furthermore, silorane-based composites exhibit excellent bonding properties to tooth structure, which allows for conservative cavity preparations and minimal removal of healthy tooth structure [12].

8.1.2.2 Applications

Silorane-based composite resins are mainly used in dentistry to restore posterior teeth. They are particularly useful in large restorations where the risk of polymerization shrinkage and stress is higher [13,14]. Silorane-based composites have shown promising clinical outcomes in terms of longevity, marginal adaptation, and color stability [15]. They are also used in esthetic restorations of anterior teeth, although methacrylate-based composites are still preferred for this indication due to their higher translucency and color-matching properties.

8.1.2.3 Limitations

Silorane-based composites have some limitations that need to be considered. They have longer curing time compared to methacrylate-based composites, which may increase the risk of contamination and patients' discomfort. Silorane-based composites are also more technique-sensitive and require careful handling and placement to achieve optimal results. Furthermore, silorane-based composites are not compatible with all bonding systems and may require specific adhesive protocols [6,14].

Silorane-based composites constitute a promising alternative to traditional methacrylate-based composites in restorative dentistry. They offer several advantages, such as lower polymerization shrinkage, higher mechanical properties, and improved wear resistance and esthetic performance. Silorane-based composites are mainly used in posterior teeth for large restorations, where their unique properties can help reduce the risk of marginal gaps and secondary caries. Although silorane-based composites have shown promising clinical outcomes, they also have some limitations, such as longer curing times, greater technique sensitivity, and specific adhesive requirements.

8.1.3 ANTIMICROBIAL POLYMERIC COMPOSITES

Dental caries, or better said tooth decay, is a global health issue. The conventional approach of treating dental caries involves removing decayed tooth structure and substituting it using dental restorative materials. However, dental restorations are not immune to bacterial colonization and subsequent infection. The use of antimicrobial polymeric composites has been proposed as a potential solution to prevent bacterial colonization and to improve the longevity of dental restorations.

Antimicrobial polymeric composites for dental restorations have been developed thanks to recent advances in material science. These composites are designed to have antibacterial properties and promote remineralization, in addition to maintaining the mechanical strength and durability required for dental restorations.

One of the primary antimicrobial agents used in these composites is chlorhexidine. Boaro et al. [16] developed an antibacterial resin-based composite that contains chlorhexidine to be used in dental applications. In their study, they demonstrated that this composite exhibits potent antibacterial activity against oral pathogens, indicating its potential as an effective material for dental restorations.

In addition to chlorhexidine, other antimicrobial agents, including quaternary ammonium compounds and silver nanoparticles have also been incorporated into polymeric composites for dental restorations. Cheng et al. [15] described the emergence of a new generation of bioactive and antimicrobial dental resins containing silver nanoparticles and quaternary ammonium salts. The study demonstrated that adding these antimicrobial agents improves the antibacterial efficacy of the composite and promotes remineralization of tooth structure.

Another approach was developed to improve dental restoration longevity. It involves the development of bioactive dental composites that promote remineralization of tooth structure. Zhang et al. [17] developed bonding agents and bioactive dental composites possessing antibacterial and remineralization properties. These composites were found to release calcium and phosphate ions, thus promoting remineralization of the tooth structure and improving dental restoration longevity.

Incorporating antimicrobial agents and bioactive compounds into dental restorative materials has revolutionized the field of dentistry. Weng et al. developed a new antibacterial resin composite to improve dental restorations [18]. The composite was found to possess excellent mechanical properties and potent antibacterial activity, making it a promising material for use in dental restorations.

In conclusion, the development of antimicrobial polymeric composites has the potential to revolutionize the field of dental restorations. These composites offer a promising solution to prevent bacterial colonization and promote remineralization, in addition to maintaining the mechanical strength and durability required for dental restorations. With the ongoing advances in material science, the future of dental restorations looks bright [19].

8.1.4 COMPOSITE WITH REMINERALIZATION AGENTS

One of the main issues facing composite restorations is the development of secondary caries, representing the leading cause of restoration failure. To overcome these limitations, recent research has focused on developing composites that restore the tooth and promote its remineralization.

One of the most studied remineralization agents is calcium phosphate nanoparticles (NaCP). These particles are small enough to penetrate into the enamel and dentin, where they release calcium and phosphate ions to promote remineralization. Xu et al. studied the input of nanocomposites containing calcium phosphate and found that the inclusion of CaP nanoparticles to the composite seriously increases its remineralization ability. This is because CaP particles can interact with the tooth structure to form a strong bond, allowing for better integration of the restoration with the surrounding tooth structure [20].

In another study, Xu et al. demonstrated the ability of nanocomposites containing remineralization agents to release fluoride (F), phosphate (PO4), and calcium (Ca) ions to inhibit dental caries. Nanocomposites are prepared using a combination of calcium silicate and resin matrix, with the addition of nanoparticles containing Ca, PO4, and F. The resulting nanocomposites exhibit excellent mechanical properties, as well as prolonged release of F, PO4, and Ca ions over an extended period [21]. In vitro studies showed that nanocomposites are able to repress the multiplication of cariogenic bacteria and to promote the remineralization of tooth enamel. These findings have shown that nanocomposites have huge potential for use in dental restorations and other applications, as well as in the prevention and treatment of dental caries [21].

Similarly, Ke Zhang et al. studied quaternary ammonium compounds and reported that these have antimicrobial properties that prevent the growth of bacteria around the restoration margins. They conducted experiments to examine how altering the length of the quaternary ammonium chain impacts the antibacterial and remineralization properties of calcium phosphate nanocomposites. Their findings revealed a noteworthy improvement in the composite's remineralization capacity with the elongation of the quaternary ammonium chain. This enhancement is attributed to the extended chains of quaternary ammonium, which can penetrate deeper into the tooth structure, resulting in more effective antimicrobial and remineralization effects. This is because longer chains of quaternary ammonium can penetrate deeper into the tooth structure, providing better antimicrobial and remineralization effects [22].

In addition to NaCP and quaternary ammonium, other remineralization agents have been investigated for their potential to enhance the remineralization ability of dental composites. Casein phosphopeptides and amorphous calcium phosphate complex (CPP-ACP) and CSP improve the remineralization ability of dental composites. CPP-ACP can help to stabilize calcium and phosphate ions, thus promoting their deposition onto the tooth surface. Zhou et al. studied the effect of CPP-ACP and CSP on artificial carious lesions, and found that both agents significantly increase the enamel surface microhardness. This finding indicates that these agents have the potential to remineralize early carious lesions and prevent the progression of caries [23].

Fluoride-releasing dental materials have also been extensively studied for their potential to prevent secondary caries. Fluoride ions can promote remineralization and inhibit the growth of bacteria, making these ions effective in preventing secondary caries. In the study of Chaudhary and al. assessing the clinical effectiveness of fluoride-releasing dental materials on caries control, they found that fluoride-releasing materials decrease the possibility of secondary caries and improve the endurance of composite restorations [24]. Cury et al. also investigated the goods of fluoride-releasing dental materials on caries control, and concluded that these materials are effective in preventing caries recurrence and enhancing the longevity of restorations [25].

In conclusion, adding remineralization agents to composite materials has shown promising results in preventing secondary caries and enhancing the longevity of restorations. Further research is required to optimize the composition and properties of these materials and evaluate their long-term clinical effectiveness. The use of remineralization agents can provide a promising solution to secondary caries and therefore improve the overall success rate of composite restorations.

8.1.5 SELF-HEALING COMPOSITES

Recent research has also focused on developing self-healing antimicrobial dental composites that can repair small cracks and defects within the restoration. Self-healing composites have gained great interest in the field of biomaterials thanks to their ability to autonomously repair damage. This innovation is inspired by the biological systems that can self-repair after injury. In recent years, self-healing composites have received significant attention in the field of dentistry as a promising solution to improve both the durability and longevity of restorative dental materials [26].

Under occlusal load, dental composites are susceptible to wear and degradation over time, leading to the need for replacement. Self-healing composites have the potential to address this issue by autonomously repairing the damage caused by wear, fatigue, and occlusal trauma.

Self-healing composites can be split into three main categories, namely capsule-based healing systems, vascular healing systems, and intrinsically healed systems. Each type utilizes a specific mechanism for repairing cracks and therefore has a different healing ability, leading to alterations in the survival rate of restorations under different circumstances [27].

Capsule-based self-healing systems trigger the healing process by unleashing the healing agents included inside individual capsules. Whenever the material is exposed to damage, the capsules are broken off and the healing agents contained within are released at the damage site to initiate the repair process.

To develop such a system, a design cycle consisting of five steps is followed. First, the healing agent is sequestered inside a capsule through a process known as encapsulation or phase separation to prevent its reaction without causing damage. Then, these capsules and the healing agents included inside are embedded into the composite material to assess its mechanical properties. After that, the system is tested for its triggering and healing abilities using mechanical trials, and optical, infrared, or scanning electron microscopy [25].

To understand the healing process, the example of epoxy composite materials, containing resin-filled microcapsules, can be studied. When sustaining damage, the capsules included inside the epoxy resin release the resin that would fill the gap resulting from the propagation of the crack. A later reaction with Grubbs catalyst would catalyze the healing resin polymerization and induce the repair of the void. This system is embedded in various composite materials, including fiber-reinforced composites. Other capsule-based formulations have been developed, such as phase-separation where the healing component is phase-separated inside the matrix rather than engulfed within a capsule, and multicapsulation where both the polymerizer and the healing resin are included within the same capsule [26,27]

Besides, vascular self-healing systems contain the healing component in capillary-like tubular structures. These systems function in the same way as capsule-based systems. Indeed, they sequester the healing material until its release is triggered by a crack. However, vascular self-healing systems differ from capsule-based systems in both the way they are processed and the way they store the healing material, i.e., they are tested in the same way for their healing ability and triggering mechanisms.

To hold the healing agent, vascular systems use network structures. Such structures are built using capillaries (hollow glass fiber tubes, channels, etc.) intertwined together to form complex "network" structures and the healing agent can be transferred through this network [28].

As their name suggests, intrinsic self-healing materials do not rely on discrete healing structures, like capsules or networks. These systems can repair themselves based on the physical properties of the composite, such as the inherent reversibility of the matrix polymer bonding.

Other mechanisms used by this type of material include thermally reversible reactions, hydrogen bonding, ionomeric coupling, molecular diffusion, or dispersed meltable thermoplastic phase. Designing these types of materials is rather simpler than the previous ones as no separate agents are required to perform the healing process. The matrix of the material should be more homogenous to eliminate compatibility issues with regard to the healing agents and their carrier structures [29]. The healing process within these materials can occur through different mechanisms, such as

- dispersed thermoplastic polymers where meltable additives carry out healing through the redispersion process.

- ionomeric self-healing, in which healing takes place via ionic segments acting as reversible cross-links that can be triggered by UV irradiation.

Clinical significance: Self-healing composites have shown promising results in dentistry. One approach to developing self-healing composites for dental applications is to incorporate microcapsules filled with a healing agent, such as resin monomer or antibacterial agent. When damage takes place, the microcapsules break open, releasing the healing agent into the affected region to initiate the repair process [29].

The use of graphene oxide is another recent development in self-healing composites. Graphene oxide has been shown to boost the mechanical properties and the self-healing ability of dental composites. Additionally, it can be functionalized with antibacterial agents, making it a promising material in the development of self-healing dental composites with antibacterial properties [29].

Furthermore, self-healing composites could be used to develop antibacterial dental materials that prevent the multiplication of bacteria and therefore minimize the risk of secondary caries. This holds special significance, especially in composite restorations, which exhibit a higher susceptibility to bacterial growth when compared to other restorative materials [30].

To conclude, Self-healing composites have emerged as a promising solution to enhance the durability and longevity of dental restorations. Recent advances in self-healing composites have shown promising results for their use in dentistry, particularly in developing restorative dental materials with self-healing and antibacterial properties. The use of self-healing composites could lead to a significant progress in the field of dentistry, thus improving the overall quality and lifespan of dental restorations. Further research is required to optimize the properties of self-healing composites in dental applications and to assess their long-term performance in vivo [31].

8.1.6   SMART COMPOSITE

8.1.6.1   Presentation and Benefits

Smart composites represent a category of composite materials with the ability to react to various external triggers, including changes in temperature, pH levels, exposure to light, or mechanical stress. These composites are engineered to release therapeutic substances, like antimicrobial agents or fluoride, in reaction to these stimuli. Additionally, they possess self-healing properties, effectively guarding against recurring caries and post-operative sensitivity. [32,33].

In recent developments within the field of intelligent dental composites, significant efforts have been dedicated to enhancing their antimicrobial attributes, maintaining dimensional stability, and fortifying their mechanical characteristics. Scientists have investigated the application of diverse antimicrobial substances, including quaternary ammonium compounds (QACs), to enhance the antibacterial qualities of smart composites. QACs have demonstrated their efficacy in combating a wide range of oral pathogens, including Streptococcus mutans, the primary culprit behind dental caries [34].

Lavanya et al. [32] explored the utilization of different fillers, such as silica nanoparticles, to enhance the dimensional stability of intelligent composites. Some research has indicated that temperature-induced expansion and contraction in dental composites may result in microleakage, potentially contributing to secondary caries.

The mechanical characteristics, encompassing strength and wear resistance, stand as pivotal factors influencing the overall performance of dental composites. Recent advancements in smart composite technology have concentrated on augmenting these attributes by integrating a range of fillers, including zirconia, within the composite matrix [34].

8.1.6.2 Applications

Smart dental composites hold promise across diverse applications within restorative dentistry. Their versatility extends to the repair of dental caries, as well as the prevention of subsequent caries development. The antimicrobial attributes inherent to smart composites render them especially valuable when addressing cavity restoration in individuals at elevated risk, such as those with a history of dental caries.

According to Maloo et al. [35], these composites find applications in dental restoration, orthodontics, and oral health monitoring. They can be employed to fabricate fillings or crowns capable of sensing alterations in the adjacent tooth structure and adapting to them. This proactive feature can serve to forestall additional damage to the tooth and enhance the overall durability of the restoration. Moreover, they offer a promising option for restoring primary teeth, with recent research demonstrating their effectiveness in preventing microleakage and presenting a feasible alternative to conventional composite restorations [36].

Finally, smart composites serve a role in monitoring oral health. Their capacity to detect shifts in oral pH levels provides a valuable indicator of potentially harmful bacterial presence. This capability can be harnessed to create individualized oral hygiene strategies and proactively mitigate the onset of dental ailments [37].

To sum up, smart dental composites are at the forefront of restorative dentistry's future. Recent strides in smart composite technology have bolstered their responsiveness to external triggers, enhanced their antimicrobial features, reinforced dimensional stability, improved mechanical properties, and bolstered their self-repair capabilities. These composites hold a wide spectrum of potential applications within restorative dentistry, encompassing the repair and prevention of dental caries, including the restoration of primary teeth. As smart composite technology continues its evolution, it is likely that smart dental composites will increasingly gain favor as a compelling choice for restorative dentistry. Nevertheless, long-term studies are still essential to confirm their enduring efficacy.

8.1.7 BULK-FILL COMPOSITE

The field of restorative dentistry has been transformed by the introduction of bulk-fill composite materials. This type of composite allows a faster and more straightforward placement method, thus eliminating the time-consuming incremental layering by allowing the placement in increments of 4 mm or more [38].

8.1.7.1 Composition

Bulk-fill composite seems not to differ greatly from regular nanohybrid and microhybrid composites with regard to the chemical composition. The primary component is the resin matrix, which is composed of dimethacrylate monomers, namely Bis-GMA, UDMA, and TEGDMA [39]. These monomers have a distinct molecular weight and chemical structure that can impact the overall properties of the composite.

Additionally to the resin matrix, filler particles are also added to enhance the mechanical properties of the composite [40]. The size, shape, and composition of these particles can affect the strength and wear resistance of the composite [41].

Glass or ceramic fillers are commonly used in bulk-fill composites to increase their radiopacity.

Additionally, photoinitiators, such as Camphorquinone (CQ) are added to initiate the polymerization reaction. Alternative initiators, like Ivocerin, have been developed to reduce the potential for color change and to polymerize the material in depth [42].

8.1.7.2 Presentation

The first generation of bulk-fill composite resins was introduced in flowable form and only used as dentin substitute. Indeed, the flowable composite resins have good adaptation on the cavity walls; however, they show great polymerization shrinkage and low mechanical properties. It is therefore recommended to apply a 2-mm capping layer of conventional resin composite when restoring areas subject to occlusal stress to ensure the longevity and durability of the restoration [43].

Currently, bulk-fill composites are available in body form, and the entire restoration can be constructed using a bulk-filling technique. These materials have different shades and are available from various manufacturers.

8.1.7.3 Clinical Performance

Bulk-fill composites can be used to restore posterior teeth having large cavities as they can be placed in a block, thus eliminating the need for layering and minimizing the risk of gaps and voids. The improved depth of cure makes it a suitable material for even deep Class I cavities [44]. Additionally, the improved handling properties of the material make it an ideal alternative for non-carious cervical lesions [45]. Bulk-fill composite is also a less invasive alternative to stainless steel crowns for pediatric patients [46]. It can also be used in combination with fiber reinforced composite for the restoration of endodontically treated teeth, reinforcing weakened tooth structure [47]. Finally, bulk-fill composite can be used as base material in the restoration of teeth with large defects, providing a strong foundation for the final restoration [48].

8.1.7.4 Limitations and Consideration

It is worth noting that bulk-fill composites have some limitations that should be kept in mind. Recent studies have demonstrated that there is negligible disparity in polymerization shrinkage between bull-fill composites and conventional filled-in layers technique.

The compressive and tensile strengths of flowable and paste-like bulk-fill composite are lower than those of conventional composite, which may result in a higher risk of fracture or failure. Additionally, due to the limited light penetration, polymerization of deep cavities may be difficult; thus, more attention and care are needed during the application process.

Additional extended-term investigations are necessary to evaluate the long-lasting durability and performance of bulk-fill composites. At last, It has been recently shown that the advantage of using bulk-fill composite primarily pertains to ergonomic benefits and time savings [38,46].

8.1.8 SONICATED BULK-FILL COMPOSITES

In recent years, dental composites have undergone considerable advances in terms of material properties and clinical performance. One such advance is the use of sonicated bulk-fill composites. These involve applying a certain sonic power to the filling composite mass when placed in the cavity, thereby improving the material's flowability without compromising the resin/filling material ratio. This innovation represents the latest generation of bulk-filled composites [38].

8.1.8.1 Composition

Similar to traditional dental composites, sonicated bulk-fill composites typically contain a resin matrix, inorganic fillers, and photoinitiators. However, the formulation of sonicated bulk-fill composites is optimized to allow deeper light penetration and more efficient polymerization, thereby reducing the risk of inadequate curing. The addition of nanofillers and pre-polymerized resin fillers in sonicated bulk-fill composites can further enhance their mechanical properties and clinical performance [49].

8.1.8.2 The Benefits of Sonic Activation

1. Enhanced mechanical characteristics: One of the primary advantages of employing sonic activation in bulk-fill composite restorations lies in the enhancement of mechanical properties. Research has indicated that sonic activation has the potential to elevate the flexural strength and elastic modulus of the composite resin, ultimately resulting in heightened durability against wear and fractures [50].
2. Enhanced polymerization depth: Another benefit of sonic activation is its ability to improve the polymerization depth of bulk-fill composite resins. This is due to the ultrasonic energy that helps to reduce oxygen inhibition and increase the conversion rate of resin [51].
3. Reduced restoration failure rates: With improved mechanical properties, polymerization depth, and by minimizing the presence of gaps between layers, it has been demonstrated that bulk-fill composite restorations incorporating sonic activation exhibit lower rates of failure when compared to conventional bulk-fill methods [52].
4. Reduced post-operative sensitivity: Sonic activation has also been shown to reduce post-operative sensitivity in patients receiving bulk-fill

composite restorations. This is likely due to the improved mechanical properties and polymerization depth, that can help to reduce microleakage and bacterial infiltration [53].

5. Increased efficiency: Sonic activation can also lead to increased efficiency in dental practice as it can reduce the time required for restoration placement and decrease the need for costly reinterventions.

8.1.8.3 Limitations and Considerations

Recent clinical investigations have demonstrated the beneficial utilization of sonicated bulk-fill composites in various clinical situations, with good clinical outcomes and patients' satisfaction. However, some potential negative effects should be considered.

This class of bulk-fill requests special instruments and has a negative effect on the mechanical properties in the first phase of resin gelation, given the sonic power of the "vibration" [54].

Some studies have found that the use of sonic activation can result in reduced bond strength between composite restorations and the dentin. This may be due to the increased heat and pressure generated by the ultrasound waves, which can cause damage to the dentin and compromise the bonding interface.

Sonicated bulk-fill composites represent an important advance in modern dentistry, offering improved handling characteristics, reduced polymerization shrinkage, and good clinical performance. Overall, while the use of sonic activation can offer many benefits for bulk-fill composite restorations, it is important for dental practitioners to carefully consider its potential negative effects. Indeed, these negative effects should be evaluated before incorporating this technique into practice as the limited long-term clinical data on bulk-fill composites, reported in many published studies, have shorter follow-up periods [55].

8.1.9 Self-adhesive Composites

Self-adhesive dental composites are gaining popularity in the field of restorative dentistry because of their esthetic appeal and strong adhesive properties. While traditional composites require multiple steps for bonding, such as etching, priming, and adhesion promoters, the use of self-adhesive composites simplifies the process as the need for a separate adhesive system is eliminated. These composites directly attach to the tooth structure, making them a convenient option for dental procedures. Herein, the properties and applications of self-adhesive composites are investigated in depth [56].

8.1.9.1 Properties

Self-adhesive composites have unique characteristics that differentiate them from ordinary composites. Their application process is simplified and they can be directly bonded to tooth structure without the need for a separate adhesive system. Self-adhesive composites and traditional composites have comparable bonding strength to the enamel and dentin [56]. Using self-adhesive composites is associated with a lower risk of post-operative hypersensitivity as they are less likely to penetrate dentinal tubules However, reduced penetration may also minimize the adhesive strength to the dentin [57].

8.1.9.2   Applications

Self-adhesive composites are versatile materials that can be utilized in various clinical scenarios, including direct restorations, core build-ups, and luting cement for indirect restorations. They can be particularly helpful in cases where moisture control is challenging, such as in pediatric dentistry or when treating patients with limited mouth opening. Additionally, they can serve as liners for deep cavities, bases for composite restorations, or even temporary restorations [58,59].

8.1.9.3   Bond Strength

Numerous investigations have explored the bonding capabilities of self-adhesive composites to both dentin and enamel. In a study by Van Meerbeek and colleagues [59], it was demonstrated that self-adhesive composites exhibit bond strength levels similar to those of traditional composites when applied to enamel and dentin. Similarly, Poitevin et al. [60] reported bond strength values that are comparable between self-adhesive composites and their traditional counterparts. Nevertheless, various factors, including moisture control, preparation techniques, aging, and the presence of a smear layer, may influence the bonding strength of self-adhesive composites to dentin [60,61]

8.1.9.4   Mechanical Properties

It has been demonstrated that self-adhesive composite cements possess mechanical properties that are equal to or even better than traditional resin cements. In the studies of Temel et al. [62], they proved that self-adhesive composite cements have greater flexural strength and less water sorption compared to traditional resin cements. Furthermore, Yu et al. reported that self-adhesive composite cements have higher fracture toughness compared to traditional resin cements [63].

8.1.9.5   Clinical Performance

Numerous clinical investigations have examined the effectiveness of self-adhesive composite cements. Weiser and Behr reported a high clinical success rate for self-adhesive composite cements used in the cementation of indirect restorations (11 cements used for the cementation of indirect restorations) [64].

8.1.9.6   Surface Preparation

Effective surface preparation plays a crucial role in influencing the bonding capabilities of self-adhesive composite resins. Various surface conditioning methods, including air abrasion, acid etching, and laser treatment, have been explored to enhance the bonding strength of these materials. It's worth noting that the ideal surface preparation protocols may vary depending on the specific type of self-adhesive composite resin and the tooth substrate under consideration [65].

Self-adhesive composites have brought a revolutionary change to the field of adhesive dentistry by simplifying the bonding process while maintaining the bond strength. These composites are an efficient and reliable alternative to traditional bonding systems. Indeed, self-adhesive composites are a game-changer in adhesive dentistry. However, more studies are necessary to optimize their clinical perform-ance and to understand their properties in depth.

8.1.10 Short Fiber Reinforced Composites

Short fiber reinforced composites (SFRCs) are a class of composite materials used in a variety of applications, including dentistry. SFRCs are composed of short fibers embedded in a matrix material, such as resin or polymer. The fibers provide strength as well as stiffness to the composite while the matrix material provides flexibility and toughness. In dentistry, SFRCs are used to perform dental restorations, such as crowns, bridges, and veneers. Compared to other types of composites, SFRCs offer several advantages.

Fiber-reinforced composite materials made of glass are the most common type of fibers used in dentistry [66] because this type of material has the ability to adhere to the resin matrix.

Glass fibers are also characterized by their transparency and optical properties due to the orientation of the fibers within the matrix, a factor to be considered when dealing with esthetic restorations [1]. Being transparent in the core with a low refraction index enables the fibers to transmit light along its length. This attribute also helps in curing the luting materials around the fiber posts [67].

With regard to restoring endodontically treated teeth, studies have shown that using SFRCs as a bulk base for core build-up enhances fracture resistance [68]. Studies also reported that placing SFRCs as a core material results in restorations showing very similar mechanical properties to those of intact teeth and superior to those of conventional composites alone [69]

In their case-series study published in 2018, Tanner et al. [70]. reported an overall survival rate of 97.2% for short fiber-reinforced composite restorations of posterior teeth with a 5-year follow-up period.

Polymerization shrinkage is one of the main reasons for conventional composite restoration failure. It can lead to the formation of gaps at the interface between the restoration material and the dental tissue, resulting in poor marginal fit or even recurrent caries.

Studies, including papers published by Tsujimoto et al. [71] and Tezvergil et al. [72] have shown that incorporation of fibers inside the matrix can lead to a decrease in shinkage stress.

In another study [73], Garoushi reported that the amount of shrinkage is strongly dependent on the orientation of the fibers. For this reason, shrinkage occurs mainly in the matrix space between individual fibers, and fibers do not shrink horizontally, suggesting that the low shrinkage ratio of fiber-reinforced restorations is due to the fact that the fibers close to the margin are directed towards that margin.

In the same study, Tsujimoto et al. also reported that SFRCs show higher fracture toughness compared to other composites, with a statistically significant difference [71].

This is because the occlusal load is distributed on multiple small structures rather than on the composite material, suggesting that fibers can mitigate the propagation of cracks due to their multidirectional architecture. Indeed, cracks can only travel short distances within the fibers.

Tsujimoto also reported that SFRCs have improved bond durability compared to conventional composites. Indeed, parameters like shear bond strength are generally higher [71].

Advances in fiber-reinforced composites have integrated the "biomimetic principles" in cavity restoration involving the restorative protocols that focus on being as minimally invasive as possible, and taking the properties of natural tooth structure as a guide for the selection of adequate materials, in a way that they "mimic" the tissue they are restoring [74]. Since different dental tissues have different properties, the biomimetic restorative protocols use different materials to match the mechanical properties of each type of tissue they are replacing.

SFRCs have been indicated as materials to replace dentine or a bulk base thanks to their mechanical properties that closely match the natural dentine. These materials are favorable in high-stress-bearing zones. This enhancement in mechanical properties has been proven in in vivo as well as in vitro studies [73,74].

According to Bijelic-Donova et al., the mechanical properties of fiber composites are significantly influenced by the material's structural aspects, including dimensions like length, diameter, and orientation [75].

Various research findings have showcased the superior mechanical properties of SFRCs in comparison to traditional composites. These investigations have encompassed parameters such as fracture toughness and fatigue limit. Furthermore, some studies have assessed flexural strength and concluded that SFRCs outperform both conventional and bulk-fill composites in this regard [75].

In short, SFRCs provide the clinician with interesting mechanical and physical properties that address and solve many shortcomings in conventional composite materials. Bonding performance, shear strength, flexural strength, marginal fit, light transmission, and shrinkage stress are among the key advantages when using SFRCs in the restoration procedure. This so-called biomimetic approach should be correctly carried out in order to boost the restoration performance.

8.1.11 FUTURE SCOPE

The advances described above in the new generations of composite resins open the door to future prospects for adhesive restorations as follows:

- reduced polymerization shrinkage and prevention of post-operative sensitivity
- the advent of injectable resin
- prevention of microcracking within restorations
- improved mechanical properties and longevity of composite resins
- prevention of caries recurrence thanks to bio-active composites and remineralizing agents contained in their formula
- simplified operating protocol

New research is opting for products that are more tolerant of moisture in the oral cavity, so can we succeed in finding a hydrophilic composite?

8.2 CONCLUSION

Dental composites have witnessed significant advancements since their debut in the 1960s. Presently, the latest generations of composites provide superior esthetics, strength, and longevity compared to their predecessors. Ongoing developments in dental composite technology have continued to enhance their performance, rendering them an appealing choice for restorative dentistry. Indeed, they have been made to minimize polymerization shrinkage, reduce the risk of post-operative sensitivity, increase mechanical strength, improve the durability of bonding interfaces, and prevent recurrent caries. Advanced low-shrink composites with expanding monomers, such as siloranes and spiro-ortho carbonates monomers have shown interesting outcomes in vitro and in vivo. Smart composites with bioactive properties and antimicrobial agents, self-healing composites, self-adhesive composites, and composites reinforced by short fiber have also shown promising clinical results. However, long-term outcomes still have to be investigated.

REFERENCES

1. Wang Z, Zhang X, Yao S, Zhao J, Zhou C, Wu J. Development of low-shrinkage dental adhesives via blending with spiroorthocarbonate expanding monomer and unsaturated epoxy resin monomer. J Mech Behav Biomed Mater. 2022 Sep;133:105308. doi: 10.1016/j.jmbbm.2022.105308. Epub 2022 Jun 9. PMID: 35709601.
2. Kostoryz EL, Tong PY, Chappelow CC, Glaros AG, Eick JD, Yourtee DM. In vitro toxicity of spiroorthocarbonate monomers designed for non-shrinking dental restoratives. J Biomater Sci Polym Ed. 2000;11(2):187–196. doi: 10.1163/156856200743 643. PMID: 10718478.
3. Marx P, Wiesbrock F. Expanding monomers as anti-shrinkage additives. Polymers (Basel). 2021 Mar 6;13(5):806. doi: 10.3390/polym13050806. PMID: 33800726; PMCID: PMC7961351.
4. Duarte María, Reyna Medina Luis, Reyes, Patricia, González, Sandra, Herrera-González, Ana María. Dental restorative composites containing methacrylic spiroorthocarbonate monomers as antishrinking matrixes. J Appl Polym Sci. 2018;136. 10.1002/app.47114.
5. Acosta Ortiz R, Reyna Medina LA, Berlanga Duarte ML, Ibarra Samaniego L, Garcia Valdez AE, García Mendez ZL, Mendez Gonzalez L. Synthesis of glycerol-derived diallyl spiroorthocarbonates and the study of their antishrinking properties in acrylic dental resins. J Mater Sci Mater Med. 2013 Aug;24(8):2077–2084. doi: 10.1007/s1 0856-013-4959-5. Epub 2013 May 28. PMID: 23712536.
6. Larson TD. Low shrinkage silorane composites. Northwest Dent. 2017 Jan;96(1):15–16. PMID: 30549745.
7. Maru VP, Kulkarni P, Chauhan R, Bapat SS. Evaluation and comparison of silorane resin composite to glass ionomer in occluso-proximal restorations of primary molars: A randomized controlled trial. J Indian Soc Pedod Prev Dent. 2022 Jul-Sep;40(3):281–287. doi: 10.4103/jisppd.jisppd_377_22. PMID: 36260469.
8. Zanatta RF, Torres CR, de Oliveira JB, Yui KC, Matuda AG, Lopes SR, Mafetano AP, Campos RP, Borges AB, Pucci CR. Minimal intervention in dentistry: which is the best approach for silorane composite restoration repairs? J Clin Exp Dent. 2021 Apr 1;13(4):e357–e362. doi: 10.4317/jced.57640. PMID: 33841734; PMCID: PMC8020319.

9. Sharifi M, Khoramian Tusi S. Comparison of microtensile bond strength of silorane-based composite with the conventional methacrylate composite to the dentin of primary teeth. J Dent Biomater. 2016 Dec;3(4):315–321. PMID: 28959759; PMCID: PMC5608044.

10. Liu C, Pan J, Lin H, Shen S. Aging of silorane- and methacrylate-based composite resins: Effects on color and translucency. Zhonghua Kou Qiang Yi Xue Za Zhi. 2015;Oct;50(10):636–639. Chinese. PMID: 26757637.

11. Abed Kahnamouei M, Gholizadeh S, Rikhtegaran S, Daneshpooy M, Kimyai S, Alizadeh Oskoee P, Rezaei Y. Effect of preheat repetition on color stability of methacrylate- and silorane-based composite resins. J Dent Res Dent Clin Dent Prospects. 2017 Fall;11(4):222–228. doi: 10.15171/joddd.2017.039. Epub 2017 Dec 13. PMID: 29354248; PMCID: PMC5768954.

12. Maghaireh GA, Taha NA, Alzraikat H. The silorane-based resin composites: A review. Oper Dent. 2017 Jan/Feb;42(1):E24–E34. doi: 10.2341/15-311-LIT. PMID: 28002691.

13. Marques IP, de Oliveira FBS, Souza JGS, Ferreira RC, Magalhães CS, França FMG, Popoff DAV. Influence of surface treatment on the performance of silorane-based composite resin in class I restorations: A randomized clinical trial. Clin Oral Investig. 2018 Dec;22(9):2989–2996. doi: 10.1007/s00784-018-2390-5. Epub 2018 Feb 16. PMID: 29453496.

14. Bastos LA, Sousa AB, Drubi-Filho B, Panzeri Pires-de-Souza Fde C, Garcia Lda F Microtensile bond strength of silorane-based composite specific adhesive system using different bonding strategies. Restor Dent Endod. 2015 Feb;40(1):23–29. doi: 10.5395/rde.2015.40.1.23. Epub 2014 Aug 25. PMID: 25671209; PMCID: PMC4320273.

15. Cheng L, Zhang K, Zhang N, Melo MAS, Weir MD, Zhou XD, Bai YX, Reynolds MA, Xu HHK Developing a new generation of antimicrobial and bioactive dental resins. J Dent Res. 2017 Jul;96(8):855–863. doi: 10.1177/0022034517709739. Epub 2017 May 22. PMID: 28530844; PMCID: PMC5502962

16. Boaro LCC, Campos LM, Varca GHC, Dos Santos TMR, Marques PA, Sugii MM, Saldanha NR, Cogo-Müller K, Brandt WC, Braga RR, Parra DF. Antibacterial resin-based composite containing chlorhexidine for dental applications. Dent Mater. 2019 Jun;35(6):909–918. doi: 10.1016/j.dental.2019.03.004. Epub 2019 Apr 5. PMID: 30955856.

17. Zhang K, Zhang N, Weir MD, Reynolds MA, Bai Y, Xu HHK. Bioactive dental composites and bonding agents having remineralizing and antibacterial characteristics. Dent Clin North Am. 2017 Oct;61(4):669–687. doi: 10.1016/j.cden.2017.05.002. PMID: 28886763; PMCID: PMC5803788

18. Weng Y, Howard L, Guo X, Chong VJ, Gregory RL, Xie D. A novel antibacterial resin composite for improved dental restoratives. J Mater Sci Mater Med. 2012 Jun;23(6):1553–1561. doi: 10.1007/s10856-012-4629-z. Epub 2012 Apr 1. PMID: 22466818.

19. Xue J, Wang J, Feng D, Huang H, Wang M. Application of antimicrobial polymers in the development of dental resin composite. Molecules. 2020 Oct 15;25(20):4738. doi: 10.3390/molecules25204738. PMID: 33076515; PMCID: PMC7587579.

20. Xu HHK, Weir MD, Sun L, Takagi S, Chow LC. Effects of calcium phosphate nanoparticles on Ca-PO4 composite. J Dent Res. 2007 Apr; 86(4):378–383.

21. Xu HHK, Weir MD, Sun L, Moreau JL, Takagi S, Chow LC, Antonucci JM. Strong nanocomposites with Ca, PO(4) and F release for caries inhibition. J Dent Res. 2010 Jan;89(1):19–28.

22. Zhang K, Cheng L, Weir MD, Bai YX, Xu HHK. Effects of quaternary ammonium chain length on the antibacterial and remineralizing effects of a calcium phosphate nanocomposite. Int J Oral Sci. 2016;8: 45–53.

23. Zhou W, Peng X, Zhou X, Bonavente A, Weir MD, Melo MA, Imazato S, Oates TW, Cheng L, Xu HHK. Novel nanocomposite inhibiting caries at the enamel restoration margins in an in vitro saliva-derived biofilm secondary caries model. Int J Mol Sci. 2020 Sep; 21(17):6369.

24. Chaudhary I, Tripathi AM, Yadav G, Saha S. Effect of casein phosphopeptide–amorphous calcium phosphate and calcium sodium phosphosilicate on artificial carious lesions: An in vitro study. Int J Clin Pediatr Dent. 2017 Jul-Sep;10(3):261–266.

25. Cury JA, De Oliveira BH, Dos Santos APP, Tenuta LMA. Are fluoride releasing dental materials clinically effective on caries control? Dent Mater. 2016 Mar;32(3):323–333.

26. Jandt KD, Sigusch BW. Future perspectives of resin-based dental materials. Dent Mater, 25(8), 1001–1006. doi:10.1016/j.dental.2009.02.009

27. Blaiszik BJ, Kramer SLB, Olugebefola SC, Moore JS, Sottos NR & White SR. Self-healing polymers and composites. Annu Rev Mater Res. 2010;40(1):179–211. doi: 10.1146/annurev-matsci-070909-104532

28. Lee MW, An S, Yoon SS, Yarin AL. Advances in self-healing materials based on vascular networks with mechanical self-repair characteristics. Adv Colloid Interface Sci. 2018 Feb;252:21–37. doi: 10.1016/j.cis.2017.12.010.

29. White SR, Sottos NR, Geubelle PH, Moore JS, Kessler MR, Sriram SR, Viswanathan S. Autonomic healing of polymer composites. Nature. 2001;409(6822):794–797. doi:10.1038/35057232.

30. Hayes SA, Zhang W, Branthwaite M, Jones FR. Self-healing of damage in fibre-reinforced polymer-matrix composites. J R Soc Interface. 2007 Apr 22;4(13):381–387. doi: 10.1098/rsif.2006.0209.

31. Luo X, Ou R, Eberly DE, Singhal A, Viratyaporn W, Mather PT. A thermoplastic/thermoset blend exhibiting thermal mending and reversible adhesion. ACS Appl Mater Interfaces. 2009 Mar;1(3):612–620. doi: 10.1021/am8001605.

32. Lavanya D, Buchi D, Mantena SR, Varma M, Rao B, Vinay Chandrappa. Recent advances in dental composites: An overview. Int J Dent Mater 2019;1(2).

33. Marhawa J, Goyal R, Sharma Y, Mohanta S. Recent advancement in composites – A review. SSRG Int J Med Sci. 2020;7(1):1–3. 10.14445/23939117/IJMS-V7I1P101.

34. Montoya C, Roldan L, Yu M, Valliani S, Ta C, Yang M, Orrego S. Smart dental materials for antimicrobial applications. Bioact Mater. 2022 Dec 9;24:1–19.

35. Maloo LM, Patel A, Toshniwal SH, Bagde AD. Smart materials leading to restorative dentistry: An overview. Cureus. 2022 Oct 28;14(10): e30789. doi: 10.7759/cureus.30789.

36. Montoya C, Roldan L, Yu M, Valliani S, Ta C, Yang M, Orrego S. Dimentional stability and microleakage of SMART dental composites in primary teeth. Bioact Mater. June 2023;(24):1–19.

37. Gupta V. Smart materials in dentistry: A review. International J Adv Res Dev. 2018;3(6):90–96.

38. Sethi K, Arora A, Malhan S, Kataria B. Recent advances in composite restoration: A review. Eur J Mol Clin Med. 2022;9(3):2182–2187.

39. Ilie N, Bucuta S, Draenert M. Bulk-fill resin-based composites: an in vitro assessment of their mechanical performance. Oper Dent. 2013 Nov-Dec;38(6):618–625.

40. Gupta R, Tomer AK, Kumari A, Perle N, Chauhan P and Rana S. Recent advances in bulkfill flowable composite resins: a review. Int J Appl Dental Sci. 2017;3(3):79–81.

41. Kim KH, Ong JL, Okuno O. The effect of filler loading and morphology on the mechanical properties of contemporary composites. J Prosthet Dent. 2002 Jun;87(6):642–649

42. Fugolin APP, Pfeifer CS. New resins for dental composites. J Dent Res. 2017 Sep;96(10):1085–1091.

43. Akarsu S, Aktuğ Karademir S. Influence of bulk-fill composites, polimerization modes, and remaining dentin thickness on intrapulpal temperature rise. Biomed Res Int. 2019 Dec 4;2019:4250284. doi: 10.1155/2019/4250284.eCollection2019.
44. Van Ende A, De Munck J, Van Landuyt KL, Poitevin A, Peumans M, Van Meerbeek B. Bulk-filling of high C-factor posterior cavities: Effect on adhesion to cavity-bottom dentin. Dent Mater. 2013 Mar;29(3):269–277.
45. Canali GD, Ignácio SA, Rached RN, Souza EM. One-year clinical evaluation of bulk-fill flowable vs. regular nanofilled composite in non-carious cervical lesions. Clin Oral Investig. 2019 Feb;23(2):889–897.
46. Gindri LD, Cassol IP, Fröhlich TT, Rocha RO. One-year clinical evaluation of class II bulk-fill restorations in primary molars: A randomized clinical trial. Braz Dent J. 2022 Nov-Dec;33(6):110–120.
47. Panitiwat P, Salimee P. Effect of different composite core materials on fracture resistance of endodontically treated teeth restored with FRC posts. J Appl Oral Sci. 2017 Mar-Apr;25(2):203–210.
48. Edrees N, Amer S, Abdelaziz KM, Alaajam W. Benefits and drawbacks of bulk-fill dental composites: A systematic review. Eur J Pharmaceut Med Res. 2017;4: 124–137.
49. Lima RBW, Troconis CCM, Moreno MBP, Murillo-Gómez F, De Goes MF. Depth of cure of bulk fill resin composites: A systematic review. J Esthet Restor Dent. 2018 Nov;30(6):492–501.
50. Abbasi M, Moradi Z, Mirzaei M, Kharazifard MJ, Rezaei S. Polymerization shrinkage of five bulk-fill composite resins in comparison with a conventional composite resin. J Dent (Tehran). 2018 Nov;15(6):365–374.
51. Zorzin J, Maier E, Harre S, Fey T, Belli R, Lohbauer U, Petschelt A, Taschner M. Bulk-fill resin composites: Polymerization properties and extended light curing. Dent Mater. 2015 Mar;31(3):293–301.
52. Hannoun Abd elgawad I, Ata Mostafa S, Abd Elhady Abdallah A. Flexural strength and depth of cure of sonic fill resin composite. Al-Azhar J Dent Sci. 2018 January;21(1):57–63.
53. Van Ende A, De Munck J, Van Landuyt K, Van Meerbeek B. Effect of bulk-filling on the bonding efficacy in occlusal Class I cavities. J Adhes Dent. 2016;18(2):119–124.
54. Sajjan GS, Dutta GS, Varma KM, Satish RK, Pulidindi AK, Kolla VB. One-year clinical evaluation of bulk-fill composite resin restorations plasticized by preheating and ultrasonics: A randomized clinical trial. J Conserv Dent. 2022 Jan-Feb;25(1):88–92.
55. Ibarra ET, Lien W, Casey J, Dixon SA, Vandewalle KS. Physical properties of a new sonicaly placed composite resin restorative material. Gen Dent. 2015;63:51–56.
56. Van Meerbeek B, De Munck J, Yoshida Y, Inoue S, Vargas M, Vijay P, Van Landuyt K, Lambrechts P, Vanherle G. Buonocore memorial lecture. Adhesion to enamel and dentin: Current status and future challenges. Oper Dent. 2003 May–Jun;28(3):215–235. PMID: 12760693.
57. De Munck J, Van Landuyt K, Peumans M, Poitevin A, Lambrechts P, Braem M, Van Meerbeek B. A critical review of the durability of adhesion to tooth tissue: Methods and results. J Dent Res. 2005 Feb;84(2):118–132. doi: 10.1177/154405910508400204. PMID: 15668328.
58. Peumans M, Van Meerbeek B, Lambrechts P, Vanherle G. Porcelain veneers: A review of the literature. J Dent. 2000 Mar;28(3):163–177. doi: 10.1016/s0300-5712 (99)00066-4. PMID: 10709338.
59. Van Meerbeek B, De Munck J, Mattar D, Van Landuyt K, Lambrechts P. Microtensile bond strengths of an etch&rinse and self-etch adhesive to enamel and dentin as a function of surface treatment. Oper Dent. 2003 Sep-Oct;28(5):647–660. PMID: 14531614.

60. Poitevin A, De Munck J, Van Ende A, Suyama Y, Mine A, Peumans M, Van Meerbeek B. Bonding effectiveness of self-adhesive composites to dentin and enamel. Dent Mater. 2013 Feb;29(2):221–230. doi: 10.1016/j.dental.2012.10.001. Epub 2012 Oct 26. PMID: 23107191.
61. Latta MA, Radniecki SM. Bond strength of self-adhesive restorative materials affected by smear layer thickness but not dentin desiccation. J Adhes Dent. 2020;22(1):79–84. doi: 10.3290/j.jad.a43932. PMID: 32030378.
62. Temel UB, Van Ende A, Van Meerbeek B, Ermis RB. Bond strength and cement-tooth interfacial characterization of self-adhesive composite cements. Am J Dent. 2017 Aug;30(4):205–211. PMID: 29178703.
63. Yu H, Yoshida K, Cheng H, Sawase T. Bonding of different self-adhesive resins to high-strength composite resin block treated with surface conditioning. J Prosthodont Res. 2019 Jul;63(3):340–346. doi: 10.1016/j.jpor.2019.01.008. Epub 2019 Feb 19. PMID: 30792147.
64. Weiser F, Behr M. Self-adhesive resin cements: A clinical review. J Prosthodont. 2015 Feb;24(2):100–108. doi: 10.1111/jopr.12192. Epub 2014 Jul 9. PMID: 25041496.
65. David C, Cardoso de Cardoso G, Isolan CP, Piva E, Moraes RR, Cuevas-Suarez CE. Bond strength of self-adhesive flowable composite resins to dental tissues: A systematic review and meta-analysis of in vitro studies. J Prosthet Dent. 2022 Nov;128(5):876–885. doi: 10.1016/j.prosdent.2021.02.020. Epub 2021 Apr 7. PMID: 33838916.
66. Vallittu PK. High-aspect ratio fillers: Fiber-reinforced composites and their aniso-tropic properties. Dent Mater. 2015 Jan;31(1):1–7. doi: 10.1016/j.dental.2014.07.009.
67. Garoushi S, Gargoum A, Vallittu PK, Lassila L. Short fiber-reinforced composite restorations: A review of the current literature. J Investig Clin Dent. 2018 Aug;9(3):e12330. doi: 10.1111/jicd.12330.
68. Gürel MA, Helvacioğlu Kivanç B, Ekıcı A, Alaçam T. Fracture resistance of premolars restored either with short fiber or polyethylene woven fiber-reinforced composite. J Esthet Restor Dent. 2016 Nov 12;28(6):412–418. doi: 10.1111/jerd.12241.
69. Ozsevik AS, Yildirim C, Aydin U, Culha E, Surmelioglu D. Effect of fibre-reinforced composite on the fracture resistance of endodontically treated teeth. Aust Endod J. 2016 Aug;42(2):82–87. doi: 10.1111/aej.12136.
70. Tanner J, Tolvanen M, Garoushi S, Säilynoja E. Clinical evaluation of fiber-reinforced composite restorations in posterior teeth – Results of 2.5 year follow-up. Open Dent J. 2018 Jun 29;12:476–485. doi: 10.2174/1874210601812010476.
71. Tsujimoto A, Barkmeier WW, Takamizawa T, Latta MA, Miyazaki M. Mechanical properties, volumetric shrinkage and depth of cure of short fiber-reinforced resin composite. Dent Mater J. 2016;35(3):418–424.
72. Tezvergil A, Lassila LV, Vallittu PK. The effect of fiber orientation on the polymerization shrinkage strain of fiber-reinforced composites. Dent Mater. 2006 Jul;22(7):610–616. doi: 10.1016/j.dental.2005.05.017.
73. Garoushi S, Säilynoja E, Vallittu PK, Lassila L. Physical properties and depth of cure of a new short fiber reinforced composite. Dent Mater. 2013 Aug;29(8):835–841. doi: 10.1016/j.dental.2013.04.016.
74. Goracci C, Cadenaro M, Fontanive L, Giangrosso G, Juloski J, Vichi A, Ferrari M. Polymerization efficiency and flexural strength of low-stress restorative composites. Dent Mater. 2014 Jun;30(6):688–694. doi: 10.1016/j.dental.2014.03.006.
75. Bijelic-Donova J, Garoushi S, Lassila LV, Keulemans F, Vallittu PK. Mechanical and structural characterization of discontinuous fiber-reinforced dental resin composite. J Dent. 2016 Sep;52:70–78. doi: 10.1016/j.jdent.2016.07.009.

9 Materials for Tissue Engineering and Their Applications in Dentistry

Subrata Mondal

Department of Mechanical Engineering, National Institute of Technical Teachers' Training and Research (NITTTR) Kolkata, Kolkata, West Bengal, India

9.1 INTRODUCTION

The human body is made up of several tissues ranging from micro to nanoscale and assembled in hierarchical order to maintain the proper function of the body. Tissue loss because of diseases, congenital abnormalities, and trauma is one of the major health care issues worldwide. When tissues are damaged, it may not always be possible to reconstruct them or have access to a donor instantly (Socci et al. 2023). Tissue engineering (TE) imparts a new approach to therapeutic medicine. A few decades ago TE was an idea; however, today it has become a possible therapy for several health-related issues (Abou Neel et al. 2014). TE is an interdisciplinary field and it combines three major disciplines namely engineering, material science, and medicine (Amiryaghoubi et al. 2020; Li, Mao et al. 2022; Petchdee et al. 2020; Socci et al. 2023). It can reconstruct biological structures in vitro or in vivo to replace damaged tissues. Tissue damage because of congenital abnormalities, trauma or disease is one of the significant global healthcare problems.

Current TE has an edge over traditional technology, as the process is aimed at selecting materials with beneficial properties to construct scaffolds that are extremely compatible with the human body. TE and regenerative medicine are interdisciplinary domains that have developed quickly in recent years (Ercal, Pekozer, and Kose 2018; Leyendecker et al. 2018; Sancilio et al. 2018; Socci et al. 2023). The primary principle of TE is to gather properties related to cells and plant them in a natural or synthetic scaffold to stimulate cell proliferation by growth factors in order to regenerate tissue or organs. Therefore, materials which are used for the TE is very important. TE materials are a class of biomaterials that need to be implanted in patients. TE has three main aspects, namely scaffold, stem cell, and growth factors. Scaffold biomaterials are categorized into three major groups such as ceramics, polymers, and composites/ nanocomposites. Safety is the top priority for this kind of biomaterials and it is directly linked to the patient's life and health (Qiu, Cui, and Wang 2019; Yasuda et al. 2005).

DOI: 10.1201/9781003404934-9

Biomaterials play a significant role in TE (Ellermann et al. 2023; Wang et al. 2023). A *biomaterial* is tailor-made to interact with the biological network on medical grounds – either for a diagnostic or a therapeutic purpose. Biomaterials include living tissue and engineered materials used for the replacement, repair, as well as stimulation of biological systems. Two key properties of biomaterials are biocompatibility and biodegradability or biostability which depends on type of applications (Li, Cui, et al. 2022; Vakil et al. 2021; Wang et al. 2014). Biomaterials have been used for centuries; however, advances in molecular biology, cell, materials chemistry, engineering and medicine have provided broader opportunity for the use of biomaterials in medicine. The role of biomaterials in TE is to provide support and induce cell growth (Keane and Badylak 2014). TE biomaterials are a class of biomedical materials that need to be implanted in a patient and are different from conventional agricultural and industrial products.

Tooth is an indispensable organ of human beings, and it consists of hard tissue containing enamel, cementum, and dentin (Fu et al. 2023; Sarna-Bos et al. 2022). The hard tissue of teeth is a complex composite material, enclosing the pulp with pulp connecting tissue. Teeth may be damaged by mechanical trauma and bacterial infection (Wanasathop et al. 2023). Bacterial infection can also affect the pulp and degenerate underlying soft tissue. Advances in materials science and engineering make it possible to engineer and regenerate damaged oral hard and soft tissues. This chapter will provide an overview of biomaterials for dental TE applications. A brief overview of dental TE is included. Various issues related to dental biomaterials such as biocompatibility of dental biomaterials and surface modification of dental implants, and various biomaterials such as ceramics, polymers, metals, composites, and nanomaterials for dental TE applications are discussed.

9.2   TISSUE ENGINEERING IN DENTISTRY

A tissue can be injured when it is exposed to various external hazards such as mechanical hazards, chemical hazards, or microbial hazards (Sugiaman et al. 2022). Various diseases can affect teeth and their surrounding tissues which lead to infection and gradual destruction and ultimate loss (Orsini, Putignano, and Mitsiadis 2019). Decay and traumatic injury to teeth can promote inflammation and eventual death of the dental pulp (Ghosh et al. 2023). With the advances of research in TE, specific materials and scaffolds are required for effective delivery of synthetic and biomolecules for the regeneration of tissues (Jazayeri et al. 2016). TE exhibits great potential for treatment of dental defects due to tumour, trauma, and other diseases (Earthman et al. 2003; Galler, D'Souza, and Hartgerink 2010; Huang 2020; Li et al. 2017; Zafar, Khurshid, and Almas 2015). TE can reconstruct biological structures in vitro or in vivo to replace damaged tissues. TE is a promising method that applies cell seed scaffold drug delivery system to reconstruct the defective tissue caused by tumours, trauma, and other diseases e.g. periodontics (Zhu et al. 2022). TE is one of the most notable areas in the interdisciplinary field of engineering, material science, and medicine that have been aggressively developed (Zamri et al. 2021). Three essential components of TE are (i) cells that can form a functional domain, (ii) a scaffold to support, and (iii) bioreactive molecules which will support the growth of the desired tissue (de Isla et al. 2010). Conductive and inductive approaches are used for the regeneration of damaged paradental and dental tissues. The conductive approach depends on the application of biomaterial in an inert way to passively expedite the ingrowth of existing growing tissue. The inductive method uses a specific biological signal to activate cells near defective areas (Grawish et al. 2020; Rai et al. 2015).

9.3 SCAFFOLD FOR DENTAL TE

Scaffold is one of the three indispensable elements in TE applications, and the other two components are bioactive molecules and stem cells (Farzin et al. 2020; Galler et al. 2011; Jazayeri et al. 2020; Moussa and Aparicio 2019; Sugiaman et al. 2023; Zhang et al. 2019). TE consists of a fabrication of biomaterial scaffold to treat or regrow damaged tissue (Figure 9.1). Scaffold design is the pivotal step in any TE for appropriate delivery of cells, biomolecules, and generating a favourable environment for cell activities and intercellular communications. Scaffolds are designed to bestow a three-dimensional domain to assist cellular processes such as migration, differentiation, and proliferation. Therefore, the scaffold must be porous enough as well as biocompatible with the host tissue for the easy transportation of nutrients and degrades proportionately with regeneration of new tissue leaving no toxic residue (de Isla et al. 2010; Grande et al. 1997; Jazayeri et al. 2020; Masaru et al. 2019). The scaffold materials require desirable composition, mechanical characteristics, and adequate physiochemical behaviour to assist biological tissue growth (Khan et al. 2021; Zheng et al. 2021). Scaffold in TE applications should be mechanically strong during the in vitro culturing in order to provide an adequate gap for cell infiltration and extracellular

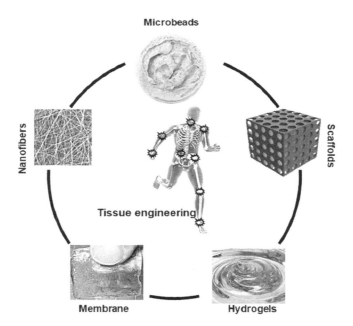

FIGURE 9.1 Different forms of biomaterials for tissue engineering applications. Reproduced from Khan et al. (2021). Open access © 2021 by the authors.

matrix. TE scaffold should impart temporary support, its mechanical characteristics should be close to that of the host tissue, and bears in vivo loading and stress condition (Pryadko, Surmeneva, and Surmenev 2021).

9.4 DENTAL BIOMATERIALS

Biomaterials are required to facilitate the revitalization of dental pulp (Sugiaman et al. 2023). A *biomaterial* is any matter that has been tailor-made to interact with biological structures on medical grounds. Requirements for materials in biomedical applications are biocompatibility, excellent resistance to alkali, acid and microorganism, and adequate dimensional stability, absorption/repellency, air permeability, biodegradability/non-biodegradability, and others depending on specific applications. The chemical nature of the biomaterials plays a significant role in its bioactive properties (Baino and Yamaguchi 2020). Biomaterials can be broadly categorized as: polymers including synthetic and natural, metal or alloy, ceramics and their composites.

9.4.1 BIOCOMPATIBILITY OF DENTAL BIOMATERIALS

Biocompatibility assessment of dental biomaterial is critical to ensure safety and to determine compliance with regulatory norms (Hadjichristou et al. 2020). Biocompatibility of biomaterial is the capacity of a material to achieve any preferred functionality without imparting any localized or systemic unfavourable effect to the beneficiary of the biomaterial (Pryadko, Surmeneva, and Surmenev 2021). Biocompatibility of biomaterial is an important issue for biomedical applications. It involves the acceptance of an artificial implant by the neighboring tissues and by the human body as a whole. Biocompatible substances should not: (i) irritate the neighboring tissue, (ii) arouse an abnormal inflammatory reaction, (iii) stimulate allergic or immunologic response, and (iv) cause cancer. Therefore, supreme biocompatibility is extremely required for a material to be utilized in TE in order to avoid a harmful influence on the living tissue. Hence, assessments of biocompatibility and cytotoxicity are essential for biomaterials (Mousavi et al. 2021). Materials used for dental TE should be compatible with oral fluid and do not exude any toxic substance, and must have enough strength and stability in the body fluid. In addition to these, the material must prevent bacterial growth and biofilm formation on the scaffold surface (Mousavi et al. 2021). In degradable implant materials, inflammatory reaction depends on factors like extent of injury, shape, size, degradation rate, and mechanical, chemical, and physical properties of implant materials (Gupta et al. 2015).

9.4.2 POLYMERS FOR DENTAL TE

Polymers as well as their composites can make cost-effective authentic biomaterials with adequate mechanical characteristics (Imran, Al Rashid, and Koc 2023; Modrak et al. 2023). Polymers used for TE can be natural (biopolymer) or synthetic type. Biopolymers are derived from bioresources, e.g., living organisms and plants, and a few examples are carbohydrate, chitin, gelatine, starch, polyhydroxyalkanoate, etc. Derived biopolymers are chemically synthesized and their raw materials are obtained from bioresources, and examples of bio-derived polymers are poly(lactic acid), poly(3

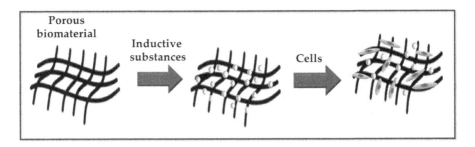

FIGURE 9.2 Schematic representation of porous scaffold for tissue engineering. Reproduced from Socci et al. (2023). Open access. © 20023 by the authors.

hydroxybutyrate), etc. (Okonkwo, Collins, and Okonkwo 2017). Polymeric biomaterials are widely chosen for the design and construction of TE scaffolds because of their wide availability, and economical and tailorable properties. Porous polymeric scaffold plays a crucial role in TE to impart a favourable surrounding (Figure 9.2) for damaged tissue restoration. Scaffolds establish the interaction of biomaterials with living cells and other biomolecules (Socci et al. 2023). Natural or synthetic polymers with appropriate biomaterial characteristics can promote tissue regeneration when paired with stem cell and growth factor to regenerate dental pulp tissue (Sugiaman et al. 2023). Natural polymers such as collagen, fibrin, chitosan, peptide-based materials, spider silk, gelatine, silk fibroin, and alginate are widely used for scaffolds of dental pulp regeneration. Apart from natural polymers, scaffolds can be developed by using synthetic polymers such as poly(glycolic acid), poly(l-lactic acid), poly (lactic acid), poly (caprolactone) and poly(d,l-lactide-coglycolide) (Ashri, Ajlan, and Aldahmash 2015; Galler et al. 2018; Hafner et al. 2017; Jazayeri et al. 2016; Sugiaman et al. 2023; Woloszyk et al. 2014). EzEldeen et al. (2021) described a chitosan-based scaffold with or without gelatine and cross-linked to 3-glycidyloxyproply trimethoxysilane for potential application in dental root TE applications. Tailor-made chitosan scaffold with tuneable properties and favourable human dental pulp stem cell response has found potential applications in regenerative dentistry.

9.4.3 CERAMICS FOR DENTAL TE

Bioceramics are a class of ceramic used for replacement and repair of damaged and diseased parts of an organ. Therefore, bioceramics should be biocompatible, degradable or stable (depending on application type), bioactive or bioinert. Different types of bioceramics with examples are schematically shown in Figure 9.3. Bioceramics are extensively used for hard TE applications. Bioceramics such as zirconia, hydroxyapatite, alumina, and bioactive glass play an important part in the design and construction of TE scaffolds with tailor-made characteristics. These biomaterials have several interesting qualities which make them ideal for hard TE, such as biocompatibility, excellent mechanical characteristic, wear resistance, corrosion resistance, and chemical stability (Kumar et al. 2023). Ceramic scaffold has advantages of appropriate porous construct and chemical texture which can promote cell

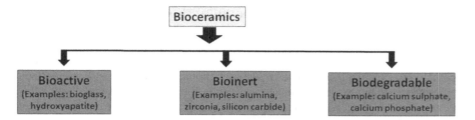

FIGURE 9.3 Different types of bioceramic materials.

differentiation and mineralization of extracellular matrix (Ohgushi H 2003). Goudouri et al. (2014) reported synthesis of Mg-based glass ceramics which can be used for an akermanite scaffold. Sol-gel technique has been employed for synthesis of Mg-based glass ceramic and scaffold has been manufactured by foam replica method. Sintering temperature is at 1350°C in order to induce crystallization of akermanite ceramic. The morphological structure of fabricated porous scaffold is depicted in Figure 9.4. Images show pores are interconnected and pore size is in the scale of several micrometers. Excellent microporous structure can help vascularization, cell penetration, and nutrient and metabolic byproduct transportation.

9.4.4 METAL OR ALLOYS FOR DENTAL TE

Metals and metal alloys such as titanium, nickel-titanium shaped memory alloy, cobalt chromium, Ti-6Al-4V, stainless steel, Co-Cr-Mo alloys, and gold are widely used for dental implants because of their corrosion resistance property, toughness, and shear and fracture resistance properties (Anusha Yarram 2019; Hanawa 2004;

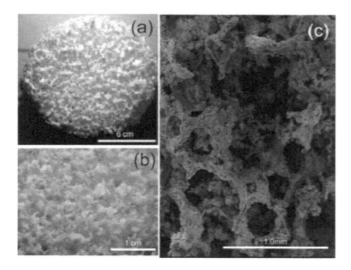

FIGURE 9.4 (a, b) Optical microscopic images of ceramic scaffold at different magnifications, (c) Scanning electron microscopic image of scaffold. Reproduced with permission from Goudouri et al. (2014) © 2013 Elsevier Ltd.

Karamian et al. 2014; Teigen and Jokstad 2012). Titanium and its alloys have been extensively applied in the area of implant dentistry due to its interesting properties, such as light weight, excellent biocompatibility, superior corrosion resistance property, and tailorable mechanical properties. Some of the applications of metallic biomaterials in dentistry include dental implants, maxilla and cranio/facial reconstruction, and external prostheses (Anusha Yarram 2019). If metals and alloys are used as biomaterials, sometimes metal ions come out from the implant biomaterials. A significant amount of metal ions released in the human body may be harmful and these may accumulate in organs, create allergies and in extreme cases they may cause cancer. Surface oxide film on metal or alloy surface plays a crucial role as an inhibitor of metal ion release. Surface oxide film covers the biomaterials and the interaction of materials with body fluid occurs at the interface. Composition of the film is important for biocompatibility of metal material. Figure 9.5 shows preferentially released metal ions and oxide film formation mechanisms. Elements which form the oxide film are hardly released, whereas preferentially released elements do not form oxide film (Hanawa 2004).

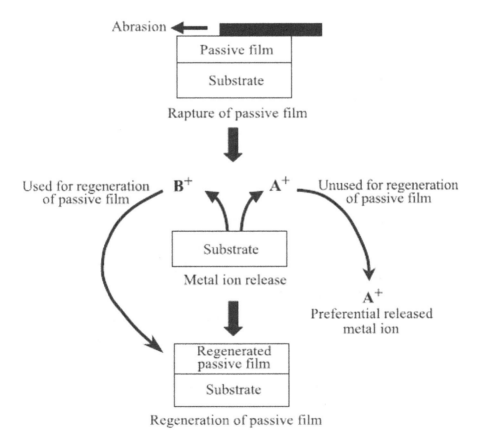

FIGURE 9.5 Schematic showing metal ion release mechanism. Reproduced with permission from Hanawa (2004) © 2004 Elsevier B. V.

9.4.5 Dental Biocomposites

Composites are defined as materials with two or more component materials which are physically and/or chemically different but remain bonded together; however, they retain their identities which can be recognized microscopically. The major component of composite materials is termed as matrix domain, while the minor component is known as reinforcement domain. Depending on the kind of matrix materials, composite materials are categorized as metal matrix composite, polymer matrix composite, and ceramic matrix composite. Whereas, depending on the size of reinforcing materials, composites can be categorized as macro composite, micro composite, and nanocomposite. Nanocomposite has reinforcing materials with at least one dimension sized between 1 and 100 nm. Composite materials used in biomedical applications should be biocompatible. Therefore, both matrix and reinforcing materials and their intermediate products should be biocompatible for biomedical applications. In order to stimulate the natural tissue construct, biomedical grade bioceramics, polymers, and other inorganic materials need to be combined for improved properties. Inorganic nanomaterial-reinforced polymer composites can be applied as scaffolds for bone TE. When compared with traditional polymer composites, nanoparticle-reinforced polymers have several improved properties, such as lighter, good mechanical properties, superior durability, and bioactive interface. Advanced and functional properties of biopolymeric composite materials are required for applications in biomedical and regenerative medicine (Ferrer et al. 2020; Khan et al. 2021). A few biomedical applications of polymer nanocomposites are as follows: (a) nano-HAp/Collagen Porous Scaffolds: Bone regeneration, (b) nano-HA/Biodegradable Polyurethane Hollow Fiber Membranes: Multichannel scaffold for bone applications, and (c) nanocarbon reinforced polymer composite: Bone applications. Gupta et al. (2015) reported a single-walled carbon nanotube-reinforced poly(lactic-co-glycolic acid) biocomposite for TE applications. The material possesses biocompatibility and has the capability to regenerate hard tissue. Another study (Mohandesnezhad et al. 2020) reported in vitro analysis of zeolite and nanohydroxyapatite (nHA) reinforced poly(lactic acid) (PLA)/poly(caprolactone) (PCL) electrospun biocomposite nanofiber for dental TE applications. Biocomposite materials were tested for growth of human dental pulp-extracted stem cells (hDPSC). The results show (Figure 9.6) that cell growth on the biocomposite nanofiber containing both nHA and zeolite was superior to that of the biocomposite which contained only nHA. All scaffold materials showed cytocompatibility of hDPSC. Reinforcement of both nHA and zeolite improved proliferation and consequently absorbance of cell. However, zeolite-reinforced biocomposite nanofiber exhibited superior cell adhesion, viability, and proliferation; therefore, this biocomposite material is an excellent candidate for dental TE application (Mohandesnezhad et al. 2020).

9.4.6 Nanomaterials for Dental TE

Nanomaterials are tiny particles with at least one dimension up to 100 nm. Nanomaterials are nowadays extensively used to enhance hard TE. Nanomaterials

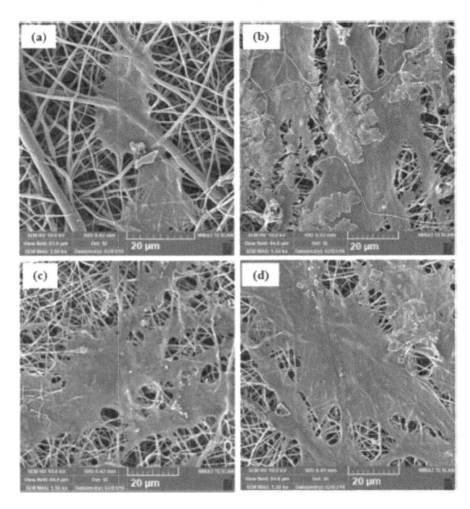

FIGURE 9.6   FESEM images for cell adhesion on nanofibers: (a) PCL-PLA, (b) PCL-PLA/ zeolite biocomposite, (c) PCL-PLA/nHA biocomposite, and (d) PCL-PLA/nHA/zeolite biocomposite. Reproduced with permission from Mohandesnezhad et al. (2020) © 2020 Elsevier B. V.

include nanofiber, nanotube, nanosheet, and nanoparticles (Li et al. 2017). Depending on the number of dimensions that are not within nanoscale range, i.e. ≤ 100 nm, nanomaterials can be categorized as 0D, 1D, 2D, and 3D nanomaterials. Nanomaterials with all dimensions up to 100 nm are named as 0D nanomaterials. One example of 0D nanomaterial is fullerene. ID nanomaterials have one dimension more than 100 nm and the remaining two dimensions within 100 nm. Carbon nanotube is an example of 1D nanomaterial. Nanomaterials with two dimensions ˃100 nm and remaining one dimension up to 100 nm is termed as 2D nanomaterials. Graphene sheet is an example of 2D nanomaterial. 3D nanomaterials are basically 0D/1D/2D containing composite, dispersion, or nonporous materials (Harish et al. 2022). Rapid progress of nanotechnology has produced different nanomaterials with a wide range of properties that can revolutionaries their applications in biomedical fields (Arzaghi et al. 2020). Nanomaterials can be applied for multiple purposes such as drug delivery (therapy), disease detection (imaging), diagnosis/monitoring (disease markers), orthopedics, TE, biosensor systems, gene therapy, and dentistry. Constructing TE scaffolds in nanoscale may lead to unforeseeable novel characteristics of the material, such as improved mechanical and physical properties, altered chemical reactivity, and other functional characteristics depending on type of nanomaterials used. Other merits of applying nanotechnology for scaffold manufacturing may include upgrading biocompatibility, enhancing contact guidance, decreasing friction, eliminating the requirement for revision surgery, modifying physical or chemical characteristics of the scaffold, and fostering tissue growth surrounding the implant.

The rapid development of fabrication processes and nanotechnological research provide an opportunity for researchers to incorporate a wide range of nanomaterials in TE, including nanocomposite, nanoporous scaffold, and nanomembranes (Cigane, Palevicius, and Janusas 2021). Novel treatment process is required to repair periodontal tissue damage due to age-related issue or traumatic damage. Some of the other applications of nanomaterials in dental TE are (a) nano reinforcement to improve mechanical characteristics of biomaterials applied in dental TE, (b) nano-coating for dental implants, (c) nano antimicrobial agent to prevent oral infection, and (d) nanoparticle containing personal care products and tooth paste for better oral health (Harish et al. 2022). Acuna et al. reported a SiO_2/gelatin/polyethylene oxide hybrid scaffold with bioactive nanoparticles which was fabricated by using electrospinning method. Scaffold materials are nontoxic, bioactive, and exhibit enhanced osteogenic differentiation and therefore, can find potential applications in dental TE (Acuna, Cohn, and Quero 2023). Bioactive glass has superior bioactive, osteoconductive, and osteogenic properties because of the resemblance of its inorganic components with dental tissue (Sujon et al. 2023). A review presented by Mousavi et al. (Mousavi et al. 2021) described various carbon-based nanomaterials for dental TE applications. They reported prospects of carbon nanotube and graphene oxide for their utilization in dental TE applications. A study has confirmed the biocompatibility of graphene oxide and carbon nanotube, and their ability to produce hard tissues (Mousavi et al. 2021). Carbon nanomaterials are divided into carbon nanotube, nanodiamond, fullerene, graphene, and carbon nano dot (Kang et al. 2021). Various nanostructured materials that can be applied in dental TE are depicted schematically in Figure 9.7.

9.4.7 Surface Modification of Dental Implants

Biomaterials are made up of various types of materials including metals or alloys, ceramics, polymers or blends, composites or nanocomposites and biological substances that replace or support the functions of various parts of the human body. One of the main issues for biomaterials is biocompatibility of material surface with native/host tissue. Biocompatibility of biomaterials can be enhanced by surface modification. Surface characteristics of implants affect the speed and strength of

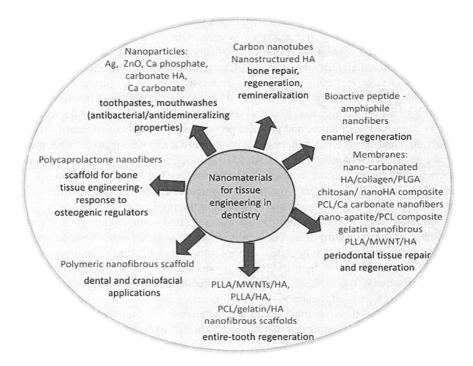

FIGURE 9.7 Nanostructure materials for tissue engineering in dentistry. Reproduced from Chieruzzi et al. (2016) © 2016 by the authors.

osseointegration which include bioactivity and crystal structure (Karamian et al. 2014). Optimization of dental implant surface by surface engineering is an interesting area of research. Based on the region, different surface properties are essential to tailor prevailing tissue response in order to stimulate osseointegration, enhance tissue bonding, and employ antibacterial effectiveness. Therefore, surface engineering is a crucial tool for continued future success of dental implants (van Oirschot et al. 2022). Various surface modifications strategies have been developed to improve the biocompatibility of biomaterials. Implant surface modification by addition and subtraction of metal can impart corrosion resistance by preventing release of metal ions and improving biocompatibility of metal with surrounding tissues (Anusha Yarram 2019). Carbon-based nanomaterials (CNM) are widely used for dental TE. Surface modification of CNM can improve antibacterial property, enhance corrosion resistance and improve biocompatibility (Figure 9.8) (Kang et al. 2021). Duailibi et al. compared oxygen containing (hydrophilic) surface with hydrogen-containing surfaces of nano-crystalline diamond film for the growth of dental stem cells. Experimental results revealed that the oxygen-terminated region contained a higher level of calcium and phosphorus. Therefore, extracellular matrix has been developed in the oxygen-terminated domain than hydrogen-terminated domain (Duailibi et al. 2013).

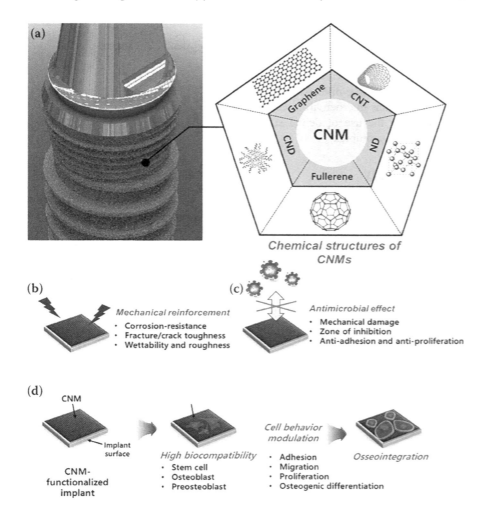

FIGURE 9.8 Schematic representation of (a) Various carbon-based nanomaterials, (b) mechanical reinforcement, (c) antibacterial property, and (d) osseointegration. Reproduced from Kang et al. (2021). Open access © 2021 by the authors.

9.5 FUTURE SCOPE

Dental TE is a novel and promising approach to repair damaged tooth or replace missing tooth or to repair damaged dental tissues. Scaffold, cell culture, and growth-stimulating factors are key components of engineered dental tissues. In vitro and in vivo research on dental TE materials are promising. Research trends and technologies positively impact the future direction of TE materials to make them a reality in dentistry. Considering the current state of the art in research, the author proposes studies in the following areas for further development:

i. Smart biomaterials for dental TE;
ii. Cellular development and differentiation on dental TE materials;
iii. Vascularization of engineered tissues;
iv. Optimization of various parameters;
v. Advanced three-dimensional bio-printing for culture and engineering of the cellular microenvironment;
vi. Explore the use of dental stem cells on the surface of biomaterials to create biocomplex.

9.6 SUMMARY

TE offers a great potential for dental defects. This chapter discussed various biomaterials such as metals or alloys, polymers, ceramics and their composites, and nanomaterials for dental TE applications. A brief overview of dental TE has been included. Scaffold for dental TE has been included. Biocompatibility and surface modifications of dental materials have been discussed. Compositions, structure-property relationships, and mechanical characteristics of biomaterials are important for their successful applications in dental TE. The relation between biocompatibility and mechanical properties of dental biomaterials depends on the combination of material, scalability, and sustainability of applied methods.

REFERENCES

Abou Neel, E. A., W. Chrzanowski, V. M. Salih, H.-W. Kim, and J. C. Knowles. 2014. "Tissue engineering in dentistry." *Journal of Dentistry* 42 (8):915–928. doi: 10.1016/j.jdent.2014.05.008.

Acuna, D., N. Cohn, and F. Quero. 2023. "Electrospun bioactive tertiary glass nanoparticles-containing silica/gelatin/polyethylene oxide hybrid membranes for potential dental bone tissue engineering applications." *Materials Letters* 337. doi: 10.1016/j.matlet.2023.133997.

Amiryaghoubi, N., N. N. Pesyan, M. Fathi, and Y. Omidi. 2020. "Injectable thermosensitive hybrid hydrogel containing graphene oxide and chitosan as dental pulp stem cells scaffold for bone tissue engineering." *International Journal of Biological Macromolecules* 162:1338–1357. doi: 10.1016/j.ijbiomac.2020.06.138.

Arzaghi, H., B. Adel, H. Jafari, S. Askarian-Amiri, A. S. Dezfuli, A. Akbarzadeh, and H. Pazoki-Toroudi. 2020. "Nanomaterial integration into the scaffolding materials for nerve tissue engineering: a review." *Reviews in the Neurosciences* 31 (8):843–872. doi: 10.1515/revneuro-2020-0008.

Ashri, N. Y., S. A. Ajlan, and A. M. Aldahmash. 2015. "Dental pulp stem cells biology and use for periodontal tissue engineering." *Saudi Medical Journal* 36 (12):1391–1399. doi: 10.15537/smj.2015.12.12750.

Baino, F., and S. Yamaguchi. 2020. "The use of simulated body fluid (SBF) for assessing materials bioactivity in the context of tissue engineering: Review and challenges." *Biomimetics* 5 (4). doi: 10.3390/biomimetics5040057.

Chieruzzi, M., S. Pagano, S. Moretti, R. Pinna, E. Milia, L. Torre, and S. Eramo. 2016. "Nanomaterials for tissue engineering in dentistry." *Nanomaterials* 6 (7). doi: 10.3390/nano6070134.

Cigane, U., A. Palevicius, and G. Janusas. 2021. "Review of nanomembranes: Materials, fabrications and applications in tissue engineering (bone and skin) and drug delivery systems." *Journal of Materials Science* 56 (24):13479–13498. doi: 10.1007/s10853-021-06164-x.

Duailibi, S. E., M. T. Duailibi, L. M. Ferreira, Kilc Salmazi, M. C. Salvadori, F. D. Teixeira, A. Pasquarelli, J. P. Vacanti, and P. C. Yelick. 2013. "Tooth tissue engineering: The influence of hydrophilic surface on nanocrystalline diamond films for human dental stem cells." *Tissue Engineering Part A* 19 (23–24):2537–2543. doi: 10.1089/ten.tea. 2012.0628.

Earthman, J. C., C. G. Sheets, J. M. Paquette, R. M. Kaminishi, W. P. Nordland, R. G. Keim, and J. C. Wu. 2003. "Tissue engineering in dentistry." *Clinics in Plastic Surgery* 30 (4):621–639. 10.1016/s0094-1298(03)00080-4.

Ellermann, E., N. Meyer, R. E. Cameron, and S. M. Best. 2023. "In vitro angiogenesis in response to biomaterial properties for bone tissue engineering: A review of the state of the art." *Regenerative Biomaterials* 10. doi: 10.1093/rb/rbad027.

Ercal, P., G. G. Pekozer, and G. T. Kose. 2018. "Dental stem cells in bone tissue engineering: Current overview and challenges." In *Cell Biology and Translational Medicine, Vol 3: Stem Cells, Bio-Materials and Tissue Engineering*, edited by K. Turksen, 113–127.

EzEldeen, M., J. Loos, Z. M. Nejad, M. Cristaldi, D. Murgia, A. Braem, and R. Jacobs. 2021. "3D-printing-assisted fabrication of chitosan scaffolds from different sources and cross-linkers for dental tissue engineering." *European Cells & Materials* 40:485–501. doi: 10.22203/eCM.v041a31.

Farzin, A., N. Bahrami, A. Mohamadnia, S. Mousavi, M. Gholami, J. Ai, and R. S. Moayeri. 2020. "Scaffolds in dental tissue engineering: A review." 7 (1):e97014. doi: 10.5812/ans.97014.

Ferrer, C. T., G. Vilarino-Feltrer, M. Rizk, H. G. Sydow, and A. Valles-Lluch. 2020. "Nanocomposites based on poly(glycerol sebacate) with silica nanoparticles with potential application in dental tissue engineering." *International Journal of Polymeric Materials and Polymeric Biomaterials* 69 (12):761–772. doi: 10.1080/00914037.2019. 1616197.

Fu, J., H. W. Zheng, Y. Y. Ou, G. B. Yang, Z. Chen, and G. H. Yuan. 2023. "AAV6-mediated gene therapy prevents developmental dentin defects in a dentinogenesis imperfecta type III mouse model." *Human Gene Therapy*. doi: 10.1089/hum.2023.008.

Galler, K. M., R. N. D'Souza, and J. D. Hartgerink. 2010. "Biomaterials and their potential applications for dental tissue engineering." *Journal of Materials Chemistry* 20 (40):8730–8746. doi: 10.1039/c0jm01207f.

Galler, K. M., R. N. D'Souza, J. D. Hartgerink, and G. Schmalz. 2011. "Scaffolds for dental pulp tissue engineering." *Advances in Dental Research* 23 (3):333–339. doi: 10.1177/0022034511405326.

Galler, K. M., F. P. Brandl, S. Kirchhof, M. Widbiller, A. Eidt, W. Buchalla, A. Gopferich, and G. Schmalz. 2018. "Suitability of different natural and synthetic biomaterials for dental pulp tissue engineering." *Tissue Engineering Part A* 24 (3-4):234–244. doi: 10. 1089/ten.tea.2016.0555.

Ghosh, S., W. Qiao, Z. B. Yang, S. Orrego, and P. Neelakantan. 2023. "Engineering dental tissues using biomaterials with piezoelectric effect: Current progress and future perspectives." *Journal of Functional Biomaterials* 14 (1). doi: 10.3390/jfb14010008.

Goudouri, O. M., E. Theodosoglou, E. Kontonasaki, J. Will, K. Chrissafis, P. Koidis, K. M. Paraskevopoulos, and A. R. Boccaccini. 2014. "Development of highly porous scaffolds based on bioactive silicates for dental tissue engineering." *Materials Research Bulletin* 49:399–404. doi: 10.1016/j.materresbull.2013.09.027.

Grande, D. A., C. Halberstadt, G. Naughton, R. Schwartz, and Ryhana Manji. 1997. "Evaluation of matrix scaffolds for tissue engineering of articular cartilage grafts." *Journal of Biomedical Materials Research* 34 (2):211–220. doi: 10.1002/(SICI)1097-4636(199702)34:2<211::AID-JBM10>3.0.CO;2-L.

Grawish, M. E., L. M. Grawish, H. M. Grawish, M. M. Grawish, and S. A. El-Negoly. 2020. "Challenges of engineering biomimetic dental and paradental tissues." *Tissue Engineering and Regenerative Medicine* 17 (4):403–421. doi: 10.1007/s13770-020-00269-1.

Gupta, A., T. A. Liberati, S. J. Verhulst, B. J. Main, M. H. Roberts, A. G. R. Potty, T. K. Pylawka, and S. F. El-Amin. 2015. "Biocompatibility of single-walled carbon nanotube composites for bone regeneration." *Bone & Joint Research* 4 (5):70–77. doi: 10.1302/2046-3758.45.2000382.

Hadjichristou, C., E. Papachristou, I. Bonovolias, and A. Bakopoulou. 2020. "Three-dimensional tissue engineering-based dentin/pulp tissue analogue as advanced bio-compatibility evaluation tool of dental restorative materials." *Dental Materials* 36 (2):229–248. doi: 10.1016/j.dental.2019.11.013.

Hafner, K., D. Montag, H. Maeser, C. Y. Peng, W. R. Marcotte, D. Dean, and M. S. Kennedy. 2017. "Evaluating adhesion and alignment of dental pulp stem cells to a spider silk substrate for tissue engineering applications." *Materials Science & Engineering C-Materials for Biological Applications* 81:104–112. doi: 10.1016/j.msec.2017.07.019.

Hanawa, T. 2004. "Metal ion release from metal implants." *Materials Science & Engineering C-Biomimetic and Supramolecular Systems* 24 (6–8):745–752. doi: 10.1016/j.msec.2004.08.018.

Harish, V., D. Tewari, M. Gaur, A. B. Yadav, S. Swaroop, M. Bechelany, and A. Barhoum. 2022. "Review on nanoparticles and nanostructured materials: Bioimaging, biosensing, drug delivery, tissue engineering, antimicrobial, and agro-food applications." *Nanomaterials* 12 (3). doi: 10.3390/nano12030457.

Huang, Q. 2020. "Research Progress of Dental Tissue Engineering Technology." 2020 International Conference on Public Health and Data Science (ICPHDS), 20-22 Nov. 2020.

Imran, R., A. Al Rashid, and M. Koc. 2023. "Material extrusion 3D printing (ME3DP) process simulations of polymeric porous scaffolds for bone tissue engineering." *Materials* 16 (6). doi: 10.3390/ma16062475.

de Isla, N., C. Huseltein, N. Jessel, A. Pinzano, V. Decot, J. Magdalou, D. Bensoussan, and J. F. Stoltz. 2010. "Introduction to tissue engineering and application for cartilage engineering." *Bio-Medical Materials and Engineering* 20 (3–4):127–133. doi: 10.3233/bme-2010-0624.

Jazayeri, H. E., M. D. Fahmy, M. Razavi, B. E. Stein, A. Nowman, R. M. Masri, and L. Tayebi. 2016. "Dental applications of natural-origin polymers in hard and soft tissue engineering." *Journal of Prosthodontics-Implant Esthetic and Reconstructive Dentistry* 25 (6):510–517. doi: 10.1111/jopr.12465.

Jazayeri, H. E., S. M. Lee, L. Kuhn, F. Fahimipour, M. Tahriri, and L. Tayebi. 2020. "Polymeric scaffolds for dental pulp tissue engineering: A review." *Dental Materials* 36 (2):E47–E58. doi: 10.1016/j.dental.2019.11.005.

Kang, M. S., H. J. Jang, S. H. Lee, J. E. Lee, H. J. Jo, S. J. Jeong, B. Kim, and D. W. Han. 2021. "Potential of carbon-based nanocomposites for dental tissue engineering and regeneration." *Materials* 14 (17). doi: 10.3390/ma14175104.

Karamian, E., M. R. K. Motamedi, A. Khandan, P. Soltani, and S. Maghsoudi. 2014. "An in vitro evaluation of novel NHA/zircon plasma coating on 316L stainless steel dental implant." *Progress in Natural Science-Materials International* 24 (2):150–156. doi: 10.1016/j.pnsc.2014.04.001.

Keane, Timothy J., and Stephen F. Badylak. 2014. "Biomaterials for tissue engineering applications." *Seminars in Pediatric Surgery* 23 (3):112–118. doi: 10.1053/j.sempedsurg.2014.06.010.

Khan, M. U. A., S. I. Abd Razak, W. S. Al Arjan, S. Nazir, T. J. S. Anand, H. Mehboob, and R. Amin. 2021. "Recent advances in biopolymeric composite materials for tissue engineering and regenerative medicines: A review." *Molecules* 26 (3). doi: 10.3390/molecules26030619.

Kumar, R., I. Pattanayak, P. A. Dash, and S. Mohanty. 2023. "Bioceramics: a review on design concepts toward tailor-made (multi)-functional materials for tissue engineering applications." *Journal of Materials Science* 58 (8):3460–3484. doi: 10.1007/s10853-023-08226-8.

Leyendecker, A., C. C. G. Pinheiro, T. L. Fernandes, and D. F. Bueno. 2018. "The use of human dental pulp stem cells for in vivo bone tissue engineering: A systematic review." *Journal of Tissue Engineering* 9. doi: 10.1177/2041731417752766.

Li, G., T. Zhou, S. Lin, S. Shi, and Y. Lin. 2017. "Nanomaterials for craniofacial and dental tissue engineering." *Journal of Dental Research* 96 (7):725–732. doi: 10.1177/0022034517706678.

Li, W. P., M. Y. Mao, N. Hu, J. Wang, J. Huang, and S. S. Gu. 2022. "In vitro evaluation of periapical lesion-derived stem cells for dental pulp tissue engineering." *FEBS Open Bio* 12 (1):270–284. doi: 10.1002/2211-5463.13336.

Li, Y., C. B. Cui, Y. Z. Li, D. W. Tan, X. W. Jia, S. H. Liu, H. P. Feng, and C. N. Feng. 2022. "Biodegradable biomaterial arterial stent in the treatment of coronary heart disease." *Journal of Biomedical Nanotechnology* 18 (1):288–292. doi: 10.1166/jbn.2022.3238.

Masaru, Murata, Okubo Naoto, Shakya Mamata, Kabir Md Arafat, Yokozeki Kenji, Zhu Bowen, Ishikawa Masahiro, Kitamura Ryuji, and Akazawa Toshiyuki. 2019. "Dentin materials as biological scaffolds for tissue engineering." In *Biomaterial-supported Tissue Reconstruction or Regeneration*, edited by Barbeck Mike, Jung Ole, Smeets Ralf, and Koržinskas Tadas, Ch. 2. Rijeka: IntechOpen.

Modrak, M., M. Trebunova, A. F. Balogova, R. Hudak, and J. Zivcak. 2023. "Biodegradable materials for tissue engineering: Development, classification and current applications." *Journal of Functional Biomaterials* 14 (3). doi: 10.3390/jfb14030159.

Mohandesnezhad, S., Y. Pilehvar-Soltanahmadi, E. Alizadeh, A. Goodarzi, S. Davaran, M. Khatamian, N. Zarghami, M. Samiei, M. Aghazadeh, and A. Akbarzadeh. 2020. "In vitro evaluation of Zeolite-nHA blended PCL/PLA nanofibers for dental tissue engineering." *Materials Chemistry and Physics* 252. doi: 10.1016/j.matchemphys.2020.123152.

Mousavi, S. M., K. Yousefi, S. A. Hashemi, M. Afsa, S. Bahrani, A. Gholami, Y. Ghahramani, A. Alizadeh, and W. H. Chiang. 2021. "Renewable carbon nanomaterials: Novel resources for dental tissue engineering." *Nanomaterials* 11 (11). doi: 10.3390/nano11112800.

Moussa, D. G., and C. Aparicio. 2019. "Present and future of tissue engineering scaffolds for dentin-pulp complex regeneration." *Journal of Tissue Engineering and Regenerative Medicine* 13 (1):58–75. doi: 10.1002/term.2769.

Ohgushi, H., J. Miyake, T. Tateishi. 2003. "Mesenchymal stem cells and bioceramics: Strategies to regenerate the skeleton." *Novartis Found Symp* 249:118–127.

van Oirschot, Baja, Y. Zhang, H. S. Alghamdi, J. M. Cordeiro, B. E. Nagay, V. A. R. Barao, E. D. de Avila, and Jjjp van den Beucken. 2022. "Surface engineering for dental implantology: Favoring tissue responses along the implant." *Tissue Engineering Part A* 28 (11–12):555–572. doi: 10.1089/ten.tea.2021.0230.

Okonkwo, P. C., E. Collins, and E. Okonkwo. 2017. "18 – Application of biopolymer composites in super capacitor." In *Biopolymer Composites in Electronics*, edited by K. K. Sadasivuni, D. Ponnamma, J. Kim, J. J. Cabibihan, and M. A. AlMaadeed, 487–503. Elsevier.

Orsini, G., A. Putignano, and T. A. Mitsiadis. 2019. "Editorial: Advances in craniofacial and dental materials through nanotechnology and tissue engineering." *Frontiers in Physiology* 10. doi: 10.3389/fphys.2019.00303.

Petchdee, S., W. Chumsing, S. Udomsom, and K. Thunsiri. 2020. "Dental pulp stem cells for tissue engineered heart valve." *Indian Journal of Animal Research* 54 (12):1554–1557. doi: 10.18805/ijar.B-1224.

Pryadko, A., M. A. Surmeneva, and R. A. Surmenev. 2021. "Review of hybrid materials based on polyhydroxyalkanoates for tissue engineering applications." *Polymers* 13 (11). doi: 10.3390/polym13111738.

Qiu, Zhi-Ye, Yun Cui, and Xiu-Mei Wang. 2019. "Chapter 1 – Natural bone tissue and its biomimetic." In *Mineralized Collagen Bone Graft Substitutes*, edited by Xiu-Mei Wang, Zhi-Ye Qiu and Helen Cui, 1–22. Woodhead Publishing.

Rai, R., R. Raval, R. V. Khandeparker, S. K. Chidrawar, A. A. Khan, and M. S. Ganpat. 2015. "Tissue engineering: Step ahead in maxillofacial reconstruction." *Journal of International Oral Health* 7 (9):138–142.

Sancilio, S., M. Gallorini, C. Di Nisio, E. Marsich, R. Di Pietro, H. Schweikl, and A. Cataldi. 2018. "Alginate/Hydroxyapatite-based nanocomposite scaffolds for bone tissue engineering improve dental pulp biomineralization and differentiation." *Stem Cells International* 2018. doi: 10.1155/2018/9643721.

Sarna-Bos, K., P. Boguta, K. Skic, D. Wiacek, P. Maksymiuk, J. Sobieszczanski, and R. Chalas. 2022. "Physicochemical properties and surface characteristics of ground human teeth." *Molecules* 27 (18). doi: 10.3390/molecules27185852.

Socci, M. C., G. Rodriguez, E. Oliva, S. Fushimi, K. Takabatake, H. Nagatsuka, C. J. Felice, and A. P. Rodriguez. 2023. "Polymeric materials, advances and applications in tissue engineering: A review." *Bioengineering-Basel* 10 (2). doi: 10.3390/bioengineering10020218.

Sugiaman, V. K., R. Djuanda, N. Pranata, S. Naliani, W. L. Demolsky, and Jeffrey. 2022. "Tissue engineering with stem cell from human exfoliated deciduous teeth (SHED) and collagen matrix, regulated by growth factor in regenerating the dental pulp." *Polymers* 14 (18). doi: 10.3390/polym14183712.

Sugiaman, V. K., Jeffrey, S. Naliani, N. Pranata, R. Djuanda, and R. I. Saputri. 2023. "Polymeric scaffolds used in dental pulp regeneration by tissue engineering approach." *Polymers* 15 (5). doi: 10.3390/polym15051082.

Sujon, M. K., Snfm Noor, M. A. Zabidi, and K. A. Shariff. 2023. "Combined sol-gel bioactive glass and beta-tricalcium phosphate for potential dental tissue engineering: A preliminary study." *Journal of the Australian Ceramic Society* 59 (2):415–424. doi: 10.1007/s41779-023-00841-7.

Teigen, K., and A. Jokstad. 2012. "Dental implant suprastructures using cobalt-chromium alloy compared with gold alloy framework veneered with ceramic or acrylic resin: A retrospective cohort study up to 18 years." *Clinical Oral Implants Research* 23 (7):853–860. doi: 10.1111/j.1600-0501.2011.02211.x.

Vakil, A. U., N. M. Petryk, E. Shepherd, and M. B. B. Monroe. 2021. "Biostable shape memory polymer foams for smart biomaterial applications." *Polymers* 13 (23). doi: 10.3390/polym13234084.

Wanasathop, A., C. Zhong, P. Nimmansophon, M. Murawsky, and S. K. Li. 2023. "Characterization of porcine gingiva for drug absorption." *Journal of Pharmaceutical Sciences* 112 (4):1032–1040. doi: 10.1016/j.xphs.2022.11.016.

Wang, L. Q., Z. H. Xu, H. Zhang, and C. P. Yao. 2023. "A review on chitosan-based biomaterial as carrier in tissue engineering and medical applications." *European Polymer Journal* 191. doi: 10.1016/j.eurpolymj.2023.112059.

Wang, S. F., X. H. Wang, F. G. Draenert, O. Albert, H. C. Schroder, V. Mailander, G. Mitov, and W. E. G. Muller. 2014. "Bioactive and biodegradable silica biomaterial for bone regeneration." *Bone* 67:292–304. doi: 10.1016/j.bone.2014.07.025.

Woloszyk, A., S. H. Dircksen, N. Bostanci, R. Muller, S. Hofmann, and T. A. Mitsiadis. 2014. "Influence of the mechanical environment on the engineering of mineralised tissues using human dental pulp stem cells and silk fibroin scaffolds." *PLoS One* 9 (10). doi: 10.1371/journal.pone.0111010.

Yarram, A., K. S. V. Ramesh, G. Narasimha Rao, S. A. Yasmeen, M. C. Suresh Sajjan, A. V. Ramaraju. 2019. "Corrosion in titanium dental implants – A review." *International Journal of Dental Materials* 1 (3):72–78.

Yasuda, H., S. Kuroda, R. Nanba, T. Ishikawa, N. Shinya, S. Terasaka, Y. Iwasaki, and K. Nagashima. 2005. "A novel coating biomaterial for intracranial aneurysms: Effects and safety in extra- and intracranial carotid artery." *Neuropathology* 25 (1):66–76. doi: 10.1111/j.1440-1789.2004.00590.x.

Zafar, M. S., Z. Khurshid, and K. Almas. 2015. "Oral tissue engineering progress and challenges." *Tissue Engineering and Regenerative Medicine* 12 (6):387–397. doi: 10. 1007/s13770-015-0030-6.

Zamri, M. F. M. A., R. Bahru, R. Amin, M. U. A. Khan, S. I. Abd Razak, S. Abu Hassan, M. R. A. Kadir, and N. H. M. Nayan. 2021. "Waste to health: A review of waste derived materials for tissue engineering." *Journal of Cleaner Production* 290. doi: 10.1016/ j.jclepro.2021.125792.

Zhang, J., H. Ding, X. F. Liu, Y. F. Sheng, X. Q. Liu, and C. M. Jiang. 2019. "Dental follicle stem cells: Tissue engineering and immunomodulation." *Stem Cells and Development* 28 (15):986–994. doi: 10.1089/scd.2019.0012.

Zheng, Z. Z., D. Eglin, M. Alini, G. R. Richards, L. Qin, and Y. X. Lai. 2021. "Visible light-induced 3D bioprinting technologies and corresponding bioink materials for tissue engineering: A review." *Engineering* 7 (7):966–978. doi: 10.1016/j.eng.2020.05.0212 095-8099.

Zhu, M. J., Z. Q. Zhao, H. H. K. Xu, Z. X. Dai, K. Yu, L. Xiao, A. Schneider, M. D. Weir, T. W. Oates, Y. X. Bai, and K. Zhang. 2022. "Effects of metformin delivery via biomaterials on bone and dental tissue engineering." *International Journal of Molecular Sciences* 23 (24). doi: 10.3390/ijms232415905.

10 Use of Bioinspired and Nanostructured Materials from Nature in Dentistry

Deepak Kumar Panda and Monalisa Mishra
Neural Developmental Biology Lab, Department of Life
Science, NIT Rourkela, Rourkela, Odisha, India

10.1 INTRODUCTION

Nature is the ultimate designer, providing creative inspiration for developing novel bio-materials, entities, and operations that function from the macro to the nano level. Nature has been a bioinspiration for human civilisation. The blueprint of biological substance is an insightful and optimised tool that nature employs for the survival of organisms and allows these organisms to thrive in challenging environments (Wang, Naleway, and Wang 2020). The evolving field of biomaterials science can be categorised into biological materials, biomaterials, and bioinspired materials. Biological materials study nature-based materials like bone, feathers, skin, etc. Biomaterials like implant materials have been used in the biomedical industry. Biomimetics is the study of bioinspired materials, including novel materials synthesis, gadgets, and structures inspired by nature. Biomimetics is a budding field that allows nanostructured materials and nanostructured device generation that provides desirable properties (Bhushan and Jung 2011, Jung 2009, Zhang et al. 2015). Computational modelling and nanotechnology can amplify this to a certain degree. Bioinspired materials can be generated by correlating and formulating the basic understanding of biological materials to solve all the queries related to engineering, marine, aerospace, medical, civil engineering, and material science. Thus, natural system-based bioinspired materials show great potential for designing next-generation advanced materials (Kumar, Mittal, and Haleem 2022) (see Figure 10.1). Despite the present-day challenges, bioinspired materials have become crucial for encouraging innovations and stepping forward in the contemporary materials-based industry. Different sectors demand lightweight, high-strength, high-toughness, multifunctional, and environmentally friendly future materials (Wang, Naleway, and Wang 2020).

DOI: 10.1201/9781003404934-10

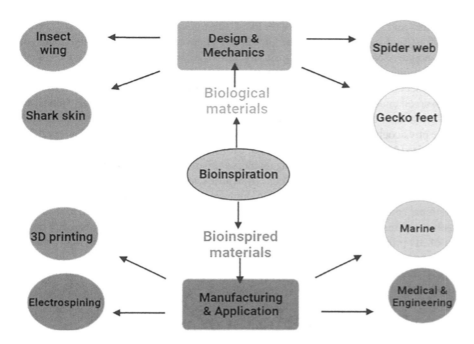

FIGURE 10.1 Bioinspired materials.

10.2 BIOINSPIRED MATERIALS FROM NATURE

Lotus and Colocasia leaves are self-cleaning and superhydrophobic because of the hierarchical roughness of micro bumps superposed with a nanostructure and the hydrophobic wax coating leaf surfaces. (Bhushan and Jung 2011, Jung 2009, Zhang et al. 2015) Gao and Jiang found that numerous small microsetae (hairs) with fine nano grooves and cuticular wax covering the pond skater's legs make the leg surfaces super hydrophobic, enabling them to skate and stride speedily on the top of the aquatic body. The spider web's strong, continuous, water-insoluble one-dimensional fibre is resistant to water, air, and solar light because of its tensile strength of 1.1 GPa. The eye of certain moths consists of hundreds of hexagonally organised nanoscopic pillars, which makes them anti-reflective to visible light (Bhushan and Jung 2011, Jung 2009). The hierarchical structure of the gecko feet helps them to adhere to walls (Wang, Naleway, and Wang 2020). Honeycomb inspires chemical engineering, mechanical engineering, nanofabrication and architecture (Zhang et al. 2015). Although Nacre material is composed chiefly of brittle minerals, its Young's modulus ranges from 70–80 GPa, tensile strength ranges from 70–100 MPa, and toughness ranges from 4–10 MPa m1/2 (Wang, Naleway, and Wang 2020). Many insects with antimicrobial surfaces have ~50–250 nm diameter nanopillars and divergent densities and heights. Natural surfaces and agents have evolved through billions of years, and a great number have generated bacterial colonisation inhibition ability (Zhang et al. 2015). Dragonfly wings have randomly distributed nanostructures that kill gram-positive bacteria like *S. aureus* and

B. subtilis and gram-negative bacteria like *P. aeruginosa* (Tripathy et al. 2017, Hasan, Crawford, and Ivanova 2013). The Cicada wings have bactericidal activity against the gram-negative bacteria *P. aeruginosa*, as reported by Ivanova et al. (2012). Despite the superhydrophobic nature of the cicada wing, bacteria's adhesion on the nanostructured surface occurs significantly, killing attached gram-negative bacteria within five minutes, as observed under microscopes. Lotus leaves, rose petals, shark skin, cactus spines, and exoskeletons of desert beetles are super wettable (superhydrophobic) surfaces, attained by the physicochemical component of the surface (Hasan, Crawford, and Ivanova 2013). Bioinspired Mercedes Benz was designed by boxfish architecture of the Zayed National Museum, Abu Dhabi, built by taking feathers as inspiration and the inspiration of a bullet train from a Kingfisher's nose (Chen, McKittrick, and Meyers 2012). These exciting functions obtained through dependable, long-lasting, and non-toxic materials provide additional benefits and have been used in various practical applications. *Salvinia molesta* has been an inspiration for designing superhydrophobic eggbeater-like structure by the use of 3D printing (see Table 10.1) (Wang, Naleway, and Wang 2020). Many natural plant and animal derived antimicrobial agents are found in nature like catechin, allicin, pomegranate, cinnamon, Furanone, chitosan, etc. which are effective for bacterial growth inhibition (see Table 10.2).

10.3   RECENT TRENDS IN THE USE OF ANTIMICROBIAL BIOINSPIRED MATERIALS IN DENTISTRY

The development and use of intelligent dental antimicrobial biomaterials have exponentially increased in the dental industry. They offer better efficacy in preventing infections and increase the durability of dental implant materials (Montoya et al. 2023). The first and foremost approach for designing antimicrobial biomaterials is to stop the accumulation of those microbes. The oral cavity contains over 700 biofilm-forming microbes that can cause periodontitis, dental caries, candidiasis, root canal infections, periimplantitis, pulpitis and soft tissue infections. The mouth is an unfriendly and adverse environment for dental materials. Microbes interfere with esterases from saliva by producing acids that cause hard tissue demineralisation, leading to direct and indirect restoration failure (Montoya et al. 2023).

10.4   TOOTH STRUCTURE, DISEASES AND ASSOCIATED MICROBES

The tooth is the toughest calcium-phosphate-based biomineral generated by humans. Different classes and types of teeth perform various functions in the mastication process. The teeth of humans have heterodont dentition (Fuller 1999).

10.4.1   HUMAN DENTITION

Humans have mainly two types of dentition, namely deciduous and permanent. Deciduous teeth are temporary and commonly known as milk teeth. There are 20 deciduous teeth in humans with four incisors, two canines, two first molars, and two second molars per arch. Permanent dentition is composed of 32 teeth with 16 permanent teeth per arch (Fuller 1999).

TABLE 10.1

Bioinspired Materials from Nature (Tripathy et al. 2017)

Naturally Occurring Surface	Surface Features	Nature	Functions	References
Brittle star	Calcitic microlenses	Mechanically strong	Highly focusing, aberration-free, birefringence-free	(Liu and Jiang 2011)
Butterfly wing	Nanostripes over microsquamas	Superhydrophobic, directional adhesion	Self-cleaning, fluorescence emission, chemical sensing capability	(Liu and Jiang 2011)
Wing of Cicada	200 nm height, 60 nm diameter (top), 100 nm diameter (base) Nanoneedles	Superhydrophobic, Contact angle of the water (CA) = 159°, Anti-reflection	Fatal to *P. aeruginosa*	(Ivanova et al. 2012)
Wing of Dragonfly	50–70 nm diameter, 240 nm height Nanograss	Superydrophobic, Contact angle of the water (CA) = 153°	Fatal to *P. aeruginosa*, *S. aureus*	(Ivanova et al. 2013)
Fish scale	Nanostructured micropapillae	Superoleophobic in water and superoleophilic in air	Drag-reduction	(Liu and Jiang 2011)
Gecko feet	Sub-micron spaced hair (spinules) like structures and radius of curvature at the tip is less than 20 nm.	Superhydrophobic, CA = 151° to 155°, reversible adhesive	Fatal to *Porphyromonas gingivalis*, *B. subtilis*, self-cleaning	(Watson et al. 2015)
Lotus leaves	Microbumps or microasperties	Superhydrophobic, low adhesive	self-cleaning	(Bhushan and Jung 2011, Liu and Jiang 2011)
Pond skater's legs	Nano-grooved needle-shaped microsetae	Robust Superydrophobic	Durable	(Bhushan and Jung 2011, Liu and Jiang 2011)
Spider web	Beta-strands, Beta-sheet nanocrystals	Water insoluble	Resistant to rain	(Bhushan and Jung 2011, Liu and Jiang 2011)
Mosquito compound eye	Hexagonally closed pack micro-ommatidia covered by nano-nipples	Superhydrophobic	Antifogging, anti-reflection	(Liu and Jiang 2011)

(Continued)

TABLE 10.1 (Continued)
Bioinspired Materials from Nature (Tripathy et al. 2017)

Naturally Occurring Surface	Surface Features	Nature	Functions	References
Moth eye	Nanoscopic pillars	Anti-reflective	Resistant to visible light	(Bhushan and Jung 2011)
Honeycomb	Hexagonal cells	Highly shearing	High specific strength	(Zhang et al. 2015)
Peacock feather	2-D photonic crystal	Superhydrophobic	Self-cleaning, Structural colour	(Liu and Jiang 2011)
Polar bear fur	Microstructure	Optical property	Thermal insulation	(Liu and Jiang 2011)
Rice leaf	Quasi 1-D microasperties	Superhydrophobic	Anisotropic wettability	(Liu and Jiang 2011)
Rose petal	Micropapillae and nanoscale creases	Superhydrophobic	High adhesion	(Liu and Jiang 2011)
Shark's skin	Micro-ribbed dermal denticles	Drag reduction	Anti-biofouling	(Liu and Jiang 2011)
Shell nacre	Multiscale structured abalone nacre	High mechanical strength and toughness	Resistant to fracture	(Wang, Naleway, and Wang 2020)
Kingfisher's nose	Less splashy	Minimal resistance	Sonic boom eliminator	(Chen, McKittrick, and Meyers 2012)
Bird feather	Serrated surface	Cool air drawer	Highly ventilated	(Chen, McKittrick, and Meyers 2012)
Box fish	Self-correcting forced carapace	Hydrodynamic stability	Efficient pitching and yawing motion	(Chen, McKittrick, and Meyers 2012)

TABLE 10.2

Natural Antimicrobial Agents and Extracts (Montoya et al. 2023)

Type	Antimicrobial Agent	Antimicrobial Mechanism
Natural agents and extract	Catechins and Gallocatechin gallate (GCG)	Inhibits cell wall biosynthesis and type II fatty-acid synthase biosynthesis of bacteria.
	Canephora or *Coffea arabica*	Inactivates enzymes of cell
	Cranberry proanthocyanidins	It affects the adhesion and coaggregation of bacteria.
	Allicin (Diallyl thiosulfate)	Thioredoxin reductase, RNA polymerase, and Alcohol dehydrogenase are inhibited.
	Isothiocyanate	Disturbs bacterial biochemical processes by reacting with the protein
	Eugenol (Clove oil)	Impair and hamper the membrane of bacteria
	Citrus aurantium/ Citrus limonum	Disrupts membrane of bacteria
	Pomegranate	Microbial enzyme and ATP synthesis inhibition
	Farsenol (Propolis)	Cell membrane permeability hindrance and membrane potential disruption.
	Cinnamon	Disrupt the membranes of bacterial cells.
	Urushiol	The shape of bacteria change and ECM structural integrity destruction.
	Curcumin	Inhibits bacterial cell growth
Compounds	Chitosan	Cell membrane permeability alteration, inhibition of DNA replication
	Catechol derivatives (PDA), (LDOPA)	Production of hydroxyl radicals due to H_2O_2 generation
	Furanone (Derived from marine algae)	Interfere with bacterial quorum sensing and swarming pathogens.

10.4.2 ANATOMY OF THE TOOTH

A tooth consists of enamel, dentin, Cementum, pulp cavity and periodontal ligament. The crown is the visible portion of the mouth. The enamel is the tooth's most challenging part and the crown's outermost layer. It contains non-living cells. Odontoblasts are dentine-forming living cells located on the pulp's surface. The central part of tooth tissue contains dentine. A bone-like structure that covers the tooth's roots and attaches the tooth to the periodontal ligament is called a Cementum. The pulp cavity comprises pure organic connective tissue embedded with blood vessels and nerves within the mouth. The periodontal ligament fixes the tooth's root to the bony alveolar socket (see Figure 10.2) (Fuller 1999).

10.4.3 DISEASES OF TOOTH AND GUM

The innate host defence system continuously monitors the colonisation of bacteria and inhibits bacterial invasion of local tissues. The newborn baby's oral cavity

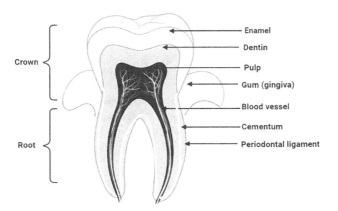

FIGURE 10.2 Anatomy of the human tooth.

bacteria are usually absent but rapidly become colonised with *Streptococcus salivarius* bacteria. *Streptococcus mutans* and *Streptococcus sanguinis* colonise the dental surface and gingiva in the first year of teeth appearance. Bacterial fermentation of the food debris accumulated on the tooth surface produces acid, leading to the build-up of a yellowish film called plaque on teeth. *S. mutans and S. sanguis* are plaque-forming bacteria (see Figures 10.3, 10.4 and Table 10.4) (Jenkinson 2011, Loesche 1986, Jakubovics 2015) (Table 10.3).

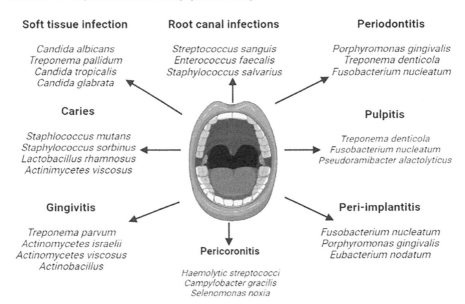

FIGURE 10.3 Pathogens associated with oral and systemic diseases of humans.

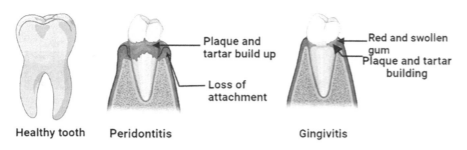

Healthy tooth   Peridontitis   Gingivitis

FIGURE 10.4   Dental diseases.

TABLE 10.3
Dental Diseases and Symptoms

Disease	Sign and Symptoms	References
Caries	Lesions, blackish discolouration on the chewing surface, the white spot near the gingival margin	(Mathur and Dhillon 2018)
Periodontitis	Bleeding while brushing the teeth, periodontal pocketing, persistent halitosis (lousy taste/ odour), red swollen tender gum, plaque, difficulty in eating	(Gasner and Schure 2022, Sehrawat et al. 2022)
Gingivitis	When touched, brushed, or even if random bleeding occurs, the gum becomes red, swollen, and easily bleeds.	(Singh and Singh 2013)
Pericoronitis	The advanced stage includes symptoms like lymphadenopathy, fever, reduced mouth opening, trouble with chewing and deglutition, halitosis, alteration of voice, or even breathing problems may be seen.	(Al Farabi Clinics and Arabia 2022)
Pulpitis	Darkening of enamel, tooth mobility, bleeding, redness of the gum, swelling of the tissue, dilated blood vessels, odontoblast layer disruption, irreversible pulpitis, and severe, continuous, and long-lasting pain are seen.	(Botirovna, Shuhratovna, and Rustambekovna 2021)
Peri-implantitis	Increased depth of the probe, bleeding on probe and suppuration, and loss of bone.	(Yi et al. 2020)

10.5   SMART DENTAL MATERIAL

Four types of intelligent, innovative biomaterials are bioinert, bioactive, bioresponsive, and autonomous. After implantation, bioinert biomaterials bring about less reaction and nominal toxicity with neighbouring tissues. A secure, chemically inactive biomaterial for crowns, oral implants, bridges, and the dental frame is Polyetheretherketone (PEEK). Bioactive materials provide beneficial therapies like

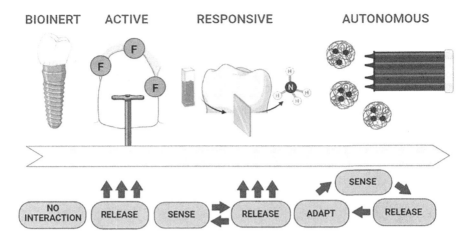

FIGURE 10.5   Smart dental materials.

antibacterial, regeneration, drug delivery, etc. (Montoya et al. 2023, Kumar, Singh, et al. 2023). Stabilising the tooth's cyclic loss and gain of minerals by fluoride-releasing compounds is an example of a bioactive material. Fluoride inhibits the adherence of bacteria and its growth and interferes with its acidogenicity and acidurance as it is toxic to bacterial cells. Surface coating or functionalization methods can upgrade bioinert to bioactive dental materials. Specific stimuli like light, temperature, changes in pH, and electrical and enzymes are sensed by stimuli-responsive or bioresponsive biomaterials, and they react by liberating a pre-programmed therapy (Montoya et al. 2023). Dental composites can be coated with NPs sensitive to pH to treat caries that release antimicrobial agents in response to acidic pH, an example of bioresponsive material. Biomaterials that are autonomous can recognise several impulses and tune their reaction correspondingly, which is the most brilliant biomaterials. Magnetically steered nanobots filled with antibacterial therapies can sterilise and treat root canals, which confers autonomous biomaterials' function. Innovative biomaterials have many implementations, such as drug delivery, tissue engineering, antimicrobial, tissue regeneration, and remineralization (see Figure 10.5) (Montoya et al. 2023).

10.6   NATURE-DERIVED BIOINSPIRED MATERIALS USED IN DENTISTRY

To treat dental disease, classic dental material should be designed to combat microbes, hinder hydrolytic degradation, encourage remineralization, firm tissue binding, and rejuvenate tooth tissues (Montoya et al. 2023). Inspired by spider silk's hierarchical nanostructure, Chen et al. have prepared a bioinspired hybrid film. They fabricated the film by launching graphene quantum dots (mimics β-sheet crystals) into polyvinyl alcohol as the matrix of the protein. The concentration of graphene quantum dots can enhance remarkable mechanical properties. To form "strong-weak" tiny features in the shell nacre, the polysaccharides, and proteins grip the calcium carbonate microtablets in conjunction. For crack propagation and energy dissipation, the organic phase is essential (Wang, Naleway, and Wang 2020). Ritchie et al. have used freeze-casted zirconia polycrystal densified with methacrylate resin as a suspension to fabricate bioinspired dental materials and, as a consequence, nacre-like lamellar and brick-and-mortar architecture composite were produced. The deformable and challenging nature of the nacre is due to the dispersion of profuse mechanical energy by sliding mechanism, bridging, and crack deflection. Barthelat et al. produced bioinspired toughened glass using lamination fabrication methods with laser engraving (Wang, Naleway, and Wang 2020).

10.7 NATURE-INSPIRED ANTIMICROBIAL DENTAL NANOPARTICLES (NPS), NANOSTRUCTURES AND COATINGS

Antibiotics such as chlorhexidine, minocycline, antimicrobial peptides (AMPs), positively charged monomers, and metallic and non-metallic fillers are some of the antimicrobial agents in biologically active therapies. Immediately after implantation, embodying antimicrobial agents inside a carrier (biomaterial) using bioactive technology are practiced to deliver the treatment. Adhesion-ensuring binding materials and dental sealants are coated with percolating antibiotics such as tetracycline, metronidazole, and chlorohexidine to prevent biofilm formation and microbial growth suppression (Montoya et al. 2023). Antibacterial Polyelectrolyte Multilayer films have been formed by Zhuk et al. by combining positively charged gentamycin, tobramycin, and polymyxin B-like antibiotics with negatively charged tannic acid (Cloutier, Mantovani, and Rosei 2015). Bioactive fillers have gained popularity among scientists to surpass the concerns related to the microbial resistance of antibiotics. Farnesol disrupts the membrane, decreases biofilm's acidogenicity, and inhibits extracellular polymeric substance synthesis, whereas myricetin kills biofilm-forming *S. mutans*. So, an antibacterial system with double nanoparticles has been used (Montoya et al. 2023). The biosynthesized AgNP from *Punica granatum* L. acted as an antioxidant and showed high microbe inhibiting ability against *B. cereus* and *V. cholera*. AgNP could be a potent anti-biofilm agent (Sahoo et al. 2022). Antimicrobial coatings prevent the colonisation of bacteria and the generation of biofilm on the surface of the implant and have successfully reduced mucositis, peri-implantitis, and implant failure. Contact and release-killing surfaces are the solutions to create antimicrobial coatings. Surface-adhered antimicrobial quaternary ammonium compounds, antimicrobial peptides, and antimicrobial enzymes are used in the contact-killing strategy (see Table 10.6). Catechols like polydopamine and dopamine are coatings that produce H_2O_2 and singlet oxygen (O_2). This leads to inhibiting bacterial adhesion, proliferation, and cell death due to oxidative stress. Catechol, an antimicrobial, biocompatible, and moist-resistant adhesion molecule, becomes a suitable coating for dental implants. Periodontitis, peri-implantitis, and caries have been treated using oxidised pectin as a coating substance, increasing mucous adhesion to soft and hard tissues. Aspect-ratio (width-to-height) of nanostructures ranging from 0.2 to 2 induce tension on the membrane of the bacteria, hastening their disruption (Montoya et al. 2023). Anti-biofouling surfaces are generated by changing the physical features of the surface,

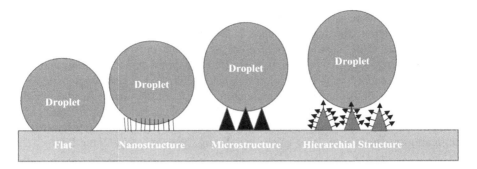

FIGURE 10.6   Interaction between droplet and surface shows less contact between droplet and surface for microstructure and significantly less for the hierarchical structure.

preventing microbial adhesion and biofilm formation (see Figure 10.6). Some of these physical changes are nature-inspired, mimicking the surface design of shark skin, dragonfly wings, cicada wings, upper surfaces of lotus and rose petals, etc. *S. mutans* attachment and colony formation were reduced compared to unmodified wires when the surface of the dental archwires were redesigned by imitating the *Colocasia esculenta* leaf surface (Wang, Naleway, and Wang 2020, Montoya et al. 2023). Resins (adhesives/sealants), nanocarriers (micelles, nano gel), and hydrogels become "smart" conveyors for antimicrobial technologies in dentistry that are sensitive to pH.

Hydrogels expand and collapse in acidic and basic pH, respectively. It has been seen that drug-free resins are sensitive to pH and have caries inhibition effects by inhibiting *S. mutans* biofilm. Carboxybetaine methacrylate-dimethylaminoethyl methacrylate copolymer P (CBMA-co-DMAEMA) is a pH-sensitive coat; when it is exposed to low pH, it delivers octapeptides that kill caries forming *S. mutans* (Montoya et al. 2023). Micelles are sensitive to pH and are employed to enclose and liberate farnesol for treating caries. Micelles released the farnesol in low pH conditions, reducing the proliferation of bacteria. To combat the formation of biofilms and to cure inflammation of periodontal ligament, dental surfaces are fabricated using pH-sensitive quaternary ammonium chitosan-liposome NPs and are found to be effective (Montoya et al. 2023).

10.7.1 NANOPARTICLES

An antimicrobial peptide called cateslytin is generated upon the breakdown of bacterial hyaluronidase-mediated hyaluronic acid/chitosan film (Cloutier, Mantovani, and Rosei 2015). The use of nanomaterials has been increasing dramatically worldwide in this era due to their phenomenal implementations in all domains. Generous metal nanoparticle synthesis, especially the synthesis of nanoparticles of Ag (AgNPs) using a natural product, has become an area of focus in nanotechnology. Natural polymers such as chitosan, starch and tannic acid have been used to synthesise silver and gold nanoparticles known from recent studies. Plants, algae, fungi, yeast, bacteria, and viruses are natural reservoirs known to be used both for the extracellular and intracellular gold, platinum, silver, and titanium nanoparticle synthesis. *Rosmarinus officinalis*, *Sesbania grandiflora*, and *Tribulus terrestris* are known to be used for the biological synthesis of nanoparticles of gold and silver (Velusamy et al. 2016). Compared to chemically synthesised NPs, plant-derived NPs exhibit more biotic potential and less detrimental complications inside the body. They have an implementation in farming, food science, nanomedicine, cosmetics and maintenance of human health. Depending on the circumstances, they are antimicrobial, antiparasitic, anti-inflammatory, pro-apoptotic, and anti-oxidative (Hano and Abbasi 2021, Marinescu et al. 2020, Singh et al. 2018). Curcumin-conjugated chitosan-gold NPs sensitive to pH showed regulated antibacterial effects against gram-positive and negative species. To treat dental caries, pHly-1, an antimicrobial peptide NP segregated from the venom of a spider, has no harmful impact on the diversity of oral microbiota and gingiva tissues (Montoya et al. 2023). Due to antimicrobial and biofilm-inhibiting properties and low bacterial strain resistance, antimicrobial peptides have been given special attention. They are naturally occurring smaller molecules consisting of 50 amino acids, generally cationic and amphipathic. There are thousands of different AMPs but only a few have been used as dental implants. Salivary protein BPIFA2 derived GL13K, a self-building, positively charged, amphipathic antimicrobial peptide, could be anchored on titanium, reducing *Porphyromonas gingivalis* and *Streptococcus gordonii*. hLF1-11 is another AMP used to coat implants and has been shown to decrease the activity of *Lactobacillus salivarius* and *Streptococcus sanguinis* (Fontelo et al. 2022). Combining the antibacterial potentiality of antimicrobial peptides and pH-sensitive nanocarriers by enclosing antimicrobial peptides into nanocarriers leads to the generation of pH-responsive AMPs with high bacterial properties. Membrane penetrating ability and lysis activity of the peptide at low pH can be increased by modifying amphipathic α-helical GH12 with histidine. C18G-His, a peptide rich in histidine, shows an equivalent response in opposition to *E. coli.*, *S. aureus*, and *P. aeruginosa* (Montoya et al. 2023). Antibacterial surfaces can be fabricated using antimicrobial peptides. A popular synthetic peptide named CM15 has been synthesised which mimics naturally present Cecropin A in moths and having antimicrobial activity (Hasan, Crawford, and Ivanova 2013) (see Table 10.6).

10.7.2 Nature-inspired Antimicrobial Dental Implants Coating Material

Replacement of body parts and their function by inserting tissues or devices into the body or placing them on the surface is defined as implants by the U.S. Food and Drug Administration 2018 (Baghdan et al. 2019). An implant integrates science and technology in multidisciplinary areas such as surface chemistry, physics, biomechanics manufacturing technologies, and nanoscale surface engineering (Duraccio, Mussano, and Faga 2015). Cracking, bending and losing its properties leads to failure of *in vivo* implant. The material's intrinsic properties include elastic moduli of the material, point of yield, tensile strength, fatigue strength, and toughness (Brunski 1988). Ideal implants are tough, biocompatible, resistant to fracture and wear and have good corrosion resistance (Zhang and Van Le 2020). Advanced dentistry aims to retain the patient's usual function, oration, health, and aesthetics despite atrophy, disease, or injury to masticatory apparatus. Replacement of single missing teeth in the anterior region has always challenged dentists' minds (Duraccio, Mussano, and Faga 2015, Kumar, Kumar, Dogra, et al. 2023). The three major types of biocompatibility of implants are biotolerant, bioinert, and bioactive. Biotolerant materials are not refuted by the host's tissue but are enclosed by a fibrous capsule. Bioinert materials provide the proximate cohesion of bone on their surface. Bioactive materials allow ossification on their surface and the formation of chemical bonds by exchanging ions with host tissue along the juncture (Barfeie, Wilson, and Rees 2015). The chief reason for post-implantation implant collapse is inadequate bone formation surrounding the biomaterial. Hence upgradations are needed, as patients need quick healing (Toledo 2013). Infection, accelerated loss of bone, formation of biofilm, and bad osseointegration (bone-to-implant contact) with implant loosening are some of the reasons behind the 5% failure in dentistry (Tomsia et al. 2011). The implant design, surgical technique, type of bone, and loading conditions of the implant influence osseointegration. Surface roughness, wettability, and chemical composition of the implant surface regulate osseointegration. Implant surface remodelling affects the bone-implant interplay. The growth of implant surface coatings induces a maximum association between the implant's surface and bone (Damerau et al. 2022). Bacterial attachment and the rate of improvement of healing can be changed by changing the surface morphology of the implant with nanoparticles. Several methods can produce various nanoparticle forms using natural or synthetic polymers, metallic implants, and ceramic implants (Baghdan et al. 2018) (see Table 10.7). American Association of Oral and Maxillofacial Surgeons states that 35–44 aged adults have not less than one tooth affected by injury or gum disease, which counts for 69%. Screw threads and porous coated designs of the solid body press-fit are important aspects of endosseous implants. It has been disclosed that minute changes in the implant form, length, and breadth could affect the success rate. The osseointegration rate and speed are affected by the surface's physical and chemical nature. Fluoride ions increase the rate of calcification of the bone. Hence, they have been coated over implants. To improve the attachment of cells, deposition of protein and mineralisation, implant surfaces are coated with immobilised molecules that osteoblasts can recognise. To promote the adsorption of protein and adhesion of cells, nanoscale modification of the implant's surface roughness has been attempted. Incorporating the growth factors and coating the biomimetic calcium phosphate accelerates the process of bone restoration (Gaviria et al. 2014). Modification of surface, use of different coatings, and the regulated liberation of antibiotics, have enhanced the osseointegration, integration of soft tissue, antibacterial property and immunomodulation of dental implants (Zhang et al. 2021). The use of dental implants to restore usual function, oration, and aesthetics has increased over the past 50 years (Elia et al. 2015). Insertion of dental implant is a standard plan of action with a 90–95% success rate. An implant surface with accumulated bacteria induces surrounding tissue inflammation, removing the infected implant and degrading bone (Baghdan et al. 2019). Alternative approaches to antibiotic treatment have been demanding due to the continuous rise in multi-resistant microbial population and decrease in the latest sanctioned antibiotics (Agel et al. 2019). Coating the implant and modifying the surface are favourable approaches that prevent implant failure. Antimicrobial implant coatings have antibiofilm forming ability advantageous over systemic antibiotics administration. Various courses of action have produced nanostructured, less bacterial adhesive, and elevated osseointegrated dental implants. The nanospray drying technique has recently been used as a one-step dental implant covering and surface modification method. It produces nanoparticles by developing narrow size tiny droplets, fewer quantities of sample, and yields more powder. The extensive use of nano spray drying was confirmed using chitin, chitosan, and curcumin with different physicochemical properties. This technique is used to produce antibacterial, biocompatible nanocoatings (Baghdan et al. 2019). Though titanium implants are a benchmark in dentistry, the tarnishing of gingiva and peri-implantitis have been reported using titanium. Possible hypersensitivity and poor aesthetics have been reported using Ti implants (Pelaez-Vargas et al. 2011). Zirconium dioxide (Zirconia) is a biologically inactive and non-absorbable metal oxide that provides superior mechanical properties to other ceramic biomaterials. It has high fracture toughness and strength of bending. Monoclinic zirconium is stable up to 1,170°C. The fracture rates of ceramic materials decreased due to the introduction of zirconia, a good alternative to titanium. Using Zirconia as an implant causes low discolouration of mucosa and better light transmission and gives a natural aesthetic appearance. Zirconia also possesses a lower rate of bacterial adhesion and lower affinity for plaque formation. Due to its less cytotoxic, high tissue compatibility, enough mucosal adhering, and high corrosion stable nature, Zirconia is a majestic material for implants. The unique ability to resist crack propagation by transforming from one crystalline phase to another has seen in Yttria stabilised tetragonal zirconia polycrystal (Y-TZP). Gaps between abutment and implant are not found in case of ceramic implants as they are made from a single piece (Reinhardt and Beikler 2014). The nacre (mother of pearl) has high strength, is resistant to fracture, favourable bone-bonding properties and, is a naturally formed composite. It can trigger differentiation of bone cell and formation of bone. The in vivo degradable nature of nacre makes it a suitable as a biological coating material. A new hope for fabricating environment-friendly and bioactive coating on dental implants arose when the titanium surface was coated with a thick, continuous, and complex topographic nacre layer. The bioactive and environment-friendly nacreous coating on titanium implants is highly tough and insensitive to cracks (Wang, Xie, and Wang 2005). Some internally cross-linked, soft and polymeric particles hydrate and dehydrate reversibly by the diffusing solvent and external stimuli behaving as Nanogels. Nanogels are biocompatible, colloid stable, high water retaining and biomolecules incorporating gel-like networks, which make them interesting to be used in the biological/biomedical field. Without changing their hydrogel nature and colloidal stability, the architectural inventiveness and the harmonious pore size of nanogels permit the integration of many molecules like inorganic nanoparticles to bio-macromolecules (Keskin et al. 2021). The criteria for nanogels among others are they should not be cytotoxic, should be non-apoptotic, and non-necrotic as they interact with tissues and cells. Biocompatibility of a biomaterial is assured when it performs its destined function without evoking any detrimental effect. Biocompatibility of nanogels are enhanced by conjugation of both nanogel and biomaterial. The generation of novel materials with inherent antimicrobial property is vital, despite the availability of antimicrobial nanogels showing antibacterial potency and slowing the emergence of multidrug-resistant bacteria (Keskin et al. 2021). Chitosan and its acetylated derivative, chitin, are harmless, bactericidal, antifungal, environmentally friendly, and biocompatible biopolymers. Chitin is the major constituent in arthropods' carapace, fungi, and yeast cell walls. Chitosan (1-4, 2-amino-2-deoxy-D-glucan) is a linear polysaccharide present primarily in the carapace of arthropods. Chitin and chitosan are hydrating agents prepared into nanofibers, gels, membranes, and nanoparticles. Uniform fibres have only been manufactured from 90% aqueous acetic acid solutions containing 7% chitosan, as chitosan is soluble in acids. Using chitosan and synthetic polymers such as Poly Vinyl Alcohol (PVA), Poly Ethylene oxide (PEO), Polyvinyl Pyrrolidine (PVP), Poly Lactic Acid (PLA), and Poly Ethylene Terephthalate (PET), electrospun chitosan amalgam nanofibrous mats have been fabricated (Agel et al. 2019). Since the biocompatibility, antibacterial and mechanical properties of the nanofibers of the chitosan were highly increased by adding PVA, PEO, PLA, PVP, and PET, amalgam fibre mats are more beneficial over the pure electrospun chitosan (Agel et al. 2019). Human Dental Pulp Stem Cells (hDPSCs) conjugated with chitosan displayed an increased rate of osseointegration and bone healing compared to xenografts in animal models (Eftekhar Ashtiani et al. 2021). In vitro and in vivo studies have observed that chitosan triggers the movement of progenitor cells and polymorphonuclear cells and intensifies blood vessel formation and extracellular tissue matrix reformation, accelerating the wound healing rate (Bumgardner et al. 2003). As it is environment-friendly, biocompatible, less inflammatory, and has good oxygen and water vapour permeability, Silk fibroin (the fibrous protein) has been used for many biological implementations. Chitosan and silk fibroin have been conjugated in formic acid and used to prepare nanofibrous scaffolds (Jayakumar et al. 2010). The fibroin protein has been modified into thin coatings, thin films, fibroin mats, fibrinogens, foams, etc. Direct settling of silk gels on adhesion-associated conductive materials has been achieved with the help of the electrogelation technique. Functionalization of dental implants with a simple and flexible system and the modulation of coating thickness and adherence are achieved by the electrogelation process, using mechanical and physical properties of the silk (Elia et al. 2015). Sericin, the silk protein, have antibacterial properties, antioxidant or anti-inflammatory behaviour. After silanization in the vapour phase, the glutaraldehyde-bound sericin coating showed notable inhibition of *S. aureus* biofilm (Ghensi et al. 2019). Photodynamic therapy (PDT) has evolved as a productive and dependable antibacterial policy. This technique uses a specific wavelength of light to activate a nontoxic photosensitiser. When the activated photosensitiser reverses the ground state, it releases energy that produces free radicals and singlet oxygen, causing cellular cytotoxicity. Photosensitisers are natural compounds used for antimicrobial PDT. It has found that bacteria are not able to generate resistance against PDT, although multi-resistant strains of bacteria are killed by PDT with the same efficacy. Curcumin is separated from the rhizomes of turmeric (*Curcuma longa*) has antioxidant, anti-inflammatory and anticancer properties. To intensify the effectiveness of curcumin and its effect against microbes, Poly Lactic-co-Glycolic Acid (PLGA) like polymers have used to produce curcumin-loaded nanoparticles. To amplify their strength and to investigate the effect of the surface charge on bacteria, chitosan-modified curcumin-loaded nanoparticles have been used. Chitosan Nanoparticles (CS.NP) and Chitosan-Curcumin Nanoparticles (CS.CUR.NP) showed a slight decrease in CFU of *Escherichia coli* without irradiation (Agel et al. 2019). Saturation of blood in the periimplant region increases by coating implants with CaP, which liberates Ca2+ and HPO_4^{2-}. Proper biomechanical fixation of dental implants is achieved by direct contact between bone and implant which is promoted by CaP coatings. Hydroxyapatite and CaP, which mimic the chemical constitution of natural bone, when coated over on Ti, enhanced the process of osseointegration (Bruschi et al. 2015) (see Table 08). Calcium Phosphate Cement (CPC), especially CaP bio-material, is advantageous in implant coating, facilitating bone healing (Eftekhar Ashtiani et al. 2021). Bioactive glass (BG), developed by Hench in 1971, is a glass ceramic that enables tight contact between bone and implant without interference of fibrous tissue. Bioactive glass is slowly absorbed by the body. Dental implants coated with silicate bioactive glass showed good osseointegration ability comparable to HA coating when inserted in human jaw bone. Collagen is a popular, harmless, environment friendly and well absorbed implant material used as dental implant coating. Tissue restoration and granulation, wound protection and infections can be improved by the use of collagen as it acts as an analgesic (Eftekhar Ashtiani et al. 2021). A less cytotoxic natural antibacterial agent, Totarol prevents biofilm formation and is effective against methicillin-resistant *Staphylococcus aureus*. Titanium disks coated with totarol incubated with human saliva and *Streptococcus gordonii were* found to kill bacteria after 24 hr., compared to the control group. Biosurfactants are also used as probable antibacterial dental implant coatings. *Pseudomonas aeruginosa* produces amphiphilic microbial surfactant such as Rhamnolipids, that can maintain the titanium surface's biocompatibility due to their low toxicity to cell and the microbial attachment restraining property. Antisense oligonucleotides (ASOs) interfere with metabolism of bacteria, preventing bacterial contamination. They target mRNA encoding genes and 23 S and 16 S rRNA's functional domain. In addition to targeting the mRNA and rRNA, non-essential biofilm-forming genes are targeted by ASOs. Vascular Endothelial Growth Factor (VEGF) and Bone Morphogenetic Proteins (BMPs) are examples of growth factors used as implant coatings. Vasculogenesis and angiogenesis are associated with VEGF signal protein. Osteoblasts and endothelial cell activation are increased by coating VEGF over the implant. BMPs are the family of growth factors that induce bone and cartilage formation, bone mesenchymal stem cells (MSCs) differentiation and can regulate the osteogenic cells. To regulate cell-matrix adhesion, extracellular matrix (ECM) protein accumulation on the surfaces of the implant is an alternative to increase the dental implant biocompatibility. FGFs induce fibroblast to secrete extracellular matrix proteins such as elastin, proteoglycans and collagen. Dong Yin et al. found that biocompatible, environmental friendly and safe Mussel Adhesive Protein (MAP) can be a possible implant coating material for titanium (Dong et al. 2020) (see Table 10.5).

TABLE 10.4
Natural Dental Implant Coating

Nano Coatings	Functional Role
Antisense Oligonucleotide	Targets mRNA, rRNA encoding genes, a functional domain of 16 s and 23 s rRNA of bacteria
Biosurfactants	Amphiphilic microbial surfactant
Bioactive glass	Enhances contact between bone and implant.
Curcumin	Inhibits *E. coli* population when conjugated with PLGA
Chitin	Progenitor cells, Polymorphonuclear cells movement, osseointegration,
Chitosan	Biocompatible, antibacterial
Collagen	Dental implant coating
Calcium phosphate	Biochemical fixation of an implant
Growth factor (BMP, VEGF)	Vasculogenesis, Angiogenesis, Bone and cartilage formation, Osteogenesis
Mussel adhesive protein coating	Coating material for Titanium
Nacreous Coating	Bone cell differentiation and bone formation
Plant-derived NPs	Antimicrobial, anti-inflammatory
Photodynamic Therapy	Kills multiple bacteria
Silk fibroin	Thin coating, fibroin mat for implant coating
Sericin	Inhibits biofilm formation
Surfactant	Antibacterial dental implant coating
Totarol	Antibacterial implant coating
Zirconia	Crack-resistant implant material, plaque inhibition

TABLE 10.5
Antibacterial Compounds in Release-Based Coatings (Cloutier, Mantovani, and Rosei 2015)

Antibacterial Compound Type	Released Compounds	Mode of Action
Antibiotics	Aminoglycosides (gentamycin, tobramycin)	Binds 30 s bacterial ribosomal subunits and inhibits protein synthesis
	Quinolones (ciprofloxacin, norfloxacin)	Inhibit replication of DNA and transcription by attacking topoisomerase II and IV.
	Penicillins (Ampicillins)	Peptidoglycan synthesis disruption by enzymatic inhibition. Effective against gram-positive and gram-negative strains
	Glycopeptides (Vancomycin)	Disrupts peptidoglycan synthesis and acts in opposition to mycobacteria and gram-positive bacteria.
	Tetracyclines (minocycline, tetracycline)	Inhibit translation

TABLE 10.5 *(Continued)*
Antibacterial Compounds in Release-Based Coatings (Cloutier, Mantovani, and Rosei 2015)

Antibacterial Compound Type	Released Compounds	Mode of Action
	Rifamycins (Rifampin)	Binds to RNA polymerase and inhibits transcription. Effective as opposed to gram-positive strains and mycobacteria.
Antimicrobial peptides (AMPS)	2000 AMPs found	Inhibit metabolic mechanism
Elements (metal and nonmetal)	Silver	Inhibits respiratory chain and formation of ROS.
	Copper	Promotes lipid peroxidation in the bacterial membrane and produce ROS and lower antioxidants
	Zinc	Inhibits enzymatic activity
	Gallium	Mimics iron
	Selenium	Generates oxidative stress to the bacterial cell.
	Halogens (Chlorine and Iodine)	Protein and nucleic acid structure and synthesis inhibited
Enzyme	Lysozyme	Hydrolyzes the glycosidic bond of peptidoglycan in the bacterial cell wall and acts against gram-positive strains.
	Acyclase	Quorum-quenching and effective against the gram-negative strain
Organic cationic compounds	Quarternary ammonium compounds	Interfere with bacterial enzymes, membrane components and intermolecular interaction.
	Chlorohexidine	Disrupts membranes by attaching to the negatively charged bacterial cell membrane used in dentistry
	Octenidine	Binds to the negatively charged bacterial cell membrane and disrupts membranes.
	Cationic surfactants (BAC, CTAB, DODAB)	Indicate cell surface potential changes from positive to negative
	Chitosans	Positively charged chitosan molecules disrupt the cell membrane.
Organic non-cationic compounds	Furanone	This inhibits quorum sensing and swamping pathways of bacteria.
	Triclosan	Binds to a bacterial enzyme that inhibits the production of fatty acids
Other non-organic compounds	Nitric oxide	Disrupts bacterial signalling
	TiO_2 and TiO_2-based nanocomposite	ROS production is photo-catalytically activated.

TABLE 10.6

Classification of Dental Implants Based on Fabrication Materials (Rasouli, Barhoum, and Uludag 2018, Kumar, Kumar, Mittal, et al. 2023)

Type	Implant Material
Metal implants	Titanium
	Titanium alloys
	Tantalum
	Gold alloys
	Stainless steel
	Cobalt chromium alloys
	Ti–6Al-4V
	Ti–Nb-Ta-Zr (TZNT)
	Mg-based alloys
	Ni-Ti shape memory alloy
Ceramic implants	Bioglass
	β–Tricalcium phosphate
	Zirconia (ZrO_2)
	Zirconia (ZrO_2)-toughened alumina (Al_2O_3)
	Alumina (Al_2O_3)
	Hydroxyapatite (HA)
Polymer implants	Polymethylmethacrylate
	Polytetrafluoroethylene
	Polyethene
	Polysulfone
	Polyurethane
	Polyether ether ketone
	Ultra-high molecular weight polythene
	High-density polyethene
	Polyacetal

TABLE 10.7

Use of Non-natural Antibacterial Nanostructures in Dental Implants (Wang, Naleway, and Wang 2020)

Type of Nanostructure	Role of Nanostructure	Application
Chitosan conjugated silver nanoparticle.	Titanium dental implant coating material.	Inhibits *S. mutants* and *P. gingivalis* attachment and biofilm generation
Zinc oxide + hydroxyapatite nanoparticle	Dental implant covering material	Anti-biofilm activity

TABLE 10.7 *(Continued)*
Use of Non-natural Antibacterial Nanostructures in Dental Implants (Wang, Naleway, and Wang 2020)

Type of Nanostructure	Role of Nanostructure	Application
Copper + zinc oxide nanoparticle	Prospective disinfectant element for implanting temporary abutment connections.	Bactericidal activity increased
Nanocomposite Titania-zinc oxide	Used as a thin film for dental implants on a Si substrate.	Hinders the population of both *S. aureus* and *E. coli*.
Nanoporous silica nanoparticles	As dental composite coating or medical implants and caries, a chlorohexidine drug.	Treatment for biofilm-related infection
Hydroxyapatite nanoparticles	As a ciprofloxacin(CipP) and gentamicin sulphate (Gs) carrier	Inhibit the bacteria *Pseudomonas aeruginosa*
Cerium oxide-incorporated calcium silicate coatings (CeO$_2$CS)	As a covering material (CeO$_2$-CS) for dental implants	Promote osteoblast differentiation, strong antimicrobial activity and good biocompatibility
Zinc oxide nanoparticles (nZnO) + nano-hydroxyapatite (nHA)	As coating materials of bone implants	Improvement of antibacterial activity
Graphene/zinc oxide nanocomposite (GZNC)	As an effective coating substance for dental implants	Inhibits the biofilms of *S. mutans*
Zn(O)nanoparticles + Porous tantalum oxide	dental implant coating material	Prevent initial colonisation forming by bacteria.
Graphene oxide (nGO) nanosheet + PMMA	As a coating material for dental implants	Hydrophilicity increased, preventing microbial adhesion
Polymethyl methyl acrylate (PMMA) + silk fibroin + polyethyleneimine	The material used in dental applications mainly as denture resins and functional material for dental restoration	Antibacterial activity and mechanical support improve
Calcium fluoride nanoparticles	Used as dental nanocomposite	Releasing of fluoride
Zinc oxide + Calcium fluoride nanoparticles	As stress bearing-sealants and sealants inhibit caries	Anti-bacterial and mechanical properties increased
Nano-hydroxyapatite	Dental restorative composites	Physical and mechanical properties enhanced.
Hydroxyapatite nanoparticles	Dental material	Anti-bacterial properties enhanced
Silver nanoparticles	As a covering on the Ti substrate	Anti-bacterial activity against *Lactobacillus salivarius*
Poly-l-lysine/sodium alginate + nano silver	As a covering material for dental implants	Cytocompatibility enhanced and prevents infection caused by bacteria

10.8 FUTURE SCOPE

Natural-system-based bioinspired materials show great potential for designing next-generation advanced materials in dentistry. These materials can be used for implant remodelling and modification of implant surfaces. Implant surface remodelling induces a maximum association between the implant surface and bone. Remodelling the implant surfaces with different bioinspired materials prevents microbial adhesion, accumulation, plaque formation, and implant failure. Bioinspired and nanostructured materials like chitin, chitosan, curcumin, farnesol, sericin, fibroin, totarol, catechol, collagen and nacre material are bactericidal, antifungal and environment-friendly nature-inspired materials, known to be effective against gram-positive and negative bacteria. Nacre materials have high strength, are resistant to fracture, and have favourable bending properties. They induce blood vessel formation and accelerate the wound healing rate. Hence, using the above-mentioned nature-inspired materials can increase the success rate of implantation and the durability of implants, bridges, dental frames, dental archwires and improve the aesthetics of the oral cavity.

10.9 CONCLUSION

NPs used in multiple dental materials have been tested clinically as antimicrobial agents. Still, the frequent use of NPs in practice is limited as they release lethal ions that cause cytotoxicity, swelling, adverse effects on the immune system, and damage to DNA in normal cells. A solid systemic immune response has been observed due to the release of NPs of titanium after decontamination from implants via lasers and ultrasonic tips. Using natural bioinspired materials such as nanoparticles, coatings, and implant materials can increase the success rate in dentistry.

ACKNOWLEDGEMENT

DKP is thankful to MHRD and NIT Rourkela for financial support. DKP is also grateful to the biorender platform for drawing images and illustrations.

REFERENCES

Agel, Michael R, Elias Baghdan, Shashank Reddy Pinnapireddy, Jennifer Lehmann, Jens Schaefer, and Udo Bakowsky. 2019. "Curcumin loaded nanoparticles as efficient photoactive formulations against gram-positive and gram-negative bacteria." *Colloids and Surfaces B: Biointerfaces* 178:460–468. 10.1016/j.colsurfb.2019.03.027.
Al Farabi Clinics, Jeddah, and Saudi Arabia. 2022. "Etiology, evaluation, and treatment of pericoronitis." *Journal of Healthcare Sciences* 2:457–462. 10.52533/JOHS.2022.21119.
Baghdan, Elias, Shashank Reddy Pinnapireddy, Hendrik Vögeling, Jens Schäfer, Alexander W Eckert, and Udo Bakowsky. 2018. "Nano spray drying: A novel technique to prepare well-defined surface coatings for medical implants." *Journal of Drug Delivery Science and Technology* 48:145–151. 10.1016/j.jddst.2018.09.008.
Baghdan, Elias, Michael Raschpichler, Walaa Lutfi, Shashank Reddy Pinnapireddy, Marcel Pourasghar, Jens Schäfer, Marc Schneider, and Udo Bakowsky. 2019. "Nano spray dried antibacterial coatings for dental implants." *European Journal of Pharmaceutics and Biopharmaceutics* 139:59–67. 10.1016/j.ejpb.2019.03.003.

Barfeie, A, J Wilson, and J Rees. 2015. "Implant surface characteristics and their effect on osseointegration." *British Dental Journal* 218 (5):E9–E9. https://www.nature.com/articles/sj.bdj.2015.171.

Bhushan, Bharat, and Yong Chae Jung. 2011. "Natural and biomimetic artificial surfaces for superhydrophobicity, self-cleaning, low adhesion, and drag reduction." *Progress in Materials Science* 56 (1):1–108. 10.1016/j.pmatsci.2010.04.003.

Botirovna, Saidmurodova Jamila, Ruzimurodova Zilola Shuhratovna, and Shaimatova Aziza Rustambekovna. 2021. "Tooth pulpitis." *Texas Journal of Medical Science* 3:40–41.

Brunski, John B. 1988. "Biomaterials and biomechanics in dental implant design." *International Journal of Oral & Maxillofacial Implants* 3 (2): 85–97. https://www.researchgate.net/profile/John-Brunski/publication/20081480_Biomaterial_and_biomechanics_in_dental_implant_design/links/0fcfd51014649d23a7000000/Biomaterial-and-biomechanics-in-dental-implant-design.pdf.

Bruschi, Michela, Doris Steinmüller-Nethl, Walter Goriwoda, and Michael Rasse. 2015. "Composition and modifications of dental implant surfaces." *Journal of Oral Implants* 2015: 1–14. 10.1155/2015/527426.

Bumgardner, Joel D, Robin Wiser, Patrick D Gerard, Patrick Bergin, Betsy Chestnutt, Mark Marini, Victoria Ramsey, Steve H Elder, and Jerome A Gilbert. 2003. "Chitosan: potential use as a bioactive coating for orthopaedic and craniofacial/dental implants." *Journal of Biomaterials Science, Polymer Edition* 14 (5):423–438. 10.1163/156856203766652048.

Chen, Po-Yu, Joanna McKittrick, and Marc André Meyers. 2012. "Biological materials: functional adaptations and bioinspired designs." *Progress in Materials Science* 57 (8):1492–1704. 10.1016/j.pmatsci.2012.03.001.

Cloutier, Maxime, Diego Mantovani, and Federico Rosei. 2015. "Antibacterial coatings: Challenges, perspectives, and opportunities." *Trends in Biotechnology* 33 (11):637–652. 10.1016/j.tibtech.2015.09.002.

Damerau, Jeanne-Marie, Susanne Bierbaum, Daniel Wiedemeier, Paula Korn, Ralf Smeets, Gregor Jenny, Johanna Nadalini, and Bernd Stadlinger. 2022. "A systematic review on the effect of inorganic surface coatings in large animal models and meta-analysis on tricalcium phosphate and hydroxyapatite on periimplant bone formation." *Journal of Biomedical Materials Research Part B: Applied Biomaterials* 110 (1):157–175. 10.1002/jbm.b.34899.

Dong, Heng, Hui Liu, Na Zhou, Qiang Li, Guangwen Yang, Li Chen, and Yongbin Mou. 2020. "Surface modified techniques and emerging functional coating of dental implants." *Coatings* 10 (11):1012. 10.3390/coatings10111012.

Duraccio, Donatella, Federico Mussano, and Maria Giulia Faga. 2015. "Biomaterials for dental implants: current and future trends." *Journal of Materials Science* 50:4779–4812.

Eftekhar Ashtiani, Reza, Mostafa Alam, Sara Tavakolizadeh, and Kamyar Abbasi. 2021. "The role of biomaterials and biocompatible materials in implant-supported dental prosthesis." *Evidence-Based Complementary and Alternative Medicine* 2021:1–9.

Elia, Roberto, Courtney D Michelson, Austin L Perera, Masly Harsono, Gray G Leisk, Gerard Kugel, and David L Kaplan. 2015. "Silk electrogel coatings for titanium dental implants." *Journal of Biomaterials Applications* 29 (9):1247–1255. 10.1177/0885328214561536.

Fontelo, Raul, Diana Soares da Costa, Manuel Gomez-Florit, Hanna Tiainen, Rui L Reis, Ramon Novoa-Carballal, and Iva Pashkuleva. 2022. "Antibacterial nanopatterned coatings for dental implants." *Journal of Materials Chemistry B* 10 (42):8710–8718. 10.1039/D2TB01352E.

Fuller, James L. 1999. *Concise dental anatomy and morphology*: University of Iowa College of Dentistry.

Gasner, Noah S, and Ryan S Schure. 2022. "Periodontal disease." In *StatPearls [Internet]*: StatPearls Publishing.

Gaviria, Laura, John Paul Salcido, Teja Guda, and Joo L Ong. 2014. "Current trends in dental implants." *Journal of the Korean Association of Oral and Maxillofacial Surgeons* 40 (2):50. 10.5125/jkaoms.2014.40.2.50.

Ghensi, Paolo, Elia Bettio, Devid Maniglio, Emiliana Bonomi, Federico Piccoli, Silvia Gross, Patrizio Caciagli, Nicola Segata, Giandomenico Nollo, and Francesco Tessarolo. 2019. "Dental implants with anti-biofilm properties: A pilot study for developing a new sericin-based coating." *Materials* 12 (15):2429. 10.3390/ma12152429.

Hano, Christophe, and Bilal Haider Abbasi. 2021. *Plant-based green synthesis of nanoparticles: Production, characterization and applications*: MDPI.

Hasan, Jafar, Russell J Crawford, and Elena P Ivanova. 2013. "Antibacterial surfaces: the quest for a new generation of biomaterials." *Trends in Biotechnology* 31 (5):295–304. 10.1016/j.tibtech.2013.01.017.

Ivanova, Elena P, Jafar Hasan, Hayden K Webb, Vi Khanh Truong, Gregory S Watson, Jolanta A Watson, Vladimir A Baulin, Sergey Pogodin, James Y Wang, and Mark J Tobin. 2012. "Natural bactericidal surfaces: Mechanical rupture of Pseudomonas aeruginosa cells by cicada wings." *Small* 8 (16):2489.

Ivanova, Elena P, Jafar Hasan, Hayden K Webb, Gediminas Gervinskas, Saulius Juodkazis, Vi Khanh Truong, Alex HF Wu, Robert N Lamb, Vladimir A Baulin, and Gregory S Watson. 2013. "Bactericidal activity of black silicon." *Nature Communications* 4 (1):2838.

Jakubovics, NS. 2015. "Saliva as the sole nutritional source in the development of multispecies communities in dental plaque." *Microbiology Spectrum* 3:263–277.

Jayakumar, R, M Prabaharan, SV Nair, and H Tamura. 2010. "Novel chitin and chitosan nanofibers in biomedical applications." *Biotechnology Advances* 28 (1):142–150. 10. 1016/j.biotechadv.2009.11.001.

Jenkinson, Howard F. 2011. "Beyond the oral microbiome." *Environmental Microbiology* 13 (12):3077–3087. 10.1111/j.1462-2920.2011.02573.x.

Jung, Yong Chae. 2009. *Natural and biomimetic artificial surfaces for superhydrophobicity, self-cleaning, low adhesion, and drag reduction* The Ohio State University.

Keskin, Damla, Guangyue Zu, Abigail M Forson, Lisa Tromp, Jelmer Sjollema, and Patrick van Rijn. 2021. "Nanogels: A novel approach in antimicrobial delivery systems and antimicrobial coatings." *Bioactive Materials* 6 (10):3634–3657. 10.1016/j.bioactmat.2021.03.004.

Kumar, Ajay, Ravi Kant Mittal, and Abid Haleem. 2022. *Advances in additive manufacturing: Artificial intelligence, nature-inspired, and biomanufacturing*: Elsevier.

Kumar, Ajay, Parveen Kumar, Ravi Kant Mittal, and Victor Gambhir. 2023. "Materials processed by additive manufacturing techniques." In *Advances in Additive Manufacturing Artificial Intelligence, Nature-Inspired, and Biomanufacturing*, 217–233. Elsevier.

Kumar, Ajay, Parveen Kumar, Namrata Dogra, and Archana Jaglan. 2023. "Application of Incremental Sheet Forming (ISF) toward biomedical and medical implants." *Handbook of Flexible and Smart Sheet Forming Techniques: Industry 4.0 Approaches. Wiley publisher*:247–263. 10.1002/9781119986454.ch13.

Kumar, Ajay, Hari Singh, Parveen Kumar, and Bandar AlMangour. 2023. *Handbook of smart manufacturing: forecasting the future of industry 4.0*: CRC Press.

Liu, Kesong, and Lei Jiang. 2011. "Bio-inspired design of multiscale structures for function integration." *Nano Today* 6 (2):155–175. 10.1016/j.nantod.2011.02.002.

Loesche, Walter J. 1986. "Role of Streptococcus mutans in human dental decay." *Microbiological Reviews* 50 (4):353–380. 10.1128/mr.50.4.353-380.1986.

Marinescu, Liliana, Denisa Ficai, Ovidiu Oprea, Alexandru Marin, Anton Ficai, Ecaterina Andronescu, and Alina-Maria Holban. 2020. "Optimized synthesis approaches of metal nanoparticles with antimicrobial applications." *Journal of Nanomaterials* 2020:1–14. 10.1155/2020/6651207.

Mathur, Vijay Prakash, and Jatinder Kaur Dhillon. 2018. "Dental caries: A disease which needs attention." *The Indian Journal of Pediatrics* 85:202–206. 10.1007/s12098-017-2381-6.

Montoya, Carolina, Lina Roldan, Michelle Yu, Sara Valliani, Christina Ta, Maobin Yang, and Santiago Orrego. 2023. "Smart dental materials for antimicrobial applications." *Bioactive Materials* 24:1–19. 10.1016/j.bioactmat.2022.12.002.

Pelaez-Vargas, A, D Gallego-Perez, M Magallanes-Perdomo, MH Fernandes, DJ Hansford, AH De Aza, P Pena, and FJ Monteiro. 2011. "Isotropic micropatterned silica coatings on zirconia induce guided cell growth for dental implants." *Dental Materials* 27 (6):581–589. 10.1016/j.dental.2011.02.014.

Rasouli, Rahimeh, Ahmed Barhoum, and Hasan Uludag. 2018. "A review of nanostructured surfaces and materials for dental implants: Surface coating, patterning and functionalization for improved performance." *Biomaterials Science* 6 (6):1312–1338. 10.1039/C8BM00021B.

Reinhardt, Belinda, and Thomas Beikler. 2014. "Dental implants." In *Advanced Ceramics for Dentistry*, 51–75: Elsevier.

Sahoo, Banishree, Lipsa Leena Panigrahi, Rohit Pritam Das, Arun Kumar Pradhan, and Manoranjan Arakha. 2022. "Biogenic synthesis of silver nanoparticle from Punica granatum L. and evaluation of its antioxidant, antimicrobial and anti-biofilm activity." *Journal of Inorganic and Organometallic Polymers and Materials* 32 (11):4250–4259. 10.1007/s10904-022-02441-7.

Sehrawat, Sonam, Ajay Kumar, Mona Prabhakar, and Jasmine Nindra. 2022. "The expanding domains of 3D printing pertaining to the speciality of orthodontics." *Materials Today: Proceedings* 50:1611–1618. 10.1016/j.matpr.2021.09.124.

Singh, Brijendra, and Ritu Singh. 2013. "Gingivitis–A silent disease." *Journal of Dental and Medical Sciences* 6:30–33. https://www.researchgate.net/profile/Brijendra-Singh-2/publication/288115367_Gingivitis_-_A_silent_Disease/links/567e514408ae051f9ae52fa5/Gingivitis-A-silent-Disease.pdf.

Singh, Jagpreet, Tanushree Dutta, Ki-Hyun Kim, Mohit Rawat, Pallabi Samddar, and Pawan Kumar. 2018. "'Green'synthesis of metals and their oxide nanoparticles: Applications for environmental remediation." *Journal of Nanobiotechnology* 16 (1):1–24. 10.1186/s12951-018-0408-4.

Toledo, Valentina Andrea Ormazabal. 2013. "Dental implant surface modifications and osteointegration." Master's thesis, Universidade Catolica Portuguesa (Portugal).

Tomsia, Antoni P, Maximilien E Launey, Janice S Lee, Mahesh H Mankani, Ulrike GK Wegst, and Eduardo Saiz. 2011. "Nanotechnology approaches for better dental implants." *The International Journal of Oral & Maxillofacial Implants* 26 (Suppl):25. https://www.ncbi.nlm.nih.gov/pmc/articles/PMC3087979/.

Tripathy, Abinash, Prosenjit Sen, Bo Su, and Wuge H Briscoe. 2017. "Natural and bioinspired nanostructured bactericidal surfaces." *Advances in Colloid and Interface Science* 248:85–104. 10.1016/j.cis.2017.07.030.

Velusamy, Palaniyandi, Govindarajan Venkat Kumar, Venkadapathi Jeyanthi, Jayabrata Das, and Raman Pachaiappan. 2016. "Bio-inspired green nanoparticles: Synthesis, mechanism, and antibacterial application." *Toxicological Research* 32:95–102. 10.5487/TR.2016.32.2.095.

Wang, Xiao-Xiang, Lei Xie, and Rizhi Wang. 2005. "Biological fabrication of nacreous coating on titanium dental implant." *Biomaterials* 26 (31):6229–6232. 10.1016/j.biomaterials.2005.03.029.

Wang, Yayun, Steven E Naleway, and Bin Wang. 2020. "Biological and bioinspired materials: structure leading to functional and mechanical performance." *Bioactive Materials* 5 (4):745–757. 10.1016/j.bioactmat.2020.06.003.

Watson, Gregory S, David W Green, Lin Schwarzkopf, Xin Li, Bronwen W Cribb, Sverre Myhra, and Jolanta A Watson. 2015. "A gecko skin micro/nano structure – A low adhesion, superhydrophobic, anti-wetting, self-cleaning, biocompatible, antibacterial surface." *Acta Biomaterialia* 21:109–122. 10.1016/j.actbio.2015.03.007.

Yi, Yuseung, Ki-Tae Koo, Frank Schwarz, Heithem Ben Amara, and Seong-Joo Heo. 2020. "Association of prosthetic features and peri-implantitis: A cross-sectional study." *Journal of Clinical Periodontology* 47 (3):392–403. 10.1111/jcpe.13251.

Zhang, Kaiqiang, and Quyet Van Le. 2020. "Bioactive glass coated zirconia for dental implants: A review." *Journal of Composites and Compounds* 2 (2):10–17. 10.29252/jcc.2.1.2.

Zhang, Qiancheng, Xiaohu Yang, Peng Li, Guoyou Huang, Shangsheng Feng, Cheng Shen, Bin Han, Xiaohui Zhang, Feng Jin, and Feng Xu. 2015. "Bioinspired engineering of honeycomb structure – Using nature to inspire human innovation." *Progress in Materials Science* 74:332–400. 10.1016/j.pmatsci.2015.05.001.

Zhang, Yifan, Karan Gulati, Ze Li, Ping Di, and Yan Liu. 2021. "Dental implant nano-engineering: advances, limitations and future directions." *Nanomaterials* 11 (10):2489. 10.3390/nano11102489.

ABBREVIATIONS

AgNP	Argentum nanoparticle
AMPs	Antimicrobial peptides
BAC	Benzyldimethyltetradecylammonium chloride
B. cereus	*Bacillus cereus*
B. subtilis	*Bacillus subtilis*
BMPs	Bone morphogenetic proteins
BPIFA	BPI fold containing family A member 2
CA	Contact angle
CaP	Calcium phosphate
CTAB	Cetyl trimethylammonium bromide
CM 15	Cercopin Mellitin 15
C18GHis	C-terminus of the human platelet factor IV protein ALWKKLLKKLLKSAKKLG
1D	1 Dimensional
3D	3 Dimensional
DNA	Deoxyribonucleic acid
DODAB	Dioctadecyldimethylammonium bromide
ECM	Extracellular matrix
FGFs	Fibroblast growth factor
GPa	Gigapascals
GH12	GH12 (Gly-Leu-Leu-Trp-His-Leu-Leu-His-His-Leu-Leu-His-NH2)
GL13K	DGL13K (Gkiiklkaslkll-NH2)
HA	Hydroxyapatite
hLF	Human lactoferrin
H_2O_2	Hydrogen peroxide
LDOPA	L-3,4-dihydroxyphenylalanine
MPa	Megapascals
mRNA	Messenger RNA
NPs	Nanoparticles
P. aeruginosa	*Pseudomonas aeruginosa*
PDA	Polydopamine
rRNA	Ribosomal RNA
RNA	Ribonucleic acid
ROS	Reactive oxygen species
S. aureus	*Staphylococcus aureus*
Ti	Titanium
TiO_2	Titanium dioxide
V. cholera	*Vibrio cholera*

11 Dentistry 4.0's Role in COVID-19
Telemedicine and Online Education

K.R. Padma
Department of Biotechnology, Sri Padmavati Mahila Visvavidyalayam (Women's University), Tirupati, Andhra Pradesh, India

K.R. Don
Department of Oral Pathology & Microbiology, Sree Balaji Dental College and Hospital, Bharath Institute of Higher Education & Research (BIHER) Bharath University, Chennai, Tamil Nadu, India

11.1 BACKGROUND OF THE STUDY

The SARS-CoV-2 virus causes the infectious disease coronavirus disease (COVID-19). SARS-CoV-2 primarily spreads by fomite, aerosol, droplet, and contact routes. According to World Health Organization (WHO) data, there were 603,525,541 confirmed cases worldwide as of 1 September 2022, and there were 6,496,790 fatalities. Nonetheless, the United States had the most instances at 90 million, followed by more than ten other countries with at least ten million confirmed cases. The Omicron variety is currently becoming more widespread on a global scale. Compared to the original COVID-19 virus and its Delta variant, it spreads more quickly although producing less severe disease. On March 11, 2020, the WHO issued a pandemic declaration. In a variety of respects, these events had a big impact on how healthcare systems were designed [1].

The COVID-19 pandemic does not, however, appear to be abating anytime soon given the current trend of growing COVID-19 instances. According to the WHO, this virus may actually spread throughout society and become an enduring sickness [2]. Dental practices will need to reorganize and adjust if these rumors are true and COVID-19 does, in fact, become endemic or pandemic in order to continue offering dental care with the least level of risk of cross-infection. Teledentistry is a cutting-edge way to continue practicing dentistry throughout and after the current pandemic.

DOI: 10.1201/9781003404934-11

The term "tele" means "remote," and it satisfies the need to keep oneself socially apart, which is the fundamental objective in order to prevent contracting the COVID-19 virus. The primary goal is to preserve social distance and avoid one-on-one interaction during the current COVID-19 outbreak, which may soon grow into a pandemic. A subset of telehealth called teledentistry consults patients and collects their clinical results using communication means. This idea is also workable for patients who live on the outskirts of the city and have limited access to dental clinics or hospitals. For virtual communication between patients and dentists, there are many different mediums available, including electronic apps, digital photos, webcam-equipped PCs, smartphones, WhatsApp, etc.

The COVID-19 epidemic and other recent rapid technology breakthroughs have ushered in a new era of oral healthcare. Smart technology and customization have opened up new possibilities for tailored treatment. Dentistry 4.0 enables creative problem-solving by providing novel manufacturing capabilities, automation, data communication, and other cutting-edge technology. Through the Internet of Dental Things (IoDT), many dental instruments and apparatus are connected [3–5].

Therefore, our review article's prime focus is to portray the Artificial Intelligence (AI) based decision-making for individualized and predictive dental care through real-time data collecting from networked smart devices supported by the cloud in the dentistry 4.0. Dentistry 4.0 will lead to business model innovation in addition to altering working practices and enhancing healthcare quality.

11.2 THE COVID-19 PANDEMIC HAS RESTRUCTURED DENTAL EDUCATION

These peculiar problems have presented difficulties for educational systems all around the world. The majority of academic programmes have been touched by these exceptional conditions. They were initially planned and authorized to be carried out through face-to-face contacts, but they have been compelled to swiftly convert to virtual programming. COVID-19 has augmented the advancements in learning through the Internet as a response; when first enrolled and accustomed to receiving instruction in person, the majority of students are now learning through distance education, which is often viewed as a challenging learning environment. Thankfully, a variety of technological tools and platforms are now available that may be utilized to work around COVID-19's issues [6] and make it simpler for students to complete their programmes [7].

Virtualization of dentistry education and education more broadly has been made possible by already-existing technology and platforms. Due to the COVID-19 epidemic, technology is changing how remote learning is imparting knowledge.

11.3 FOLLOWING EXPOSURE TO CORONAVIRUS PANDEMIC CHALLENGES, POSSIBILITIES, AND KNOWLEDGE IN DENTISTRY EDUCATION

In 2019, Wuhan, China, experienced the emergence of a novel disease known as The Coronavirus Disease (COVID-19) [8]. It has spread globally and turned into a pandemic [9,10]. It presented a genuine challenge to medical professionals around

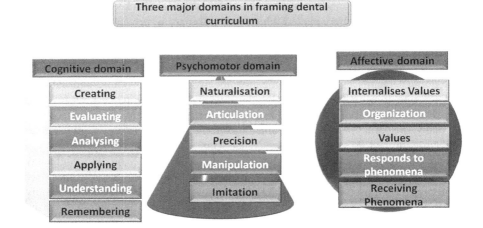

FIGURE 11.1   Illustrates the major domains in dental curriculum.

the world and undoubtedly had an impact on dental professionals in practice, research, and dental education. Due to the confinement and shutdown brought on by the COVID-19 pandemic, universities and dental colleges were obliged to stop clinical training and switch to online distance learning programmes. All dental colleges and institutions make every effort to provide students with the greatest education available in order to guarantee that dental students meet the standards of the Dental Council. The three learning areas of the dentistry curriculum are emotional, psychomotor, and cognitive (Figure 11.1). The COVID-19 pandemic has had an impact on each of the three dentistry curricular categories. Learning digitally has been the only option for continuing education throughout the globe for the past few months [11]. This study aimed to review how COVID-19 outbreaks affected the three areas of knowledge and dental research and education nationally.

Each domain and level of dentistry education, from application to admission to graduation and certification, have been significantly impacted by the COVID-19 epidemic. Each dental college was forced to quickly evaluate its capabilities in a number of areas after the lockdown measures were put in place, as the abrupt suspension of academic and clinical activities required the identification of the kinds of curriculum modifications that would be practical and effective [12,13]. In order to guarantee the ongoing remote dissemination of curriculum content, timely implementation and execution were consequently necessary [14]. Inevitably faculty members and students had to adapt quickly to the new circumstances, which in many cases included creating an entirely online dental programme [15,16]. It was important to be liberated from the usual limits and rules to permit the execution of innovative as well as speedy modifications fashion particularly throughout the COVID-19 pandemic, which unavoidably led to difference in curriculum changes across diverse institutes within the country.

Nowadays, the vast majority of dentistry institutions employ synchronous (in-person delivery) and asynchronous mode (on request) online training approaches to swap out any educational materials. in-class, or "virtualizable" curricular components [17,18]. In order to accomplish this, professors used a range of technical platforms with teleconferencing and file-sharing capabilities, which made it easier to conduct group discussions, deliver virtual lectures, and increase student involvement [19]. The way that their curriculum is taught at dentistry colleges all across the world has changed dramatically as a result of COVID-19. The safety of the faculty, staff, and students, continuity and maintenance of the standards of dental instruction along with adherence to the regulations and policies issued by the organizations for governance were all taken into consideration when these adjustments were made in accordance with the contingency plans that were established [20]. Table 11.1 lists the general adjustments made by dental institutions around the world in response to the COVID-19 outbreak.

TABLE 11.1
Dental College's Adoption of Changes as a Result of COVID-19

S.No.	Changes Observed or Applied	Discipline
		Programme Delivery Methods
1	Didactic features	Online mode of presentation
2	External rotations	Annulled
3	Practical elements	–
4	Virtualize	Online delivery
5	If not virtualizable	shifted to a different teaching strategy that accomplishes the same objectives of learning, like case-specific discussions in groups or procedural videos
6	Assessment	–
7	Tools employed	Multiple-choice tests, research papers, virtual oral exams, OSCEs, and video production are some of the options available.
8	Examination security	Automated plagiarism detection, identity authentication, and third-party proctoring
9	Admission interviews & meetings	Online conduction
10	Clinical features	Substituted with alternative instructional methods that meet related learning objectives; examples include case-based group discussions, procedural films, and telemedicine
11	Basic and Clinical Research	Temporarily canceled
12	Elective care	Rescheduled
13	Urgent Assistance	Offered through teledentistry or on-campus
14	Mode of delivery	Online
15	Writing and publication during Covid-19	Increased

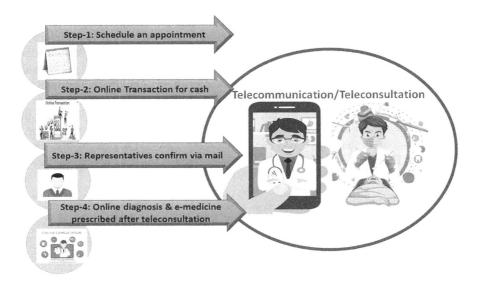

FIGURE 11.2　Telecommunication/teleconsultation-based digital technology during COVID-19.

11.4　TELECONSULTATION AND TELEDIAGNOSIS

Teleconsultation is essentially the use of electromagnetic technology for communications or communication between patients and dentists. This form of consultation has made it simple to consult people who have intellectual and physical limitations. Additionally, it has helped elderly patients and prisoners [21,22]. Teleconsultation has been a blessing for the common populace during the quarantine and lockdown. Not only that, but it also reduces the amount of time needed to travel to a dentist (see Figure 11.2).

Telediagnosis, as the name implies, is the practice of making diagnoses or conducting examinations using images and data transmitted to the dentist via technology. Smartphones are advised for the diagnosis of dental caries [23,24]. Additionally, WhatsApp and mobile phones can be used to research dental lesions that could be cancerous. Mobile Mouth Screening Anywhere (MeMoSA®) has been developed by Haron et al. [25] to detect oral cancer, however, they also discovered that it was advantageous for patients who had little access to medical professionals. It is advised to employ telediagnosis in this pandemic to avoid having close contact with the patients.

11.5　TELEDENTISTRY'S ROLE IN CARE FOR PATIENT

Teledentistry is the practice of looking for information on the Internet that may be of use to a patient. Some people might compare it to taking online continuing education courses. Web browsing and remote learning are actually these two activities.[26] For dental consultation and treatment planning, however, teledentistry blends telecommunications and dentistry and includes transferring clinical data and images over significant distances [27]. Cook introduced the concept of "teledentistry" and described it as "the practice of using video-conferencing technologies to diagnose and provide advice about treatment over a distance" in 1997 [28]. Teledentistry is a cutting-edge method of treating access issues and dentistry that doesn't necessitate personal contact with a dental expert. Dental technology has developed more slowly than those of other medical specialties in terms of communication and information. The swift adoption of teledentistry by the dental community during the COVID-19 pandemic offers a great chance to research how it can be used for both immediate and ongoing dental treatment while also providing a safe environment to give patients excellent care and lower the likelihood of infection.

During and after the COVID-19 epidemic, dentists can treat patients with urgent dental issues by using online teledentistry consultation to offer the necessary guidance, follow up on a patient's condition repeatedly, and offer the proper advice. For dental services to efficiently deliver improved triage services to individuals who require them, it is essential that they have the option of online interaction assistance right away. The recovery and restoration stage of the COVID-19 epidemic as well as future outbreaks will be handled more easily by using an online consulting service. Consequently, dental clinics will have the ability to able to manage the delays of patients who are at present struggling to receive care and prioritizing those who demand immediate therapy, which will assist in the gradual reintroduction of routine dental care [29–31].

11.6 THE APPLICATION OF DENTAL 4.0 TECHNOLOGIES HAS MADE A POSITIVE CONTRIBUTION THROUGHOUT THE COVID-19 PANDEMIC

Since the infectious agent COVID-19 is primarily transmitted through droplets and aerosols, it is logical to presume that dental hygiene might have experienced one of the greatest rates of mortality [32]. Nevertheless, when the number of fatalities in England and Wales between March and December 2020 was reviewed, there was insufficient proof that COVID-19 triggered a greater number of deaths among dentists. This eventually resulted in an understanding that the rigorous safety measures kept in place were possibly the reason for the low incidence of illness among dentists. Pre-screening before visiting the clinic is advised by the American Dental Association (ADA) and the majority of European dental organizations limiting only one person in the area of waiting at one time, keeping an eye on staff and patient temperature levels, cleaning hands and cleansing them, providing patients with access to sanitizers, disinfecting surfaces, providing medical staff with personal protection equipment, providing patients with disposable shoe covers, using UV lamps and other air purifiers, washing hands after touching objects, and washing hands following touching objects that have been handled (see Figure 11.3).

Conservative procedures including coronal restorations and root canal fillings had a large decline during the COVID-19 epidemic but a considerable rise in surgical operations was also observed. The decline in patients was countered in the ensuing months by an increase in the number of treatments performed per visit [33,34]. The execution of numerous treatment techniques was also advised to undergo a number of adjustments. For instance, manual tools rather than rotary ones were used to treat carious lesions with mechanochemical methods. Similar to how manual scaling was chosen over ultrasonic scaling for periodontal treatments.

FIGURE 11.3 During COVID-19 pandemic dental doctors followed safety protocols for dental patients.

The COVID-19 pandemic's restricted restrictions had a number of negative repercussions, some of which have been successfully mitigated via telemedicine. There are no standard protocols for aerosol-generating operations, according to a number of publications [35]. This can be explained by telemedicine's illogical adoption as a form of continuous education in medicine. For instance, dental experts in the UK modified how they handled clinical situations and created a triage system utilizing remote consultations. To reduce danger of transmission, only advice, analgesia, and first-line antibiotic prescription were permitted as options for therapy.

11.7 DENTISTRY 4.0 IMPLEMENTATION PROBLEMS AND DIFFICULTIES IN THE COVID-19 PANDEMIC DENTAL HEALTHCARE

The way that their curriculum is taught at dentistry colleges all across the world has changed dramatically as a result of COVID-19. These adjustments were made in accordance with the contingency plans that were established, keeping in mind the safety of the teachers, staff, and students, as well as preserving the standard of dentistry education and adhering to the rules and regulations imposed by governing organizations [36]. New technologies are emerging swiftly in the current environment, causing significant change. The COVID-19 pandemic is driving up demand for these technologies. Numerous dental innovations have been developed as a result of the COVID-19 outbreak to help people maintain good oral health. The use of numerous auxiliary software by these technologies helps us reach a higher level of digitization. Connected sensors in dental equipment provide precise information and prompt alarms. During the COVID-19 outbreak, virtual technologies offered a variety of dentistry-related training opportunities, enhancing the method of instruction and education [37–40].

The suggested dentistry 4.0 philosophy for healthcare is in agreement with the bulk of the problems that are commonly identified in the dental field. But there are

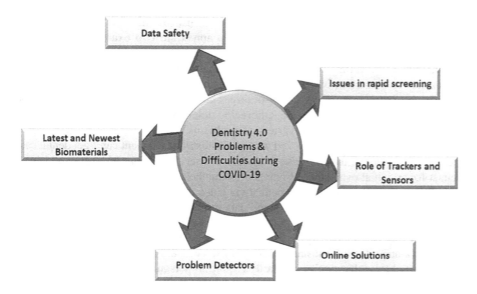

FIGURE 11.4 Problems and difficulties faced during the implementation of Dentistry 4.0 technology.

still some other issues and challenges that need to be handled in the long run. When attempting to implement the suggested dental approach, particularly in light of the COVID-19 outbreak, it is imperative to pay closer concentration to the security, privacy, and protection of the patient's data. Utilizing the most cutting-edge smart biomaterials for dental care is a further area of concentration for this field's future development [41–43]. Due to the fact that smart sensors and trackers are still in their beginning in this field, considerable effort needs to be made to study more comprehensive insights into their accuracy and proper functioning, especially in some common and difficult activities [44–46]. Figure 11.4 displays the numerous issues and challenges found when implementing Dentistry 4.0 for dentistry during the challenging COVID-19 timeframe.

11.8 ISSUES WITH DENTISTS AND PATIENTS ON EMBRACING TELEDENTISTRY

Dentistry is a fairly hands-on profession, but as the world becomes more digital, teledentistry services are playing a bigger part in routine practice. Teledentistry uses digital audio and visual communication techniques to provide services over distance [47]. Such amenities can be real-time (synchronous) or asynchronous (known as "store-and-forward"), wherein the patient provides information or leaves a message that the dentist assesses later. By using remote patient monitoring, which electronically communicates patient data to a healthcare provider for additional assistance, dentists can participate in teledentistry [48,49].

The monitoring of saliva pH levels and the use of mandibular advancement devices by patients to treat obstructive sleep apnea are two examples of this. By communicating with patients digitally, dentists may assess patients, reassure them, calculate how much time will be spent in the chair, and make any required referrals. In contrast to medicine, where telemedicine is better developed, dentistry is still in its infancy. During the COVID-19 outbreak access to medical services must be improved and some dentists are embracing teledentistry. As a result, they are coming up with solutions to a variety of problems.

Access to care could be improved with teledentistry. If a patient can't get dental care right away in person, they can use a teledentistry service to chat with an experienced dentist for an initial evaluation. While addressing their dental issue over the phone, the patient can communicate with the dentist via video chat. Dental practitioners and their patients can communicate and exchange data throughout an encrypted way thanks to teledentistry-specific technology. Environment that complies with the Health Insurance Portability and Accountability Act (HIPAA) is now available to people who exist in isolated countryside places distant from a dentist's office. Patients can also get answers to dental problems that don't necessarily require in-person care.

The healthcare sector now needs to be fully, unwaveringly, and strategically aligned as a result of the usage of teledentistry. Thankfully, there is currently almost enough network connectivity, digital technology, and a variety of platforms to make teledentistry a possibility. For a contemporary digital strategy to control the epidemic, however, a large portion of the world was probably still unprepared [50].

11.9 DENTISTRY 4.0 TECHNOLOGIES AND ONLINE DENTAL EDUCATION RESOURCES, ACTIVITIES, AND PLATFORMS

Globally clinical dental education has faced a number of difficulties as a result of the COVID-19 epidemic. Dental schools have to use a number of strategies to offer a secure ambiance for their faculty, students, and clients as a result of the peculiar circumstances. Even though blended education, virtual reality simulators (VRS), and simulated classrooms have all been widely adopted as cutting-edge educational tools, dental students have expressed a desire to bring back on-site practical lessons so they can improve their clinical skills in front of actual patients. Undergraduate dental education (UDE) may need to undergo considerable organizational changes, appropriate curriculum updates, and novel teaching techniques in order to uphold an excellent caliber throughout the COVID-19 pandemic confinement.

In order to give competent instruction in our curriculum in light of the current epidemic, we need to look at how various online education and hybrid approaches have been successfully embraced and applied. Due to the fast growing need for the digitalized environment during COVID-19, primarily because of protection and health concerns, online education has certainly become mainstream. The fact that online education encompasses more than only the electronic dissemination of either asynchronous or synchronous learning materials ought to be highlighted, because this is a crucial point to keep in mind. The course material has to be updated to take into account the possibility that dentistry modules and courses will one day be provided wholly online or in a blended learning environment that combines traditional in-person instruction with online instruction [51].

Without a doubt, dental simulation facilities have evolved into a successful method for instructing undergraduate students safely while also significantly enhancing their pre-clinical services, minimizing the need for clinical supervision by instructors' time, and encouraging a more learner-centered methodology to the challenging technical and clinical services involved in providing clinical oral healthcare during the pandemic's peak [52,53]. But there isn't a true patient connection, which is an important part of dental care, and, perhaps more importantly, only a few colleges of dentistry have the Virtual Reality System software or the on-campus expertise necessary for tactile machinery to be deployed in a timely manner.

Dentistry 4.0 brings about significant innovation and improvement in the field. This strategy is to produce various dentistry components, which is very helpful in the current environment. The frequency of the patient's routine checkups is reduced by smart gadgets like telehealth management systems. The scan and image of any anomalies, such as fractured teeth, are analysed using AI-based technology. There are technologies that can assess how you brush your teeth, extending their life. The following list of Dentistry 4.0 technologies' notable accomplishments:

- Utilizing technologies from Dentistry 4.0 to enhance the quality of care
- Dental 4.0 technologies are being used in the digital manufacture of dental components.
- Implementing the applications for Dentistry 4.0 advancements for quality control.
- Smart dentistry is making use of Dentistry 4.0 technologies during the COVID-19 epidemic.
- Dentistry 4.0 protocols to assist with treatment throughout the COVID-19 pandemic.

11.10   FUTURE SCOPE OF TELEDENTISTRY

Partner organizations from every state are persuaded to work together to prevent the effective and evidence-based use of teledentistry during the present pandemic and subsequent upcoming outbreaks. It is important to define the standards for screening for unacceptable behavioral patterns. The regulations for compensation, state-by-state licencing, and data privacy issues should be revised. Dentists should have an in-depth knowledge of the principles and technological advances of teledentistry.

11.11   CONCLUSION

This work is meant to serve as a reference for researchers, clinicians (or dental hospitals), and industry in visualizing the next generation of dentistry in order to adapt, further develop and implement smart dental appliances with a strong emphasis on preventive care and increasing the efficacy of curative care. It provides a brief overview of the technological underpinnings necessary to realize this notion as well as information on the many Dentistry 4.0 application possibilities. We discuss the development of a new business model as a result of the realization of such an idea. Dentistry 4.0's definition and requirements have been the exclusive focus of the research for the present avatar. To fully describe the different use cases, further work must be done. The current overview leads to the conclusion that teledentistry can prove to be very beneficial for ongoing dental educational initiatives during the COVID-19 outbreak. An approach that was less frequently taken in the past has now become possible due to the current scenario. All necessary components of dental education can be delivered with the aid of teledentistry. Teledentistry can also be utilized in routine dental procedures, which is advantageous because it reduces the need for patient and dentist consultations. As a result, these technologies provide highly automated and computerized management systems, which minimize the need for human involvement. As time goes on, we hope that these technologies can shorten dental procedures, reduce the COVID-19 epidemic's need for dental care, and ultimately improve dental care.

ACKNOWLEDGMENTS

Dr. K.R. Padma and Dr. K.R. Don solely drafted the paper. All the authors are thankful to the Department of Biotechnology Sri Padmavati Mahila Visvavidyalayam (Women's) University, Tirupati-India. and the Department of Oral Pathology and Microbiology, Sri Balaji Dental College and Hospital, Bharath Institute of Higher Education and Research (BIHER) Bharath University, Chennai, Tamil Nadu.

REFERENCES

1. Chan HF, Brumpton M, Macintyre A, Arapoc J, Savage DA, et al. How confidence in health care systems affects mobility and compliance during the COVID-19 pandemic. PLoS One (2020); 15: 10
2. BBC News. Coronavirus may never go away, WHO warns. BBC News; 2020.
3. Dobrzański LA, Dobrzański LB. Dentistry 4.0 concept in the design and manufacturing of prosthetic dental restorations. Processes (2020); 8 (5): 525.
4. Ahmadi H, Ebrahimi A, Ghorbani F. The impact of COVID-19 pandemic on dental practice in Iran: a questionnaire-based report. BMC Oral Health (2020); 20(1): 1–9.
5. Pemmada R, Zhu X, Dash M, Zhou Y, Ramakrishna S, Peng X, Thomas V, Jain S, Nanda HS. Science-based strategies of antiviral coatings with viricidal properties for the COVID-19 like pandemics. Materials (2020); 13(18): 4041.
6. Ting DSW, Carin L, Dzau V, Wong TY. Digital technology and COVID-19. Nat Med (2020); 26(4): 459–461. 10.1038/s41591-020-0824-5.
7. Carmo RDOS, Franco AP. Da docência presencial à docência online: aprendizagens de professores universitários na educa-ção a distância. Educação Rev (2019); 35:e210399. 10.1590/0102-4698210399.
8. Patel N. Impact on dental economics and dental healthcare utilization in COVID-19: an exploratory study. J Adv Oral Res (2020); 11: 128–136. 10.1177/2320206820941365.
9. Hattar S, AlHadidi A, Sawair FA, Alraheam IA, El-Ma'aita A, Wahab FK. Impact of COVID-19 pandemic on dental academia. Students' experience in online education and expectations for a predictable practice (PREPRINT). Res Sq (2020), 10.21203/rs.3.rs-54480/v1.

10. Princeton B, Santhakumar P, Prathap L. Awareness on preventive measures taken by health care professionals attending COVID-19 patients among dental students. Eur J Dent (2020); 14: S105–S109. 10.1055/s-0040-1721296.

11. Ammar N, Aly NM, Folayan MO, et al. Behavior change due to COVID-19 among dental academics-The theory of planned behavior: stresses, worries, training, and pandemic severity. PLoS One (2020); 15: e0239961. 10.1371/journal.pone.0239961.

12. Elangovan S, Mahrous A, Marchini L. Disruptions during a pandemic: gaps identified and lessons learned. J Dent Educ (2020); 84(11): 1270–1274. 10.1002/jdd.12236 [PMID: 32500586]

13. Alon E, Amato R Evaluation of endodontic competency in the COVID-19 era: Problem, solution and results. J Dent Educ (2020). 10.1002/jdd.12237 [PMID: 32462660]

14. Martins MD, Carrard VC, Dos Santos CM, Hugo FN. COVID-19-Are telehealth and tele-education the answers to keep the ball rolling in Dentistry? Oral Dis (2020). 10.1111/odi.13527 [PMID: 32615648]

15. Eachempati P, Ramnarayan K. Covido-pedago-phobia. Med Educ (2020); 54(8): 678–680. 10.1111/medu.14257 [PMID: 32473029]

16. Iyer P, Aziz K, Ojcius DM. Impact of COVID-19 on dental education in the United States. J Dent Educ (2020); 84(6): 718–722. 10.1002/jdd.12163 [PMID: 32342516]

17. Peres K, Reher P, Castro R, Vieira A. COVID-19-related challenges in dental education: experiences from Brazil, the USA, and Australia. Pesqui Bras Odontopediatria Clín Integr (2020); 20(suppl 1).

18. Wu DT, Wu KY, Nguyen TT, Tran SD. The impact of COVID-19 on dental education in North America – Where do we go next? Eur J Dent Educ (2020); 24(4): 825–827.

19. Chaple-Gil AM, Afrashtehfar KI. Telegram Messenger: a suitable tool for teledentistry. J Oral Res (2020); 9(1): 4–6. 10.17126/joralres.2020.001

20. Emami E. COVID-19: Perspective of a dean of dentistry. JDR Clin Trans Res (2020); 5(3): 211–213. 10.1177/2380084420929284 [PMID: 32401587].

21. Spivack, E. Teledentistry: remote observation of patients with special needs. Gen Dent (2020); 68(3): 66–70.

22. Tynan, A, Deeth, L, McKenzie, D, Bourke, C, Stenhouse, S, Pitt, J, Linneman, H. An integrated approach to oral health in aged care facilities using oral health practitioners and teledentistry in rural Queensland. Aus J Rural Health (2018); 26(4): 290–294.

23. AlShaya, MS, Assery, MK, Pani, SC. Reliability of mobile phone teledentistry in dental diagnosis and treatment planning in mixed dentition. J Telemed Telecare (2020); 26(1–2), 45–52.

24. Kohara, EK, Abdala, CG, Novaes, TF, Braga, MM, Haddad, AE, Mendes, FM. Is it feasible to use smartphone images to perform telediagnosis of different stages of occlusal caries lesions?. PLoS One (2018); 13(9): e0202116.

25. Haron, N, Zain, RB, Ramanathan, A, Abraham, MT, Liew, CS, Ng, KG, Cheong, SC. m-Health for early detection of oral cancer in low-and middle-income countries. Telemed e-Health (2020); 26(3): 278–285.

26. Clark GT Teledentistry: what is it now, and what will it be tomorrow? J Calif Dent Assoc (2000); 28: 121–127.

27. Bhambal A, Saxena S, Balsaraf SV. Teledentistry: potentials unexplored. J Int Oral Health (2010); 2: 1–6.

28. Fricton J, Chen H. Using teledentistry to improve access to dental care for the underserved. Dent Clin North Am (2009); 53: 537–548.

29. Khan SA, Omar H. Teledentistry in practice: literature review. Telemed J E Health (2013); 19: 565–567. 10.1089/tmj.2012.0200

30. Irving M, Stewart R, Spallek H, Blinkhorn A. Using teledentistry in clinical practice as an enabler to improve access to clinical care: a qualitative systematic review. J Telemed Telecare. (2018); 24: 129–146. 10.1177/1357633X16686776

31. Talla, PK, Levin, L, Glogauer, M, Cable, C, Allison, PJ. Delivering dental care as we emerge from the initial phase of the COVID-19 pandemic: teledentistry and face-to-face consultations in a new clinical world. Quintessence Int. (2020): 51: 672–677.

32. Devlin, H, Soltani, P. COVID-19 and dentistry. Encyclopedia (2021); 1: 496–504.

33. Meethil, AP, Saraswat, S, Chaudhary, PP, Dabdoub, SM, Kumar, PS. Sources of SARS-CoV-2 and other microorganisms in dental aerosols. J Dent Res (2021); 100: 817–823.

34. Nijakowski, K, Cie´slik, K, Łaganowski, K, Gruszczy´nski, D, Surdacka, A. The impact of the COVID-19 pandemic on the spectrum of performed dental procedures. Int J Environ Res Public Health (2021); 18: 3421.

35. Luchian, I, Moscalu, M, Goriuc, A, Nucci, L, Tatarciuc, M, Martu, I, Covasa, M. Using salivary MMP-9 to successfully quantify periodontal inflammation during orthodontic treatment. J Clin Med (2021); 10: 379.

36. Bennardo F, Buffone C, Fortunato L, Giudice A. COVID-19 is a challenge for dental education-A commentary. Eur J Dent Educ (2020); 24(4): 822–824. 10.1111/eje.12555 [PMID: 32542796]

37. Kumar MS, Raut RD, Narwane VS, Narkhede BE Applications of industry 4.0 to overcome the COVID-19 operational challenges. Diabetes Metab Syndr (2020); 14(5): 1283–1289.

38. Shafiq SI, Sanin C, Toro C, Szczerbicki E. Virtual engineering object (VEO): toward experience-based design and manufacturing for industry 4.0. Cybern Syst (2015); 46(1–2): 35–50.

39. Shadmi E, Chen Y, Dourado I, Faran-Perach I, Furler J, Hangoma P, Hanvoravongchai P, Obando C, Petrosyan V, Rao KD, Ruano AL. Health equity and COVID-19: global perspectives. Int J Equity Health (2020); 19(1): 1–6 Dec.

40. Khader Y, Al Nsour M, Al-Batayneh OB, Saadeh R, Bashier H, Alfaqih M, Al-Azzam S. Dentists' awareness, perception, and attitude regarding COVID-19 and infection control: cross-sectional study among Jordanian dentists. JMIR Public Health Surveill (2020) 6 (2): e18798.

41. Singh RP, Javaid M, Kataria R, Tyagi M, Haleem A, Suman R. Significant applications of virtual reality for COVID-19 pandemic. Diabetes Metab Syndr (2020).

42. Maspero C, Abate A, Cavagnetto D, El Morsi M, Fama A, Farronato M. Available technologies, applications and benefits of teleorthodontics. A literature review and possible applications during the COVID-19 pandemic. J Clin Med (2020); 9 (6): 1891.

43. da Costa CB, Peralta FD, Ferreira de Mello AL. How has teledentistry been applied in public dental health services? An integrative review. Telemed e-Health (2020); 26(7): 945–954.

44. Sallam M, Dababseh D, Yaseen A, Al-Haidar A, Ababneh NA, Bakri FG, Mahafzah A. Conspiracy beliefs are associated with lower knowledge and higher anxiety levels regarding COVID-19 among students at the University of Jordan. Int J Environ Res Pub Health (2020); 17(14): 4915.

45. Javaid M, Haleem A, Singh RP, Haq MI, Raina A, Suman R. Industry 5.0: Potential applications in COVID-19. J Ind Integr Manag (2020) 2050022.

46. Cavalheiro MN, Fonseca VR, Zeigelboim BS, Costa DF, de Lima LV, Bozzo MK, de Cássia Tonochi R, Hartmann BC. Evaluating the quality of rigid optic video laryngoscopy image taken through dental protection cap and its feasibility as additional barrier method against COVID-19. J Voice (2020).

47. "Facts About Teledentistry." American TeleDentistry Association, americanteledentistry.org/facts-about-teledentistry/. Accessed 30 April (2020).

48. "ADA Policy on Teledentistry." American Dental Association, ada.org/en/about-the-ada/ada-positions-policies-and-statements/statement-on-teledentistry. Accessed 30 April (2020).
49. State Telehealth Laws & Reimbursement Policies. Center for Connected Health Policy, 2019.
50. Omboni S. Telemedicine During the covid-19 in Italy: a missed opportunity? Telemed J E Health (2020); 26(8): 973–975. 10.1089/tmj.2020.0106
51. Jeganathan S and Fleming PS. Blended learning as an adjunct to tutor-led seminars in undergraduate orthodontics: a randomised controlled trial. Br Dent J (2020); 228(5): 371–375. 10.1038/s41415-020-1332-1
52. Liu X, Zhou J, Chen L, Yang Y, et al. Impact of COVID-19 epidemic on live online dental continuing education. Eur J Dent Educ (2020). 10.1111/eje.12569
53. Liu L, Zhou R, Yuan S, Sun Z, et al. Simulation training for ceramic crown preparation in the dental setting using a virtual educational system. Eur J Dent Educ (2020); 24(2): 199–206. 10.1111/eje.12485

12 The Era of Telemedicine

Current Applications

Deepika Dahiya, Manisha Khanna,
Namrata Dogra, and Archana Jaglan
Department of Orthodontics, Shri Guru Gobind Singh
Tricentenary University, Budhera, Gurugram, Haryana, India

12.1 INTRODUCTION

The potential for teletechnology to provide a simple, quick, and secure method of delivering and sharing health information has drawn greater interest in the professions of medicine and dentistry. There are many public health concerns related to the current coronavirus illness (COVID-19) pandemic spread. There is now a pressing need to address the difficulty in obtaining dental treatment. The application of technologies to support the fulfilment of health objectives in this particular period of crisis has the potential to change how health services are delivered globally. Over the past few decades, the Internet has become increasingly popular as a source of information. Recent developments have enhanced patient treatment both locally and for people who live in remote areas without access to medical facilities or dentist offices. A branch of the science of telemedicine associated with dentistry called as "Teledentistry" handles the full process of networking, sharing digital information, distant consultations, workup, and analysis.

The use of technologies to facilitate the attainment of health goals in this particular environment has the potential to alter how health services are provided worldwide. Smartphones have contributed significantly to big data and that adds more efficiency to machine learning [1]. This uses deep networks to detect the disease by retrieving or extracting the information from the images provided and also give information about the clinical applications in the medical fields [2].

The Internet has gained prominence as a source of knowledge during the past few decades. Timely follow-up visits are necessary for some continuing treatments, like orthodontic therapies, and/or emergency cases, including conditions that must be identified and treated right away to prevent more serious repercussions [3–5].

This method has a wide range of clinical uses, from community dentistry to special needs dentistry. Additionally, teledentistry apps can be especially helpful in developing nations like India where access to oral health services is restricted by distance.

Teledentistry may be highly helpful to dental patients in aspects of consultation, triaging, and providing dental emergency medication given the existing social

DOI: 10.1201/9781003404934-12

distance, mobility restrictions, and compromised healthcare systems. This helps keep the dentists as well as the patients well versed with the new technologies like 3D printing and smart materials like polymers, ceramics, composites etc. [6]. Teledentistry is a great resource for teaching dental students as well as giving practising dentists ongoing updates.

12.2 TYPES OF TELEDENTISTRY

Teledentistry is the practice of providing dental care remotely using information and communication technology. Teledentistry is a technique used by dentists to conduct consultations, exams, educational sessions, and even treatments. Here are a few prevalent teledentistry techniques.

12.2.1 TWO-WAY INTERACTIVE TECHNOLOGY: SYNCHRONOUS

In synchronous teledentistry, patient and the dentist converse in real time. Both the dentist and the patient use a camera, speaker, and microphone in synchronous teledentistry. Each device connects to the internet and communicates with the others. You can converse, see, and hear each other in this manner [7].

This is the most used form of teledentistry; with this technology, patients can consult with their dentist from anywhere in the world by using simple or advanced telecommunications, internet connections, and video conferencing as shown in Figure 12.1. With the aid of modern technology, ordinary dentists can quickly confer with experts in any particular case and then organise treatment accordingly [8,9].

12.2.2 STORES AND FORWARDS: ASYNCHRONOUS

The literal opposite of synchronous teledentistry is asynchronous teledentistry. The dentist and patient do not engage in real time when using the asynchronous method. Instead, the patient writes down the necessary dental details and gives them to their dentist. Following a study and assessment of the data, the dentist contacts the patient.

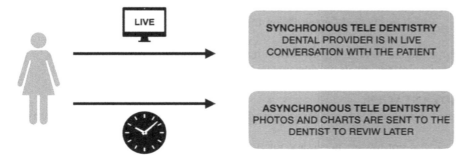

FIGURE 12.1 Types of teledentistry: *synchronous* where the dentist converses with the patient in real time; *asynchronous* where data is sent for analysis and treated accordingly.

Let's say that you are experiencing a dental issue. You might photograph the tooth and send it to the dentist for analysis as shown in Figure 12.1. After that, the dentist will contact you with suggestions. For instance, the dentist might suggest a medication or plan some tests for more analysis [7]. All data is gathered and kept using this approach before being distributed to consultation practitioners from diverse locations. With this technique, all necessary information is recorded, including the patient's history, their family history, pictures, radiographs, and more [8,9].

ADVANTAGES
Additionally, asynchronous teledentistry provides advantages. Here are a few examples:

1. If necessary, the dentist can quickly share the data gathered with other professionals.
2. It is not necessary for the dentist and their patient to have the same schedule. For instance, the patient can gather the essential data at night and send it to the dentist for review in the morning.

Your consultation will be based on the type of data your dentist will gather. In some circumstances, a medical or dental expert may be required to obtain further information from you [7].

12.2.3 MOBILE HEALTH

Teledentistry for mobile health (mHealth) depends on portable communication tools. Cell phones are the primary devices, although there are also tablet computers, personal digital assistants (PDAs), and wearable gadgets (like smartwatches).

Most mHealth applications let users collect data without the help of dentists. mHealth solutions come in the following varieties as depicted in Figure 12.2:

1. A patient uses an app to monitor their treatment for a persistent dental issue like dental cavities or gingivitis.
2. Digital reminders are used by patients, for instance, to remember to take their prescription while they are healing after dental surgery.
3. A patient monitors sporadic symptoms with the help of smartphone apps, such as cyclical dental discomfort.

For additional analysis, some mHealth systems send patient information back to the dentist. Certain situations don't necessitate further dental care.

ADVANTAGES:
There are several advantages to mHealth solutions. Here are a few illustrations:

1. It's not always necessary for the dentist and their patient to synchronise their schedules.
2. The majority of individuals already own the required technology, including cell phones.

FIGURE 12.2 Mobile health or M health as a portable communication tool.

3. Wearable technology is one example of a type of mHealth solution that can work in the background even when the patient is not actively using it.

The teledentistry subcategory of mHealth is expanding. Every day, new applications and solutions are released. Even some dentists have their own proprietary solutions.

12.3 ROLE OF TELEDIAGNOSIS AND TELECONSULTATION IN DENTISTRY

The increasing adoption of online dental appointments and practices will help reduce the pressure now being placed on global health care delivery networks. As a result, emergency departments will be less busy [10]. In the COVID-19 surge, teledentistry may be used to develop a screening procedure in which medical practitioners can consult with a stable patient via online video conferencing. The implementation of such programmes might be an effective and affordable strategy for protecting the safety of both patients and medical personnel during the outbreak. With the use of this technique, tension at healthcare institutions could be reduced. [10,11].

12.3.1 Oral Medicine and Public Health

In the application of such technology, oral health continues to be ignored. There has been a lot of international interest in the health programme m-Oral Health, which focuses on oral health. The following four essential elements make up the m-Oral Health strategy [12]:

1. m-Oral Health Literacy
2. m-Oral Health Training
3. m-Oral Health Early Detection
4. m-Oral Health Surveillance

12.3.1.1   m-Oral health Literacy

The ability to access, process, and comprehend fundamental oral health information using telecommunications technologies like video conferencing, messaging, and mobile apps is referred to as tele oral health literacy. In their discussion of the COVID-19 pandemic's financial effects on the dental sector, Vujicic et al. draw attention to the potential contribution of teledental care to increasing access to oral healthcare, fostering tele oral health literacy, and other areas [13]. In order to increase access to dental treatment and oral health outcomes for rural and underserved groups, Divaris K. et al. investigate the efficacy of tele oral health promotion initiatives. The study emphasises how tele oral health promotion could raise oral health literacy and lessen gaps in access to care [14]. The relevance of addressing oral health literacy through telecommunication technologies is stressed by LEE JY et al. in their systematic evaluation of the research on the ethical consequences of poor oral health literacy [15]. In an underserved community, Park SE et al. investigate the impact of teleconsultation services on dental anxiety, pain, and oral health-related quality of life. According to the study, teleconsultation services have the potential to increase tele oral health literacy and foster access to oral healthcare [16].

In general, tele oral health education has the potential to increase oral health literacy among marginalised communities, decrease inequities in oral health outcomes, and enhance access to dental treatment.

12.3.1.2   Tele Oral Health Training

Using technology like video conferencing, webinars, and online training modules, tele oral health training is a technique for delivering oral health education and training remotely. This method makes it possible for people to get oral health education no matter where they live, which can be especially crucial for those who reside in distant or underserved locations where access to dental care and oral health education may be constrained. Aspects of tele oral health training include the following:

ACCESSIBILITY: For those who might encounter obstacles to receiving conventional in-person training, such as transportation or time constraints, tele oral health training can expand accessibility to oral health education and training.

FLEXIBILITY: Individuals can attend tele oral health training at their own pace and on their own schedule, which can be very useful for professionals who are busy or for those who have other commitments.

TECHNOLOGY: Tele oral health instruction makes use of online training modules and video conferencing, both of which have varying degrees of difficulty and usability. The target audience should be kept in mind while creating effective tele oral health training programmes, as well as the technology that is available to them.

INTERACTIVITY: Interactive elements like live Q&A sessions and discussion forums can be included in tele oral health training to improve engagement and learning.

EVALUATION: To make sure that tele oral health training programmes are achieving the intended aims and objectives, it is crucial to assess their performance. Assessing changes in oral health-related knowledge, attitudes, and behaviours might be part of this.

In summary, tele oral health education is a viable strategy to broaden access to oral health instruction and training, especially in rural or underserved areas. Programmes for tele oral health training that are effective should be created with the target audience in mind, take advantage of technology that is now available, and incorporate interactive elements and evaluation [17–19].

12.3.1.3 Tele Oral Health for Early Detection

The capacity to identify oral health issues early on, when they are most treatable, is one of the main benefits of tele oral health for early recognition. For instance, remote monitoring of oral health issues can assist dentists in spotting early indications of oral cancer, tooth decay, and gum disease. This makes it possible for prompt intervention and treatment, which can stop more harm and problems [20].

Furthermore, tele oral health can be utilised to deliver preventative treatment, such as oral hygiene instruction and guidance on healthy behaviours, which can assist patients retain good oral health and avert future issues.

12.3.1.4 Tele Oral Health Surveillance

Tele oral monitoring is a potent tool for keeping tabs on oral health trends, spotting possible epidemics, and enhancing population health in general. Even in remote or underserved locations, dentists and public health officials may obtain and analyse data on oral health in real-time with the help of technology like digital health records, mobile applications, and remote monitoring equipment. Dental professionals and public health officials can spot oral health condition trends, including shifts in the prevalence of caries or gingivitis, and respond rapidly to outbreaks or epidemics with the aid of tele oral health surveillance. By monitoring the spread of infectious diseases like oral thrush or herpes, for instance, tele oral wellness surveillance can help with early detection and treatment [20].

In underserved or distant areas where access to dental care may be limited, tele oral health surveillance can also be utilised to enhance the delivery of preventative care and health education. Dentists and other dental specialists can offer patients individualised advice on oral hygiene routines and healthy behaviours through remote consultations, which can help stop oral health issues before they start. In general, tele oral health surveillance is a useful tool for enhancing community oral health, enabling early outbreak diagnosis and response, and guaranteeing that patients receive the care they require, when they require it.

12.4 DIGITAL ORAL HEALTH RECORDS AND DIGITAL SURVEYS AND QUESTIONNAIRES

A comprehensive model for health economic policy is the type of population-derived health data at the personalised level of information and data. The Internet of medical things (IoMT), which is made possible by the exponential growth in the use of digital devices like smartphones, laptops, smartwatches, and online applications, allows for the collection of health data from patients who participate in online forums, surveys, and research projects. It aids in illness surveillance, treatment prognosis, prevention programme design, research initiation, and surveying.

Limitation: There are still a lot of obstacles to overcome before technology can be fully integrated into dentistry. A central digitalisation would continue to be contested in a large country like India with such wide-ranging linguistic and cultural diversity. Uncertain factors include the disparity in digital literacy across people of different demographics, including gender, location, and financial position. Unfortunately, pricing also acts as a deterrent to the adoption of technological breakthroughs for the promotion of oral health in some regions and segments of society. Conclusion It is important to create digital technologies that will increase community oral health care access. It presents a chance to enhance healthy behaviour, lower risk factors linked to oral and other non-communicable illnesses, and help lessen disparities in oral health. It can facilitate the implementation of comprehensive healthcare and contribute to the realisation of the 2030 Sustainable Development Agenda, which aims to leave no one behind.

12.4.1 BENEFITS TO ELDERLY

An unexpected benefit of this service development was the successful community-based patient management of several elderly patients. This was only possible with the remote supervision of the consultant who ensured consistency of approach, assessed urgency/priority, assisted with diagnosis, and agreed appropriate treatment. He was available for further advice when required and where there were concerns the patient could be referred again. Because of this, the vast majority (65%) of the patients in the community group completely avoided hospital-based care. The need for expensive transportation was avoided, accompanying staff time was greatly decreased, and patient anxiety was addressed by offering locally based assessments. In fact, a patient was best served when the basic diagnostic and information gathering were carried out at home (75%), especially if the patient was severely weak, disoriented, or ill.

12.5 TELEPERIODONTICS

One of the most frequent causes of tooth loss in adult populations is periodontal disease, a silent disease of the supporting tissues of the teeth that affects the whole world's population. The lifespan of the teeth in the oral cavity can be extended with prompt detection and diagnosis. Those who reside in rural or underserved locations are among those whose communities have the greatest need for dental care [21,22].

General dentists may be enlisted to diagnose and treat simple periodontal issues in situations where a periodontist is not accessible for consultation. All teledentistry applications work to increase efficiency, reach marginalised populations, enhance service quality, and lessen the burden of oral diseases [23].

12.5.1 Teleconsultation

A periodontist can be consulted for advice on the best course of action after receiving all the relevant data (including a radiograph of the affected area, an intraoral photo, and any charting and health history information) from a general dentist through the internet. After the lesion has healed, the general dentist can recommend the proper antibiotics as recommended by the periodontist and refer the patient to an expert for periodontal surgery (if necessary). These straightforward teledentistry consultations not only reduce the patient's travel time, but also ease their discomfort and prepare the area for treatment. The technology would make easy multidisciplinary consultations possible if a patient with medical problems were seen in a teleperiodontics dentistry practice, boosting the idea of holistic health care.

12.5.2 Telediagnosis

A periodontist can help with the diagnosis of particular lesions if the general practitioner is unable to do so. This will aid in providing prompt care for the issue up until the patient needs to see a periodontist.

12.5.3 Teletreatment

The periodontist can recommend several emergency and non-emergency medications to the practising dentist who would properly provide the necessary care.

12.5.4 Telemonitoring/support

Patients who are not in the same place as the healthcare professional are monitored using telemonitoring. A patient would often have many monitoring devices at home, and the results of these devices will be communicated to the healthcare professional by telephone. After various treatments, such as periodontal surgery, telemonitoring may serve as a useful platform for patient monitoring. Patients might receive supportive periodontal care from different parts of the world. The frequency of periodontal care visits can also be significantly decreased by telemonitoring them live. Telemonitoring is a practical solution for patients to avoid travel and handle some of the most fundamental tasks in self-care. This would help with the monitoring and treatment of acute oral disorders and other oral lesions linked to broader illnesses. The main goal would be to get and supply some more modern or uncommon medications, which are typically unattainable in remote areas.

12.6 TELEORTHODONTICS

Instead of direct personal interaction, teleorthodontics uses web consultations to deliver orthodontic care and treatment. Orthodontists frequently consult with one another online and exchange digital copies of patient records. Typically, tele-orthodontic consultations and treatments are carried out without the involvement of general dentists. They have also been mentioned in connection with general dentists, albeit less frequently [24,25–34]. Currently, teleorthodontics is carried out via technology including high-speed internet access, digital films and photographs, smartphones, and websites.

MSN, Skype, and other communication services are recommended by Costa et al. as being effective for in-patient treatment; nevertheless, a poll reveals that WhatsApp Messenger is the most popular option [26]. With the aid of ongoing virtual interaction, this also aids in developing and maintaining a strong patient-clinician connection [27].

Teledentistry in orthodontics basically refers to the use of telecommunications technology to provide remote dental care and orthodontic services. It leverages digital tools and communication platforms to enable orthodontists to diagnose, treat, monitor, and consult with patients without the need for in-person visits.

Some key aspects and benefits of teledentistry in orthodontics:

12.6.1 TELECONSULTATIONS

Teledentistry allows orthodontists to conduct virtual consultations with patients, where they can evaluate their orthodontic needs, review their medical history, and discuss treatment options. This initial assessment helps determine whether a patient requires in-person orthodontic care or if their concerns can be addressed remotely.

12.6.2 TELETREATMENT PLANNING

Orthodontists can use telecommunication platforms to create treatment plans and discuss them with patients. Through video conferencing, they can visually demonstrate treatment objectives, explain the process, and answer any questions. This helps patients understand their treatment options and make informed decisions. Digital scanners can also be successfully used in efficient treatment planning, custom appliance fabrication, clear aligner technology and orthognathic surgical simulation motivating the patient. [28]

12.6.3 TELEMONITORING PROGRESS

Teledentistry enables remote monitoring of patients' progress throughout their orthodontic treatment as seen in Figure 12.3. Patients can submit regular updates, including photos or videos of their teeth, which orthodontists can review remotely. This allows orthodontists to assess treatment progress, make adjustments if necessary, and provide guidance and support to patients from a distance.

TELE- ORTHODONTICS

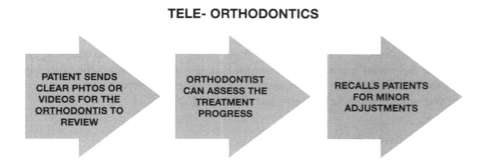

FIGURE 12.3 Telemonitoring done by assessing the treatment progress by photos and videos sent by the patient.

12.6.4 TELEFOLLOW-UP

Patients frequently require routine follow-up visits after completing orthodontic treatment to guarantee long-term stability. These follow-up appointments can be facilitated through teledentistry, which lowers the number of in-person visits while preserving the ability of orthodontists to track the progress and resolve any issues [29].

Through teledentistry, orthodontists can advise patients on proper oral hygiene techniques, healthy eating habits, and aftercare instructions. Orthodontists can provide advice on preserving dental health during orthodontic treatment and address any worries or issues patients may experience through virtual visits or pre-recorded films. Teledentistry does away with the requirement that patients visit the orthodontist's office for each consultation. Patients with restricted mobility or who reside in distant places will especially benefit from this. Additionally, it lessens the inconvenience and expense of in-person sessions, making orthodontic treatment more affordable and practical for patients. Teledentistry can boost orthodontic offices' productivity by streamlining administrative procedures and shortening wait times. By scheduling more patients in a given amount of time, it enables orthodontists to focus their in-person meetings on situations that require hands-on treatment.

It's important to note that while teledentistry can be beneficial in certain situations, it may not be suitable for all orthodontic cases. Some complex orthodontic issues may require in-person evaluations and treatment. Orthodontists evaluate each patient's unique needs to determine the appropriateness of teledentistry for their specific case.

12.7 ORAL SURGERY

Teledentistry, which involves the use of telecommunication technology to provide dental care and consultation remotely, has the potential to be a useful tool in oral surgery.

12.7.1 Teleconsultation

Teledentistry can be used to conduct virtual consultations between oral surgeons and patients prior to surgery. During these consultations, the oral surgeon can evaluate the patient's condition, review medical history, and discuss the procedure with the patient. This can help to ensure that the patient is prepared for the surgery and that any questions or concerns are addressed [30].

12.7.2 Telediagnosis

Evaluation and assessment: Teleconsultation allows oral surgeons to remotely evaluate and assess patients. Through video calls or teleconferencing, the surgeon can review the patient's medical history, perform a visual examination of the oral cavity, and discuss the patient's symptoms and concerns. This evaluation helps determine the appropriateness of the surgical procedure and enables the surgeon to plan the surgery accordingly.

Patient education and informed consent: Teledentistry provides an opportunity for oral surgeons to educate patients about the surgical procedure, potential risks, and expected outcomes. They can explain the steps involved, discuss the post-operative care requirements, and address any questions or concerns the patient may have [31]. This helps the patient make informed decisions and provide informed consent for the surgery. It also plays an important in patient education and motivation, presurgical discussion among the surgeons, and performing mock surgeries to estimate treatment outcomes [32].

Preoperative instructions: Oral surgeons can provide preoperative instructions to patients. They can explain the necessary preparations, such as fasting requirements, medications to be discontinued, and specific instructions for the day of surgery. This ensures that patients receive clear instructions and are adequately prepared for the procedure.

Screening and risk assessment: During teleconsultation, oral surgeons can screen patients for any potential contraindications or risks associated with the surgery. They can assess the patient's overall health, medications, and any pre-existing conditions that might affect the surgery or anaesthesia. This screening process helps identify high-risk patients and ensures that appropriate measures are taken to minimise complications [33].

Planning and coordination: Teledentistry allows oral surgeons to collaborate with other healthcare professionals involved in the patient's care. They can discuss the treatment plan, share diagnostic images or records, and coordinate with other specialists if necessary. This facilitates comprehensive care and ensures that all aspects of the patient's oral health are considered before surgery.

It is important to note that Teledentistry has its limitations, and not all oral surgery cases may be suitable for remote evaluation. However, in many situations, preoperative teleconsultation can streamline the process, enhance patient communication, and optimise patient care before the actual surgery takes place.

12.7.3 TELEMONITORING

Post-operative follow-up: Teledentistry can be used to monitor patients remotely after surgery. Oral surgeons can check in with patients via video call to assess their recovery, evaluate the healing process, and answer any questions or concerns the patient may have.

Post-operative follow-up for oral surgery patients via teledentistry can be a valuable tool to monitor patients' recovery remotely.

Assessing healing progress: Oral surgeons can visually assess the healing progress of the surgical site. Patients can use video calls to show their oral cavity, allowing the surgeon to examine the incisions, check for any signs of infection or complications, and evaluate the overall healing process.

Addressing patient concerns: Teledentistry enables patients to communicate any concerns or questions they may have after the surgery. The oral surgeon can address these concerns, provide reassurance, and offer guidance on post-operative care. This remote communication helps to alleviate patient anxiety and ensures that they receive appropriate support during the recovery period.

Medication management: Oral surgeons can discuss and adjust medication prescriptions remotely. They can evaluate the patient's pain levels, review any medication side effects, and provide recommendations for pain management or adjusting medication dosages if necessary.

Post-operative instructions: Oral surgeons can provide detailed post-operative instructions to patients. They can explain proper wound care, oral hygiene practices, dietary restrictions, and any specific precautions that need to be taken during the recovery period [34]. This remote guidance ensures that patients understand and adhere to the post-operative instructions correctly.

Scheduling in-person visits if needed: During teleconsultation, if the surgeon identifies any concerns or complications that require in-person evaluation, they can schedule an in-office visit accordingly. This allows for a timely response to any issues while minimising unnecessary trips to the clinic.

It's important to note that while teledentistry can be beneficial for post-operative follow-up, it may not be suitable for all cases. Some patients may require in-person visits for more thorough assessments or procedures such as suture removal. The decision to utilise teledentistry for post-operative follow-up should be made on a case-by-case basis, taking into consideration the specific needs and circumstances of each patient [35].

Second opinions: Teledentistry can be used to obtain second opinions from other oral surgeons or specialists. This can be particularly helpful in complex cases or situations where a patient is unsure about their treatment plan.

12.8 PEDODONTICS

Children's dental health affects their overall health as well as their social, physical, and mental development. Paediatric dentists can make better use of information and technology advancements to increase access to oral health care and modify oral health behaviours. Oral health education and promotion campaigns have been able to attract the public's attention and reach a sizable audience thanks to mobile technology, the internet, and mHealth applications.

Digital technology is easier for children to use than it is for adults, and they use it more frequently. Dental professionals frequently use social networking tools to communicate with their patients. This is also seen in the COVID-19 pandemic case. The current health crisis has therefore presented new problems to dentists and motivated new priorities, such as guaranteeing patient safety, controlling and decreasing contamination hazards, and improving treatment efficacy to boost productivity and effectiveness. As a result, new methods, tools, and applications for digital health have emerged [36].

12.8.1 TELECONSULTATION AND DIAGNOSIS

Teledentistry can be a new approach to continuing dental treatment that supports long-distance oral clinical care, professional health-related education, and is patient-related both now and in the future. This new technology can significantly reduce the shortage of paediatric dental specialists in areas with insufficient healthcare services, ensure patient safety during the pandemic, provide dental care for paediatric patients, and promote good health management [37].

They are handy to use since they can be accessed immediately from a smartphone, removing the need for a second device. They may also be customised to provide feedback and particular reminders for developing new behaviours or routines.

Teledentistry, which allows access to patients' dental state based on an electronic database and their medical history, is a good tool for routine systematic dental check-ups and examinations in children, adolescents, and adults [38,39].

Teledentistry has successfully bridged this gap, where the patient is no longer afraid of the pain and discomfort, assisting in the early detection of caries and enhancing patient education and motivation for dental treatment, from the fear of their first dental visits to the phobia of needles and scalpels.

12.8.2 TELEMANAGEMENT/MONITORING

Teledentistry can be used in conjunction with in-person clinical practices in child dentistry to improve patient care. In areas with few healthcare facilities, this technology can significantly help with better patient management. This approach might result in ensuring safety during the epidemic. It can offer paediatric patients safe dental care management.

Collaboration between different professionals can also be a part of teleconsultation. Interdisciplinary participation can happen more quickly for conditions that need multidisciplinary team management since electronic patient records are available [40].

By lowering the number of dental visits during the pandemic, mobile game applications help reduce face-to-face contact by giving kids an interactive option to control their conduct. These programmes can combine behaviour modification strategies including tell-show-do, encouraging visualisations before visits, diversion, and modelling.

Video modelling is beneficial in improving children's coping abilities in stressful situations while also acting as a therapeutic influence in the management of anxiety [41,42].

While Simsek et al., 2020 [43] used YouTube to describe oral habits, authors like Zotti et al., 2016 [44], Scheerman et al., 2019 [45], and Lotto et al., 2020 [46] used common social medial applications like WhatsApp and telegram for oral health education, patient communication via photographs or text messages. They showed significant improvements in early childhood caries management and overall compliance with dental hygiene among preschoolers from low socioeconomic backgrounds.

Patil et al., 2017 [47] discovered that using a mobile application called "my little dentist" successfully reduced anxiety and enhanced positive behaviour among the subjects. Paediatric dentists can use this technology for patient and parent education, monitoring preventative care and post-treatment follow-up, assessment of dental development, diagnosis of dental illnesses, treatment planning, and behaviour coaching before appointments to lessen anxiety in young patients. Despite its shortcomings, teledentistry can be a strategy for addressing access disparities and providing long-term dental healthcare for the young population. This requires collaboration between health authorities and paediatric dentists.

12.9 PROSTHODONTICS

Prosthodontics is one field of dentistry where teledentistry, or the delivery of dental care remotely via telecommunications technology, has attracted a lot of interest and adoption. Dental prostheses like crowns, bridges, dentures, and dental implants are the subject of prosthodontics, which also deals with their design, production, and fitting. Depending on the treatment, the provision of prosthodontic care to senior patients may be urgent or emergency. Provisional restoration debonding, denture adjustments or repairs, prosthetic fractures, and screw loosening in implant prostheses are a few examples of emergencies in prosthodontics [48–50].

12.9.1 TELECONSULTATIONS AND TREATMENT PLANNING

Prosthodontists can conduct virtual consultations and treatment planning over the internet thanks to teledentistry. Prosthodontists can evaluate a patient's dental health, go over treatment choices, and develop a unique treatment plan via video conference or telephone consultations.

Ignatius E. et al. looked into the use of videoconferencing for diagnosis and treatment planning for patients needing prosthetic or oral rehabilitation treatment and found that it could increase the availability of dental specialist services in sparsely populated areas [51].

Prosthodontists can evaluate patients from a distance before implanting dental prostheses thanks to teledentistry. In order to analyse oral health, appraise the remaining teeth, and design the best prosthetic solution, patients might take intraoral photographs and send them to their prosthodontist. Similar to this, there aren't many resources available for teaching patients about prosthodontic treatments, oral hygiene habits, and dental prosthetic care. To help patients comprehend the treatment process and make wise decisions, prosthodontists might provide films, animations, and other instructional resources.

Practical obstacles make it difficult for elderly patients who reside in nursing homes, private homes, or institutions to get to the dentist. These patients could now be treated through domiciliary dental care services like mobile dentistry [52,53].

In order to provide prompt care, mobile dentistry enables the transfer of tools, supplies, and equipment from the dental office to the patients' location [54].

12.9.2 TELEMONITORING

Teledentistry enables prosthodontists to follow up with patients remotely after dental prostheses have been fitted and address any problems they may have. Patients can send photos of their prosthesis for evaluation or report their complaints, enabling prompt action if required as depicted in Figure 12.4.

This allows for effective communication between prosthodontists and dental labs in addition to between prosthodontists and patients. Dental technicians can safely access digital photos and impressions of patients' oral structures, enabling precise manufacturing of dental prostheses.

Teledentistry, on the other hand, can be a useful tool for triaging patients, cutting down on pointless visits, increasing access to care, and boosting interaction and cooperation between prosthodontists and clients.

12.9.3 TELEMANAGEMENT

It might be able to employ a teledentistry model with the suggested questions as outlined in this brief message to examine and manage such patients. Social media and technological advancements have made communication simple, and they can be utilised as a useful tool to manage senior patients in times like pandemic outbreaks. Additionally, the recommended questionnaire used in conjunction with the teledentistry paradigm is crucial when dealing with older patients [55].

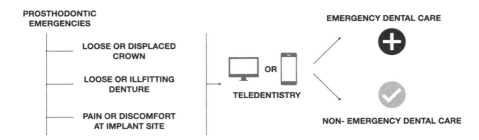

FIGURE 12.4 Common prosthodontic problems faced by patients can be evaluated as emergent or non emergent on the basis of photographs or any other information sent by the patient

12.10 TELEENDODONTICS

Although endodontics is one of several dental disciplines to which teledentistry can be applied, it is crucial to be aware that remote endodontic therapy has some limits.

Teledentistry can be used in endodontics for a number of reasons and purposes, including the following:

12.10.1 TELECONSULTATIONS

Through the use of teledentistry, endodontists can analyse and consult with patients who may need a root canal procedure or who have issues with their tooth pulp or periapical tissues from a distance. Patients can describe their symptoms using video conferencing, and endodontists can make initial diagnoses and recommendations. For instance, it can be utilised to detect root canal orifices at a distance, indicating that experienced dentists can assist younger colleagues in the detection of root canal orifices by remotely identifying root canals [56]. The diagnosis of periapical lesions of the anterior teeth can be accomplished with success using teledentistry based on the internet as a telecommunication medium, lowering the costs of distant trips and making immediate assistance available [57].

12.10.2 TELEDIAGNOSIS

Initial screenings can be done through teledentistry, and patients can be prioritised according to their symptoms. Endodontists can prioritise cases based on the urgency of the procedure by remotely examining patients. This can assist in making the best use of few resources and guarantee that people who need care get it quickly. Endodontics specialists who are remote consultants are notified of the request via their mobile devices, and they then download the digital photos and related anamnestic information. They determine the diagnosis and recommend a course of action, after which they put this information online on a server that notifies the dentist who requested the consultation about the response they have got [58]. In assessing periapical lesions, Baker and colleagues (2000) found no statistically significant difference between locally viewed photos and those relayed via a videoconferencing system and viewed on a monitor screen [59].

12.10.3 PATIENT EDUCATION

Teledentistry platforms allow endodontists to instruct patients through the internet about endodontic procedures, available treatments, and oral hygiene habits. They can answer any concerns or questions patients may have, give instructional materials, and describe treatment options. This improves patient comprehension and compliance.

12.10.4 TELEMONITORING AND FOLLOW-UP

Teledentistry can be used for remote follow-up appointments after endodontic operations for monitoring and follow-up. In addition to receiving post-operative instructions, patients can communicate their progress and report any problems or concerns. By eliminating the need for pointless in-person appointments, this can save time both the patient and the endodontist.

Despite the advantages, it's critical to recognise the teledentistry in endodontics limitations. Many procedures necessitate in-person visits, including the physical inspection of teeth, diagnostic tests, and performing root canal therapy. Additionally, difficulties with remote evaluations may arise from the absence of tactile feedback and restricted access to some diagnostic instruments.

12.11 ADVANTAGES OF TELEDENTISTRY IN COVID-19 LOCKDOWN

12.11.1 Management of Preliminary Emergencies

By providing the patient with the appropriate antibiotic therapy and home care instructions, the dentist can treat primary emergencies. By doing so, the treatment could be continued until the lockdown was released.

12.11.2 Assisting with Expert Consultations

Without having to go to a dentist during the lockdown, teledentistry is an effective way to get a specialist's opinion. This makes it easier for the patient's treatment plan to be formed more quickly and effectively.

12.11.3 Follow-up Visits can be Avoided

The dentist can receive a proper follow-up for the patients with the use of images taken by the patient of the site of infection after performing emergency treatments like extractions or emergency access opening in cases of swelling.

12.12 PITFALLS OF TELEDENTISTRY

There are still a lot of obstacles to overcome before technology can be fully integrated into dentistry. A central digitalisation would continue to be contested in a large country like India with such wide-ranging linguistic and cultural diversity. Uncertain factors include the disparity in digital literacy across people of different demographics, including gender, location, and financial position. Unfortunately, pricing also acts as a deterrent to the adoption of technological breakthroughs for the promotion of oral health in some regions and segments of society. Even while teledentistry is a godsend for dentists in these trying times, nothing compares to the precision of a clinical diagnosis of the patient. The most critical diagnostic procedures, including palpation and percussion, cannot be carried out via teledentistry.

Only the diagnostic and preventive procedures benefit from teledentistry. A patient must visit the clinic for operations like extractions, endodontic treatments, and restorations if he needs therapy.

12.12.1 Online Assessment

Clinical photography serves as the basis for the diagnosis, which may change based on in-person interactions [60]. The proper representation on intraoral photos or videos might not match what's truly there. It is unable to use further diagnostic tools like percussion and palpation.

12.12.2 Teledental Care is Compliant with HIPAA

A telehealth service must have all required controls, such as access restrictions, audit controls, and complete end-to-end encryption, to ensure that Protected Health Information (PHI) may be delivered securely in order to be deemed HIPAA-compliant. Additionally, a BAA must be in place to guarantee that any outside vendors handling PHI for a health care provider will only use the information in a secure manner [61].

12.12.3 Cybersecurity Liability

The risk of cyber threats rises along with the demand for cyber liability insurance as workplaces switch from in-person to virtual visits. Data may be significantly at risk during Internet communications. As previously mentioned, a specific computer with stringent firewalls and cyber security measures must be used for patient interactions. However, there is still a potential of unauthorised access to a computer system, therefore patients need to be informed of this possibility. Computers can be compromised in cyberattacks, and data can be stolen or used as a launchpad for more attacks [62]. These assaults may result in unintended HIPAA violations or privacy invasions. Cyber liability covers crisis response costs, including those associated with identifying and contacting affected patients, investigating the system to ascertain the reason for the system hack, providing credit/identity monitoring services to patients whose information was compromised, and recovering and/or replacing data, in addition to claims made against the provider due to the release of personal information [63].

Six "telemedicine barriers" were highlighted in the 1994 Western Governors' Association Telemedicine Action Report as potential obstacles to the adoption of this means of delivering healthcare:

1. issues with infrastructure planning and development;
2. issues with telecommunications regulations;
3. issues with reimbursement for telemedicine services due to a lack of or inconsistent policies;
4. issues with licensure and credentialing due to conflicting interests with regard to ensuring quality of care, regulating professional activities, and implementing health policies;
5. issues with medical malpractice liability due to a lack of certification; and
6. issues with telemedicine reimbursement due to a lack of or inconsistent policies [57,58]

12.13 TELEEDUCATION

Another frontier of teledentistry is distance learning, which aims to improve knowledge of dentistry and achieve new levels of science and information transfer. Teledentistry is the practice of providing dental care, education, and consultation remotely using communication and information technologies. Teledentistry has gained popularity as a technique for dental education as e-learning has grown.

The following are some applications of teledentistry in online education:

Remote education: Dental professionals and students can receive interactive workshops, webinars, and online courses thanks to teledentistry. This enables everyone, regardless of location, to access educational resources and get immediate feedback from subject-matter experts.

Virtual Consultation: Teledentistry can be utilised to assist patients who are unable to physically visit a dental clinic with virtual consultations. To connect with a dentist or dental hygienist and get advice on oral health issues, patients can use video conferencing capabilities.

Clinical Supervision: During clinical rotations, dental professionals and students can be remotely supervised using teledentistry. As a result, supervisors are able to keep an eye on and assess the clinical performance of their students' or colleagues' without really being there.

Continuing Learning: Dental professionals can receive continuing education through the use of teledentistry. Remote delivery of online workshops, webinars, and courses enables professionals to stay up-to-date with the most recent findings, technology, and best practices [64–67].

12.14 FUTURE IMPLICATIONS

Inadequate health infrastructure and clinical services, a lack of qualified doctors, the absence of specialist care, the late discovery of an illness, and the prolonged wait for patients to be transported to urban healthcare facilities are just a few of the constraints and barriers that prevent effective dental care in rural India. Dentistry has seen a significant transformation as a result of technology. Another drawback is the delivery of dental services by inexperienced primary healthcare professionals. Additionally, patients prioritise their major medical conditions over dental issues, and they typically only visit a dentist in an emergency (typically severe pain). The most ignored oral condition is periodontal disease since it is a silent disease, and patients typically do not respond till their teeth are exfoliated. Additionally, patients frequently self-medicate due to the prevalence of superstitions, unfounded nonscientific cures, and misunderstandings regarding dental therapy.

Additionally, patients are not aware of the different preventive practices that could otherwise lessen the burden of the condition. The Indian Space Research Organisation (ISRO) [64] has successfully carried out a number of telemedicine/

telehealth projects, which are of great social relevance to the nation because they enable specialty healthcare to the remote, rural, and underserved population.

ISRO has successfully used INSAT satellites to connect a number of hospitals and healthcare facilities in remote rural areas with speciality hospitals in cities. Thus, effective linkage between patients at the far end and the specialised medical professionals in urban centres has been established.

12.15 CONCLUSION

In conclusion, teledentistry is a profession that makes use of communications technology to deliver dental services and care remotely. It has a number of advantages, including improved patient convenience, expanded access to dental care, and the capacity to deliver remote consultations, treatment planning, and oral health instruction. Teledentistry offers the potential to increase access to dental care, especially for people with limited mobility or who live in underserved areas. It's crucial to keep in mind, though, that some dental treatments and procedures can still call for a trip to a dental office. Depending on the location, teledentistry may be subject to different laws and insurance policies. In the field of dentistry, teledentistry has become a vital technology that has the ability to supplement traditional in-person therapy and improve patient outcomes.

REFERENCES

1. Rajendra P, Kumari M, Rani S, Dogra N, Boadh R, Kumar A, Dahiya M. Impact of artificial intelligence on civilization: Future perspectives. Mater Today: Proc, 2022 Jan 1;56:252–256.
2. Singhal A, Phogat M, Kumar D, Kumar A, Dahiya M, Shrivastava VK. Study of deep learning techniques for medical image analysis: A review. Mater Today: Proc, 2022 Jan 1;56:209–214.
3. Nichols K Teledentistry overview: United States of America. Telemed e-Health, 2019;7:9–12.
4. Daniel SJ, Kumar S. Teledentistry: A key component in access to care. J Evid Based Dent Pract, 2014;14:201–208.
5. Achmad H, Tanumihardja M, Ramadhany YF. Teledentistry as a solution in dentistry during the covid-19 pandemic period: A systematic review. Int J Pharm Res, 2020;12(2):272–278.
7. Fornaini C, & Rocca P. Relevance of teledentistry: Brief report and future perspectives. Front Dent, 2022;19:1–6. 10.18502/fid.v19i25.10596
6. Handbook of manufacturing: forecasting future of industry 4.0
8. Bhambal A, Saxena S, Balsaraf SV. Teledentistry: Potentials unexplored. J Int Oral Health, 2010;2(3):1–6.
9. Baheti MJ, Bagrecha SD, Toshniwal NG, Misal A. Teledentistry: A need of the era. Int J Dent Med Res, 2014;1(2):80–91.
10. Abbas B, Wajahat M, Saleem Z, Imran E, Sajjad M, Khurshid Z. Role of teledentistry in COVID-19 pandemic: A nationwide comparative analysis among dental professionals. Eur J Dent, 2020;14(1):116–122.
11. Nassani MZ, Al-Maweri SA, AlSheddi A, Alomran A, Aldawsari MN, Aljubarah A, Almuhanna AM, Almutairi NM, Alsalhani AB, Noushad M. Teledentistry—knowledge, practice, and attitudes of dental practitioners in Saudi Arabia: A nationwide web-based survey. InHealthcare, 2021;9(12):1682–1684.

12. Global m-OralHealth Workshop. Accessedfrom https://moralhealth.bhbm.org/site/les-comities/.
13. Vujicic M, Suda KJ. COVID-19 and dentistry's economic shock. J Am Dent Assoc, 2020;151(10):743–745. doi:10.1016/j.adaj.2020.08.001
14. Divaris K, Lee JY, Baker AD, et al. The use of tele oral health promotion to improve access to dental care in rural and underserved populations: A systematic review. Telemed J E Health, 2018;24(4):269–277. doi:10.1089/tmj.2017.0067
15. Lee JY, Divaris K. The ethical imperative of addressing oral health literacy: A systematic review of evidence. J Dent Educ. 2012;76(4):409–418.
16. Park SE, Lee JY, Kim S, Kim S. Effects of teleconsultation service on dental anxiety, pain, and oral health-related quality of life in underserved population. Telemed J E Health, 2021;27(4):345–352. doi:10.1089/tmj.2020.0085
17. "Tele-oral Health Promotion in Rural Schools: An Interventional Study" by the Journal of Telemedicine and Telecare.
18. Oral Health Education and Promotion Through Telemedicine Technologies" by the Journal of Dental Education.
19. Telehealth: Delivering Dental Education and Training Using Technology" by the American Dental Education Association (ADEA).
20. Shulman JD. Using telehealth for oral health assessments in rural and remote areas. J Am Dent Assoc, 2017 Feb;148(2):81–82. doi: 10.1016/j.adaj.2016.12.011. PMID: 28126420.
21. Allukian M, Jr The neglected epidemic and the surgeon general's report: A call to action for better oral health. Am J Public Health, 2000;90:843–845. [PMC free article] [PubMed] [Google Scholar]
22. Beetstra S, Derksen D, Ro M, Powell W, Fry DE, Kaufman A. A "health commons" approach to oral health for low-income populations in a rural state. Am J Public Health, 2002;92:12–13. [PMC free article] [PubMed] [Google Scholar]
23. Khan SA, Omar H. Teledentistry in practice: Literature review. Telemed J E Health, 2013;19:565–567. [PubMed] [Google Scholar]
24. Berndt J, Leone P, King G. Using teledentistry to provide interceptive orthodontic services to disadvantaged children. Am J Orthod Dentofac Orthop, 2008;134(5):700–706.
25. Mandall NA, O'Brien KD, Brady J et al. Teledentistry for screening new patient orthodontic referrals. Part 1: A randomised controlled trial. Br Dent J, 2005;199(10):659–662.
26. daCosta, ALP, Silva, AA, Pereira, CB. Teleortodontia: Ferramentadeauxílioàpráti caclínicaeàeducação continuada. Dental Press J Orthod, 2011;16:15–21.
27. Caprioglio, A, Pizzetti, GB, Zecca, PA et al. Management of orthodontic emergencies during 2019-NCOV. Prog. Orthod, 2020;21:10.
28. Sehrawat S, Kumar A, Grover S, Dogra N, Nindra J, Rathee S, Dahiya M, Kumar A. Study of 3D scanning technologies and scanners in orthodontics. Mater Today: Proc, 2022 Jan 1;56:186–193.
29. Mani Dr. SA, Manerikar Dr. R, Mani Dr. A, Sachdeva Dr. S, Goyal Dr. A. Teleorthodontics: Future trend and beyond. Ann Rom Soc Cell Biol, 2020;24(2):884–888.
30. La Touche S, Hill K. Teledentistry in oral and maxillofacial surgery. Oral Maxillofac Surg Clin North Am, 2020 Nov; 32(4): 469–475. doi: 10.1016/j.coms.2020.07.002. PMID: 33092711.
31. Nibali L, Agudio G, Cabras M, Di Tanna GL, Rizzo M, Cocchi D, Marconcini S. Teledentistry in oral and maxillofacial surgery: A narrative review. J Clin Med, 2021 Mar 26;10(7):1405. doi: 10.3390/jcm10071405. PMID: 33810513; PMCID: PMC8037434.
32. Sehrawat S, Kumar A, Prabhakar M. Substitute for orthognathic surgery using bioprinted bone scaffolds in restoring osseous defects. In Advances in Additive

Manufacturing Artificial Intelligence, Nature-Inspired, and Biomanufacturing 2023 Jan 1 (pp. 335–347). Elsevier.

33. Kamath DG, Dhinakarsandrasarma P. Telemedicine in oral and maxillofacial surgery: A systematic review of the literature. J Maxillofac Oral Surg, 2020 Dec;19(4):545–552. doi: 10.1007/s12663-020-01377-6. Epub 2020 Jun 20. PMID: 33520223; PMCID: PMC7792476.

34. Nalliah RP, Allareddy V, Elangovan S. Telemedicine in oral and maxillofacial surgery: A primer for the practicing surgeon. J Oral Maxillofac Surg, 2019 Dec;77(12):2522–2531. doi: 10.1016/j.joms.2019.06.015. Epub 2019 Jun 21. PMID: 31326488.

35. Elangovan S, Mahrous A, Chambrone L. Telemedicine in dentistry: A review of the literature. J Dent. 2017 Jul;62:1–11. doi: 10.1016/j.jdent.2017.04.001. Epub 2017 Apr 6. PMID: 28392269

36. Kui A, Popescu C, Labuneţ A et al. Is teledentistry a method for optimizing dental practice, even in the post-pandemic period? An integrative review. Int J Environ Res Public Health, 2022;19(13):7609.

37. Harrel SK and Molinari J. Aerosols and splatter in den-tistry: A brief review of the literature and infection control implications. J Am Dent Assoc, 2004;135(4):429–437.

38. Daniel SJ and Kumar S. Teledentistry: A key componentin access to care. J Evid Based Dent Pract 2014;14 (Suppl), 201–208.

39. Mariño R and Ghanim A. Teledentistry: A systematic review of the literature. J Telemed Telecare, 2013;19(4): 179–183.

40. Schleyer TK, Thyvalikakath TP, Spallek H, Dziabiak MP, Johnson LA. From information technology to informatics: The information revolution in dental education. J Dent Educ, 2012;76:142e53.

41. Melamed BG, Hawes RR, Heiby E, Glick J. Use of filmed modeling to reduce uncooperative behavior of children during dental treatment. J Dent Res, 1975;54:797e801.

42. Paryab M, Arab Z. The effect of filmed modeling on the anxious and cooperative behavior of 4-6 years old children during dental treatment: A randomized clinical trial study. Dent Res J, 2014;11:502e7.

43. Simsek H, Buyuk SK, Ç etinkaya E. YouTubeTM as a source of information on oral habits. J Indian Soc Pedod Prev Dent, 2020;38:115e8.

44. Zotti F, Dalessandri D, Salgarello S, Piancino M, Bonetti S, Visconti L, et al. Usefulness of an app in improving oral hygiene compliance in adolescent orthodontic patients. Angle Orthod, 2016;86:101e7.

45. Scheerman JFM, Hamilton K, Sharif MO, Lindmark U, Pakpour AH. A theory-based intervention delivered by an online social media platform to promote oral health among Iranian adolescents: a cluster randomized controlled trial. Psychol Health, 2020;35:449e66.

46. Lotto M, Strieder AP, Ayala Aguirre PE, Oliveira TM, Andrade Moreira Machado MA, Rios D, et al. Parental-orientededucational mobile messages to aid in the control of early childhood caries in low socioeconomic children: A randomized controlled trial. J Dent, 2020;101:e103456.

47. Patil VH, Vaid K, Gokhale NS, Shah P, Mundada M, Hugar SM. Evaluation of effectiveness of dental apps in management of child behaviour: A pilot study. Int J Pedod Rehabil, 2017;2:14e8.

48. Issrani R, Ammanagi R, Keluskar V. Geriatric dentistry – meet the need. Gerodontology, 2012;29:e1–e5. doi: 10.1111/j.1741-2358.2010.00423.

49. Barenghi L, Barenghi A, Cadeo C, Di Blasio A Innovation by computer- aided design/computer-aided manufacturing technology: A look at infection prevention in dental settings. BioMed Res Int, 2019;2019:6092018. doi: 10.1155/2019/6092018.

50. Batista AUD, Silva PLPD, Melo LA, Carreiro ADFP. Prosthodontic practice during the COVID-19 pandemic: Prevention and implications. Braz Oral Res, 2021;35:e049. doi: 10.1590/1807-3107bor-2021.vol35.0049.
51. Ignatius E, Perälä S, Mäkelä K. Use of videoconferencing for consultation in dental prosthetics and oral rehabilitation. J Telemed Telecare, 2010;16(8):467–470.
52. Henry RG, Ceridan B. Delivering dental care to nursing home and homebound patients. Dent Clin North Am, 1994;38:537–551.
53. Bee JF. Portable dentistry: A part of general dentistry's service mix. Gen Dent, 2004;52:520–526.
54. Mallineni SK, Bhumireddy JC, Nuvvula S. Dentistry for children during and post COVID-19 pandemic outbreak. Child Youth Serv Rev, 2021;120:105734. doi: 10.1016/j.childyouth.2020.105734.
55. Aldhuwayhi S, Shaikh SA, Thakare AA, Mustafa MZ, Mallineni SK. Remote management of prosthodontic emergencies in the geriatric population during the pandemic outbreak of COVID-19. Front Med (Lausanne), 2021 Jul 28;8:648675.
56. Brullmann D, Schmidtmann I, Warzecha K, D'Hoedt B. Recognition of root canal orifices at a distance – a preliminary study of teledentistry. J Telemed Telecare, 2011;17(3):154–157.
57. Zivkovic D, Tosic G, Mihailovic B, et al. Diagnosis of periapical lesions of the front teeth using the internet. PONS Med J, 2010;7:138–143.
58. Chang SW, Plotkin DR, Mulligan R, Polido JC, Mah JK, Meara JG. Teledentistry in rural California: A USC initiative. J Calif Dent Assoc, 2003;31: 601–608.
59. Baker WP 3rd, Loushine RJ, West LA, Kudryk LV, Zadin-sky JR. Interpretation of artificial and in vivo periapical bone lesions comparing conventional viewing versus a video con- ferencing system. J Endod, 2000;26(1): 39–41
60. Deshpande S, Patil D, Dhokar A, Bhanushali P, Katge F. Teledentistry: A boon amidst COVID-19 lockdown—a narrative review. Int J Telemed Appl, 2021 Feb 16;2021:1–6.
61. U.S. Department of Health and Human Services. Are the following entities considered "business associates" under the HIPAA Privacy Rule: US Postal Service, United Parcel Service, delivery truck line employees and/or their management?. Available at: https://www.hhs.gov/hipaa/for-professionals/faq/245/are-entities-business-associates/index.html. [Accessed 27 August 2020].
62. MedPro Group. Cyber liability. Available at: https://www.server2.medpro.com/proxy-storage/documents/42470/42583/Cyber_Coverage_Dental_Slick. pdf. [Accessed 27 August 2020].
63. Western Governors Association Telemedicine Reports 1998. See http://www.westgov.org/wga/publicat/combar4.htm (last checked 31 October 2004).
64. Elangovan, S, Allareddy, V, Singh, P, Elsy, J. The use of teledentistry in dental education: A review of the literature. J Dent Educ, 2016;80(12): 1499–1507.
65. Estai, M, Bunt, S, Kanagasingam, Y, Tennant, M, Kruger, E. Applications of teledentistry: A literature review and update. J Telemed Telecare, 2017;23(10): 828–840.
66. Kruger, E, Tennant, M, Short, SD. Distance education and teledentistry in the Pacific: A model for continuing professional development and sustainable education. Front Public Health, 2017;5: 322.
67. Platin, E, Helgeson, MJ, Elangovan, S. Teledentistry in dental education during the COVID-19 pandemic: A review of the literature. J Dent Educ, 2021;85(3): 295–301.

13 Virtual Reality Distraction as an Effective and Intelligent Tool for Effective Behaviour Management

Shruti Sharma
Department of Conservative Dentistry and Endodontics,
SGT University, Budhera, Gurugram, Haryana, India

13.1 INTRODUCTION

Medical and dental procedures frequently cause discomfort, worry, and agony [1].

In particular, these sensations not only can they negatively impact patient comfort levels during medical treatments, but they are also linked to unfavourable outcomes like efforts to flee, poor recuperation, disturbed sleeping and eating patterns [2].

Additionally, since anxiety and pain can cause patients to put off seeking medical and dental attention, treatments are required to deal with these issues in patients [3].

Because it prevents cooperation and increases the failure rate of dental treatments, several nations regard dental anxiety and fear as one of the major public health challenges [4].

According to studies conducted in numerous nations throughout the world, prevalence ranges from 3 to 43%. In Thailand, 23.6% of 12-year-olds report having dental anxiety [5].

Children's dental fear and anxiety can be brought on by a variety of factors. According to past studies, characteristics that enhance dental anxiety and terror include young age and female gender [6].

Sibling presence and family structure are major factors in children's dental phobia and anxiety, according to a study by Wu and Gao [7]. In addition, childhood dental phobia and anxiety were connected to greater rates of tooth deterioration, toothaches, and extractions.

This consequence will cause children's oral health issues to worsen over time, making treatment more challenging. As a result of this reinforcement, kids become more fearful and anxious [8].

DOI: 10.1201/9781003404934-13

It is important for the success of therapy that children cooperate with dental professionals in order to reduce their concerns and anxiety [9]. Dental anxiety and terror management techniques can be either pharmaceutical or non-pharmacological. Inhalation, sedative (nitrous oxide), intravenous, and oral sedatives are all examples of pharmacological techniques for reducing anxiety and panic during dental procedures. The hazards and unfavourable side effects of this sedative include headache, nausea, rash, lethargy, confusion and dizziness [4].

Additionally, this raises the associated cost of dental care. Patients value a management strategy that does not use drugs. This is due to the possibility that using the medicine carries unwelcomed risks [9]. Diversion and environment modification of the clinic is appropriate, painless and quick method to alleviate anxiety.

Numerous non-pharmacological techniques use cognitive-behavioural strategies to divert children's attention from frightening and uncomfortable procedures. Children are subjected to cognitive interventions to divert their attention from pain caused by the procedure. These methods support the child's right to take full part in the operation. The most common intervention utilised in the dental operatory to divert kids' attention from the unpleasant stimuli is distraction [10].

13.2 ANXIETY

Although dental procedures are typically thought to be stressful and anxiety-inducing [11–13]. It is commonly acknowledged that psychological stress may have physiological consequences on several physiological systems, similar to those brought on by physical obstacles [14]. The hypothalamus-pituitary-adrenocortical axis is activated, which results in a stimulation of the adrenal cortex and release of cortisol [15,16].

It has been experimented that the level of cortisol in saliva closely resembles serum cortisol levels and accurately represents HPA activity [17].

Estimating salivary cortisol levels in kids has become a possible biological indicator of stress-related behaviours [18].

To assess the efficacy of interventions, salivary cortisol levels have been used by many researchers [19,20]. No studies have been done to assess the effect of distraction techniques on cortisol levels of saliva in children undergoing invasive dental procedures. The Diagnostic and Statistical Manual for Mental Health Disorders, Fifth Edition (DSM-5) now divides anxiety disorders into around a dozen distinct categories.

The most common types of anxiety disorders are agoraphobia, panic disorder, social anxiety disorder, and generalised anxiety disorder (GAD). In the most recent revision of the DSM, which no longer includes PTSD in the category of anxiety disorders, PTSD is now categorised under Trauma and Stressor-Related Disorders. A corresponding modification has been made to the most current edition of the International Classification of Diseases (ICD-11; World Health Organisation). Putting PTSD and anxiety disorders into distinct diagnostic groups based on how their symptoms present clarifies and ensures consistency in professional practice, which can be a vital step in approving and delivering evidence-based therapy care.

13.3   DISTRACTION

Distraction is a cognitive behavioural method that is based on the idea that people have a finite amount of attentional capacity. The idea is that there is a larger chance of pain diversion the more engaging the distraction strategy, integrating visual, auditory, and tactile clues. Distraction techniques include both passive and active measures [21]. Virtual reality has recently gained popularity as a cutting-edge distraction method in clinical research trials.

The logic behind incorporating distraction techniques for pain reduction is that "pain perception has a considerable psychological component" and if the attention is taken away, a person's feeling of pain similarly diminishes. To compete with signals from unpleasant stimuli, "An adequate measure of attention which involves multiple sensory modalities (kinesthetic, visual and auditory) and active emotional involvement of patient are required [22], in order to combat with signals from stimuli which is unpleasant [23,24].

These include non invasive techniques such as employing cards used for distraction, seeing cartoons, bubbles forming, listening to soothing audio, watching kaleidoscope, and donning virtual reality (VR) glasses. These techniques increase the patient's tolerance to pain while not completely eliminating the pain. Non-pharmacological techniques are accepted as trustworthy and affordable, and they aid in the dentist's independent practice [25].

13.4   INCIDENCE

According to some estimates, up to one-third of people will have an anxiety disorder at some point in their lives, with the recent COVID-19 pandemic being a major contributor to the increase in prevalence of anxiety-related symptoms.

13.5   VIRTUAL REALITY

Virtual reality (VR) is termed as "a computer-human interface" that enables the user to interact and participate dynamically with the virtual reality world, which is a environment synthesised by computer. Distraction caused by virtual reality is more better because it offers more immersive images in front of the user. The real-world (visual, aural, or both) stimuli may be blocked off depending on the particular kind of VR device being utilised.

Full immersion, or the sensation of being there in the virtual environment, can be achieved through VR [26]. Importantly, because less attention is available for pain perception, greater immersion is associated with greater pain relief. Children are particularly drawn to VR since they are frequently completely engrossed in imaginative play [27]. VR can not only provide distraction but also exposure, which reduces pain and anxiety. In order to boost patients' comfort and familiarity with the medical processes and environs, VR exposure has recently been used in a more prophylactic manner.

There is one such VR system named VR system (i-glasses 920HR, Ilixco Inc., Menlo Park, CA, USA) (Figure 13.1). The system comprises eyeglasses which project the required virtual images in front of the child's eyes and have occluding

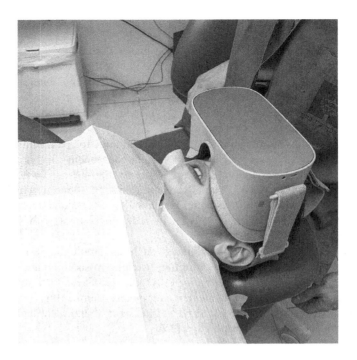

FIGURE 13.1　Virtual reality glasses worn by patient.

eyepads which block out the child's visual field from the projected images in the dentist office setting. To reduce noise from the dental operatory, the device also has earphones that transmits noises from the virtual environment [28].

13.6　APPLICATION OF VIRTUAL REALITY

McCahill et al. carried out s systematic study that found the usage of VR to be effective in anxiety reduction in kids between the ages of 4 and 7. According to Caruso et al., VR was safe to use and helped patients between the ages of 6 and 10 feel less anxious and afraid [29–31].

For children, videos of dental significance can be chosen. For example, the clinician can choose a video in which the significance of routine toothbrushing is emphasised in a Spiderman video. Children prefer to see familiar and colourful creatures, animals or cartoons. This also prevents the onset of anxiety and dread which children under the age of 8 years get after seeing unfamiliar things [32].

Therefore, it would be easier to keep their attention for a longer period of time if the clinician showed them cartoon characters they would recognise and enjoy. Distraction operates via the attention process. A distraction's ability to lessen discomfort is inversely correlated with how much concentration it requires. Prior to six, the main emphasis was on patient pain and distress [33]. The practise of paying attention is how distraction works. The degree of discomfort that a distraction can alleviate is inversely related to the degree of attention that it needs.

13.7 MECHANISM

There are a number of reasons why VR distraction can lessen anxiety and pain perception. There is a hypothesis that there is a psychological component of pain and it elicits attention.

The focus is diverted (distracted) by changing how pain is experienced, which reduces the pain's severity. VR alters the way people perceive pain signals and even decreases the brain activity associated with pain [33].

The fear-inspiring appearance of the dental equipment and the patient's vigilant attention to every detail of the process being carried out are the two main sources of stress associated with dental treatments in children in paediatric dentistry. As a result, the total blockage of the patient's visual fields by the VR device and the subsequent success of the distraction approach are to blame for the good effects of VR distraction on the pain felt by the study's participants.

Pain has historically been characterised as a strong demand on one's attentional resources and as an automatic access to consciousness [34–36]. Pain is still a controlled process even though it is a reaction to unpleasant stimuli. Therefore, the perception of pain may be influenced by any task involving an equivalent or greater amount of cognitive resources. Therefore, any task requiring an equivalent or greater amount of cognitive resources may affect how pain is perceived. After the development of the gate control theory, the phenomena of pain relief by distraction appeared.] This theory proposes that nociceptive signals must pass through a "gate" mechanism in the spinal cord before they may reach the brain directly from the site of injury.

An indication is felt to be more or less painful depending on how wide open the gate is. Many things could cause the gate to open or close. Some of them are sensory; for example, if someone cuts oneself and immediately immerses the affected area in water, large-diameter spinal cord fibres are activated, and activity of fibres with small diameter are reduced and the gate is closed, producing pain relief.

The connected emotion with pain, the experiences related to it and the attention given to it are behavioural and psychological aspects that could affect whether the gate opens or closes.

Given recent research on the neuromatrix, the significance of psychological elements in the perception of pain has grown [37,38]. The neuromatrix is a large neural network that represents the brain's hallmark for experiencing pain. According to the biopsychosocial model, pain can be defined as a conglomeration of sensation and cognition, mediated through regions in the brain. This network is thought to mediate the pain experience itself [39]. Parallel networks play a role in the affective-motivational (A), sensory-discriminative (S), and evaluative-cognitive (E) aspects of the pain experience in the original model. According to this theory, pain is a multisystem output that is intended to cause action, with the main objective being the recovery of the brain's homoeostatic regulatory system.

The concept of the neuromatrix has been largely questioned by recent research; intensity of pain can be separated from the neuromatrix's degree of response, and the neuronal architecture of the neuromatrix appears responsive to non-nociceptive stimuli [40]. To explain how many components, such as cognitive and emotional factors, affect the final sensation of pain, the concept of a complex pain network is still essential [41]. The review by Linton and Shaw found that psychological elements that contribute to pain sensation should be acknowledged and addressed separately from physiological reasons [42]. Because pain perception necessitates focusing cognitive resources on the painful stimulus, attention is especially crucial. The expectation about pain, circumstances around the pain, patient's attitude and cognitive attitude are the factors which affect the experience and management of pain. Additionally, there is a significant impact of emotional activations on pain perception.

Negative emotions like dread and anxiety are not the only ones that are brought on by pain; emotions also actively modulate the perception of pain (for example, they are linked to increased self-reported pain) [43,44].

In the absence of painful stimuli, anticipatory anxiety associated with challenging future circumstances may directly generate pain experiences [45]. Numerous strategies designed to lessen pain during dental procedures are based on distraction techniques since distraction and other psychological factors influence the feeling of pain [46]. While experiencing pain, patients are working on other things. When patients devote their cognitive and attentional resources to the distractor stimuli, they experience a significant reduction in pain. To date, several items and activities have been employed in distraction tactics to engage patients' attentional systems and aid in pain management.

Virtual reality (VR) has recently become a creative and effective distraction technique. In virtual reality, a patient is completely submerged in a simulated setting via utilising a head-mounted display, noise-cancelling or noise-reduction headphones, and a tracking system of the head that helps the patient to move naturally in the environment of virtual reality. Additionally, VR can be interactive, allowing the user to take actions in the virtual world [47]. There have already been a number of evaluations of the effectiveness of VR-based analgesia and some of these evaluations acknowledge the significance of patient's characteristics and subjective experiences when evaluating the efficacy of VR in reduction of pain [48–50].

Keeping in mind the relation of pain with psychology, the aspects related to psychology must be taken into account to increase its effectiveness. Because of this, clinicians and researchers have used distraction in various ways, varying its intensity and tailoring their approaches to various types of pain in various circumstances.

The technology that each VR method uses varies as well, and the user's cognitive and emotional traits can actively influence their experience in a VR simulator [51]. The expectations, feelings, and level of participation of the user all affect how well VR works and how effective it is.

13.8   IMMERSION/PRESENCE

The terms presence and immersion are occasionally used interchangeably. The physical and sensory stimulation that the virtual environment offers, as well as the level of perceptual realism that the virtual system can produce, are what are referred to as immersion [52–55]. In a virtual environment, a false sense of presence is felt. An individual using virtual reality may feel more or less immersed in the environment they are engaging with [56–58]. Although it may not only be defined in terms of science, presence can be compared to immersion psychologically.

The user's mindset, setup of narrative backdrop of virtual reality,personality attributes, all significantly impact the user's perception of "being there," even if technological developments in VR equipment also have an impact [59,60]. Because of this, users' feelings of presence are commonly used as a gauge for the "ecological validity" of VR implementations [61,62].

The best way to gauge presence is undoubtedly up for dispute. Self-report questionnaires are the most popular way to measure presence in previous studies, while behavioural responses, physiological correlates, and qualitative interviews have also been taken into account [63–66]. When describing how immersed they felt in the virtual environment, On a scale, users are asked to rank their level of presence.

There are also numerous approved questionnaires for assessing presence. The effects of VR-aided analgesia were examined by Gutierrez-Martinez and colleagues in a group of 37 volunteers who had their hands placed in cold pressors to simulate experimentally generated pain.

All participants took part in two sessions back-to-back, one utilising virtual reality (VR; Surreal World, a display of surroundings in three dimensions, with intriguing imagery). The second group used a blank screen. Compared to the control condition, the VR session led to a noticeable decrease in discomfort. The authors discovered a substantial inverse relationship between presence ratings and subjective pain ratings: The more a VR user feels present, the more their attention is drawn to the VR world, which reduces their perception of discomfort. Tse and associates (72 participants with artificially induced pain) and Hoffman et al. (11 people with burn wounds) reached comparable conclusions [67,68].

Presence assessments were positively connected with a rise in pain threshold, or, "the degree of immersion"(Tse et al). Furthermore, Sharar et al. weighed presence in the VR environment across three distinct investigations involving participants of various ages [69]. It's interesting to note that youngsters rated presence (and the "realness" of the scene was perceived) higher than adults.

Several research investigated patients who were already in pain as opposed to creating pain artificially. In 12 soldiers with burn injuries from warfare, Maani et al. evaluated and compared VR to a control condition without VR; in 20 children with discomfort from intravenous implantation, Gold et al. utilised a similar methodology.

For Gold and colleagues to analyse their virtual environment (Street Luge) for potential applications, a high level of presence is very important.

In a 5-day research with repeated sessions, Schmitt et al. examined the combination of VR with conventional pharmaceutical pain management. A total of 54 young patients with burn injuries participated. They found that starting on the first day and continuing throughout the future therapeutic sessions, the VR condition significantly reduced pain ratings. On the first day of therapy, presence evaluations were similarly impacted, and this effect persisted throughout the experiment.

Wender et al. compared the use of non interactive VR and interactive VR with 21 patients (in experimentally created pain environment) in an effort to evaluate the significance of interactivity in the analgesic effect of VR. When compared to noninteractive VR, interactive VR demonstrated a 75% increase in the perceived analgesic effect [25]. The presence ratings for interactive and noninteractive VR were not significantly different [70].

Hoffman and associates discovered, however, the exact opposite. In comparison to low-technology VR, noninteractive high-technology VR exhibited greater pain reduction and higher presence evaluations in 39 students with experimentally produced pain. The study done by Chan et al. is the only exception, where the subjects did not distinguish between VR and non VR and the feeling of presence did not correlate with pain ratings [71].

13.9   FUN

It is evident that emotional involvement is intimately tied to a sense of perceived realism and presence in VR, and that users' emotional responses are vital to a virtual environment's effective operation. Because of this, a lot of studies think about the idea of "fun" and assess joyful feelings and enjoyment in virtual application [72].

Since fun has been considered in numerous user experience studies, some usability experts now refer to their profession as "funology" [73–75]. Hoffman and associates discovered a positive correlation between presence assessments and pain relief.

Fun has been taken into account in several user experience studies to this point to the point where some usability specialists refer to their field as "funology." Hoffman and associates discovered a positive correlation between presence assessments and pain relief.

Participants in the VR condition in research by Sharar et al. and Schmitt et al. reported much more enjoyment compared to those who took part in a non-VR condition, ratings. Wender et al. questioned 21 healthy participants to rate how much enjoyment they had when experiencing the most recent painful experience while using interactive versus noninteractive virtual reality. Comparatively to participants in the noninteractive VR condition, participants in the interactive VR condition expressed considerably higher levels of fun. All of these research point to the fact that a key factor in how well virtual reality (VR) works as a painkiller is the participants' perception of fun.

13.10   STATE ANXIETY AND TRAIT ANXIETY

The management of pain is significantly influenced by the negative patient emotions. The well-known issue of anticipatory anxiety affects people undergoing inconvenient or painful medical treatments [76,77].

The usefulness of VR may change depending on whether a person has trait or state anxiety. Tse et al. used a tourniquet approach to apply controlled pain to 72 subjects. Prior to the test, participants' ratings of their anxiety on a single Likert scale (ranging from 1 to 10 in terms of anxiety) were contrasted with the degree to which their pain threshold had increased as a result of the VR stimulation. Right scales should be used to assess anxiety in patients before the use of VR, e.g., STAI, as those with lower anxiety levels showed superior progress in pain reduction [78]. Actually, the STAI questionnaire was only utilised by Van Twillert et al. to evaluate both trait and state anxiety [79].

Patients having burn injuries (N = 19) were either not distracted. In VR and TV environments, there was a slight decrease in state anxiety (2%), but it wasn't very noticeable.

13.11   PRESENCE

The most significant psychological aspect that is directly related to the VR experience may be presence. Positive analgesic effects appear to be associated with a high level of presence. Although it may not directly impact pain per se, the impression of presence may make VR distracting from a perceptual perspective. Researchers can find out if people think of their virtual representation as an environment by measuring presence. Recent accounts make a significant connection between presence and focus [80]. They can watch, listen to, and interact with items there while having experiences.

In conclusion, virtual reality (VR) is a very rich stimulation that can also help individuals forget about their discomfort, but for VR to be successful, users must experience it physically. For the purpose of keeping track of interventions based on VR, it is crucial to quantify presence.

Since the feeling of "being there" typically results from a variety of distinct aspects of the experience, a single inquiry may not be sufficient to fully assess the sense of presence. The participant may be prevented from appreciating the complexity of his or her sensations if presence is reduced to a single inquiry. For instance, the Witmer and Singer Presence Questionnaire examines a variety of factors, including perceived control, involvement, realism of the representation done virtually, and quality of interface.

LessiteR et al. Proposed ITC SOPI, in comparison, takes into account other factors such as user characteristics and potential adverse consequences that affect the sensation of presence. Comparing virtual surroundings is necessary.

Is one device type superior to another? Does a basic exploratory design distract more people than a narrative or cinematic VR experience? Are there changes in how different types of VR content are received based on gender or age? Given its close linkages to efficacy, measuring the presence experience with the appropriate methods could be a crucial element in the context of studies with comparable goals but concentrate on different VR genres.

13.12   FUN AND ANXIETY

Here, we integrate the emotions of enjoyment and worry into a single part. The effectiveness of VR-based analgesia was associated with both enjoyment and anxiety, and their responses were always assessed separately. The relationship between pain and anxiety in therapeutic settings is already established. Scientific evidence confirmed this widely held belief: Anxiety levels have been found to predict the intensity of pain [1,81]. The many components of pain perception, such as pain threshold, pain discrimination, and pain severity, are also intensified by worry. Ploghaus and associates have proposed a potential theory to explain how anxiety impacts pain [82].

The authors assessed the activation responses to painful heat stimulation in a functional magnetic resonance imaging experiment while adjusting the perceived pain's intensity by varying either the physical intensity or the degree of fear. According to the anxiety modulation, imaging data identified distinct activity in the hippocampus in response to similar noxious stimuli. To put it another way, anticipatory worry serves as a prime, enlisting the hippocampus to intensify the unpleasant experience and prepares the person to act in an adaptive manner in the event of the worst-case scenario.

Anxiety (and other emotional responses in general) can directly alter how pain feels, but experience of presence also influences how successful virtual reality (VR) is as a tool for distraction.

Although there is a substantial body of research on how emotions affect how virtual environments are perceived (and vice versa), more recent methods that look at the complete emotional response rather than merely predetermined emotional categories have methodological and theoretical advantages [83–86]. In particular, dimensional theories of emotions aid in better understanding of confusing and complicated effects [87]. These models have also shown to be particularly beneficial for the study of practical cyberpsychology [88]. According to Russell's approach, an emotion modifies the "core affect," a neurophysiological section, that corresponds to the mixture of arousal (low/high intensity) and valence (positive/negative) [89].

The full emotional response can be measured without forcing participants into predesigned categories using adaptive self-report methods [90]. Psychophysiological measurements may also enable researchers to monitor emotions more accurately during the experimental activities. Future studies on VR-based analgesia may use comparable tools and make mention of dimensional models of emotions to address intriguing research concerns. How intensely do feelings feel throughout therapy, and how may a strong or weak feeling affect how patients respond? Is the pleasant emotion of fun more prevalent during pain management than the negative emotion of anxiety? Can these feelings coexist, and if so, how?

13.13   FUTURE SCOPE

The potential for behaviour control through the use of virtual reality (VR) distraction is bright in the future and has the ability to have a big impact on a number of industries, including healthcare, education, therapy, and more. Here are a few crucial facets of its potential future:

13.13.1   Pain Management and Healthcare

VR distraction has previously showed potential in the treatment of pain, particularly in patients undergoing severe medical procedures. We may expect more VR applications intended specifically to minimise pain perception during medical treatments to be developed and adopted in the future.

13.13.2 Therapy and Mental Health

VR therapy is gaining popularity in the treatment of anxiety, PTSD, and phobias. As VR technology advances and becomes more widely available, it will be able to be utilised for a broader spectrum of mental health therapies, providing immersive and regulated environments for therapy.

13.13.3 Training and Education

Immersive learning experiences can be improved using VR. It may be utilised for behaviour management in educational settings in the future. VR simulations, for example, can teach children and adults alike about consequences and decision-making in a safe virtual environment. Additionally, the newest invention, additive manufacturing (AM)-based technology, has lately been used in medical and oral healthcare. Three-dimensional printing has demonstrated enormous promise in the development of medical equipment and appliances. AM explains how it may help dental professionals improve their surgical abilities, aid in patient motivation and education, and train medical experts about its utility in understanding medical anomalies, as well as the customised production of dental products [91].

13.13.4 Behavioural Therapy (BT)

VR can be used in behavioural therapy to imitate difficult events and help people learn and practise coping techniques in a safe environment. This can be especially effective for people who have autism, ADHD, or behavioural difficulties.

13.13.5 Treatment for Addiction

By simulating circumstances that stimulate cravings and teaching people how to cope with them, virtual reality can play a part in addiction treatment programmes. It can be used to help manage substance abuse-related behaviour.

13.13.6 Correctional Rehabilitation

VR can be used to help offenders get back on their feet. It may imitate real-world circumstances and educate offenders valuable life and employment skills, hence lowering recidivism rates.

13.13.7 ASD (Autism Spectrum Disorder)

VR has shown promise in assisting people with ASD in developing social and communication skills. It can be used to provide safe and regulated conditions for social interaction practice.

13.13.8   WORKFORCE MANAGEMENT AND CORPORATE TRAINING

VR can be used in business settings to train staff in a variety of scenarios, such as dispute resolution, stress management, and customer service, in order to enhance behaviour and interpersonal skills.

13.13.9   ENTERTAINMENT AND GAMING

VR innovation will continue to be driven by the game sector. Game makers will most likely produce more immersive and interactive experiences that can influence behaviour indirectly by affecting choices and actions within the virtual environment.

13.13.10   CONSIDERATIONS FOR ETHICAL BEHAVIOUR

As virtual reality becomes more integrated into behaviour control, there will be ethical concerns about privacy, consent, and the possibility of manipulation. To ensure ethical use, regulations and rules will need to evolve.

13.13.11   DEVELOPMENT AND RESEARCH

Continuous advancements in artificial intelligence (AI), machine learning and virtual reality (VR) will lead to a better, sophisticated and adaptive VR systems for behaviour management. Furthermore, a novel technique termed as DNA computing along with AI would also help research enthusiasts and academicians for medical and dental research [92].

13.13.12   ACCESSIBILITY

VR technology and software advancements will most certainly make VR more affordable and accessible, allowing it to reach a wider audience.

To summarise, the use of VR distraction as an effective and intelligent tool for behaviour management has a promising future. As technology progresses and our awareness of its potential uses grows, virtual reality (VR) is likely to become a vital part of a variety of fields targeted at enhancing behaviour and decision-making in people of all ages and backgrounds. However, it will be critical to address ethical concerns and guarantee that this technology is used responsibly and fairly.

13.14   CONCLUSION

A startling number of psychological factors have an impact on how painful we feel. The neuromatrix theory states that pain is a combination of affect, cognition, and sensation that is processed by various parts of the brain. Additionally, it appears that external stimuli that divert attention from unpleasant occurrences can lessen the perception of pain.

Pharmacological treatments were once the main focus of patient pain and anxiety management.

The frequency of visits from patients who avoid going to the dentist would undoubtedly rise if pain and discomfort during dental and periodontal operations were reduced. The most challenging component of managing dental patients is seen to be their fear-related behaviours, which can make it difficult to provide quality dental care [93]. The level of discomfort felt at the dentist has been linked to dental work anxiety [66].

In addition, it can be inferred that VR focuses the patient's awareness, which lessens their experience of pain [94]. By diverting attention away from an uncomfortable medical setting and into an engrossing world of virtual reality while also triggering higher emotional and cognitive centres of the nervous system, VR can considerably reduce a patient's subjective experience of pain.

REFERENCES

1. Ploghaus, Alexander, Charvy Narain, Christian F. Beckmann, Stuart Clare, Susanna Bantick, Richard Wise, Paul M. Matthews, J. Nicholas P. Rawlins, and Irene Tracey. "Exacerbation of pain by anxiety is associated with activity in a hippocampal network." *Journal of Neuroscience* 21, no. 24 (2001): 9896–9903.
2. Meentken, Maya G., Ingrid M. Van Beynum, Jeroen S. Legerstee, Willem A. Helbing, and Elisabeth MWJ Utens. "Medically related post-traumatic stress in children and adolescents with congenital heart defects." *Frontiers in Pediatrics* 5 (2017): 20.
3. Wong, M. L., K. S. Chia, W. M. Yam, G. R. Teodoro, and K. W. Lau. "Willingness to donate blood samples for genetic research: a survey from a community in Singapore." *Clinical Genetics* 65, no. 1 (2004): 45–51.
4. Beena, J. P. "Dental subscale of children's fear survey schedule and dental caries prevalence." *European Journal of Dentistry* 7, no. 02 (2013): 181–185.
5. Samnieng, Patcharaphol. "Prevalence of dental fear and its relationship with oral health in children." *International Journal of Clinical Preventive Dentistry* 9, no. 1 (2013): 1–5.
6. Rajwar, Anju Singh, and Mridula Goswami. "Prevalence of dental fear and its causes using three measurement scales among children in New Delhi." *Journal of Indian Society of Pedodontics and Preventive Dentistry* 35, no. 2 (2017): 128–133.
7. Wu, Lingli, and Xiaoli Gao. "Children's dental fear and anxiety: exploring family related factors." *BMC Oral Health* 18 (2018): 1–10.
8. Armfield, Jason M., and L. J. Heaton. "Management of fear and anxiety in the dental clinic: a review." *Australian Dental Journal* 58, no. 4 (2013): 390–407.
9. Aitken, Jennifer Creem, Stephen Wilson, Daniel Coury, and Amr M. Moursi. "The effect of music distraction on pain, anxiety and behavior in pediatric dental patients." *Pediatric Dentistry* 24, no. 2 (2002): 114–118.
10. Srouji, Rasha, Savithiri Ratnapalan, and Suzan Schneeweiss. "Pain in children: assessment and nonpharmacological management." *International Journal of Pediatrics* 2010 (2010).
11. Ship, Irwin I., and Carl L. White. "Physiologic response to dental stress." *Oral Surgery, Oral Medicine, Oral Pathology* 13, no. 3 (1960): 368–376.
12. Edmondson, H. D., B. Roscoe, and M. D. Vickers. "Biochemical evidence of anxiety in dental patients." *British Medical Journal* 4, no. 5831 (1972): 7–9.

13. Shannon, Ira L., Gerald M. Isbell, John R. Prigmore, and Warren R. Hester. "Stress in dental patients: II. The serum free 17-hydroxycorticosteroid response in routinely appointed patients undergoing simple exodontia." *Oral Surgery, Oral Medicine, Oral Pathology* 15, no. 9 (1962): 1142–1146.

14. Takai, Noriyasu, Masaki Yamaguchi, Toshiaki Aragaki, Kenji Eto, Kenji Uchihashi, and Yasuo Nishikawa. "Effect of psychological stress on the salivary cortisol and amylase levels in healthy young adults." *Archives of Oral Biology* 49, no. 12 (2004): 963–968.

15. Sapolsky, Robert M., Lewis C. Krey, and Bruce S. McEwen. "The neuroendocrinology of stress and aging: the glucocorticoid cascade hypothesis." *Science of Aging Knowledge Environment* 2002, no. 38 (2002): cp21–cp21.

16. Al'Absi, M., and D. K. Arnett. "Adrenocortical responses to psychological stress and risk for hypertension." *Biomedicine & Pharmacotherapy* 54, no. 5 (2000): 234–244.

17. Schmidt, Nola A. "Salivary cortisol testing in children." *Issues in Comprehensive Pediatric Nursing* 20, no. 3 (1997): 183–190.

18. Padmanabhan, Vivek, Kavita Rai, and A. M. Hedge. "Stress responses in children during endodontic treatment." *Journal of Pediatric Dentistry* 1 (2013): 14–18.

19. Miller, Craig S., Jeffrey B. Dembo, Donald A. Falace, and Alan L. Kaplan. "Salivary cortisol response to dental treatment of varying stress." *Oral Surgery, Oral Medicine, Oral Pathology, Oral Radiology, and Endodontology* 79, no. 4 (1995): 436–441.

20. Shahrbanian, Shahnaz, Xiaoli Ma, Najaf Aghaei, Nicol Korner-Bitensky, Keivan Moshiri, and Maureen J. Simmonds. "Use of virtual reality (immersive vs. non immersive) for pain management in children and adults: a systematic review of evidence from randomized controlled trials." *European Journal of Experimental Biology* 2, no. 5 (2012): 1408–1422.

21. Aminabadi, Naser Asl, Leila Erfanparast, Azin Sohrabi, Sina Ghertasi Oskouei, and Armaghan Naghili. "The impact of virtual reality distraction on pain and anxiety during dental treatment in 4–6 year-old children: a randomized controlled clinical trial." *Journal of Dental Research, Dental Clinics, Dental Prospects* 6, no. 4 (2012): 117.

22. Slifer, Keith J., Cindy L. Tucker, and Lynnda M. Dahlquist. "Helping children and caregivers cope with repeated invasive procedures: how are we doing?." *Journal of Clinical Psychology in Medical Settings* 9 (2002): 131–152.

23. Leventhal, Howard. "I know distraction works even though it doesn't!." *Health Psychology* 11, no. 4 (1992): 208–209.

24. Sevil, I. N. A. L., and Nejla CANBULAT. "Use of distraction methods in procedural pain management in children." *Journal of Health Sciences and Professions* 2, no. 3 (2015): 372–378

25. Hoffman, Hunter G., Sam R. Sharar, Barbara Coda, John J. Everett, Marcia Ciol, Todd Richards, and David R. Patterson. "Manipulating presence influences the magnitude of virtual reality analgesia." *Pain* 111, no. 1–2 (2004): 162–168.

26. Lillard, A. S. "Pretend play skills and the childs theory of mind. *Child Development* 64, no. 2 (1993): 348–371.

27. Shetty, Vabitha, Lekshmi R. Suresh, and Amitha M. Hegde. "Effect of virtual reality distraction on pain and anxiety during dental treatment in 5 to 8 year old children." *Journal of Clinical Pediatric Dentistry* 43, no. 2 (2019): 97–102.

28. McCahill, Robyn J., Cate Nagle, and Patricia Clarke. "Use of virtual reality for minor procedures in the emergency department: a scoping review." *Australasian Emergency Care* 24, no. 3 (2021): 174–178.

29. Caruso, Thomas J., Chloe O'Connell, Jimmy J. Qian, Tiffany Kung, Ellen Wang, Susan Kinnebrew, Molly Pearson, Madison Kist, Maria Menendez, and Samuel T. Rodriguez. "Retrospective review of the safety and efficacy of virtual reality in a pediatric hospital." *Pediatric Quality & Safety* 5, no. 2 (2020).

30. Gold, Jeffrey I., Alexis J. Kant, and Seok Hyeon Kim. "Virtual anesthesia: the use of virtual reality for pain distraction during acute medical interventions." In *Seminars in Anesthesia, Perioperative Medicine and Pain*, vol. 24, no. 4, pp. 203–210. WB Saunders, 2005.

31. Jameson, Eleanor, Judy Trevena, and Nic Swain. "Electronic gaming as pain distraction." *Pain Research and Management* 16 (2011): 27–32.

32. Morris, Linzette Deidré, Quinette Abegail Louw, and Lynette Christine Crous. "Feasibility and potential effect of a low-cost virtual reality system on reducing pain and anxiety in adult burn injury patients during physiotherapy in a developing country." *Burns* 36, no. 5 (2010): 659–664.

33. Cioffi, Delia. "Beyond attentional strategies: a cognitive-perceptual model of somatic interpretation." *Psychological Bulletin* 109, no. 1 (1991): 25.

34. Shallice, Tim, and PaulBurgess. "Supervisory control of action and thought selection." In A. D. Baddeley & L. Weiskrantz (Eds.), Attention: Selection, awareness, and control: A tribute to Donald Broadbent.Clarendon Press/Oxford University Press. (1993): 171–187.

35. Melzack, Ronald, and Patrick D. Wall. "Pain Mechanisms: A New Theory: A gate control system modulates sensory input from the skin before it evokes pain perception and response." *Science* 150, no. 3699 (1965): 971–979. 46. Melzack R. Gate control theory. On the evolution of pain concepts. Pain Forum 1996; 5:128–138.

36. Katz, Joel, and Ronald Melzack. "Pain 'memories' in phantom limbs: review and clinical observations." *Pain* 43, no. 3 (1990): 319–336.

37. Melzack, R. "From the gate to the neuromatrix." *Pain* 82, Suppl 1 (1999): S121–S126.

38. Ploghaus, Alexander, Irene Tracey, Joseph S. Gati, Stuart Clare, Ravi S. Menon, Paul M. Matthews, and J. Nicholas P. Rawlins. "Dissociating pain from its anticipation in the human brain." *Science* 284, no. 5422 (1999): 1979–1981.

39. Iannetti, Gian Domenico, and André Mouraux. "From the neuromatrix to the pain matrix (and back)." *Experimental Brain Research* 205 (2010): 1–12.

40. Legrain, Valéry, Gian Domenico Iannetti, Léon Plaghki, and André Mouraux. "The pain matrix reloaded: a salience detection system for the body." *Progress in Neurobiology* 93, no. 1 (2011): 111–124.

41. Linton, Steven J., and William S. Shaw. "Impact of psychological factors in the experience of pain." *Physical Therapy* 91, no. 5 (2011): 700–711.

42. Craig, Arthur D. "A new view of pain as a homeostatic emotion." *Trends in Neurosciences* 26, no. 6 (2003): 303–307.

43. Sullivan, Michael JL, William Stanish, Heather Waite, Maureen Sullivan, and Dean A. Tripp. "Catastrophizing, pain, and disability in patients with soft-tissue injuries." *Pain* 77, no. 3 (1998): 253–260.

44. Lyons, Ian M., and Sian L. Beilock. "When math hurts: math anxiety predicts pain network activation in anticipation of doing math." *PloS One* 7, no. 10 (2012): e48076.

45. McCaul, Kevin D., and James M. Malott. "Distraction and coping with pain." *Psychological Bulletin* 95, no. 3 (1984): 516.

46. Shahrbanian, Shahnaz, Xiaoli Ma, Nicol Korner-Bitensky, and Maureen J. Simmonds. "Scientific evidence for the effectiveness of virtual reality for pain reduction in adults with acute or chronic pain." *Annual Review of Cybertherapy and Telemedicine* (2009): 40–43.

47. Wismeijer, Andreas AJ, and Ad JJM Vingerhoets. "The use of virtual reality and audiovisual eyeglass systems as adjunct analgesic techniques: a review of the literature." *Annals of Behavioral Medicine* 30, no. 3 (2005): 268–278.

48. Mahrer, Nicole E., and Jeffrey I. Gold. "The use of virtual reality for pain control: A review." *Current Pain and Headache Reports* 13 (2009): 100–109.

49. Malloy, Kevin M., and Leonard S. Milling. "The effectiveness of virtual reality distraction for pain reduction: a systematic review." *Clinical Psychology Review* 30, no. 8 (2010): 1011–1018.

50. Gorini, Alessandra, Claret S. Capideville, Gianluca De Leo, Fabrizia Mantovani, and Giuseppe Riva. "The role of immersion and narrative in mediated presence: the virtual hospital experience." *Cyberpsychology, Behavior, and Social Networking* 14, no. 3 (2011): 99–105.

51. Bohil, Corey J., Bradly Alicea, and Frank A. Biocca. "Virtual reality in neuroscience research and therapy." *Nature Reviews Neuroscience* 12, no. 12 (2011): 752–762.

52. Biocca, Frank. "The cyborg's dilemma: Progressive embodiment in mediated environments." *Journal of Computer-Mediated Communication* 3, no. 2 (1997): JCMC324.

53. Sanchez-Vives, Maria V., and Mel Slater. "From presence to consciousness through virtual reality." *Nature Reviews Neuroscience* 6, no. 4 (2005): 332–339.

54. Slater, Mel, and Sylvia Wilbur. "A framework for immersive virtual environments (FIVE): Speculations on the role of presence in virtual environments." *Presence: Teleoperators & Virtual Environments* 6, no. 6 (1997): 603–616.

55. Coelho, Carlos, Jennifer Tichon, Trevor J. Hine, Guy Wallis, and Giuseppe Riva. "Media presence and inner presence: the sense of presence in virtual reality technologies." *From communication to presence: Cognition, emotions and culture towards the ultimate communicative experience* 11 (2006): 25–45.

56. Riva, Giuseppe. "Is presence a technology issue? Some insights from cognitive sciences." *Virtual Reality* 13 (2009): 159–169.

57. Riva, Giuseppe, John A. Waterworth, Eva L. Waterworth, and Fabrizia Mantovani. "From intention to action: The role of presence." *New Ideas in Psychology* 29, no. 1 (2011): 24–37.

58. Baños, Rosa María, Cristina Botella, Mariano Alcañiz, Víctor Liaño, Belén Guerrero, and Beatriz Rey. "Immersion and emotion: their impact on the sense of presence." *Cyberpsychology & Behavior* 7, no. 6 (2004): 734–741.

59. Bowman, Doug A., and Ryan P. McMahan. "Virtual reality: how much immersion is enough?." *Computer* 40, no. 7 (2007): 36–43.

60. Gee, James Paul. "Glued to games: how video games draw us in and hold us spellbound." *American Journal of Play* 4, no. 4 (2012): 510.

61. Juan, M. Carmen, Rosa Baños, Cristina Botella, David Pérez, Mariano Alcañiz, and Carlos Monserrat. "An augmented reality system for the treatment of acrophobia: the sense of presence using immersive photography." *Presence* 15, no. 4 (2006): 393–402.

62. Riva, G., F. Davide, and W. A. IJsselsteijn. "Measuring presence: Subjective, behavioral and physiological methods." *Being there: Concepts, effects and measurement of user presence in synthetic environments* 5 (2003): 110–118.

63. Meehan, Michael, Sharif Razzaque, Brent Insko, Mary Whitton, and Frederick P. Brooks. "Review of four studies on the use of physiological reaction as a measure of presence in stressfulvirtual environments." *Applied Psychophysiology and Biofeedback* 30 (2005): 239–258.

64. Slater, Mel, Andrea Brogni, and Anthony Steed. "Physiological responses to breaks in presence: A pilot study." In *Presence 2003: The 6th annual international workshop on presence*, vol. 157. Cleveland, OH: Citeseer, 2003.

65. Garau, Maia, Doron Friedman, Hila Ritter Widenfeld, Angus Antley, Andrea Brogni, and Mel Slater. "Temporal and spatial variations in presence: qualitative analysis of interviews from an experiment on breaks in presence." *Presence: Teleoperators and Virtual Environments* 17, no. 3 (2008): 293–309.

66. Sharar, Sam R., Gretchen J. Carrougher, Dana Nakamura, Hunter G. Hoffman, David K. Blough, and David R. Patterson. "Factors influencing the efficacy of virtual reality

distraction analgesia during postburn physical therapy: preliminary results from 3 ongoing studies." *Archives of Physical Medicine and Rehabilitation* 88, no. 12 (2007): S43–S49.

67. Hoffman, Hunter G., David R. Patterson, Eric Seibel, Maryam Soltani, Laura Jewett-Leahy, and Sam R. Sharar. "Virtual reality pain control during burn wound debridement in the hydrotank." *The Clinical Journal of Pain* 24, no. 4 (2008): 299–304.

68. Tse, Mimi MY, Jacobus KF Ng, Joanne WY Chung, and Thomas KS Wong. "The effect of visual stimulation via the eyeglass display and the perception of pain." *CyberPsychology & Behavior* 5, no. 1 (2002): 65–75.

69. Wender, Regina, Hunter G. Hoffman, Harley H. Hunner, Eric J. Seibel, David R. Patterson, and Sam R. Sharar. "Interactivity influences the magnitude of virtual reality analgesia." *Journal of Cyber Therapy and Rehabilitation* 2, no. 1 (2009): 27.

70. Chan, Engle Angela, Joanne WY Chung, Thomas KS Wong, Angela SY Lien, and Jiu Yung Yang. "Application of a virtual reality prototype for pain relief of pediatric burn in Taiwan." *Journal of Clinical Nursing* 16, no. 4 (2007): 786–793.

71. Riva, Giuseppe, Fabrizia Mantovani, Claret Samantha Capideville, Alessandra Preziosa, Francesca Morganti, Daniela Villani, Andrea Gaggioli, Cristina Botella, and Mariano Alcañiz. "Affective interactions using virtual reality: the link between presence and emotions." *Cyberpsychology & Behavior* 10, no. 1 (2007): 45–56.

72. MacFarlane, Stuart, Gavin Sim, and Matthew Horton. "Assessing usability and fun in educational software." In *Proceedings of the 2005 conference on Interaction design and children*, pp. 103–109. 2005.

73. Shneiderman, Ben. "Designing for fun: how can we design user interfaces to be more fun?." *Interactions* 11, no. 5 (2004): 48–50.

74. Carroll, John M. "Beyond fun." *Interactions* 11, no. 5 (2004): 38–40.

75. Jacobsen, Paul B., Dana H. Bovbjerg, and William H. Redd. "Anticipatory anxiety in women receiving chemotherapy for breast cancer." *Health Psychology* 12, no. 6 (1993): 469.

76. Lim, Chi Ching, M. Kamala Devi, and Emily Ang. "Anxiety in women with breast cancer undergoing treatment: a systematic review." *International Journal of Evidence-Based Healthcare* 9, no. 3 (2011): 215–235.

77. Spielberger, Charles D. "State-trait anxiety inventory for adults." [Database record]. APA PsycTests. (1983): 77. https://doi.org/10.1037/t06496-000

78. van Twillert, Björn, Marco Bremer, and Albertus W. Faber. "Computer-generated virtual reality to control pain and anxiety in pediatric and adult burn patients during wound dressing changes." *Journal of Burn Care & Research* 28, no. 5 (2007): 694–702.

79. Nordahl, Rolf, and Dannie Korsgaard. "Distraction as a measure of presence: using visual and tactile adjustable distraction as a measure to determine immersive presence of content in mediated environments." *Virtual Reality* 14 (2010): 27–42.

80. Kain, Zeev N., Ferne Sevarino, Gerianne M. Alexander, Sharon Pincus, and Linda C. Mayes. "Preoperative anxiety and postoperative pain in women undergoing hysterectomy: a repeated-measures design." *Journal of Psychosomatic Research* 49, no. 6 (2000): 417–422.

81. van den Hout, Johanna HC, Johan WS Vlaeyen, Ruud MA Houben, Aukje PM Soeters, and Madelon L. Peters. "The effects of failure feedback and pain-related fear on pain report, pain tolerance, and pain avoidance in chronic low back pain patients." *Pain* 92, no. 1–2 (2001): 247–257.

82. Han, Kiwan, Jeonghun Ku, Kwanguk Kim, Hee Jeong Jang, Junyoung Park, Jae-Jin Kim, Chan Hyung Kim, Min-Hyung Choi, In Young Kim, and Sun I. Kim. "Virtual reality prototype for measurement of expression characteristics in emotional situations." *Computers in Biology and Medicine* 39, no. 2 (2009): 173–179.

83. Macedonio, Mary F., Thomas D. Parsons, Raymond A. Digiuseppe, Brenda A. Weiderhold, and Albert A. Rizzo. "Immersiveness and physiological arousal within panoramic video-based virtual reality." *Cyberpsychology & Behavior* 10, no. 4 (2007): 508–515.

84. Miyahira, Sarah D., Raymond A. Folen, Melba Stetz, Albert Rizzo, and Michelle M. Kawasaki. "Use of immersive virtual reality for treating anger." *Studies in Health Technology and Informatics* 154 (2010): 82–86.

85. Barrett, Lisa Feldman. "Discrete emotions or dimensions? The role of valence focus and arousal focus." *Cognition & Emotion* 12, no. 4 (1998): 579–599.

86. Eerola, Tuomas, and Jonna K. Vuoskoski. "A comparison of the discrete and dimensional models of emotion in music." *Psychology of Music* 39, no. 1 (2011): 18–49.

87. Riva, Giuseppe, Rosa M. Baños, Cristina Botella, Brenda K. Wiederhold, and Andrea Gaggioli. "Positive technology: using interactive technologies to promote positive functioning." *Cyberpsychology, Behavior, and Social Networking* 15, no. 2 (2012): 69–77.

88. Russell, James A. "Core affect and the psychological construction of emotion." *Psychological Review* 110, no. 1 (2003): 145.

89. Bradley, Margaret M., and Peter J. Lang. "Measuring emotion: the self-assessment manikin and the semantic differential." *Journal of Behavior Therapy and Experimental Psychiatry* 25, no. 1 (1994): 49–59.

90. O'Shea, Robert M., Norman L. Corah, and William A. Ayer. "Sources of dentists' stress." *Journal of the American Dental Association (1939)* 109, no. 1 (1984): 48–51.

91. Bhardwaj, Amit, Anurag Bhatnagar, and Ajay Kumar. "Current trends of application of additive manufacturing in oral healthcare system." In *Advances in Additive Manufacturing Artificial Intelligence, Nature-Inspired, and Biomanufacturing*, pp. 479–491. Elsevier, 2023.

92. Kumar, Tarun, and Suyel Namasudra. "Introduction to DNA computing." In *Advances in Computers*, vol. 129, pp. 1–38. Elsevier, 2023.

93. McNeil, Daniel W., Anthony R. Au, Michael J. Zvolensky, Deborah Rettig McKee, Iven J. Klineberg, and Christopher CK Ho. "Fear of pain in orofacial pain patients." *Pain* 89, no. 2–3 (2001): 245–252.

94. Morris, Linzette Deidré, Quinette Abegail Louw, and Karen Grimmer-Somers. "The effectiveness of virtual reality on reducing pain and anxiety in burn injury patients: a systematic review." *The Clinical Journal of Pain* 25, no. 9 (2009): 815–826.

14 Sustainable and Innovative Techniques for Improving Dental Health

Towards Effective Behavior Management

Lakhloufi Soraya and Labjar Najoua
Laboratory of Spectroscopy, Molecular Modeling, Materials, Nanomaterials, Water and Environment, (LS3MN2E-CERNE2D), ENSAM, Mohammed V University in Rabat, Morocco

Labjar Houda
Faculty of Sciences and Technology, University Hassan II Casablanca, Mohammedia, Morocco

El Hajjaji Souad
Laboratory of Spectroscopy, Molecular Modeling, Materials, Nanomaterials, Water and Environment, (LS3MN2E-CERNE2D), Department of Chemistry, Faculty of Sciences, Mohammed V University in Rabat, Morocco

14.1 INTRODUCTION

Dental practitioners are always looking for new and creative methods to improve the patient experience and achieve better oral health results. Effective behavior management is essential in this process, and technology breakthroughs like artificial intelligence (AI) are increasingly being used in dentistry operations [1]. In recent years, there have been several sustainable and innovative non-pharmacological techniques that have emerged as effective ways to manage patient behavior during dental procedures. These techniques include audio-visual distraction, virtual reality, dental apps, and digital games. Addressing dental anxiety can indeed promote better oral health outcomes, improve patient experience, and promote overall health and

DOI: 10.1201/9781003404934-14

well-being. Dental anxiety is a prevalent psychological condition that impacts a considerable number of individuals globally, spanning across different age groups and backgrounds. Dental fear is considered a significant public health issue worldwide due to its impact on individuals' oral health and overall quality of life. The prevalence of this problem ranges from 5% to 61% in children and from 1% to 52% in adults, encompassing individuals with varying degrees of dental anxiety, from mild to severe [2]. It is often associated with negative dental experiences at the dentist such as pain or discomfort and embarrassment about the state of one's teeth during dental procedures. Some people may also have a general anxiety disorder that manifests itself during dental appointments [3,4]. Consequently, individuals who experience dental anxiety may choose to evade dental treatments, which can have negative consequences on their oral well-being. The influence of dental anxiety on oral health can be substantial. Individuals with dental anxiety might skip regular dental check-ups and cleanings, which can result in the emergence of dental issues such as tooth decay, gum disease, and potential loss of teeth. Delaying treatment can make these problems worse, resulting in more complex and expensive dental treatments, such as root canals or tooth extractions. These procedures can be more invasive and painful, further reinforcing a person's dental anxiety and making it more difficult to seek care in the future [5,6]. For individuals with severe dental anxiety, seeking the help of a mental health professional may be beneficial. Therapeutic interventions and counseling offer individuals the opportunity to recognize and confront the underlying origins of their anxiety, enabling them to formulate effective techniques for handling their symptoms when visiting the dentist [7]. For this an effective management is essential during dental procedures to ensure a positive experience for patients and to achieve the best possible outcomes. Dental procedures can be uncomfortable and even painful, which can cause anxiety and fear in some patients. This is particularly true for individuals who have had negative experiences with dental care in the past, or who have underlying conditions such as autism or anxiety disorders that can make it difficult to tolerate dental procedures [8].

Effective behavior management is a critical aspect of dental care that can help alleviate fears and make dental procedures more comfortable for patients. This can include a variety of techniques, such as distraction techniques (listening to music or watching a movie during the procedure), relaxation techniques (deep breathing or guided imagery), and communication techniques (explaining each step of the procedure and giving the patient control over the pace of the procedure). In addition to improving the patient experience, effective behavior management can also help dental professionals achieve better outcomes. Patients who are anxious or uncooperative during dental procedures may be more difficult to treat, which can lead to longer procedures, increased risk of complications, and suboptimal outcomes. By keeping patients calm and cooperative, dental professionals can provide higher quality care and achieve better outcomes. Effective behavior management also helps reduce the risk of injury during dental procedures. Some procedures involve the use of sharp or powerful instruments that can cause injury if the patient moves suddenly or unexpectedly. By keeping patients still and relaxed, dental professionals can reduce the risk of accidental injury. Effective behavior management is critical for ensuring that dental procedures are safe, comfortable, and effective. Patients who have positive experiences during dental procedures are more likely to comply with follow-up care instructions and to maintain regular dental appointments [9]. This can lead to better oral health outcomes and a reduced need for more invasive or expensive procedures in the future. By prioritizing effective behavior management, dental professionals can help their patients maintain good oral health over time. To address this issue, it is important to explore sustainable and innovative techniques to improve dental health, including effective behavior management during dental procedures. This section presents a summary of dental anxiety and its influence on oral health, along with emphasizing the significance of efficient behavior management. Within this chapter, we will examine the utilization of non-pharmacological behavioral strategies as a viable and progressive method for enhancing dental well-being. Specifically, our focus will be on the implementation of audio-visual distraction, virtual reality distraction, dental applications, and digital games as effective techniques for managing behavior. We will also examine the evidence supporting the effectiveness of these techniques, as well as the benefits of sustainable dentistry for patients and the environment. Finally, we discuss considerations for integrating non-pharmacological techniques into dental practice, including training requirements for dentists and patient education and communication. Through the examination of these subjects, our aim is to equip dentists with the necessary knowledge and resources to incorporate sustainable and innovative strategies for efficient behavior management within their professional settings.

14.2   NON-PHARMACOLOGICAL BEHAVIOR MANAGEMENT TECHNIQUES

Dental anxiety poses a significant obstacle when it comes to receiving necessary dental care. Traditional methods of behavior control, such as pharmaceutical sedation, can be expensive and carry potential adverse consequences. Traditional techniques for behavior control in dentistry generally entail the use of pharmaceutical medications to treat patient anxiety and terror. These medicines, which might vary from moderate sedatives to complete anesthesia, are commonly supplied orally or intravenously [10]. These methods have demonstrated their effectiveness in alleviating patient anxiety, although they are not devoid of drawbacks. One of the biggest disadvantages of traditional behavior control procedures is the possibility of negative side effects. Nausea, vomiting, dizziness, and headaches are some of the symptoms. Patients may also develop more severe adverse effects, such as respiratory depression and cardiovascular problems, in certain circumstances. These dangers are especially serious for individuals who have pre-existing medical issues or are taking other drugs. The expense of traditional behavior control measures is another disadvantage. These techniques can be highly costly, especially for people who do not have insurance. Furthermore, some patients may require multiple appointments or extended recovery periods, raising the overall cost. Traditional therapy approaches do not address the underlying cause of the patient's anxiety and fear. Patients who use these methods may still suffer stress and terror during subsequent dental sessions, perpetuating a cycle of medication dependency.

Despite these disadvantages, traditional behavior control approaches continue as a significant instrument in addressing patient apprehension and distress. Pharmacological medicines may be the most effective alternative for delivering a comfortable and stress-free dental treatment for some people. However, it is critical

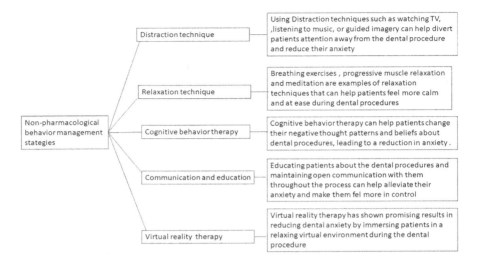

FIGURE 14.1   Non-pharmacological behavior management strategies.

for dental professionals to consider alternative approaches and tailor treatment plans to each patient's unique needs. As a result, we may strive toward a future in which all patients can get necessary dental treatment without fear or worry. Traditional behavior control strategies have been widely employed in dentistry practice, but they may be expensive and have possible undesirable side effects. Non-pharmacological behavior control strategies have gained popularity in recent years as a safe and cost-effective option. These methods include distraction, relaxation, and other efforts to make patients feel more at ease during dental operations. In recent times, there has been a growing interest in non-pharmacological approaches to address dental anxiety and aid patients in coping with it. Figure 14.1 provides an overview of the different non-pharmacological behavior management strategies that are accessible to help individuals effectively manage their dental anxiety.

Non-pharmacological behavior management techniques have become increasingly popular in recent times as a safe and cost-efficient alternative for alleviating anxiety and stress levels associated with medical procedures. These techniques are well-known and widely used across all age groups, but they are particularly helpful for children who may experience heightened anxiety and fear during medical procedures. Many research studies have centered around the efficacy of non-pharmacological strategies for managing children's behavior. These techniques include audio-visual distraction, virtual reality distraction, dental apps, and digital games [11]. According to recent studies, non-pharmacological behavior management techniques have become increasingly popular among dental professionals for patients of all ages, but particularly in children. Numerous research studies have been carried out to examine the ways in which these approaches can enhance the dental experience for youngsters and alleviate their treatment-related anxiety and fear. These techniques include the tell-show-do technique, distraction techniques such as audio-visual glasses or videos, role modeling, and positive reinforcement. Moreover, the dentist's engagement with the child is of utmost importance for the effective outcome of dental procedures. Employing a blend of traditional techniques and advanced technology like audio-visual glasses, dental professionals can establish a favorable rapport with young patients and alleviate their apprehension [12–15]. Besides addressing dental anxiety among children, there has been research conducted on non-pharmacological approaches to managing dental anxiety in adult patients [16]. Various approaches are employed to address the issue, which involve psychotherapeutic behavioral methods such as muscle tension reduction, guided mental imagery, physiological tracking, biofeedback techniques, hypnotherapy, acupuncture, diversion, and emotional desensitization. The goal of these therapies is to alter the patient's perception and response, using non-invasive techniques that have minimal or no adverse effects. The selection of these methods depends on the individual's anxiety levels and specific clinical circumstances. It is important to recognize patient-specific needs and provide effective treatment to reduce negative perceptions and clinical stress, leading to more comfortable and successful treatments. Non-pharmacological strategies play a pivotal role in addressing dental anxiety among adult patients, as various methods have been utilized and proven effective in reducing anxiety levels and enhancing the overall well-being of patients [17–21].

14.2.1 Audio-Visual Distraction as a Behavior Management Technique

Audio-visual distraction is a behavior management technique which can be employed to assist in the management of dental-related anxiety. This method involves employing video-recorded cartoons, audio-recorded stories, and video games to divert patients' attention during dental procedures. Studies have shown that distraction techniques are equally effective compared to relaxation-based methods and more effective than no intervention at all. Recent technological advancements have shown promising results in the use of virtual reality (VR) head-mounted display devices (HMD) as a means of distraction. These devices have demonstrated significant reductions in anxiety and pain perception among children when they are shown videos through virtual glasses. Implementing audio-visual distraction can assist patients in focusing on the positive aspects of dental care, making it especially beneficial for children who may find dental treatments stressful or frightening [22–25].

14.2.2 Virtual Reality Distraction as a Behavior Management Technique

Virtual reality distraction is a non-pharmacological technique that involves the use of immersive technology to create a relaxing and engaging environment for patients during dental procedures. The technique uses a virtual reality headset to transport the patient to a different environment, such as a beach or forest, to distract them from the dental procedure. The virtual reality setting can be tailored according to the patient's preferences, allowing them to engage with the environment using handheld controllers. Virtual reality distraction has surfaced as a potentially effective non-pharmacological technique for addressing dental anxiety in both adult and pediatric individuals. Extensive research has demonstrated the effectiveness of virtual reality distraction in alleviating anxiety and mitigating pain perception among patients of different age groups, including adults and children [26–28].

14.2.3 Dental Apps as a Behavior Management Technique

Dental apps are mobile applications that can be downloaded onto smartphones or tablets to provide patients with information about oral health and dental procedures. These apps can also help patients manage their dental appointments and track their oral health progress. Some dental apps also include features such as virtual reality distraction and relaxation exercises to help patients manage dental anxiety. As a behavior management technique, dental apps can be used to help patients overcome dental anxiety by providing them with information and tools to manage their oral health. One illustration of this is that dental applications have the capacity to furnish patients with details regarding dental treatments, encompassing insights into what one can anticipate throughout the procedure and how to make the necessary preparations. This information can help patients feel more informed and in control, which can reduce anxiety. Dental apps can also help patients manage their dental appointments by sending reminders and allowing patients to schedule appointments directly from their mobile device [29]. This can help reduce the stress and anxiety associated with scheduling and attending dental appointments. Dental applications have the potential to serve as a valuable resource for individuals in maintaining their oral well-being and alleviating dental procedure-related stress.

14.2.4 Digital Games as a Behavior Management Technique

Digital games have been used as a behavior management technique for dental anxiety in some studies. The idea is that playing a game on a mobile device or tablet can distract patients from their anxiety and make the dental experience more enjoyable. Using digital games can be especially beneficial for children who are more susceptible to dental anxiety. Employing digital games can create a sense of ease and comfort for children during dental procedures, ultimately resulting in improved treatment results. Some dental apps offer relaxation techniques, such as guided meditation or breathing exercises, to help patients calm their nerves before and during dental procedures. These techniques can be used in conjunction with digital games to help patients manage their anxiety [30,31]. Additionally, dental apps can provide educational resources to help patients understand the dental procedures they will undergo, which can help alleviate anxiety. Digital games and relaxation techniques can be effective behavior management techniques for dental anxiety. However, Additional investigation is required to ascertain the efficacy of these methodologies and identify optimal means of their integration within the dental field [32].

14.3 EFFECTIVENESS OF NON-PHARMACOLOGICAL BEHAVIOR MANAGEMENT TECHNIQUES

Non-pharmacological strategies for managing dental anxiety have been receiving more and more attention as an alternative approach. These techniques can include cognitive behavioral therapy, relaxation techniques, distraction techniques, positive reinforcement, and clear communication [17]. To investigate the effectiveness of these techniques, a systematic and rigorous approach is necessary [33]. When assessing the effectiveness of non-pharmacological methods in addressing dental anxiety, it is imperative to take into account various essential stages and significant elements that require thorough examination. Firstly, the population to be studied must be defined, followed by the non-pharmacological behavior management techniques that will be studied. The control group must also be defined, along with the outcomes of interest, such as anxiety and pain levels. Prior to commencing a research study, it is crucial to conduct a thorough examination of the pertinent literature to inform the design of the research. The most highly regarded approach to study design involves utilizing a randomized controlled trial, where individuals are assigned randomly to either an intervention group or a control group. The collection and analysis of data should be carried out, and conclusions should be drawn based on the study's findings, aiming to provide insights for future practice and research endeavors. To ensure a thorough and reliable study on the efficacy of non-pharmacological behavior management techniques for dental anxiety, it is crucial to consider these steps and important aspects. Establishing rapport and trust between the dental team and the patient is an effective approach in managing dental anxiety without medication. A constructive dialogue can be initiated using organized formats to explore collaborative measures that can enhance the patient's comfort during dental treatment [34]. From a clinical perspective, it is possible to motivate patients by suggesting that they write a "letter to the dentist." In this letter, they can outline techniques that they believe would personally benefit them, such as listening to music, taking regular breaks, or using a predetermined stop signal. The clinician and patient can then collaborate and agree upon the list of techniques. Recent studies have shown the effectiveness of using standardized communication tools to empower adolescents and young adults, allowing them to feel more engaged in the decision-making process regarding their healthcare [34].

Many research investigations have been conducted to assess the effectiveness of non-pharmacological approaches in the management of dental fear and anxiety. These techniques can be classified into the following categories:

14.3.1 Evidence Supporting the Effectiveness of Audio-Visual Distraction

The utilization of audio-visual distraction techniques has been identified as an efficient non-pharmacological strategy for addressing dental anxiety. As such, several studies have investigated its effectiveness as a behavior management technique for dental anxiety. The research conducted in these studies presents proof that audio-visual distraction is beneficial, with different techniques of distraction being mentioned, Comprising the application of archived animations, auditory narratives, and interactive digital entertainment [35]. Research has shown that distraction methods are just as potent as relaxation-oriented techniques and surpass the efficacy of no intervention whatsoever. In a recent comprehensive analysis and meta-review exploring the effectiveness of employing auditory and audio-visual diversion strategies to mitigate discomfort and unease in young dental patients, it has been established that both auditory and audio-visual approaches are validated means of diminishing pain and anxiety in the context of dental procedures for children. The research revealed that combining audio and visual distractions proved significantly more efficient than relying solely on audio distractions [36]. This is consistent with another study that showed audio-visual distraction techniques to be an effective non-pharmacological approach to managing dental anxiety [34]. Audio-visual distraction techniques involve utilizing video-recorded cartoons, audio-recorded stories, and video games as a means of diverting patients' attention during dental procedures. Recent technological progress has shown encouraging results in employing head-mounted virtual reality displays for the purpose of distraction. These devices have shown encouraging results in terms of reducing anxiety and perceptions of pain among children who are exposed to videos through virtual glasses. In a randomized controlled clinical trial conducted with 4–5-year-old children, it was found that virtual reality distraction proved effective in alleviating pain and anxiety experienced during dental treatment. Additionally, the implementation of stop signals is another commonly employed technique that has shown efficacy in reducing pain and alleviating discomfort in individuals receiving dental treatments, along with its successful application in diverse healthcare scenarios.

14.3.2 EVIDENCE SUPPORTING THE EFFECTIVENESS OF VIRTUAL REALITY DISTRACTION

Numerous research studies have indicated that using virtual reality (VR) as a means of diversion has proven to be an effective and unobtrusive approach to reducing anxiety and easing discomfort associated with dental procedures. For example, Wiederhold et al. [37] conducted an investigation which showed that using virtual reality (VR) as a distraction technique was effective in reducing anxiety and pain during dental procedures. Similarly, Fakhruddin et al. [38] It was observed that employing audio-visual distraction eyewear along with computerized administration of anesthesia during pulp therapy for apprehensive pediatric patients resulted in a decrease in dental apprehension. Numerous other investigations have similarly demonstrated the advantageous outcomes of virtual reality (VR) in the management of pain, alleviating anxiety, and influencing behavior in diverse medical procedures, including the treatment of burns, traumatic injuries, dental interventions, and administering injections. The fundamental principle behind the incorporation of virtual reality (VR) hinges on the notion that the experience of pain is heavily influenced by psychological factors. By redirecting attention away from the unpleasant stimuli towards the virtual environment, VR has the ability to significantly alleviate a patient's subjective experience of pain [26,39].

14.3.3 EVIDENCE SUPPORTING THE EFFECTIVENESS OF DENTAL APPS

The evidence supporting the effectiveness of dental apps for promoting dental health and reducing anxiety in patients is discussed in several subsections of recent studies. Research studies and findings have demonstrated the positive impact of using dental apps, such as dental game apps, to reduce anxiety levels in children during dental check-ups, educate them about proper dental care practices, and increase their knowledge of dental hygiene [40,41]. The main evidence comes from a study that found playing a dental game app reduced anxiety levels and increased children's knowledge of dental hygiene. Other studies also support the use of dental apps for education and anxiety reduction in pediatric patients. The evidence suggests that dental apps can be effective tools for promoting dental health and reducing anxiety in children. The use of dental game apps and other types of dental apps can help to educate children about proper dental care practices, increase their knowledge of dental hygiene, and reduce their anxiety levels during dental check-ups [42,43].

14.3.4 EVIDENCE SUPPORTING THE EFFECTIVENESS OF DIGITAL GAMES

Serious video games, also referred to as educational games or therapeutic games, are created with the intention of instructing particular skills or aiding in the treatment of mental health conditions. These games have the potential to be utilized in the management of various disorders, such as anxiety, depression, Attention Deficit Hyperactivity Disorder (ADHD), and Autism Spectrum Disorder (ASD) [44]. Several research investigations have been conducted to evaluate the effectiveness of using immersive video games in mitigating dental anxiety in individuals. These studies offer substantiated evidence that digital games, particularly serious games, have a significant impact on reducing anxiety levels. Exergames have shown similar efficacy to conventional workouts in reducing anxiety, and interactive computer-based cognitive-behavioral therapy (CBT) games have also been found to have comparable effects; this situation arises because biofeedback games have demonstrated superior efficacy in contrast to both the absence of intervention and traditional video games. Nonetheless, it's crucial to note that the quality of the available evidence ranged from very limited to modest, and a substantial proportion of the studies included exhibited a high overall risk of bias. As a result, although serious games show promise in reducing anxiety levels, Healthcare professionals and decision-makers must exercise prudence in their interpretation of these findings. It is advisable to view serious games as a supplementary method rather than a substitute for existing interventions, pending the emergence of more dependable and robust evidence [45,46].

14.4   SUSTAINABLE DENTISTRY

Sustainable dentistry is an emerging field focused on minimizing the ecological impact of dental procedures, while simultaneously promoting long-term oral health. Its primary goal is to implement environmentally friendly practices within dental clinics without compromising the quality of care provided to patients. By adopting sustainable approaches, such as using eco-friendly materials, reducing waste generation, and implementing energy-efficient technologies, dental professionals can contribute to a greener future while ensuring the well-being of their patients' oral health. With increased knowledge of the environmental effects of human activities, the dentistry sector is realizing the need to implement sustainable practices. Sustainable dentistry involves minimizing dental offices' carbon footprints, decreasing waste, preserving resources, and encouraging eco-friendly products and procedures [47]. This can be achieved through the use of eco-friendly materials and technologies, such as digital X-rays, reusable or compostable dental products, and biodegradable dental materials [48]. Sustainable dentistry also emphasizes the use of energy-efficient and low-emission technologies, such as LED lighting and high-efficiency HVAC systems, to reduce energy consumption and carbon emissions [49]. Sustainable dentistry prioritizes the use of safe and non-toxic dental materials and practices to promote public health. This is because some dental materials, such as those containing mercury or other toxic substances, can pose health risks to both patients and dental professionals. By using safer and more natural alternatives, such as composite fillings and ceramic restorations, sustainable dentistry aims to minimize exposure to harmful substances and reduce associated health risks [50–52]. Figure 14.2 illustrates the four key rationales for adopting sustainable dental practices environmental, public health, economic, and ethical responsibility [53]. The significance of minimizing waste and pollution in dental practices is emphasized in the context of environmental concerns. This rationale emphasizes the need for dental professionals to use sustainable materials and practices to minimize the negative impact on the environment [54,55]. Public health reasons, focuses on the importance of promoting public health by using safe and non-toxic dental materials and minimizing exposure to harmful substances. By adopting sustainable dentistry practices, dental professionals can reduce the risk of health problems for both patients and dental professionals [56]. The economic reasons emphasize the financial benefits of sustainable dentistry practices, such as reducing costs associated with waste management and increasing efficiency in dental practices [57]. The Ethical responsibility, emphasizes the importance of

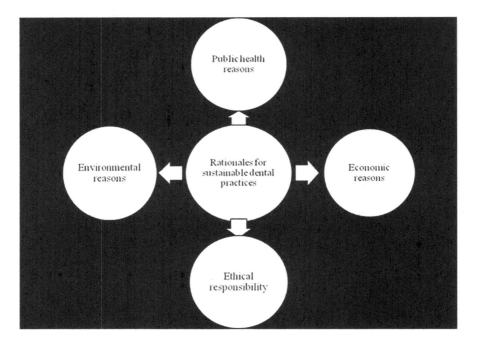

FIGURE 14.2   Rationales for sustainable dental practices.

ethical responsibility in dental practices, including promoting social and environmental justice [58]. Figure 14.2 highlights the importance of adopting sustainable dentistry practices for the benefit of the environment, public health, economics, and ethical responsibility [59]. By understanding these rationales, dental professionals can make informed decisions that promote sustainability and contribute to a healthier and more sustainable future.

14.4.1 THE USE OF NON-PHARMACOLOGICAL BEHAVIOR MANAGEMENT TECHNIQUES AS A SUSTAINABLE APPROACH AND BENEFITS OF SUSTAINABLE DENTISTRY FOR PATIENTS AND THE ENVIRONMENT

Utilizing non-pharmacological strategies for managing behavior is an efficient and long-lasting method that can minimize the requirement for sedation or other pharmaceuticals when undergoing dental treatments. As a result, this can contribute positively to environmental conservation efforts by decreasing the production and disposal of such substances [60]. Additionally, non-pharmacological techniques can also help to minimize the amount of waste generated during dental procedures, as fewer disposable items may be needed.

To advance the cause of eco-friendly dentistry, it is imperative to reduce the ecological footprint associated with dental care, specifically concerning the transportation of both dental staff and patients. One practical strategy is to promote active travel and carpooling among employees, while also minimizing the frequency of patient appointments and implementing appropriate recall intervals. Additionally, the use of remote consultations and digital technology can significantly reduce the need for travel to conferences and meetings. Another essential aspect of sustainable dentistry is sustainable procurement, ensuring that the materials and products used align with environmental sustainability principles [54]. Manufacturers should enhance their transparency regarding the materials and techniques employed in their products and packaging. By taking these practical steps, the dental profession can contribute to a more sustainable approach to dentistry and reduce its impact on the environment. In addition to the environmental benefits, sustainable dentistry can also lead to improved oral health for patients. Prevention strategies, such as promoting a diet low in sugar and emphasizing efficient oral hygiene practices, play a crucial role in minimizing the necessity for sedation or other medications during dental procedures. By doing so, these strategies actively contribute to ensuring the safety of patients [54]. In the field of dentistry, a comparison is being made between Non-Pharmacological Behavior Management Techniques and Sustainable Dentistry. This analysis aims to explore the similarities and differences between these two aspects and their impact on the dental profession. Dental professionals can adopt a holistic approach to dental care that considers both patient well-being and environmental sustainability. Both approaches aim to improve dental care while minimizing the environmental impact of dental practices. Table 14.1 outlines the key features of each approach and highlights how they contribute to improving dental care while minimizing the environmental impact of dental practices.

TABLE 14.1

Comparison of Non-pharmacological Behavior Management Techniques and Benefits of Sustainable Dentistry in Dentistry

	Non-pharmacological Behavior Management Techniques	Sustainable Dentistry
Definition	Techniques that do not involve the use of medication to manage patient behavior during dental procedures	An approach to dentistry that minimizes the environmental impact of dental practices
Examples	Tell-show-do technique, distraction techniques, positive reinforcement	Reduced carbon footprint, energy efficiency, waste reduction, improved oral health
Environmental Impact	Reduces the need for sedation or other medications, which can have negative environmental impact due to their production and disposal	Reduces the carbon footprint of dental services, promotes energy efficiency, and reduces waste generated during dental procedures
Patient Safety	Reduces the need for sedation or other medications, which can pose risks to patient safety	Improves patient safety by reducing the use of harmful substances and encouraging prevention strategies
Waste Reduction	Fewer disposable items may be needed during dental procedures	Reuse and recycle where appropriate to reduce waste generated by dental practices
Travel Reduction	Remote consultations reduce the need for staff and patients to travel	Promote active travel and lift sharing among employees to reduce the carbon footprint of dental services
Oral Health Improvement	Encourages prevention strategies such as a low sugar diet and efficient oral hygiene	Promotes oral health through prevention strategies and reduced use of harmful substances
Transparency and Sustainable Procurement	Manufacturers should be more transparent about the materials and methods used in their products and packaging	Sustainable procurement reduces the environmental impact of dental practices by choosing environmentally friendly products and materials

To summarize, the practice of eco-friendly dentistry holds the potential to enhance the well-being of both patients and the environment. This can be achieved by mitigating the ecological footprint of dental procedures, prioritizing patient safety, and advancing the overall quality of oral health results. Through the implementation of non-pharmacological methods for behavior management and adopting sustainable practices such as reducing travel, promoting sustainable procurement, and embracing digital technology, dental practices can become more environmentally friendly and sustainable [55].

14.5   IMPLEMENTING NON-PHARMACOLOGICAL BEHAVIOR MANAGEMENT TECHNIQUES IN DENTAL PRACTICE

The implementation of non-pharmacological behavior management techniques in dental practice involves utilizing non-medication methods to manage patient behavior during dental treatments. Examples of such strategies include utilizing positive reinforcement, diversion techniques, nonverbal communication, allowing or restricting parental presence, using protective stabilizing measures, employing voice control, and incorporating magic tricks [61]. The purpose of using these strategies is to create a good and comfortable environment for patients, especially children, during dental appointments, allowing them to feel calmer and more cooperative throughout treatment. Dental practitioners may collaborate with patients to create tailored behavior management programs that combine these strategies as well as the patient's views and opinions about dental care.

Non-pharmacological methods of managing behavior have demonstrated effectiveness in reducing dental anxiety and enhancing patient cooperation during dental procedures. Therefore, it is important to implement these techniques in dental practice to improve patient outcomes and provide a more positive dental experience for patients [62]. One of the methods that can be used is verbal and non-verbal communication. Dental professionals can use a calm and reassuring tone of voice, explain the procedure in simple terms, and use positive reinforcement to encourage patients. They can also use non-verbal communication such as a gentle touch or a smile to help patients feel more comfortable [63]. Utilizing positive reinforcement is an additional approach to effectively handle dental anxiety. This method entails providing patients with rewards as an incentive for exhibiting desirable behavior throughout the procedure, such as remaining calm and cooperating by following instructions to open their mouth when requested. Rewards can be as simple as verbal praise or a small toy or sticker [64]. Parent's presence/absence during the dental visit can also be a factor in managing dental anxiety. Research has shown that the presence of a parent may not always be beneficial, and in some cases, children may feel more comfortable without their parent present. Dental professionals should discuss this with parents and determine the best approach for each individual child [18].

Modeling presents itself as an alternative approach in handling dental anxiety. It entails providing patients with a visual representation or demonstration that illustrates the procedure they will undergo. This can help patients understand what will happen during the procedure and reduce their anxiety [65]. Systematic desensitization is a technique that involves gradually exposing patients to the dental procedure in a controlled and safe environment. This can be done using virtual reality or other digital solutions, such as the CARL system. The effectiveness of this approach in alleviating dental fear among adult patients has been demonstrated [13,66].

It is essential to incorporate non-pharmacological behavior management strategies in dental practices to effectively address dental anxiety and enhance patient outcomes. Dental practitioners have at their disposal several techniques to assist patients in feeling at ease during dental treatments. These techniques encompass various forms of communication, both verbal and non-verbal, the application of positive reinforcement, taking into account the involvement of parents, utilizing modeling strategies, and employing systematic desensitization. These approaches aim to create a more comfortable environment for patients during dental procedures. By using these techniques, dental professionals can provide a more positive dental experience for their patients and improve their oral health outcomes. Research has demonstrated that non-pharmacological strategies have the capacity to alleviate apprehension related to dental care and enhance patient compliance during dental procedures [48]. The significance of proficient communication with patients plays a crucial role in addressing dental anxiety and fostering favorable results in patient care. Various forms of communication, both verbal and non-verbal, including the implementation of techniques such as the Tell-Show-Do method, have been found to be effective in this regard [67]. The utilization of voice control and the implementation of positive reinforcement have shown efficacy in effectively addressing dental anxiety in individuals of all age groups, including both children and adults [68]. However, communication can pose significant difficulties in procedures involving the use of a cofferdam. In order to tackle this issue, digital solutions such as the CARL system and the "touch n'tell" system have proven to be successful in alleviating dental anxiety among adults. The CARL system employs systematic desensitization techniques to aid patients in acquiring relaxation methods and navigating the injection process. Research has shown its effectiveness in diminishing dental anxiety among adult patients. On the other hand, the "touch n'tell" system enables patients to communicate with dental professionals throughout the procedure, fostering a greater sense of comfort and reducing anxiety levels. This approach has proven to be successful in alleviating dental fear among grown-ups [69]. By using these digital solutions [70], dental professionals can improve communication with patients and reduce dental anxiety in adults. These remedies have the potential to give patients a feeling of authority during the process and enhance their level of ease, resulting in a more favorable dental encounter. In addition, studies have shown that computer-based and online solutions such as cognitive-behavioral therapy (CBT) can be highly effective in alleviating dental anxiety. In particular, among adult individuals experiencing moderate levels of anxiety, this is especially noticeable [71,72]. Dental professionals should consider using digital solutions such as the CARL system and the "touch n'tell" system to alleviate dental phobia among adult individuals. Establishing good communication with patients and utilizing non-pharmacological strategies like positive reinforcement, modeling, and systematic desensitization can greatly enhance the dental experience for patients. These techniques contribute to a more positive atmosphere, leading to improved oral health outcomes.

14.5.1 Considerations for Integrating Non-pharmacological Techniques into Dental Practice

Incorporating non-pharmacological techniques into dental procedures can serve as an effective approach to alleviating pain, anxiety, and associated negative emotions commonly experienced by patients. However, there are a number of factors to consider before introducing these procedures to dental practice [73]. Patient selection is a crucial factor when considering the use of non-pharmacological approaches. Not all patients may be suitable candidates for these techniques, so it is important to identify those who may benefit from them. Patients who have a history of trauma, anxiety, or fear of dental procedures, for example, may be appropriate candidates for non-pharmacological approaches. When selecting patients for non-pharmacological procedures, it is also important to consider other factors such as age, medical history, and the type of surgery involved [74,75]. In recent studies, a specific age group of children, namely those aged 8–12 years [33,62,68,69], were found to highly accept positive reinforcement and distraction techniques. Dental practitioners may consider incorporating these techniques into their practice to create a positive and comfortable environment for children. However, the use of reassuring touch and parental presence/absence should be used with caution and only with the consent of the child and parent. It is crucial for dental professionals to collaborate with children in order to create customized behavior management strategies, while also valuing their perspectives and opinions when it comes to dental procedures. Furthermore, it is essential for dental professionals to have a comprehensive understanding of the potential advantages and disadvantages associated with various dental techniques. They should exercise caution and employ these techniques judiciously based on individual patient needs and circumstances. Although protective stabilization, voice control, and magic tricks were also evaluated, their acceptability varied among children. The ultimate goal is to create a positive and stress-free experience for children during dental visits. By carefully selecting appropriate patients and utilizing the most acceptable non-pharmacological techniques, dental practitioners can provide effective and comfortable dental care for their patients.

Another factor to consider is employee training. Non-pharmacological approaches, such as relaxation techniques, guided imagery, and cognitive-behavioral therapy, should be taught to dental staff members. They should also be familiar with the data supporting these treatments and how to apply them into dental practice. Staff members should possess the ability to identify patients who could potentially derive advantages from these therapies and provide suitable suggestions [76]. In order to promote the utilization of non-pharmacological interventions in dental practices, it is recommended to furnish suitable equipment and resources. These may include relaxation CDs or movies, comfortable seating arrangements, and calming lighting. Furthermore, the dental office should have access to proper training materials and tools to ensure that its team is appropriately trained to execute these approaches. Another essential factor is informed consent. Patients should be thoroughly informed about the non-pharmacological procedures being utilized, as well as the possible advantages and hazards associated with them. Before using any non-pharmacological approaches, informed permission should be acquired. Patients should be given detailed information on how to use these approaches as well as what to expect throughout the operation [77,78]. Non-pharmacological procedures should not be used in place of pharmacological techniques when necessary. To give a holistic approach to patient care, they should be utilized in concert with pharmacological treatments such as local anesthetic or nitrous oxide. Non-pharmacological treatments should be used with caution in the dental practice, and they should be incorporated with other therapy strategies.

Non-pharmacological approaches must be evaluated and monitored to ensure their efficacy and safety. The success of these strategies should be examined and tracked on a regular basis using patient input, clinical results, and staff observations. Based on this finding any required changes to the treatment plan should be implemented. Non-pharmacological approaches must be carefully integrated into dental practice, which involves careful consideration of patient selection, staff training, equipment and resources, informed consent, integration with pharmacological procedures, and continuing assessment and monitoring. Non-pharmacological approaches, when applied effectively, can provide an effective and safe alternative or complement to pharmacological procedures in dental treatment [18,31,62,64,79].

14.6 CONCLUSION AND FUTURE DIRECTIONS

The area of non-pharmacological behavior management approaches in dentistry has evolved dramatically in recent years, and this section has offered an overview of the numerous techniques available and their usefulness in decreasing dental anxiety and terror. Various methods such as positive reinforcement, diversion strategies, and the use of virtual reality have shown significant advantages in alleviating dental phobia and enhancing patient contentment. However, certain treatments, such as protective stabilization, may raise ethical considerations and should be utilized only in severe instances and with the permission of the patient and/or their parents.

Addressing dental anxiety is critical for enhancing patient experience and encouraging improved oral health outcomes. Dental fear or anxiety can result in individuals delaying necessary dental treatment, potentially resulting in negative consequences for their oral health such as tooth decay, gum disease, and tooth loss. Moreover, it can negatively impact the patient's overall experience and increase the likelihood of complications during dental procedures. As a result, establishing long-term and novel non-pharmacological strategies for regulating patient behavior during dental treatments is critical. Not only will this improve the patient experience, but it will also help to avoid dental illnesses and boost general health and well-being. Dental practitioners must acknowledge the relevance of dental anxiety and endeavor to provide a good and peaceful environment throughout dental operations.

Implementing sustainable behavior management approaches in dental practice brings both possibilities and obstacles. While non-pharmacological treatments can increase patient satisfaction and lessen sedation concerns, they may necessitate more money, training, and time. Further investigation is required to evaluate the extended-term effectiveness and economic viability of these methods, along with identifying the most suitable patient demographics and situations for their implementation.

Future directions for research in sustainable and innovative techniques for improving dental health include personalized, technology-based interventions like virtual reality and gamification [80,81], as well as exploring the use of non-pharmacological techniques in more complex procedures and special patient populations, such as individuals with intellectual or developmental disabilities.

Additionally, researchers could investigate the use of artificial intelligence (AI) in behavior management and further explore the effectiveness of digital tools for dental anxiety reduction [82]. Research endeavors could be carried out to assess the prolonged efficacy of these methods in fostering improved oral health results and the general well-being of patients over an extended period.

REFERENCES

1. J. Ma, L. Schneide, S. Lapuschkin, R. Achtibat, M. Duchrau, J. Krois, F. Schwendicke, and W. Samek. 2022. "Towards Trustworthy AI in Dentistry," J. Dent. Res., vol. 101, no. 11, pp. 1263–1268, doi: 10.1177/00220345221106086.
2. I. K. M. And, and F. K. Kahabuka. 2019. "Dental Anxiety and Its Consequences to Oral Health Care Attendance and Delivery," in Anxiety Disorders - From Childhood to Adulthood reaction, pp. 36–49. doi: 10.5772/intechopen.82175.
3. F. Ahmed, I. A. Quddus, M. O. Sharif, and K. Ahmed. 2016. "Dental Anxiety: Understanding Is the Key to Effective Management," Dent. Update, vol. 43, no. 9, pp. 883–890, doi: 10.12968/denu.2016.43.9.883.
4. B. H. Hassan, M. M. Abd El Moniem, S. S. Dawood, A. A. Alsultan, A. I. Abdelhafez, and N. M. Elsakhy. 2022. "Dental Anxiety and Oral-Health-Related Quality of Life among Rural Community-Dwelling Older Adults," Int. J. Environ. Res. Public Health, vol. 19, no. 7643, pp. 1–13, doi: 10.3390/ijerph19137643.
5. A. Badran, K. Keraa, and M. M. Farghaly. 2023. "The Impact of Oral Health Literacy on Dental Anxiety and Utilization of Oral Health Services among Dental Patients: A Cross Sectional Study," BMC Oral Health, vol. 23, no. 1, pp. 1–12, doi: 10.1186/s12903-023-02840-3.
6. S. Khan, S. Sultan, and H. Khan. 2022. "Impact of Dental Anxiety on Oral Health QOL among Dental Patients: Exploring Mediating Effect of Cynical Hostility," Pakistan J. Humanit. Soc. Sci., vol. 10, no. 2, pp. 541–545, doi: 10.52131/pjhss.2022.1002.0218.
7. L. Svensson, M. Hakeberg, U. Wide, L. Svensson, M. Hakeberg, and U. Wide. 2018. "Dental Pain and Oral Health-Related Quality of Life in Individuals with Severe Dental Anxiety Dental Anxiety," Acta Odontol. Scand., vol. 76, no. 6, pp. 401–406, doi: 10.1080/00016357.2018.1473892.
8. K. Strøm, A. Rønneberg, A. B. Skaare, I. Espelid, and T. Willumsen. 2015. "Dentists' Use of Behavioural Management Techniques and Their Attitudes Towards Treating Paediatric Patients with Dental Anxiety," Eur Arch Paediatr Dent, no. 123, pp. 1–7, doi: 10.1007/s40368-014-0169-1.
9. V. D. Anil Gupta, Charu M. Marya, and Hind Pal Bhatia. 2014. "Behaviour Management of an Anxious Child," Stomatol. Balt. Dent. Maxillofac. J., vol. 16, no. May, pp. 3–6.
10. P. Kasemkhun, A. Smutkeeree, and V. Jirarattanasopha. 2022. "A Retrospective Comparison of Dental Treatment under General Anesthesia versus Non-pharmacological Approach in Patient with Special Health Care Needs," J. Dent. Sci., vol. 17, no. 3, pp. 1238–1243, doi: 10.1016/j.jds.2021.11.019.
11. R. P. Anthonappa, P. F. Ashley, D. L. Bonetti, G. Lombardo, and P. Riley. 2017. "Non-pharmacological Interventions for Managing Dental Anxiety in Children," Cochrane Database Syst. Rev., vol. 2017, no. 6, pp. 1–15, doi: 10.1002/1465185 8.CD012676.
12. M. V. da Silva, S. K. Bussadori, E. M. Santos, and K. M. Rezende. 2021. "Behaviour Management of the Contemporary Child in Paediatric Dentistry: An Overview of the Research," Pesqui. Bras. Odontopediatria Clin. Integr., vol. 21, pp. 1–12, doi: 10.1590/PBOCI.2021.090.

13. J. M. Armfield, and L. J. Heaton. 2013. "Management of Fear and Anxiety in the Dental Clinic: A Review," Aust. Dent. J., vol. 58, no. 4, pp. 390–407, doi: 10.1111/adj.12118.

14. L. R. Costa, C. B. Bendo, A. Daher, E. Heidari, R. Sá Rocha, A. P. de Sousa Costa Moreira, L. S. Moura, A. Banerjee, J. Tim Newton, and M. T. Hosey. 2020. "A Curriculum for Behaviour and Oral Healthcare Management for Dentally Anxious Children—Recommendations from the Children Experiencing Dental Anxiety: Collaboration on Research and Education (CEDACORE)," Int. J. Paediatr. Dent., vol. 30, no. 5, pp. 556–569, doi: 10.1111/ipd.12635.

15. C. Lewis. 2020. "Child Behaviour Management: Non-pharmacological Strategies," CLINCAL, Dental Health, vol. 59, no. 5 of 6, pp. 34–36.

16. D. P. Appukuttan. 2016. "Strategies to Manage Patients with Dental Anxiety and Dental Phobia: Literature Review," Clin. Cosmet. Investig. Dent., vol. 8, pp. 35–50, doi: 10.2147/CCIDE.S63626.

17. B. Hoffmann, K. Erwood, S. Ncomanzi, V. Fischer, D. O. Brien, and A. Lee. 2022. "Management Strategies for Adult Patients with Dental Anxiety in the Dental Clinic: A Systematic Review," Aust. Dent. J., vol. 67, no. 1, pp. 3–13, doi: 10.1111/adj.12926.

18. B. Abbas, A. Irfan Qureshi, M. Waseem, and A. Talaat. 2023. "Effect of Parental Dental Anxiety Level on Acceptance of Non-Pharmacological Behavior Management Strategies used in Pediatric Dentistry," Eur. J. Dent. Oral Heal., vol. 4, no. 1, pp. 5–9, doi: 10.24018/ejdent.2023.4.1.231.

19. J. M. Bernson, M. L. Elfström, and M. Hakeberg. 2013. "Dental Coping Strategies, General Anxiety, and Depression among Adult Patients with Dental Anxiety but with Different Dental-Attendance Patterns," Eur. J. Oral Sci., vol. 121, no. 3 PART2, pp. 270–276, doi: 10.1111/eos.12039.

20. H. Kassem El Hajj, Y. Fares, and L. Abou-Abbas. 2021. "Assessment of Dental Anxiety and Dental Phobia among Adults in Lebanon," BMC Oral Health, vol. 21, no. 1, pp. 1–11, doi: 10.1186/s12903-021-01409-2.

21. R. Mishra, A. K. Singh, and P. Singh. 2019. "A Comparison of Audio and Audio-Visual Distraction Techniques in Managing Dental Anxiety in Pediatric Patients: A Clinical Study," Orig. Res. Artic., vol. 88, no. 3, pp. 88–91, doi: 10.21276/ijmrp.2019.5.3.019.

22. I. Mishra, S. Deep, and A. Agrawal. 2022. "Comparative Evaluation of Audio, Audiovisual and Virtual Reality Distraction Techniques on Dentally Anxious Children," Baba Farid Univ. Dent. J., vol. 12, no. 1, pp. 24–27, doi: 10.5958/2230-7273.2022.00016.3.

23. A. Delgado, S. M. Ok, D. Ho, T. Lynd, and K. Cheon. 2021. "Evaluation of Children's Pain Expression and Behavior Using Audio Visual Distraction," Clin. Exp. Dent. Res., vol. 7, no. 5, pp. 795–802, doi: 10.1002/cre2.407.

24. N. Mahajan, B. Kotwal, A. Gupta, B. Kaul, R. K. Gupta, and S. Kaul. 2022. "Comparative Evaluation of an Audiovisual Distraction Aid and Print Format Entertainment on Pain Perception, Anxiety and Children Behavior in the Dental Setting," Int. J. Clin. Pediatr. Dent., vol. 15, no. 1, pp. 54–59, doi: 10.5005/jp-journals-10005-2329.

25. T. Hussain, S. J. Bajwa, S. Ghani, B. Alam, M. A. Khan, and A. Durrani. 2021. "Dental Anxiety Measurement of Children in Abbottabad Using Audio Visual System," Pakistan J. Med. Heal. Sci., vol. 15, no. 7, pp. 1633–1636, doi: 10.53350/pjmhs211571633.

26. J. J. Cheruvatoor, and L. Kaini. 2021. "Use of Virtual Reality (VR) as an Audio-Visual Distraction Tool in the Reduction of Dental Anxiety during Local Anesthesia," J. Pharm. Res. Int., vol. 33, no. June, pp. 102–108, doi: 10.9734/jpri/2021/v33i31B31696.

27. A. Cunningham, O. McPolin, R. Fallis, C. Coyle, P. Best, and G. McKenna. 2021. "A Systematic Review of the Use of Virtual Reality or Dental Smartphone Applications as Interventions for Management of Paediatric Dental Anxiety," BMC Oral Health, vol. 21, no. 1, pp. 1–12, doi: 10.1186/s12903-021-01602-3.

28. R. Moussa, A. Alghazaly, N. Althagafi, R. Eshky, and S. Borzangy. 2022. "Effectiveness of Virtual Reality and Interactive Simulators on Dental Education Outcomes: Systematic Review," Eur. J. Dent., vol. 16, no. 1, pp. 14–31, doi: 10.1055/s-0041-1731837.

29. H. A. Shah, N. Swamy, K. M. Pedodontics, S. Kulkarni, M. Pedodontics, S. Choubey, S. Harsh, and N. S. Kv. 2017. "Evaluation of Dental Anxiety and Hemodynamic Changes (Sympatho-Adrenal Response) during Various Dental Procedures Using Smartphone Applications v/s Traditional Behaviour Management Techniques in Pediatric Patients," Int. J. Appl. Res., vol. 3, no. 5, pp. 429–433, [Online]. Available: https://www.allresearchjournal.com/archives/?year=2017&vol=3&issue=5&part=G&ArticleId=3709

30. S. M. Alaki, R. A. Al-Raddadi, and H. J. Sabbagh. 2023. "Children's Electronic Screen Time Exposure and Its Relationship to Dental Anxiety and Behavior," J. Taibah Univ. Med. Sci., vol. 18, no. 4, pp. 778–786, doi: 10.1016/j.jtumed.2022.12.021.

31. H. Shukla, S. Kulkarni, M. B. Wasnik, N. Rojekar, D. Bhattad, and P. Kolekar. 2021. "Acceptance of Parents for Behavior Management Technique with Reference to Previous Dental Expertise and Dental Anxiety," Int. J. Clin. Pediatr. Dent., vol. 14, no. S2, pp. S193–S198, doi: 10.5005/jp-journals-10005-2115.

32. J. Zhao, K. Zhou, and Y. Ding. 2022. "Digital Games-Based Learning Pedagogy Enhances the Quality of Medical Education: A Systematic Review and Meta-Analysis," Asia-Pacific Educ. Res., vol. 31, no. 4, pp. 451–462, doi: 10.1007/s40299-021-00587-5.

33. M. N. Al-Halabi, N. Bshara, and Z. AlNerabieah. 2018. "Effectiveness of Audio Visual Distraction Using Virtual Reality Eyeglasses versus Tablet Device in Child Behavioral Management during Inferior Alveolar Nerve Block," Anaesthesia, Pain Intensive Care, vol. 22, no. 1, pp. 55–61.

34. J. Hare, G. Bruj-milasan, and T. Newton. 2018. "An Overview of Dental Anxiety and the Non-pharmacological Management of Dental Anxiety," Prim. Dent. J., vol. 7, no. 4, pp. 36–39.

35. S. Allani, and J. V. Setty. 2018. "Effectiveness of Distraction Techniques in the Management of Anxious Children in the Dental Operatory Effectiveness of Distraction Techniques in the Management of Anxious Children in the Dental Operatory," J. Dent. Med. Sci., vol. 15, no. 10, pp. 69–73, doi: 10.9790/0853-1510026973.

36. K..Milind Gurav, N. Kulkarni, V. Shetty, V. Vinay, P. Borade, S. Ghadge, and K. Bhor. 2022. "Effectiveness of Audio and Audio-Visual Distraction Aids for Management of Pain and Anxiety in Children and Adults Undergoing Dental Treatment – A Systematic Review and Meta-Analysis," J. Clin. Pediatr. Dent., vol. 46, no. 2, pp. 86–106, doi: 10.17796/1053-4625-46.2.2.

37. M. D. Wiederhold, V. Reality, K. Gao, and S. Francisco. 2014. "Clinical Use of Virtual Reality Distraction System to Reduce Anxiety and Pain in Dental Procedures," Cyber Psychology, Behavior, Soc. Netw., vol. 17, no. 6, pp. 359–365, doi: 10.1089/cyber.2014.0203.

38. K. S. Fakhruddin, E. B. Hisham, and M. O. Gorduysus. 2015. "Effectiveness of Audiovisual Distraction Eyewear and Computerized Delivery of Anesthesia during Pulp Therapy of Primary Molars in Phobic Child Patients," Eur. J. Dent., vol. 9, no. 4, pp. 470–475, doi: 10.4103/1305-7456.172637.

39. A. Constantini Leopardi, A. Adanero Velasco, M. Espí Mayor, and M. Miegimolle Herrero. 2023. "Effectiveness of Virtual Reality Goggles as Distraction for Children in Dental Care—A Narrative Review," Appl. Sci., vol. 13, no. 3, pp. 1–10, doi: 10.3390/app13031307.

40. D. Jurusan, K. Gigi, and P. Kemenkes. 2022. "The Dentist Mobile Game Playing Method on Reducing Anxiety Level at the Dental," Indones. J. Care's Oral Heal., vol. 6, no. 2, pp. 292–302.

41. I. Montenegro and A. Marinho. 2021. "A Novel Mobile App Intervention to Reduce Dental Anxiety in Infant Patients," Telemed. J. e-Health., vol. 27, no. 6, pp. 694–699, doi: 10.1089/tmj.2020.0138.

42. V. H. Patil, K. Vaid, N. S. Gokhale, P. Shah, M. Mundada, and S. M. Hugar. 2017. "Evaluation of Effectiveness of Dental Apps in Management of Child Behaviour: A Pilot Study," Int. J. Pedod. Rehabil., vol. 2, no. 1, pp. 14–18, doi: 10.4103/ijpr.ijpr.

43. G. Derbala, A. Khalil, and R. Soliman. 2022. "Effectiveness of Smart Phone Application in Reducing Anxiety During Pediatric Dental Procedures: A Randomized Controlled Trial," Alexandria Dent. J., vol. 47, no. 2, pp. 196–204, doi: 10.21608/adjalexu.2021.73371.1190.

44. A. Vahed. 2016. "Dental Technology: Digital and Board Games for Dental Technicians," in Why Games Are Good for Business – How to Leverage the Power of Serious Games, Gamification and Simulations, no. 4, pp. 84–87.

45. P. Environmental, and Y. Bozok. 2023. "Being a Child in the Digital World: Balancing Anxiety Levels," Public Environ. Occup. Heal. /, vol. 14, no. 1, pp. 68–75.

46. A. A. Abd-alrazaq, W. C. Medicine-qatar, D. Alhuwail, and L. M. Akhu-zaheya. 2022. "The Effectiveness of Serious Games in Alleviating Anxiety: Systematic Review and Meta-analysis," JMIR Serious Games, vol. 10, no. 1, pp. 1–22, doi: 10.2196/29137.

47. L. A. Dobrzanski. 2020. "The Concept of Sustainable Development of Modern Dentistry," Processes, vol. 8, no. December, pp. 1–86, doi: 10.3390/pr8121605.

48. Bhardwaj, A., Bhatnagar, A., and Kumar, A. 2023. Chapter 29 – Current Trends of Application of Additive Manufacturing in Oral Healthcare System, in Advances in Additive Manufacturing (eds. Kumar, A., Mittal, R. K., and Haleem, A.), Elsevier, pp. 479–491. 10.1016/B978-0-323-91834-3.00010-7

49. N. Martin, M. Sheppard, G. P. Gorasia, P. Arora, M. Cooper, and S. Mulligan. 2021. "Awareness and Barriers to Sustainability in Dentistry: A Scoping Review," J. Dent., vol. 112, p. 103735, doi: 10.1016/j.jdent.2021.103735.

50. B. Duane. 2023. "Sustainable Dentistry Making a Difference", no. 4, Springer, pp. 1–231.

51. D. D. Simpson. 2011. "A Framework for Implementing Sustainable Oral Health Promotion Interventions," J. Public Health Dent., vol. 71, no. SUPPL. 1, pp. 584–594, doi: 10.1111/j.1752-7325.2011.00234.x.

52. M. Al-Qarni, N. V. Shakeela, M. A. Alamri, and Y. A. Alshaikh. 2016. "Awareness of Eco-Friendly Dentistry among Dental Faculty and Students of King Khalid University, Saudi Arabia," J. Clin. Diagnostic Res., vol. 10, no. 10, pp. ZC75–ZC78, doi: 10.7860/JCDR/2016/21560.8663.

53. B. Duane, R. Stancliffe, F. A. Miller, J. Sherman, and E. Pasdeki-Clewer. 2020. "Sustainability in Dentistry: A Multifaceted Approach Needed," J. Dent. Res., vol. 99, no. 9, pp. 998–1003, doi: 10.1177/0022034520919391.

54. G. J. Wilson, S. Shah, and H. Pugh. 2020. "What Impact Is Dentistry Having on the Environment and How Can Dentistry Lead the Way?," Fac. Dent. J., vol. 11, no. 3, pp. 110–113, doi: 10.1308/rcsfdj.2020.96.

55. B. Duane, D. Ramasubbu, S. Harford, I. Steinbach, J. Swan, K. Croasdale, and R. Stancliffe. 2019. "Environmental Sustainability and Waste within the Dental Practice," Br. Dent. J., vol. 226, no. 8, pp. 611–618, doi: 10.1038/s41415-019-0194-x.

56. M. Glick, O. Monteiro da Silva, and G. K. Seeberger. 2012. "FDI Vision 2020: Shaping the Future of Oral Health," Int. Dent. J., vol. 62, no. 6, pp. 278–291, doi: 10.1111/idj.12009.

57. M. Antoniadou, T. Varzakas, and I. Tzoutzas. 2021. "Circular Economy in Conjunction with Treatment Methodologies in the Biomedical and Dental Waste Sectors," Circ. Econ. Sustain., vol. 1, no. 2, pp. 563–592, doi: 10.1007/s43615-020-00001-0.

58. C. M. Mörch, S. Atsu, W. Cai, X. Li, S. A. Madathil, X. Liu, V. Mai, F. Tamimi, M. A. Dilhac, and M. Ducret. 2021. "Artificial Intelligence and Ethics in Dentistry: A Scoping Review," J. Dent. Res., vol. 100, no. 13, pp. 1452–1460, doi: 10.1177/0022 0345211013808.

59. N. Martin, L. Smith, and S. Mulligan. 2021. "Sustainable Oral Healthcare and the Environment: Mitigation Strategies," Dent. Update, vol. 48, no. 7, pp. 524–531, doi: 10.12968/DENU.2021.48.7.524.

60. S. Arora, S. Mittal, and V. Dogra. 2017. "Eco-Friendly Dentistry: Need of Future. An Overview," J. Dent. Allied Sci., vol. 6, no. 1, p. 22, doi: 10.4103/2277-4696.205446.

61. J. Rosiak, and J. Szymańska. 2018. "Non-pharmacological Methods of Fighting Dental Anxiety," J. Pre-Clinical Clin. Res., vol. 12, no. 4, pp. 145–148, doi: 10. 26444/jpccr/99771.

62. N. B. Nagaveni, K. Muzammil, and T. P. Poornima. 2023. "Evaluation of Children' S Perception of Non- Pharmacological Behaviour Management Techniques – An Innovative Study," Int. J. Pedod. Rehabil., vol. 8, no. 1, pp. 36–43.

63. S. Cianetti, L. Paglia, R. Gatto, A. Montedori, and E. Lupatelli. 2017. "Evidence of Pharmacological and Non-pharmacological Interventions for the Management of Dental Fear in Paediatric Dentistry: A Systematic Review Protocol," BMJ Open, vol. 7, no. 8, pp. 1–6, doi: 10.1136/bmjopen-2017-016043.

64. R. A. Baakdah, J. M. Turkistani, A. M. Al-Qarni, A. N. Al-Abdali, H. A. Alharbi, J. A. Bafaqih, and Z. S. Alshehri. 2021. "Pediatric Dental Treatments with Pharmacological and Non-pharmacological Interventions: A Cross-Sectional Study," BMC Oral Health, vol. 21, no. 1, pp. 1–9, doi: 10.1186/s12903-021-01555-7.

65. G. Z. Wright, and A. Kupietzky. 2014. "Non-Pharmacologic Approaches in Behavior Management," in Behavior Management in Dentistry for Children: Second Edition, no. 2, pp. 63–91. doi: 10.1002/9781118852446.ch6.

66. A. De Jongh, P. Adair, and M. Meijerink-Anderson. 2005. "Clinical Management of Dental Anxiety: What Works for Whom?," Int. Dent. J., vol. 55, no. 2, pp. 73–80, doi: 10.1111/j.1875-595X.2005.tb00037.x.

67. B. Yeptho, B. J. Emmanuel, D. Shekhawat, J. Raja, and V. S. Inda. 2021. "A Review on Non-pharmacological Behavior Shaping in Pediatric Dentistry Emphasized on Tell-Show-Do and It's Modifications," J. Adv. Clin. Res. Insights, vol. 8, no. 4, pp. 91–93, doi: 10.15713/ins.jcri.339.

68. E. Guanabara, K. Ltda, E. Guanabara, and K. Ltda. 2013. "An Exploratory Study Investigating Children's Perceptions of Dental Behavioural Management Techniques," Int. J. Paediatr. Dent., vol. 23, no. 4, pp. 297–309.

69. C. Campbell. 2017. "A Comprehensive Analysis of the Evidence on Non-pharmacological Interventions in the Management of Dental Anxiety: A Linked Series of Systematic Reviews." PhD diss. In Dental Fear and Anxiety in Pediatric Patients: Practical Strategies to Help Children Cope, pp. 1–252.

70. T. Joda, M. M. Bornstein, R. E. Jung, M. Ferrari, T. Waltimo, and N. U. Zitzmann. 2020. "Recent Trends and Future Direction of Dental Research in the Digital Era," Int. J. Environ. Res. Public Health, vol. 17, no. 6, pp. 1–8, doi: 10.3390/IJERPH17061987.

71. H. S. Gomes, K. A. Viana, A. C. Batista, L. R. Costa, M. T. Hosey, and T. Newton. 2018. "Cognitive Behaviour Therapy for Anxious Paediatric Dental Patients: A Systematic Review," Int. J. Paediatr. Dent., vol. 28, no. 5, pp. 422–431, doi: 10.1111/ipd.12405.

72. H. Matsuoka, I. Chiba, Y. Sakano, A. Toyofuku, and Y. Abiko. 2017. "Cognitive Behavioral Therapy for Psychosomatic Problems in Dental Settings," Biopsychosoc. Med., vol. 11, no. 1, pp. 1–7, doi: 10.1186/s13030-017-0102-z.

73. S. Momen. 2016. "Special Care Dentistry," British Dental Journal, vol. 220, no. 3, p. 89, doi: 10.1038/SJ.BDJ.2016.67.

74. T. O. Hussein, and D. Akşit-Bıçak. 2022. "Management of Post-Traumatic Dental Care Anxiety in Pediatric Dental Practice—A Clinical Study," Children, vol. 9, no. 8, pp. 1–13, doi: 10.3390/children9081146.

75. E. Heidari, J. T. Newton, and A. Banerjee. 2020. "Minimum Intervention Oral Healthcare for People with Dental Phobia: A Patient Management Pathway," Br. Dent. J., vol. 229, no. 7, pp. 417–424, doi: 10.1038/s41415-020-2178-2.

76. O. Felemban, R. Baamer, Z. Bukhari, K. Baghlaf, M. Aldajani, and O. Sijini. 2022."Variation in the Use of Basic Behavioral Management Techniques in General and Pediatric Dental Practice: A Cross-sectional Study," J. Adv. Oral Res., vol. 13, no. 2, pp. 225–233, doi: 10.1177/23202068221103983.

77. M. Shindova. 2022. "Knowledge and Attitudes of Dental Practitioners Regarding the Use of Behaviour Management Techniques for Paediatric Dental Patients," Folia Med. (Plovdiv)., vol. 64, no. 1, pp. 128–133, doi: 10.3897/folmed.64.e64416.

78. A. Kumar, and J. Intern. 2022. "How to Manage Dental Anxiety and Fear among Paediatric Patients," Int. J. Curr. Sci., vol. 12, no. 4, pp. 544–555.

79. K. Swarna, Gs. Prathima, M. Suganya, A. Sanguida, and A. Selvabalaji. 2019. "Recent Advances in Non-Pharmacological Behaviour Management Techniques in Children-An Overview," IOSR J. Dent. Med. Sci. e-ISSN, vol. 18, no. December, pp. 18–21, doi: 10.9790/0853-1805101821.

80. R. Monterubbianesi, V. Tosco, F. Vitiello, G. Orilisi, F. Fraccastoro, A. Putignano, and G. Orsini. 2022. "Augmented, Virtual and Mixed Reality in Dentistry: A Narrative Review on the Existing Platforms and Future Challenges," Appl. Sci., vol. 12, no. 2, pp. 1–14, doi: 10.3390/app12020877.

81. S. Fahim, A. Maqsood, G. Das, N. Ahmed, S. Saquib, A. Lal, A. A. Ghaffar Khan, and M. Khursheed Alam. 2022 "Augmented Reality and Virtual Reality in Dentistry: Highlights from the Current Research," Appl. Sci., vol. 12, no. 8, doi: 10.3390/app12083719.

82. A. Kumar, R. K. Mittal, and A. Haleem eds. 2022. Advances in Additive Manufacturing: Artificial Intelligence, Nature-Inspired, and Biomanufacturing. Elsevier.

15 A Mobile Application for Malocclusion Classification and Segmentation in Dental Images Using a Deep Learning Ensemble

Sanya Sinha
Department of Electronics and Communication Engineering, Birla Institute of Technology Mesra Patna Campus, Patna, Bihar, India

Nilay Gupta
Center for Artificial Intelligence, ZHAW School of Engineering, Zurich, Switzerland

15.1 INTRODUCTION

Malocclusion is a dental condition in which the teeth do not align properly when the jaws are closed [1]. This can lead to several dental and health problems, including difficulty chewing, speech problems, and even jaw pain [2]. They may give rise to multifaceted issues, such as impaired biting and mastication, potentially culminating in inadequate nutritional absorption and digestion [3]. Furthermore, malocclusions may detrimentally impact speech patterns, given that teeth and tongue are crucial in proper pronunciation. In addition, these anomalies can result in discomfort in the jaw, neck, and head regions due to a lack of alignment of the teeth and jaw. Besides, crooked teeth can impede optimal oral hygiene practices, predisposing one to dental caries, periodontal ailments, and other dental complications.

A range of factors can lead to malocclusions, such as genetic inheritance, developmental abnormalities, and oral habits [4]. The genetic makeup of an individual can notably influence malocclusion development as the teeth, jaw, and facial structure's form and size are innate characteristics that can impact tooth alignment. Additionally, individuals with a family history of malocclusions are at higher risk of developing similar

DOI: 10.1201/9781003404934-15

issues [5]. Malocclusions can also stem from developmental challenges, such as abnormal jaw growth. Premature loss of baby teeth, facial or mouth injury, or extended thumb or pacifier sucking habits in childhood can contribute to these issues. Additionally, oral habits such as tongue jabbing, pollex lapping and breathing through the mouth can bring about changes in the teeth and jaw's position over time, leading to misalignment. Other possible contributors to malocclusions include jaw or mouth tumors, facial or dental injuries, and specific medical conditions, such as cleft palate or lip.

Overall, an amalgamation of inherent and ecological features can influence the development of malocclusions, and early detection and treatment are essential for preventing further dental and health problems [6].

There exists a diversity of malocclusions based on the orientation of overlap, ranging from overbite, underbite, crossbite, open bite, crowding, spacing, to misplaced midline. Overbite entails an excessive overlapping of the frontal teeth along the upper and lower jaws, while underbite denotes protrusion of the lower front teeth beyond the upper front teeth [7]. Crossbites ensue when the teeth in the upper jaw bite against the teeth in the lower jaw, and open bite arises when an orifice exists between the teeth in the upper and lower jaws even when the jaws are closed [8]. Crowding transpires when the available space in the dental arches is insufficient to accommodate all teeth, resulting in overlapping or twisting of the teeth. Spacing, which can be caused by missing teeth or smaller-than-average teeth, occurs when there is excessive space between teeth [9]. Lastly, a misplaced midline arises when the center of the upper front teeth does not align with the center of the lower front teeth. Based on the relationship between the upper and lower teeth, malocclusions can be classified into three classes: Class I malocclusions occur when the teeth are relatively straight, but the upper teeth slightly overlap the lower teeth, causing an uneven bite. Class II malocclusions occur when the upper teeth significantly overlap the lower teeth, resulting in an overbite. This type of malocclusion is further divided into two subtypes: division 1, where the upper teeth are excessively protruding, and division 2, where the upper central teeth are more vertical. Class III malocclusions occur when the lower teeth protrude past the upper teeth, resulting in an underbite [10]. This type of malocclusion is also known as a prognathic jaw, meaning that the lower jaw is more prominent than the upper jaw. Identifying the class of malocclusion is critical in planning the appropriate orthodontic treatment. Radiographs, CT scans, and other imaging techniques can be used to detect malocclusions [11]. X-rays and panoramic radiographs are commonly used to evaluate the relationship between teeth and jaws, while cone-beam-computed tomography (CBCT) is more commonly used to provide more circumspective information about the teeth and the surrounding orthodontic structures [12]. These imaging techniques can help orthodontists identify the type and severity of malocclusions, as well as determine the best treatment plan to correct them. In addition, digital models and teeth images can also be useful in diagnosing and planning the orthodontic line of treatment. (Figure 15.1 and 15.2)

The quality of the image clicked is largely subjective and heavily dependent on external environmental factors such as even illumination, controlled brightness, artifacts, and manual imaging discrepancies [13]. Lack of adequate imaging produces poor quality images unfit for clinical diagnosis. Therefore, a better approach for malocclusion detection would be to segment out the dental skeleton explicitly. This would enable the orientation of the teeth to be observed irrespective of the original image's quality [14]. Several segmentation algorithms can be used to segment out individual teeth and assess

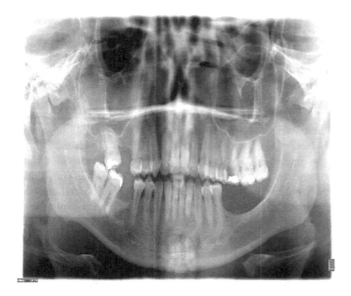

FIGURE 15.1 A dental radiograph (X-ray).

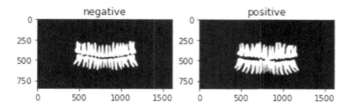

FIGURE 15.2 Segmented tooth region ground truth of negatively and positively maloccluded radiographic images.

their alignment to detect malocclusions. For the purpose of classifying and segmenting 15 distinct classes of dental concerns, Muresan et al. suggested semantic segmentation technique driven by deep learning [15]. Oktay et al. suggested AlexNet-based architecture to categorize orthodontic structures into inclusive X-ray radiographs [16]. In order to recover structures with high/low curvature, Yamany et al. created an image segmentation technique and shaped a 2D image by encoding the surface perpendicular and curvature information. [17]. After segmentation has been performed on dental images, the skeletal arrangement can be clinically analyzed to predict the presence of malocclusions. Manual detection of malocclusions from radiographs is a time-consuming process with subjective accuracy rates. This inadequacy paved the way for computer-aided diagnosis (CAD) of malocclusions [18]. Automated detection provides a standardized method for malocclusion analysis, thus allowing more consistent diagnosis and treatment planning. Moreover, CAD can detect minute deviations from normalcy that might have evaded manual orthodontic scans [19–22]. This provides results free from variability and occlusive manual discrepancies that might unnecessarily lengthen the course of treatment. By performing image analysis on voluminous datasets, CAD successfully proves to be a boon for oral health.

Through this paper, a novel dental image segmentation and detection instrument driven by a deep learning mechanism is proposed. The segmentation has been performed on the TUFTS Dental database (TDD) [23]. TDD includes a series of abnormality detection binary masks, a mask for eye tracking, and a thorough analysis of the initial outcomes for the improvement of dental radiography image quality and tooth segmentation. Here, we have performed tooth-wise, panoramic image segmentation by leveraging a U-Net model built on top of a VGG16 backbone [24]. The U-Net architecture is an integrated CNN. [25]. There are two paths in this architecture: a contraction path and an extension path. Operations involving convolution have been performed in the Contraction path followed by a maximum pooling operation layer to calculate the highest-valued patch in the network. Transposed convolution or up sampling is performed in the expansion part. Two 3×3 convolutions layers, ReLu activation and maximum pooling operations make up the UNet architecture, which is then followed by contractive down sampling. To reduce the number of feature canals, a transposed convolution operation was performed in the up sampling path. The UNet architecture also includes skip connections to spatially recover the features lost during up sampling. VGG16 is a DNN model that is widely used for image classification tasks [26]. The VGG16 architecture, as the name suggests consists of 16 trainable layers. These include 13 fully convolutional layers and 3 fully-connected layers. The convolutional layers use small 3×3 filters and have a single pixel value for a stride, which allows the network to learn complex features in the images. The first convolutional layer takes in the input image, and the subsequent layers down sample the spatial dimensions of the feature maps while increasing the number of channels. It was trained on the ImageNet dataset, and achieved state-of-the-art performance at the time of its release. In the proposed work, a novel UNet-VGG16 backbone has been leveraged wherein the VGG16 contractor extracts the topographical traits from the images while the UNet decoder performs segmentation on the extracted features. This would generate precisely segmented dental skeletons which would further ease clinical diagnosis. A computer-aided ensemble is suggested that would automatically segment individual teeth in mandibular dental skeletons and classify the segmented outputs as maloccluded or unaffected [27]. This would reduce significant amounts of essential clinical time that could result in misdiagnosis or underdiagnosis. We propose a ResNet50-based classifier [28] to distinguish between maloccluded and unaffected dental skeletons. This ensemble is computationally efficient and easy to develop into a user-friendly application to democratize effective oral healthcare from the comfort of one's home.

15.2 RELATED WORK

Dental imaging involves various modalities to capture different types of images of the teeth, jaws, and surrounding structures. Here are some common modalities used in dental imaging:

1. CBCT: CBCT is a specialized form of computed tomography that generates 3D images of the teeth, jawbone, and facial structures. It is particularly useful for complex dental procedures such as implant planning, and to assess the relationship between teeth and surrounding anatomical structures [29].

2. Digital Imaging: Digital imaging systems use electronic sensors instead of traditional X-ray films. This includes Digital Intraoral and Digital Panoramic Systems for advanced, high-resolution dental imaging [30].
3. Magnetic Resonance Imaging (MRI): MRI can help evaluate conditions such as temporomandibular joint disorders, tumors, or abnormalities affecting the head and neck region [31].
4. Ultrasonography: Ultrasound imaging is used in dental practice for assessing the temporomandibular joint, salivary glands, or oral soft tissues to provide information about the structural and functional aspects of these areas [32].
5. Optical Coherence Tomography (OCT): OCT is a non-surgical imaging method that employs electromagnetic radiation to produce detailed sample images of tissues. It is used in dental applications for examining tooth structures, assessing periodontal tissues, and detecting dental caries [33].
6. X-ray Radiography: X-ray imaging is an extensively-employed modality in dentistry [34]. It includes two subcategories:
   • Intraoral X-rays: These are taken from inside the mouth and include bitewing, periapical, and occlusal X-rays. The bitewise X-rays are responsible for representing minute details about teeth in both the maxilla and the mandible, while the periapical X-rays denote the entire instance of a tooth. They provide detailed images of individual teeth, tooth roots, and the supporting bone.
   • Extraoral X-rays: These are taken externally from regions outside the mouth. Panoramic and cephalometric X-rays are examples of extraoral X-rays. [35]. They ensure a circumspective overview of the entire jaw region.

X-ray radiographs evolved to become one of the most widely used methods of dental imaging. This was courtesy of their effectivity in detecting tooth decay and infection at early stages, thus allowing for expedited treatment. X-rays provide detailed images of teeth, tooth roots, and surrounding bone structures to enable dentists to assess conditions, identify abnormalities, and evaluate dental infections, bone loss, or fractures. They also help visualize tooth roots and impacted teeth, and provide valuable information about supporting structures like the jawbone and periodontal tissues, aiding in treatment planning. Modern digital X-ray systems reduce radiation exposure while maintaining high diagnostic quality [36]. These X-ray radiographs are cost-effective and widely accessible, making them a preferred choice in dental practices. However, the selection of imaging modalities depends on specific clinical needs, and in complex cases, additional modalities like CBCT or MRI may be used for comprehensive evaluation.

X-ray radiograph analysis is largely subjective and varies based on the dentist's experiences, patient-to-patient tooth structure, and poor image quality, among other factors. Therefore, significant contributions were suggested in the AI-enabled, computer-aided diagnosis landscape [37].

15.2.1 TRADITIONAL METHODS

Lurie *et al.* [38] and Modi et al. [39] proposed a region-based dental image segmentation methodology which relies on performing pixel intensity-based segmentation. A number of threshold-based segmentation techniques [40–42] were proposed in notable works.

The reasoning behind applying intensity thresholds in image segmentation begins with selecting a specific threshold value. When assigning pixels to regions, pixels with intensities exceeding the threshold are assigned to one region, while pixels with intensities lesser than the prescribed standard are assigned to an adjacent region. [43,44]. Global thresholding methods often prove ineffective when an image displays significant variations in hue and brightness, leading to numerous pixel intensities unable to be correctly classified. A problem-solving approach driven by a "shading function" can be used to correctly estimate the non-uniform intensity pattern. In such cases, variable thresholding emerges as a viable solution. Wang et al. [45] presented a variable thresholding-based benchmarking for dental image segmentation. A clustering methodology is adopted when the primary incentive is grouping correlated data points into a single cluster. Alsmadi et al. [46] leveraged fuzzy C-means clustering on panoramic dental X-ray radiographs. Boundary-based edge segmentation encapsulates a group of traditional edge detection mechanisms which perform image segmentation by detecting discontinuities in colors and pixel intensities. Razali et al. [41] proposed sobel and canny-based edge detection for medical images. Ali et al. and Hasan et al. [47,48] proposed a more refined method for edge-driven segmentation in bitewing X-ray images by introducing the active contourlet model which uses geometrical variations to detect changes in the image's topology. Watershed segmentation is a marker-based segmentation algorithm that mathematically segments the different regions in an image based on the image's inherent morphology. Li et al. [49] presented a marker-controlled watershed segmentation algorithm for bitewing X-ray images.

15.2.2 Deep Learning-Based Methods

A major drawback faced by traditional segmentation methods includes manual feature learning and extraction. This is a lengthy process heavily dependent on the subject knowledge of the developer. Deep learning-based methodologies can mechanically absorb relevant characteristics from images, eliminating the need for manual feature engineering [50,51]. This ability to learn high-level features allows deep learning models to capture complex patterns and variations in the data, which traditional methods often struggle with. An added advantage of deep learning (DL) methods includes high adaptability and the capacity to handle a wide range of data types, including images, videos, and even 3D data. They excel while working on large, multi-modal datasets with complex patterns. Traditional methods, on the other hand, often require domain-specific knowledge and manual tuning to handle different data types effectively. The ability of DL models to capture intricate details and semantic context has led to significant improvements in segmentation accuracy compared to traditional methods.

Koch et al. [52] proposed a U-Net segmentation method for panoramic radiograph segmentation by combining vanilla U-Net with fully convolutional networks (FCN). This integrated approach relied on the exploitation of the symmetrical orientation of teeth to bootstrap segmentation accuracy. Kong et al. [53] proposed an efficient encoder-decoder network (EEDNet) to segment panoramic X-ray images by leveraging an Inception-ResNet block in the feature centrifuge. Cui et al. proposed TSegNet [54], which is an efficient tooth segmentation model based on the SegNet neural network cascaded with a distance-aware centroid detector. KCNet was proposed by Lin et al. [55], a lightweight knowledge network for all-inclusive X-ray segmentation. Yu et al. proposed a bilateral segmentation approach in orthodontic dental structures by leveraging the BiseNet [56] neural network architecture. While these methods performed significantly, not much literature has been found on exploiting the segmented outputs for disease detection in the tooth region.

15.2.3 Deep Learning for Malocclusion Detection

Harun et al. proposed a dental malocclusion detection model using the frame-cut-out method for restructuring and CNNs for the detection phase. Aljabri et al. [57] projected a comparative study for canine detection and impaction classification based on advanced deep models like DenseNet-121 [58], VGG16 [59] and Inception V3 [60]. Kim et al. [61] suggested the 3D CBCT image modality for malocclusion classification and detection. Harun et al. [62] proposed a computationally-efficient, lightweight ensemble for the diagnosis of orthodontic abstractions. Talaat et al. [63] created a technique centered on "You Only Look Once" (YOLO) algorithm to detect multiple instances of malocclusive teeth in intraoral clinical images. This model was dispatched into an AI-driven, computationally efficient ensemble for accurately detecting and grading. Song et al. used a contextually-driven CNN ensemble [64] on the ISBI 2015 challenge dental X-ray image dataset. Despite the advent of such modern methods of malocclusion detection, orthodontists still heavily rely on Edward Angle's classification methodology for classifying the three types of malocclusions.

15.3   PROPOSED WORK

15.3.1 Dataset

The Tufts Dental Dataset (TDD) [23] is a multi-modal dataset of panoramic dental radiography images that have been labeled by experts to identify abnormalities in teeth. The dataset consists of 1000 panoramic X-ray radiograph images. The anatomical position, outlying characteristics, radiodensity, influence on the surrounding assembly, and the grade of the anomaly were used as the five separate criteria for categorizing these radiography images. The TDD dataset includes various components such as a mask for tooth segmentation, a mask for abnormality identification, a mask indicating the ROI in the maxillomandibular area, an eye-tracking gaze map, and a documented account that delivers minutiae about the detected abnormality. These different components can be illustrated as:

a. Tooth Segmentation Mask: The TDD contains precise and detailed dental segmentation masks for the overall teeth region. These provide accurate teeth boundaries that can be used by dental researchers to study tooth-specific features and appearances.

b. Abnormality Mask: Abnormality Masks in the TDD highlight areas of the dental images that have diseases or anomalies. These masks make it possible to localize and identify specific dental problems, which helps in the development of algorithms for automatic anomaly detection.

c. Maxillomandibular ROI Mask: The maxillomandibular region refers to the anatomical jaw area encompassing the maxilla and the lower jaw mandible. The ROI inside the maxillomandibular region of dental images can be determined by TDD masks. With the aid of this ROI mask, analysis can be focused on a region where dental anomalies and anomalous attributes are more likely to be present.

d. Eye-Tracking Gaze Map: TDD's eye-tracking gaze maps reveal the parts of the dental photos that draw the most attention visually. This information can be helpful for figuring out how individuals perceive dental images and what gaze patterns they follow to help with dental imaging system design and provide guidance for the generation of automated analysis algorithms.

e. Text Description of Abnormality: Textual descriptions of the discovered abnormalities in the dental pictures are included in TDD and provide comprehensive information about them. These descriptions enable more thorough study and research by providing further insights into the nature, traits, and implications of the observed dental diseases.

These provisions in the TDD allow the seamless amalgamation of radiology and orthodontics with artificial intelligence-based computer-aided analysis. (Figure 15.3)

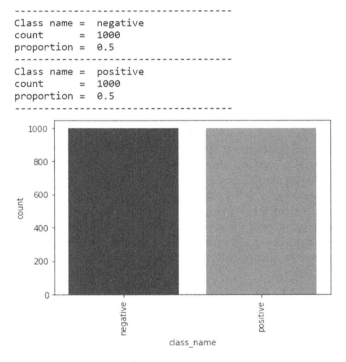

FIGURE 15.3 Dataset distribution.

15.3.2 SEGMENTATION

The U-Net is a CNN architecture for semantic segmentation tasks, which are aimed at identifying and classifying different objects or regions within an image.

In this model, we propose a U-Net model based on the VGG16 backbone [24]. VGG16 is a DNN model extensively used for image cataloging tasks. The proposed model leverages VGG16 as a potent feature extractor. Thus, VGG16 layers can be used to model the contracting path of the U-Net VGG neural network. The convolutional base of VGG16 consists of 3 convolutional layers of size 3 × 3, a single stride and padding to maintain spatial dimensions; superseded by a non-linear activation function, ReLU. The number of filters in each layer increases with depth. The filters chosen in this model are 64, 128, 256 and 512. After each set of convolutional layers, a max-pooling layer with a 2 × 2 window and double stride is applied to reduce the spatial dimensions by half. This is replicated for the 3 consecutive blocks of convolution to perform consistent downsampling. The outputs of the convolutional layers are amalgamated and flattened into a one-dimensional feature vector. A bridge is added to the neural network model to connect the encoder to the decoder. It typically consists of convolutional layers that help in maintaining spatial information and capturing more abstract features.

The network's decoder structure is like the UNet architecture. It is made up of up-convolutional layers (also known as transpose convolutions or deconvolutions) that steadily increase spatial dimensions while decreasing channel count. Skip connections concatenate feature vectorial distributions from the separate levels in the expander after the up-convolutional layers. These skip connections aid in the recovery of spatial details as well as the integration of low abstraction and high abstraction elements. The expanding path and the contracting path are the two fundamental components of the U-Net design. While the expanding path is a series of transposed convolutional layers that gradually increase the input's spatial dimensions, the contracting path is a sequence of convolutional layers that gradually decrease the input's spatial dimensions. The convolutional blocks that make up the contracting path are separated by batch normalization layers, ReLU activation functions, and 2 × 2 max pooling operations. Each convolutional block is made up of two 3 × 3 convolutions. The incentive behind using convolutional blocks is to abstract and capture features at different spatial scales, while the downsamplers increase the receptive field of the subsequent convolutional layers. The expanding path is constructed of a chain of unsampling blocks, each of which consists of a transposed convolution (also known as a deconvolution) that doubles the spatial dimensions of the input, followed by two 3 × 3 convolutions, a chain operation using the matching feature orientation from the contracting path, a batch normalizing layer, and a ReLU activation function are all added together. The concatenation operation allows the network to preserve spatial information and high-level features from the contracting path. The U-Net architecture also has a balanced skip connection that connects the corresponding layers of the contracting and expanding paths. These skip connections allow the network to recover fine-grained details and spatial information that might have been lost during the downsampling operation. The final step in the algorithm involves passing the output of the expanding path via a 1 × 1 convolutional layer with a sigmoid activation function. A likelihood projection of the input image's size is generated. The likelihood that a given pixel in the input image is part of the object of interest is represented by each pixel in the likelihood projection.

This segmentation algorithm is trained in Python using the Keras API with Tensorflow on an Intel Core i7 with NVIDIA Tesla Pascal 100 GPU with 16GB of RAM. An input training shape of $256 \times 256 \times 3$ is used to train the image-based model on 150 epochs using the Adam v.2 optimizer with patience of 5 virtues and 25860163 trainable parameters.

15.3.3 MALOCCLUSION DETECTION

Once the tooth regions have been segmented from the original radiographic images, the segmented outputs can be used for detecting malocclusions in the teeth. There are 400 training images in an orthodontically confirmed training subset of the TDD, 219 of which are positive (maloccluded) and 181 of which are negative. Neural network models, however, are frequently data-hungry. Naturally, the model performs better when it has been trained on more data. Therefore, a data augmenter has been used to analyze and rectify the class imbalance to return robust results by minimizing the equivalence bias. Image transformations are used to augment the dataset to strengthen the size of the dataset and balance the classes accordingly. Here are the commonly used image transformations in data augmentation: (Figure 15.4)

a. Rotation: Rotating an image involves rotating it by a certain or a random angle within a specified range. This transformation helps the model become invariant to the orientation of objects within the image.
b. Translation: Translation shifts an image horizontally and/or vertically. To make the model more resistant to adjustments in object position within the image, minor translations are applied at random.
c. Scaling: Scaling involves resizing an image by zooming in or zooming out. It helps the model handle variations in object size and distance from the camera.
d. Flipping: Flipping helps the model learn features that are invariant to flips. Horizontal flipping can be suitable in scenarios where left-right symmetry exists, while vertical flipping can be beneficial for top-bottom symmetry.
e. Shearing: Shearing transforms an image by tilting it along one axis while keeping the other axis unchanged. It introduces distortions that make the model more robust to shear transformations in real-world scenarios.
f. Elastic Deformations: These deformations simulate local deformations by distorting the image using a grid-based deformation approach. It introduces random local distortions to improve the model's ability to handle deformations or fluctuations in shape.
g. Random Cropping: Randomly cropping inconsequential parts of images helps the model focus on specific regions of interest. It also simulates object occlusion or incomplete views, making the model more robust to such scenarios.

These image transformations can be combined and applied with appropriate parameters to create multiple augmented samples from each original image. The augmented training dataset has a total of 2000 images with 1000 images belonging

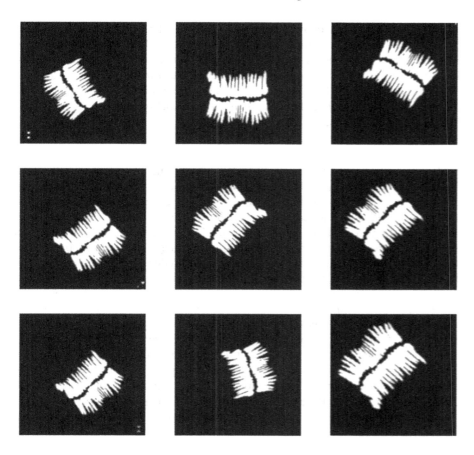

FIGURE 15.4   Results of data augmentation.

to each class. The train-to-test dataset size ratio is kept at 8:2. This means that out of the 2000 images in the training dataset, 1600 images are present in the training subset while 400 images are in the testing subset.

Once the dataset has been augmented, a neural network classifier is leveraged to segregate the segmented dental image samples as positively or negatively maloccluded. The classifier used in this model is ResNet50 [28]. ResNet-50 is a DNN architecture that has been widely used for image classification tasks. "ResNet" stands for "Residual Network," which refers to the use of residual blocks in the network's design. Residual blocks are a key component that allow the network to traverse deep roots while mitigating the problem of vanishing gradients commonly faced by binary classifiers. As the name suggests, ResNet-50 consists of 50 convolutional layers, including residual blocks, pooling layers, fully connected layers, and a sigmoid layer for binary classification. The network is organized in a hierarchical manner, where the input image passes through multiple layers. The initial convolution layers of ResNet-50 perform basic low-level feature extraction, such as detecting edges, corners, and textures. These convolution layers have a kernel size 3 × 3 and filters ranging from 64 to 512. These layers are followed by a string of residual blocks containing multiple convolutional layers for a more inclusive, minute-level feature extraction. These Residual blocks employed in the ResNet-50 architecture utilize "skip" connections. These connections skip out the layers in the network that might cause the derivative (gradient) to disappear. The skip connections allow the gradient to bypass (or "skip") one or more layers, enabling the network to learn residual mappings.

$$y = \mathcal{F}(x, \{W_i\}) + W_s x \qquad (15.1)$$

Mathematically, a skip connection in ResNet-50 adds the input of a residual block directly to its output. Through this method, the gradient can flow through the skip connection without passing through multiple nonlinear activation functions that might cause the gradient to reduce unprecedentedly and ultimately vanish. By using these connections for identity mapping, the model can learn the difference between the input and the desired output, facilitating the training of deeper networks. After convolution layers, pooling layers are employed to reduce spatial dimensions and capture the most salient features by identifying the highest-valued patch. Pooling layers downsample the feature maps, retaining the most important information while reducing computational complexity. Fully-connected layers are used after downsampling layers to vectorize the learned features and perform classification by mapping the features to the output classes. The final layer of the architecture uses the sigmoid activation function to predict the probability of belongingness of each class. In this model, we are classifying segmented outputs into two classes: negative malocclusions and positive malocclusions. This is a standard binary classification problem; therefore, the Binary Cross Entropy loss function has been used as a feedback signal to update the model's parameters based on the discrepancy between the predicted output and the actual target variable's values. The model is trained for 200 epochs using the Adam v.2 optimizer with a patience of 5 virtues and 14677825 trainable parameters in Python using the Keras API on TensorFlow 2.0 on an Intel Core i7 processor with an NVIDIA Tesla Pascal 100 GPU and 16GB RAM. The complete model architecture can be viewed in Figure 15.5.

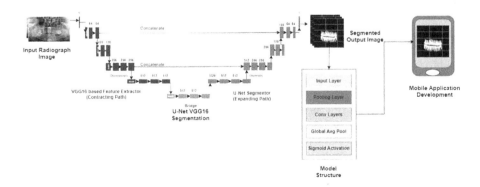

FIGURE 15.5 Methodology architecture.

15.3.4 MOBILE APPLICATION DEVELOPMENT

The fully-trained model can be shipped into production by shaping a web-based/mobile-based application around it. This application would enable dental patients to test themselves for malocclusions from the comfort of their houses without paying visits to the dentist. This automation can be brought into effect using application description provided through Flask or Django. In this method, we have used Microsoft Power Apps to effectively model an application for malocclusion segmentation and detection by exploiting our ensemble. The User-Interface (UI) can be viewed in Figure 15.6. The UI can be improvised accordingly to ensure unbiased accessibility to oral and dental health

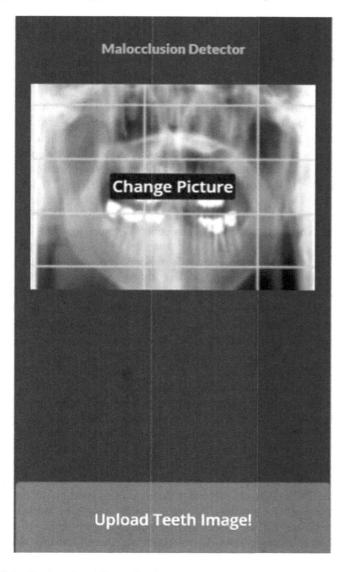

FIGURE 15.6   Deployed mobile application.

through AI intervention. To measure the effectivity of the suggested ensemble, its performance is compared with that of other up-to-the-minute methods.

15.4 RESULTS AND DISCUSSION

To gauge the performance of our model, it has been compared with various other updated technologies that have been predominantly used in the past for segmenting dental skeletons and detecting the presence of malocclusions in them. The performance of the model is validated in multiple steps. First, the segmentation module is validated on the 100 test images. Secondly, the classifier module is validated on 400 test images in the augmented dataset.

15.4.1 QUALITATIVE ANALYSIS

The performance of the segmentation module can be visually perceived by plotting the original ground truth (real label) against the segmented result. A high extent of similarity between the predicted output and the real label would indicate better model performance. This is because the ground truth is the binary mask of the tooth region that has been explicitly extracted. Severe cutting-edge segmentation techniques have been juxtaposed with the proposed ensemble to stalwartly back the claims of robustness and the effectivity of the proposed technique. The methods compared with the proposed model are TsegNet [54], BiseNet [56], KCNet [55] and EEDNet [53]. It can be visually attested to how TSegNet returns a distorted output with unevenness in the tooth structures. The segmentation product of BiseNet is heavily warped with multiple instances of inaccurate pixel intensity reproduction as several locations outside the tooth region have also been predicted as dental structures. KCNet did a better job than the former two models. However, it failed to perfectly encapsulate the dimensional difference between the upper jaw and lower jaw counterparts of each tooth. EEDNet returned a satisfactory output but failed to copy the exact girth of the teeth in the output, thus reducing the overall segmentation accuracy. Therefore, it is concluded that the performance of the proposed ensemble reigns superior with negligible incorrect pixel intensity localization, clear tooth wise segmentation and almost perfect dimensional reproduction as was seen in the ground truth. (Figure 15.7)

After qualitatively assessing the performance of the segmentation module, the performance of the classification module needs to be attested. To ensure compatibility and enhanced user satisfaction, our proposed classifier has been juxtaposed to other modern classification algorithms. DenseNet 121 [58], VGG16 [59], Inception V3 [60], and Cut outs-based, contextually-driven CNNs [62]. To perceive the performance of the models visually, we have leveraged Grad-CAMs.

Grad-CAM (Gradient-weighted Class Activation Mapping) is a cutting-edge map scheme used for analyzing and comprehending the internal workings and adeptness mechanisms of CNNs. It assists in locating the areas of an input image that significantly influence the predictions provided by the network. Grad-CAM analysis is typically performed on CNNs that use global average pooling (GAP) layers to extract spatial minutiae. This is because GAP layers retain spatial information and allow for the generation of class activation maps. Grad-CAM analysis is used to enhance

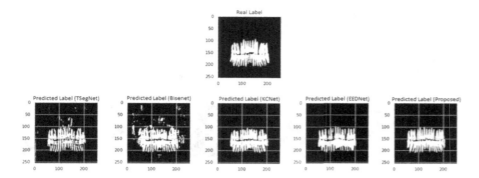

FIGURE 15.7 Real label vs predicted labels of the five compared models.

the interpretability of CNNs in vision related tasks. By visualizing the regions of an input image that are most relevant to the network's predictions, Grad-CAM provides insights into the model's heuristic process. This technique finds applications in model interpretability, enabling researchers and practitioners to understand which parts of the image the network focuses on and providing explanations for its behavior. Grad-CAM analysis also aids in model debugging by identifying potential issues or biases in the network's predictions, leading to improvements in model performance and reliability. To emphatically highlight the model's performance, the Grad-CAM analysis has been done on the original input radiograph which contains a larger domain of gray values as compared to the segmented binary masks. Through Fig. 4.1 of a maloccluded radiograph, it is seen that the cut-out-driven contextual CNN performed poorly and highlighted insignificant regions while developing the class activation map. It fails to demarcate between the different tooth regions which contributed towards the malocclusion's detection. DenseNet-121 and VGG16, albeit performed better than the contextual CNN, still failed to effectively capture the local features contributing towards the malocclusion. Inception V3 did a fairly good job in recognizing the critical regions of interest, however, the extent of attention applied towards the malocclusive teeth was less than anticipated. The proposed model beats all the aforementioned methods by directing exactly the required amount of attention (mapped in red and yellow)to the malocclusive teeth appearing throughout the jaw region. This emphasizes the computational resilience and computational efficiency of the proposed ensemble.

The effectivity of the proposed method can also be attested to by analyzing negatively maloccluded images through Grad-CAMs. Unlike in positively mal-occluded images, instead of analyzing anomalous tooth segments, the perfect alignment of a single jaw needs to be validated. The contextual method merely analyzes the anomalous teeth and fails to address the problem at hand. The outputs of DenseNet and VGG16 identify the entire jaw of teeth, which is not a concrete proof to support claims of malocclusion deprivation. The proposed model does a phenomenal job at identifying tooth region alignment by entirely interpreting the teeth orientation in the lower jaw, along with the hinge separating the mandible from the upper jaw. This provides all the required evidentiary support required to validate the non-prevalence of malocclusions. (Figures 15.8–15.10)

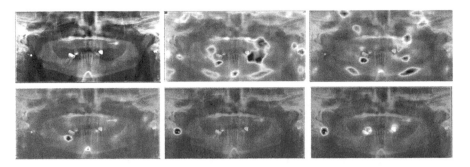

FIGURE 15.8   Grad-CAMs for maloccluded samples.

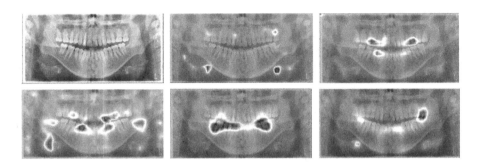

FIGURE 15.9   Grad-CAMs for non-maloccluded samples.

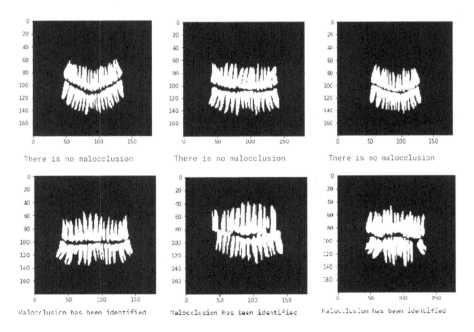

FIGURE 15.10   Results for the deployed model showcasing segmentation predictions.

15.4.2 QUANTITATIVE ANALYSIS

The performance of the model can also be perceived in quantifiable numeric metric values. Several performance metrics have been leveraged to effectively measure the performance of the model. For the segmentation module, the performance metrics used are:

- Dice coefficient: Dice coefficient is a statistical measure used to assess the similarity or overlap between two sets or samples [65]. The Dice coefficient is defined as twice the intersection of two sets divided by the sum of their sizes. In terms of formula, it can be expressed as:

$$\text{Dice coefficient} = \frac{(2 * |A \cap B|)}{(|A| + |B|)} \tag{15.2}$$

where A and B are the two sets being compared, $|A|$ represents the size (cardinality) of set A, and $|B|$ represents the size of set B. The intersection of sets A and B, denoted as $A \cap B$, represents the elements that are common to both sets. Dice coefficient is often used as a measure of agreement or accuracy between the segmented regions and ground truth annotations. It provides a quantification of how well the segmentation algorithm performs in capturing the true object boundaries or regions of interest. Higher values of the Dice coefficient indicate better agreement or similarity between the segmentation and ground truth.

- IOU (Intersection over Union), or Jaccard index, is a metric used to evaluate the overlap between two bounding boxes or segmentation masks [66]. It is commonly used in tasks such as object detection and instance segmentation. The IOU score is calculated by dividing the area of intersection between two regions by the area of their union. An IOU score of 1 indicates perfect overlap, meaning the predicted and ground truth regions are identical. A score of 0 indicates no overlap or complete dissimilarity between the regions. In terms of formula, it can be expressed as:

$$\text{IOU} = \frac{\text{Area of Intersection}}{\text{Area of Union}} \tag{15.3}$$

- Accuracy: A standard criterion for assessing a classification model's performance is accuracy. It counts the number of examples in a dataset that were successfully predicted as a percentage of all the instances. By dividing the number of accurate forecasts by the total number of predictions made, accuracy is obtained. For example, if a model correctly classifies 90 out of 100 instances in a dataset, the accuracy would be 90%. In formula form, it can be expressed as:

$$Accuracy = \frac{\text{(Number of Correct Predictions)}}{\text{(Total Number of Predictions)}} \tag{15.4}$$

- Precision: In binary classification tasks, precision is a performance indicator frequently used to assess how accurately a model predicts the positive outcomes. Out of all the positive predictions made by the model, it quantifies the percentage of real positive forecasts. By dividing the total number of true positives (TP) by the total number of true positives and false positives (FP), precision is determined. In formula form, it can be expressed as:

$$Precision = \frac{TP}{TP + FP} \tag{15.5}$$

True positives (TP) represent the instances that are correctly predicted as positive by the model, while false positives (FP) represent the instances that are incorrectly predicted as positive. (Table 15.1)

It can be quantifiably estimated that the proposed hybrid U-Net model returns drastically better results than the other DL-based models. It has the highest values of dice coefficient, IoU score, Accuracy and Precision. EEDNet and KCNet follow closely with the 2nd and 3rd best results for all the metrics. However, TSegNet and BiseNet proved ineffective, as they returned the poorest performance metrics in each of the scenarios. These quantitative metrics further back the claims presented by the quantitative analysis, thus proving the resilience and efficiency of the proposed model. (Figs 15.12 and 15.13)

The detection module can be quantifiably evaluated using a different set of performance metrics. The metrics are: (Table 15.2)

- Sensitivity, sometimes referred to as Recall or genuine Positive Rate, is the share of genuine positive predictions that come true out of all instances of positive data that really exist. It measures how well the model can identify positive occurrences. By dividing the total number of true positives (TP) by the sum of true positives and false negatives (FN), the sensitivity is determined. In formula form, it can be expressed as:

TABLE 15.1

Comparison of Performance Metrics for the Segmentation Models

Model Name	Dice Coefficient	IoU Score	Accuracy	Precision
TSegNet [54]	0.7823	0.5865	0.6882	0.6789
BiseNet [56]	0.7463	0.5674	0.5947	0.6645
KCNet [55]	0.8388	0.7973	0.7332	0.7156
EEDNet [53]	0.8872	0.7996	0.7451	0.8956
Hybrid U-Net VGG16 (Proposed)	**0.8956**	**0.8909**	**0.8562**	**0.9882**

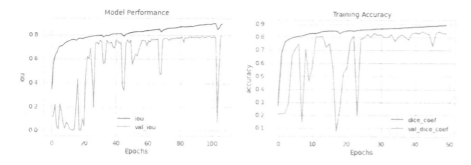

FIGURE 15.11 Model performance and training accuracy for the proposed model.

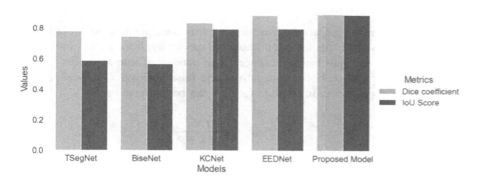

FIGURE 15.12 Dice coefficient and IoU of the models.

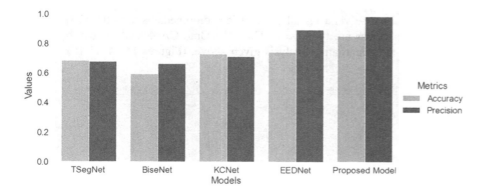

FIGURE 15.13 Accuracy and precision of the models.

TABLE 15.2

Comparison of Performance Metrics for the Detection Models

Model Name	Accuracy	Sensitivity	Specificity	Precision
Contextual CNN [62]	0.7654	0.7790	0.7567	0.7432
DenseNet-121 [58]	0.7543	0.8320	0.7956	0.8567
VGG16 [59]	0.7432	0.8543	0.8926	0.8657
InceptionV3 [60]	0.9345	0.9546	0.9435	0.9675
Proposed Model	0.9900	1.0000	0.9978	0.9875

$$Senstivity = \frac{TP}{TP + FN} \qquad (15.6)$$

- The percentage of accurate negative predictions relative to all actual negative events in the dataset is known as specificity. It measures how well the model can spot bad occurrences. The number of true negatives (TN) divided by the total of true negatives and false positives (FP) is used to calculate specificity. In formula form, it can be expressed as:

$$Specificity = \frac{TN}{TN + FP} \qquad (15.7)$$

The proposed model returns the best possible output in all the metrics. Inception V3 is the 2nd best model and returns an accuracy of 93% with the sensitivity and specificity scores of 95.4% and 94.3% respectively. DenseNet-121 and VGG16 return comparable, yet unsatisfactory output results with a deviation of 14% and 15% from the proposed model's accuracy respectively. Contextual CNN had the poorest performance vis-à-vis all the metrics combined. Its sensitivity, specificity and precision values are the lowest. Thus, the Grad-CAM analysis can be further validated by the quantitative analysis given above. (Figures 15.14–15.16)

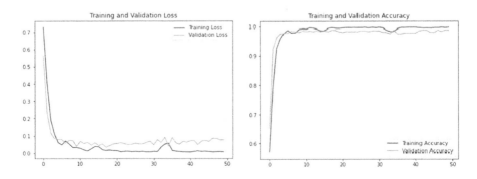

FIGURE 15.14 Training and validation loss and accuracy.

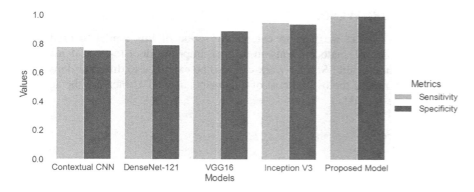

FIGURE 15.15 Sensitivity and specificity of the models.

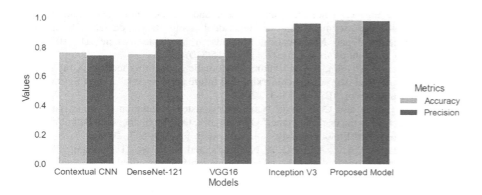

FIGURE 15.16 Accuracy and precision of the models.

15.5 CONCLUSION

In this paper, we propose a deep learning-based ensemble to effectively segment and predict the presence of malocclusions in teeth by analyzing panoramic, extraoral X-ray dental images. The developed model is then dispatched into a Flask-based environment to develop a user-friendly application. We found quantitatively that our proposed model was able to outperform several state-of-the-art segmentation techniques such as TSegNet and KCNet, and detection techniques such as DenseNet-121, VGG16 and Inception V3 in terms of performance metrics such as dice coefficient, Jaccard index, accuracy, precision, sensitivity, and specificity. The performance of the model can also be qualitatively analyzed by critically examining the Grad-CAM activation heatmaps which capture important features in the X-ray radiograph that were primarily taken into consideration by the proposed model while formulating decisions.

15.6 FUTURE WORK

In our future works, we plan to extend the scope of this model to predict the different classes of malocclusions to further improve door-to-door dentistry to democratize oral health. Similar work can also be extended to different domains of healthcare to reduce the overall cost of diagnosis , as well as increase the accuracy of predictions [67,68].

REFERENCES

1. A. Rana, G. Yauney, L. C. Wong, O. Gupta, A. Muftu, and P. Shah, "Automated segmentation of gingival diseases from oral images," In 2017 IEEE Healthcare Innovations and Point of Care Technologies (HIPOCT), vol. 6, pp. 144–147, IEEE, Nov 2017.
2. X. Xu, C. Liu, and Y. Zheng, "3D tooth segmentation and labelling using deep convolutional neural networks," IEEE Trans. on Visualization and Computer Graphics, vol. 25, no. 7, pp. 2336–2348, 2018.
3. H. C. Kang, C. Choi, J. Shin, J. Lee, and Y. G. Shin, "Fast and accurate semiautomatic segmentation of individual teeth from dental CT images," Computational and Mathematical Methods in Medicine. Article ID 810796, 12 pages, 2015. http://dx.doi.org/10.1155/2015/810796
4. G. Silva, L. Oliveira, and M. Pithon, "Automatic segmenting teeth in X-ray images: Trends, a novel data set, benchmarking and future perspectives," Expert Systems with Applications, vol. 107, pp. 15–31, 2018.
5. C. H. Huang, and C. Y. Hsu, "Computer-assisted orientation of dental periapical radiographs to the occlusal plane," Oral Surgery, Oral Medicine, Oral Pathology, Oral Radiology, and Endodontology, vol. 105, no. 5, pp. 649–653, 2008.
6. R. Indraswari, A. Z. Arifin, D. A. Navastara, and N. Jawas, "Teeth segmentation on dental panoramic radiographs using decimation-free directional filter bank thresholding and multistage adaptive thresholding," In 2015 International Conference on Information & Communication. Technology and Systems (ICTS), pp. 49–54, IEEE, September 2015.
7. M. K. Alsmadi, "A hybrid Fuzzy C-Means and Neutrosophic for jaw lesions segmentation," Ain Shams Engineering Journal, vol. 9, no. 4, pp. 697–706, 2018.
8. T. M. Tuan, "Dental segmentation from X-ray images using semisupervised fuzzy clustering with spatial constraints," Engineering Applications of Artificial Intelligence, vol. 59, pp. 186–195, 2017.
9. K. Anuradha, and K. Sankaranarayanan, "Detection of oral tumor based on marker controlled watershed algorithm," International Journal of Computer Applications, vol. 52, no. 2, 2012.
10. A. Agrawal, and R. K. Bhogal, "A review–edge detection techniques in dental images," In International Conference on ISMAC in Computational Vision and Bio-Engineering, pp. 1359–1378, Springer, Cham., May 2018.
11. O. Ronneberger, P. Fischer, and T. Brox, "U-net: Convolutional networks for biomedical image segmentation," InMedical image computing and computer-assisted intervention–MICCAI 2015: 18th international conference, Munich, Germany, Proceedings, part III (pp. 234-241). Springer International Publishing. October 2015: 234–241.
12. M. Drozdzal, E. Vorontsov, G. Chartrand, S. Kadoury, and C. Pal, "The importance of skip connections in biomedical image segmentation," In Deep learning and data labeling for medical applications, pp. 179–187, Springer, 2016.

13. G. Jader, J. Fontineli, M. Ruiz, K. Abdalla, M. Pithon, and L. Oliveira, "Deep instance segmentation of teeth in panoramic X-ray images," In 2018 31st SIBGRAPI Conference on Graphics, Patterns and Images (SIBGRAPI), pp. 400–407, IEEE, October 2018.

14. A. Koschan, "Perception-based 3D triangle mesh segmentation using fast marching watersheds," in Proceedings of the IEEE Conference on Computer Vision and Pattern Recognition, pp. II-27–II-32, 2003.

15. M. P. Muresan, R. Barbura, and S. Nedevschi, "Teeth detection and dental problem classification in panoramic X-ray images using deep learning and image processing techniques," pp. 457–463, 2020. 10.1109/ICCP51029.2020.9266244.

16. A. Betul Oktay. "Tooth detection with convolutional neural networks," 2017 Medical Technologies National Congress (TIPTEKNO), Trabzon, Turkey, 2017.

17. S. Yamany, and A. Farag, "Surfacing signatures: An orientation independent free-form surface representation scheme for the purpose of objects registration and matching," Pattern Analysis and Machine Intelligence, IEEE Transactions on, vol. 24, pp. 1105–1120, 2002.

18. Y. Lee, S. Lee, A. Shamir, D. Cohen-Or, and H. P. Seidel, "Intelligent mesh scissoring using 3D snakes," in Proceedings of the Pacific Conference on Computer Graphics and Applications, pp. 279–287, 2004.

19. Y. Lee, S. Lee, A. Shamir, D. Cohenor, and H. Seidel, "Mesh scissoring with minima rule and part salience," Computer Aided Geometric Design, vol. 22, no. 5, pp. 444–465, 2005.

20. L. Fan, M. Meng, and L. Liu, "Sketch-based mesh cutting," Graphical Models Image Process Computer Vision, Graphics, and Image Processing., vol. 74, no. 6, pp. 292–301, 2012.

21. M. Meng, L. Fan, and L. Liu, "A comparative evaluation of foreground/background sketch-based mesh segmentation algorithms," Computer Graphics, vol. 35, no. 3, pp. 650–660, 2011.

22. Z. Ji, L. Liu, Z. Chen, and G. Wang, "Easy mesh cutting," Computer Graphics Forum, vol. 25, no. 3, pp. 283–291, 2006.

23. K. Panetta, R. Rajendran, A. Ramesh, S. P. Rao, and S. Agaian, "Tufts dental database: A multimodal panoramic X-Ray dataset for benchmarking diagnostic systems," in IEEE Journal of Biomedical and Health Informatics, vol. 26, no. 4, pp. 1650–1659, April 2022.

24. Q. Yang, and X. Ji, "Automatic pixel-level crack detection for civil infrastructure using Unet++ and deep transfer learning," in IEEE Sensors Journal, vol. 21, no. 17, pp. 19165–19175, 1 Sept.1, 2021.

25. J. S. Suri et al., "UNet deep learning architecture for segmentation of vascular and non-vascular images: A microscopic look at UNet components buffered with pruning, explainable artificial intelligence, and bias," in IEEE Access, vol. 11, pp. 595–645, 2023.

26. J. Duan, and X. Liu, "Online monitoring of green pellet size distribution in haze-degraded images based on VGG16-LU-Net and haze judgment," in IEEE Transactions on Instrumentation and Measurement, vol. 70, pp. 1–16, 2021, Art no. 5006316.

27. O. K. Au, Y. Zheng, M. Chen, P. Xu, and C. Tai, "Mesh segmentation with concavity-aware fields," IEEE Transactions on Visualization and Computer Graphics, vol. 18, no. 7, pp. 1125–1134, Jul. 2012.

28. Z. J. Xu, R. F. Wang, J. Wang, and D. H. Yu, "Parkinson's disease detection based on spectrogram-deep convolutional generative adversarial network sample augmentation," in IEEE Access, vol. 8, pp. 206888–206900, 2020.

29. Y. Chen, H. Du, Z. Yun, S. Yang, Z. Dai, L. Zhong, Q. Feng, and W. Yang, "Automatic segmentation of individual tooth in dental CBCT images from tooth surface map by a multi-task FCN," IEEE Access, vol. 8, pp. 97296–97309, 2020.

30. Y. Wang, S. Asafi, O. Van Kaick, H. Zhang, D. Cohenor, and B. Chen, "Active co-analysis of a set of shapes," ACM Transactions on Graphics, vol. 31, no. 6, 2012, Art. no. 165.

31. H. Benhabiles, G. Lavoue, J. Vandeborre, and M. Daoudi, "Learning boundary edges for 3D-mesh segmentation," Computer Graphics Forum, vol. 30, no. 8, pp. 2170–2182, 2011.

32. J. Park, Y. Kim, J. Kim, and T. K. Song, "Continuous wave dental Doppler ultrasound system for measuring pulp blood flow," 2021 IEEE Biomedical Circuits and Systems Conference (BioCAS), Berlin, Germany, pp. 1–5, 2021.

33. M. Grzegorzek, M. Trierscheid, D. Papoutsis, and D. Paulus, "A multi-stage approach for 3D teeth segmentation from dentition surfaces," in Proceedings on the International Conference on Signal and Image Processing, pp. 521–530, 2010.

34. D. Milošević, M. Vodanović, I. Galić, and M. Subašlć, "A comprehensive exploration of neural networks for forensic analysis of adult single tooth X-ray images," in IEEE Access, vol. 10, pp. 70980–71002, 2022.

35. T. Yuan, W. Liao, N. Dai, X. Cheng, and Q. Yu, "Single-tooth modeling for 3D dental model," Journal of Biomedical Imaging, 2010: 1–14.

36. Y. Kumar, R. Janardan, B. E. Larson, and J. Moon, "Improved segmentation of teeth in dental models," Computer-Aided Design and Applications, vol. 8, no. 2, pp. 211–224, 2013.

37. T. Kronfeld, D. Brunner, and G. Brunnett, "Snake-based segmentation of teeth from virtual dental casts," Computer-Aided Design and Applications, vol. 7, no. 2, pp. 221–233, 2013.

38. A. Lurie, G. M. Tosoni, J. Tsimikas, and F. Walker Jr, "Recursive hierarchic segmentation analysis of bone mineral density changes on digital panoramic images," Oral Surgery, Oral Medicine, Oral Pathology and Oral Radiology, vol. 113, no. 4, pp. 549–558, 2012.

39. C. K. Modi, and N. P. Desai, "A simple and novel algorithm for automatic selection of ROI for dental radiograph segmentation," In 2011 24th Canadian Conference on Electrical and Computer Engineering (CCECE) (pp. 000504–000507). IEEE, 2011, May.

40. P. L. Lin, P. W. Huang, P. Y. Huang, and H. C. Hsu, "Alveolar bone-loss area localization in periodontitis radiographs based on threshold segmentation with a hybrid feature fused of intensity and the H-value of fractional Brownian motion model," Computer Methods and Programs in Biomedicine, vol. 121, no. 3, pp. 117–126, 2015.

41. N. S. Ahmad, Z. M. Zaki, and W. Ismail, "September. Region of adaptive threshold segmentation between mean, median and otsu threshold for dental age assessment," In 2014 International Conference on Computer, Communications, and Control Technology (I4CT), pp. 353–356, IEEE, 2014.

42. R. Indraswari, A. Z. Arifin, D. A. Navastara, and N. Jawas, "Teeth segmentation on dental panoramic radiographs using decimation-free directional filter bank thresholding and multistage adaptive thresholding," In 2015 International Conference on Information & Communication Technology and Systems (ICTS), pp. 49–54, IEEE, 2015, September.

43. J. W. H. Tangelder, and R. C. Veltkamp, "A survey of content-based 3D shape retrieval methods," Multimedia Tools Applications, vol. 39, no. 3, 2008, Art. no. 441.

44. R. Litman, A. Bronstein, M. Bronstein, and U. Castellani, "Supervised learning of bag-of-features shape descriptors using sparse coding," Computer Graphics Forum, vol. 33, no. 5, pp. 127–136, 2014.

45. C. W. Wang, C. T. Huang, J. H. Lee, C. H. Li, S. W. Chang, M. J. Siao, T. M. Lai, B. Ibragimov, T. Vrtovec, O. Ronneberger, and P. Fischer, "A benchmark for comparison of dental radiography analysis algorithms," Medical Image Analysis, vol. 31, pp. 63–76, 2016.
46. M. K. Alsmadi, "A hybrid Fuzzy C-Means and Neutrosophic for jaw lesions segmentation." Ain Shams Engineering Journal, vol. 9, no. 4, 2018.
47. R. B. Ali, R. Ejbali, and M. Zaied, "GPU-based segmentation of dental x-ray images using active contours without edges." In 2015 15th International Conference on Intelligent Systems Design and Applications (ISDA), pp. 505–510. IEEE, 2015.
48. Md M. Hasan, W. Ismail, R. Hassan, and A. Yoshitaka, "Automatic segmentation of jaw from panoramic dental X-ray images using GVF snakes." In 2016 World Automation Congress (WAC), pp. 1–6. IEEE, 2016.
49. H. Li, G. Sun, H. Sun, and W. Liu, "Watershed algorithm based on morphology for dental X-ray images segmentation," In 2012 IEEE 11th International Conference on Signal Processing, vol. 2, pp. 877–880. IEEE, 2012.
50. C. H. Shen, H. Fu, K. Chen, and S. M. Hu, "Structure recovery by part assembly," ACM Transactions on Graphics, vol. 31, no. 6, pp. 1–11, 2012.
51. X. Xie, K. Xu, N. J. Mitra, D. Cohen-Or, and B. Chen, "Sketchto-design: Context-based part assembly," Computer Graphics Forum, vol. 32, no. 8, pp. 233–245, 2013.
52. FCN with U-Net – T. L. Koch, M. Perslev, C. Igel, and S. S. Brandt, "Accurate segmentation of dental panoramic radiographs with U-NETS," 2019 IEEE 16th International Symposium on Biomedical Imaging (ISBI 2019), Venice, Italy, pp. 15–19, 2019.
53. EED-Net – Z. Kong et al., "Automated maxillofacial segmentation in panoramic dental X-ray images using an efficient encoder-decoder network," in IEEE Access, vol. 8, pp. 207822–207833, 2020.
54. TSegNet – Z. Cui, C. Li, N. Chen, G. Wei, R. Chen, Y. Zhou, D. Shen, and W. Wang, "TSegNet: An efficient and accurate tooth segmentation network on 3D dental model," Medical Image Analysis, vol. 69, pp. 101949, 2021, ISSN 1361-8415.
55. KCNet – S. Lin, X. Hao, Y. Liu, et al., "Lightweight deep learning methods for panoramic dental X-ray image segmentation," Neural Computation and Applications, vol. 35, pp. 8295–8306, 2023.
56. J. Zhang, K. Yang, C. Ma, S. Reiß, K. Peng, and R. Stiefelhagen, "Bending reality: distortion-aware transformers for adapting to panoramic semantic segmentation," In: Proceedings of the IEEE/CVF Conference on Computer Vision and Pattern Recognition, pp 16917–16927, 2022.
57. M. Aljabri, S. S. Aljameel, N. Min-Allah, J. Alhuthayfi, L. Alghamdi, N. Alduhailan, R. Alfehaid et al., "Canine impaction classification from panoramic dental radiographic images using deep learning models." Informatics in Medicine Unlocked, vol. 30, 2022: 1–10.
58. A. Gurses, and A. B. Oktay, "Tooth restoration and dental work detection on panoramic dental images via CNN," 2020 Medical Technologies Congress (TIPTEKNO), Antalya, Turkey, pp. 1–4, 2020, doi: 10.1109/TIPTEKNO50054.2020.9299272.
59. S. Ji, W. Li, B. Zhang, L. Zhou, and C. Duan, "Bucket teeth detection based on faster region convolutional neural network," in IEEE Access, vol. 9, pp. 17649–17661, 2021.
60. D. Saini, R. Jain, and A. Thakur, "Dental caries early detection using convolutional neural network for tele dentistry," 2021 7th International Conference on Advanced Computing and Communication Systems (ICACCS), Coimbatore, India, pp. 958–963, 2021.
61. V. G. Kim, W. Li, N. J. Mitra, S. Chaudhuri, S. Diverdi, and T. Funkhouser, "Learning part-based templates from large collections of 3D shapes," ACM Transactions on Graphics, vol. 32, no. 4, 2013, Art. no. 70.

62. M. F. Harun, A. A. Samah, M. I. A. Shabuli, H. A. Majid, H. Hashim, N. A. Ismail, S. M. Abdullah, and A. Alias, "Incisor malocclusion using cut-out method and convolutional neural network," Progress in Microbes and Molecular Biology, vol. 5, no. 1, pp. 1–16, 2022.

63. S. Talaat, A. Kaboudan, W. Talaat, B. Kusnoto, F. Sanchez, M. H. Elnagar, C. Bourauel, and A. Ghoneima, "The validity of an artificial intelligence application for assessment of orthodontic treatment need from clinical images," In Seminars in Orthodontics (Vol. 27, No. 2, pp. 164–171). WB Saunders, 2021, June.

64. Y. Song, X. Qiao, Y. Iwamoto, and Y. Chen, "Automatic cephalometric landmark detection on X-ray images using a deep-learning method," Applied Sciences, vol. 10, no. 7, p. 2547, 2020. 10.3390/app10072547

65. P.-S. Wang, Y. Liu, Y.-X. Guo, S. Chun-Yu, and X. Tong, "O-CNN: Octree-based convolutional neural networks or 3D shape analysis," ACM Transactions on Graphics, vol. 36, no. 4, 2017, Art. no. 72.

66. C. Farabet, C. Couprie, L. Najman, and Y. Lecun, "Learning hierarchical features for scene labeling," IEEE Transactions on Pattern Analysis and Machine Intelligence, vol. 35, no. 8, pp. 1915–1929, Aug. 2013.

67. A. Singhal, M. Phogat, D. Kumar, A. Kumar, M. Dahiya, and V. K. Shrivastava, "Study of deep learning techniques for medical image analysis: A review," Materials Today: Proceedings, vol. 56, Part 1, pp. 209–214, 2022.

68. A. Bhardwaj, A. Bhatnagar, and A. Kumar, "Chapter 29 – Current trends of application of additive manufacturing in oral healthcare system," Editor(s): Ajay Kumar, Ravi Kant Mittal, Abid Haleem, In Additive manufacturing materials and technologies, advances in additive manufacturing, Elsevier, pp. 479–491, 2023.

16 Doctor's Assistive System Using Augmented Reality Glass

A. Reethika
Department of Electronics and Communication Engineering, Sri Ramakrishna Engineering College, Coimbatore, Tamil Nadu, India

P. Kanaga Priya
Department of Computer Science and Engineering, KPR Institute of Engineering and Technology, Coimbatore, Tamil Nadu, India

M.S. Cholaathiraj
Department of Artificial Intelligence and Machine Learning, Bannari Amman Institute of Technology, Sathyamangalam, Tamil Nadu, India

16.1 INTRODUCTION

In today's quick-paced world, technology is very crucial to the medical industry. The desire for innovative technology that may make doctors' jobs easier and more effective is greatest among surgeons. They quickly adopt new technology, enabling them to improve surgical outcomes and patient satisfaction. The field of augmented reality (AR) is quickly evolving and is widely accessible. As a result, they are applied to improve healthcare systems. To warn the surgeon if anything is strange about the patient, We are developing a technology that provides the surgeon with important patient data via an automated augmented reality glass. By showing pertinent digital information in the context of the actual world, augmented reality is a highly visual, interactive approach to connecting employees and enhancing corporate outcomes. The use of glasses or other devices to detect the physical environment and deliver additional information about the immediate surroundings is known as augmented reality. Researchers now have more opportunities to study the interactions between people and computers in both virtual and real environments because of augmented reality (AR). the real-time visualization of the human body is known as augmented reality in healthcare. Many different industries, including those in healthcare, entertainment, business, and education, are implementing augmented reality (AR). Future developments in AR are anticipated to be significant in

DOI: 10.1201/9781003404934-16

the healthcare industry. Physicians may gather information and keep track of their patient's health using augmented reality technology, which can be very beneficial. In terms of real-time data-based diagnosis and therapy, health practitioners can benefit from adopting augmented reality. Real-time digital patient data is provided using AR glass. A surgeon may inspect secret bodily activities and enhance the patient's therapy by using AR glasses. It continuously assesses the patient's health throughout the operation. This method minimizes unanticipated medical mishaps and is very helpful to surgeons. In a shorter length of time, it delivers precise findings. With the use of AR, surgeons may obtain patient imaging data and have a centralized view of their patient's data. Since it is challenging to physically evaluate a patient's wellness during surgery, the suggested method, the system must carefully monitor the bodily parameters. Nowadays, getting the right results will be very helpful for surgeons. The main goal is to use AR technology to measure metrics, assess patients' health, and produce notifications on augmented reality glasses in the event of any aberrant circumstances. To do this, sensors that gather and analyze data are inserted into the patient's body. The doctor's AR glasses then receive the data remotely. An alarm to the AR glasses is promptly delivered to the physician if the individual's health status is out of the ordinary. The doctor's course of action may depend on the patient's present state of health. Based on that they may take appropriate measures. Doctors have access to the past of several patients at any moment.

- Medical Training: Using augmented reality technology has the potential to expand the reach and efficacy of medical education in a variety of domains, from operating MRI scanners to carrying out intricate surgeries.
- Repair & Maintenance: Repairing and maintaining sophisticated machinery is one of the most prevalent industrial uses of AR. Repair and maintenance personnel are starting to employ augmented reality (AR) headsets and glasses while performing their tasks to provide them vital information on the spot, propose potential remedies, and point out potential issue spots, whether it be a vehicle motor or an MRI machine. The strength of this use case will only increase as machine-to-machine IoT technology develops and becomes capable of providing data straight to augmented reality headsets.
- Using virtual reality and augmented reality healthcare has progressed the medical pitch to the point where physicians can readily diagnose patients virtually. Both medical professionals and patients are aware that accuracy is crucial during surgery. AR can now help surgeons do operations more quickly. AR healthcare applications have the potential to save lives and provide patients with excellent treatment, Regardless of whether they are carrying out a minimally invasive surgery or detecting a liver tumor.

AR Display: It is clear that AR system displays have advanced during the past ten years. Some HMDs are now as big and heavy as a pair of sunglasses due to the shrinking of the HMD.

- Low brightness and low contrast are still the main issues with AR screens.
- The screens' low resolution (800 × 600 at most).
- The restricted field of vision.

Since the see-through items are not opaque, they cannot obscure the real things behind them in the majority of optical see-through displays. Depending on the background, this can obstruct the view. The written information shown in the area of vision may also seem highly hazy and hard to read. Furthermore, virtual things are always projected onto the display's plane even while the user is concentrating on actual, tangible items existing in the actual world. The user could nevertheless see the virtual item incorrectly even when it has been accurately calculated and projected.

Handheld devices: The mobile user can access a wide range of services using many different types of devices as terminals. Most of the gadgets that are currently on the market have several restrictions. Others have no or extremely restricted connectivity capabilities, while others have very modest screens and memory. To provide highly powerful and adaptable user terminals, certain new devices are being created and some are already on the market that combine the advantages of mobile phones with those of portable computers and GPS receivers. Since they can display data, information, and images while the user is looking at the actual environment, near-eye augmented reality devices can be utilized as portable head-up displays.

16.2 LITERATURE REVIEW

The use of virtual objects in conjunction with the real environment is known as augmented reality (AR) impression that they are coexisting in the same place. Clinical care utilizes AR because it offers a vision of the patients' interior anatomy without any intrusive treatments. AR is used in many healthcare settings and is intended for learners of all skill levels. However, this study lacks learning theories to inform the development of AR [1,2]. Therefore, in this project, we give surgeons a concrete example of how augmented reality may be used in operations by donning translucent glasses; they can be alerted when any parameters exceed the threshold values.

The software architecture for control is illustrated by receiving input data from the vehicle's ultrasonic sensors, processing it, and then transmitting it to higher levels within the system. The program operates by utilizing data obtained from ultrasonic sensors as its inputs [3]. A possible limitation of this solution is a bottleneck in computational power, particularly once a big volume of data from several sensors in one location needs to be handled at a judicious distance of period. We advise a certain degree of optimization as a result. Since just one sensor value is considered in this instance, it might become problematic if more sensors are placed nearby [4,5]. Therefore, we offer a networked architecture to read information from many types of sensors, including respiratory sensors, heartbeat sensors, and temperature sensors.

Developed augmented reality, and automobile assistance systems. After reading this research, we decided to apply a similar strategy for assisting physicians. Spatial augmented reality (SAR) technology can be employed in various devices, such as handheld gadgets, head-mounted displays (HMDs), smart glasses, stationary augmented reality and smart contact lenses. Image-guided surgery and robot-assisted surgery0 are0two important medical0applications. As0a result, there 0is a lot of research being done to include AR in tools that take advantage of the surgeon's intuitive ability [6,7]. Smart glasses, Handheld devices, smart lenses, stationary AR systems, displays on the head, and can all benefit from augmented reality technology. Image-guided surgery and robotic surgery are two crucial applications in the field of medicine.

A system called ARAV was developed to continuously track a patient's vital signs. This essay discusses many ideas and methods for moving patients from the lab to the operating room in the trauma room [8]. The ARAV (Augmented Reality Aided Vertebroplasty) project aims to implement augmented reality technology in surgical settings for performing vertebroplasty procedures. This involves introducing new strategies and ideas for incorporating AR technology into the operating theater. It uses real-time visualization of US slices that are simulated from CT [9].

The construction business is the topic of this study, which examines 120 papers from significant journal and conference databases between 2005 and 2011. All of the augmented reality prototyping toolkits are divided into five sections in the study: 2D marker-based AR for PC and camera, 3D object recognition-based AR for mobile, marker-less tools, and GPS compass-based AR [10–13]. Similar to how it is for rendered objects, the display specs also restrict the picture quality for the real view. Since actual and virtual objects have the same color gamut, brightness, resolution, accommodation, range of vision, etc., [14]. They may be combined more smoothly than with optical overlays. Since the production of the augmentation is already handled by the computer, as opposed to the actual overlay of light in the eye, the overlay is not user-dependent. An optical see-through system's final picture is typically unknown [15]. With optical overlays, a validation without contact is virtually ever feasible.

Over 75% of illnesses in China are chronic, according to data from the Ministry of Health, and have an annual mortality rate of about 85.5% when diabetes and cardiovascular diseases are taken into account. Internet healthcare typically concentrates on chronic high-risk diseases and sub-healthy groups because of the significant number of sub-healthy groups, as well as the complex and expensive nature of chronic diseases [16–18]. Therefore, IoT-based human health monitoring has become increasingly popular. China's aging population and rising standard of life are to blame for the country's sub-healthy population's rise in chronic ailments. As a result, the Chinese people have a fundamental demand for healthcare facilities and services that are effective, convenient, secure, and reliable. Establishing a health monitoring system is crucial to enable remote and real-time monitoring of health status [19]. To effectively handle the present difficulties encountered by networks, companies, and governments worldwide, IoT technology integrates the Internet and smart sensing devices. A new method of using smart systems and intelligent devices to analyze data for diverse purposes has resulted from the emergence of IoT. The fundamental IoT framework with a generalized architecture is suggested in this article [20].

Using ground-breaking technology, the Doctors Assistive System (DAS) with Augmented Reality Glass has the power to completely change the healthcare sector. Augmented reality technology, which can superimpose virtual things over the real world, has already shown promise in industries including gaming, education, and entertainment [21,22]. However, the employment of this technology in healthcare, particularly with the Doctors Assistive System, has the potential to significantly enhance patient outcomes and transform medical practices.

16.3 IMPORTANCE OF DOCTORS ASSISTIVE SYSTEM USING AUGMENTED REALITY GLASS

Using ground-breaking technology, the Doctors Assistive System with Augmented Reality Glass has the power to completely change the healthcare sector. Augmented reality technology, which can superimpose virtual things over the real world, has already shown promise in industries including gaming, education, and entertainment. However, the employment of this technology in healthcare, particularly with the Doctors Assistive System, is likely to greatly improve patient outcomes then transform medical practices.

Doctors Assistive System's use of Augmented Reality Glass has several major advantages, including its capacity to improve the precision and accuracy of medical treatments. The device enables more precise diagnosis and treatments by giving clinicians real-time data and a thorough, 3D image of the patient's anatomy. This can therefore result in better patient outcomes and a lesser need for additional procedures or therapies. The capability of this technology to lower medical errors is another significant advantage. The technology can help to ensure that errors are discovered before they have a chance to influence patient outcomes by providing clinicians with pertinent medical information and notifications throughout procedures. Particularly in high-risk operations like surgery, this can be helpful.

Additionally, by giving patients a more engaging and participatory experience, the Doctors Assistive System with Augmented Reality Glass can significantly increase patient satisfaction. The device can help patients feel less anxious and have a better knowledge of their health and treatment plan by enabling them to view their anatomy and medical procedures in real time. The Doctors Assistive System with Augmented Reality Glass is significant because it can boost patient outcomes, streamline medical operations, and eliminate errors. As this technology advances, The healthcare industry might undergo a major transformation as a result, and patient lives could be improved globally.

16.4 A DISCUSSION OF HOW DOCTORS ASSISTIVE SYSTEM CAN IMPROVE PATIENT EXPERIENCE

The Doctors Assistive System using Augmented Reality Glass has the potential to greatly improve the patient experience in several ways. Here are some of the key ways that this technology can enhance the patient experience:

- Improved Communication: The Doctors Assistive System can facilitate better communication between doctors and patients by providing visual aids to help explain medical conditions, procedures, and treatments. By doing so, patients can acquire a better comprehension of their healthcare concerns and consequently make well-informed decisions about their treatment.
- Enhanced Education: The use of AR technology can also enhance patient education by providing interactive and immersive experiences that can assist people in better understanding their medical issues and procedures. This can improve patient engagement and adherence to treatment plans.

- Increased Comfort: The use of AR technology can also increase patient comfort by providing distraction and relaxation during medical procedures. For example, patients undergoing dental procedures can use the Doctors Assistive System to watch videos or play games to help distract them from any discomfort or anxiety.
- Faster Diagnosis and Treatment: The Doctors Assistive System can help doctors to make faster and more accurate diagnoses, leading to earlier treatment and improved outcomes for patients.
- Improved Access to Care: The use of AR technology can improve access to care by allowing doctors to remotely consult with patients or provide telemedicine services. This can be particularly beneficial for patients in rural or remote areas who may not have access to specialist care.

Overall, the Doctors Assistive System using Augmented Reality Glass has the potential to greatly enhance the patient experience by improving communication, education, comfort, and access to care. As this technology continues to evolve and become more widely adopted in healthcare, we can expect to see even more innovative applications emerge that further improve the patient experience.

16.5   SYSTEM IMPLEMENTATION

Innovative opportunities for surgical training are presented by AR and VR's application in the medical industry, notably in the virtual surgical environment. However, there is still some uncertainty surrounding the implementation of real-time improvements during surgical procedures. This is because present methods make it difficult to continuously check the patient's parameters.

Our proposed system utilizes AR technology to display real-time patient data to doctors during surgery. This is achieved by using semi-transparent AR glasses, which provide a view of the real-world while also displaying data collected by sensors linked to the body of the patient. The data is analyzed and wirelessly transmitted to the doctor's AR glasses, which will alert them if any abnormal conditions occur. This system is easy to use during surgery and ensures that doctors have constant access to the patient's health parameters, such as their heartbeat rate. The sensors attached to the body of the sufferer collect real-time data, then processed and transmitted wirelessly to the AR glasses worn by the doctors.

The system mentioned can be applied during surgeries in hospital operating rooms. The system's transmitter consists of sensors, a NodeMCU module, and wireless AR glasses. The patient's body is equipped with the sensors, and their readings are processed and stored in the Internet of Things (IoT) before being shown on the AR wearable glasses. The doctors collect and authenticate the data in real time, confirming its high dependability. The method makes it simple to keep an eye on the patient's internal processes and respond swiftly to any potential problems.

This approach seeks to assess numerous health markers using augmented reality before uploading the results to the Internet of Things. Patient data is safely transported across many databases and is accessible using AR Glasses, which is one of the system's standout advantages. Using augmented reality (AR) technology, surgeons can now learn about the interior organs' concealed functions and the adjustments needed for fine-needle biopsies. Virtual things are in real-time superimposed on actual objects to increase realism. AR provides critical digital information in addition to bringing digital items into the real world. Additionally, medical images can be interpreted and used in significant services provided by AR technology.

16.6 METHODOLOGY

The Node MCU Wi-fi board is connected to an external power supply and the heartbeat, respiratory, and temperature sensors are connected to it. These sensors collect patient values, and the temperature values are displayed on an LCD board that will alert if the temperature goes beyond the set threshold. All sensor values are then transmitted wirelessly. The heartbeat, pressure, and temperature sensors are coupled with the microprocessor, and an external power supply is also provided. After the patient is admitted, the microcontroller is fed the patient's information through the sensors. This data is then saved and passed to the doctor's microcontroller from the microprocessor AR glasses using a wireless transmitter. The WIFI receiver present on the doctor's AR glasses receives the data. This is useful for the doctor during surgery, as they can prioritize the treatment of critical patients.

After the wireless transmitter sends the patient data, it is received by a wireless receiver and then displayed on an AR glass. This allows for continuous monitoring of the patient's health during surgery and provides real-time data to the surgeons. By utilizing AR technology, doctors can accurately diagnose and treat patients, while receiving patient information faster and with greater precision. These sensors are attached to the patient during surgery, and the WIFI transmitter collects patient information and transmits it to the AR goggles. Through the goggles, the doctor can see this data and assess the patient's status to see if it is critical or average. The doctor will give the patient greater attention if they are critical, rather than moving on to other patients if they are judged normal.

Body factors such as heartbeat, temperature, blood oxygen flow, and breathing rate are measured using the sensors. The OLED lens shows information about the patient's pressure, temperature, and heartbeat. The Node MCU microcontroller receives the analog outputs from the sensors as inputs and processes them. Figure 3.8 depicts the information on the webpage where we can get the patient report. This AR glass, which is semi-transparent glass, may be worn during surgery and brings innovations to the medical industry. Using Arduino software, the processed digital outputs are sent via the WiFi protocol to the wireless transceiver. The receiver component of the device comprises an OLED display and a wifi module, and its output is shown on the wearable glass utilizing augmented reality.

16.6.1 TEMPERATURE SENSOR

A temperature sensor is an instrument that measures temperature by converting it into an electrical signal. This can be achieved through the use of a thermocouple or an RTD (Resistance Temperature Detector). A thermocouple consists of two different metals that generate an electrical voltage that is indirectly proportional to changes in temperature.

On the other hand, an RTD is a variable resistance that changes the electrical resistance indirectly proportional to changes in temperature, in a precise and almost linear manner. With an accuracy of ±5°C, the DS18B20 temperature sensor runs over a one to one interface and is able to measure temperatures between −55°C and +125°C. This waterproof sensor has numerous uses in various industries. There is no need for an external power source because the sensor can draw power straight from the data line. It can resist high temperatures and communicate via a single-wire bus protocol that connects to an internal processor using a single data line.

16.6.2 RESPIRATORY SENSOR

During surgery, a respiration sensor is used to monitor the rate of breathing. It is a sensor made to keep track of both regular and emergency breathing patterns in the patient. The breathing rate is calculated by determining how many breaths an individual takes in a minute, which remains normally monitored when the patient is at rest. However, if the patient is experiencing fever, illness, or other medical conditions, their respiration rate may increase. If the rate falls outside of the acceptable range of 12–25 breaths per minute, an "ALERT" message will be displayed on the AR glasses.

16.6.3 HEARTBEAT SENSOR

When a finger is placed on it, the heartbeat sensor is created to produce a digital output of the heartbeat. The detector is in operation when the beat LED lights are in rhythm with each heartbeat. By directly coupling this digital output to the microcontroller, the BPM rate may be calculated. It works on the principle that each pulse modifies the amount of modulated light. For detecting the patients' heartbeat rates, MAX30100 utilized a sensor. This sensor module is utilized to find the signal from the heartbeat. For detecting the patients' heartbeat rates, MAX30100 utilized a sensor. Using a finger, this sensor module can find the heartbeat signal. By placing your finger on this module, you can't reach the output of this sensor. Placing a finger on the heartbeat sensor results in the display of a digital value. Each rate is indicated by an LED blinking in this module, which determines each rate per minute and displays the value automatically while connected to the controller. It functions by altering light passes on the finger to find blood flow.

16.6.4 PULSE OXIMETRY SENSOR

This is a small, portable gadget that detects the body's oxygen saturation level as well as pulse rate. The device emits infrared light into the capillaries of the finger, and the oxygen saturation level is determined by measuring the amount of light reflected by the blood gases. The device can measure how much oxygen is being carried by the 0ed blood cells by analyzing the oxygen saturation level. The amount of oxygen in the blood is closely monitored by the body. SpO_2 readings of 95% or higher are regarded as normal, whereas readings of 92 percent or lower show low blood saturation. Chest pain, rapid heartbeat, and shortness of breath are all signs of inadequate saturation. It demonstrates that a healthy pulse rate normally ranges from

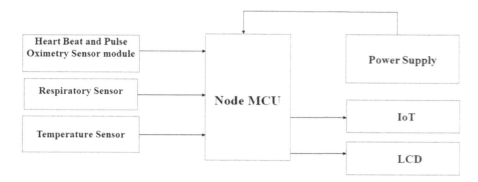

FIGURE 16.1 Block diagram for transmitter section.

FIGURE 16.2 Block diagram for the receiver section.

40 to 100 beats per minute (BPM) and that any abnormalities in blood oxygen levels are serious threats to general well-being and must be reported right away to a doctor.

16.7 BLOCK DIAGRAM

Figures 16.1 and 16.2. depict the generalized block diagram for the transmitter and receiving part. Using a wireless transmitter, real-time patient data is gathered and shown through AR glasses. A blood oximeter, a breathing sensor, a temperature sensor, and a heartbeat sensor that measures the finger pulse are just a few of the sensors that make up the system and collect input values. The respiratory sensor tracks the patient's breathing rate while the finger-detection. The heart rate is determined by the cardiac sensor through the analysis of the body's blood flow. The patient's current body temperature is measured by the temperature sensor. The embedded C programming is done on the Node MCU module, which then processes the input values. The doctor's wireless AR glasses get the processed data to display.

16.8 FLOW CHART

A breakdown of the flowchart is seen in Figure 16.3. can be found below. First, patients' heart rates, respiration rates, pulse rates, and temperatures are tracked using biomedical sensors (Step 1). The PIC microcontroller is then given these measured data to process further (Step 2). The controller (Step 3) compares these processed values to the designated threshold values. An alert notification is sent to the doctor if the temperature climbs above 102 F or falls below 95 F, the breathing rate exceeds 25 breaths per minute or falls below 12 breaths per minute, or the heart rate exceeds 100 bpm or falls below 60 bpm, go to step 4 instead any combination of these conditions. The final step (Step 5) shows the word "ALERT" on the screen.

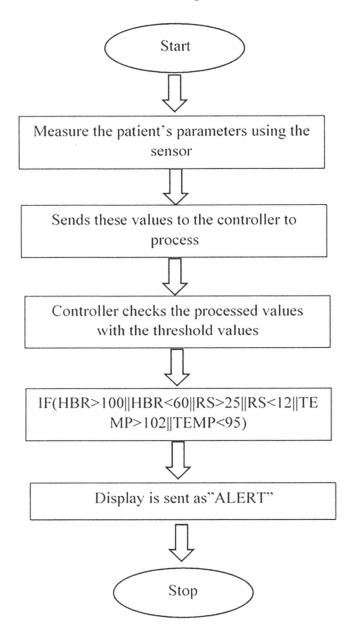

FIGURE 16.3 Process flow of proposed approach (DAS).

16.9 CIRCUIT DIAGRAM

Figures 16.4 and 16.5. below show the complete circuit connection.

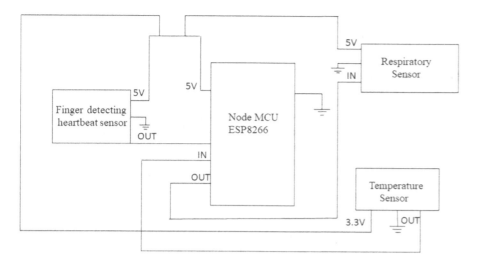

FIGURE 16.4 Circuit connection for transmitter kit.

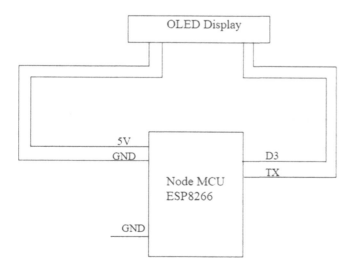

FIGURE 16.5 Circuit connection for receiver kit.

16.10 SOFTWARE REQUIREMENTS

16.10.1 INTERNET OF THINGS (IoT)

Almost any devices that can be linked to the internet and remotely monitored are considered to be part of the (IoT). To enhance productivity, gain customer insights, and improve service, various industries are quickly implementing IoT technology. Here, information about the patient's health is uploaded to an IoT webpage powered by ubidots IoT applications. We can save and retrieve data conveniently because there are many patient records kept in the cloud.

16.10.2 UBIDOTS

The IoT is an infrastructure of interconnected computing devices, physical objects, digital and mechanical gear, people, and animals that may exchange data over a network without needing to interact with one another or with computers. An IoT data analytics and visualization business is Ubidots. We transform sensor data into knowledge that is relevant for commercial choices, machine-to-machine communication, academic research, and maximizing the efficient use of global resources.

16.10.3 API AND SDKs

To help with the integration of hardware with their cloud service utilizing different protocols such as HTTP, MQTT, TCP, UDP, or custom/industrial protocols, Ubidots provides more than 200 trustworthy libraries, SDKs, and tutorials. The onboarding process for any number of devices is made simpler by Ubidots Device Types. The look, device attributes, and set variables are automatically produced for each new device. Ubidots devices are virtual representations of data sources that use a connection protocol to send sensor data to the Ubidot's cloud. Ubidot's libraries do away with the necessity for manual request submission.

16.10.4 LOGIN PAGE

An Ubidots device is a virtual representation of a source of data. or simply an asset that transmits sensor data to the ubidots cloud using a connection protocol. The libraries of Ubidots eliminsate the need to manually submit these requests. Username and Password are required on this login page to access the patient record. The login page is represented in Figure 16.6.

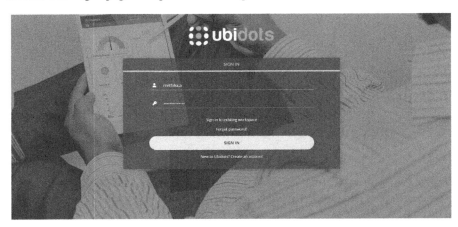

FIGURE 16.6 Login page.

16.10.5 HOME PAGE

The heartbeat, temperature, amount of breathing and oxygen flow of the patient are all detailed on this home screen, along with the date and time shown in Figure 16.7.

The patient's report is available for download at any time. Date-wise monitoring of the patient's data is possible, as shown in Figure 16.8. Instead of providing values in the event of an abnormal state, it displays the message "ALERT" as an alarm. Temperature levels exceeding 40°C fall within the range of abnormal values. The range of abnormal heartbeat and breathing rates exceeds 75 bpm and 100 breaths per minute bpm, respectively. Alerts are delivered for emergency purposes using the input values entered into Gmail, and they also display which value has been elevated above the required level.

FIGURE 16.7 Home page.

FIGURE 16.8 Downloading the patient's report.

16.11 RESULTS AND DISCUSSIONS

16.11.1 EXPERIMENTAL RESULTS

16.11.2 TRANSMITTER SECTION

When the kit receives the power supply, the breathing, temperature, and respiratory oximetry sensors are then connected to the Node MCU Wifi module. The temperature, heartbeat, and respiration values are shown on the LCD. The WiFi module connects to the internet, and the IoT stores the processed values. Both devices' Tx and Rx pins are linked to the Node MCU. The output based on sensors is displayed using an LCD and augmented reality goggles. The hardware representation is shown in Figure 16.9.

As seen in Figure 16.10., the IoT portal also updates the patient's vital signs. We have access to patient records that can be downloaded, as well as a health graph. Through a webpage, the sensed values are shown.

16.11.3 RECEIVER SECTION

The assistive system for doctors is created in this project. Continuously keeping an eye on the patient's vital signs will be beneficial to the doctors. The doctor's AR glass receives an alarm message if this parameter rises above the threshold values. If we choose to use The notification will contain any aberrant parameter values in

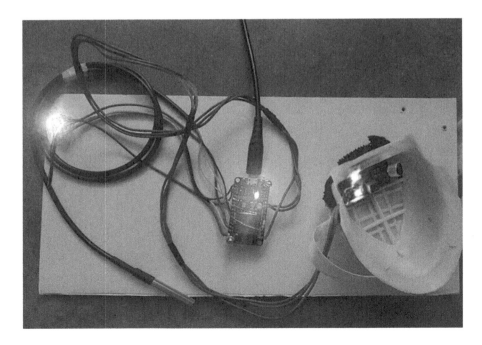

FIGURE 16.9 Hardware setup.

Vifi-IOTLogs   ◌   ☰ Datalogs   ✎ DigitalOutput   ☼ DigitalInput

how 10 ⬦ entries   Search

LogID	DATA	Logdate	L
1	ECG_=000_PX=067_Pres=000ECG_=000_PX=075_Pres=000ECG_=000_PX=071_Pres=000ECG_=000_PX=069_Pres=000ECG_	03/18/2021	1
2	ECG_=000_PX=072_Pres=000	03/18/2021	1
3	ECG_=000_PX=069_Pres=481	03/18/2021	1
5	ECG_=000_PX=071_Pres=000	03/18/2021	1
8	ECG_=000_PX=071_Pres=000	03/18/2021	1
10	ECG_=000_PX=068_Pres=000	03/1	1

howing 1 to 6 of 6 entries   Previous

FIGURE 16.10   Patient health status uploaded in IoT webpage.

real-time, unlike the prototype shown in Figure 16.11, where it is only displayed as "ALERT" from Table 16.1.

The Node MCU controller receives the analog outputs from the sensors as inputs and processes them. This AR glass, which is semi-transparent glass, may be worn during surgery and brings innovation to the medical industry. Using Arduino

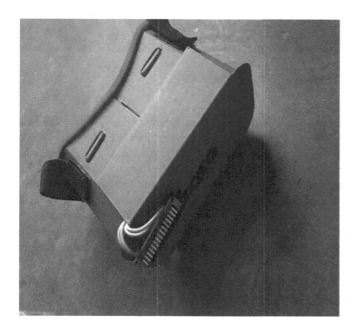

FIGURE 16.11   AR glass prototype.

TABLE 16.1
Threshold Parameters

Condition	Result
HBR>100, HBR<60	ALERT
RS>12, RS>25	ALERT
TEMP>102, TEMP<95	ALERT

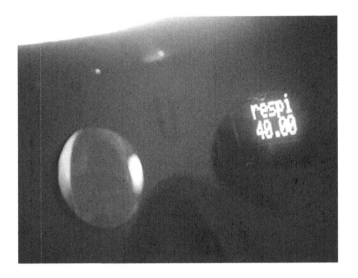

FIGURE 16.12　The output of wearable glass.

software, the processed digital outputs are sent via the WiFi protocol to the wireless transceiver. The receiver component included an OLED display and a node MCU Wifi Module, which displayed data from the database. The patient's information is gathered by the WI-FI transmitter and sent to the goggle. Through the goggle, the doctor can now observe details about the patient. The doctors determine if a patient is critical or normal after reviewing the medical data. The result produced on the wearable glass employing augmented technologies is shown in Figure 16.12.

There are several advantages of this technology, including low power consumption, higher efficiency, and the ability to minimize errors and multitask simultaneously.

16.12　FUTURE DEVELOPMENTS IN THE FIELD OF AUGMENTED REALITY HEALTHCARE TECHNOLOGY

Numerous potential future breakthroughs could further alter how healthcare is provided in the realm of augmented reality (AR), which is quickly developing. A few of the most exciting areas for study and development in augmented reality healthcare technology are listed below:

- Enhancing Haptic input: One of the difficulties with AR technology is that it can be challenging to give users haptic input. But researchers are looking into ways to get over this restriction, such as employing force feedback gadgets or wearable haptic interfaces. These developments may enable medical professionals to use augmented reality (AR) technology to have a more lifelike and immersive experience.
- Integration of Artificial Intelligence: The incorporation of AI into AR healthcare technologies is a separate topic of study. Real-time analysis of patient data or medical picture data using AI algorithms could give doctors immediate feedback and insights. This might facilitate surgical procedures or possibly help doctors identify illnesses more quickly and accurately.
- Wearable AR gadgets: The latest crop of AR gadgets, like the Doctors Assistive System, is frequently large and needs a separate computer to run. However, scientists are attempting to create wearable, more compact gadgets that are simple to incorporate into routine clinical practice. This might improve the usability and accessibility of AR technology for both patients and clinicians.
- Remote Medical Consultations: With the help of augmented reality (AR) technology, doctors might consult with patients or other healthcare providers in real time from anywhere in the world. When medical resources are limited or there is an urgent need for consultation, this could be especially helpful.
- Training and Education using Augmented Reality: Lastly, medical professionals and students could be trained using AR technology in a more immersive and participatory way. For doctors and surgeons to practice complex procedures or for medical students to learn about anatomy and physiology, augmented reality simulations may offer a safe and regulated environment.

Overall, there are several possible advances for augmented reality (AR) healthcare technologies that could significantly enhance patient outcomes and revolutionize the way healthcare is provided. In the upcoming years, we may anticipate the emergence of more cutting-edge applications and use cases as technology advances.

16.13   CHALLENGES AND LIMITATIONS OF USING DOCTORS ASSISTIVE SYSTEM IN HEALTHCARE

While the Doctors Assistive System using Augmented Reality Glass offers many potential benefits for healthcare providers and patients, some challenges and limitations need to be considered. Here are some of the key challenges and limitations of using the Doctors Assistive System in healthcare:

- Cost: The Doctors Assistive System can be expensive to implement, and not all healthcare organizations may have the budget or resources to adopt this technology.

- Training: Healthcare professionals may require extensive training to effectively use the Doctors Assistive System, which could be time-consuming and costly for organizations.
- Accuracy and Reliability: While the Doctors Assistive System is designed to improve accuracy and reliability in medical procedures, there is still a risk of errors or malfunctions that could potentially harm patients.
- Security and Privacy: Patient security and privacy are issues that are raised by the usage of AR technology in healthcare. It is the responsibility of healthcare organizations to safeguard patient data and that there are adequate safeguards in place to prevent unauthorized access.
- Regulatory Compliance: Healthcare organizations must comply with various regulations and standards, such as HIPAA, when implementing the Doctors Assistive System. Failure to comply with these regulations could result in legal and financial consequences.
- Ethical Considerations: The use of AR technology in healthcare raises ethical considerations, such as the potential for dehumanizing the patient experience or the risk of bias in the interpretation of medical data.
- Integration with Existing Systems: The Doctors Assistive System may not be compatible with existing healthcare systems, such as Electronic Health Records (EHRs), which could make it difficult to integrate into clinical workflows.

Despite these challenges and limitations, the potential benefits of the Doctors Assistive System using Augmented Reality Glass in healthcare make it an exciting area of research and development. By addressing these challenges, healthcare organizations can maximize the potential of AR technology to improve patient outcomes and transform the way healthcare is delivered.

16.14 CONCLUSION AND FUTURE TRENDS

16.14.1 Conclusion

Based on real-time patient data, this initiative develops an assistive system for doctors. Augmented reality has the potential to display patient information and imaging data, potentially saving lives and reducing medical mistakes. When performing surgery, it will be very beneficial for the surgeons. The presentation of the most crucial information to the surgeon can lead to a decrease in the chances of invasive surgery. It dramatically raises the standard of care. Doctors receive the digital outputs through augmented reality glasses through wireless data transmission and notifications in the event of an abnormal situation. This information can be kept for future use. The necessary action can be taken by the doctor, considering the patient's state of health at the moment.

16.14.2 Future Trends

Surgeons drive the most possible use of AR, for example a cutting-edge computer-human interaction gets even better results. Access to important data has been enhanced because of this technology. Real-time human body visualization through augmented reality offers enormous potential for the healthcare industry. The surgeons can perform their work much better thanks to it. Students will have the opportunity to simulate surgical procedures in a digital setting rather than performing them on real patients. Future AR glasses may become more straightforward, secure, and economical. utilizing cutting-edge methods to get greater results. Currently, there are several techniques for surgeons to see the area in which they work. However, among the many techniques available, augmented reality (AR) is one of the most widely used, as it can display a 3D visualization of the patient's anatomy during surgical procedures. Accuracy and results are probably going to improve from the surgeon's perspective. It enables medical professionals to quickly recognize, assess, and dissect clinically important structures. The best way to experience digital information will be with augmented reality.

REFERENCES

1. M. Tröbinger and A. Costinescu, et al, "A dual doctor-patient twin paradigm for transparent remote examination, diagnosis, and rehabilitation", 2021 IEEE/RSJ International Conference on Intelligent Robots and Systems (IROS), volume no. 8, 124–130, 2021.
2. A. Ranieri and A. Ruggiero, "Complementary role of conversational agents in e-health services", 2022 IEEE International Conference on Metrology for Extended Reality, Artificial Intelligence and Neural Engineering (MetroXRAINE), volume no. 10, 22–45, 2022.
3. N. Torabi and V. C. M. Leung, "Cross-layer design for prompt and reliable transmissions over body area networks", IEEE Journal of Biomedical and Health Informatics, vol. 18, no. 4, pp. 1303–1316, Jul. 2014.
4. J. P. Kolengadan, S. J. Dsouza and M. M. Ramya, "Development of interactive visual recognition assistant bot", 2023 International Conference on Artificial Intelligence and Knowledge Discovery in Concurrent Engineering (ICECONF), volume no. 19, 80–96, 2023.
5. E. D. Rekow. "Digital dentistry: The new state of the art—Is it disruptive or destructive?", Dental Materials, vol. 36, no. 1, 9–24, 2020.
6. D. Schmalstieg, T. Langlotz, and M. Billinghurst, "Augmented reality 2.0", Institute for Computer Graphics and Vision, University Graz of Technology, Graz, Austria, vol. 16, no. 4, pp. 303–316, 2019.
7. K. Proniewska, D. Dołe ga-Dołe gowsk, and D. Dudek, "A holographic doctors' assistant on the example of a wireless heart rate monitor", Bio-Algorithms and Med-Systems, vol. 14, no. 2, pp. 1–5, Aug. 2018.
8. E. Murphy-Chutorian and M. M. Trivedi, "Head pose estimation in computer vision: A survey", IEEE Transactions on Pattern Analysis and Machine Intelligence, vol. 31, no. 4, pp. 607–626, Apr. 2019.
9. G. Jha, L. S. Sharma, and S. Gupta, "Future of augmented reality in healthcare department", In Proceedings of Second International Conference on Computing, Communications, and Cyber-Security: IC4S 2020 2021 (pp. 667–678). Springer Singapore, volume no. 05, no. 4, 1230–1236, 2021.
10. S. Benila, N. Naveen, and R. P. Kumar, "Augmented reality based doctor's assistive system", i-Manager's Journal on Digital Signal Processing, vol. 9, no. 1, pp. 30, 2021.
11. C. Gieber, J. Knode, A. Gruenewald, T. J. Eiler, V. Schmuecker, and R. Brueck, "SkillsLab+-Augmented reality enhanced medical training", In 2021 IEEE International Conference on Artificial Intelligence and Virtual Reality (AIVR) 2021 Nov 15 (pp. 194–197). IEEE, 2021

12. A. Bhardwaj, A. Bhatnagar, and A. Kumar, "Current trends of application of additive manufacturing in oral healthcare system", Book: Advances in Additive Manufacturing Artificial Intelligence, Nature-Inspired, and Biomanufacturing (pp. 479–491). 2023.

13. A. Kumar, R. K. Mittal, and A. Haleem, "Advances in additive manufacturing: Artificial intelligence, nature-inspired, and biomanufacturing". Elsevier, 2022.

14. T. K. Huang, C. H. Yang, Y. H. Hsieh, J. C. Wang, and C. C. Hung, "Augmented reality (AR) and virtual reality (VR) applied in dentistry", The Kaohsiung Journal of Medical Sciences, vol. 4, pp. 257–281, 2018.

15. G. Pellegrino, C. Mangano, R. Mangano, A. Ferri, V. Taraschi, and C. Marchetti, "Augmented reality for dental implantology: A pilot clinical report of two cases", BMC Oral Health, vol. 19, no. 1, pp. 1–8, Dec. 2019.

16. A. Privorotskiy, V. A. Garcia, L. E. Babbitt, J. E. Choi, and J. P. Cata, "Augmented reality in anesthesia, pain medicine and critical care: A narrative review", Journal of Clinical Monitoring and Computing, vol. 17, pp. 1–7, Apr. 2021.

17. A. Sharma, R. Mehtab, S. Mohan, and M. K. Mohd Shah, "Augmented reality–an important aspect of Industry 4.0", Industrial Robot: The International Journal of Robotics Research and Application, Apr 21, vol. 49, no. 3, pp. 428–441, 2022.

18. G. Kalra, Y. K. Rajoria, et al, "Study of fuzzy expert systems towards prediction and detection of fraud case in health care insurance", Materials Today: Proceedings, vol. 56, pp. 477–480, 2022.

19. R. Monterubbianesi, V. Tosco, F. Vitiello, G. Orilisi, F. Fraccastoro, A. Putignano, and G. Orsini, "Augmented, virtual and mixed reality in dentistry: A narrative review on the existing platforms and future challenges", Applied Sciences, Jan 15, vol. 12, no. 2, pp. 877, 2022.

20. C. Gsaxner, U. Eck, D. Schmalstieg, N. Navab, and J. Egger, "Augmented reality in oral and maxillofacial surgery", In Computer-Aided Oral and Maxillofacial Surgery, Jan 1 (pp. 107–139). Academic Press, 2021.

21. W. S. Khor, B. Baker, K. Amin, A. Chan, K. Patel, and J. Wong, "Augmented and virtual reality in surgery—the digital surgical environment: Applications, limitations and legal pitfalls", Annals of Translational Medicine, vol. 30, pp. 130–180, 2016.

22. Y. El Miedany and Y. El Miedany, "Virtual reality and augmented reality", Rheumatology Teaching: The Art and Science of Medical Education, vol. 07, pp. 330–340, 2019.

Index

Note: Locators in *italics* represent figures and **bold** indicate tables in the text.